Second Edition
Blue Book of Tactical Firearms

by S.P. Fjestad
Edited by John B. Allen and David Kosowski

$24.95
Publisher's Softcover
Suggested List Price

$49.95
Publisher's Deluxe Hardcover
Suggested List Price

Second Edition *Blue Book of Tactical Firearms*
by S.P. Fjestad

Publisher's Note:

This book is the result of nonstop and continuous firearms research obtained by attending and/or participating in trade shows, gun shows, auctions, and also communicating with contributing editors, gun dealers, collectors, company historians, and other knowledgeable industry professionals worldwide each year. This book represents an analysis of prices for which tactical firearms have actually been selling during that period at an average retail level. Although every reasonable effort has been made to compile an accurate and reliable guide, gun prices may vary significantly (especially auction prices) depending on such factors as the locality of the sale, the number of sales we were able to consider, and the economic conditions during the time period this information and pricing were compiled. Accordingly, no representation can be made that the guns listed may be bought or sold at prices indicated, nor shall the author or publisher be responsible for any error made in compiling and recording such prices and related information.

Orders Only: 800-877-4867, ext. 3 (domestic only)
Phone No.: 952-854-5229
Fax No.: 952-853-1486
General Email: support@bluebookinc.com
Web site: www.bluebookinc.com

Published and printed in the United States of America

ISBN 10: 1-936120-00-3
ISBN 13: 978-1-936120-00-0

Distributed in part to the book trade by Ingram Book Company and Baker & Taylor.

Distributed throughout Europe by *Deutsches Waffen Journal*
Rudolf-Diesel-Strasse 46
Blaufelden, D-74572 Germany
Fax No.: 011-497-7953-9787-882
Website: www.dwj.de

TABLE OF CONTENTS

GENERAL INFORMATION

While many of you have probably dealt with our company for years, it may be helpful for you to know a little bit more about our operation, including information on how to contact us regarding our various titles, software programs, and other informational services.

Blue Book Publications, Inc.
8009 34th Avenue South, Suite 175
Minneapolis, MN 55425 USA
Phone No.: 952-854-5229 • Orders Only (domestic and Canada): 800-877-4867
Fax No.: 952-853-1486 (available 24 hours a day)
Web site: www.bluebookinc.com
General Email: support@bluebookinc.com - we check our email at 9am, 12pm, and 4pm M - F (excluding major U.S. holidays). Please refer to individual email addresses listed below with phone extension numbers.

To find out the latest information on our products, including availability and pricing, consumer related services, and up-to-date industry information (blogs, trade show recaps with photos/captions, upcoming events, feature articles, etc.), please check our web site, as it is updated on a regular basis. Surf us - you'll have fun!

Since our phone system is equipped with voice mail, you may also wish to know extension numbers which have been provided below:

Extension 10 - Beth Schreiber	beths@bluebookinc.com	Extension 17 - Zachary R. Fjestad	zachf@bluebookinc.com
Extension 11 - Katie Sandin	katies@bluebookinc.com	Extension 18 - Tom Stock	toms@bluebookinc.com
Extension 12 - John Andraschko	johnand@bluebookinc.com	Extension 19 - Cassandra Faulkner	cassandraf@bluebookinc.com
Extension 13 - S.P. Fjestad	stevef@bluebookinc.com	Extension 22 - Kelsey Fjestad	kelseyf@bluebookinc.com
Extension 15 - Clint Schmidt	clints@bluebookinc.com	Extension 27 - Shipping	
Extension 16 - John Allen	johna@bluebookinc.com		

Office hours are: 8:30am - 5:00pm CST, Monday - Friday.

Additionally, an after-hours message service is available for ordering. All orders are processed within 24 hours of receiving them, assuming payment and order information is correct. Depending on the product, we typically ship either FedEx, UPS, Media Mail, or Priority Mail. Expedited shipping services are also available domestically for an additional charge. Please contact us directly for an expedited shipping quotation.

All correspondence regarding technical information/values on guns or guitars is answered in a FIFO (first in, first out) system. That means that letters, faxes, and email are answered in the order in which they are received, even though some people think that their emails take preference over everything else. Please refer to our policy regarding gun questions and appraisals on page 6 for more information on telephone questions regarding firearms.

Online subscriptions for the *Blue Book of Gun Values, Blue Book of Tactical Firearms, Blue Book of Modern Black Powder Arms, Blue Book of Airguns, Blue Book of Pool Cues, Blue Book of Electric Guitars, Blue Book of Acoustic Guitars,* and the *Blue Book of Guitar Amplifiers* are available.

As this edition goes to press, the following titles/products are currently available, unless otherwise specified:

Blue Book of Gun Values, 31st Edition by S.P. Fjestad
Blue Book of Tactical Firearms, 2nd Edition by S.P. Fjestad
3rd Edition *The Book of Colt Firearms* by R.L. Wilson
Blue Book Pocket Guide for Colt Dates of Manufacture by R.L. Wilson
Black Powder Revolvers - Reproductions & Replicas by Dennis Adler
Black Powder Long Arms & Pistols - Reproductions & Replicas by Dennis Adler
6th Edition *Blue Book of Modern Black Powder Arms* by John Allen
Ammo Encyclopedia, 2nd Edition by Michael Bussard
Gianfranco Pedersoli – Master Engraver by Dag Sundseth, edited by S.P. Fjestad & Elena Micheli-Lamboy
Firmo & Francesca Fracassi – Master Engravers by Elena Micheli-Lamboy & Stephen Lamboy
Giancarlo & Stefano Pedretti – Master Engravers by Elena Micheli-Lamboy & Stephen Lamboy
8th Edition *Blue Book of Airguns* by Dr. Robert Beeman & John Allen
American Gunsmiths, 2nd Edition by Frank Sellers
Parker Gun Identification & Serialization, compiled by Charlie Price and edited by S.P. Fjestad
Blue Book of Pool Cues, 3rd Edition, by Brad Simpson
Blue Book of Electric Guitars, 12th Edition, by Zachary R. Fjestad
Blue Book of Acoustic Guitars, 12th Edition, by Zachary R. Fjestad
Blue Book of Guitar Amplifiers, 3rd Edition, by Zachary R. Fjestad, edited by S.P. Fjestad
Blue Book of Guitars, 12th Edition CD-ROM
Blue Book of Guitar Amplifiers, 3rd Edition CD-ROM

The Gibson Flying V, 2nd Edition by Larry Meiners & Zachary R. Fjestad
Gibson Amplifiers 1933-2008 – 75 Years of the Gold Tone by Wallace Marx Jr.
The Nethercutt Collection - The Cars of San Sylmar by Dennis Adler

If you would like to get more information about any of the above publications/products, simply check our web site: www.bluebookinc.com.

We would like to thank all of you for your business in the past – you are the reason we are successful. Our goal remains the same – to give you the best products, the most accurate and up-to-date information for the money, and the highest level of customer service available in today's marketplace. If something's right, tell the world over time. If something's wrong, please tell us immediately – we'll make it right.

MEET THE STAFF

Many of you may want to know what the person on the other end of the telephone/fax/email looks like, so here are the faces that go with the voices and emails.

S.P. Fjestad - Author/Publisher

Co-editors John B. Allen (l), and David Kosowski (r), contemplate yet another iron sight image.

Cassandra Faulkner
Executive Editor

Tom Stock
CFO

John Andraschko
Technology Director

Clint Schmidt
Art Director

Beth Schreiber
Operations Manager

Katie Sandin
Operations

Kelsey Fjestad
Operations/Proofing

Zachary R. Fjestad
Author/Editor Guitar &
Amp Division

GUN QUESTIONS/APPRAISALS POLICY

Whether we wanted it or not, Blue Book Publications, Inc. has ended up in the driver's seat as the clearing house for gun information. Because the volume of gun questions now requires full-time attention, we have developed a standardized policy that will enable us to provide you with the service you have come to expect from Blue Book Publications, Inc. To that end, we have extended all of these services to our website (www.bluebookinc.com).

To ensure that the research department can answer every gun question with an equal degree of thoroughness, a massive firearms library of well over 1,100 reference books, thousands of both new and old factory brochures, price sheets, and dealer inventory listings are maintained and constantly updated. It's a huge job, and we answer every question like we could go to court on it.

POLICY FOR GUN QUESTIONS

The charge is $10 per gun value question, payable by a major credit card. All gun questions are answered on a first-come, first-served basis. All pricing requests will be given within a value range only. If the firearm needs to be identified first, the charge is $15 per gun question. Gun question telephone hours are 1:00 p.m. to 5:00 p.m., M-F, CST, no exceptions please. You must provide us with all the necessary gun information if you want an accurate answer. Our goal is to answer most telephone gun questions in less than 5 business days, unless we're away attending trade/gun shows.

APPRAISAL INFORMATION

Written appraisals will be performed only if the following criteria are met:

We must have good quality photos with a complete description, including manufacturer's name, model, gauge or caliber, barrel length, and other pertinent information. On some firearms (depending on the trademark and model), a factory letter may be necessary. Our charge for a written appraisal is 2% of the appraised value, minimum of $20 per gun. For email appraisals please refer to www.bluebookinc.com. Please allow 2-3 weeks response time per appraisal request.

ADDITIONAL SERVICES

Individuals requesting a photocopy of a particular page or section from any edition for insurance or reference purposes will be billed at $5 per page, up to 5 pages, and $3.50 per page thereafter. Please direct all gun questions and appraisals to:

Blue Book Publications, Inc.
Attn: Research Dept.
8009 34th Ave. S., Suite 175
Minneapolis, MN 55425 USA
Phone: 952-854-5229, ext. 16 • Fax: 952-853-1486 • www.bluebookinc.com
Email: guns@bluebookinc.com
Use "Firearm Inquiry" in the subject line or it may get deleted.

ACKNOWLEDGEMENTS

The publisher would like to express his thanks to the following people and companies:

David Kosowski	Jeff Swisher and Angela Harrel – H&K USA	Glock
John B. Allen		Remington
G. Brad Sullivan	Eyck Pflaumer – Umarex	Smith & Wesson
Bud Fini – SIG Arms	Artur Prewo – Schwaben Arms GmbH	McMillian Group International
Randy Luth and crew – DPMS Panther Arms	Dr. Leonardo M. Antaris	DSA, Inc.
	Michael Tenny – Cheaper Than Dirt	PTR 91, Inc.
Michael Kassner – K.B.I., Inc.	Midway USA	Olympic Arms
Mark Westrom – Armalite	Benelli USA	FNH USA

CREDITS

Front cover design and layout – S.P. Fjestad and Clint H. Schmidt
Front Cover – Heckler & Koch MR556 semi-auto rifle courtesy of H&K USA.
Back Cover Firearms – (top down, left to right) Remington Model 870™ Tactical Desert Recon, Springfield Armory XD (X-Treme Duty) Service Model, and Taurus Model 45-410 Judge
Back Cover Knives – (top down, left to right) Spyderco Model Endura II (C10TS), SOG Flash-2 Camo (CFSA-98), Benchmade Mel Pardue Model 3550SBT
Printing – Bang Printing, Brainerd, MN
Manuscript Supervision – Cassandra Faulkner
Proofing – David Kosowski, John Allen, Kelsey Fjestad, and Cassandra Faulkner

FOREWORD
by S.P. Fjestad

Welcome to the 2nd Edition *Blue Book of Tactical Firearms*, now expanded to almost 400 pages! If someone would have told me 20 years ago that I'd be publishing a separate book on tactical firearms (a term not in use at the time), I would have bet a lot of money against it. Tactical guns continue to be the dominant configuration in today's firearms marketplace, even though most of the artificial demand is a direct result of fear created by potential anti-gun legislation brought on by the current Obama administration.

Let's take the gloves off and talk about this previous black sheep configuration. Originally dubbed "assault weapons" during the 1960s, the moniker was established in an effort to describe black, synthetic stocked, full auto rifles/carbines with parkerized metal finishes that were primarily used by the military. However, it wasn't long before this term bled over to the semi-auto civilian counterparts. Initially, the short list of these rifles and pistols was H&K Models 91 and 93, Galil AR/ARM, Uzis (pistols also), CETMEs, AR-15s (beginning in 1963), and even the low rent AK-47s after the Vietnam War. It's no secret that this initial batch of civilian, semi-auto "assault weapons" made little impact in the U.S. firearms marketplace, which at the time was dominated by traditional sporting and hunting guns. I remember turning down a mint H&K91 for $500 during 1982 from my old boss at Investment Rarities, where it had seen limited use by company security personnel. After all, what was I going to use it for? It certainly would have been the dark knight in my gun cabinet at the time, surrounded by Winchester Model 12s and 21s, Browning A5s and Superposed, and a few Remingtons.

These semi-auto "assault weapons" continued to establish a toehold in the semi-auto firearms marketplace during the 1970s-1980s. Sales were being made primarily to private companies for security, law enforcement and police departments who didn't require full auto capability, and some civilians who also had an interest in this new configuration. Looking back, the original owners of these initial black guns may have been ahead of their time. Today's tactical bad boys loaded with accessories compared to an early AR-15 look like Darth Vader next to Snow White!

The firearms industry, which never adopted the "assault weapons" term, especially after the Bush Ban of 1989, began using the term "paramilitary firearms", a softer, more politically correct description. Paramilitary design defined civilian firearms whose appearances generally resembled features and configurations of military firearms, except that rifles/carbines were semi-auto only and sported such features as flash suppressors, folding/collapsible stocks, high capacity magazines, bayonet lugs, etc.

The biggest reason these early "assault weapons" caught on wasn't because of a normal demand for these black guns. What really turbo charged sales was when the Bush Ban was enacted in 1989. Nothing sells guns faster than fear of impending anti-gun legislation, and this was proven again during the political negotiations for the Crime Bill of 1994. Paramilitary design terminology went out of vogue during the past five years, and now has been replaced by tactical firearms, which may eventually give way to simply defense guns. Certainly, the press still uses the "assault weapon" term, even though it is inaccurate and out-of-date.

So what will be the future of tactical firearms? The answer depends entirely on what type of anti-gun laws/ordnances federal, state, city,

Author/Publisher S.P. Fjestad at recent IWA Show in Nuremberg, Germany, shown with semi-auto MP5 clone. Tactical weapons continue to be the primary driving force in the firearms industry currently.

and local government may pass. We all know the crazy demand created for tactical firearms and ammunition that began shortly before Obama was elected. I've used this analogy before, but I am going to use it again because it directly applies to this situation. Do you think the liquor stores were busy the week before Prohibition started?

What's unfortunate this time, as compared to the anti-gun legislation of 1989 and 1994, is the firearms industry today has become dependant on tactical firearms. In effect, the tail is now wagging the dog. Most sporting firearms are simply not selling very well as the recession continues to curb consumer spending on anything that is not vital with day-to-day living. One thing that can't be ignored however is the amount of tactical firearms that have already been sold in America during the past 25 years – a figure that some writers guesstimate at over 10 million. So there will always be a marketplace for this configuration, even if someday it may be only for used guns.

In closing, I would like to thank John B. Allen and David Kosowski for taking the extra time to make this 2nd Edition even more of a tactical source guide, not just a pricing guide with related information. Don't forget, we now have a mobile application that allows you to get all the information in this book, plus images, on your mobile device. Thanks again for supporting this newest publication from Blue Book Publications, Inc. The entire staff continues to be committed to making our products and services better.

Sincerely,

S.P. Fjestad
Author & Publisher
Blue Book of Tactical Firearms

HOW TO USE

The values listed in this Second Edition of the *Blue Book of Tactical Firearms* are based on the national average retail prices gathered from gun shows, dealers, and auction sites. This is not a wholesale pricing guide (there is no such thing). More importantly, do not expect to walk into a gun/pawn shop or trade/gun show and think that the proprietor/dealer should pay you the retail price listed within this text for your gun(s). Resale offers on most models could be anywhere from close to retail to up to 50% less than the values listed, depending on condition, availability and overall supply/demand economics. Prices paid by dealers will be dependent upon locality, desirability, dealer inventory, and potential profitability. In other words, if you want to receive 100% of the price (retail value), then you have to do 100% of the work (become the retailer, which also includes assuming 100% of the risk).

Percentages of original finish, (condition factors with corresponding prices/values, if applicable) are listed between 60% and 100%. Please consult the Photo Percentage Grading System (PPGS), available at no charge online at www.bluebookinc.com or also included in the *Blue Book of Gun Values*.

Included in this Second Edition is the most extensive Glossary ever compiled for tactical firearms, sights, and optics. Combined with the Anatomy illustrations, this will help you out immensely in determining correct terminology on the wide variety of tactical firearms available in today's marketplace. Also see Abbreviations for more detailed information about both nomenclature and terminology abbreviations.

This book contains three unique Trademark Indexes – one for current tactical firearms manufacturers, importers, and distributors, one for accessories, and another for ammunition. These Trademark Indexes are actually a source book unto themselves, and include the most recent emails, websites, and other pertinent contact information for these companies. No other publication has anything like it, and you could research online for days before getting this much up-to-date information!

The Index might be the fastest way to find the make/model you are looking for. To find a model in this text, first look under the name of the manufacturer, trademark, brand name, and in some cases, the importer. Next, find the correct category name (if any), which are typically Pistols, Revolvers, Rifles and Shotguns. In some cases, models will appear with MSRs only after the heading/category description.

Once you find the correct model or sub-model, determine the specimen's percentage of original condition, and find the corresponding percentage column showing the value of a currently manufactured model or the value on a discontinued model.

For the sake of simplicity, the following organizational framework has been adopted throughout this publication.

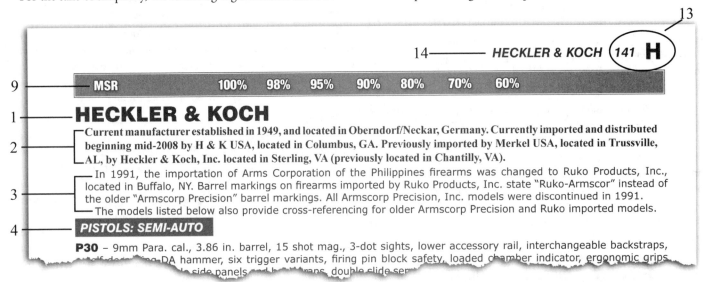

1. Manufacturer Name or Trademark - brand name, importer, trademark or manufacturer is listed alphabetically in uppercase bold face type.

2. Manufacturer Status - This information is listed directly beneath the manufacturer/trademark heading, providing current status and location along with importer information for foreign trademarks.

3. Manufacturer Description - These notes may appear next under individual heading descriptions and can be differentiated by the typeface. This will be specific information relating to the trademark or models.

4. Category Name - (normally, in alphabetical sequence) in upper case (inside a screened gray box), referring to various tactical configurations, including Pistols, Revolvers, Rifles, and Shotguns.

5. Category Note - May follow a category name to help explain the category, and/or provide limited information on models and current MSRs.

6. Value Additions/Subtractions – Value add ons or subtractions may be encountered directly under individual price lines or in some cases, category names, and are typically listed in either dollar amounts or percentages. These individual lines appear bolder than other descriptive typeface. On many guns less than 15 years old, these add/subtract adjustments will reflect the last factory MSRs (manufacturer's suggested retail price) for that option, and need to be either added or subtracted to ascertain the original MSR..

7. Model Name and Description – Model Name appears flush left, is bold faced in all upper-case letters, either in chronological order (normally) or alphabetical order (sometimes, the previous model name and/or close sub variation will appear at the end in parentheses). Model descriptions follow and usually start out with caliber/gauge, type of action, barrel length, important features, weight, and year(s) of manufacture/importation.

8. Value line – This pricing information will follow directly below the model name and description. The information appears in descending order from left to right with the values corresponding to a condition factor shown in the Grading Line near the top of the page. A pricing line with an MSR automatically indicates the gun is currently manufactured, and the MSR

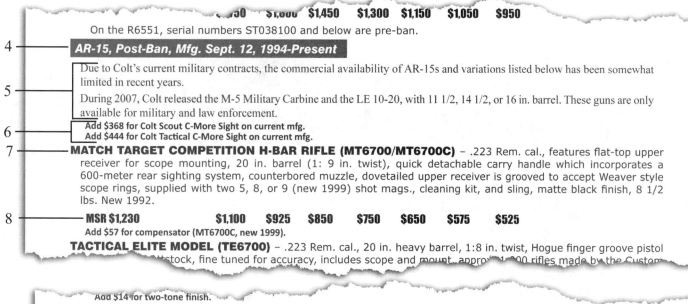

4 — **AR-15, Post-Ban, Mfg. Sept. 12, 1994-Present**

5 — Due to Colt's current military contracts, the commercial availability of AR-15s and variations listed below has been somewhat limited in recent years.

During 2007, Colt released the M-5 Military Carbine and the LE 10-20, with 11 1/2, 14 1/2, or 16 in. barrel. These guns are only available for military and law enforcement.

6 — Add $368 for Colt Scout C-More Sight on current mfg.
Add $444 for Colt Tactical C-More Sight on current mfg.

7 — **MATCH TARGET COMPETITION H-BAR RIFLE (MT6700/MT6700C)** – .223 Rem. cal., features flat-top upper receiver for scope mounting, 20 in. barrel (1: 9 in. twist), quick detachable carry handle which incorporates a 600-meter rear sighting system, counterbored muzzle, dovetailed upper receiver is grooved to accept Weaver style scope rings, supplied with two 5, 8, or 9 (new 1999) shot mags., cleaning kit, and sling, matte black finish, 8 1/2 lbs. New 1992.

8 — **MSR $1,230**   **$1,100**   **$925**   **$850**   **$750**   **$650**   **$575**   **$525**

Add $57 for compensator (MT6700C, new 1999).

TACTICAL ELITE MODEL (TE6700) – .223 Rem. cal., 20 in. heavy barrel, 1:8 in. twist, Hogue finger groove pistol ...stock, fine tuned for accuracy, includes scope and mount, appro... ...000 rifles made by the Custom...

Add $14 for two-tone finish.

MODEL P239 – .357 SIG, 9mm Para., or .40 S&W (new 1998) cal., compact personal size, double action or double action only, black Nitron or two-tone stainless steel slide and aluminum alloy frame, firing pin block safety, 3.6 in. barrel, 7 or 8 (9mm Para. only) shot mag., fixed sights, approx. 29 oz. New 1996.

MSR $840   **$735**   **$625**   **$525**   **$450**   **$375**   **$325**   **$295**

6 — Add $75 for Siglite night sights.
Add $305 for Crimson Trace laser grips and night sights (mfg. 2007).
Add $135 for two-tone stainless slide with night sights.
Add $75 for .357 SIG cal. with night sights.

11 — This model was also available as a Custom Shop Limited Edition during May, 2004 (MSR was $673).

10 — * *Model P239 SAS* – 9mm Para. (new 2008) or .40 S&W cal., 3.6 in. barrel, 7 shot mag., DAK trigger, smooth dehorned stainless steel slide, Siglite night sights, contrast rear sight, light-weight black hard anodized frame, black Nitron or two-tone finish, rounded trigger guard, checkered/carved wood grips, designed for snag-free profile for concealed carry, Generation II features became standard 2009, 29 1/2 oz. Mfg. by Custom Shop beginning June, 2005.

MSR $1,005   **$885**   **$750**   **$625**   **$550**   **$475**   **$425**   **$350**

6 — Add $45 for two-tone finish.

MODEL P245 – .45 ACP cal., compact model featuring 3.9 in. barrel, traditional double action, includes 6 and 8 shot mag., blue, two-tone (disc. 2005), Ilaflon (mfg. 2000 only), or K-Kote (disc. 1999) finish, approx. 30 oz. Mfg. 1999-2006.

                     $695   **$585**   **$495**   **$440**   **$400**   **$350**   **$310**   Last MSR was $840. — 12

Add $75 for Siglite night sights.
Add $56 for two-tone or K-Kote finish (disc.).
Add $50 for Ilaflon finish (mfg. 2000 only).

...9mm Para., .357 SIG, .40 S&W or .45 ACP cal., DAO, choice of 4.7 (full size), 3.9 (Compact), or 3.1... ...teel fra... ...olym... ...shell...

(Manufacturer's Suggested Retail) is shown left of the 100% column. 100% price on a currently manufactured gun also assumes not previously sold at retail. In some cases, N/As (Not Applicable) are listed and indicate that either there is no MSR on this particular model or the condition factor is not frequently encountered, and the value is not predictable. On a currently manufactured gun, the lower condition specimens will bottom out at a value, and a lesser condition gun value will approximate the lowest value listed. Recently manufactured 100% specimens without boxes, warranties, etc., that are currently manufactured must be discounted slightly (5%-20%, depending on the desirability of make and model).

9. Grading Line – The 100%-60% grading line will normally appear at or near the top of each page.

10. Sub-model Name - Variations within a model appear as sub-models, and they are differentiated from model names because they are preceded by a bullet, indented, and are in upper and lower case type, and are usually followed by a short description.

11. Model Note - Model notes and other pertinent information may follow price lines and value additions/subtractions. These appear in different type, and should be read since they contain both important and other critical, up-to-date information.

12. On many discontinued models and sub-models, a line may appear at the end of the price line, indicating the last manufacturer's suggested retail price (MSR).

13. Alphabetical Designator/Page Number – Capital letter indicating which alphabetical section you are in and the page number you are on.

14. Manufacturer Heading/Continued Heading – Continued Headings may appear at the top of the page, indicating a continuation of information for the manufacturer/trademarks from the previous page.

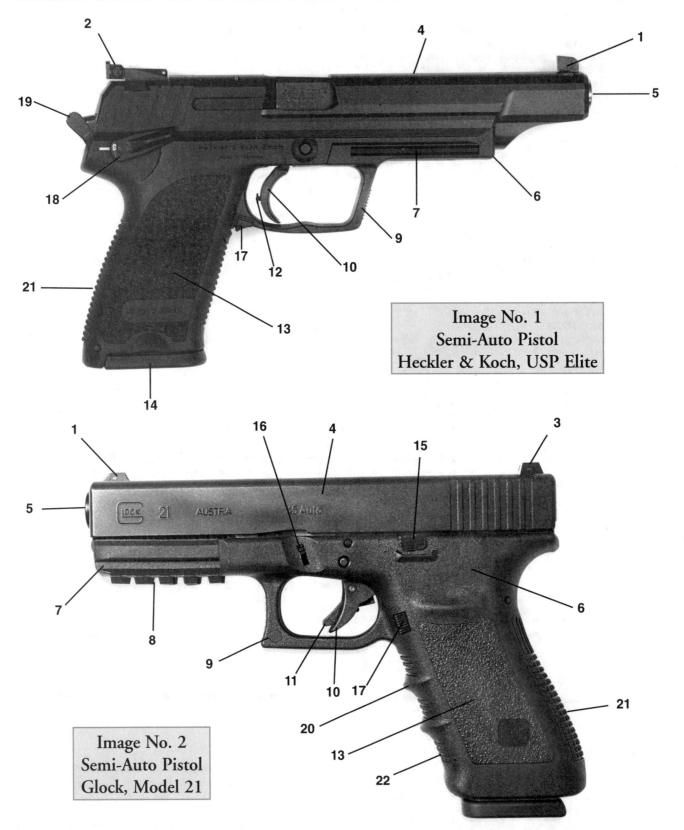

Image No. 1
Semi-Auto Pistol
Heckler & Koch, USP Elite

Image No. 2
Semi-Auto Pistol
Glock, Model 21

1.	Fixed blade front sight	9.	Trigger guard	17.	Magazine release
2.	Adj. rear sight	10.	Trigger	18.	Safety/decocking lever
3.	Fixed rear sight	11.	Trigger safety	19.	Hammer
4.	Slide	12.	Trigger overtravel stop	20.	Contoured finger grooves
5.	Barrel muzzle	13.	Grip frame	21.	Checkered rear grip frame
6.	Frame	14.	Magazine	22.	Checkered front grip frame
7.	Accessory/equipment rail	15.	Slide stop		
8.	Picatinny rail	16.	Takedown lever		

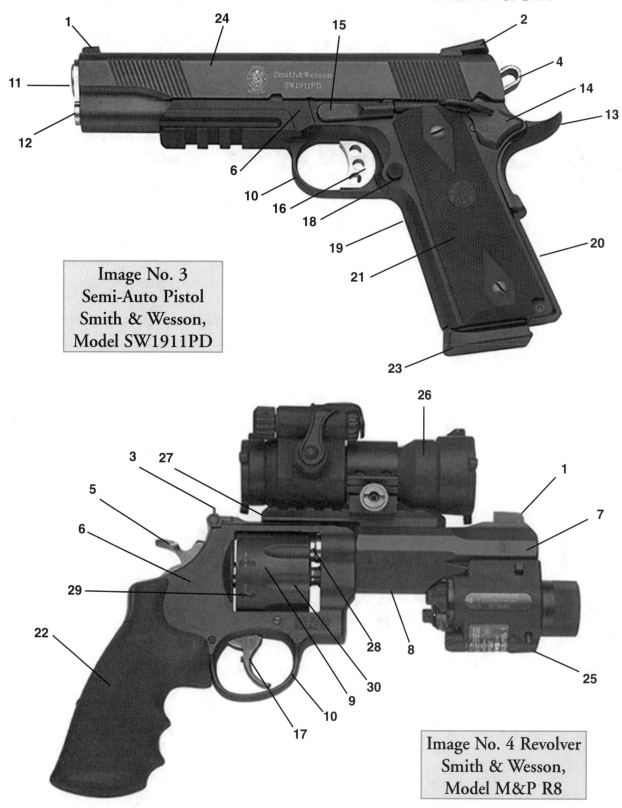

Image No. 3
Semi-Auto Pistol
Smith & Wesson,
Model SW1911PD

Image No. 4 Revolver
Smith & Wesson,
Model M&P R8

1. Fixed blade front sight	11. Barrel muzzle	21. Grip
2. Low profile combat rear sight	12. Recoil spring guide rod	22. Finger grooved grip
3. Adj. blade rear sight	13. Beavertail grip safety	23. Magazine
4. Skeletonized hammer	14. Safety lever	24. Slide with front and rear serrations
5. Hammer with full spur	15. Slide stop lever	25. Flashlight (accessory)
6. Frame	16. Skeletonized trigger	26. Reflex sight
7. Barrel	17. Trigger with over travel stop	27. Picatinny rail
8. Barrel lug	18. Magazine release	28. Breech end of barrel
9. Cylinder	19. Checkered front grip strap	29. Cylinder stop notch
10. Trigger guard	20. Checkered rear grip strap	30. Cylinder flute

ANATOMY OF A TACTICAL BOLT ACTION RIFLE

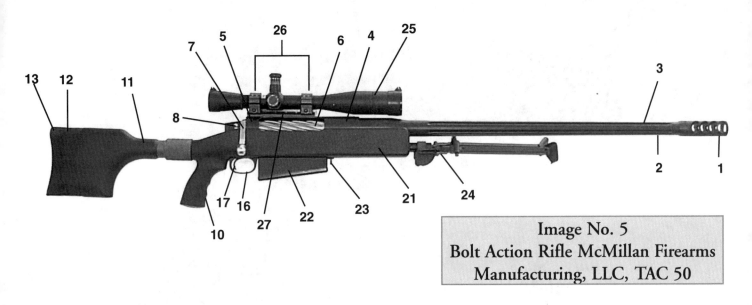

Image No. 5
Bolt Action Rifle McMillan Firearms
Manufacturing, LLC, TAC 50

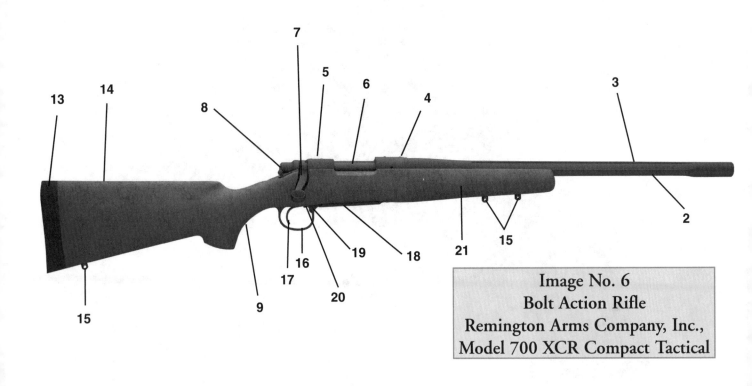

Image No. 6
Bolt Action Rifle
Remington Arms Company, Inc.,
Model 700 XCR Compact Tactical

1.	Muzzle brake	10.	Full pistol grip	19.	Floorplate release
2.	Barrel	11.	Takedown buttstock	20.	Bolt release lever
3.	Barrel fluting	12.	Buttstock spacers	21.	Forend
4.	Front receiver ring	13.	Buttpad	22.	Detachable box magazine
5.	Rear receiver bridge	14.	Buttstock	23.	Magazine release
6.	Bolt	15.	Sling swivel stud	24.	Detachable military style bipod
7.	Bolt handle	16.	Trigger guard	25.	Variable power scope w/target turrets
8.	Safety	17.	Trigger	26.	Scope rings
9.	Semi-pistol grip	18.	Hinged floorplate	27.	Picatinny rail (scope base)

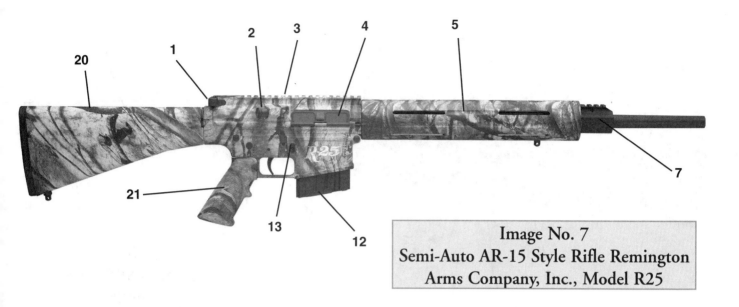

Image No. 7
Semi-Auto AR-15 Style Rifle Remington
Arms Company, Inc., Model R25

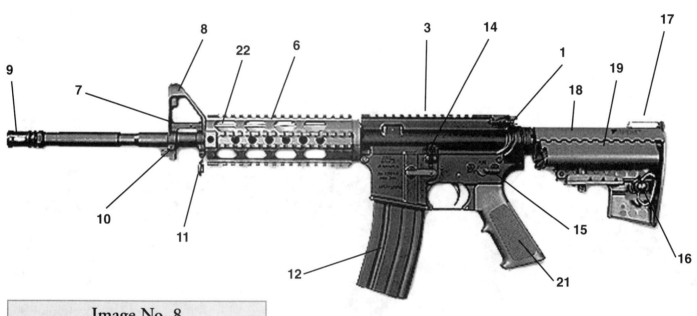

Image No. 8
Semi-Auto AR-15/M4 Style Rifle
DSA Inc., ZM-4 Carbine

1. Charging handle	9. Flash suppressor	17. Single point sling attachment
2. Forward bolt assist	10. Bayonet mounting lug	18. Collapsible stock
3. Flat-top upper w/Picatinny rail	11. Front sling swivel	19. Cheekpiece
4. Ejection port dust cover	12. Detachable box magazine	20. Fixed buttstock
5. Free floating forearm	13. Magazine release button	21. Pistol grip
6. Quad rail forearm	14. Bolt release lever	22. Gas tube
7. Gas block w/Picatinny rail	15. Safety lever	
8. A2 style front sight	16. Rear sling swivel	

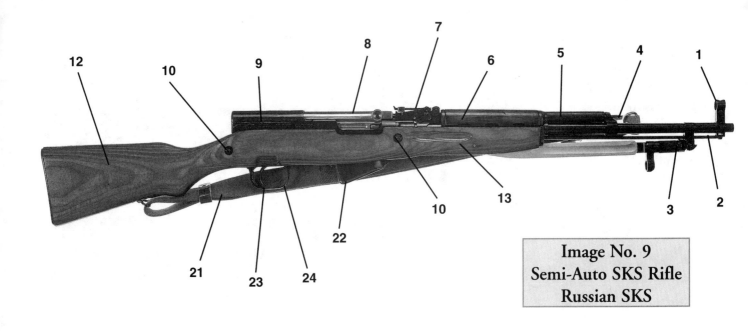

Image No. 9
Semi-Auto SKS Rifle
Russian SKS

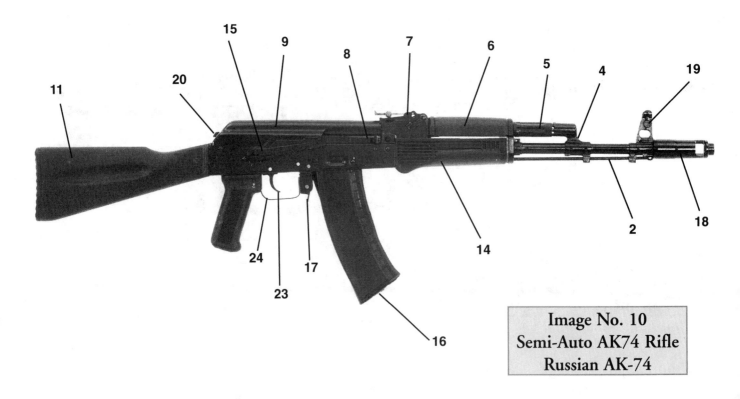

Image No. 10
Semi-Auto AK74 Rifle
Russian AK-74

1.	Hooded adjustable front sight	9.	Receiver cover	17.	Magazine release lever
2.	Cleaning rod	10.	Stock reinforcing cross bolts	18.	Flash suppressor
3.	Non-detachable folding bayonet	11.	Fixed buttstock	19.	Adjustable front sight
4.	Gas block	12.	Buttstock	20.	Takedown button
5.	Gas tube	13.	Forend	21.	Sling
6.	Handguard	14.	Forearm	22.	Non-detachable box magazine
7.	Rear tangent adjustable sight	15.	Safety lever	23.	Trigger
8.	Bolt	16.	Detachable box magazine	24.	Trigger Guard

Image No. 11
Semi-Auto HK Style Rifle
PTR 91 Inc., Model PTR-91

Image No. 12
Semi-Auto AR-15 Style Rifle
Olympic Arms Inc., OA-93 Carbine

1.	Flash suppressor	7.	Free floating forearm	13.	Adjustable diopter rear sight
2.	Hooded front sight	8.	Shell deflector	14.	Stamped sheet metal receiver
3.	Charging handle	9.	Skeleton side folding stock	15.	Fire control group
4.	Bipod mounting adapter	10.	Adjustable cheekpiece	16.	Accessory and optics rail
5.	Bipod	11.	Sling attachment bar		
6.	Ventilated forearm	12.	Adjustable LOP (length of pull) buttpad		

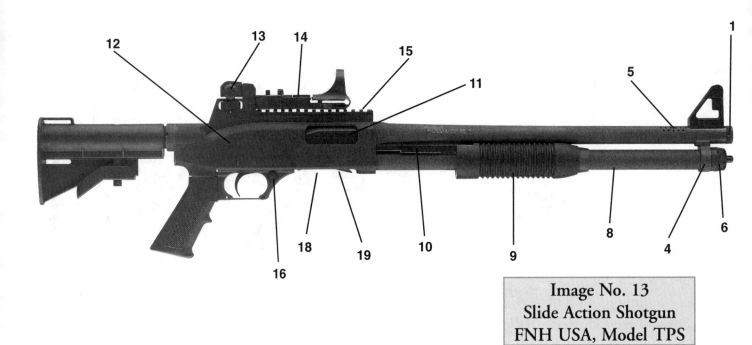

Image No. 13
Slide Action Shotgun
FNH USA, Model TPS

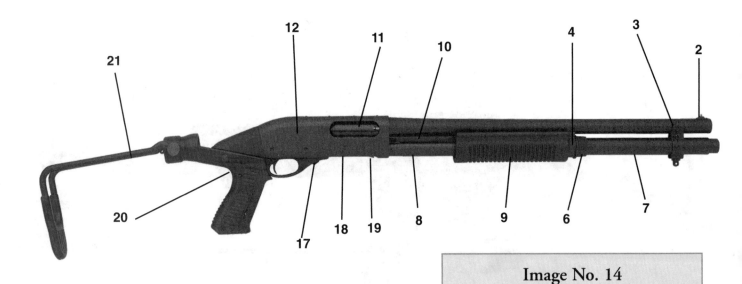

Image No. 14
Slide Action Shotgun
Remington Arms Company, Inc.,
Model 870 TAC-3

1. Removable choke tube	8. Magazine tube	15. Picatinny rail
2. Bead front sight	9. Forearm	16. Safety button
3. Barrel band	10. Action bar	17. Action release button
4. Forward magazine tube barrel band	11. Bolt	18. Loading port
5. Barrel porting	12. Receiver	19. Carrier
6. Magazine end cap	13. Back up iron sights	20. Recoil absorbing pistol grip
7. Magazine tube extension	14. Reflex sight	21. Top folding wire butt stock

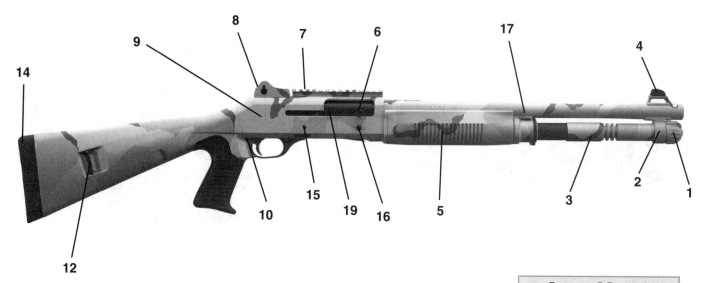

Image No. 15
Semi-Auto Shotgun
Benelli, M4 Tactical

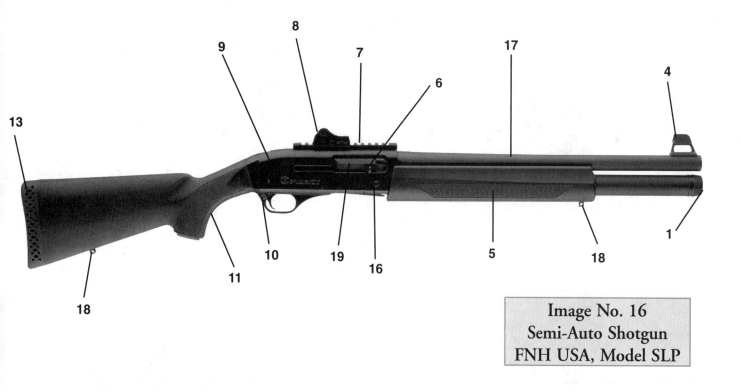

Image No. 16
Semi-Auto Shotgun
FNH USA, Model SLP

1. Magazine end cap	8. Adjustable ghost-ring rear sight	15. Takedown pin
2. Forward magazine tube barrel band	9. Receiver	16. Action release button
3. Magazine tube extension	10. Safety	17. Fixed choke barrel
4. Elevated front sight	11. Semi-pistol grip	18. Sling swivel stud
5. Forearm	12. Side mount sling bar	19. Ejection port w/charging handle slot
6. Charging handle	13. Ventilated recoil pad	
7. Picatinny rail	14. Solid recoil pad	

OPEN SIGHT ILLUSTRATIONS

Low Profile Handgun Combat Sights

Flip-Up Aperture Rear Sight

AR-15 Style Front Sight

AK Style Tangent Rear Sight

Adjustable Hooded Rifle Front Sight

Rifle or Shotgun Ghost Ring Rear Sight

OPEN SIGHT ILLUSTRATIONS

Elevated Rifle or Shotgun Front Sight

Shotgun Front or Mid-Bead Sights

Rail Mounted Laser Sight

Internal Guide Rod Laser Sight

Grip Mounted Laser Sight

OPTICAL SIGHT ILLUSTRATIONS

Compact Fixed Power Scope

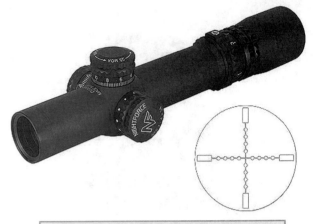

Compact Adjustable Power Scope with Mil-Dot Reticle

Full Size Fixed Power Scope with Mil-Dot Reticle and Target Turrets

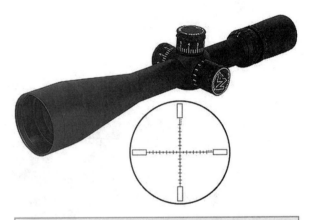

Full Size Adjustable Power Scope with Duplex Reticle and Target Turrets

Tube Style Reflex Dot Sight

Tubeless Style Reflex Dot Sight

Compact Reflex Dot Sight

GLOSSARY

1989 BUSH BAN

Refers to the U.S. Federal executive branch study and resulting regulations which banned the importation of firearms which did not meet "sporting criteria", i.e. certain paramilitary semi-auto only rifles and shotguns. The study was undertaken in response to the Stockton, CA tragedy in which an AK-47 type rifle was criminally used by a so-called "mass murderer." The Federal regulation, U.S.C. Title 18, Section 922r, applies to imported firearms and to firearms assembled in the U.S. using imported components. It is important to note that even though the Assault Weapon Ban (which applied to U.S. manufactured firearms, not imports) has expired, Section 922r remains in effect, and has the force of U.S. Federal law, regardless of its presedential origin as opposed to U.S. Senate and House of Representatives legislation. Also see Section 922r.

A2 STYLE FRONT SIGHT

A variation of an elevated front sight, so named because of its use on the U.S. Military M16A2 Rifle. See Image No. 8.

ACCESSORY/EQUIPMENT RAIL

See Picatinny rail. See Image Nos. 1 & 11.

ACCOUTREMENT

All equipment carried by soldiers on the outside of their uniform, such as buckles, belts, or canteens, but not weapons.

ACTION

The heart of the gun, including receiver, bolt, or breech block feeding and firing mechanism.

ACTION BAR

A firearm component which connects the forearm or gas operating system to the breechblock or bolt. Also called an operating rod. See Image No. 14.

ACTION RELEASE BUTTON

A fire control part on a pump shotgun which allows a user to unlock and move the forearm rearwards, thereby opening the action for inspection, extracting a live shell, or loading a shell through the ejection port. See Image No. 14.

ADJUSTABLE BLADE REAR SIGHT

A rear sight component which can be moved within the sight's body. Most adjustable blades move only side-to-side for windage adjustments, elevation adjustments are made by vertical movement of the sight body to which the blade is attached. See Image No. 10.

ADJUSTABLE CHOKE

A device built into the muzzle of a shotgun enabling changes from one choke to another.

ADJUSTABLE FRONT SIGHT

A sight which can be moved horizontally or vertically, to make windage or elevation adjustments. See Image No. 10.

ADJUSTABLE L.O.P. (LENGTH OF PULL)

A buttstock or buttpad which can be moved along its internal attachment part(s) to reduce or increase the firearm's L.O.P. See Image No. 11.

ADJUSTABLE SIGHT

A rear sight's aperture or sight blade, a front sight's post or reticle, and optical sights reticle, or the entire sight unit, which can be moved horizontally or vertically in relation to the sight body or the firearm; so that the line of sight and bullet trajectory coincide at a desired range.

APERTURE SIGHT

A sight consisting of a hole or aperture located in an assembly through which the sight and target are aligned. Aperture sights may be adjustable, and both front or rear sights.

ASSAULT RIFLE

Refers to a military or law enforcement rifle/carbine capable of select-fire (semi-auto or full auto).

ASSAULT SHOTGUN

Refers to a shotgun manufactured by contract for the military or law enforcement with a barrel shorter than 18 inches, usually a semi-auto or slide action configuration.

ASSAULT WEAPONS

Please refer to individual listings.

ASSAULT WEAPONS BAN

Popular title for the Violent Crime Control and Law Enforcement Act of 1994, Public Law 103-322. See Violent Crime Control and Law Enforcement Act of 1994, Public Law 103-322.

AUTO LOADING/LOADER

See Semi-automatic.

BACKSTRAP

Those parts of the revolver or pistol frame that are exposed at the rear of the grip.

BACK UP IRON SIGHT(S)

Flip up or fixed iron sights which are not the primary sight system. They are used if the primary optical sight system fails, and usually co-witness (optic sight picture and back up sight picture share the same zero).

BARREL

The steel tube (may be wrapped in a sleeve of synthetic material) that a projectile travels through.

BARREL BAND

A metal band, either fixed or adjustable, which attaches to and secures the stock, forend, magazine tube, or accessories to the barrel.

BARREL FLUTING

Lengthwise grooves cut into the barrel's exterior surface to reduce weight and increase cooling surface area. See Image No. 6.

BARREL LUG

An integral or removable full- or partial-length metal formation under and parallel to the barrel, usually semi-circular and intended to counter the effects of recoil by adding forward weight. See Image No. 4.

BARREL PORTING

Slots, vents, or circular opening machined into a firearm's barrel near the muzzle which allow propellant gasses to escape upwards and partially reduce muzzle jump. See Image No. 13.

BARREL THROAT

The breech end of a barrel which is chambered and somewhat funneled for the passage of a bullet from cartridge case mouth into the barrel. Also known as a forcing cone.

BATTUE

A ramped fixed rear sight assembly located on the back of the barrel, allowing quick target acquisition.

BAYONET MOUNTING LUG

A metal form, projecting from the barrel or other forward component of a weapon, which allows a bayonet to be easily and quickly attached or removed without tools. See Image No. 8

BEAD FRONT SIGHT

See Image No. 14.

BEAN BAG ROUND

A special impact munition shotshell loaded with a lead shot filled cloth bag projectile.

BEAVERTAIL FOREND

A wider than normal forend.

BEAVERTAIL GRIP SAFETY

A grip safety lever with an extended and upward flaring tang; designed to allow a high firing grip and prevent the hammer spur from striking the web of the shooter's hands (popularly known as "hammer bite"). A grip safety is usually spring-loaded in the "on" position and must be depressed completely by the user's hand to fire the pistol. See Image No. 3.

BIPOD

A two-legged accessory, usually detachable with folding extendable legs, which supports the firearm and allows for greater accuracy compared to unsupported firing positions. See Image No. 11.

BIPOD MOUNTING ADAPTER

An adapter with a Picatinny rail interface on its upper surface and a sling swivel stud on its lower surface; enabling a bipod with a sling swivel stud attachment design to be mounted on a Picatinny rail.

BLIND MAGAZINE

A box magazine which is completely concealed within the action and is not accessible from the bottom of the action.

BLUING

The chemical process of artificial oxidation (rusting) applied to gun parts so that the metal attains a dark blue or nearly black appearance.

BOLO

A special impact munition shotshell loaded with three rubber projectiles interconnected by three high strength 5.5 ft. cords. The projectiles wrap around the target in the same manner as the traditional South America bola hand-thrown weapon.

BOLT (REVOLVER)

The metal stud which rises and falls from a revolver's frame to lock the cylinder and correctly align the chamber to be fired with the barrel bore.

BOLT (RIFLE)

An assembly of reciprocating metal components (with or without a projecting handle) which support and move the cartridge, lock the action, fire, unlock, and extract the fired cartridge case.

BOLT RELEASE LEVER

A component part which allows a firearm's bolt to be removed from its receiver or frame. Also, with respect to semi-auto rifles, the lever assembly which usually holds the bolt open after the last round has been fired, and when pressed allows the bolt to move forward to its "in battery" firing position. See Image Nos. 6 & 8.

BORE

Internal dimensions of a barrel (smooth or rifled) that can be measured using the Metric system (i.e. millimeters), English system (i.e. inches), or by the Gauge system (see gauge). On a rifled barrel, the bore is measured across the lands. Also, it is a traditional English term used when referring to the diameter of a shotgun muzzle (gauge in U.S. measure).

BOX MAGAZINE

A boxlike ammunition feeding device for a firearm, which allows cartridges to be stacked one on top of the other. Most box magazines are removable for reloading.

BRADY ACT/BILL

See Brady Handgun Violence Prevention Act.

BRADY HANDGUN VIOLENCE PREVENTION ACT

1998 Federal legislation which established the National Instant Criminal Background Check System (NICS). Also commonly known as the Brady Bill, or the Brady Act. See National Instant Criminal Background Check System.

BREAK OPEN

A type of action where the barrels pivot on a hinge pin, allowing access to the chamber(s) in the breech. Configurations include: single shot, SxS, O/U, combination guns, drillings, and vierlings.

BREECH

The firearm components which support the cartridge as it is chambered, fired, and extracted.

BUCKHORN SIGHT

An "iron" rear sight with curved opposing horn shaped blades and a "u" or "v" notch.

BULL BARREL

A heavier, thicker than normal barrel with little or no taper.

BUTT PAD

A rubber or synthetic composition part attached to the buttstock's end; intended to absorb recoil energy, prevent damage to the buttstock, and vary length of pull. May be fixed, solid or ventilated, or adjustable (horizontally, vertically, cant). See Image No. 5.

BUTTPLATE

A protective plate, usually steel, attached to the back of the buttstock.

BUTTSTOCK

The portion of a stock which is positioned against the user's shoulder; also known as the butt. On AR-15/M16 style or similar long guns, the separate component which is attached to the rear of the receiver.

BUTTSTOCK SPACERS

Rubber or synthetic components attached between the buttstock and buttpad primarily to change L.O.P.; there may be some reduction of perceived recoil. See Image No. 5.

CALIBER

The diameter of the bore (measured from land to land), usually measured in either inches or millimeters/centimeters. It does not designate bullet diameter.

CAMO (CAMOUFLAGE)

Refers to a patterned treatment using a variety of different colors/designs which enable a gun to blend into a particular outdoors environment. In most cases, this involves a film or additional finish applied to a gun's wood and/or metal parts (i.e. Mossy Oak Break-Up, Advantage Timber, Realtree Hardwoods, etc.).

CARRIER

A part in repeating firearms with tubular under-barrel magazines, which elevates a cartridge within the receiver to a position where it can be moved into the chamber. Also called a lifter, or shell/cartridge elevator. See Image No. 13.

CASE COLORS

See Color Case Hardening.

CENTERFIRE

A self-contained cartridge where the detonating primer is located in the center of the case head.

CHAMBER

Rear part of the barrel that has been reamed out so that it will contain a cartridge. When the breech is closed, the cartridge is supported in the chamber, which aligns the primer with the firing pin and bullet with the bore.

CHAMBER THROAT

The area in the barrel which is directly forward of the chamber and tapers to bore diameter. Also called throat.

CHARGING HANDLE

A semi-auto firearm component which is manipulated to cycle the action, but which does not fire the cartridge. Also called cocking handle, cocking knob, or operating handle. See Image Nos. 11 & 15.

CHECKERING

A functional decoration consisting of pointed pyramids cut into the wood or metal surfaces of a firearm. Generally applied to the pistol grip and forend/forearm areas, affording better handling and control. See Image Nos. 1 & 3.

CHEEKPIECE

An elevated section of the upper buttstock on which the shooter's cheek rests when holding a rifle or shotgun in firing position. It may be integral to the buttstock, or a separate component. Adjustable cheekpieces may be moved in one or more ways: up, down, fore, aft, or side-to-side. May or may not be adjustable. See Image No. 11.

CHOKE

The muzzle constriction on a shotgun which controls the spread of the shot.

CHOKE TUBES

Interchangeable screw-in devices allowing different choke configurations (i.e., cylinder, improved cylinder, improved modified cylinder, modified, full). While most choke tubes fit flush with the end of the barrel, some choke tubes now also protrude from the end of the barrel. Most recently made shotguns usually include three to five choke tubes with the shotgun.

CLEANING ROD

A metal or synthetic rod used to clean the bore with patches and/or brushes which attach to the rod. Also may be used to clear bore obstructions or stuck cases. See Image No. 9, an example of a one piece rod designed expressly for and stored "on board" that rifle. Note: one piece rods are considered to be superior to multiple piece "sectional" rods, and far superior to "pull-through" metal chains.

CLIP

A metal or synthetic material formed/shaped to hold cartridges in readiness to be loaded into a magazine or chamber. A clip is NOT a magazine (i.e., stripper clips for most variations of the Mauser Broomhandle, M1 Garand). Also known as a stripper or cartridge clip.

COCKING INDICATOR

Any device by which the act of cocking a gun is moved into a position where it may be seen or felt, in order to notify the shooter that the gun is cocked. Typical examples are the pins found on some high-grade hammerless shotguns, which protrude slightly when they are cocked, and also the exposed cocking knobs on bolt-action rifles. Exposed hammers found on some rifles and pistols are also considered cocking indicators.

COLOR CASE HARDENING

A method of hardening steel and iron while imparting colorful swirls as well as surfaces figure. Normally, the desired metal parts are put in a crucible packed with a mixture of charcoal and finely ground animal bone to temperatures in the 800o C. – 900oC. range, after which they are slowly cooled. Then they are submerged into cold water, leaving a thin, colorful protective finish.

COLLAPSIBLE STOCK

Mostly used in reference to a buttstock which can be shortened or lengthened along its fore to aft axis. Also applies in theory to top-folding, under-folding, and side folding buttstocks; all of which when folded reduce the weapon's length. See Image No. 8.

COMB

The portion of the stock on which the shooter's cheek rests.

COMBINATION GUN

Generally, a break-open shotgun-type configuration which is fitted with at least one shotgun barrel and one rifle barrel. Such guns may be encountered with either two or three barrels, and less frequently with as many as four or five, and have been known to chamber for as many as four different calibers.

COMPENSATOR

Slots, vents, or ports machined into firearm's barrel near its muzzle, or a muzzle device, which allow propellant gasses to escape upwards and partially reduce muzzle jump/recoil. Also see MUZZLE BRAKE.

CRANE

In a modern solid-frame, swing-out cylinder revolver, the U-shaped yoke on which the cylinder rotates, and which holds the cylinder in the frame. The crane/yoke is the weakest part of a revolver's mechanism.

CRIME BILL

Popular title for the Violent Crime Control and Law Enforcement Act of 1994, Public Law 103-322. See Violent Crime Control and Law Enforcement Act of 1994, Public Law 103-322.

CRIMP

A turning in of the case mouth to affect a closure or to prevent the bullet from slipping out of the case mouth. Various crimps include: roll crimp, pie crimp, star or folded crimp, rose crimp, stab crimp, and taper crimp.

CROSSBOLT

A transverse metal bolt which reinforces and prevents damage to the stock from recoil or abusive handling. See Image No. 9.

CROWNING

The rounding or chambering normally done to a barrel muzzle to insure that the mouth of the bore is square with the bore axis and that its edges are countersunk below the surface to protect it from impact damage. Traditionally, crowning was accomplished by spinning an abrasive-coated brass ball against the muzzle while moving it in a figure-eight pattern, until the abrasive had cut away any irregularities and produced a uniform and square mouth.

CRYOGENIC TEMPERING

Computer controlled cooling process that relieves barrel stress by subjecting the barrel to a temperature of -310 degrees F for 22 hours.

CURIO/RELIC

Firearms which are of special interest to collectors by reason of some quality other than that which is normally associated with firearms intended for sporting use or as offensive or defensive weapons. Must be older than 50 years.

CYLINDER

A rotating cartridge holder in a revolver. The cartridges are held in chambers and the cylinder turns, either to the left or the right, depending on the gun maker's design, as the hammer is cocked. See Image No. 4.

CYLINDER ARM

See Crane.

CYLINDER FLUTE

A weight-reduction and decorative groove on the exterior surface of a revolver cylinder. Usually longitudinal but sometimes circumferential. See Image No. 4.

CYLINDER STOP NOTCH

A small groove machined into the rear surface of a revolver cylinder; it allows the cylinder stop stud or bolt to lock cylinder chambers in alignment w/the barrel bore. See Image No. 4.

DETACHABLE MILITARY STYLE BIPOD

A bipod designed for severe/heavy use and greater durability, with a Picatinny rail or other type of quick attach/detach mounting system.

DIOPTER REAR SIGHT

An aperture rear sight; usually the size of the aperture can be adjusted by means of an iris disc (similar to a camera lens), or by rotating a disc or drum which has a limited number of differently sized apertures. See Image Nos. 5 and 11.

DOUBLE ACTION

The principle in a revolver or auto-loading pistol wherein the hammer can be cocked and dropped by a single pull of the trigger. Most of these actions also provide capability for single action fire. In auto loading pistols, double action normally applies only to the first shot of any series, the hammer being cocked by the slide for subsequent shots.

DOUBLE ACTION ONLY

A firing mode which does not allow for single action cocking/short trigger pull; a DAO firearm can only fire when the trigger is completely pulled through its travel distance. Many new DAO firearms are hammerless.

DOUBLE-SET TRIGGER

A device consisting of two triggers; one to cock a mechanism which spring-assists the other trigger, substantially lightening trigger pull.

DOVETAIL

A flaring machined or hand-cut slot that is also slightly tapered toward one end. Cut into the upper surface of barrels and sometimes actions, the dovetail accepts a corresponding part on which a sight is mounted. Dovetail slot blanks are used to cover the dovetail when the original sight has been removed or lost; this gives the barrel a more pleasing appearance and configuration.

DRILLED & TAPPED

Refers to screw holes that are drilled into the top of a receiver/frame, allowing scope bases, blocks, rings, or other sighting devices to be rigidly attached to the gun.

EJECTION PORT

An opening or window in a semi-automatic firearm's slide or receiver through which fired cartridge cases are ejected, or an unfired cartridge unloaded from the firearm. May have an extending narrow opening for charging handle clearance. See Image No. 15

EJECTION PORT DUST COVER

A spring loaded hinged thin metal cover on many tactical semi-auto rifles which prevents dust, debris, or liquids from entering the receiver. See Image No. 7.

EJECTOR

A mechanical device used to eject cartridges or fixed cases from a revolver cylinder, or in a semi-auto firearm, from the breech and out through the ejection port.

ELECTRO-OPTICAL SIGHT

An optical sight (see definition) with the addition of electronic battery powered components which illuminate a reticle (least complex), or which generate a reticle/optional reticles. Electro optical sights may be: magnifying, non-magnifying, full-tube convention optical, or reflex types (see REFLEX SIGHT). See Image Nos. 4 & 13.

ELEVATED FRONT SIGHT

A sight blade attached to or part of a base which raises the blade a considerable distance above the barrel's bore line. See Image No. 15.

ETCHING

A method of decorating metal gun parts, usually done by acid etching or photo engraving.

EXPRESS SIGHTS

A front sight post with bead; and a rear sight with one or more "folding leaf" blades, each for a specific range. A very popular system for dangerous game rifles.

EXTRACTOR

A part which removes a cartridge or empty case from a firearm's chamber(s).

EYE RELIEF

The distance interval from an optical sight ocular lens and the shooter's eye when the image completely fills the lens. Eye relief changes as magnification is changed on variable power scope.

FAILURE TO FEED

A semi- or fully automatic firearm stoppage due to a cartridge which has exited the magazine but then becomes misaligned and cannot complete its forward movement into the firearm's chamber.

FAILURE TO EJECT

A semi- or fully automatic firearm stoppage where the fired and extracted cartridge case is only partially ejected from the firearm, and is then trapped in the ejection port as the slide or bolt moves forward. The case mouth often projects upward, hence the popular alternate term "stovepipe".

FAILURE TO EXTRACT

Mainly relevant to semi-automatic or fully automatic firearms, a stoppage due to a cartridge case which was not removed from the chamber by the firearm's extractor.

FIELD OF VIEW

The horizontal dimension of an optical sight's image at a specific range. Field of view decreases as magnification increases.

FIBER OPTIC SIGHT

An iron sight with fiber optic light gathering rods or cylinders; the rod ends are perceived as glowing dots and enhance sight visibility and contrast.

FINGER GROOVES

Concave rounded cut-outs in a firearm's front grip or forearm surface which position the user's fingers for an optimal grip, improve recoil control, and prevent slipping. See Image Nos. 1, 2 & 4.

FIT AND FINISH

Terms used to describe over-all firearm workmanship.

FIRE CONTROL GROUP

All components necessary to cause a cartridge to be fired; may be a self-contained assembly, easily disassembled or not user-serviceable, detachable, modular/interchangeable, and may or may not include a safety, bolt release, or other parts. See Image No. 11.

FIRING PIN

That part of a gun which strikes the cartridge primer, causing detonation. Also called a striker.

FIXED BUTTSTOCK

A non-adjustable buttstock; generally a separate component which attaches to the receiver, and not the shoulder end of a traditional stock. See Image No. 7.

FLAT-TOP UPPER

An AR-15/M16 style or other tactical semi-auto rifle with a literally flat receiver top. The majority of flat-top uppers have an extended Picatinny rail for mounting iron sights, optical sights, and other accessories, which provides much more versatility than the original "carry handle" receiver design. See Image No. 7.

FLASH SUPPRESSOR/HIDER

A muzzle attachment which mechanically disrupts and reduces muzzle flash. It does not reduce muzzle blast or recoil. See Image Nos. 8 & 12.

FLASHLIGHT (ACCESSORY)

On tactical weapons most illumination devices are high-intensity multi-function (on, strobe, momentary on, spot/flood, etc.) "weapon lights" which can be used either defensively or offensively. See Image No. 4.

FLOATING/FREE FLOATED BARREL

A barrel bedded to avoid contact with any point on the stock. Also see FREE FLOATING FOREARM.

FLOORPLATE

The base or bottom of a box magazine.

FLOOR PLATE RELEASE

A lever or button which is actuated to open the bottom of an internal non-detachable magazine. Typically found on bolt-action rifles and allows the magazine to be unloaded without working the bolt. See Image No. 6.

FOLDING BUTTSTOCK

An articulated buttstock which rotates on a hinge at the buttstock/receiver joint; similar to a collapsing stock in that it reduces the firearm's overall length. May fold alongside, over, or under the receiver. See Image No. 14.

FORCING CONE

Forward part of the chamber in a shotgun where the chamber diameter is reduced to bore diameter. The forcing cone aids the passage of shot into the barrel.

FOREARM

In this text, a separate piece of wood, or synthetic material in front of the receiver and under the barrel used for hand placement when shooting. See Image Nos. 14 & 16.

FOREND/FORE-END

Usually the forward portion of a one-piece rifle or shotgun stock (in this text), but can also refer to a separate piece of wood.

FORWARD BOLT ASSIST

A button, usually found on AR-15 type rifles, which may be pushed or struck to move the bolt carrier fully forward so that the extractor has completely engaged the cartridge rim and the bolt has locked. Mainly used to close/lock the bolt when the rifle's chamber and receiver are excessively fouled or dirty. See Image No. 7.

FRAME

See RECEIVER.

FREE FLOATING FOREARM

A forearm which does not contact the barrel at any point, as it attaches and places mechanical stress only on the receiver. An accuracy enhancement for AR-15/M16 style rifles, which by their modular design, are not able to have a conventionally free floated barrel in a one-piece stock. See Image Nos. 7 & 12.

FREE RIFLE

A rifle designed for international-type target shooting. The only restriction on design is an 8 kilogram (17.6 lbs.) maximum weight.

FRONT STRAP

That part of the revolver or pistol grip frame that faces forward and often joins with the trigger guard. In target guns, notably the .45 ACP, the front strap is often stippled to give shooter's hand a slip-proof surface.

FULL PISTOL GRIP

A rifle or shotgun grip extending below the receiver and buttstock; shaped and held like a handgun grip. See Image No. 5.

GAS BLOCK

A metal component which channels propellant gases from the rifle bore into a gas cylinder or gas tube; the gas is used to cycle the rifle's action. See Image No. 7.

GAS PORT

An opening in the barrel wall which allows propellant gas to flow into a firearm's gas operating system, or to reduce recoil impulse.

GAS VENT

A small diameter hole in a firearm's action which allows gas to escape from the breech; a safety feature which prevents high pressure gas from injuring a shooter if a cartridge case ruptures upon firing. Also a hole in a gas operated firearm's gas cylinder which allows gas to bleed off after its use.

GAUGE/GA.

A unit of measure used to determine a shotgun's bore. Determined by the amount of pure lead balls equaling the bore diameter needed to equal one pound (i.e., a 12 ga. means that 12 lead balls exactly the diameter of the bore weigh one pound). In this text, .410 is referenced as a bore (if it was a gauge, it would be a 36 ga.).

GAUGE VS. BORE DIAMETER

10-Gauge = Bore Diameter of .775 inches or 19.3mm

12-Gauge = Bore Diameter of .729 inches or 18.2mm

16-Gauge = Bore Diameter of .662 inches or 16.8mm

20-Gauge = Bore Diameter of .615 inches or 15.7mm

28-Gauge = Bore Diameter of .550 inches or 13.8mm

36-Gauge = Bore Diameter of .410 inches or 12.6mm

GHOST RING SIGHT

Actually a front and rear sight system with a very large diameter rear aperture sight; its optical design is intended to focus the shooter's eye on the front sight and thereby cause the rear sight to appear as an unfocused blurred "ghostly" ring surrounding the front sight. A very useful sight where faster target acquisition and wider field of view are required. See Image No.15.

GRIP

The handle used to hold a handgun, or the part of a stock directly behind and attached to the frame/receiver of a long gun.

GRIP FRAME

The front, rear, and both sides of a one-piece synthetic polymer frame handgun which are gripped by a shooter's hands. There are no grips (see def.) but checkering, stippling, contouring, grooves, and finger grooves may be "molded-in" to its surface. See Image No. 1.

GRIPS

Can be part of the frame or components attached to the frame which improve accuracy, handling, control, and safety of a handgun. Many currently manufactured semi-auto handguns have a grip frame (see definition) instead of grips.

GRIPSTRAP(S)

Typically refers to the front and back metal that attaches to a handgun frame and supports the grips/stocks.

GROOVED FRONT GRIP FRAME

See Image No. 1.

GROOVES

The spiral cuts in the bore of a rifle or handgun barrel that give the bullet its spin or rotation as it moves down the barrel. Also the parallel cuts in grips, grip frames, stocks, slides, or other components, which aid in grasping, controlling, and manipulating a firearm.

HAMMER

A part of a gun's fire control group. May or may not have a firing pin attached.

HAMMER WITH FULL SPUR

An external hammer with an elongated rearward projection; the spur facilitates cocking or lowering the hammer without firing. See Image No. 4.

HAMMERLESS

Some "hammerless" firearms do in fact have hidden hammers, which are located in the action housing. Truly hammerless guns, such as the Savage M99, have a firing mechanism that is based on a spring-activated firing pin.

HALF COCK

A position of an external hammer in a hammer activated firing mechanism which serves as a manual safety.

HANDGUARD

A wooden, synthetic, or ventilated metal part attached above the barrel and ahead of the receiver to protect the shooter's hand from the heat generated during semi-auto rapid firing. See Image Nos. 9 & 10.

HANGFIRE

A ten or less millisecond delay of propellant ignition and firing after the primer has been struck by the firing pin or striker. Not technically a misfire or a squib load, as the cartridge does fire.

HEEL

Back end of the upper edge of the butt stock at the upper edge of the buttplate or recoil pad.

HINGED FLOORPLATE

An internal box magazine floorplate which can be opened but not intended to be detachable. The magazine spring is normally attached to the inner side of this floorplate type. See Image No. 6.

HOODED FRONT SIGHT

A front sight post blade, etc. surrounded by an arch or tunnel. The hood prevents glare-induced aiming errors, and damage to the sight. See Image Nos. 9 & 11.

IRON SIGHTS

A generic term for front or rear sights which do not use optical lens (magnifying or non-magnifying) components.

LAMINATED STOCK

A gunstock made of many layers of wood glued together under pressure. After drying/curing the laminations become very strong, preventing damage from moisture, heat, and warping.

LANDS

Portions of the bore left between the grooves of the rifling in the bore of a firearm. In general, the grooves are usually twice the width of the land. Land diameter is measured across the bore, from land to land.

LASER SIGHT

An aiming system which projects a beam of laser light onto the target. Usually mounted so the beam is parallel to the barrel bore but not a "traditional" front or rear sight as the shooter does not look through the laser apparatus.

LENS COATINGS

Metallic coatings which increase light transmission, image brightness, and color rendition. Also used to improve abrasion resistance and filter out unwanted or harmful light.

LIMP WRIST(ING)

A vernacular term for the cause of a failure to feed stoppage; this occurs when a shooter holds a recoil operated semi-auto pistol so loosely during firing the slide loses velocity and energy sufficient to cycle the pistol's action, because the frame also moves rearwards. Recoil operated pistols cycle reliably only when their frames are held relatively motionless during slide travel.

LOW PROFILE COMBAT REAR SIGHT

A handgun sight which has no sharply angled projections, sloping surfaces, beveled/rounded edges, and a very short vertical dimension. Its advantages are: very fast sight picture acquisition, rugged/reliable, and essentially snag free. See Image No. 3.

M1913 PICATINNY RAIL

Original designation for a Picatinny rail. Also see PICATINNY RAIL.

MAGAZINE (MAG.)

The container (may be detachable) which holds cartridges under spring pressure to be fed into the gun's chamber. A magazine is NOT a clip.

MAGAZINE END CAP

A removable cover on the muzzle end of a tubular magazine. See Image Nos. 13 & 16.

MAGAZINE RELEASE

A button, lever, or other part which is pressed to unlock and allow a detachable magazine to be withdrawn or fall free from a firearm's magazine well. See Image Nos. 1 & 7.

MAGAZINE TUBE

The circular cross-section body of a tubular magazine; cartridges or shotshells are held "in line" end-to-end. Most often found on shotguns. See Image No. 14.

MAGAZINE TUBE EXTENSION

An accessory which increases the cartridge capacity of a tubular magazine; usually consists of a special end cap, tube, follower, and extended spring. See Image Nos. 14 & 15.

MAGNIFICATION ADJUSTMENT RING

On a variable power telescopic sight main tube, the ring which is turned to change magnification level.

MAGNUM (MAG.)

A modern cartridge with a higher-velocity load or heavier projectile than standard.

MAINSPRING

The spring that delivers energy to the hammer or striker.

MAIN TUBE

The central component of a telescopic sight, usually machined aluminum.

METALLIC SIGHTS

See IRON SIGHTS.

MICROMETER SIGHT

A windage and elevation adjustable sight with very precise and small increments of adjustment.

MID-BEAD SIGHT/MIDDLE SIGHT

An additional bead sight, smaller than the front bead, located in the middle of a shotgun barrel.

MIL-DOT

A reticle with dots spaced center-to-center one milradian apart; the distance to an object of known dimension may be calculated based upon the number of milradians which are subtended by the target's known dimension.

MILRADIAN

The horizontal angle subtended by one unit of measurement at 1,000 units distance. Also called a "mil".

MINUTE OF ANGLE

1/60 of a degree of angle; 1.047" at 100 yards. Also a unit of accuracy measurement.

MISFIRE

Failure of the primer to detonate after being struck a normal blow by the firing pin; failure of a properly initiated primer to ignite the propellant powder.

MONTE CARLO STOCK

A stock with an elevated comb used primarily on scoped rifles.

MUZZLE

The forward end of the barrel where the projectile exits.

MUZZLE BRAKE

A recoil-reducing device attached to the muzzle. Also see COMPENSATOR. See Image No. 5.

NATIONAL INSTANT CRIMINAL BACKGROUND CHECK SYSTEM (NICS)

A Check System which an FFL must, with limited exceptions, contact for information on whether receipt of a firearm by a person who is not licensed under 18 U.S.C. 923 would violate Federal or state law.

NICS CHECK

See National Instant Criminal Background Check System.

NIGHT SIGHTS

Iron sights with radioactive tritium gas capsules; the capsules are inserted into recesses in the sight body with their end facing the shooter. The tritium glow provides sight alignment and aiming reference in low-light/no-light conditions.

NON-DETACHABLE BOX MAGAZINE

A rectangular magazine which is never removed during normal use or maintenance of the firearm. It may extend beyond/below the receiver or stock, may be high capacity, and generally is loaded from its top (single cartridges or stripper clips). See Image No. 9.

NON-DETACHABLE FOLDING BAYONET

An articulated bayonet which cannot be removed by the end user. Normally "locked" into its fully folded or extended position. See Image No. 9.

OBJECTIVE LENS

A telescopic sights front, usually larger, lens which may be adjustable to reduce parallax error.

OCULAR LENS

The rear lens of a telescopic sight, normally adjustable by rotation to focus the sight image.

OPEN SIGHT

A simple rear iron sight with a notch – the shooter aims by looking through the notch at the front sight and the target.

OPTICAL SIGHT

A generic term for a sight which has one or more optical lenses through which the weapon is aimed. Optical sights usually magnify the target image, but there are many non- magnifying optical sights.

OVERTRAVEL STOP

A part attached to a trigger's rear surface, or to the inside surface of a trigger guard, which prevents any rearward movement of the trigger after the sear has released the hammer, striker, or firing pin. See Image No. 1 & 4.

PARALLAX

The predominating telescopic sight problem, caused when the target image is not focused on the reticle plane. An indicator of parallax is the apparent shift of the reticle aiming point on the target when the shooter's head moves relative to the scope.

PARAMILITARY

Typically refers to a firearm configured or styled to resemble a military weapon with one or more of the military weapon's configurations or features, EXCEPT FOR automatic or selective fire capability. Paramilitary firearms may be slide action (primarily shotguns), bolt action, or semi-automatic (most handguns and rifles).

PARKERIZING

Matte rust-resistant oxide finish, usually dull gray or black in color, found on military guns.

PEEP SIGHT

A vernacular alternative term for an aperture rear sight.

PICATINNY RAIL

A serrated flat rail typically located on the top of a frame/slide/receiver, but may also be located on the sides and bottom of other components, allowing different optics/sights/accessories to be used on the gun. It was developed at the U.S. Army's Picatinny arsenal. Picatinny rail dimensions are as follows: locking slot width: .206 in., slot center spacing: .394 in., and slot depth: .118 in. Similar to a Weaver rail, except for the size of the standardized slots. See Image Nos. 2, 4, 5, 13 & 16.

POLYGONAL

Rifling without sharp edged lands and grooves. See RIFLING.

POST-BAN

See 1989 BUSH BAN, and Section 922r.

PRE-BAN

See 1989 BUSH BAN, and Section 922r.

PROOFMARK

Proofmarks are usually applied to all parts actually tested, but normally appear on the barrel (and possibly frame), usually indicating the country of origin and time-frame of proof (especially on European firearms). In the U.S., there is no federalized or government proof house, only the manufacturer's in-house proofmark indicates that a firearm has passed its internal quality control standards per government specifications.

PRIMER

Small metal cup filled with explosive primer compound, fitted in the head of a centerfire cartridge case. When struck by a firing pin, it ignites the powder charge.

PRIMER RING

Refers to a visible dark ring around a firing pin hole created by the impact of centerfire ammunition primers on the breech or bolt face when a cartridge is fired.

QUAD RAIL FOREARM

A rifle forearm with upper, lower, and lateral Picatinny rails which allow attachment of multiple accessories. See Image No. 8.

RAMP FRONT SIGHT

A front sight blade with a sloped rear facing surface.

REAR TANGENT ADJUSTABLE SIGHT

An open iron sight commonly found on military rifles; adjustable for elevation only with a spring tensioned sight leaf and a sliding adjustment piece. See Image No. 10.

RECEIVER

That part of a rifle or shotgun (excluding hinged frame guns) that houses the bolt, firing pin, mainspring, trigger group, and magazine or ammunition feed system. The barrel is threaded or pressed into the somewhat enlarged forward part of the receiver, called the receiver ring. At the rear of the receiver, the butt or stock is fastened. In semiautomatic pistols, the frame or housing is sometimes referred to as the receiver.

RECEIVER BRIDGE

The upper rear portion of a bolt action rifle receiver which crosses over the bolt hole.

RECEIVER COVER

A detachable or hinged part on some semi-auto rifles which is removed or opened for access and disassembly of other action components (recoil spring and guide, bolt, bolt carrier, etc.) See Image No. 9.

RECEIVER RING

The forward cylindrical portion of a bolt-action rifle receiver; the barrel attaches to the receiver via the ring. See Image No. 6.

RECOIL ABSORBING BUTTSTOCK

A buttstock with internally mounted components which absorb and dissipate recoil energy before that energy is transmitted to the shooter's body. Depending on the recoil absorbing design, it may or may not move in relation to the buttstock. Configurations include fixed buttstock, various buttstock types w/pistol grip, and pistol grip only designs. See Image No. 14.

RECOIL SPRING GUIDE ROD

A metal or synthetic rod which positions the recoil spring within the firearm's receiver or slide, and prevents binding/dislocation of the spring during its compression or expansion. See Image No. 3.

RED DOT SIGHT

See REFLEX SIGHT.

REFLEX SIGHT

An optical sight which generates reticle image upon a partially curved objective lens; the reticle appears superimposed in the field of view and focused at infinity. Most reflex sights are non-magnifying and battery powered. Fiber optic light collectors or tritium may also be used to generate the reticle. Reflex sights are adjustable and virtually parallax free. Popularly known as "red dot" sights; they are NOT laser sights.

RELIC

See listing under Curio/Relic.

REMOVABLE CHOKE TUBE

A shotgun component which screws in/out of the barrel muzzle; available in many levels of shot constriction (choke) and provides versatility not possible with fixed choke barrels. See Image No. 13.

RETICLE

The shapes, lines, marks, etc. which provide an aiming reference when using an optical sight. Reticles may be illuminated electronically, with tritium, or with fiber optics, and are available in a multitude of designs for many differing requirements.

RIB

A raised sighting plane affixed to the top of a barrel.

RIFLING

The spirally cut grooves in the bore of a rifle or handgun barrel. The rifling causes the bullet to spin, stabilizing the bullet in flight. Rifling may rotate to the left or the right, the higher parts of the bore being called lands, the cuts or lower parts being called the grooves. Many types exist, such as oval, polygonal, button, Newton, Newton-Pope gain twist, parabolic, Haddan, Enfield, segmental, etc. Most U.S.-made barrels have a right-hand twist, while British gun makers prefer a left-hand twist. In practice, there seems to be little difference in accuracy or barrel longevity.

RIMFIRE

A self-contained metallic cartridge with its priming compound evenly distributed within the cartridge, but only in the rim. The priming compound is detonated only if the firing pin strikes the rim of the case head.

RINGS

See SCOPE RINGS.

SAFETY

A mechanism(s) in/on a gun that prevents it from firing. Many different types and variations. See Image No. 16.

SAFETY/DECOCKING LEVER

An operating lever (may be ambidextrous) which has two functions: engaging or disengaging the safety, and lowering the hammer without firing a chambered cartridge. See Image No. 1.

SAFETY LEVER

An external lever which causes the other parts of a safety mechanism to engage or disengage, when it is moved. May be manual, automatically engaged, ambidextrous, and located on the frame, receiver, slide or bolt. See Image No. 8.

SCOPE MOUNT(S)

Metal components which attach an optical sight to a firearm, i.e. rings and bases.

SCOPE RINGS

Metal mounts used to attach an optical sight to a gun's frame/receiver or scope base. See Image No. 5.

SEAR

The pivoting part in the fire control group or lock mechanism of a gun. The sear is linked to the trigger, and may engage the cocking piece or the firing pin.

SECTION 922r

A 1989 Federal regulation which established sporting criteria for centerfire weapons, either imported, or assembled from imported and domestic components. Firearms which do not meet the criteria are "banned", i.e. non-importable as of the regulation's effective date. Also the source of the popular terms "pre-ban" and post-ban". Due to the complexity of this regulation readers are advised to refer to the actual text of the regulation and contact the BATFE. See 1989 BUSH BAN.

SEE-THROUGH MOUNT

Optical sight mounts which allow the firearm's iron sights to be used, via openings in the bases.

SELECTIVE FIRE

Describes a firearm which has more than one firing mode; which is controlled, or "selected", by the user.

Most often used in reference to fully automatic firearms which can fire in semi-auto, burst, or full auto mode.

SEMI-PISTOL GRIP

A downward curving integral portion of a stock or buttstock which is similar to a handgun's grip/grip frame. See Image No. 6.

SHELL DEFLECTOR

A protrusion of the receiver near the ejection port which is positioned and shaped to deflect an ejected case away from the shooter's body. Especially appreciated by left handers when firing a semi-auto with right side ejection. See Image No. 12.

SHORT ACTION

A rifle action designed for short overall length cartridges.

SHOTSHELL

Self-contained round of ammunition used in shotguns, generally either brass and paper (older mfg.) or brass/steel and plastic (newer mfg.).

SIGHT ALIGNMENT

Horizontal and vertical centering of the front sight in the rear sight notch or aperture while aiming.

SIGHT(S)

Any part or device which allows a firearm to be aimed, versus merely pointed, at a target. There are two main systems: "iron" and optical. Iron sights are now made of substances other than iron and in many variations. Optical sights have a lens, or lenses, which may or may not magnify the target image.

SIGHT LEAF

The vertical rear surface of an iron rear sight; may have a notch or aperture and may be adjustable.

SIGHT PICTURE

What the shooter sees when the front and rear sights are in alignment and "on target".

SIGHT RAMP

A sight base which slopes upward toward the muzzle.

SINGLE ACTION

A firearms design which requires the hammer to be manually cocked for each shot. Also an auto loading pistol design which requires manual cocking of its mechanism for the first shot only.

SINGLE POINT SLING ATTACHMENT

A loop, bar, or stud for attaching a carry sling to only one place on the weapon. Typically the weapon is retained close to the body, even if both hands are not grasping the weapon. See Image No. 8.

SINGLE TRIGGER

One trigger on a double-barrel gun. It fires both barrels individually by successive pulls.

SKELETON STOCK

A fixed, folding, or collapsible buttstock; usually made of heavy wire or metal tubing in a stock outline shape, with no center. A buttpad may be attached. See Image No. 12.

SKELETONIZED HAMMER

A hammer with circular or other shaped holes in its main body and/or spur; for weight-reduction and decorative purposes. See Image No. 3.

SKELETONIZED TRIGGER

A trigger with various sized and shaped holes; the reduced weight improves trigger function. See Image No. 3.

SLIDE

The reciprocating (in relation to the frame) part of a semi-automatic handgun which holds the breech, firing pin, extractor, barrel, recoil-spring and its guide rod, and other action parts.

SLIDE STOP

Usually a lever on the frame of semi-auto handguns, which can be moved to lock the slide in its open position. See Image Nos. 2 & 3.

SLIDE SERRATIONS

Multiple patterned grooves machined into the surfaces of a slide which provide an improved grasping surface for manipulating the slide. See Image No. 3.

SLING

A leather (traditional), fabric, or synthetic strap attached to a firearm so that it can be more easily carried by the user. Usually length adjustable, attached with swivels to a stud on the firearm, and may be used to stabilize the user and firearm in certain shooting positions. See Image No. 9.

SLING ATTACHMENT BAR

An alternative to the sling swivel; one end of the sling looped around the bar, or one end with a snap hook is attached to the bar. See Image No. 11.

SLING SWIVELS

Metal loops affixed to the gun to which a carrying strap is attached. See Image Nos. 6 & 8.

SLING SWIVEL STUD

A metal stud on a firearm for attaching a sling swivel, or other accessories, such as bipods or monopods. See Image Nos. 6 & 16.

SOLID RECOIL PAD

A solid buttpad which is attached to the buttstock; made of recoil absorbing rubber or synthetics. See Image No. 15.

SPECIAL IMPACT MUNITIONS

A class or type of firearm ammunition loaded with one or more projectiles; when fired at a human target the projectiles have a low probability of causing serious injury or death. For example: bean bag, baton, tear gas, and rubber ball rounds. A sub-class of SIMs is known as SPLLAT, or special purpose less lethal anti terrorist munitions.

SQUIB LOAD

A cartridge with no propellant, or so little propellant, that when fired in a semi-auto the action does not cycle; and in any type of firearm a squib load most likely results in the projectile remaining in and completely obstructing the barrel's bore.

STAMPED SHEET METAL RECEIVER

A receiver manufactured out of sheet metal which has been cut, stamped into a three-dimensional shape, and welded. An economical alternative to milling a receiver from a solid block of metal. See Image No. 11.

STIPPLING

The process and finished result of roughening a firearm surface with a pointed tool; it creates an improved gripping area when applied to stocks, grips, etc.

STOCK

Traditionally the single piece wood, metal, or synthetic firearm component part which all other components are attached, and which allow the user to hold and operate the firearm.

STOCKS

Older terminology used to describe handgun grips (see Grips).

STOPPAGE

A malfunction of either the firearm's mechanism or its ammunition which causes it to stop firing. Primarily used in the context of semi-automatic or fully automatic weapons, and of a temporary nature. Common stoppages are: failure to extract, failure to eject, failure to feed, limp-wristing (a shooter induced mechanical stoppage), misfire, and squib load. Also known as a "jam".

SUPPRESSOR

A mechanical device, usually cylindrical and detachable, which alters and decreases muzzle blast and noise. Commonly referred to, in error, as a silencer, it acts only on the sound of the firearms discharge. It does not have any effect on the sounds generated by: the firearm's moving parts, a supersonic bullet in flight, or the bullet's impact.

TACTICAL

An imprecise term referring to certain features on handguns, rifles, and shotguns that are not NFA regulated. Before 2000, a tactical gun generally referred to a rifle or carbine designed for military or law enforcement. In today's marketplace, tactical refers to certain features of both handguns and long arms.

TACTICAL REVOLVERS

Tactical revolvers have at least three of the following factory/manufacturer options or features: non-glare finish (generally but there may be exceptions), Mil Std 1913 Picatinny or equivalent rail(s), combat style grips (wood or synthetic), fixed or adjustable low profile primary sights (can be tritium or illuminated night sights), auxiliary aiming/sighting/illumination equipment, compensators or barrel porting, as well as combat triggers and hammers.

TACTICAL RIFLES

Semi-auto, bolt action, or slide action rifles that have at least two of the following factory/manufacturer options or features: magazine capacity over ten rounds, non-glare finish (generally but there may be exceptions), Mil Std 1913 Picatinny or equivalent rail(s), mostly synthetic stocks which may be fixed, folding, collapsible, adjustable, or with/without pistol grip, most have sling attachments for single, traditional two, or three point slings, tritium night sights, and some Assault Weapon Ban characteristics, such as flash suppressors, detachable magazines, bayonet lugs, etc.

TACTICAL SEMI-AUTO PISTOLS

Tactical semi-auto pistols have at least three of the following factory/manufacturer options or features: magazine capacity over ten rounds, non-glare finish (generally but there may be exceptions), Mil Std 1913 Picatinny or equivalent rail(s), combat style grips (wood or synthetic), fixed or adjustable low profile primary sights (can be tritium or illuminated night sights), auxiliary aiming/sighting/illumination equipment, and compensators or barrel porting.

TACTICAL SHOTGUNS

Semi-auto or slide action shotguns have at least two of the following factory/manufacturer options or features: higher capacity (than sporting/hunting shotguns) magazines, or magazine extensions, non-glare finish (generally but there may be exceptions), Mil Std 1913 Picatinny or equivalent rail(s), mostly synthetic stocks which may be fixed, folding, collapsible, adjustable, or with/without pistol grip, most have sling attachments for single, traditional two, or three point slings, some Assault Weapon Ban characteristics, such as bayonet lugs, or detachable "high capacity" magazines, rifle, tritium night sights, or ghost ring sights (usually adjustable), and short (18-20 inches) barrels with fixed cylinder choke.

TAKE DOWN

A gun which can be easily disassembled into at least two sections for carrying or shipping.

TAKE DOWN BUTTON

A disassembly control; pressing the button opens or allows removal of one or more parts. See Image No. 10.

TAKE DOWN LEVER

A disassembly control; pressing the lever opens or allows removal of one or more parts. See Image No. 2.

TAKE DOWN PIN

A transverse pin in a receiver which is moved or withdrawn completely to allow disassembly of the firearm. Most often found in shotguns (pump or semi-auto). See Image No. 15.

TANG(S)

Usually refers to the extension straps (upper and lower) of a rifle or shotgun receiver/frame to which the stock/grips are attached.

TELESCOPIC SIGHT

An optical sight which magnifies the target image; may have fixed or variable levels of magnification.

THUMBHOLE STOCK (CRIME BILL)

An adaptation of the sporter thumbhole stock design which removed a weapon from "semi-auto assault weapon"

legal status. The thumbhole was/is very large and provides the functionality of a true pistol grip stock.

THUMBHOLE STOCK (SPORTER)

A sporter/hunting stock with an ergonomic hole in the grip; the thumb of the shooter's trigger hand fits into the hole which provides for a steadier hold.

TOP STRAP

The upper part of a revolver frame, which often is either slightly grooved - the groove serving as rear sight - or which carries at its rearward end a sight (which may or may not be adjustable).

TRIGGER

Refers to a release device (mechanical or electrical) in the fire control system that starts the ignition process. Usually a curved, grooved, or serrated piece of metal which is pulled rearward by the shooter's finger, and which releases the sear or hammer.

TRIGGER GUARD

Usually a metal or synthetic band which encloses the trigger to provide both protection to the trigger and prevent an accidental discharge.

TRIGGER SAFETY

A trigger assembly component which must be depressed or otherwise moved before the trigger can be pulled completely through to fire the weapon. Most often a pivoting blade in the center of a trigger which protrudes from the face of the trigger when it is engaged/"on" and automatically resets itself. See Image No. 2.

TURRETS

Cylinders on an optical sight's main tube which hold adjustment knobs or screws. A turret is dedicated to one of several functions: windage, elevation, parallax, reticle type, reticle illumination, or ranging.

UNLOAD

To remove all ammunition/cartridges from a firearm or magazine.

UNSERVICEABLE FIREARM

A firearm that is damaged and cannot be made functional in a minimal amount of time.

UPPER ASSEMBLY

For a semi-auto pistol this includes the barrel and slide assembly, for AR style rifles it includes the barrel, bolt and receiver houuosing.

VARIABLE POWER OPTICAL SIGHT

A optical sight with a multiple magnification levels, most common are 3-9 power general purpose scopes.

VENTILATED

Denotes a component with holes, slots, gaps, or other voids which reduce weight, promote cooling, have a structural purpose, or are decorative. See Image Nos. 11 & 16.

VENTILATED RIB

A sighting plane affixed along the length of a shotgun barrel with gaps or slots milled for cooling and reduced weight.

VERNIER

Typically used in reference to a rear aperture (peep) sight. Usually upper tang mounted, its aperture is adjusted for elevation by a very precise vernier screw.

VIOLENT CRIME CONTROL AND LAW ENFORCEMENT ACT OF 1994, PUBLIC LAW 103-322

On September 13, 1994, Congress passed the Violent Crime Control and Law Enforcement Act of 1994, Public Law 103-322. Title IX, Subtitle A, Section 110105 of this Act generally made it unlawful to manufacture, transfer, and possess semiautomatic assault weapons (SAWs) and to transfer and possess large capacity ammunition feeding devices (LCAFDs). The law also required importers and manufacturers to place certain markings on SAWs and LCAFDs, designating they were for export or law enforcement/ government use. Significantly, the law provided that it would expire 10 years from the date of enactment. Accordingly, effective 12:01 am on September 13, 2004, the provisions of the law ceased to apply and the following provisions of the regulations in Part 478 no longer apply:

- Section 478.11- Definitions of the terms "semiautomatic assault weapon" and "large capacity ammunition feeding device"
- Section 478.40- Entire section
- Section 478.40a- Entire section
- Section 478.57- Paragraphs (b) and (c)
- Section 478.92- Paragraph (a)(3) – [NOTE: Renumbered from paragraph (a)(2) to paragraph (a)(3) by TD ATF – 461 (66 FR 40596) on August 3, 2001]
- Section 478.92- Paragraph (c)
- Section 478.119- Entire section- [NOTE: An import permit is still needed pursuant to the Arms Export Control Act- see 27 CFR 447.41(a)]
- Section 478.132- Entire section
- Section 478.153- Entire section

NOTE: The references to "ammunition feeding device" in section 478.116 are not applicable on or after September 13, 2004.

NOTE: The references to "semiautomatic assault weapons" in section 478.171 are not applicable on or after September 13, 2004.

Information from ATF Online - Bureau of Alcohol, Tobacco and Firearms, an official site of the U.S. Department of Justice.

WAD

A shotgshell component in front of the powder charge and has a cup or flat surface that the

shot charge rests on. Various types of wads exist with the most common a column of plastic.

WADCUTTER BULLET

A flat nose bullet typically used for target shooting because it cuts an even hole in paper targets.

WEAVER-STYLE RAIL

A mounting rail system similar in dimensions and use as the Picatinny Rail. Weaver-style grooves

are .180" wide and do not always have consistent center-to-center widths. Most Weaver-style accessories

will fit the Picatinny system however Picatinny accessories will not fit the Weaver-style system.

Also see PICATINNY RAIL.

YOKE

See CRANE.

YOUTH DIMENSIONS

Usually refers to shorter stock dimensions and/or lighter weight enabling youth/women to shoot and carry a lighter, shorter firearm.

ZERO

The sight or scope settings of elevation and windage which make the point of aim and point of impact

in proper relation to each other at a given range.

ABBREVIATIONS

*	Banned due to 1994-2004 Crime Bill (may be current again)
A2	AR-15 Style/Configuration w/ fixed carry handle
A3	AR-15 Style/Configuration w/ detachable carry handle
ACOG	Advanced Combat Optical gunsight
ACP	Automatic Colt Pistol
adj.	Adjustable
AE	Automatic Ejectors or Action Express
AK	Avtomat Kalashnikova
AP	Armor Piercing
API	Armor Piercing Incendiary
APIT	Armor Piercing Incendiary Tracer
appts.	Appointments
AO	Adjustable Objective (Optics)
AR	Automatic Rifle
ATK	Alliant Techsystems Inc.
AWB	Assault Weapons Ban
B	Blue
BAC	Browning Arms Company
BATFE	Bureau of Alcohol, Tobacco, Firearms, and Explosives
BAN/CRIME BILL ERA	Mfg. between Nov. 1989 - Sept. 12, 2004
BBL	Barrel
BMG	Browning Machine Gun
BOSS	Ballistic Optimizing Shooting System
BP	Buttplate or Black Powder
BR	Bench Rest
BUIS	Back Up Iron Sight(s)
C/B 1994	Introduced because of 1994 Crime Bill
c.	Circa
cal.	Caliber
CCA	Colt Collectors Association
CF	Centerfire
CH	Cross Hair
CIP	Commission Internationale Permanente des Armes A Feu
COMM.	Commemorative
COMP	Compensated/Competition
C-R	Curio-Relic
CYL/C	Cylinder
DA	Double Action
DAO	Double Action Only
DCM	Director of Civilian Marksmanship
DISC or disc.	Discontinued
DN	Dynamit Nobel
DWM	Deutsche Waffen und Munitionsfabriken
EJT	Ejectors
EXC	Excellent
EXT	Extractors
F	Full Choke
F&M	Full & Modified
FA	Forearm
FAL	Fusil Automatique Leger
FC/FED	Federal Cartridge Company
FDL	Fleur-de-lis
FE	Fore End
FFL	Federal Firearms License
FIRSH	Free Floating Integrated Rail System Handguard
FMJ	Full Metal Jacket
FN	Fabrique Nationale
FP	Flat Point (Projectile)
FPE	Foot Pounds Energy
FPS	Feet Per Second
FS	Front Sight
ft-lbs.	Foot Pounds
g.	Gram
ga.	Gauge
GAP	Glock Automatic Pistol
gr.	Grain
GCA	Gun Control Act
GOVT	Government
HB	Heavy Barrel
HC	Hard Case
HK	Heckler und Koch
HMR	Hornady Magnum Rimfire
HP	Hollow Point
I	Improved
IC	Improved Cylinder
ICORE	International Confederation of Revolver Enthusiasts
IM	Improved Modified
IMI	Israel Military Industries
in.	Inch
intro.	Introduced
IPSC	International Practical Shooting Confederation
IR	Illuminated Reticle (Optics)
IR	Infrared (Optics)
ISSF	International Shooting Sports Federation
ISU	International Shooting Union
L	Long
lbs.	Pounds
LC	Long Colt
LCAFD	Large Capacity Ammunition Feeding Device
LEM	Law Enforcement Model
LEO	Law Enforcement Only
LER	Long Eye Relief (Optics)
LOP	Length of Pull
LPI	Lines Per Inch
LR	Long Range
LR	Long Rifle
LT	Long Tang or Light
M (MOD.)	Modified Choke
M-4	Newer AR-15/M16 Carbine Style/ Configuration
M&P	Military & Police
Mag.	Magnum Caliber
mag.	Magazine
MC	Monte Carlo
MFG or Mfg.	Manufactured/manufacture
mil.	Milradian
mil-dot	Milradian Dot (Optic Reticle)
MIL SPEC	Mfg. to Military Specifications
MK	Mark
mm	Millimeter
MOA	Minute of Angle
MR	Matted Rib
MSR	Manufacturer's Suggested Retail
MV	Muzzle Velocity
N	Nickel
N/A	Not Applicable or Not Available
NATO	North Atlantic Treaty Organization
NIB	New in Box
NICS	National Instant Criminal Background Check System
NM	National Match
no.	Number
NRA	National Rifle Association
NSSF	National Shooting Sports Foundation
NV	Night Vision
O/U	Over and Under
OA	Overall
OAL	Overall Length
OB	Octagon Barrel
OBO	Or Best Offer
OCT	Octagon
OEG	Occluded Eye Gunsight
oz.	Ounce
Para.	Parabellum
PFFR	Percantage of factory finish remaining
PG	Pistol Grip
POR/P.O.R.	Price on Request
POST-'89	Paramilitary mfg. after Federal legislation in Nov. 1989
POST-BAN	Refers to production after Sept. 12, 2004
PPC	Pindell Palmisano Cartridge
PPC	Police Pistol Competition
PPD	Post Paid
PRE-'89	Paramilitary mfg. before Federal legislation in Nov. 1989
PRE-BAN	Mfg. before September 13, 1994 per C/B or before Nov. 1989.
psi/PSI	Pounds Per Square Inch
QD	Quick Detachable
RAS	Rail Adapter System
RB	Round Barrel/Round Butt
RCM	Ruger Compact Magnum
RCMP	Royal Canadian Mounted Police
REC	Receiver
REM	Remington
REM. MAG.	Remington Magnum
RF	Rimfire
RFM	Rim Fire Magnum
RK	Round Knob
rpm	Rounds Per Minute
RR	Red Ramp
RS	Rear Sight
RSUM	Remington Short Ultra Magnum
RUM	Remington Ultra Magnum
RWS	Rheinisch-Westfalische Sprengstoff
S	Short
S&W	Smith & Wesson
S/N	Serial Number
SA	Single Action
SAAMI	Sporting Arms and Ammunition Manufacturers' Institute
SAUM	Short Action Ultra Magnum
SAW	Squad Automatic Weapon
SAW	Semiautomatic Assault Weapon
SB	Shotgun butt or Steel backstrap
ser.	serial
SG	Straight Grip
SIG	Schweizerische Industriegesellschaft
SIM	Special Impact Munition
SJ	Semi-Jacketed (Projectile)
SK	Skeet
sq.	Square
SMG	Submachine Gun
SMLE	Short Magazine Lee Enfield Rifle
SOCOM	Special Operations Command
SOPMOD	Special Operations Peculiar Modification
SPC	Special Purpose Cartridge
SPEC	Special
SPG	Semi-Pistol Grip
Spl.	Special
SPLLAT	Special Purpose Low Lethality Anti Terrorist (Munition)
SR	Solid Rib
SS	Single Shot or Stainless Steel
SSA	Super Short Action
SST	Single Selective Trigger
ST	Single Trigger
STANAG	Standardization Agreement (Nato)
SWAT	Special Weapons Assault Team
SWAT	Special Weapons and Tactics
SxS	Side by Side
TBA	To be Announced
TD	Take Down
TDA	Traditional Double Action
TGT	Target
TH	Target Hammer
TS	Target Stocks
TSOB	Scope mount rail Weaver type
TT	Target Trigger
UIT	Union Internationale de Tir
UMC	Union Metallic Cartridge (Company)
USAMU	U.S. Army Marksmanship Unit
USPSA	United States Practical Shooting Association
var.	Variable
VAT	Value Added Tax
VG	Very Good
VR	Ventilated Rib
w/	with
w/o	without
WBY	Weatherby
WC	Wad Cutter
WCF	Winchester Center Fire
WD	Wood
WFF	Watch For Fakes
WIN	Winchester
WO	White Outline
WRA	Winchester Repeating Arms Co.
WRM	Winchester Rimfire Magnum
WSL	Winchester Self-Loading
WSM	Winchester Short Magnum
WSSM	Winchester Super Short Magnum
WSUM	Winchester Short Ultra Magnum
wt.	Weight
WW	World War
X (1X)	Extra Full Choke Tube
XX (2X)	Extra Extra Full Choke Tube

NATIONAL RIFLE ASSOCIATION OF AMERICA

Help NRA Fight *for* You

JOIN TODAY

NRA membership is regularly $35 per year. But if you act today, we'll sign you up for a full year of NRA membership for just $25!

Name: _____

First   Last   M.I.

Address: _____

City: _____ State: _____ Zip: _____ D.O.B. _____/_____/_____

Phone: _____ E-mail: _____

Magazine choice: ❑ *American Rifleman*   ❑ *American Hunter*   ❑ *America's 1ST Freedom*   XR012415

Please enclose $25 for your One-Year Membership

❑ Check or money order enclosed, payable to: "NRA"   ❑ Please charge my: ❑ *VISA*   ❑ *MasterCard*   ❑ *AMERICAN EXPRESS*   ❑ *DISCOVER*

Card Number [ ]   Exp. Date [ ][ ] / [ ][ ]
                                                          MO   YR

Signature: _____

NRA

Freedom through Strength

To join instantly call 1-800-672-0004

Mail application with payment to:
National Rifle Association of America
c/o Recruiting Programs Department
11250 Waples Mill Road
Fairfax, VA 22030

Contributions, gifts or membership dues made or paid to the National Rifle Association of America are not refundable or transferable and are not deductible as charitable contributions for Federal income tax purposes. International memberships: add $5 for Canadian and $10 for all other countries. Please allow 4 - 6 weeks for membership processing. This membership offer can not be combined with any other discounts or offers.

GRADING CRITERIA

The old, NRA method of firearms grading – relying upon adjectives such as "Excellent" or "Fair" – has served the firearms community for a many years. Today's dealers/collectors, especially those who deal in modern guns, have turned away from the older subjective system. There is too much variance within some of the older subjective grades, therefore making accurate grading difficult.

Most dealers and collectors are now utilizing what is essentially an objective method for deciding the condition of a gun: THE PERCENTAGE OF ORIGINAL FACTORY FINISH(ES) REMAINING ON THE GUN. After looking critically at a variety of firearms and carefully studying the Photo Percentage Grading System™ (available free of charge on our website: www.bluebookinc.com or on pages 33-110 in the 31st Edition of the *Blue Book of Gun Values*), it will soon become evident if a specific a gun has 98%, 90%, 70% or less finish remaining. Remember, sometimes an older gun described as NIB can actually be 98% or less condition, simply because of the wear accumulated by taking it in and out of the box and handling it too many times. Every gun's unique condition factor – and therefore the price – is best determined by the percentage of original finish(es) remaining, with the key consideration being the overall frame/receiver finish. The key word here is "original", for if anyone other than the factory has refinished the gun, its value as a collector's item has been diminished, with the exception of rare and historical pieces that have been properly restored. Every year, top quality restorations have become more accepted, and prices have gone up proportionately with the quality of the workmanship. Also popular now are antique finishes, and a new question has come up, "what is 100% antique finish on new reproductions?" Answer – a gun that started out as new, and then has been aged to a lower condition factor to duplicate natural wear and tear.

It is important to remember that most tactical firearms have either a parkerized, phosphated, matte black, or camouflaged finish which is very durable and resistant to wear and extreme weather conditions. Because of this, observing wear on the breech block, internal firing mechanism, and in the barrel may be the only way to accurately determine condition as these black/camo wonders get used, since most of them are all going to look 98% or better from the outside!

Every gun's unique condition factor – and therefore the price – is best determined by the percentage of original finish(es) remaining, with the key consideration being the overall frame/receiver finish. The key word here is "original", for if anyone other than the factory has refinished the gun, its value as a collector's item has been diminished, with the exception of rare and historical pieces that have been properly restored.

Note where the finishes of a firearm typically wear off first. These are usually places where the gun accumulates wear from holster/case rubbing, and contact with the hands or body over an extended period of time. A variety of firearms have been shown in four-color to guarantee that your "sampling size" for observing finishes with their correct colors is as diversified as possible.

It should be noted that the older a collectible firearm is, the smaller the percentage of original finish one can expect to find. Some very old and/or very rare firearms are sought by collectors in almost any condition!

For your convenience, NRA Condition Standards are listed on page 37. Converting from this grading system to percentages can now be done accurately. Remember the price is wrong if the condition factor isn't right!

GRADING SYSTEM CONVERSION GUIDELINES

New/Perfect   100% condition with or without box. 100% on currently manufactured firearms assumes NIB (New In Box) condition and not sold previously at retail.

Mint   typically 98%-99% condition, depending on the age of the firearm. Probably sold previously at retail, and may have been shot occasionally.

Excellent   95%+ - 98% condition (typically).

Very Good   80% - 95% condition (all parts/finish should be original).

Good   60% - 80% condition (all parts/finish should be original).

Fair   20% - 60% condition (all parts/finish may or may not be original, but must function properly and shoot).

Poor   under 20% condition (shooting not a factor).

NRA CONDITION STANDARDS

The NRA conditions listed below have been provided as guidelines to assist the reader in converting and comparing condition factors. In order to use this book correctly, the reader is urged to examine these images of NRA condition standards. Once the gun's condition has been accurately assessed, only then can values be accurately ascertained.

NRA MODERN CONDITION DESCRIPTIONS

New - not previously sold at retail, in same condition as current factory production.

Perfect - in new condition in every respect.

Excellent - new condition, used but little, no noticeable marring of wood or metal, bluing near perfect (except at muzzle or sharp edges).

Very Good - in perfect working condition, no appreciable wear on working surfaces, no corrosion or pitting, only minor surface dents or scratches.

Good - in safe working condition, minor wear on working surfaces, no broken parts, no corrosion or pitting that will interfere with proper functioning.

Fair - in safe working condition, but well worn, perhaps requiring replacement of minor parts or adjustments which should be indicated in advertisement, no rust, but may have corrosion pits which do not render article unsafe or inoperable.

NRA ANTIQUE CONDITION DESCRIPTIONS

Factory New - all original parts; 100% original finish; in perfect condition in every respect, inside and out.

Excellent - all original parts; over 80% original finish; sharp lettering, numerals and design on metal and wood; unmarred wood; fine bore.

Fine - all original parts; over 30% original finish; sharp lettering, numerals and design on metal and wood; minor marks in wood; good bore.

Very Good - all original parts; none to 30% original finish; original metal surfaces smooth with all edges sharp; clear lettering, numerals and design on metal; wood slightly scratched or bruised; bore disregarded for collectors firearms.

Good – less than 20% original finish, some minor replacement parts; metal smoothly rusted or lightly pitted in places, cleaned or reblued; principal lettering, numerals and design on metal legible; wood refinished, scratched, bruised or minor cracks repaired; in good working order.

Fair – less than 10% original finish, some major parts replaced; minor replacement parts may be required; metal rusted, may be lightly pitted all over, vigorously cleaned or reblued; rounded edges of metal and wood; principal lettering, numerals and design on metal partly obliterated; wood scratched, bruised, cracked or repaired where broken; in fair working order or can be easily repaired and placed in working order.

Poor – little or no original finish remaining, major and minor parts replaced; major replacement parts required and extensive restoration needed; metal deeply pitted; principal lettering, numerals and design obliterated, wood badly scratched, bruised, cracked or broken; mechanically inoperative, generally undesirable as a collector's firearm.

PPGS – FIREARMS GRADING MADE EASY

During the past 20 years, the firearms industry has adopted the Photo Percentage Grading System™ (PPGS) as the standard for accurately grading firearms condition factors. The newest PPGS appears in the 31st Edition of the *Blue Book of Gun Values*, and has not been included in this text, as much of it does not apply to tactical firearms. However, if you are interested in seeing the color PPGS, please visit www.bluebookinc.com and click on the Firearms home page, then on the Photo Percentage Grading System™ link.

If you carefully study all the images, and thoroughly read the accompanying captions, the color images will help you accurately determine condition better than anything that's ever been printed or written. This revised Photo Percentage Grading System™ (PPGS) includes images of both NRA new and antique condition factors, in addition to all the 100%-10% percentage conditions for revolvers, pistols, rifles, and shotguns.

Condition factors pictured (indicated by PPGS-o-meters), unless otherwise noted, refer to the percentage of a gun's remaining finish(es), including blue, case colors, nickel, or another type of original finish remaining on the frame/receiver. On older guns, describing the receiver/frame finish accurately is absolutely critical to ascertain an accurate grade, which will determine the correct value.

Additional percentages of condition may be used to describe other specific parts of a gun (i.e. barrel, wood finish, plating, magazine tube, etc.). Percentages of patina/brown or other finish discoloration factors must also be explained separately when necessary, and likewise be interpolated accurately. **With antiques, the overall percentage within this text is NOT an average of the various condition factors, but, again, refers to the overall original condition of the frame/receiver. Being able to spot original condition has never been more important, especially when the prices get into four, five, and six figures.** Remember, the price is wrong if the condition factor isn't right.

Now, more than ever, it takes well-trained senses of sight, hearing, touch, and smell, and a corresponding connection to the most powerful computer ever built, a trained human brain, to accurately fingerprint a gun's correct condition factor. Regardless of how much knowledge you've accumulated from books, websites, auction catalogs, dealer listings, etc., you're still in potential danger as a buyer if you can't figure out a gun's condition factor(s) accurately. More than anything else, an older gun's overall condition must "add up" (i.e., a crispy looking Steyr Aug should not have a worn out bore).

While the Photo Percentage Grading System™ certainly isn't meant to be the Last Testament on firearms grading, it hopefully goes a lot further than anything else published on the subject. Once you've accumulated the experience necessary to grade guns accurately, a ten-second "CAT scan" is usually all the time that is needed to zero in on each gun's unique condition factor.

Sincerely,

S.P. Fjestad
Author & Publisher - *Blue Book of Tactical Firearms*

A SECTION

A.A. ARMS INC.

Previous manufacturer located in Monroe, NC until 1999.

MSR	100%	98%	95%	90%	80%	70%	60%

CARBINES: SEMI-AUTO

AR9 CARBINE – similar action to AP9, except has carbine length barrel and side-folding metal stock. Banned 1994.

	$750	$625	$550	$475	$400	$350	$300

PISTOLS: SEMI-AUTO

AP9 MINI-SERIES PISTOL – 9mm Para. cal., semi-auto blowback tactical design, phosphate/blue or nickel finish, 2 barrel lengths, 10- (C/B 1994) or 20*-shot mag. Disc. 1999, parts cleanup during 2000.

	$425	$375	$325	$275	$225	$200	$175	Last MSR was $245.

Add $20 for nickel finish.
Add $200 for AP9 long barrel Target Model (banned 1994).

A & B HIGH PERFORMANCE FIREARMS

Previous competition pistol manufacturer located in Arvin, CA.

PISTOLS: SEMI-AUTO

OPEN CLASS – 9mm Para. or .38 Super cal., single action, competition M1911-styled action, STI frame, Ultimatch or Hybrid compensated barrel, Caspian slide, C-More scope, blue or chrome finish.

	$2,800	$2,300	$1,875	$1,600	$1,375	$1,000	$750	Last MSR was $2,800.

A.R. SALES

Previous manufacturer located in South El Monte, CA, circa 1968-1977.

RIFLES: SEMI-AUTO

MARK IV SPORTER – .308 Win. cal., semi-auto, M-14 style action, adj. sights. Approx. 200 mfg.

	$725	$650	$575	$500	$450	$400	$350

AKS (AK-47, AK-74, & AKM COPIES)

Select fire tactical design rifle originally designed in Russia (initials refer to Avtomat Kalashnikova, 1947). The AK-47 was officially adopted by Russia in 1949. Russian-manufactured select fire AK-47s have not been manufactured since the mid-1950s. Semi-auto AK-47 and AKM clones are currently manufactured by several arsenals in China including Norinco and Poly Technologies, Inc. (currently illegal to import), in addition to being manufactured in other countries including the Czech Republic, Bulgaria, Russia, Egypt, and Hungary. On April 6th, 1998, recent "sporterized" variations (imported 1994-1998) with thumbhole stocks were banned by presidential order. Beginning in 2000, AK-47s were being assembled in the U.S., using both newly manufactured and older original military parts and components.

AK-47s are not rare - over 100 million have been manufactured by Russia and China since WWII.

AK/AK-47/AKM HISTORY & RECENT IMPORTATION

Since the early 1950s, the AK/AK-47/AKM series of select fire rifles has been the standard issue military rifle of the former Soviet Union and its satellites. It continues to fulfill that role reliably today. The AK series of rifles, from the early variants of the AK-47 through the AKM and AK-74, is undoubtedly the most widely used military small arms design in the world. Developed by Mikhail Kalashnikov (the AK stands for Avtomat Kalashnikova) in 1946, the AK went into full production in 1947 in Izhevsk, Russia. In 1953, the milled receiver was put into mass production. Since then, variants of the original AK-47 have been manufactured by almost every former Soviet bloc country and some free world nations, including Egypt. The AK action is the basis for numerous other weapons, including the RPK (Ruchnoy Pulemyot Kalashnikova).

The AK-47 was replaced in 1959 by the AKM, and retained the same basic design. The rifle was simply updated to incorporate easier and more efficient production methods, using a stamped, sheet metal receiver that was pinned and riveted in place, rather than a milled receiver. Other changes included a beavertail forearm, muzzle compensator, and an anti-bounce device intended to improve controllability and increase accuracy.

The AK was designed to be, and always has been, a "peasant-proof" military weapon. It is a robust firearm, both in design and function. Its record on the battlefields around the world is impressive, rivaled only by the great M1 Garand of the U.S. or bolt rifles

MSR	100%	98%	95%	90%	80%	70%	60%

such as the English Mark III Enfield. The original AK-47 prototypes are on display in the Red Army Museum in Moscow.

All of the current semi-auto AK "clones" are copies of the AKM's basic receiver design and internal components minus the full-auto parts. The Saiga rifle (see separate listing), manufactured by the Izhevsk Machining Plant, in Izhevsk, Russia, is the sole Russian entry into this market. It is available in the standard 7.62x39 mm, 5.45x39 mm (disc.) and 20 gauge or .410 bore. Molot (hammer) JSC also exports semi-automatic AKs to the U.S. under the trade name Vepr. (see separate listing). Both the Saiga and Vepr. are imported and distributed by Robinson Armaments. Molot was the home of the PPSh-41 sub-machine gun during WWII, and also manufactured the RPK and the RPK-74. Other AK European manufacturers include companies in the Czech Republic, Bulgaria, and the former Yugoslavia. The Egyptian-made Maahdi AK clones were also available in the U.S. market.

Interest in the Kalashnikov design is at an all-time high due to the availability of high quality military AK-74, AKS-74, AKS-74U, and RPK-74 parts kits. Some models, such as those produced by Marc Krebs, are of very high quality. Currently, it is hard to go to a gun show or page through a buy/sell firearms magazine and not see a variety of parts, accessories, and high capacity magazines available for many of the AK variants. For shooters, the value represented by these guns is undeniable for the price point.

Values for almost all of the imported AK clones are based solely on their use as sporting or target rifles. Fit and finish varies by country and importer. Most fall on the "low" side. Interest peaked prior to the passage of the 1994 Crime Bill and both AK clones and their "high capacity" magazines were bringing a premium for a short period of time in 1993 and 1994. However, interest waned during 1995-97, and the reduced demand lowered prices. In November of 1997, the Clinton Administration instituted an "administrative suspension" on all import licenses for these types of firearms in order to do a study on their use as "sporting firearms."

On April 6th, 1998, the Clinton Administration, in the political wake of the Jonesboro tragedy, banned the further import of 58 "assault-type" rifles, claiming that these semi-automatics could not be classified as sporting weapons - the AK-47 and most related configurations were included. During 1997, firearms importers obtained permits to import almost 600,000 reconfigured rifles - approximately only 20,000 had entered the country when this ban took effect. When the ban began, applications were pending to import an additional 1,000,000 guns. Previously, thumbhole-stocked AK Sporters were still legal for import, and recent exporters included the Czech Republic, Russia, and Egypt.

PISTOLS: SEMI-AUTO, AK-47 VARIATIONS

AK-47 PISTOLS – 7.62x39mm, or .223 Rem. cal., patterned after the AK-47 rifle/carbine, barrel length approx. 12 1/4, but can vary according to mfg., typically wood furniture, 5 to 30 shot mag. (depends on configuration), adj. rear sight, pistol grip, parkerized finish most common, recent Romanian mfg., approx. 5 lbs.

$375	$325	$295	$275	$250	$225	$200

RIFLES: SEMI-AUTO, AK-47, AK-74, & AKM MODELS

"AK-47" technically designates the original select fire (semi-automatic or fully automatic), Russian-made military rifle with a milled receiver. Recent semi-automatic "clones" normally have stamped receivers and are technically designated AKMs. Recently manufactured AK-47 clones refer to rifles with milled receivers. Chinese importation stopped during late 1990.

Also refer to separate listings under Poly Technologies, Inc., Norinco, Federal Ordnance, B-West, K.B.I., Sentinel Arms, American Arms, Inc., and others who have imported this configuration.

AK-47 (AKM) – 7.62x39mm (most common cal., former Russian M43 military), 5.45x39mm (Romanian mfg. or Saiga/MAK - recent mfg. only), or .223 Rem. cal., semi-auto Kalashnikov action, stamped (most common) or milled receiver, typically 16 1/2 in. barrel, 5-shot, 10-shot, or 30*-shot (C/B 1994) mag., wood or synthetic stock and forearm except on folding stock model, recent importation (1994-early 1998) mostly had newer "sporterized" fixed stocks with thumbholes, may be supplied with bayonet, sling, cleaning kit, patterned after former military production rifle of China and Russia.

* **AK-47 Pre-1998 Mfg./Importation** – 7.62x39mm (most common cal., former Russian M43 military), 5.45x39mm (Romanian mfg. or Saiga/MAK - recent mfg. only), or .223 Rem. cal., semi-auto Kalashnikov action, stamped (most common) or milled receiver, typically 16 1/2 in. barrel, 5-shot, 10-shot, or 30*-shot (C/B 1994) mag., wood or synthetic stock and forearm except on folding stock model, recent importation (1994-early 1998) mostly had newer "sporterized" fixed stocks with thumbholes, may be supplied with bayonet, sling, cleaning kit, patterned after former military production rifle of China and Russia.

	100%	98%	95%	90%	80%	70%	60%
Romanian mfg.	$450	$395	$350	$325	$295	$275	$250
Yugoslavian mfg.	$795	$725	$675	$575	$450	$425	$400
Hungarian mfg.	$795	$725	$675	$575	$450	$425	$400
Czech mfg.	$795	$725	$675	$575	$450	$425	$400
Bulgarian mfg.	$795	$725	$675	$575	$450	$425	$400
Egyptian mfg.	$650	$600	$550	$450	$400	$365	$335

Add 20% for milled receiver.

MSR		100%	98%	95%	90%	80%	70%	60%

Add 10% for chrome-lined barrel.
Add 10% for older folding stock variations.
Add 10%-15% for 5.45x39 mm cal. on Eastern European mfg. (non-recent import).

* ***AK-47 Post 1998 Mfg./Importation*** – most AK-47s manufactured/imported after 1998 utilize plastic/synthetic furniture, stamped receivers, and folding/telescoping stocks which have different components and construction from those rifles/carbines produced before 1998. Recent U.S. assembly refers to an original stamped European (mostly FEG) or milled receiver with U.S. assembly, using either new parts or matched, older unused original Eastern European-manufactured parts (BATF 922.R compliant). This newest generation of AK-47s typically have features as described above, and cannot be sold in several states. Check city and state laws regarding high capacity magazine compliance.

Most recently imported and/or assembled AK-47s are currently selling in the $375 - $475 range. Additional AK-47 listings can be found under current individual manufacturers and importers listed separately in this text (i.e., Arsenal Inc., Century International, Interarms, etc.).

AK-74 – 5.45x39mm cal., semi-auto action based on the AKM, imported from Bulgaria and other previous Eastern bloc countries, in addition to recent assembly in the U.S., using FEG receivers, Bulgarian parts sets, and additional U.S.-made components.

	100%	98%	95%	90%	80%	70%	60%
Bulgarian mfg.	$700	$650	$600	$525	$450	$400	$350
Recent U.S. assembly	$650	$575	$500	$425	$350	$300	$275

A M A C

See the "Iver Johnson" section in this text. AMAC stands for American Military Arms Corporation. Manufactured in Jacksonville, AR. AMAC ceased operations in early 1993.

A.M.S.D. (ADVANCED MILITARY SYSTEM DESIGN)

Current manufacturer located in Geneva, Switzerland. Currently distributed beginning 2010 by Loki Weapon Systems, located in Coalgate, OK.

RIFLES: BOLT ACTION

A.M.S.D. manufactures the OM 50 Nemesis tactical rifle in a variety of configurations and options. The base rifle features a 27 1/2 in. barrel, high performance muzzle brake, bipod, box mag., Picatinny top and side rails, adj. folding stock, adj. two-stage trigger, extended forend, adj. ground spike, scope rings, field cleaning kit, tool kit, and fitted storage case. A variety of options are available, including barrel length, stock, and finish. A.M.S.D. also manufactures a Tacten rifle in .338 Lapua cal., with tactical stock, bipod, two 10 shot mags., muzzle brake, two-stage trigger, cleaning kit and case. A variety of Picatinny rail options are available, as well as scopes. Prices are POR. Please contact the distributor directly for pricing and U.S. availability (see Trademark Index).

AMP TECHNICAL SERVICE GmbH

Previous manufacturer located in Puchheim, Germany. Previously imported and distributed 2001-2004 by CQB Products, located in Tustin, CA.

RIFLES: BOLT ACTION

DSR-1 – .300 Win. Mag., .308 Win., or .338 Lapua cal., bolt action, bull pup design with in-line stock, receiver is made from aluminum, titanium, and polymers, internal parts are stainless steel, two-stage adj. trigger, 4- or 5-shot mag., 25.6 Lothar Walther fluted barrel with muzzlebrake and vent. shroud, includes bipod, ambidextrous 3-position safety, 13 lbs. Imported 2002-2004.

$7,295	$6,300	$5,200	$4,100	$3,000	$2,500	$2,000	Last MSR was $7,795.

Add $100 for .300 Win. Mag. cal.
Add $300 for .338 Lapua cal.

AR-7 INDUSTRIES, LLC

Previous manufacturer 1998-2004, and located in Geneseo, IL. Previously located in Meriden, CT, from 1998 to early 2004.

In February 2004, AR-7 Industries LLC was purchased by ArmaLite, Inc., and recent manufacture was in Geneseo, IL.

RIFLES: BOLT ACTION

AR-7 TAKEDOWN – .22 LR cal., bolt action variation of the AR-7 Explorer rifle, similar takedown/storage configuration, 2 1/2 lbs. Advertised 2002 only.

While advertised during 2002, this model was never manufactured.

MSR	100%	98%	95%	90%	80%	70%	60%

RIFLES: SEMI-AUTO

AR-7 EXPLORER RIFLE – .22 LR cal., takedown barrelled action stores in synthetic stock which floats, 8-shot mag., aperture rear sight, 16 in. barrel (synthetic sleeve with steel liner), black matte finish on AR-7, silvertone on AR-7S (disc. 2000), camouflage finish on AR-7C, two-tone (silver receiver with black stock and barrel) on AR-7T (disc. 2000), walnut finish on AR-W (mfg. 2001-2002), stowed length 16 1/2 in., 2 1/2 lbs. Mfg. late 1998-2004.

	$175	$150	$125	$110	$100	$90	$80	Last MSR was $200.

Add $15 for camouflage or walnut finish.

This model was also previously manufactured by Survival Arms, Inc. and Charter Arms - see individual listings for information.

AR-7 SPORTER (AR-20) – .22 LR cal., 16 1/2 in. steel barrel with vent. aluminum shroud, metal skeleton fixed stock with pistol grip, 8 (new 2001) or 16 shot "flip clip" (optional) mag., 3.85 lbs. Mfg. late 1998-2004.

	$175	$150	$125	$110	$100	$90	$80	Last MSR was $200.

Add $100 for sporter conversion kit (includes aluminum shrouded barrel, pistol grip stock, and 16 shot flip clip).

This model was also previously manufactured by Survival Arms, Inc. - see individual listing for information.

AR-7 TARGET – .22 LR cal., 16 in. bull barrel with 7/8 in. cantilever scope mount, tube stock with pistol grip, 8-shot mag., 3-9x40mm compact rubber armored scope was optional, 5.65 lbs. Mfg. 2002-2004.

	$195	$175	$150	$125	$105	$95	$80	Last MSR was $210.

Add $60 for compact scope.

ACCU-MATCH INTERNATIONAL INC.

Previous handgun and pistol parts manufacturer located in Mesa, AZ circa 1996.

PISTOLS: SEMI-AUTO

ACCU-MATCH PISTOL – .45 ACP cal., patterned after the Colt Govt. 1911, competition pistol features stainless steel construction with 5 1/2 in. match grade barrel with 3 ports, recoil reduction system, 8-shot mag., 3-dot sight system. Approx. 160 mfg. 1996 only.

	$795	$700	$625	$550	$450	$375	$325	Last MSR was $840.

ACCURACY INTERNATIONAL LTD.

Current rifle manufacturer located in Hampshire, England since 1978, with offices in Fredericksburg, VA. Currently distributed by Mile High Shooting Accessories, located in Broomfield, CO, SRT Supply, located in St. Petersburg, FL, and Tac Pro Shooting Center, located in Mingus, TX. Previously imported by Accuracy International North America, located in Orchard Park, NY until circa 2005, and 1998-2005 in Oak Ridge, TN. Also previously imported until 1998 by Gunsite Training Center, located in Paulden, AZ.

RIFLES: BOLT ACTION

In addition to the models listed below, Accuracy International also makes military and law enforcement rifles, including the SR98 Australian, G22 German, and the Dutch SLA.

On Models AE, AW, AWP, and AWM listed below, many options and configurations are available which will add to the base prices listed.

Add $255 for Picatinny rail on all currently manufactured rifles (standard on Model AE and AW50).

AE MODEL – .308 Win. cal., similar to AWP Model, 5-shot mag., 20 or 24 in. stainless barrel, Harris bipod attachment point, four sling attachment points, Picatinny rail, approx. 8 1/2 lbs. Importation began 2002.

MSR $3,369	$3,150	$2,650	$2,325	$1,950	$1,675	$1,425	$1,200

Add $307 for adj. cheekpiece or $422 for folding stock.
Add $333 for 20 in. barrel with threaded standard muzzle brake.

AW MODEL – .243 Win. (new 2000), .308 Win., or .338 Lapua cal., precision bolt action featuring 20, 24, 26, or 27 in. 1:12 twist stainless steel barrel with or w/o muzzle brake, 3-lug bolt, 10-shot detachable mag., green synthetic folding (military/LE only) thumbhole adj. stock, AI bipod, 14 lbs. Importation began 1995.

MSR $5,587	$5,150	$4,400	$3,800	$3,300	$2,750	$2,150	$1,800

Add $376 for AW-F Model (disc. 2002).
Add $339 for fluted barrel.

AWP MODEL – similar to AW Model, except has 20 or 24 in. barrel w/o muzzle brake, 15 lbs. Imported 1995-2007.

	$4,250	$3,650	$3,150	$2,650	$2,150	$1,800	$1,500	Last MSR was $4,600.

Add $310 for AWP-F Model (disc. 2002).

AWM MODEL (SUPER MAGNUM) – .300 Win. Mag. or .338 Lapua cal., 6-lug bolt, 26 or 27 in. 1:9/1:10 twist stainless steel fluted barrel with muzzle brake, 5-shot mag., 15 1/2 lbs. Imported 1995-2009.

	$5,600	$5,100	$4,675	$3,800	$2,950	$2,500	$1,750	Last MSR was $5,900.

MSR	100%	98%	95%	90%	80%	70%	60%

Add $100 for .338 Lapua cal.
Add $324 for AWM-F Model (disc. 2002).

PALMAMASTER – .308 Win. cal., available with either NRA prone or UIT style stock, 30 in. stainless steel fluted barrel, designed for competition shooting, laminated stock. Disc. 2002.

| | $2,600 | $2,350 | $2,100 | $1,900 | $1,700 | $1,500 | $1,250 | Last MSR was $2,850. |

CISMMASTER – .22 BR, 6mm BR, .243 Win., .308 Win., 6.5x55mm, or 7.5x55mm cal., designed for slow and rapid fire international and military shooting competition, 10-shot mag., 2-stage trigger. Disc. 2002.

| | $3,175 | $2,850 | $2,600 | $2,350 | $2,100 | $1,900 | $1,700 | Last MSR was $3,480. |

VARMINT RIFLE – .22 Middlested, .22 BR, .22-250 Rem., .223 Rem., 6mm BR, .243 Win., .308 Win., or 7mm-08 Rem. cal., features 26 in. fluted stainless steel barrel. Mfg. 1997-2002.

| | $3,200 | $2,725 | $2,350 | $1,950 | $1,675 | $1,475 | $1,300 | Last MSR was $3,650. |

AW50 – .50 BMG, advanced ergonomic design, features built-in anti-recoil system, 5-shot mag., adj. third supporting leg, folding stock, 27 in. fluted barrel with muzzle brake, Picatinny rail, approx. 30 lbs. New 1998.

| MSR $13,096 | $12,500 | $10,500 | $8,750 | $7,500 | $6,250 | $4,950 | $3,750 | |

ACTION ARMS LTD.

Previous firearms importer and distributor until 1994, located in Philadelphia, PA.

Only Action Arms Models AT-84S, AT-88S, and the Model B Sporter will be listed under this heading. Galil, Timberwolf, and Uzi trademarks can be located in their respective sections.

CARBINES: SEMI-AUTO

MODEL B SPORTER – 9mm Para. cal., patterned after the original Uzi Model B Sporter, 16.1 in. barrel, fires from closed bolt, thumbhole stock with recoil pad, 10-shot mag., adj. rear sight, 8.8 lbs. Limited importation from China 1994 only.

| | $695 | $625 | $550 | $475 | $435 | $385 | $335 | Last MSR was $595. |

ACTION LEGENDS MFG., INC.

Previous manufacturer, importer, and distributor until circa 2006 and located in Houston, TX.

RIFLES

MODEL 888 M1 CARBINE – .22 LR or .30 Carbine cal., 18 in. barrel, mfg. from new original M1 parts and stock and unused GI parts, 10-, 15-, or 30-shot mag., choice of birch or walnut stock, parkerized finish, metal or wood handguard, 5 1/2 lbs.

| | $675 | $625 | $550 | $495 | $425 | $375 | $325 | Last MSR was $650. |

Add $11 for .22 LR cal.
Add $31 for walnut/metal forearm or $47 for walnut/wood forearm.

MODEL 1903 SPRINGFIELD – .30-06 cal., 24 in. barrel, bolt action, mfg. from new and original GI parts, 5-shot mag., parkerized finish, wood stock, canvas sling.

While previously advertised at a $950 MSR, only a few prototypes were manufactured.

ADCO SALES INC.

Current importer of Diamond shotguns manufactured by Vega in Istanbul, Turkey, and accessory manufacturer established circa 1981, and currently located in Woburn, MA. Dealer sales.

SHOTGUNS: SLIDE ACTION

All Adco slide action shotguns were manufactured in Turkey.

MARINER MODEL – 12 ga., 3 in. chamber, choice of 18 1/2 plain or 22 in. VR barrel with chokes, 5-shot mag., black synthetic stock and forearm. Imported 2003-2006.

| | $250 | $225 | $200 | $175 | $150 | $135 | $110 | Last MSR was $319. |

ALCHEMY ARMS COMPANY

Previous manufacturer located in Auburn, WA, 1999-circa 2006.

PISTOLS: SEMI-AUTO

SPECTRE STANDARD ISSUE (SI) – 9mm Para., .40 S&W, or .45 ACP cal., single action full size design, hammerless firing mechanism, linear action trigger, keyed internal locking device, aluminum receiver with 4 1/2 in. match grade

MSR	100%	98%	95%	90%	80%	70%	60%

stainless steel barrel and slide, tactical rail, various silver/black finishes, lowered ejection port, 10-shot double column mag, 32 oz. Mfg. 2000-2006.

	$675	$585	$525	$465	$415	$350	$300	Last MSR was $749.

SPECTRE SERVICE GRADE (SG & SGC) – similar to Spectre Standard Issue, except does not have tactical rail and rounded trigger guard, SGC is Commander style with 4 in. barrel and weighs 27 oz. Mfg. 2000-2006, SGC mfg. 2001-2006.

	$675	$585	$525	$465	$415	$350	$300	Last MSR was $749.

SPECTRE TITANIUM EDITION (TI/TIC) – similar to Spectre Series, except features a titanium slide with aluminum receiver, 22 (TIC is Commander style) or 24 oz. Mfg. 2000-2006.

	$895	$775	$675	$575	$500	$450	$395	Last MSR was $999.

ALEXANDER ARMS LLC

Current manufacturer located in Radford, VA. Law enforcement, military, dealer, and consumer sales.

RIFLES: SEMI-AUTO

Add $130 for Shilen barrel.

.50 BEOWULF – .50 Beowulf cal., AR-15 styling, shoots 300-400 grain bullet at approx. 1,800 feet per second, forged upper and lower receiver, 7-shot mag., rotary locking bolt and gas delay mechanism, various configurations include Entry, Over Match kit, Over Match Plus kit, Over Match Tactical kit, Precision Entry, Precision kit, AWS, and Law Enforcement (POR). New 2002.

* *Beowulf Overwatch .50* – similar to .50 Beowulf, except has 24 in. stainless steel barrel, extended range model, shoots 334 grain bullet at approx. 2,000 feet per second, 9 1/4 lbs. Mfg. 2004-2005.

	$1,550	$1,355	$1,160	$1,055	$850	$695	$540	Last MSR was $1,789.

* *Beowulf Entry 16* – .50 Beowulf cal., 16 in. barrel, mid length hand guard, Picatinny rail, 7 shot mag., black or coyote brown stock.

MSR $1,250	$1,195	$1,045	$895	$800	$655	$540	$420

* *Beowulf Precision 16* – .50 Beowulf cal., 161/2 in. chromemoly barrel, composite free float hand guards, Picatinny rail, low profile gas block, 7 shot mag., black stock.

MSR $1,350	$1,295	$1,135	$970	$880	$710	$585	$455

* *Beowulf AWS 16 (Advanced Weapons System)* – .50 Beowulf cal., 16 in. barrel, four rail hand guard system, Picatinny rail, black stock, 7 shot mag., includes soft carry bag.

MSR $1,450	$1,375	$1,200	$1,025	$930	$755	$615	$480

* *Beowulf Overmatch Plus* – .50 Beowulf cal., 16 1/5 in. chromemoly barrel, flattop receiver, detachable iron sights, mid-length hand guard, Picatinny rail, 7 shot mag., rear carry handle, black stock.

MSR $1,450	$1,375	$1,200	$1,025	$930	$755	$615	$480

* *Beowulf 24 Overwatch* – .50 Beowulf cal., 24 in. barrel, full length free float handguard, standard trigger and buttstock, Picatinny rail. Disc. 2009.

	$1,775	$1,555	$1,330	$1,200	$975	$800	$620	Last MSR was $1,789.

GENGHIS – 5.45x39mm cal., M-4 styling with 16 in. stainless steel barrel, forged upper and lower receiver, 10-shot mag., various configurations with last MSRs included Entry ($1,066 MSR), Over Match kit ($1,158 MSR), Over Match Plus kit ($1,267 MSR), and Over Match Tactical kit ($1,372 MSR). Mfg. 2002-2005.

6.5 GRENDEL – 6.5 Grendel cal., M-4 styling with 18 1/2, 19, 20, or 24 in. stainless steel barrel, 10-shot mag. New 2004.

* *Grendel Overwatch 6.5* – 6.5 Grendel cal., 24 in. stainless steel barrel with match chamber, extremely accurate, forged and hard anodized upper and lower receiver. Mfg. 2004-disc.

	$1,375	$1,200	$1,030	$935	$755	$620	$480	Last MSR was $1,499.

* *Grendel 19.5 Entry* – 6.5 Grendel cal., 19 1/2 in. stainless steel fully lapped threaded barrel, composite free float hand guard, Picatinny rail, 10 shot mag., black stock.

MSR $1,469	$1,450	$1,270	$1,085	$985	$795	$650	$505

* *Grendel 24 Overwatch* – 6.5 Grendel cal., 24 in. stainless steel fully lapped threaded barrel, compsite free float hand guard, Picatinny rail, low profile gas block, black stock.

MSR $1,499	$1,495	$1,300	$1,120	$1,015	$820	$675	$525

MSR	100%	98%	95%	90%	80%	70%	60%

* *Grendel AWS* – 6.5 Grendel cal., 19 1/2 or 24 in. stainless steel fully lapped threaded barrel, four rail hand guard, Picatinny rail, 10 shot mag., black stock.

| MSR $1,499 | $1,495 | $1,310 | $1,120 | $1,015 | $820 | $675 | $525 |

Add $50 for 24 in. barrel.

* *Grendel Hunter* – 6.5 Grendel cal., 19 1/2 in. stainless steel fully lapped threaded barrel, flat top receiver, full length military hand guard, Picatinny rail, black or coyote brown stock, 10 shot mag., standard trigger.

| MSR $1,370 | $1,325 | $1,195 | $1,025 | $930 | $750 | $615 | $480 |

* *Grendel Tactical 16* – 16 in. threaded barrel, A2 flash hider, M4 style or folding stock, with or w/o rail.

| MSR $1,100 | $1,100 | $960 | $825 | $750 | $600 | $495 | $385 |

Add $157 for mid-length rail handguard.

This model is also available with a 14 1/2 in. barrel for law enforcement only (Tactical 14).

* *Grendel Ultralight* – 16 in. fully fluted rifled barrel, integral flash hider, vented free float and Enidine buffer, M4 folding stock.

| MSR $2,100 | $1,975 | $1,730 | $1,480 | $1,345 | $1,085 | $890 | $690 |

GDMR – 16, 20, or 24 in. barrel, PRS OD Green or black stock, full tactical model, LaRue four rail hand guard, sight base, bipod mount, Magpul rail covers, tactical single stage trigger, Troy fold up front and rear back up iron sights.

| MSR $3,650 | $3,375 | $2,885 | $2,470 | $2,240 | $1,810 | $1,485 | $1,155 |

GSR – 20, 24, or 28 in. threaded (except 28 in.) barrel, composite vented hand guard system, black or Dark Earth stock, long range precision rifle.

| MSR $3,100 | $3,100 | $2,710 | $2,325 | $2,110 | $1,700 | $1,395 | $1,085 |

ALPINE INDUSTRIES

Previous manufacturer located in Los Angeles, CA.

Alpine Industries was a commercial M1 carbine manufacturer which produced approximately 17,000 guns between 1962-1965. Guns were made with newly manufactured cast receivers and military surplus parts, including some from England.

AMERICAN ARMS, INC.

Previous importer and manufacturer located in North Kansas City, MO, until 2000. American Arms imported various Spanish shotguns (Indesal, Lanber, Norica, and Zabala Hermanos), Italian shotguns including F. Stefano, several European pistols and rifles, and Sites handguns (1990-2000) mfg. in Torino, Italy. This company also manufactured several pistols in North Kansas City, MO. For more information and pricing on Norica airguns previously imported by American Arms, please refer to the *Blue Book of Airguns* **by Dr. Robert Beeman & John Allen (also available online).**

In late 2000, TriStar Sporting Arms, Ltd. acquired the parts inventory for some models previously imported by American Arms, Inc. Original warranties from American Arms do not apply to TriStar Sporting Arms, Ltd.

RIFLES: SEMI-AUTO

MODEL ZCY 308 – .308 Win. cal., gas operated semi-auto AK-47 type action, Yugoslavian mfg. Imported 1988 only.

| | $775 | $650 | $550 | $450 | $400 | $375 | $350 | Last MSR was $825. |

MODEL AKY 39 – 7.62x39mm cal., gas operated semi-auto AK-47 type action, teakwood fixed stock and grip, flip up Tritium front and rear night sights, Yugoslavian mfg. Imported 1988-1989 only.

| | $650 | $550 | $495 | $440 | $395 | $350 | $300 | Last MSR was $559. |

This model was supplied with sling and cleaning kit.

* *Model AKF 39 Folding Stock* – 7.62x39mm cal., folding stock variation of the Model AKY-39. Imported 1988-89 only.

| | $725 | $625 | $550 | $475 | $425 | $375 | $325 | Last MSR was $589. |

EXP-64 SURVIVAL RIFLE – .22 LR cal., semi-auto, takedown rifle stores in oversize synthetic stock compartment, 21 in. barrel, 10-shot mag., open sights, receiver grooved for scope mounting, cross bolt safety, 40 in. overall length, 7 lbs. Imported 1989-90 only.

| | $150 | $135 | $125 | $115 | $105 | $95 | $85 | Last MSR was $169. |

AMERICAN CLASSIC

Current trademark of pistols distributed by Eagle Imports, Inc., located in Wanamassa, NJ.

MSR	100%	98%	95%	90%	80%	70%	60%

PISTOLS: SEMI-AUTO

COMMANDER – .45 ACP cal., 4 1/4 in. barrel, 8 shot mag., blue or chrome finish, steel frame and slide, SA, Novak rear sight, dovetail front sight, flared and lowered ejection port, extended slide stop, beavertail grip safety, combat hammer, combat trigger, rear slide serrations, diamond cut checkered mahogany grips, approx. 36 oz. New 2010.

MSR $575	$485	$425	$360	$320	$290	$270	$250

Add $95 for hard chrome finish.

TROPHY – .45 ACP cal., 5 in. barrel, 8 shot mag., hard chrome finish, steel frame and slide, SA, dovetail fiber optic front sight, adj. Novak rear sight, flared and lowered ejection port, ambidextrous thumb safety, reverse plug recoil system with full length guide rod, beveled mag well, combat hammer and trigger, front and rear slide serrations, diamond cut checkered mahogany grips, checkered main spring housing, approx. 38 oz. New 2010.

MSR $775	$675	$595	$550	$495	$450	$425	$375

AMERICAN INTERNATIONAL CORP.

Previous manufacturer and importer located in Salt Lake City, UT, circa 1972-1984. American International was a wholly owned subsidiary of ARDCO (American Research & Development). ARDCO's previous name was American Mining & Development. American International imported firearms from Voere, located in Kufstein, Austria. American Arms International (AAI) was another subsidiary of ARDCO.

In 1979, after American International Corp. had dissolved, AAI resumed production using mostly Voere parts. After running out of Voere parts, late production featured U.S. mfg. receivers (can be recognized by not having a pivoting barrel retainer slotted on the bottom of the receiver). American Arms International declared bankruptcy in 1984.

CARBINES: SEMI-AUTO

AMERICAN 180 AUTO CARBINE (M-1) – .22 LR cal., a specialized design for tactical use, 177 round drum mag., 16 1/2 in. barrel, aperture sight, high impact plastic stock and forearm, aluminum alloy receiver with black finish. Semi-auto variation mfg. 1979-c.1984. Total Voere production (denoted by A prefix serial number) between 1972 and 1979 was 2,300 carbines (includes both full and semi-auto versions). Later mfg. was marked either M-1 (semi-auto) or M-2 (fully auto). "B" serial number prefix was introduced in 1980, and barrel markings were changed to "Amer Arms Intl, SLC, UT."

		$725	$600	$475	$375	$350	$325	$295

Add $550 for Laser Lok System - first commercially available laser sighting system.
Add approx. $300 for extra drum mag. and winder (fragile and subject to breakage).

AMERICAN PRECISION ARMS

Current manufacturer established in 2001, and located in Jefferson, GA.

In addition to rifles, American Precision Arms offers a shotgun modification service on customer supplied Remington 870s. Prices begin at $1,395. Please contact the company directly for more information on the wide lineup of available options and configurations (see Trademark Index).

RIFLES: BOLT ACTION

Current tactical models include the .308 Raven ($3,395 MSR), Revelation Tactical Rifle ($3,995 MSR), and the Genesis Tactical Rifle ($2,450 MSR). Hunting models include the Revelation Hunter ($3,450 MSR), and the Genesis Hunter ($2,450 MSR). All MSRs are considered base price. Many options and custom services are also available.

RIFLES: SEMI-AUTO

Current models include the Lycan ($3,450 MSR), the Urban Sniper ($2,450 MSR), and the Urban Sniper .308 ($3,098 MSR). All MSRs are considered base price. Many options and custom services are also available.

RIFLES: TARGET

American Precision Arms also builds custom target rifles per customer's specifications. All models are POR, and a wide variety of options are available

AMERICAN SPIRIT ARMS

Current manufacturer located in Scottsdale, AZ.

PISTOLS: SEMI-AUTO

American Spirit Arms offers a 5.56 NATO cal. pistol in either flat top ($1,070 MSR) or A2 fixed carry handle ($1,075 MSR) configuration. A 9mm Para. cal. pistol is also available in flat top ($1,170 MSR) or fixed carry handle ($1,170 MSR) configuration.

MSR	100%	98%	95%	90%	80%	70%	60%

RIFLES/CARBINES: SEMI-AUTO

American Spirit Arms manufactures a wide variety of semi-auto carbines and rifles based on the AR-15, M16, and the M4 in 5.56 NATO, .223 Rem., 9mm Para., and .308 Win. cal. A complete line of options, accessories and parts are available. Base models are listed. Please contact the company directly regarding pricing for options and accessories (see Trademark Index).

ASA-M4A3 CARBINE – 5.56 NATO cal., flat top with 16 in. barrel, collapsible stock, with (ASA-M4A3G) or without gas block.

MSR $1,000	$875	$775	$675	$575	$500	$450	$400

ASA-A2 RIFLE – 5.56 NATO cal., 20 in. barrel, fixed carry handle, fixed (A2) buttstock.

MSR $1,000	$875	$775	$675	$575	$500	$450	$400

ASA-M4A2 CARBINE – 5.56 NATO cal., 16 in. barrel, fixed carry handle, collapsible stock.

MSR $1,000	$875	$775	$675	$575	$500	$450	$400

ASA-A320G RIFLE – 5.56 NATO cal., flat top with gas block, 20 in. barrel, fixed buttstock.

MSR $1,000	$875	$775	$675	$575	$500	$450	$400

ASA-DISSIPATOR CARBINE – 5.56 NATO cal., fixed carry handle, 16 in. barrel, with (A2) or w/o (A3G) gas block, fixed buttstock, dissipator CAR length gas system.

MSR $1,050	$900	$795	$675	$575	$500	$450	$400

ASA-9mm CARBINE – 9mm Para. cal., fixed carry handle, 16 in. barrel, collapsible stock.

MSR $1,350	$1,150	$1,000	$875	$750	$625	$500	$450

ASA-9mm A3G CARBINE – 9mm Para. cal., 16 in. barrel, flat top, gas block, collapsible stock.

MSR $1,350	$1,150	$1,000	$875	$750	$625	$500	$450

ASA-BULL A3 CARBINE – 5.56 NATO cal., 16 in. bull barrel, flat top, fixed buttstock.

MSR $1,350	$1,150	$1,000	$875	$750	$625	$500	$450

ASA-BULL A3 RIFLE – 5.56 NATO cal., 24 in. bull barrel, fixed buttstock.

MSR $1,350	$1,150	$1,000	$875	$750	$625	$500	$450

ASA-BULL SIDE CHARGER RIFLE/CARBINE – .223 Rem. cal., 16 (carbine) or 24 (rifle) in. bull barrel, side charger, fixed buttstock.

MSR $1,600	$1,375	$1,175	$1,000	$875	$775	$675	$575

ASA-308 SIDE CHARGER CARBINE/RIFLE – .308 Win. cal., flat top side charger, 16 (carbine) or 24 in. bull barrel, fixed buttstock.

MSR $2,199	$1,895	$1,700	$1,500	$1,300	$1,100	$925	$750

Add $200 for 24 in. barrel.

AMERICAN SPIRIT ARMS CORP.

Previous rifle and components manufacturer 1998-2005, and located in Tempe, AZ. Previously located in Scottsdale, AZ.

RIFLES: SEMI-AUTO

Add $25 for green furniture, $65 for black barrel finish, $75 for fluted barrel, $125 for porting, $119 for two-stage match trigger, and $55 for National Match sights on .223 cal. models listed below.

ASA 24 IN. BULL BARREL FLATTOP RIFLE – .223 Rem. cal., patterned after AR-15, forged steel lower receiver, forged aluminum flattop upper receiver, 24 in. stainless steel bull barrel, free floating aluminum handguard, includes Harris bipod. Mfg. 1999-2005.

	$850	$700	$625	$550	$500	$450	$400	Last MSR was $950.

ASA 24 IN. BULL BARREL A2 RIFLE – similar to ASA Bull Barrel Flattop, except features A2 upper receiver with carrying handle and sights. Mfg. 1999-2005.

	$875	$725	$650	$565	$500	$450	$400	Last MSR was $980.

OPEN MATCH RIFLE – .223 Rem. cal., 16 in. fluted and ported stainless steel match barrel with round shroud, flattop without sights, forged upper and lower receiver, two-stage match trigger, upgraded pistol grip, individually tested, USPSA/IPSC open class legal. Mfg. 2001-2005.

	$1,350	$1,100	$950	$825	$725	$650	$525	Last MSR was $1,500.

LIMITED MATCH RIFLE – .223 Rem. cal., 16 in. fluted stainless steel match barrel with round shroud with staggered

MSR	100%	98%	95%	90%	80%	70%	60%	

hand grip, National Match front and rear sights, two-stage match trigger, upgraded pistol grip, individually tested, USPSA/IPSC open class legal. Mfg. 2001-2005.

	$1,175	$975	$825	$725	$650	$525	$475	Last MSR was $1,300.

DCM SERVICE RIFLE – .223 Rem. cal., 20 in. stainless steel match barrel with ribbed free floating shroud, National Match front and rear sights, two-stage match trigger, pistol grip, individually tested. Mfg. 2001-2005.

	$1,175	$975	$825	$725	$650	$525	$475	Last MSR was $1,300.

ASA 16 IN. M4 RIFLE – .223 Rem. cal., features non-collapsible stock and M4 handguard, 16 in. barrel with muzzle brake, aluminum flattop upper receiver. Mfg. 2002-2005.

	$795	$700	$625	$525	$450	$400	$350	Last MSR was $905.

ASA 20 IN. A2 RIFLE – .223 Rem. cal., features A2 receiver and 20 in. National Match barrel. Mfg. 1999-2005.

	$765	$640	$565	$500	$425	$350	$300	Last MSR was $820.

ASA CARBINE WITH SIDE CHARGING RECEIVER – .223 Rem. cal., features aluminum side charging flattop upper receiver, M4 handguard, 16 in. NM barrel with slotted muzzle brake. Mfg. 2002-2004.

	$865	$750	$650	$565	$500	$450	$400	Last MSR was $970.

C.A.R. POST-BAN 16 IN. CARBINE – .223 Rem. cal., non-collapsible stock, Wilson 16 in. National Match barrel. Mfg. 1999-2005.

	$775	$650	$575	$500	$450	$400	$350	Last MSR was $830.

ASA 16 IN. BULL BARREL A2 INVADER – .223 Rem. cal., similar to ASA 24 in. Bull Barrel rifle, except has 16 in. stainless steel barrel. Mfg. 1999-2005.

	$860	$725	$630	$550	$500	$450	$400	Last MSR was $955.

ASA 9MM A2 CAR CARBINE – 9mm Para. cal., forged upper and lower receiver, non-collapsible CAR stock, 16 in. Wilson heavy barrel w/o muzzle brake, with birdcage flash hider (pre-ban) or muzzle brake (post-ban), includes 9mm conversion block, 25 shot modified Uzi mag. Mfg. 2002-2005.

	$860	$725	$630	$550	$500	$450	$400	Last MSR was $950.

Add $550 per extra 25 shot mag.

ASA 9MM FLATTOP CAR RIFLE – 9mm Para. cal., similar to A2 CAR Rifle, except has flattop w/o sights. Mfg. 2002-2005.

	$860	$725	$630	$550	$500	$450	$400	Last MSR was $950.

ASA 16 IN. TACTICAL RIFLE – .308 Win. cal., 16 in. stainless steel air gauged regular or match barrel, side charging handle, Hogue pistol grip, guaranteed 1/2 in. MOA accuracy, individually tested, 8 3/4 lbs. Mfg. 2002-2005.

	$1,475	$1,200	$995	$850	$750	$650	$525	Last MSR was $1,675.

Add $515 for Match Rifle (includes fluted and ported barrel, 2 stage trigger, and hard chromed bolt and carrier).

ASA 24 IN. MATCH RIFLE – .308 Win. cal., 24 in. stainless steel air gauged match barrel with or w/o fluting/porting, side charging handle, Hogue pistol grip, guaranteed 1/2 in. MOA accuracy, individually tested, approx. 12 lbs. Mfg. 2002-2005.

	$1,475	$1,200	$995	$850	$750	$650	$525	Last MSR was $1,675.

Add $515 for Match Rifle (includes fluted and ported barrel, 2 stage trigger, and hard chromed bolt and carrier).

AMERICAN TACTICAL IMPORTS

Current importer located in Rochester, NY.

American Tactical Imports offers a wide variety of products, including Turkish-made semi-auto pistols, as well as tactical pistols and semi-auto carbines manufactured by German Sports Guns GmbH (see separate listing). The company also imports ammunition, knives, and other tactical gear.

CARBINES/RIFLES: SEMI-AUTO

ATI also imports a variety of tactical style semi-auto carbines and rifles. Please contact the company directly for pricing and model availability (see Trademark Index).

PISTOLS: SEMI-AUTO

Semi-auto pistols include the Arsan 2000L Models (mfg. in Turkey), the American Tactical Series, including Models HP9, C-40, C-45, CS9, and FS9. Other tactical pistols include the AT Series. Please contact the company directly regarding pricing and U.S. availability (see Trademark Index).

SHOTGUNS: SEMI-AUTO

American Tactical Imports offers a Model T14 chambered in .410 ga. with 3 in. chamber. The design is based on the AR-15, and includes a detachable 5 shot mag., with 20 in. barrel. Please contact the company directly for pricing and availability (see Trademark Index).

MSR	100%	98%	95%	90%	80%	70%	60%

AMTEC 2000, INC.

Previous trademark incorporating Erma Werke (German) and H & R 1871 (U.S.) companies located in Gardner, MA until 1999. Amtec 2000, Inc. previously imported the Erma SR 100 rifle (see listing in Erma Suhl section).

REVOLVERS

5 SHOT REVOLVER – .38 S&W cal., 5 shot double action, swing-out cylinder, 2 or 3 in. barrel, transfer bar safety, Pachmayr composition grips, high polish blue, matte electroless nickel, or stainless steel construction, fixed sights, approx. 25 oz., 200 mfg. 1996-99, all were distributed and sold in Europe only (no U.S. pricing).

ANZIO IRONWORKS CORP.

Current manufacturer established during 2000, and located in St. Petersburg, FL. Anzio Ironworks has been making gun parts and accessories since 1994. Dealer and consumer sales.

RIFLES: BOLT ACTION

.50 BMG SINGLE SHOT TAKEDOWN MODEL – .50 BMG cal., modified bullpup configuration, tube stock with 2 in. buttpad, 17 in. barrel with match or military chambering and muzzle brake, automatic ambidextrous safety and decocking mechanism, takedown action allowing disassembly in under 25 seconds, adj. target trigger, inclined sight mounting rail, cased, 25 lbs. Mfg. 2000-2002.

	100%	98%	95%	90%	80%	70%	60%	
	$4,200	$4,000	$3,500	$2,350	$2,000	$1,800	$1,600	Last MSR was $2,500.

Add $150 for 29 in. barrel or $1,050 for 29 in. barrel assembly.

.50 BMG SINGLE SHOT TITANIUM TAKEDOWN MODEL – .50 BMG cal., modified bullpup configuration, tube stock, 16 in. barrel with match or military chambering and muzzle brake, automatic ambidextrous safety and decocking mechanism, interrupted thread lockup, takedown action allowing disassembly in under 12 seconds, adj. target trigger, Picatinny rail mount, cased, 11 lbs. Limited mfg. 2002 only.

	100%	98%	95%	90%	80%	70%	60%	
	$5,700	$5,000	$4,000	$3,500	$3,500	$3,000	$2,500	Last MSR was $3,200.

Add $250 for 29 in. barrel, $350 for custom barrel length to 45 in., or $1,050 for 29 in. barrel assembly.

.50 BMG SINGLE SHOT MODEL LTD. – .50 BMG cal., laminated wood stock, butter knife bolt handle, bolt complete with ejector and extractor, parkerized finish, inclined sight mounting rail, 17 in. barrel with match or military chambering and muzzle brake, 21 lbs. Limited mfg. 2002 only.

	100%	98%	95%	90%	80%	70%	60%	
	$2,500	$2,200	$1,950	$1,675	$1,400	$1,200	$1,000	Last MSR was $2,750.

Add $150 for 29 in. barrel or $250 for custom barrel length to 45 in.

.50 BMG SINGLE SHOT MODEL – .50 BMG cal., 29 1/2 in. Lothar Walther match grade barrel, AR-15 trigger and safety, fixed metal buttstock with shrouded barrel and optional muzzle brake, 22 lbs. Mfg. 2003-2006.

	100%	98%	95%	90%	80%	70%	60%	
	$1,800	$1,625	$1,400	$1,200	$1,000	$900	$800	Last MSR was $1,995.

SINGLE SHOT MODEL W/TAKEDOWN BARREL – .50 BMG or .338 Lapua cal., similar to single shot model, except features a 20 minute inclined sight mounting rail, heavier receiver, match grade stainless steel takedown barrel with clamshell muzzle brake, .5 MOA guaranteed. New 2005.

MSR $4,200	$3,675	$3,150	$2,750	$2,400	$2,100	$1,900	$1,700

Add $500 for .338 Lapua cal.

.50 BMG LIGHTWEIGHT REPEATER MODEL – .50 BMG cal., lightweight model with 18 in. Lothar Walther fluted target barrel with 3 (standard) or 5 shot detachable mag., titanium muzzle brake, scope rail, bipod, and sling, 13 1/2 lbs. New 2003.

MSR $4,995	$4,500	$3,950	$3,300	$2,775	$2,350	$2,125	$1,850

Add $705 for takedown model.

ANZIO .50 BMG STANDARD REPEATER – .50 BMG cal., 18 or 26 in. barrel, similar to .50 Lightweight Repeater Model, except does not have barrel/receiver fluting, and is not available with titanium muzzle brake/bolt handle. New 2004.

MSR $3,995	$3,475	$2,850	$2,400	$2,000	$1,750	$1,500	$1,350

MAG. FED RIFLE – 14.5x114mm, 20mm Vulcan (requires $200 transfer tax in states where legal), or Anzio .20-50 cal., single shot or repeater, 49 in. match grade fluted take down barrel, detachable 3 shot box mag., titanium firing pin, bipod, scope rail, customer choice of Duracoat color finish, oversized bolt handle. New 2008.

MSR $11,900	$11,900	$9,950	$8,750	$8,000	$7,250	$6,500	$5,750

Add $1,100 for handguard, freefloating barrel, and adj. bipod.
Add $3,200 for muzzle brake.
Subtract $2,100 for single shot.

MSR	100%	98%	95%	90%	80%	70%	60%

ARLINGTON ORDNANCE

Previous importer located in Westport, CT until 1996. Formerly located in Weston, CT.

CARBINES & RIFLES: SEMI-AUTO

M1 GARAND RIFLE – .30-06 cal., imported from Korea in used condition, various manufacturers, with import stamp. Imported 1991-96.

	$825	$750	$675	$550	$500	$475	$450

Add $40 for stock upgrade (better wood).

* ***Arsenal Restored M1 Garand Rifle*** – .30-06 or .308 Win. cal., featured new barrel, rebuilt gas system, and reinspected components. Imported 1994-1996.

	$850	$700	$650	$600	$575	$550	$500

Add 5% for .308 Win. cal.

TROPHY GARAND – .308 Win. cal. only, action was original mil-spec., included new barrel and checkered walnut stock and forend, recoil pad. Imported 1994-1996.

	$925	$825	$725	$675	$575	$525	$475	Last MSR was $695.

T26 TANKER – .30-06 or .308 Win. cal., included new barrel and other key components, updated stock finish. Imported 1994-1996.

	$850	$700	$650	$600	$575	$550	$500

.30 CAL. CARBINE – .30 Carbine cal., 18 in. barrel, imported from Korea in used condition, various manufacturers, with import stamp. Imported 1991-1996.

	$725	$650	$575	$525	$475	$425	$400

Add approximately $55 for stock upgrade (better wood).

MODEL FIVE CARBINE – while advertised, this model never went into production.

ARMALITE

Previous manufacturer located in Costa Mesa, CA, approx. 1959-1973.

RIFLES: SEMI-AUTO

AR-7 EXPLORER – .22 LR cal., 16 in. aluminum barrel with steel liner, aperture rear sight, take down action and barrel store in hollow plastic stock in either brown (rare), black, or multi-color, gun will float, designed by Gene Stoner, mfg. 1959-73 by Armalite, 1973-90 by Charter Arms, 1990-97 by Survival Arms located in Cocoa, FL, and by AR-7 Industries, LLC, located in Meriden, CT, 1998-2004. Current mfg. beginning 1997 by Henry Repeating Arms Co. located in NJ.

Black/Multi-color stock	$325	$285	$250	$225	$185	$165	$145
Brown stock	$450	$375	$325	$260	$220	$195	$175

Some unusual early Costa Mesa AR-7 variations have been observed with ported barrels, extendable wire stock, hooded front sight, and hollow pistol grip containing a cleaning kit, perhaps indicating a special military contract survival weapon.

AR-7 CUSTOM – similar to AR-7 Explorer, only with custom walnut stock including cheekpiece, pistol grip. Mfg. 1964-70.

	$325	$300	$265	$235	$200	$190	$180

AR-180 – .223 Rem. cal., semi-auto, gas operated, 18 1/4 in. barrel, folding stock. Manufactured by Armalite in Costa Mesa, CA, 1969-1972, Howa Machinery Ltd., Nagoya, Japan, 1972 and 1973, and by Sterling Armament Co. Ltd., Dagenham, Essex, England.

Sterling Mfg.	$1,750	$1,600	$1,450	$1,300	$1,225	$1,125	$1,050
Howa Mfg.	$2,100	$1,900	$1,800	$1,650	$1,500	$1,300	$1,150
Costa Mesa Mfg.	$2,100	$1,900	$1,800	$1,650	$1,500	$1,300	$1,150

ARMALITE, INC.

Current manufacturer located in Geneseo, IL. New manufacture began in 1995 after Eagle Arms, Inc. purchased the ArmaLite trademarks. The ArmaLite trademark was originally used by Armalite (no relation to ArmaLite, Inc.) during mfg. in Costa Mesa, CA, approx. 1959-1973 (see Armalite listing above). Dealer and distributor sales.

MSR	100%	98%	95%	90%	80%	70%	60%

PISTOLS: SEMI-AUTO

MODEL AR-24 (ULTIMATE) – 9mm Para. cal., full size (24-15 w/4.67 in. barrel) or compact (24K-13 w/ 3.89 in. barrel) frame, blowback action, 10, 13 (compact only), or 15 shot mag., 3-dot sights with fixed or adj. rear sight, black parkerized finish, checkered polymer grips, includes case and two magazines, 35 oz. Mfg. by Sarzsilmaz in Turkey. Importation began 2007.

MSR $550	$475	$425	$375	$325	$275	$250	$225

Add $81 for Model AR-24-10C/15C Tactical Custom pistol with C-suffix (full or compact size), adj. rear sight and checkered grip straps.

RIFLES: BOLT ACTION

AR-30M – .300 Win. Mag., .308 Win., or .338 Lapua cal., scaled down AR-50, repeater, Shilen modified single stage trigger, w/o muzzle brake, 5 shot detachable mag., 26 in. barrel, 12 lbs. New 2003.

MSR $1,742	$1,575	$1,350	$1,125	$1,000	$900	$800	$700

Add $140 for .338 Lapua cal.

AR-50A1 (AR-50) – .50 BMG cal., single shot bolt action with octagonal receiver integrated into a skeletonized aluminum stock with adj. cheekpiece and recoil pad, 30 in. tapered barrel w/o sights and sophisticated muzzle brake (reduces felt recoil to approx. .243 Win. cal.), removable buttstock, right or left-hand action, single stage trigger, 33.2 lbs. New 1999.

MSR $3,359	$3,195	$2,925	$2,600	$2,400	$2,175	$2,000	$1,875

Add $336 for left-hand action (disc. 2009).

During 2004, this model was produced with a special commemorative stamp notation on the left side of the receiver.

RIFLES: SEMI-AUTO

All ArmaLite semi-auto rifles have a limited lifetime warranty. Some previously manufactured models had stainless steel barrels and NM triggers at an additional charge. Descriptions and pricing are for currently manufactured models.

Beginning 2009, a forward bolt assist became standard on all AR-10A4 upper receivers.

Add $97-$107 for A4 carry handle assembly.
Add $150 for 100% Realtree Hardwoods or Advantage Classic camo finish (disc.).

AR-10 SERIES – semi-auto tactical design, various configurations, with or w/o sights and carry handle, choice of standard green, black (new 1999), or camo finish, supplied with two 10 shot mags. (until 2004), current mfg. typically ships with one 10 round and one 20 round mag., two-stage NM trigger became standard during 2008. New late 1995.

* ***AR-10B Rifle*** – .308 Win. cal., patterned after the early Armalite AR-10 rifle, featuring tapered M16 handguards, pistol grip, distinctive charging bolt on top inside of carry handle (cannot be used to mount sighting devices), original brown color, 20 in. barrel, 9 1/2 lbs. Mfg. 1999-2008.

	$1,495	$1,225	$1,075	$975	$875	$750	$675	Last MSR was $1,698.

* ***AR-10T Rifle*** – .243 Win. (disc. 2003, reintroduced 2009), .260 Rem. (new 2009), .300 RSUM (mfg. 2004-2008, Ultra Mag Model), 7mm-08 Rem. (new 2009), .308 Win., or .338 Federal (new 2009) cal., features 20 (.308 Win.), 22 (.338 Federal), or 24 (disc. 2008) in. stainless heavy barrel, two-stage NM trigger, smooth green or black finish, black fiberglass (disc. 2008) or aluminum handguard tube, stock, and pistol grip, flattop receiver with Picatinny rail, w/o sights or carry handle, forward bolt assist became standard in 2009, includes two 10 shot mags. and hard case, 9 1/2 - 10 1/2 lbs.

MSR $1,892	$1,625	$1,325	$1,125	$995	$875	$750	$675

Add $214 for .300 RSUM cal. (disc. 2008).
Add $20 for .338 Federal cal.
Add $250 for Lothar Walther barrel (disc.).

* ***AR-10T Carbine (Navy Model)*** – .308 Win. cal., similar to AR-10T Rifle, except has 16 in. stainless barrel and match trigger, 8 1/2 lbs. Disc. 2004.

	$1,825	$1,525	$1,275	$1,075	$995	$875	$750	Last MSR was $2,080.

* ***AR-10 National Match*** – .308 Win. cal., 20 in. stainless steel barrel, forged flattop receiver with Picatinny rail and forward assist, stainless steel flash supressor, two-stage NM trigger, 10 shot mag., Mil Std. 1913 rail handguard, extended elevation NM sights, 10.4 lbs. Limited mfg. 2009.

	$2,100	$1,850	$1,600	$1,425	$1,200	$1,000	$775	Last MSR was $2,365.

* ***AR-10A4 Rifle (SPR - Special Purpose Rifle)*** – .243 Win. (disc. 2003) or .308 Win. cal., features 20 in. chrome-lined 1:10 twist barrel, removable front sight, green or black furniture, flash suppressor, Picatinny rail, w/o carry handle, includes one 10 shot mag., one 20 shot mag., sling, and hard case, approx. 9 lbs.

MSR $1,557	$1,350	$1,075	$900	$800	$700	$600	$525

MSR	100%	98%	95%	90%	80%	70%	60%

* **AR-10A4 Carbine** – .308 Win. cal., similar to AR-10A4 Rifle, except has 16 in. barrel, 8.4-9 lbs.

MSR $1,557	$1,350	$1,075	$900	$800	$700	$600	$525

Add $414 for SIR System (Selective Integrated Rail System, mfg. 2004-2006).

* **AR-10A2 Infantry Model Rifle** – .243 Win. (disc. 2003) or .308 Win. cal., features 20 in. chrome-lined 1:10 barrel, green or black finish, includes fixed stock, A2 front sight, flash suppressor, tactical two-stage trigger, forged lower receiver, carry handle, includes one 10 shot mag., one 20 shot mag., sling, and hard case, 9.8 lbs.

MSR $1,561	$1,350	$1,100	$925	$800	$700	$600	$525

* **AR-10A2 Carbine** – .308 Win. cal., similar to AR-10A2 Rifle, except has 16 in. barrel and six-position collapsible stock with extended tube, includes one 10 shot mag., one 20 shot mag., sling, and hard case, 9 lbs.

MSR $1,561	$1,350	$1,100	$925	$800	$700	$600	$525

Add $74 for 4-way quad rail on front of forearm (mfg. 2004-2008).

* **AR-10SOF (Special Operation Forces) Carbine** – .308 Win. cal., available in either A2 or A4 configurations, fixed tube stock, 16 in. barrel, black finish only. Mfg. 2003-2004.

	$1,250	$1,075	$900	$800	$700	$600	$525	Last MSR was $1,503.

Add $52 for A2 configuration (includes Picatinny rail).

* **AR-10 Super SASS Carbine/Rifle** – .308 Win. cal., adj. gas system, AAC suppressor (military or law enforcement), mock AAC (disc.) or A2 flash suppressor, 20 in. ceramic coated stainless steel barrel, floating quad rail system with rail covers, Magpul adj. buttstock, 20 shot mag., black finish, two-stage NM trigger, available with various accessories, includes one 10 shot mag., one 20 shot mag., USMC quick adjust sling, and sling swivel mount, 12 lbs.

MSR $3,078	$2,575	$2,225	$1,950	$1,600	$1,300	$1,100	$995

M4A1C CARBINE – features 16 in. chrome-lined 1:9 twist heavy barrel with National Match sights and detachable carrying handle, grooved barrel shroud, 7 lbs. Disc. 1997.

	$1,000	$825	$750	$635	$500	$450	$415	Last MSR was $935.

M4C CARBINE – similar to M4A1C Carbine, except has non-removable carrying handle and fixed sights, 7 lbs. Disc. 1997.

	$900	$750	$700	$550	$500	$450	$415	Last MSR was $870.

M15 RIFLE/CARBINE VARIATIONS – .223 Rem. cal. standard unless otherwise noted, various configurations, barrel lengths, sights, and other features.

* **M15A2/A4 National Match Rifle** – .223 Rem. cal. w/Wylde chamber, features 20 in. stainless steel NM sleeved 1:8 twist barrel with NM sights and NM two-stage trigger, grooved barrel shroud, black or green furniture, flash suppressor, with or w/o detachable carrying handle, includes one 30 shot mag., USMC quick adjust sling, and hard case, 9 lbs.

MSR $1,388	$1,175	$1,025	$875	$775	$675	$595	$525

* **M15A4 National Match SPR** – .223 Rem. cal. w/Wylde chamber, similar to M15A2 National Match, except has forged flattop receiver with Picatinny rail and NM detachable carry handle, includes one 30 shot mag., USMC quick adjust sling, and hard case, approx. 9 lbs.

MSR $1,413	$1,195	$1,035	$875	$775	$675	$595	$525

* **M15A2 Golden Eagle** – similiar to M15A2 National Match Rifle, except has 20 in. heavy barrel, 9.4 lbs. Limited mfg. 1998 only.

	$1,200	$975	$850	$750	$675	$595	$525	Last MSR was $1,350.

* **M15A2 Service Rifle** – 5.56 NATO cal., includes 20 in. chrome-lined 1:9 twist barrel, green or black finish, forged A2 receiver, fixed stock, A2 front sight, tactical two-stage trigger, flash suppressor, carrying handle, includes one 30 shot mag., sling, and hard case, 8.2 lbs.

MSR $1,150	$975	$800	$700	$600	$500	$450	$415

* **M15A2 Carbine** – similar to M15A2 Service Rifle, except has six-position collapsible stock with G.I. diameter extension tube, and 16 in. barrel, includes one 30 shot mag., sling, and hard case, 7 lbs.

MSR $1,150	$975	$800	$700	$600	$500	$450	$415

* **M15A4 SPR (Special Purpose Rifle)** – 5.56 NATO cal., includes 20 in. chrome-lined H-Bar 1:9 twist barrel, green or black finish, gas block with rail, forged flattop receiver with Picatinny rail, tactical two-stage trigger, flash suppressor, includes one 30 shot mag., sling, and hard case, 7.8 lbs.

MSR $1,060	$925	$775	$675	$575	$500	$450	$415

* **M15A4 Carbine** – .223 Rem., 6.8 SPC (new 2009), or 7.62x39mm (new 2009) cal., similar to M15A4 Special Purpose Rifle, except has 16 in. barrel and six-position collapsible stock with G.I. diameter extension tube, includes one 10 shot mag., one 20 shot mag., sling, and hard case, 7 lbs.

MSR $1,060	$925	$775	$675	$575	$500	$450	$415

MSR	100%	98%	95%	90%	80%	70%	60%

Add $47 for 6.8 SPC or 7.62x39mm cal.
Subtract $60 for fixed front sight w/detachable carry handle (disc.).

* **M15A4 CBA2K** – 5.56 NATO cal., features 16 in. double lapped chrome lined barrel, flash suppressor, two-stage tactical trigger, forged flattop receiver with Picatinny rail, A2 front sight, 8 in. mid-length handguard, forged lower receiver, six-position collapsible stock with G.I. diameter extension tube, includes one 30 shot mag., sling, and hard case, 7 lbs. New 2008.

MSR $1,017	$995	$900	$800	$700	$600	$500	$450

* **M15A4 SPR II National Match (Special Purpose Rifle)** – similar to M15A4 SPR, except has triple lapped rifled barrel, strengthed free floating barrel sleeve and two-stage match trigger, green or black furniture. Mfg. 2003-2005.

	$1,250	$1,050	$875	$800	$700	$600	$500	Last MSR was $1,472.

* **M15SOF (Special Operation Forces) Carbine** – .223 Rem. cal., available in either A2 or A4 configurations, fixed tube stock, 16 in. barrel, black finish only. Mfg. 2003-2004.

	$950	$775	$675	$600	$525	$475	$450	Last MSR was $1,084.

Add $69 for A2 configuration (includes Picatinny rail).

* **M15ARTN** – .223 Rem. cal., 20 in. stainless steel barrel, National Match trigger, green or black finish. Mfg. 2004-2007.

	$1,130	$925	$825	$700	$600	$500	$450	Last MSR was $1,322.

* **M15A4T Rifle (Eagle Eye)** – .223 Rem. cal. w/Wylde chamber, 20 or 24 (disc. 2009) in. stainless steel 1:8 twist heavy barrel, two-stage NM trigger, smooth green or black fiberglass (disc. 2008) or lightweight aluminum hand guard, Picatinny front sight rail but w/o sights and carrying handle, black or green furniture, includes one 10 shot mag. and hard case, 8.6 lbs. Disc. 2005, reintroduced 2007.

MSR $1,296	$1,195	$900	$800	$700	$600	$525	$500

* **M15A4T Carbine (Eagle Eye)** – features 16 in. stainless steel 1:9 twist heavy barrel, picatinny rail, smooth fiberglass handguard tube, two-stage trigger, 7.1 lbs. Mfg. 1997-2004.

	$1,225	$995	$850	$775	$675	$595	$525	Last MSR was $1,383.

* **M15A4 Predator** – similar to M15A4T Eagle Eye, except has 1:12 twist barrel. Disc. 1996.

	$1,215	$985	$850	$750	$675	$595	$525	Last MSR was $1,350.

* **M15A4 Action Master** – includes 20 in. stainless steel 1:9 twist barrel, two-stage trigger, muzzle brake, Picatinny flattop design w/o sights or carrying handle, 9 lbs. Disc. 1997.

	$1,100	$975	$850	$750	$650	$550	$495	Last MSR was $1,175.

LEC15A4CBK (LAW ENFORCEMENT CARBINE) – 5.56 NATO cal., 16 in. double lapped chrome lined threaded barrel, forged flattop receiver with Picatinny rail, flash suppressor, A2 front sight, 6 in. handguard, tactical two-stage trigger, six position collapsible stock with G.I. diameter extension tube, includes one 30 shot mag., sling, and hard case, 6 1/2 lbs. New 2009.

MSR $975	$895	$825	$725	$650	$575	$525	$475

AR-180B – .223 Rem. cal., polymer lower receiver with formed sheet metal upper, standard AR-15 trigger group/magazine, incorporates the best features of the M15 (lower group with trigger and mag. well) and early AR-180 (gas system, which keeps propellant gas outside of the receiver) rifles, 19.8 in. barrel with integral muzzle brake, 6 lbs. Mfg. 2003-2007.

	$750	$675	$600	$525	$475	$425	$400	Last MSR was $750.

For more information on the original ArmaLite AR-180 and variations, please refer to the previous ArmaLite listing.

ARMAMENT TECHNOLOGY

Previous firearms manufacturer located in Halifax, Nova Scotia, Canada 1988-2003.

Armament Technology discontinued making bolt action rifles in 2003. Currently, the company is distributing optical rifle sights only.

RIFLES: BOLT-ACTION

AT1-C24 TACTICAL RIFLE – .308 Win. or .300 Win. Mag. (disc. 2000) cal., similar to AT1-M24, except has detachable mag., adj. cheekpiece, and buttstock adj. for LOP, includes 3.5-10x30mm tactical scope and Mil-Spec shipping case, 1/2" MOA guaranteed, available in left-hand action, 14.9 lbs. Mfg. 1998-2003.

	$4,095	$3,650	$2,775	$2,250	$1,825	$1,500	$1,275	Last MSR was $4,195.

MSR	100%	98%	95%	90%	80%	70%	60%

AT1-C24B TACTICAL RIFLE – .308 Win. cal., similar to AT1-C24, except is not available in left-hand, 15.9 lbs. Mfg. 2001-2003.

| | $4,250 | $3,750 | $2,850 | $2,300 | $1,850 | $1,525 | $1,300 | Last MSR was $4,695. |

AT1-M24 TACTICAL RIFLE – .223 Rem. (new 1998), .308 Win., or .300 Win. Mag. (disc. 2000) cal., bolt action, tactical rifle with competition tuned right-hand or left-hand Rem. 700 action, stainless steel barrel, Kevlar reinforced fiberglass stock, Harris bipod, matte black finish, competition trigger, 1/2" MOA guaranteed, 14.9 lbs. Disc. 2003.

| | $4,350 | $3,850 | $2,850 | $2,350 | $1,900 | $1,600 | $1,350 | Last MSR was $4,495. |

ARMAMENT TECHNOLOGY CORP.

Previous manufacturer located in Las Vegas, NV between 1972 and 1978.

RIFLES: SEMI-AUTO

In addition to the models listed below, ATC also manufactured the "Firefly II", a select fire pistol.

M-2 FIREFLY – 9mm Para. cal., unique gas delayed blowback action, tactical configuration, collapsible stock, very limited mfg., 4 3/4 lbs.

| | $695 | $625 | $550 | $475 | $395 | $350 | $295 |

ARMITAGE INTERNATIONAL, LTD.

Previous manufacturer until 1990 located in Seneca, SC.

PISTOLS: SEMI-AUTO

SCARAB SKORPION – 9mm Para. Cal., tactical design patterned after the Czech Model 61, direct blow back action, 4.63 in. barrel, matte black finish, 12 shot (standard) or 32 shot (optional) mag., 3 1/2 lbs. Mfg. in U.S. 1989-90 only.

| | $695 | $625 | $550 | $500 | $425 | $375 | $325 | Last MSR was $400. |

Add $45 for threaded flash hider or imitation suppressor.

Only 602 Scarab Skorpions were manufactured during 1989-90.

ARMORY USA L.L.C.

Previous manufacturer/importer until 2008, and located in Houston, TX. Previous company name was Arsenal USA LLC.

RIFLES: SEMI-AUTO

Armory USA, LLC produced a variety of AK-47/AKM/AK-74 semi-auto rifles. Early rifles used Bulgarian milled receivers, later versions were built using sheet metal receivers made in Hungary by FEG.

During 2004, Armory USA began production of 1.6 mm thick U.S. made AK receivers, which were sold as both receivers and complete rifles. Production of 1 mm thick receivers began in Jan. 2005. Models not listed here may have been assembled by other manufacturers using these receivers. During 2004, Armory USA began assembling rifles at a new factory in Kazanlak, Bulgaria. Some components were made in the U.S., in compliance with the BATFE.

Please refer to the Arsenal USA listing for pre-2004 manufactured/imported rifles.

MODEL SSR-56-2 – 7.62x39mm cal., Armory USA made 1.6mm receiver wall thickness, Poly-Tec barrel assembly, Bulgarian internal parts. Approx. 400 mfg. during 2004.

| | $750 | $700 | $675 | $650 | $600 | $500 | $475 | Last MSR was $500. |

MODEL AMD-63-2 UP – 7.62x39mm cal., Armory USA made 1.6mm receiver wall thickness, Hungarian parts, underfolding buttstock. Approx. 125 mfg. 2004.

| | $950 | $900 | $850 | $800 | $700 | $650 | $600 | Last MSR was $600. |

Add $200 for milled receiver.

MODEL SSR-85C-2 – 7.62x39mm cal., assembled in Bulgaria, marked "ISD Ltd", blond wood and black polymer furniture. Imported 2004-2006.

| | $795 | $750 | $700 | $650 | $600 | $525 | $475 | Last MSR was $550. |

Add $100 for sidefolding buttstock (Model SSR-85C-2 SF).

MODEL SSR-74-2 – 5.45x39mm cal., assembled in Bulgaria, marked "ISD Ltd", blond wood and black polymer furniture. Imported 2005-2008.

| | $775 | $725 | $695 | $625 | $600 | $525 | $475 | Last MSR was $550. |

ARMS RESEARCH ASSOCIATES

Previous manufacturer until 1991, located in Stone Park, IL.

MSR	100%	98%	95%	90%	80%	70%	60%

CARBINES: SEMI-AUTO

KF SYSTEM – 9mm Para. cal., tactical design carbine, 18 1/2 in. barrel, vent. barrel shroud, 20- or 36-shot mag., matte black finish, 7 1/2 lbs., select fire NFA class III transferable only.

	$395	$350	$300	$275	$250	$230	$210	Last MSR was $379.

ARMS TECH LTD.

Current manufacturer established in 1987, and located in Phoenix, AZ.

RIFLES: BOLT ACTION

Current models include the SMIR, TTR-50, TTR-700, SBA 2000, USR, USR-K, Voyager, and the Overwatch. Arms Tech Ltd. also offers a wide variety of options and accessories. Please contact the company directly for more information, including pricing, options, and availability (see Trademark Index).

RIFLES: SEMI-AUTO

Current models include the Urban Support Rifle for the civilian marketplace, and several models available for military/law enforcement. Please contact the company directly for more information, including pricing and availability (see Trademark Index).

SUPER MATCH INTERDICTION POLICE MODEL – .243 Win., .300 Win. Mag., or .308 Win. (standard) cal., features 22 in. free floating Schnieder or Douglas air gauged stainless steel barrel, gas operation, McMillan stock, updated trigger group, detachable box mag., 13 1/4 lbs. Limited mfg. 1996-98.

	$3,950	$3,650	$3,300	$3,000	$2,750	$2,350	$2,000	Last MSR was $4,800.

SHOTGUNS: SLIDE ACTION

Currently, Arms Tech Ltd. offers two shotgun models - the Hammer, and the Alpha Entry, utilizing the Rem. 870 action. Both have folding stocks. Please contact the company directly regarding pricing and availability for these two models (see Trademark Index).

ARMSCOR

Current trademark of firearms manufactured by Arms Corporation of the Philippines (manufacturing began 1952) established in 1985 (Armscor Precision - API). Currently imported and distributed beginning 1999 by Armscor Precision International (full line), located in Pahrump, NV. Previously imported 1995-1999 by K.B.I., Inc. located in Harrisburg, PA, by Ruko located in Buffalo, NY until 1995 and by Armscorp Precision Inc. located in San Mateo, CA until 1991.

In 1991, the importation of Arms Corporation of the Philippines firearms was changed to Ruko Products, Inc., located in Buffalo, NY. Barrel markings on firearms imported by Ruko Products, Inc. state "Ruko-Armscor" instead of the older "Armscorp Precision" barrel markings. All Armscorp Precision, Inc. models were discontinued in 1991.

The models listed below also provide cross-referencing for older Armscorp Precision and Ruko imported models.

PISTOLS: SEMI-AUTO

All semi-auto pistols were discontinued during 2008, and currently Armscor manufactured pistols can be found under the Rock Island Armory trademark.

M-1911-A1 FS (FULL SIZE STANDARD) – .45 ACP cal., patterned after the Colt Govt. Model, 7-shot mag. (2 provided), 5 in. barrel, parkerized (disc. 2001), blue (new 2002), two-tone (new 2002), or stainless steel (new 2002), skeletonized combat hammer and trigger, front and rear slide serrations, hard rubber grips, 38 oz. Imported 1996-97, reintroduced 2001-2008.

	$350	$300	$280	$260	$240	$220	$200	Last MSR was $399.

Add $31 for two-tone finish.
Add $75 for stainless steel.

This model was also available in a high capacity configuration (Model 1911-A2 HC, 13 shot mag., $519 MSR).

M-1911-A1 MS (COMMANDER) – .45 ACP cal., Commander configuration with 4 in. barrel, otherwise similar to M-1911 A1 Standard, rear slide serrations only. Imported 2001-2008.

	$360	$300	$280	$260	$240	$220	$200	Last MSR was $408.

Add $37 for two-tone finish.
Add $90 for stainless steel.

M-1911-A1 CS (OFFICER) – .45 ACP cal., officer's configuration with 3 1/2 in. barrel, checkered hardwood grips, 2.16 lbs. Imported 2002-2008.

	$370	$310	$285	$265	$245	$220	$200	Last MSR was $423.

Add $52 for two-tone finish.
Add $105 for stainless steel.

MSR	100%	98%	95%	90%	80%	70%	60%

RIFLES: SEMI-AUTO

M-1600 – .22 LR cal., 10- or 15- (disc.) shot mag., 18 in. barrel, copy of the Armalite M16, ebony stock, 5 1/4 lbs.

No MSR	$180	$150	$130	$110	$100	$80	$70

* **M-1600R** – similar to M-1600, except has stainless steel retractable buttstock and vent. barrel hood, 7 1/4 lbs. Importation disc. 1995, reintroduced 2008.

No MSR	$155	$135	$115	$105	$85	$70	$55

M-AK22(S) – .22 LR cal., copy of the famous Russian Kalashnikov AK-47 rifle, 18 1/2 in. barrel, 10- or 15- (disc.) shot mag., mahogany stock and forearm, 7 lbs.

No MSR	$185	$160	$140	$125	$100	$85	$65

* **M-AK22(F)** – similar to M-AK22, except has metal folding stock, and 30-shot mag. Disc. 1995.

	$275	$240	$205	$185	$150	$125	$95	Last MSR was $299.

SHOTGUNS: SLIDE ACTION

M-30 DG (DEER GUN) – 12 ga. only, law enforcement version of M-30, 20 in. plain barrel, iron sights, 7-shot mag., approx. 7 lbs. Importation disc. 1999, resumed during 2001.

	$165	$140	$120	$100	$85	$75	$70	Last MSR was $195.

M-30SAS1 – 12 ga. only, riot configuration with 20 in. barrel and vent. barrel shroud, and Speedfeed 4-shot (disc.) or regular synthetic buttstock and forearm, 6-shot mag., matte finish, 8 lbs. Imported 1996-1999 and 2001-2008.

	$180	$155	$130	$110	$95	$85	$75	Last MSR was $211.

Add $56 for Speedfeed stock (new 2002).

M-30 R6/R8 (RIOT) – 12 ga. only, similar to M-30DG, except has front bead sight only, 5- or 7-shot mag., cyl. bore. Imported disc. 1999, reintroduced 2001-2008.

	$155	$135	$110	$90	$80	$75	$70	Last MSR was $181.

Add $7 for 7 shot mag.

M-30BG – 12 ga. only, 18 1/2 in. barrel, 5-shot mag., polymer pistol grip and forearm. Importation began 2004.

Retail pricing is not available on this model.

M-30F/FS – similar to M-30BG, except has additional folding metal stock unit. Disc. 2008.

	$180	$155	$130	$110	$95	$85	$75	Last MSR was $211.

M30 C (COMBO) – 12 ga., 20 in. barrel, 5-shot mag., unique detachable black synthetic buttstock which allows pistol grip only operation. Disc. 1995.

	$210	$175	$145	$120	$100	$90	$80	Last MSR was $289.

M30 RP (COMBO) – 12 ga. only, same action as M-30 DG, interchangeable black pistol grip, 18 1/4 in. plain barrel w/front bead sight, 6 1/4 lbs. Disc. 1995.

	$210	$175	$145	$120	$100	$90	$80	Last MSR was $289.

ARMSCORP USA, INC.

Previous manufacturer and importer located in Baltimore, MD. Currently Armscorp USA deals in parts only.

PISTOLS: SEMI-AUTO

HI POWER – 9mm Para. cal., patterned after Browning design, 4 2/3 in. barrel, military finish, 13-shot mag., synthetic checkered grips, spur hammer, 2 lbs. mfg. in Argentina, imported 1989-90 only.

	$395	$350	$295	$275	$250	$225	$200	Last MSR was $450.

Add $15 for round hammer.
Add $50 for hard chrome finish w/combat grips (disc. 1989).

RIFLES: SEMI-AUTO

M-14 RIFLE (NORINCO PARTS) – .308 Win. cal., 20-shot mag., mfg. M-14 using Norinco parts, wood stock. Mfg. 1991-92 only.

	$1,225	$1,150	$1,050	$975	$875	$775	$675	Last MSR was $688.

M-14R RIFLE (USGI PARTS) – .308 Win. cal., 10- (C/B 1994) or 20*-shot mag., newly manufactured M-14 using original excellent condition forged G.I. parts including USGI fiberglass stock with rubber recoil pad. Mfg. 1986-2006.

	$1,925	$1,675	$1,400	$1,275	$1,125	$1,000	$850	Last MSR was $1,895.

MSR	100%	98%	95%	90%	80%	70%	60%

Add $80 for medium weight National Match walnut stock (M-14RNS).
Add $25 for G.I. buttplate (disc.).
Add $45 for USGI birch stock (M-14RNSB, disc.).

M-14 BEGINNING NATIONAL MATCH – .308 Win. cal., mfg. from hand selected older USGI parts, except for new receiver and new USGI air gauged premium barrel, guaranteed to shoot 1 1/4 in. group at 100 yards. Mfg. 1993-96.

	$2,050	$1,650	$1,350	$1,225	$1,125	$1,025	$925	Last MSR was $1,950.

M-14 NMR (NATIONAL MATCH) – .308 Win. cal., built in accordance with A.M.T.U. mil. specs., 3 different barrel weights to choose from, NM rear sight system, calibrated mag., leather sling, guaranteed 1 in. MOA. Mfg. 1987-2006.

	$2,675	$2,125	$1,750	$1,400	$1,200	$1,075	$950	Last MSR was $2,850.

M-21 MATCH RIFLE – .308 Win. cal., NM rear lugged receiver, choice of McMillan fiberglass or laminated wood stock, guaranteed 1 MOA accuracy.

	$3,475	$2,900	$2,325	$2,000	$1,650	$1,350	$1,175	Last MSR was $3,595.

T-48 FAL ISRAELI PATTERN RIFLE – .308 Win. cal., mfg. in the U.S. to precise original metric dimensions (parts are interchangeable with original Belgium FAL), forged receiver, hammer forged chrome lined mil-spec. 21 in. barrel (standard or heavy) with flash suppressor, adj. front sight, aperture rear sight, 10 lbs. Imported 1990-92.

	$1,650	$1,475	$1,300	$1,150	$1,075	$975	$875	Last MSR was $1,244.

This model was guaranteed to shoot within 2.5 MOA with match ammunition.

* ***T-48 FAL L1A1 Pattern*** – .308 Win. cal., fully enclosed forend with vents, 10 lbs. Imported 1992 only.

	$1,675	$1,500	$1,325	$1,175	$1,100	$1,000	$900	Last MSR was $1,181.

Add $122 for wood handguard sporter model (limited supply).

T-48 BUSH MODEL – similar to T-48 FAL, except has 18 in. barrel, 9 3/4 lbs. Mfg. 1990 only.

	$1,625	$1,450	$1,325	$1,175	$1,025	$925	$850	Last MSR was $1,250.

FRHB – .308 Win. cal., Israeli mfg. with heavy barrel and bipod. Imported 1990 only.

	$2,175	$1,900	$1,600	$1,425	$1,325	$1,225	$1,175	Last MSR was $1,895.

FAL – .308 Win. cal., Armscorp forged receiver, 21 in. Argentinian rebuilt barrel, manufactured to military specs., supplied with one military 20-shot mag., aperture rear sight, 10 lbs. Mfg. 1987-89.

	$1,800	$1,575	$1,425	$1,250	$1,125	$1,025	$925	Last MSR was $875.

Subtract $55 if without flash hider.
Add $75 for heavy barrel with bipod (14 lbs.).
Add $400 (last retail) for .22 LR conversion kit.

This model was guaranteed to shoot within 2.5 MOA with match ammunition.

* ***FAL Bush Model*** – similar to FAL, except has 18 in. barrel with flash suppressor, 9 3/4 lbs. Mfg. 1989 only.

	$2,200	$2,050	$1,925	$1,825	$1,750	$1,500	$1,250	Last MSR was $900.

* ***FAL Para Model*** – similar to FAL Bush Model, except has metal folding stock, leaf rear sight. Mfg. 1989 only.

	$2,400	$2,150	$1,050	$1,950	$1,750	$1,650	$1,550	Last MSR was $930.

* ***FAL Factory Rebuilt*** – factory (Argentine) rebuilt FAL without flash suppressor in excellent condition with Armscorp forged receiver, 9 lbs. 10 oz. Disc. 1989.

	$1,675	$1,450	$1,195	$1,025	$950	$775	$695	Last MSR was $675.

Add 20% for heavy barrel variation manufactured in Argentina under license from F.N.

M36 ISRAELI SNIPER RIFLE – .308 Win. cal., gas operated semi-auto, bullpup configuration, 22 in. free floating barrel, Armscorp M14 receiver, 20-shot mag., includes flash suppressor and bipod, 10 lbs. Civilian offering 1989 only.

	$3,050	$2,650	$2,425	$2,200	$2,050	$1,925	$1,750	Last MSR was $3,000.

ARSENAL, BULGARIA

Current manufacturer located in Bulgaria. Currently imported by Arsenal, Inc., located in Las Vegas, NV. Previously imported exclusively in 1994-96 by Sentinel Arms located in Detroit, MI. For currently imported models, please refer to the Arsenal, Inc. listing.

The artillery arsenal in Rousse began operating in 1878, and was managed by Russian officers until 1884, when a Bulgarian was appointed the director. In 1891, the factory was transferred to Sofia, and was renamed the Sofia Artillery Arsenal until the entire facility was moved to Kazanlak in 1924. At that point, the name was changed to the

MSR	100%	98%	95%	90%	80%	70%	60%

State Military Factory. After WWII, the arsenal diversified into civilian production, and its Cold War security name was "Factory 10". In 1958, the first AK-47 under Russian license came off the assembly line, and in 1982, the one millionth AK-47 had been manufactured.

RIFLES: SEMI-AUTO

BULGARIAN SA-93 – 7.62x39mm cal., Kalashnikov with hardwood thumbhole stock, 16.3 in. barrel, 5-shot detachable mag., 9 lbs. Disc. 1996.

	$800	$715	$625	$550	$600	$475	$450

* *Bulgarian SA-93L* – 7.62x39mm cal., similar to Bulgarian SA-93 except has 20 in. barrel, with or without optics, 9 lbs. Disc. 1996.

	$795	$725	$650	$595	$550	$495	$450

Add $145 with optics.

BULGARIAN SS-94 – 7.62x39mm cal., Kalashnikov action, thumbhole hardwood stock, 5-shot detachable mag., 9 lbs. Disc. 1996.

	$625	$550	$475	$425	$375	$350	$325

ARSENAL INC.

Current importer of non-military Arsenal 2000 JSCo (Bulgarian Arsenal), established during 2001 and located in Las Vegas, NV. Dealer and distributor sales.

RIFLES: SEMI-AUTO

Arsenal Inc. is the exclusive licensed manufacturer of various Arsenal Bulgaria AK style/design rifles which conform 100% to Arsenal Bulgaria specifications and manufacturing procedures. Models are built on forged and milled receivers with CNC technology, and feature solid, under-folding or side-folding stock.

SA M-5 SERIES – .223 Rem. cal., patterned after the AK-47, 16.3 in. barrel, black (SA M-5) or green (SA M-5G, disc. 2005) synthetic furniture with pistol grip, approx. 8.1 lbs. Mfg. 2003-2009.

	$710	$620	$530	$480	$390	$320	$250	Last MSR was $800.

Add $75 for SA M-5 R with scope rail (new 2007).
Add $10 for SA M-5G (disc. 2005).
Add $75 for SA M-5S with scope rail (limited edition, disc. 2005).
Add $80 for SA M-5SG (disc. 2005).

SA M-7 SERIES – 7.62x39mm cal., milled receiver, also available in carbine, otherwise similar to SA M-5, R Series witrh scope rail became standard 2009. New 2003.

MSR $1,065	$950	$830	$710	$645	$520	$425	$330

Add $35 for SA M-7S with scope rail.
Add $5 for SA M-7G with OD green furniture.
Add $40 for SA M-7SG with scope rail.
Subtract approx. 15% if w/o scope rail.

SA M-7 CLASSIC – 7.62x39mm cal., features blonde wood stock, pistol grip and forearm, double stack magazine, heavy barrel and slanted gas block, Warsaw Pact buttstock, less than 200 mfg. 2001-2002, reintroduced 2007-2008.

	$795	$695	$595	$540	$435	$360	$280	Last MSR was $1,200.

SA M-7 A1/SA M-7 A1 R – 7.62x39mm cal., milled receiver, front sight gas block w/bayonet lug, 24mm flash hider, cleaning rod, accessory lug, black polymer furniture, NATO buttstock. Mfg. 2007-2009.

	$850	$745	$635	$580	$465	$380	$295	Last MSR was $960.

Add $75 for SA M-7 A1 R w/scope rail.

SA M-7 SF – 7.62x39mm cal., U.S. mfg., milled receiver, front sight gas block with bayonet lug, 24mm flash hider, cleaning rod, accessory lug, black polymer furniture, right hand side folding stock, ambidextrous safety, scope rail. Mfg. 2007-2009.

	$1,025	$895	$770	$695	$565	$460	$360	Last MSR was $1,300.

SA M-7 SFC/SA M-7 SFK – 7.62x39mm cal., U.S. mfg., milled receiver, front sight/gas block combination with 24mm thread protector, cleaning rod, black polymer furniture, right hand side folding tubular buttstock, ambidextrous safety, scope rail, SA M-7 SFK model with short gas system and laminated wood Krinkov handguards became standard 2009. New 2007.

MSR $1,575	$1,325	$1,160	$995	$900	$730	$595	$465

MSR	100%	98%	95%	90%	80%	70%	60%	

SA RPK-7 – 7.62x39mm cal., paddle style buttstock, folding bi-pod, no scope rail, otherwise similar to SA RPK-5 (S). Limited edition 2003-2005, reintroduced 2007-2009.

| | $995 | $870 | $745 | $675 | $545 | $450 | $350 | Last MSR was $1,250. |

Add $75 for SA RPK-7 R with scope rail.

SA RPK-5 (S) – .223 Rem. cal., features blonde wood stock, RPK heavy barrel, 14mm muzzle threads, pistol grip and forearm, 23 1/4 in. barrel with folding tripod, approx. 11 lbs. Limited edition 2003-2005, reintroduced 2007-2009.

| | $1,075 | $940 | $800 | $730 | $590 | $485 | $375 | Last MSR was $1,250. |

Add $75 for SA RPK-5 R model with scope rail.

SAS M-7 – 7.62x39mm cal., U.S. mfg., authentic semi-auto version of Bulgarian model AR M1F with vertical gas block and BATFE-approved fixed metal underfolding-style stock. Mfg. 2004-2007.

| | $1,075 | $940 | $800 | $730 | $590 | $485 | $375 | Last MSR was $1,250. |

SAS M-7 CLASSIC – 7.62x39mm cal., U.S. mfg., authentic semi-auto version of Russian 1953 Model AKS-47 with slant gas block and BATFE-approved fixed metal underfolding-style stock, blond furniture, heavy barrel. Limited edition 2001-2002, reintroduced 2007-2009.

| | $1,000 | $875 | $750 | $680 | $550 | $450 | $350 | Last MSR was $1,275. |

SLR 101 S – 7.62x39mm cal., similar to SA M-7, except has thumbhole synthetic stock, available in black (SLR 101SB1) or OD Green (SLR 101SG1). Mfg. 2003-2005.

| | $595 | $550 | $500 | $450 | $400 | $350 | $325 | Last MSR was $410. |

Add $100 for SLR 101SB1.
Add $110 for SLR 101SG1.

SLR 101SB/SG – 7.62x39mm cal., double stack mag., side mount scope rail, 16 in. barrel, standard military stock configuration. Mfg. 2004-2005.

| | $725 | $635 | $545 | $495 | $400 | $325 | $255 | Last MSR was $655. |

Add $45 for SG Model with green polymer stock.

SLR-105 SERIES – 5.45x39.5mm cal., stamped receiver, cleaning rod, black polymer furniture, NATO buttstock. Mfg. 2007-2009.

| | $695 | $650 | $600 | $550 | $475 | $425 | $350 | Last MSR was $475. |

Add $50 for SLR-105 R with scope rail.
Add $150 for SLR-105 A1 model with front sight gas block, bayonet lug, and 24mm muzzle brake.
Add $200 for SLR-105 A1 R model with scope rail.

SLR-106 SERIES – 5.56 NATO cal., stamped receiver, left-side folding stock, 24mm muzzle brake, bayonet lug, accessory lug, stainless steel heat shield, two-stage trigger. Mfg. 2007-2009.

| | $795 | $725 | $650 | $575 | $500 | $450 | $395 | Last MSR was $800. |

Add $79 for SLR-106 FR with scope rail.
Add $99 for Desert Sand stock.
Add $199 for SLR-106 U Model with combination short-stroke gas block and front sight system and black furniture.
Add $80 for SLT-106 U Model with scope rail (SLR-106 UR).
Add $179 for SLR-106 Model with removable muzzle attachment.
Subtract $50 for original metal left-hand side folding stock.

SLR-107 SERIES – 7.62x39mm cal., stamped receiver, left-side folding stock, 24mm flash hider, bayonet lug, accessory lug, stainless steel heat shield, two-stage trigger. Mfg. 2008-2009.

| | $795 | $725 | $650 | $575 | $500 | $450 | $395 | Last MSR was $799. |

Add $80 for SLR-107 FR with scope rail.

Add $326 for SLR-107 UR Model with combination short-stroke gas block and front sight system and black furniture and scope rail.
Add $180 for SLR-107 CR Model with removable muzzle attachment.

ARSENAL USA LLC

Previous manufacturer/importer from 1999-2004, and located in Houston, TX. During September 2004, Arsenal USA LLC changed its name to Armory USA L.L.C. Please refer to the Armory USA L.L.C. listing for recently manufactured rifles.

RIFLES: SEMI-AUTO

MODEL SSR-99 – 7.62x39mm cal., Bulgarian milled receiver and parts, black polymer furniture. Less than 300 mfg. 1999-2000.

| | $825 | $750 | $700 | $650 | $600 | $550 | $500 | Last MSR was $600. |

MODEL K-101 – .223 Rem. cal., Bulgarian milled receiver and parts, black polymer furniture. Less than 200 mfg. 1999-2000.

| | $875 | $775 | $700 | $650 | $600 | $550 | $500 | Last MSR was $600. |

MSR	100%	98%	95%	90%	80%	70%	60%

MODEL SSR-99P – 7.62x39mm cal., Bulgarian milled receiver and parts, with rare Polish grenade launching variant parts, Polish wood furniture. Less than 500 mfg. 1999-2001.

	$875	$775	$700	$650	$600	$550	$500	Last MSR was $600.

MODEL SSR-85B – 7.62x39mm cal., Hungarian FEG receiver and Polish AKM parts, blond Hungarian wood furniture, small number produced using ITM U.S. made receiver. Approx. 1,200 mfg. 2000-2003.

	$875	$775	$700	$650	$600	$550	$625	Last MSR was $450.

MODEL AMD-63 – 7.62x39mm cal., Hungarian FEG receiver and Polish AKM parts, unique metal lower handguard with pistol grip. 200 mfg. 2000-2003.

	$875	$775	$700	$650	$600	$550	$500	Last MSR was $600.

MODEL SSR-56 – 7.62x39mm cal., Hungarian FEG receiver, Poly-Tec barrel assembly and Bulgarian internal parts. Approx. 500 mfg. 2002-2003.

	$775	$700	$650	$600	$550	$500	$450	Last MSR was $450.

ASP

Previously manufactured customized variation of a S&W Model 39-2 semi-auto pistol (or related variations) manufactured by Armament Systems and Procedures located in Appleton, WI.

PISTOLS: SEMI-AUTO

ASP – 9mm Para. cal., compact double action semi-auto, see-through grips with cut-away mag. making cartridges visible, Teflon coated, re-contoured lightened slide, combat trigger guard, spurless hammer, and mostly painted Guttersnipe rear sight (no front sight), supplied with 3 mags., 24 oz. loaded. Approx. 3,000 mfg. until 1981.

	$1,500	$1,275	$1,050	$875	$775	$695	$625

Add $200 for Tritium filled Guttersnipe sight.

This pistol is marked "ASP" on the magazine extension.

AUSTRALIAN AUTOMATIC ARMS PTY. LTD.

Previous manufacturer located in Tasmania, Australia. Previously imported and distributed by California Armory, Inc. located in San Bruno, CA.

PISTOLS: SEMI-AUTO

SAP – .223 Rem. cal., semi-auto tactical design pistol, 10 1/2 in. barrel, 20-shot mag., fiberglass stock and forearm, 5.9 lbs. Imported 1986-93.

	$795	$700	$600	$550	$500	$475	$450	Last MSR was $799.

RIFLES: SEMI-AUTO

SAR – .223 Rem. cal., semi-auto tactical design rifle, 16 1/4 or 20 in. (new 1989) barrel, 5- or 20-shot M-16 style mag., fiberglass stock and forearm, 7 1/2 lbs. Imported 1986-89.

	$1,250	$1,000	$900	$800	$775	$750	$700	Last MSR was $663.

Add $25 for 20 in. barrel.

This model was also available in a fully automatic version (AR).

SAC – .223 Rem. cal., semi-auto tactical design carbine, 10 1/2 in. barrel, 20-shot mag., fiberglass stock and forearm, 6.9 lbs. New 1986.

This model was available to NFA class III dealers and law enforcement agencies only.

SP – .223 Rem. cal., semi-auto, sporting configuration, 16 1/4 or 20 in. barrel, wood stock and forearm, 5 or 20 shot M-16 style mag., 7 1/4 lbs. Imported late 1991-93.

	$850	$750	$650	$600	$550	$500	$475	Last MSR was $879.

Add $40 for wood stock.

AUSTRALIAN INTERNATIONAL ARMS

Current manufacturer and exporter located in Brisbane, Australia. Previously, Australian International Arms worked in cooperation with ADI Limited Lithgow, formerly Small Arms Factory, known for its SMLE No. I MKIII and L1A1 rifles. AIA now outsources the manufacture of its designs and specifications. Currently imported in North America by Marstar Canada, located in Ontario, Canada. Previously imported and distributed until 2004 by Tristar Sporting Arms, Ltd., located in N. Kansas City, MO.

MSR	100%	98%	95%	90%	80%	70%	60%

RIFLES: BOLT ACTION, ENFIELD SERIES

M10-A1 – 7.62x39mm cal., redesigned and improved No. 4 MK2 action, parkerized finish, all new components, teak furniture with No. 5 Jungle Carbine style stock with steel or brass buttplate, 20 in. chrome lined barrel with muzzle brake, adj. front sight, 10 shot mag., Picatinny rail, 8.3 lbs. Importation began 2007.

As this edition went to press, prices had yet to be established on this model.

* **M10-A2** – 7.62x39mm cal., similar to M10A2, except has No. 8 style forend, Monte Carlo stock, and 16.1 in. chrome lined barrel. Limited importation 2003-2004 by Tristar.

	$750	$700	$600	$525	$450	$375	$300	Last MSR was $659.

M10-B1 – .308 Win. cal., redesigned and improved No. 4 MK2 action, matte blue finish, all new components, teak furniture with sporter carbine style stock and steel buttplate, 22 in. barrel, adj. front sight, 10 shot mag., Picatinny rail, 8.3 lbs. Importation began 2006.

MSR $675	$575	$500	$425	$350	$300	$275	$250

* **M10-B2** – .308 Win. cal., similar to M10-B1, except has brass buttplate, gloss blue finish, 25 in. chrome lined bull barrel, and bipod stud, 10.5 lbs. Importation began 2006.

MSR $760	$650	$525	$425	$350	$300	$275	$225

* **M10-B3** – .308 Win. cal., similar to M10-B1, except has chrome steel buttplate, gloss blue finish, and 22 in. lightweight barrel, 7 1/2 lbs. Limited importation began 2006.

MSR $1,000	$900	$800	$700	$600	$500	$425	$350

NO.4 MK IV – .308 Win. cal., parkerized finish, 25.2 in. chrome lined medium weight barrel, teak furniture with steel buttplate, 9.1 lbs. Prototype only imported by Tristar. Limited importation beginning 2006.

	$575	$500	$425	$350	$300	$275	$250	Last MSR was $675.

Add $440 for walnut stock, glass bedding, target barrel, elevated Picatinny rail, and accessories (disc.).

M 42 – .308 Win. cal., 27.6 in. barrel with mahogany stock and extra cheekpiece, blue printed action, bright metal/barrel finish, includes Picatinny rail, 8.2 lbs. Imported 2003-2004.

	$1,125	$950	$800	$650	$550	$450	$350	Last MSR was $1,295.

AUTO-ORDNANCE CORP.

Current manufacturer with facilities located in Worcester, MA, and corporate offices in Blauvelt, NY. Auto-Ordnance Corp. became a division of Kahr Arms in 1999. Auto-Ordnance Corp. was a division of Gun Parts Corp. until 1999. Previously located in West Hurley, NY. Consumer, dealer, and distributor sales.

Auto-Ordnance Corp. manufactures an exact reproduction of the original 1927 Thompson sub-machine gun. They are currently available from Kahr Arms in semi-auto only since production ceased on fully automatic variations (Model 1928 and M1) in 1986 (mfg. 1975-1986 including 609 M1s). All current models utilize the Thompson trademark, are manufactured in the U.S., and come with a lifetime warranty.

PISTOLS: SEMI-AUTO

During 1997, Auto Ordnance discontinued all calibers on the pistols listed below, except for .45 ACP cal. or 9mm Para. Slide kits were available for $179. Also, conversion units (converting .45 ACP to .38 Super or 9mm Para.) were available for $195.

All current Auto Ordnance 1911 Models include a spent cartridge case, plastic carrying case, and cable lock.

1911 COMPETITION – .38 Super (1996 only) or .45 ACP cal., competition features included compensated barrel, commander hammer, flat mainspring housing, white 3-dot sighting system, beavertail grip safety, black textured wraparound grips. Mfg. 1993-1996.

	$530	$415	$375	$330	$300	$285	$270	Last MSR was $636.

Add $10 for .38 Super cal.

1911 THOMPSON CUSTOM – .45 ACP cal., stainless steel or aluminum (Lightweight model, mfg. 2005-2007) construction, Series 80 design, 5 in. barrel, Thompson bullet logo on left side of double serrated slide, 7-shot mag., grip safety, checkered laminate grips with medallion, skeletonized trigger, combat hammer, low profile sights, 31 1/2 (Lightweight) or 39 oz. New 2004.

MSR $813	$695	$575	$485	$415	$350	$300	$275

* **1911 A1 WWII Parkerized** – .45 ACP cal., no frills variation of the 1911 A1, military parkerizing, G.I. detailing with military style roll stamp, plastic or checkered walnut (disc. 2001, reintroduced 2007) grips, and lanyard loop. New 1992.

MSR $627	$495	$395	$315	$275	$235	$225	$215

Add $35 for wood grips (new 2007).

MSR	100%	98%	95%	90%	80%	70%	60%

RIFLES: SEMI-AUTO

The Auto-Ordnance Thompson replicas listed below are currently supplied with a 15, 20, or 30 shot stick mag. Tommy Guns are not currently legal in CA or CT.

Add the following for currently manufactured Thompson 1921 A-1 models:
Add $70 for 20 or 30 shot stick mag.
Add $68 for 10 shot stick mag.
Add $193 for 10 shot drum mag. (they resemble the older 50 shot L-type drum) - new 1994.
Add $299 for 50* shot drum mag. or $577 for 100* shot drum mag. (mfg. 1990-93, reintroduced 2006).
Add $157 for factory violin case or $181 for hard case.

THOMPSON M1 CARBINE (.45 ACP CAL.) – .45 ACP cal., combat model, 16 1/2 in. smooth barrel w/o compensator, 30 shot original surplus mag., side-cocking lever, matte black finish, walnut stock, pistol grip, and grooved horizontal forearm, current mfg. will not accept drum mags., 11 1/2 lbs. New 1986.

MSR $1,334	$1,050	$850	$625	$525	$425	$375	$325

* *Thompson M1-C Lightweight* – similar to M1 Carbine, except receiver is made of a lightweight alloy, current mfg. accepts drum mags., 9 1/2 lbs. Mfg. 2001-2002, reintroduced 2005.

MSR $1,206	$1,075	$925	$825	$725	$625	$525	$425

During 2006, this model incorporated a large machined radius on the bottom of the receiver to improve magazine insertion.

AUTO-ORDNANCE M1-CARBINE (.30 CAL.) – .30 Carbine cal., birch or walnut (standard beginning 2008) stock, 18 in. barrel, all new parts, parkerized receiver, metal handguard, aperture rear sight, and bayonet lug, 10 (new 2005) or 15-shot mag., 5.4 lbs. New 2004.

MSR $899	$775	$625	$500	$450	$400	$350	$300

* *Auto-Ordnance M1 Carbine Paratrooper* – .30 Carbine cal., similar to .30 cal. M1 Carbine, except has folding stock, walnut handguard, parkerized finish, 15 shot mag. New 2008.

MSR $1,084	$895	$775	$675	$575	$475	$375	$325

* *Auto-Ordnance M1 Carbine Tactical* – .30 Carbine cal., similar to .30 cal. M1 carbine, except has black polymer folding stock, metal handguard, 15 shot mag. New 2008.

MSR $860	$700	$575	$475	$375	$325	$300	$275

AUTO-ORDNANCE 1927 A-1 STANDARD – .45 ACP cal., 16 in. plain barrel, solid steel construction, standard military sight, walnut stock and horizontal forearm. Disc. 1986.

	$570	$490	$430	$360	$315	$290	$270	Last MSR was $575.

THOMPSON 1927 A-1 DELUXE CARBINE – 10mm (mfg. 1991-93) or .45 ACP cal., 16 1/2 in. finned barrel with compensator, includes one 30 shot original surplus mag., current mfg. accepts drum mags., solid steel construction, matte black finish, adj. rear sight, walnut stock, pistol grip, and finger grooved forearm grip, 13 lbs.

MSR $1,420	$1,100	$975	$800	$675	$550	$495	$450

Add $433 for detachable buttstock and horizontal foregrip (new 2007).

During 2006, design changes included a more authentic spherical cocking knob, improved frame to receiver fit, and a large machined radius at the bottom of the receiver to help with magazine insertion.

* *Thompson 1927 A-1C Lightweight Deluxe* – .45 ACP cal., similar to 1927 A-1 Deluxe, except receiver made of a lightweight alloy, currently shipped with 30 shot stick mag. (where legal), current mfg. accepts drum mags., 9 1/2 lbs. New 1984.

MSR $1,286	$1,075	$950	$800	$700	$600	$500	$425

Add $413 for 100 shot drum mag.

* *Thompson 1927 A-1 Presentation Walnut Carbine* – .45 ACP cal., similar to 1927 A-1 Deluxe, except has presentation grade walnut buttstock, pistol grip, and foregrip, supplied with plastic case. Limited mfg. 2003.

	$850	$675	$525	$425	$350	$325	$295	Last MSR was $1,121.

* *Thompson 1927 A-1 Deluxe .22 LR Cal.* – .22 LR cal., very limited mfg., 30-shot mag. standard.

	$1,100	$995	$925	$800	$700	$650	$575

THOMPSON 1927 A-1 COMMANDO – .45 ACP cal., 16 1/2 in. finned barrel with compensator, 30-shot mag., black finished stock and forearm, parkerized metal, black nylon sling, 13 lbs. New 1997.

MSR $1,393	$1,095	$975	$800	$675	$550	$495	$450

During 2006, this model incorporated a spherical cocking knob.

MSR	100%	98%	95%	90%	80%	70%	60%

THOMPSON SBR – .45 ACP cal., 10 1/2 in. finned barrel, closed bolt, blue metal finish, pistol grip forearm, 30-shot mag., 12 lbs. New 2004.

MSR $2,053	$1,825	$1,600	$1,375	$1,150	$975	$850	$725

Add $503 for detachable buttstock and horizontal foregrip (new 2007).

This carbine model may only be shipped from the factory to an NFA Class II manufacturer or NFA Class III dealer.

THOMPSON M1 SBR – .45 ACP cal., 10 1/2 in. barrel, closed bolt, blue metal finish, regular forearm, 30-shot mag., 12 lbs. New 2004.

MSR $1,970	$1,750	$1,500	$1,300	$1,125	$925	$800	$700

This carbine model may only be shipped from the factory to an NFA Class II manufacturer or NFA Class III dealer.

1927 A5 PISTOL/CARBINE – .45 ACP cal., 13 in. finned barrel, alloy construction, overall length 26 in., 10- (C/B 1994) shot mag., 7 lbs. Mfg. disc. 1994.

	$1,050	$925	$825	$750	$650	$600	$500	Last MSR was $765.

1927 A3 · .22 CAL. – .22 LR cal., 16 or 18 in. finned barrel with compensator, alloy frame and receiver, fixed or detachable walnut stock, pistol grip, and forearm pistol grip, 7 lbs. Mfg. disc. 1994.

	$995	$875	$750	$650	$550	$500	$450	Last MSR was $510.

NOTES

B SECTION

BAIKAL

Current trademark of products manufactured by the Russian Federal State Unitary Plant "Izhevsky Mechanichesky Zavod" (FSUP IMZ). Baikal SxS and O/U hunting guns (including air guns) were imported and distributed exclusively 2005-2009 by U.S. Sporting Goods (USSG), located in Rockledge, FL. Many Baikal shotguns and rifles were marketed domestically by Remington under the Spartan Gunworks trademark until 2008. See listings under Spartan Gunworks for more information.

Previously imported from late 1998 until 2004 by European American Armory Corp., located in Sharpes, FL, and from 1993-1996 by Big Bear, located in Dallas, TX.

Please contact the importer directly for more information and pricing on Baikal firearms (see Trademark Index).

Baikal (the name of a lake in Siberia) was one of the key holding companies from the former Soviet Union, specializing in the production of firearms, and science intensive, complex electronic equipment.

The company was founded in 1942 as part of the Russian National Defense Industry. At that time, the plant produced world renowned Tokarev TT pistols. Upon conclusion of WWII, the company expanded its operation to include non-military firearms (O/U, SxS, and single barrel shotguns). FSUP IMZ is one of the world's largest manufacturers of military and non-military firearms. The total amount of guns produced by the FSUP IMZ is 680,000 units per year. The products range from various smoothbore guns, including slide action and self-loading models, rifled and combination guns, to a full array of sporting, civil, and combat pistols, including the internationally famous Makarov pistol. Since 2000, Baikal has produced a new pistol for the Russian Army which was developed by the enterprise designers and named after the group's leader - the Yarygin pistol.

FSUP IMZ features efficient manufacturing capacity and the unique intellectual potential of its qualified engineers-and-technicians staff. The FSUP IMZ is also undertaking the task of reintroducing the world to the "Russian Custom Gunsmith". There is a gunsmith school at the factory area for custom, one-of-a-kind hand engraved shotguns and rifles. The guns produced by the school feature high-quality assembly, attractive appearance, and high functional quality according to the best traditions of Russian gunmakers.

In the past, Baikal shotguns have had limited importation into the U.S. 1993 marked the first year that Baikals were officially (and legally) imported into the U.S. because of Russia's previous export restrictions. In prior years, however, a few O/Us have been seen for sale and have no doubt been imported into this country one at a time. Currently produced Baikals are noted for their good quality at low-level costs.

MSR	100%	98%	95%	90%	80%	70%	60%

RIFLES: SEMI-AUTO

MP161K – .17 HMR, .22 LR, or .22 Mag. cal., 19 1/2 in. accurized barrel, grey polymer thumbhole pistol grip stock with adj. LOP and cheekpiece height, 10 shot mag., integral Picatinny rail, adj. open sight, loaded chamber indicator, trigger guard mounted bottom safety, blue recoil pad and inserts in the forend. Importation began 2009.

MSR $542	$475	$415	$355	$325	$260	$215	$165

BARRETT FIREARMS MANUFACTURING, INC.

Current rifle manufacturer established in 1982, and located in Murfreesboro, TN. Dealer direct sales.

RIFLES: BOLT ACTION

MODEL 90 – .50 BMG cal., 29 in. match grade barrel with muzzle brake, 5 shot detachable box mag., includes extendible bi-pod legs, scope optional, 22 lbs. Mfg. 1990-1995.

	$3,450	$2,950	$2,400	$2,150	$1,875	$1,600	$1,500	Last MSR was $3,650.

Add $1,150 for Swarovski 10X scope and rings.

MODEL 95M – .50 BMG cal., 29 in. match grade barrel with high efficiency muzzle brake, 5 shot detachable box mag., includes extendible bi-pod legs, M19 optics rail, scope optional, includes carrying case, 22 1/2 lbs. New 1995.

MSR $6,825	$6,500	$6,000	$5,495	$4,995	$3,950	$2,900	$2,425

MODEL 98B – .338 Lapua cal., 20 in. unfluted or 27 in. fluted barrel, includes two 10 shot detachable mags., adj. stock, Harris bipod, monopod, accessory rail, two sling loops, adj. trigger, ergonomic bolt handle, black finish, air/watertight case, 13 1/2 lbs. New 2009.

MSR $5,040	$4,750	$4,250	$3,750	$3,350	$2,950	$2,675	$2,400

Add $1,366 for Leupold scope and cleaning kit.

MODEL 99 – .416 Barrett (.32 in. barrel only) or .50 BMG cal., single shot bolt action, 25 (disc.) or 29 in. lightweight fluted, or 32 in. heavy barrel with muzzle brake, straight through design with pistol grip and bi-pod, M1913 optics rail, black, brown, or silver finish, 21-25 lbs. New 1999.

MSR $4,410	$4,100	$3,650	$3,275	$2,850	$2,500	$2,175	$1,900

MSR	100%	98%	95%	90%	80%	70%	60%

Add $210 for .416 Barrett cal. with 32 in. heavy barrel.
Add $315 for Bushnell scope.

RIFLES: SEMI-AUTO

MODEL 82 RIFLE – .50 BMG cal., semi-auto recoil operation, 33-37 in. barrel, 11 shot mag., 2,850 FPS muzzle velocity, scope sight only, parkerized finish, 35 lbs. Mfg. 1982-1987.

$4,350	$3,950	$3,450	$2,700	$2,150	$1,800	$1,500

Last MSR for consumers was $3,180 in 1985.

This model underwent design changes after initial production. Only 115 were mfg. starting with ser. no. 100.

MODEL 82A1 – .416 Barrett (new 2010) or .50 BMG cal., tactical design w/short recoil operating system, variant of the original Model 82, back-up iron sights, fitted hard case, 20 or 29 (new late 1989) or 33 (disc. 1989) in. barrel, 10 shot detachable mag., 32 1/2 lbs. for 1989 and older mfg., approx. 30 lbs. for 1990 mfg. and newer. Current mfg. includes elevated M1913 optics rail, watertight case, and cleaning kit.

MSR $9,345	$9,000	$8,500	$7,750	$6,750	$6,000	$5,500	$5,000

Add $315 for .416 Barrett cal. (new 2010).
Add $1,175 for Leupold scope.
Add $375 for pack-mat backpack case (new 1999).
Add $275 for camo backpack carrying case (disc.).
Add $1,325 for Swarovski 10X scope and rings (disc.).

This model boasts official U.S. military rifle (M107) status following government procurement during Operation Desert Storm. In 1992, a new "arrowhead" shaped muzzle brake was introduced to reduce recoil.

MODEL 98 – .338 Lapua Mag. cal., 10 shot box mag., 24 in. match grade barrel with muzzle brake, bi-pod, 15 1/2 lbs.

While advertised during mid-1999, this model was never produced.

MODEL M468 – 6.8 Rem. SPC cal., aluminum upper and lower receiver, 16 in. barrel with muzzle brake, 5, 10, or 30 shot mag., dual spring extractor system, folding front and rear sight, gas block, two-stage trigger, integrated rail system, choice of full or telescoping 4-position stock, 8 lbs. Mfg. 2005-2008.

$2,400	$2,050	$1,675	$1,375	$1,175	$995	$875

Last MSR was $2,700.

Add $1,590 for Model M468 upper conversion kit.

MODEL REC7 – 6.8 Rem. SPC cal., aluminum upper and lower receiver, 16 in. chrome lined barrel, 30 shot mag., folding front and ARMS rear sight, single stage trigger, ARMS selective integrated rail system, telescoping stock, 7.62 lbs. New 2008.

MSR $2,520	$2,475	$2,100	$1,700	$1,375	$1,175	$995	$875

BENELLI

Current manufacturer established in 1967, and located in Urbino, Italy. Benelli USA was formed during late 1997, and is currently importing all Benelli shotguns and rifles. Benelli pistols (and air pistols) are currently imported by Larry's Guns, located in Gray, ME beginning 2003. Company headquarters are located in Accokeek, MD. Shotguns were previously imported 1983-1997 by Heckler & Koch, Inc., located in Sterling, VA. Handguns were previously imported until 1997 by European American Armory, located in Sharpes, FL, in addition to Sile Distributors, Inc., until 1995, located in New York, NY, and Saco, located in Arlington, VA.

For more information on Benelli air pistols, please refer to the *Blue Book of Airguns* by Dr. Robert Beeman and John Allen (also available online)

RIFLES: SEMI-AUTO

MR1 CARBINE/RIFLE – .223 Rem. cal., self-adjusting gas operation (similar to the Benelli M4 shotgun used by the Marines) with rotating bolt head featuring three lugs, accepts AR-15 type mags., 5 shot mag., 12 1/2 (law enforcement only), 16, or 20 (Europe only) in. barrel, regular or pistol grip (12 1/2 or 16 in. barrel only), rifle sights, includes Picatinny rail, push button safety on trigger guard, black finish, approx. 8 lbs. New late 2009.

MSR $1,299	$1,150	$995	$850	$725	$650	$550	$450

SHOTGUNS: SEMI-AUTO, 1985-OLDER

Benelli semi-auto 3rd generation (inertia recoil) shotguns were imported starting in the late 1960s. The receivers were mfg. of light aluminum alloy - the SL-80 Model 121 had a semi-gloss, anodized black finish, the Model 123 had an ornate photo-engraved receiver, the Model Special 80 had a brushed, white nickel-plated receiver, and the Model 121 M1 had a matte finish receiver, barrel, and stock. All 12 ga. SL-80 Series shotguns will accept 2 3/4 or 3 in. shells, and all SL-80 Series 12 ga. Models have interchangeable barrels (except the 121 M1) with 4 different model receivers (121, 121 M1, 123, and Special 80). All 4 models had fixed choke barrels.

MSR	100%	98%	95%	90%	80%	70%	60%

The SL-80 Series shotguns were disc. during 1985, and neither H&K nor Benelli USA has parts for these guns. Some misc. parts still available for the 12 ga. from Gun Parts Corp. (see Trademark Index for more information).

Approx. 50,000 SL-80 series shotguns were mfg. before discontinuance - choke markings (located on the side or bottom of the barrel) are as follows: * full choke, ** imp. mod., *** mod., **** imp. cyl. SL-80 series guns used the same action (much different than current mfg.) and all had the split receiver design. Be aware of possible wood cracking where the barrel rests on the thin area of the forend and also on the underside of the buttstock behind trigger guard. When buying or selling an SL-80 Series shotgun, be aware that when comparing the SL-80 Series with the newer action Benellis (post 1985), there is a big difference between the action, design changes, and actual selling prices in today's marketplace. The SL80s are much lower priced than current production Benellis.

Since the late 1980s, the Benelli SL-80 series marketplace has dropped sharply, and relatively few guns have been traded during the new millennium. There has been an increasing number of SL-80 guns for sale which had unresolved mechanical problems. Parts are scarce and high priced. Wood and trigger assembly groups for most models are no longer available. In 2005, there was an increase in the number of SL-80 guns sold which were "new-in-the-box". Sales of "used guns" continue to be poor, especially if less than 98% condition. Buyers clearly have become more discriminating when considering the purchase of a SL-80 series shotgun.

100% values within this section assume NIB condition.

Subtract 5% for "SACO" importation (Saco was located in Arlington, VA).

SL-80 SERIES MODEL 121 M1 POLICE/MILITARY – 12 ga. only, similar in appearance to the Super 90 M1, hardwood stock, 7 shot mag., matte metal and wood finish, most stocks had adj. lateral sling attachment inside of buttstock, 18 3/4 in. barrel. Disc. 1985.

	$395	$350	$300	$275	$240	$210	$185

Since many of this model were sold to the police and military, used specimens should be checked carefully for excessive wear and/or possible damage.

SHOTGUNS: SEMI-AUTO, 1986-NEWER

Unless indicated otherwise, all currently manufactured Benelli shotguns utilize a red fiber optic sight, and are equipped with a patented Benelli keyed chamber lock. As of 2008, Benelli had manufactured approx. 2 million shotguns in many configurations.

100% values within this section assume NIB condition.

M1 DEFENSE (SUPER 90) – similar to Super 90 Slug, except has pistol grip stock, 7.1 lbs. Disc. 1998.

	$685	$525	$395	$325	$300	$270	$250	Last MSR was $851.

Add $41 for ghost-ring sighting system.

M1 PRACTICAL (SUPER 90) – 12 ga. only, 3 in. chamber, 26 in. plain barrel with muzzle brake, designed for IPSC events, extended 8 shot mag. tube, oversized safety, speed loader, larger bolt handle, mil spec adj. ghost-ring sight and Picatinny rail, black regular synthetic stock and forearm, matte metal finish, includes 3 choke tubes, 7.6 lbs. Mfg. 1998-2004.

	$925	$825	$750	$625	$525	$450	$400	Last MSR was $1,285.

M1 TACTICAL (SUPER 90) – 12 ga. only, 3 in. chamber, 18 1/2 in. barrel, fixed rifle or ghost-ring sighting system, available with synthetic pistol grip or standard buttstock, includes 3 choke tubes, 5 shot mag., 6.7 - 7 lbs. Mfg. 1993-2004.

	$725	$650	$575	$450	$375	$335	$300	Last MSR was $975.

Add $50 for ghost-ring sighting system.
Add $50-$65 for pistol grip stock.

* ***M1 Tactical M*** – similar to M1 Tactical, except has military ghost-ring sights and standard synthetic stock, 7.1 lbs. Mfg. 1999-2000.

	$725	$595	$435	$375	$315	$275	$250	Last MSR was $960.

Add $10 for pistol grip stock.

M1 ENTRY (SUPER 90) – 12 ga. only, 14 in. barrel, choice of synthetic pistol grip or standard stock, choice of rifle or ghost-ring sights, 5 shot mag. (2 shot extension), approx. 6.7 lbs. Mfg. 1992-2006.

	$810	$675	$585	$450	$395	$340	$310

Add $15 for synthetic pistol grip stock.
Add $65 for ghost-ring sighting system.

This model required special licensing (special tax stamp) for civilians, and was normally available to law enforcement/military only.

M2 PRACTICAL – 12 ga. only, 3 in. chamber, 26 in. compensated barrel with ghost ring sights, designed for IPSC competition, 8 shot mag., Picatinny rail. Limited importation 2005.

	$1,095	$900	$800	$650	$550	$475	$425	Last MSR was $1,335.

MSR	100%	98%	95%	90%	80%	70%	60%

M2 TACTICAL – 12 ga. only, 3 in. chamber, 18 1/2 in. barrel with choice of pistol grip, regular stock, or ComforTech stock configuration, matte finish, 5 shot mag., AirTouch checkering pattern on stock and forearm, open rifle or ghost ring sights, 6.7-7 lbs. New 2005.

MSR $1,329	$1,200	$975	$850	$725	$625	$525	$450

Add $110 for ghost ring sights w/ComforTech stock.
Subtract $110 for tactical open rifle sights.

M3 CONVERTIBLE AUTO/PUMP (SUPER 90) – 12 ga. only, 3 in. chamber, defense configuration incorporating convertible (fingertip activated) pump or semi-auto action, 19 3/4 in. cyl. bore barrel with ghost ring or rifle (disc. 2007) sights, 5 shot mag., choice of standard black polymer stock or integral pistol grip (disc. 1996, reintroduced 1999), approx. 7.3 lbs. New 1989.

MSR $1,549	$1,350	$1,175	$1,050	$925	$850	$775	$700

Add $110 for folding stock (mfg. 1990-disc.) - only available as a complete gun.
Add $340 for Model 200 Laser Sight System with bracket (disc.).
Subtract approx. 10% for rifle sights (disc. 2007).

M4 TACTICAL – 12 ga. only, consumer version of the U.S. Military M4, 3 in. chamber, includes auto-regulating gas operating (ARGO) system, dual stainless self cleaning pistons, 4 shot mag., matte black phosphated metal standard, or 100% Desert camo coverage (except for pistol grip, new 2007), 18 1/2 in. barrel with ghost ring sights, pistol grip, or non-collapsible (disc. 2004) stock and forearm, Picatinny rail, approx. 7.8 lbs. Importation began late 2003.

MSR $1,799	$1,600	$1,400	$1,200	$1,050	$925	$850	$750

Add $120 for 100% desert camo coverage (new 2007).

M1014 LIMITED EDITION – similar to M4, except only available with non-collapsible stock, U.S. flag engraved on receiver, 8 lbs. Limited edition of 2,500 mfg. 2003-2004.

	$1,375	$1,100	$950	$825	$725	$650	$600	Last MSR was $1,575.

* ***Super Black Eagle II Slug*** – 12 ga. only, 3 in. chamber, 24 in. barrel with rifled bore and adj. sights, includes Picatinny rail, choice of satin walnut stock and forearm or black synthetic stock, ComforTech became standard 2007, or 100% camo coverage of Timber HD (disc. 2008) or APG HD, approx. 7.4 lbs. New 2004.

MSR $1,719	$1,525	$1,300	$1,100	$875	$700	$600	$525

Add $160 for 100% camo treatment.
Add $50 for black synthetic ComforTech stock and forearm.

SHOTGUNS: SLIDE-ACTION

All currently manufactured Benelli shotguns are equipped with a patented Benelli keyed chamber lock.

100% values within this section assume NIB condition.

* ***Nova Tactical (Special Purpose Smooth Bore)*** – 12 ga. only, 3 1/2 in. chamber, similar action to Nova, features 18 1/2 in. cyl. bore barrel with choice of rifle or ghost ring (new 2000) sights, black synthetic stock and forearm only, 7.2 lbs. New 1999.

MSR $409	$350	$285	$260	$230	$210	$200	$190

Add $40 for ghost ring sights.

* ***Nova Entry*** – 12 ga. only, 14 in. barrel, choice of ghost ring or open rifle sights, black synthetic stock and forearm, 4 shot mag., approx. 6.9 lbs. Importation began 2003.

This model is available to law enforcement or military only.

* ***SuperNova Tactical*** – features 18 in. barrel with choice of ComforTech or pistol grip synthetic stock, matte finish or Desert camo (new 2007, pistol grip only), choice of rifle or ghost ring sights. New 2006.

MSR $489	$415	$350	$300	$250	$225	$200	$185

Add $10 for pistol grip stock.
Add $20 for ghost ring sights.
Add $130 for Desert camo w/pistol grip and ghost ring sights (new 2007).

* ***SuperNova Slug*** – 12 ga., 3 1/2 in. chamber, features 24 in. rifled bore drilled and tapped barrel with adj. rifle sights, black synthetic or 100% coverage APG HD camo stock and forearm, 8.1 lbs. New 2007.

MSR $719	$625	$525	$425	$365	$310	$275	$240

Add $110 for 100% camo coverage.
Add $10 for Field & Slug combo with extra 26 in. Field barrel (mfg. 2007 only).

BERETTA

Current manufacturer located in Brescia, Italy since 1526. The company name in Italy is Fabbrica d'Armi Pietro Beretta. Beretta U.S.A. Corp. was formed in 1977 and is located in Accokeek, MD. Beretta U.S.A. Corp. has been importing Beretta Firearms exclusively since 1980. 1970-1977 manufacture was imported exclusively by Garcia. Distributor and dealer direct sales.

MSR	100%	98%	95%	90%	80%	70%	60%

Beretta is one of the world's oldest family owned industrial firms, having started business in 1526. In addition to Beretta owning Benelli, Stoeger, and Franchi, the company also purchased Sako and Tikka Companies in late 1999, Aldo Uberti & Co. in 2000, Burris Optics in 2002, and Steiner International Optics. Beretta continues to be a leader in firearms development and safety, and shooters attest to the reliability of their guns worldwide.

For more information and current pricing on both new and used Beretta precision airguns, please refer to the *Blue Book of Airguns* by Dr. Robert Beeman & John Allen (also available online).

PISTOLS: SEMI-AUTO, RECENT AND CURRENT MFG.

On Beretta's large frame pistols, alphabetical suffixes refer to the following: F Model - double/single action system with external safety decocking lever, G Model - double/single action system with external decocking only lever, D Model - double action only without safety lever, DS Model - double action only with external safety lever. The models in this section appear in numerical sequence.

MODEL PX4 STORM – 9mm Para, .40 S&W, or .45 ACP (new 2007) cal., single/double action, 3.2 (Compact model) 4 in. barrel, polymer frame, locked breech with rotating barrel system, matte black finish with plastic grips, Pronox (disc.) or Super Luminova 3-dot night sights, 9, 10, 12, 14, 15, or 17 shot mag. (varies due to caliber), accessory rail on lower frame, approx. 27 1/2 oz. New mid-2005.

MSR $600	$495	$450	$395	$350	$300	$275	$250

Add $50 for .45 ACP cal. (new 2007).
Add $435 for PX4 Storm SD .45 ACP w/extended barrel and brown polymer frame.

The trigger mechanism of this gun can be customized to four different configurations: Type F (single/double action decocker and manual safety), Type D (DAO with spurless hammer, LE only), Type G (single/double action decocker with no manual safety, LE only), or Type C (constant action, spurless hammer, LE only). Values are for Type F model only.

* *Model PX4 Storm Sub-Compact* – 9mm Para. or .40 S&W cal., 10 or 13 (9mm Para. cal. only) shot mag., similar to Model PX4 Storm, except has sub-compact frame with 3 in. barrel, includes three backstraps, 26 oz. New 2007.

MSR $600	$485	$415	$350	$315	$285	$250	$225

Pistols: Semi-Auto, Model 92 & Variations - 4.9 in. barrel

MODEL 90-TWO TYPE F – 9mm Para. or .40 S&W cal., 4.9 in. barrel, single/double action, matte metal finish, removable single piece wraparound grip in two sizes, internal recoil buffer and captive recoil sping guide assembly, low profile fixed sights, 10, 12 (.40 S&W cal.), or 17 (9mm Para. cal.) shot mag., lower accessories rail with cover, 32 1/2 oz. Mfg. 2006-2009.

	$600	$525	$450	$375	$330	$300	$275	Last MSR was $700.

MODEL 92F WITH U.S. M9 MARKED SLIDE/FRAME – 9mm Para. cal., 217 mfg. with special serial no. range, "BER" prefix, government assembly numbers on frame, slide, hammer, mag. etc. Mfg. for the Armed Forces Reserve shooters, identical to military M9, except for serial number.

	$1,750	$1,525	$1,350	$1,100	$950	$825	$700	

M9A1 – 9mm Para. cal., SA/DA, features accessory rail on lower frame and serrated grip straps, 10 or 15 shot mag., 3-dot sights, 35.3 oz. Mfg. 2006-2009.

	$615	$525	$440	$395	$340	$315	$285	Last MSR was $725.

Pistols: Semi-Auto, Model 92 & Variations - 4.7 in. barrel

MODEL 92FS INOX TACTICAL – 9mm Para. cal., 4.7 in. barrel, features satin matte finished stainless steel slide and alloy frame, rubber grips, Tritium sights. Mfg. 1999-2000.

	$695	$560	$480	$425	$375	$325	$295	Last MSR was $822.

RIFLES: SEMI-AUTO, RECENT MFG.

BM-59 M-1 GARAND – with original Beretta M1 receiver, only 200 imported into the U.S.

	$3,200	$2,900	$2,400	$1,800	$1,500	$1,300	$1,175	Last MSR was $2,080.

BM-62 – similar to BM-59, except has flash suppressor and is Italian marked.

	$3,200	$2,900	$2,400	$1,800	$1,500	$1,300	$1,175	

AR-70 – .222 Rem. or .223 Rem. cal., semi-auto tactical design rifle, 5-, 8-, or 30-shot mag., diopter sights, epoxy finish, 17.72 in. barrel, 8.3 lbs.

	$1,925	$1,675	$1,375	$1,150	$1,025	$850	$750	Last MSR was $1,065.

1989 Federal legislation banned the importation of this model into U.S.

MSR	100%	98%	95%	90%	80%	70%	60%

CX4 STORM CARBINE – 9mm Para. (92 Carbine), .40 S&W (96 Carbine) or .45 ACP (8045 Carbine) cal., blowback single action, Giugiaro design featuring tactical styling with one-piece matte black synthetic stock with thumbhole, rubber recoil pad and stock cheekpiece, top, bottom, and side Picatinny rails, ghost ring sights, 16.6 in. hammer forged barrel, reversible crossbolt safety, mag. button, bolt handle, and ejection port, 8- (.45 ACP cal.), 10, 11 (8000 and 8040 models, new 2005), 15 (92 or 96 carbine, new 2005), or 17 (92 Carbine) shot mag. (accepts Models 92, 96, 8000, 8040, and 8045 pistol mags.), 29.7 in. overall length, 5 3/4 lbs. New mid-2003.

MSR $915	$795	$625	$550	$495	$450	$395	$350

Add $95 for 92 Carbine package (includes scope, 9mm Para., (disc. 2005) or .40 S&W cal).
Add $50 for top rail (only available in 9mm Para. or .40 S&W cal., mfg. 2006-2007).

This model is available in many variations - 8045 (.45 ACP), 92 Carbine (8000, 9mm Para.), 92 Carbine package (w/ scope), and 96 Carbine (8040, .40 S&W).

RX4 STORM CARBINE – .223 Rem. cal., gas operating system, available in collapsible five position telescoping stock or sporter style stock with optional pistol grip, black matte finish, ghost ring sights, includes 5 and 10 shot AR-15 style magazines. Limited importation 2007-2008.

	$1,100	$925	$800	$700	$600	$525	$450	Last MSR was $1,100.

While advertised, only a few samples were brought into the U.S.

SHOTGUNS: SEMI-AUTO

It is possible on some of the following models to have production variances occur including different engraving motifs, stock configurations and specifications, finishes, etc. These have occurred when Beretta changed from production of one model to another. Also, some European and English distributors have sold their excess inventory through Beretta U.S.A., creating additional variations/configurations that are not normally imported domestically. While sometimes rare, these specimens typically do not command premiums over Beretta's domestic models.

The following Beretta semi-auto models have been listed in numerical sequence, if possible, disregarding any alphabetical suffix or prefix.

BERETTA CHOKES AND THEIR CODES (ON REAR LEFT-SIDE OF BARREL)

* designates full choke (F).

** designates improved modified choke (IM).

*** designates modified choke (M).

**** designates improved cylinder choke (IC).

***** designates cylinder bore (CYL).

FK designates skeet (SK).

Note: values are for unaltered guns.

QUICK REFERENCE GUIDE FOR CURRENT CHOKES

MC3 - includes three Mobilchokes. MC6 - includes six Mobilchokes. MCF - Mobilchoke Field. MCS - Mobilchoke Sport. MCS2 - Mobilchoke Sport 2. MCS2 - Mobilchoke Sport 2. OBF - Optima Bore Field. OBF-HP - Optima Bore Field. OBSP - Optima Bore Sporting. OBS - Optima Bore Sport. OBSK - Optima Bore Skeet. OBTR - Optima Bore Trap. OBTS - Optima Bore Trap Single. OCF - Optima Choke Field. OBSP-HP - Optima Bore Sporting HP.

Subtract 10% on the following factory multi-choke models if w/o newer Beretta Optima-chokes (12 ga. only, became standard 2003).

* **Model 1200 Riot** – 12 ga. only, 2 3/4 or 3 in. chamber, 20 in. cyl. bore barrel with iron sights, extended mag. Imported 1989-90 only.

	$400	$375	$350	$295	$250	$225	$200	Last MSR was $660.

* **Model 1201 FP (Riot)** – 12 ga., riot configuration featuring 18 (new 1997) or 20 (disc. 1996) in. cylinder bore barrel, 5 shot mag, choice of adj. rifle sights (disc.), Tritium sights (disc. 1998) or ghost ring (new 1999, Tritium front sight insert) sights, matte wood (disc.) or black synthetic stock and forearm, matte metal finish (disc.), 6.3 lbs. Mfg. 1991-2004.

	$725	$595	$500	$400	$300	$250	$200	Last MSR was $890.

Add $80 for Tritium sights (mfg. 1997-98).
Add $45 for pistol grip configuration (Model 1201 FPG3 - mfg. 1994 only).

TX4 STORM – 12 ga., 3 in. chamber, 18 in. barrel with Optimabore HP cylinder choke, 5 shot mag., matte black finish, alloy receiver with integral Picatinny rail, black synthetic stock, ghost ring rear sight, post front sight, includes plastic case, approx. 6.4 lbs. New 2010.

MSR $1,450	$1,200	$995	$850	$725	$625	$525	$450

MSR	100%	98%	95%	90%	80%	70%	60%

BERSA

Current manufacturer established circa 1958 and located in Ramos Mejia, Argentina. Currently distributed exclusively by Eagle Imports, Inc. located in Wanamassa, NJ. Previously imported and distributed before 1988 by Rock Island Armory located in Geneseo, IL, Outdoor Sports Headquarters, Inc. located in Dayton, OH, and R.S.A. Enterprises, Inc. located in Ocean, NJ. Distributor sales only.

PISTOLS: SEMI-AUTO

BP9/BP40CC SERIES – 9mm Para. or .40 S&W cal., DAO, 6 or 7 shot mag., matte black or duo-tone finish, polymer frame and grips, slide, frame, and trigger checkering, ambidextrous mag. release, alloy steel slide, M1913 Picatinny rail, 21 1/2 oz. New 2010.

MSR $427	$375	$325	$295	$275	$250	$225	$195

Add $13 for duo-tone finish.

BINGHAM, LTD.

Previous manufacturer located in Norcross, GA circa 1976-1985.

RIFLES: SEMI-AUTO

PPS 50 – .22 LR cal. only, blowback action, 50 round drum mag., standard model has beechwood stock. Disc. 1985.

	$250	$225	$195	$180	$145	$135	$125	Last MSR was $230.

Add 15% for deluxe model with walnut stock.
Add 20% for Duramil model with chrome finish and walnut stock.

This model was styled after the Soviet WWII Model PPSh Sub Machine Gun.

AK-22 – .22 LR cal. only, blowback action, styled after AK-47, 15 shot mag. standard, 29 shot mag. available. Standard model had beechwood stock. Disc. 1985.

	$250	$225	$195	$180	$145	$135	$125	Last MSR was $230.

Add $20 for Deluxe model with walnut stock.

GALIL-22 – .22 LR cal. only, patterned after Galil semi-auto tactical design rifle. Disc.

	$250	$225	$195	$180	$145	$135	$125

FG-9 – 9mm Para. cal., blowback action, semi-auto tactical design carbine, 20 1/2 in. barrel.

While advertised during 1984, this gun never went into production.

BLACKHEART INTERNATIONAL LLC

Current manufacturer located in Philippi, WV.

RIFLES: SEMI-AUTO

BHI offers four semi-auto AR-15 style rifles - the BHI-15 (A) (MSR $1,120), the BHI-15 (S) (MSR $1,500), the BHI SPR (Special Purpose Rifle), and the BHI Executive Package. BHI also offers two bolt action models - the BBG Tactical, and the BBG Olympic Hunter. Please contact the company directly for more information, including pricing and available options (see Trademark Index).

BLASER

Currently manufactured by Blaser Jagdwaffen GmbH in Isny im Allgäu, Germany. Currently imported and distributed beginning late 2006 by Blaser USA, located in San Antonio, TX. Previously located in Stevensville, MD. Previously imported and distributed 2002-2006 by SIG Arms located in Exeter, NH, and circa 1988-2002 by Autumn Sales Inc. located in Fort Worth, TX. Dealer sales.

The Blaser Company was founded in 1963 by Horst Blaser. In 1986, the company was taken over by Gerhard Blenk. During 1997, the company was sold to SIG. In late 2000, SIG Arms AG, the firearms portion of SIG, was purchased by two Germans named Michael Lüke and Thomas Ortmeier, who have a background in textiles. Today the Lüke & Ortmeier group includes independently operational companies such as Blaser Jadgwaffen GmbH, Mauser Jagdwaffen GmbH, J.P. Sauer & Sohn GmbH, SIG-Sauer Inc., SIG-Sauer GmbH and SAN Swiss Arms AG.

Blaser currently makes approx. 20,000 rifles annually, with most being sold in Europe. Blaser also manufactures a fine O&U shotgun line since 2004 and established Blaser USA Inc., located in San Antonio TX since 2008.

RIFLES: BOLT ACTION

The R-93 rifle system's biggest advantage is its component interchangeability. Both barrels and bolt heads/assemblies can be quickly changed making the R-93 a very versatile rifle platform. Many special orders and features are available; please contact Blaser USA directly for additional information, including pricing and availability (see Trademark Index).

MSR	100%	98%	95%	90%	80%	70%	60%

Add $337 for left-hand action available on currently manufactured R-93 models.

Add $1,663 for rimfire conversion kit (.17 HMR, .22 LR, or .22 Mag. cal., includes barrel, magazine, bolt assembly, and bolt catch insert, new 2008).

Add $1,036 per extra R-93 barrel with standard taper (includes mag.).

Add $931 for semi-weight configuration on currently manufactured standard R-93 models.

Add $600 for match grade configuration on currently manufactured standard R-93 models.

Beginning late 2006, Blaser began offering graded wood between grades 3-11. There are many ways in which to upgrade wood, so please contact the importer directly regarding wood upgrade pricing based on the model selected.

R-93 TACTICAL 2 – .223 Rem. (new 2010), .300 Win. Mag., .308 Win. or .338 Lapua cal., fluted barrel with muzzle brake, 4 or 5 shot mag., Picatinny rails on top of receiver and forearm over barrel, straight pull, ambidextrous pistol grip polymer stock with adj. buttplate and cheekpiece, black finish throughout, includes bipod, 12 lbs. Importation began 2007.

MSR $4,469	$3,950	$3,550	$2,975	$2,600	$2,150	$1,850	$1,550

Add $324 for .338 Lapua cal.

Add $1,688 per interchangable barrel.

Add $299 per individual bolt head.

This model is distributed by Sig Arms, located in Exeter, NH.

BLUEGRASS ARMORY

Current rifle manufacturer located in Ocala, FL. Previously located in Richmond, KY. Consumer direct sales.

During 2010, Bluegrass Armory was purchased by Good Times Outdoors.

RIFLES: BOLT ACTION

VIPER MODEL – .50 BMG cal., single shot action with 3-lug bolt, 29 in. chrome moly steel barrel with muzzle brake, one-piece frame with aluminum stock (choice of gray, OD green, or black), incorporates Picatinny rail, includes detachable bi-pod, right or left hand, approx. 24 lbs. New 2003.

MSR $4,200	$3,950	$3,550	$3,100	$2,750	$2,300	$1,775	$1,525

Add $100 for OD Green or grey finish.

BOBCAT WEAPONS INC.

Previous manufacturer from April, 2003-circa 2006 and located in Mesa, AZ. During late 2006, the company name was changed to Red Rock Arms. Please refer to the R section for current information and pricing.

RIFLES: SEMI-AUTO

BW-5 MODEL – 9mm Para cal., tactical design, stamped steel or polymer (Model BW-5 FS) lower receiver, roller lock bolt system with delayed blowback, 16 1/2 in. stainless steel barrel, choice of black, desert tan, OD green, or camo stock, pistol grip, and forearm, Model BW-5 FS has fake suppressor, paddle mag. release and 8 7/8 in. barrel, 10 shot mag., approx. 6.4 lbs. Mfg. 2003-2006.

	$1,175	$995	$875	$800	$725	$650	$575	Last MSR was $1,350.

Add $275 for Model BW-5 FS.

BOHICA

Previous manufacturer and customizer located in Sedalia, CO, circa 1993-1994.

RIFLES: SEMI-AUTO

M16-SA – .223 Rem., .50 AE, or various custom cals., AR-15 style, 16 or 20 in. barrel, A-2 sights, standard handguard, approx. 950 were mfg. through September 1994.

	$1,375	$1,225	$1,000	$850	$725	$600	$525

Add $100 for flat-top receiver with scope rail.

Add $65 for two-piece, free floating handguard.

In addition to the rifles listed, Bohica also manufactured a M16-SA Match variation (retail was $2,295, approx. 10 mfg.), a pistol version of the M16-SA in both 7 and 10 in. barrel (retail was $1,995, approx. 50 mfg.), and a limited run of M16-SA in .50 AE cal. (retail was $1,695, approx. 25 mfg.).

BREN 10 (PREVIOUS MFG.)

Previous trademark manufactured 1983-1986 by Dornaus & Dixon Ent., Inc., located in Huntington Beach, CA.

Bren 10 magazines played an important part in the failure of these pistols to be accepted by consumers. Originally, Bren magazines were not shipped in some cases until a year after the customer received his gun. The complications arising around manufacturing a reliable dual caliber magazine domestically led to the downfall of this company. For this reason, original Bren 10 magazines are currently selling for $125-$150 if new (watch for fakes).

MSR	100%	98%	95%	90%	80%	70%	60%

PISTOLS: SEMI-AUTO

Note: the Bren 10 shoots a Norma factory loaded 10mm auto. cartridge. Ballistically, it is very close to a .41 Mag. Bren pistols also have unique power seal rifling, with five lands and grooves. While in production, Bren pistols underwent (4) engineering changes, the most important probably being re-designing the floorplate of the magazine, thus preventing mag. shifting while undergoing recoil.

100% values in this section assume NIB condition. Add 5% for extra original factory mag. Subtract 10% without box/manual.

BREN 10 MILITARY/POLICE MODEL – 10mm cal. only, semi-auto selective double action design, 5 in. barrel, 11 shot, has all black finish, "83MP" ser. no. prefix. Mfg. 1984-86.

	100%	98%	95%	90%	80%	70%	60%	
	$2,650	$2,300	$2,100	$1,850	$1,250	$900	$700	Last MSR was $550.

BREN 10 SPECIAL FORCES MODEL – 10mm cal. only, commercial version of the military pistol submitted to the U.S. gov't. Model D has dark finish. Model L has light finish, "SFD" ser. no. prefix on Model D, "SFL" ser. no. prefix on Model L. Disc. 1986.

	100%	98%	95%	90%	80%	70%	60%	
Dark finish - Model D	$2,575	$2,250	$2,100	$1,850	$1,450	$975	$600	
Light finish - Model L	$3,300	$2,975	$2,750	$2,100	$1,650	$1,050	$675	Last MSR was $600.

BREN 10 (CURRENT MFG.)

Current trademark manufactured beginning 2010 by Vltor Mfg., located in Tucson, AZ. Distributed exclusively by Sporting Products, LLC, located in W. Palm Beach, FL.

PISTOLS: SEMI-AUTO

SM SERIES – 10mm or .45 ACP cal., 5 in. barrel, stainless steel frame with blue slide, 10 (SM45) or 15 (SM10) shot mag., two-tone finish, synthetic grips, approx. 500 (SM10) or 300 (SM45) mfg. New mid-2010.

MSR $1,200	$1,095	$995	$875	$750	$650	$550	$450

SMV SERIES – 10mm or .45 ACP cal., 5 in. barrel, stainless steel frame, hard chrome slide, 10 (SMV10) or 15 (SMV15) shot mag., black synthetic grips, approx. 500 (SMV10) or 300 (SMV45) mfg. New mid-2010.

MSR $1,299	$1,175	$1,050	$925	$800	$700	$600	$495

SFD45 – .45 ACP cal., 4 in. barrel, matte black finished frame and slide, synthetic grips, 10 shot mag., approx. 500 mfg. New mid-2010.

MSR $1,100	$995	$895	$800	$700	$600	$500	$425

SFL45 – .45 ACP cal., 4 in. barrel, matte finished stainless steel frame, hard chrome slide, 10 shot mag., synthetic grips, two-tone finish, approx. 200 mfg. New mid-2010.

MSR $1,200	$1,095	$995	$875	$750	$650	$550	$450

BRILEY

Current trademark of choke tubes manufactured by Briley Manufacturing Inc., and located in Houston, TX. Briley has produced both pistols and rifles, including those listed, in addition to manufacturing a complete line of top quality shotgun barrel tubes and chokes since 1976. Additionally, beginning late March, 2006, Briley Manufacturing began importing and distributing Mauser Models 98 and 03 bolt action rifles from Germany. Please refer to the Mauser section for more information.

PISTOLS: SEMI-AUTO

PLATE MASTER – 9mm Para. or .38 Super cal., features 1911 Govt. length frame, Briley TCII titanium barrel compensator, Briley scope mount, and other competition features, hot blue finish. Mfg. 1998-2004.

	100%	98%	95%	90%	80%	70%	60%	
	$1,675	$1,325	$1,075	$895	$775	$625	$575	Last MSR was $1,895.

Add $175 for hard chrome finish.

EL PRESIDENTE – 9mm Para. or .38 Super cal., top-of-the-line competition model with Briley quad compensator with side ports, checkered synthetic grips and front grip strap, squared off trigger guard. Mfg. 1998-2004.

	100%	98%	95%	90%	80%	70%	60%	
	$2,250	$1,925	$1,625	$1,325	$1,075	$875	$750	Last MSR was $2,550.

Add $175 for hard chrome finish.

BROLIN ARMS, INC.

Previous importer of handguns (FEG mfg.), rifles (older Mauser military, see Mauser listing), shotguns (Chinese mfg.), and airguns from 1995 to 1999. Previously located in Pomona, CA, until 1999, and in La Verne, CA until 1997.

MSR	100%	98%	95%	90%	80%	70%	60%

PISTOLS: SEMI-AUTO, SINGLE ACTION

PATRIOT SERIES MODEL P45 COMP – .45 ACP cal., similar to Legend Series Model L45, except has one-piece match 4 in. barrel with integral dual port compensator, 7 shot mag., Millett or Novak combat sights (new 1997), test target provided, choice of blue or satin (frame only) finish, 38 oz. Mfg. 1996-97 only.

| | $585 | $475 | $415 | $365 | $325 | $285 | $250 | Last MSR was $649. |

Add $70 for Novak combat sights (new 1997).
Add $20 for T-tone finish (frame only).

* *Patriot Series Model P45C (Compact)* – .45 ACP cal., similar to Model P45 Comp, except has 3 1/4 in. barrel with integral conical lock-up system, 34 1/2 oz. Mfg. 1996-97.

| | $610 | $495 | $425 | $375 | $325 | $285 | $250 | Last MSR was $689. |

Add $70 for Novak combat sights.
Add $20 for T-tone finish (frame only).

* *Patriot Series Model P45T* – features standard frame with compact slide, 3 1/4 in. barrel, 35 1/2 oz. Mfg. 1997 only.

| | $620 | $500 | $425 | $375 | $325 | $285 | $250 | Last MSR was $699. |

Add $60 for Novak combat sights (new 1997).
Add $10 for T-tone finish (frame only).

TAC 11 – .45 ACP cal., 5 in. conical barrel w/o bushing, beavertail grip safety, 8 shot mag., T-tone or blue finish, Novak low profile combat or Tritium sights, black rubber contour grips, 37 oz. Mfg. 1997-98.

| | $595 | $485 | $425 | $365 | $325 | $285 | $250 | Last MSR was $670. |

Add $90 for Tritium sights (disc. 1997).

* *Tac 11 Compact* – similar to Tac 11, except has shorter barrel. Mfg. 1998 only.

| | $610 | $495 | $435 | $365 | $325 | $285 | $250 | Last MSR was $690. |

Add $60 for hard-chrome finish.

PISTOLS: SEMI-AUTO, DOUBLE ACTION

The following models had limited manufacture 1998 only.

TAC SERIES SERVICE MODEL – .45 ACP cal., full sized double action service pistol, single/double action, 8 shot single column mag., front and rear slide serations, combat style trigger guard, royal or satin blue finish, low profile 3-dot sights. Mfg. 1998 only.

| | $360 | $315 | $285 | $260 | $240 | $220 | $200 | Last MSR was $400. |

Add $20 for royal blue finish.

TAC SERIES FULL SIZE MODEL – 9mm Para., .40 S&W, or .45 ACP cal., similar to Tac Series Service Model, except longer barrel, checkered walnut or plastic grips, 8 (.45 ACP only) or 10 shot mag. Mfg. 1998 only.

| | $360 | $315 | $285 | $260 | $240 | $220 | $200 | Last MSR was $400. |

Add $20 for royal blue finish.

TAC SERIES COMPACT MODEL – 9mm Para. or .40 S&W cal., shortened barrel/slide with full size frame, 10 shot mag. Mfg. 1998 only.

| | $360 | $315 | $285 | $260 | $240 | $220 | $200 | Last MSR was $400. |

Add $20 for royal blue finish.

TAC SERIES BANTAM MODEL – 9mm Para. or .40 S&W cal., super compact size, single/double action with concealed hammer, all steel construction, 3-dot sights. Mfg. 1998 only.

| | $360 | $315 | $285 | $260 | $240 | $220 | $200 | Last MSR was $399. |

BANTAM MODEL – 9mm Para. or .40 S&W cal., single or double action, super compact size, concealed hammer, all steel construction, 3-dot sights, royal blue or matte finish. Limited mfg. by FEG 1999 only.

| | $360 | $315 | $285 | $260 | $240 | $220 | $200 | Last MSR was $399. |

SHOTGUNS: SEMI-AUTO

MODEL SAS-12 – 12 ga. only, 2 3/4 in. chamber, 24 in. barrel with IC choke tube, 3 (standard) or 5 shot (disc. late 1998) detachable box mag., synthetic stock and forearm, gas operated. Mfg. 1998-99.

| | $445 | $385 | $335 | $300 | $280 | $260 | $240 | Last MSR was $499. |

Add $39 for extra 3 or 5 (disc.) shot mag.

SHOTGUNS: SLIDE ACTION

Brolin shotguns were manufactured in China by Hawk Industries, and were unauthorized copies of the Remington Model 870. Most of these slide action models were distributed by Interstate Arms, and it is thought that Norinco or China North Industries

MSR	100%	98%	95%	90%	80%	70%	60%

were connected to the manufacturer during the importation of these shotguns.

LAWMAN MODEL – 12 ga. only, 3 in. chamber, action patterned after the Rem. Model 870 (disc. 1998) or the Ithaca Model 37 (new 1999) 18 1/2 in. barrel, choice of bead, rifle (disc. 1998), or ghost ring (disc. 1998) sights, matte (disc. 1998), nickel (disc. 1997), royal blue (new 1998), satin blue (new 1998) or hard chrome finish, black synthetic or hardwood stock and forearm, 7 lbs. Mfg. in China 1997-99.

	$165	$155	$145	$135	$125	$115	$105	Last MSR was $189.

Add $20 for nickel finish (disc. 1997).
Add $20 for hard chrome finish.
Add $20 for ghost ring sights.

ED BROWN CUSTOM, INC.

Current rifle manufacturer established during 2000 and located in Perry, MO. During 2009, the rifle division was transferred to Ed Brown Products, Inc.

Please refer to Ed Brown Products, Inc. for currently manufactured rifles.

RIFLES: BOLT ACTION

702 LIGHT TARGET (TACTICAL) – .223 Rem. or .308 Win. cal., features Ed Brown short repeater action, aluminum trigger guard and floorplate, 21 in. match grade barrel, includes Talley scope mounts, approx. 8 3/4 lbs. Disc. 2005.

	$2,495	$2,185	$1,870	$1,695	$1,370	$1,125	$875	Last MSR was $2,495.

A3 TACTICAL – various cals., top-of-the-line sniper weapon, 26 in. heavyweight match grade hand lapped barrel, Shilen trigger, McMillan fiberglass A-3 tactical stock, 11 1/4 lbs. Disc. 2008.

	$2,995	$2,620	$2,245	$2,035	$1,645	$1,350	$1,050	Last MSR was $2,995.

ED BROWN PRODUCTS, INC.

Current manufacturer established during 1988 located in Perry, MO. Consumer direct sales.

PISTOLS: SEMI-AUTO

The following MSRs represent each model's base price, with many options available at additional charge.
Add $75 for ambidextrous safety.
Add $200 for Generation III black coating (mfg. 2007-2009).

EXECUTIVE ELITE – .45 ACP cal., M1911 style, 5 in. barrel, choice of all blue, stainless blue, or full stainless slide/barrel, features Hardcore components, flared and lowered ejection port, Commander style hammer, 25 LPI checkering on front and rear grip strap, beveled mag. well, fixed 3-dot night sights, checkered cocobolo wood grips, 34 oz. New 2004.

MSR $2,395	$2,395	$2,095	$1,795	$1,630	$1,315	$1,080	$840

EXECUTIVE CARRY – .45 ACP cal., similar to Executive Elite, except has 4 1/4 in. barrel and Bobtail grip, 34 oz. New 2004.

MSR $2,645	$2,645	$2,315	$1,985	$1,800	$1,455	$1,190	$925

SPECIAL FORCES – .45 ACP cal., M1911 style, 7 shot mag, 5 in. barrel, Commander style hammer, special ChainLink treatment on front and rear grip straps, checkered diamond pattern cocobolo grips, 3-dot night sights, Generation III black coating applied to all metal surfaces, 38 oz. New 2006.

MSR $2,195	$2,195	$1,920	$1,645	$1,490	$1,205	$990	$770

SPECIAL FORCES LIGHT RAIL – .45 ACP cal., 5 in. barrel, forged Government style frame with integral light rail, chainlink treatment on forestrap amd mainspring housing, fixed 3-dot night sights, traditional square cut cocking serrations, diamond cut wood grips, approx. 40 oz. New 2009.

MSR $2,295	$2,295	$2,010	$1,720	$1,560	$1,260	$1,035	$805

SPECIAL FORCES CARRY – .45 ACP cal., 4 1/2 in. Commander style barrel, single stack bobtail frame, chainlink treatment on forestrap and mainspring housing, fixed dovetail 3-dot night sights, diamond cut wood grips, approx. 35 oz. New 2009.

MSR $2,445	$2,445	$2,140	$1,835	$1,660	$1,345	$1,100	$855

RIFLES: BOLT ACTION

The following MSRs represent each model's base price, with many options available at additional cost. Beginning 2006, all M-702 actions were disc. in favor of Ed Brown's new Model 704 controlled feed action with spring-loaded extractor integral with the bolt. All currently manufactured rifles have stainless steel barrels and the entire rifle is coated with Generation III black coating (new 2007).

MSR	100%	98%	95%	90%	80%	70%	60%

A5 TACTICAL – .300 Win. Mag. or .308 Win. cal., features adj. McMillan A-5 tactical stock, 5 shot detachable mag., black finish, Shilen trigger, 12 1/2 lbs. New 2008.

MSR $4,495	$4,495	$3,935	$3,370	$3,055	$2,470	$2,025	$1,575

M40A2 MARINE SNIPER – .30-06 or .308 Win. cal., 24 in. match grade barrel, special McMillan GP fiberglass tactical stock with recoil pad, Woodlands camo is molded into stock, this model is a duplicate of the original McMillan Marine Sniper rifle used in Vietnam, except for the Ed Brown action, 9 1/4 lbs. New 2002.

MSR $3,695	$3,695	$3,235	$2,770	$2,515	$2,030	$1,665	$1,295

BROWN PRECISION, INC.

Current manufacturer established in 1968, and located in Los Molinos, CA. Previously manufactured in San Jose, CA. Consumer direct sales.

Brown Precision Inc. manufactures rifles primarily using Remington or Winchester actions and restocks them using a combination of Kevlar, fiberglass and graphite (wrinkle finish) to save weight. Stock colors are green, brown, grey, black, camo brown, camo green, or camo grey. Chet Brown pioneered the concept of the fiberglass rifle stock in 1965. He started blueprinting actions and using stainless steel match grade barrels on hunting rifles in 1968, and became the first custom gunmaker to use high tech weather-proof metal finishes on hunting rifles.

RIFLES: BOLT ACTION

Brown Precision will also stock a rifle from a customer supplied action. This process includes a Brown Precision stock, custom glass bedding, recoil pad, stock finish, etc. Prices begin at $895.

LAW ENFORCEMENT SELECTIVE TARGET – .308 Win. cal., Model 700 Varmint action with 20, 22, or 24 in. factory barrel, O.D. green camouflage treatment. Disc. 1992.

	$995	$870	$745	$675	$545	$450	$350	Last MSR was $1,086.

This model could have been special ordered with similar options from the Custom High Country Model, with the exception of left-hand action.

TACTICAL ELITE – various cals. and custom features, customized per individual order. New 1997.

MSR $4,895	$4,400	$3,850	$3,300	$2,990	$2,420	$1,980	$1,540

Add $675 for 3 way adj. buttplate.
Subtract $900 if action is supplied by customer.

THE UNIT – .270 Win., .300 Win. Mag., .300 Wby. Mag., .338 Win. Mag., 7mm-08 Rem., 7mm Rem. Mag., or 7mm STW cal., Rem. 700 BDL or Win. Mod. 70 controlled feed action, various lengths match grade stainless steel barrel with cryogenic treatment, Teflon or electroless nickel finish, Brown Precision Kevlar or graphite reinforced fiberglass stock, includes 60 rounds of custom ammo. Limited mfg. 2001 only.

	$3,225	$2,820	$2,420	$2,195	$1,775	$1,450	$1,130	Last MSR was $3,795.

Add $500 for Win. Model 70 Super Grade action with controlled round feeding.
Add $200 for left-hand action.
Subtract $600 if action was supplied by customer.

BROWNING

Current manufacturer with U.S. headquarters located in Morgan, UT. Browning guns originally were manufactured in Ogden, UT, circa 1880. Browning firearms are manufactured by Fabrique Nationale in Herstal and Liège, Belgium. Beginning 1976, Browning also contracted with Miroku of Japan and A.T.I. in Salt Lake City, UT to manufacture both long arms and handguns. In 1992, Browning (including F.N.) was acquired by GIAT of France. During late 1997, the French government received $82 million for the sale of F.N. Herstal from the Walloon business region surrounding Fabrique Nationale in Belgium.

The category names within the Browning section have been arranged in an alphabetical format: - PISTOLS (& variations), RIFLES (& variations), SHOTGUNS (& variations), SPECIAL EDITIONS, COMMEMORATIVES & LIMITED MFG.

The author would like to express his sincere thanks to the Browning Collector's Association, including members Rodney Hermann, H.M. Shirley, Richard Spurzem, Jim King, Bert O'Neill, Jr., Anthony Vanderlinden, and Gary Chatham for continuing to make their important contributions to the Browning section.

PISTOLS: SEMI-AUTO, F.N. PRODUCTION UNLESS OTHERWISE NOTED

PRO-9/PRO-40 – 9mm Para or .40 S&W cal., single/double action, 4 in. barrel, 10, 14 (.40 S&W cal. only), or 16 (9mm Para. cal. only) shot mag., ambidextrous decocking and safety, black polymer frame with satin stainless steel slide, under barrel accessory rail, interchangeable backstrap inserts, fixed sights only, 30 (9mm Para.) or 33 oz. Mfg. in the U.S. by FNH USA 2003-2006.

	$525	$430	$370	$350	$315	$295	$260	Last MSR was $641.

Please refer to FNH USA handgun listing for current manufacture.

MSR	100%	98%	95%	90%	80%	70%	60%

SHOTGUNS: SEMI-AUTO, A-5 1903-1998 MFG.

BROWNING CHOKES AND THEIR CODES (ON REAR LEFT-SIDE OF BARREL)

* designates full choke (F).

*- designates improved modified choke (IM).

** designates modified choke (M).

**- designates improved cylinder choke (IC).

**$ designates skeet (SK).

*** designates cylinder bore (CYL).

INV. designates barrel is threaded for Browning Invector choke tube system.

INV. PLUS designates back-bored barrels.

Miroku manufactured A-5s can be determined by year of manufacture in the following manner: RV suffix - 1975, RT - 1976, RR - 1977, RP - 1978, RN - 1979, PM - 1980, PZ - 1981, PY - 1982, PX - 1983, PW - 1984, PV - 1985, PT - 1986, PR - 1987, PP - 1988, PN - 1989, NM - 1990, NZ - 1991, NY - 1992, NX - 1993, NW - 1994, NV - 1995, NT - 1996, NR - 1997, NP - 1998.

Browning resumed importation from F.N. in 1946. On November 26, 1997, Browning announced that the venerable Auto-5 would finally be discontinued. Final shipments were made in February, 1998. Over 3 million A-5s were mfg. by F.N. in all configurations between 1903-1976. 1976-1998 mfg. was by Miroku.

NOTE: Barrels are interchangeable between older Belgian A-5 models and recent Japanese A-5s mfg. by Miroku, if the gauge and chamber length are the same. A different barrel ring design and thicker barrel wall design might necessitate some minor sanding of the inner forearm on the older model, but otherwise, these barrels are fully interchangeable.

NOTE: The use of steel shot is recommended ONLY in those recent models manufactured in Japan - NOT in the older Belgian variations.

Recoil operation, scroll engraved receiver, 1946-1951 mfg. has safety in front of triggerguard. 1951-1976 mfg. has crossbolt safety behind the trigger. Post-war 16 ga. imports by Browning are chambered for 2 3/4 in., and have either a horn (disc. 1964) or plastic (1962-1976) buttplate, high luster wood finish (disc. 1962) or glossy lacquer (1962-1976) finish. Walnut buttstock has either round knob pistol grip (disc. 1967) or flat knob (new 1967). In today's A-5 marketplace, 16 and 20 ga. guns with shorter barrels and open chokes are more desirable than a 30 in. 12 ga. gun with full choke barrel.

The publisher would like to thank Mr. H.M. Shirley, Jr. for his contributions to the A-5 section.

Add 10%-15% for NIB condition on Belgian mfg. A-5 models only, depending on desirability.

Add 10-15% for the round knob (rounded pistol grip knob on stock, pre-1967 mfg.) variation on FN models only, depending on desirability.

Add $200-$375 per additional barrel, depending on the gauge, barrel length, choke, and condition (smaller gauge open chokes are the most desirable).

AUTO-5 POLICE CONTRACT – 12 ga. only, 5 or 8 (factory extended) shot mag., black enamel finish on receiver and barrel, can be recognized by the European "POL" police markings below serial number, 24 in. barrel. Imported in limited quantities during 1999.

	100%	98%	95%	90%	80%	70%	60%
5 shot mag.	N/A	$550	$525	$495	$450	$400	$375
8 shot mag.	N/A	$1,200	$995	$895	$795	$750	$650

BRÜGGER & THOMET

Curret manufacturer located in Thun, Switzerland. Currently imported by D.S.A., located in Barrington, IL.

Brugger & Thomet manufactures a wide variety of high quality tactical style semi-auto pistols and rifles. Currently imported models include the TP-9 semi-auto tactical pistol with a MSR of $1,250. Please contact the importer directly for more information (see Trademark Index).

BUDISCHOWSKY

Previous manufacturer located in Mt. Clemens, MI.

PISTOLS: SEMI-AUTO

SEMI-AUTO PISTOL – .223 Rem. cal., 11 5/8 in. barrel, 20 or 30 shot mag., fixed sights, a novel tactical designed type pistol.

	100%	98%	95%	90%	80%	70%	60%
	$470	$415	$385	$360	$305	$250	$220

RIFLES: SEMI-AUTO

PARAMILITARY DESIGN RIFLE – .223 Rem. cal., semi-auto, 18 in. barrel, wood tactical stock.

	100%	98%	95%	90%	80%	70%	60%
	$505	$440	$415	$385	$330	$275	$250

PARAMILITARY DESIGN RIFLE W/FOLDING STOCK

	100%	98%	95%	90%	80%	70%	60%
	$575	$500	$450	$425	$395	$360	$330

MSR		100%	98%	95%	90%	80%	70%	60%

BULLSEYE GUN WORKS

Previous manufacturer located in Miami, FL circa 1954-1959.

CARBINES

Bullseye Gun Works initially started as a gun shop circa 1954, and several years later, they started manufacturing M1 carbines using their own receivers and barrels. Approx. 2,000 - 2,500 were manufactured with their name on the receiver side until the company was reorganized as Universal Firearms Corporation circa late 1950s. Values are typically in the $200 - $350 range, depending on originality and condition.

BUL TRANSMARK LTD.

Current manufacturer located in Tel Aviv, Israel. Previously imported 2003-early 2010 by K.B.I., located in Harrisburg, PA. Previously imported and distributed in North America during 2009 by Legacy Sports International, located in Reno, NV, and during 2002 by EAA Corp., located in Sharpes, FL. Previously imported and distributed 1997-2001 by International Security Academy (ISA) located in Los Angeles, CA, and from 1996-1997 by All America Sales, Inc. located in Memphis, TN. Dealer sales only.

PISTOLS: SEMI-AUTO

Please refer to the Charles Daly section in this text for most recent information and prices on Charles Daly imported Bul Transmark pistols (domestic imports were marked Charles Daly 2004-early 2010). Non-domestic Bul Pistols are typically marked Bul M-5 on left side of slide except for the Cherokee and Storm models. M-5 frame kits were previously available at $399 retail.

BUL CHEROKEE – 9mm Para. cal., full size polymer frame, integral Picatinny rail, DA, exposed hammer, double stack 17 shot mag., black polymer finger groove grips, squared off triggerguard, includes hard case, cleaning kit and two mags. Imported 2009.

		$495	**$435**	**$370**	**$335**	**$270**	**$225**	**$175**	Last MSR was $575.

* **Bul Cherokee Compact** – 9mm Para. cal., similar to the Cherokee, except is compact polymer frame. Imported 2009.

		$495	**$435**	**$370**	**$335**	**$270**	**$225**	**$175**	Last MSR was $575.

BUSHMASTER FIREARMS INTERNATIONAL LLC

Currently manufactured by Bushmaster Firearms/Quality Parts Company located in Windham, ME. The previous company name was Bushmaster Firearms, and the name changed after the company was sold on April 13, 2006 to Cerberus. Older mfg. was by Gwinn Arms Co. located in Winston-Salem, NC 1972-1974. The Quality Parts Co. gained control in 1986. Distributor, dealer, or consumer direct sales.

During 2003, Bushmaster purchased Professional Ordnance, previous maker of the Carbon 15 Series of semi-auto pistols and rifles/carbines. Carbon 15s are still made in Lake Havasu City, AZ, but are now marked with Bushmaster logo. For pre-2003 Carbon 15 mfg., please refer to the Professional Ordnance section in this text.

Bushmaster formed a custom shop during 2009, and many configurations are now available by special order only. Please contact Bushmaster directly for more information and availability on these special order guns.

PISTOLS: SEMI-AUTO

BUSHMASTER PISTOL – .223 Rem. cal., top bolt (older models with aluminum receivers) or side bolt (most recent mfg.) operation, steel frame on later mfg., 11 1/2 in. barrel, parkerized finish, adj. sights, 5 1/4 lbs.

		$650	**$550**	**$450**	**$400**	**$375**	**$350**	**$300**	Last MSR was $375.

Add $40 for electroless nickel finish (disc. 1988).
Add $200 for matte nickel finish (mfg. circa 1986-1988).

This model uses a 30 shot M-16 mag. and the AK-47 gas system.

During 1985-1986, a procurement officer for the U.S. Air Force ordered 2,100 of this model for pilot use with a matte nickel finish. Eventually, this officer was retired or transferred, and the replacement officer turned down the first batch, saying they were "too reflective". Bushmaster then sold these models commercially circa 1986-1988.

CARBON-15 TYPE P21S/TYPE 21 – .223 Rem cal., ultra lightweight carbon fiber upper and lower receivers, 7 1/4 in. "Profile" stainless steel barrel, quick detachable muzzle compensator, ghost ring sights, 10 or 30 (new late 2004) shot mag., A2 pistol grip, also accepts AR-15 type mags., Stoner type operating sytem, tool steel bolt, extractor and carrier, 40 oz. New 2003 (Bushmaster mfg.).

MSR $1,080		**$975**	**$850**	**$725**	**$600**	**$525**	**$475**	**$425**	

Subtract approx. $200 if without full-length barrel shroud and Picatinny rail (Type 21, disc. 2005).

CARBON-15 TYPE 97/TYPE P97S – similar to Professional Ordnance Carbon 15 Type 20, except has fluted barrel,

MSR	100%	98%	95%	90%	80%	70%	60%

Hogue overmolded pistol grip and chrome plated bolt carrier, Type 97S has full length barrel shroud, upper and lower Picatinny rail, 46 oz. New 2003 (Bushmaster mfg.).

MSR $1,130	$1,050	$875	$750	$650	$550	$500	$450

Subtract approx. $100 if w/o full length barrel shroud and lower Picatinny rail.

CARBON-15 9MM – 9mm Para. cal., blow-back operation, carbon fiber composite receiver, 7 1/2 in. steel barrel with A1 birdcage flash hider, A2 front sight, full-length Picatinny optics rail, Neoprene foam sleeve over buffer tube, 10 or 30 shot mag., 4.6 lbs. New 2006.

MSR $1,055	$950	$850	$775	$700	$650	$600	$550

RIFLES: SEMI-AUTO

All currently manufactured Bushmaster rifles are shipped with a hard plastic lockable case. Most Bushmaster barrels are marked "5.56 NATO", and can be used safely with either 5.56 NATO (higher velocity/pressure) or .223 Rem. cal. ammo.

During 2006, Bushmaster began offering a complete gas piston upper receiver/barrel assembly for $995 MSR (A2 type).

BUSHMASTER RIFLE – .223 Rem. cal., semi-auto, top bolt (older models with aluminum receivers) or side bolt (current mfg.) operation, steel frame (current mfg.), 18 1/2 in. barrel, parkerized finish, adj. sights, wood stock, 6 1/4 lbs., base values are for folding stock model.

	$675	$625	$550	$500	$475	$425	$400	Last MSR was $350.

Add $40 for electroless nickel finish (disc. 1988).
Add $65 for fixed rock maple wood stock.

This model uses a 30 shot M-16 mag. and the AK-47 gas system.

* ***Bushmaster Rifle Combination System*** – includes rifle with both metal folding stock and wood stock with pistol grip.

	$750	$675	$625	$575	$525	$475	$350	Last MSR was $450.

XM15-E2S/A-2/A-3 TARGET RIFLE – .223 Rem. cal., semi-auto patterned after the Colt AR-15, 20, 24, or 26 in. Govt. spec. match grade chrome lined or stainless steel (new 2002) barrel, 10 or 30 shot mag., manganese phosphate or Realtree Camo (20 in. barrel only, mfg. 2004 - late 2006) barrel finish, rear sight adj. for windage and elevation, cage flash suppressor (disc. 1994), approx. 8.3 lbs. Mfg. began 1989 in U.S.

MSR $1,095	$925	$800	$700	$600	$550	$475	$425

Add $50 for fluted barrel or $40 for stainless steel barrel (mfg. 2002-2009).
Add $10 for 24 in. or $25 for 26 in. (disc. 2002) barrel.
Add $100 for A-3 removable carry handle.
Add $60 for Realtree Camo finish (disc.).

* ***XM15-E2S/A-2/A-3 Shorty Carbine*** – similar to above, except with fixed or telescoping buttstock and 11 1/2 (disc. 1995), 14 (disc. 1994), or 16 in. barrel with (disc. 1994) or w/o suppressor, approx. 7.4 lbs. Mfg. began 1989.

MSR $1,150	$1,025	$925	$825	$725	$625	$475	$425

Add $40 for fluted barrel.
Add $10 for Dissipator models (features lengthened handguard).
Add $100 for A-3 removable carry handle.

This model does not have the target rear sight system of the XM15-E2S rifle.

* ***M4 Post-Ban Carbine (XM15-E2S)*** – 16 in. barrel, features fixed or telestock (new late 2004) tubular stock, pistol grip, phosphate or desert camo (stock, pistol grip, and forearm only) finish, M4 carbine configuration with permanently attached Izzy muzzle brake, 30 shot mag. became standard in late 2004. New 2003.

MSR $1,300	$1,175	$1,025	$900	$825	$725	$625	$525

Add $35 for desert camo finish (disc. 2005).
Add $85 for A3 removable carrying handle.
Subtract $55 for M4 Patrolman Carbine with A2 birdcage flash suppressor, collapsible stock, and 30 round magazine.

* ***E2 Carbine*** – .223 Rem. cal., features 16 in. match chrome barrel with new M16A2 handguard and short suppressor, choice of A1 or E2 sights. Mfg. 1994-95.

	$895	$825	$725	$650	$600	$550	$500

Add approx. $50 for E2 sighting system.

AK CARBINE – .223 Rem. cal., 17 in. barrel featuring AK-47 style muzzle brake, tele-stock standard, choice of A2 or A3 configuration, ribbed oval forearm, approx. 7 1/2 lbs. New 2008.

MSR $1,215	$1,075	$950	$850	$750	$650	$550	$500

Add $85 for A3 removable carryhandle.

6.8mm SPC/7.62x39mm CARBINE – 6.8mm SPC or 7.62x39mm (new 2010) cal., 16 in. M4 profile barrel with Izzy muzzle brake, six-position telescoping stock, gas operated, available in A2 or A3 configuration, 26 shot mag., includes

MSR	100%	98%	95%	90%	80%	70%	60%

black web sling, extra mag. and lockable carrying case, approx. 7 lbs. New late 2006.

| **MSR $1,330** | **$1,195** | **$995** | **$875** | **$775** | **$675** | **$600** | **$550** |

Add $100 for A3 configuration.

.450 CARBINE/RIFLE – .450 Bushmaster cal., 16 (carbine) or 20 in. chromemoly steel barrel, 5 shot mag., AR type gas operating system, forged aluminum receiver, A2 pistol grip, solid A2 buttstock with trapdoor, A3 flattop upper receiver with Picatinny rail, 8 1/2 lbs. New 2008.

| **MSR $1,390** | **$1,275** | **$1,100** | **$925** | **$825** | **$725** | **$650** | **$575** |

DISSIPATOR CARBINE – .223 Rem. cal., 16 in. heavy barrel with full length forearm and special gas block placement (gas block system is located behind the front sight base and under the rifle length handguard), A2 or A3 style with choice of solid buttstock or six-position telestock, 30 shot mag., lockable carrying case. New late 2004.

| **MSR $1,240** | **$1,075** | **$950** | **$850** | **$750** | **$650** | **$550** | **$475** |

Add $25 for tele-stock.
Add $50 for fluted barrel (disc. 2005).
Add $115 for A3 removable carrying handle.

SUPERLIGHT CARBINE – .223 Rem. cal., 16 in. lightweight barrel, choice of fixed, tele-style, or stub stock with finger groove pistol grip, A2 or A3 type configuration, black finish, 5.8 - 6 1/4 lbs. New 2004.

| **MSR $1,250** | **$1,075** | **$950** | **$850** | **$750** | **$650** | **$550** | **$475** |

Add $25 for tele-style stock.
Add $100 for A-3 removable carry handle.

MODULAR CARBINE – .223 Rem. cal., 16 in. barrel with flash suppressor, includes many Bushmaster modular accessories, such as skeleton tele-stock and four-rail free floating tubular forearm, rear flip up and detachable sight, 10 or 30 (new late 2004) shot mag., 6.3 lbs. New 2004.

| **MSR $1,780** | **$1,600** | **$1,275** | **$1,075** | **$950** | **$850** | **$750** | **$650** |

O.R.C. (OPTICS READY) CARBINE – .223 Rem. cal., 16 in. barrel with A2 birdcage suppressor, receiver length Picatinny rail with risers ready for optical sights, six position telestock, oval M4 type forearm, 6 lbs. New 2008.

| **MSR $1,180** | **$1,025** | **$900** | **$800** | **$700** | **$600** | **$500** | **$450** |

GAS PISTON CARBINE – .223 Rem. cal., features gas piston operating system similar to AK-47s and FALs, 16 in. M4 profile barrel with flash suppressor, tele-stock, ribbed oval forearm with flip-up sight. New 2008.

| **MSR $1,850** | **$1,695** | **$1,400** | **$1,175** | **$975** | **$850** | **$750** | **$650** |

V-MATCH COMPETITION RIFLE – .223 Rem. cal., top-of-the line match/competition rifle, flattop receiver with extended aluminum barrel shroud, choice of 20, 24, or 26 (disc. 2002) in. barrel, 8.3 lbs. New 1994.

| **MSR $1,115** | **$1,025** | **$900** | **$750** | **$650** | **$575** | **$515** | **$465** |

Add $50 for fluted barrel.
Add $10 for 24 in. or $25 for 26 (disc. 2002) in. barrel.
Add $117 for A-3 removable carry handle.

* **V-Match Commando Carbine** – similar to V-Match Competition Rifle, except has 16 in. barrel. New 1997.

| **MSR $1,105** | **$1,025** | **$900** | **$750** | **$650** | **$575** | **$515** | **$465** |

Add $50 for fluted barrel.
Add $117 for A-3 removable carry handle.

VARMINTER – .223 Rem. cal., includes DCM 24 in. extra heavy fluted or stainless steel varmint barrel, competition trigger, rubberized pistol grip, flattop receiver with mini-risers (adds 1/2 in. height for scope mounting), free floating vented tube forearm, 5 shot mag, controlled ejection path. New 2002.

| **MSR $1,360** | **$1,175** | **$1,050** | **$875** | **$750** | **$625** | **$550** | **$500** |

Add $5 for non-fluted stainless steel barrel.

The stainless variation includes an adj., ergonomic pistol grip.

PREDATOR – .223 Rem. cal., includes DCM 20 in. extra heavy fluted or stainless steel (disc. 2006) varmint barrel, competition trigger, rubberized pistol grip, flattop receiver with mini-risers (adds 1/2 in. height for scope mounting), free floating vented tube forearm, 10 shot mag, controlled ejection path, 8 lbs. New 2006.

| **MSR $1,350** | **$1,175** | **$1,050** | **$875** | **$750** | **$625** | **$550** | **$500** |

The stainless variation included an adj., ergonomic pistol grip.

DCM COMPETITION RIFLE – .223 Rem. cal., includes DCM competition features such as modified A2 rear sight, 20 in. extra heavy 1 in. diameter competition barrel, custom trigger job, and free-floating hand guard. Mfg. 1998-2005.

| | **$1,375** | **$1,125** | **$975** | **$875** | **$800** | **$725** | **$650** | *Last MSR was $1,495.* |

MSR	100%	98%	95%	90%	80%	70%	60%

DCM-XR COMPETITION RIFLE – .223 Rem. cal., features dual aperature rear sight and competition ground for clarity front sight, 20 in. extra heavy competition barrel, free-floating ribbed forearm, competition trigger, choice of A2 solid or A3 removable carry handle, 13.5 lbs. New 2008.

| MSR $1,150 | $985 | $875 | $775 | $700 | $625 | $550 | $500 |

Add $100 for A3 removable carry handle.

M17S BULLPUP – .223 Rem. cal., semi-auto bullpup configuration featuring gas operated rotating bolt, 10 (C/B 1994) or 30* shot mag., 21 1/2 plain or 22 (disc.) in. barrel with flash-hider (disc.), glass composites and aluminum materials, phosphate coating, 8 1/4 lbs. Mfg. 1992-2005.

| | $700 | $650 | $525 | $475 | $425 | $400 | $385 | Last MSR was $765. |

CARBON-15 R21 – .223 Rem. cal., ultra lightweight carbon fiber upper and lower receivers, 16 in. "Profile" stainless steel barrel, quick detachable muzzle compensator, Stoner type operating system, tool steel bolt, extractor and carrier, optics mounting base, fixed tube stock, 10 or 30 (new late 2004) shot mag., also accepts AR-15 type mags., 3.9 lbs. Mfg. 2003-2009 (Bushmaster mfg.).

| | $900 | $800 | $700 | $600 | $500 | $450 | $400 | Last MSR was $990. |

* **Carbon-15 Lady** – .223 Rem. cal., 16 in. barrel, includes overall tan finish (except for barrel) and webbed tube stock with recoil pad, chrome/nickel plating on small parts, supplied with soft case, 4 lbs. Mfg. 2004-2006.

| | $875 | $775 | $675 | $575 | $500 | $450 | $400 | Last MSR was $989. |

CARBON-15 R97/97S – .223 Rem. cal., ultra lightweight carbon fiber upper and lower receivers, Stoner type operating system, hard chromed tool steel bolt, extractor and carrier, 16 in. fluted stainless steel barrel, quick detachable muzzle compensator, optics mounting base, 10 or 30 (new late 2004) shot mag., quick detachable stock, also accepts AR-15 type mags., 3.9 or 4.3 (Model 97S) lbs. New 2003 (Bushmaster mfg.).

| MSR $1,300 | $1,175 | $1,025 | $900 | $825 | $725 | $625 | $525 |

Subtract approx. $175 without Picatinny rail and "Scout" extension, double walled heat shield foregrip, ambidextrous safety, and multi-carry silent sling (Model Type 97, disc. 2005).

CARBON-15 .22 LR – .22 LR cal., similar to Carbon-15 R21, 16 in. barrel, Picatinny rail, 10 shot mag., fixed stock, approx. 4.4 lbs. Disc. 2009.

| | $685 | $575 | $485 | $415 | $350 | $300 | $265 | Last MSR was $790. |

Bushmaster also made a Carbon-15 .22 rimfire upper receiver/barrel assembly, which is exclusively designed for Bushmaster lower receivers - last MSR was $387 (new 2005).

CARBON-15 9MM – 9mm Para. cal., blow-back operation, carbon fiber composite receiver, 16 in. steel barrel with A1 birdcage flash hider, A2 front sight and dual aperture rear sight, Picatinny optics rail, collapsible stock, 10 or 30 shot mag, 5.7 lbs. New 2006.

| MSR $1,080 | $975 | $875 | $775 | $700 | $650 | $600 | $550 |

CARBON-15 TOP LOADING RIFLE – .223 Rem. cal., blow-back operation, carbon fiber composite receiver, 16 in. M4 profile barrel with Izzy suppressor, A2 front sight and dual aperture rear sight, Picatinny optics rail, collapsible stock, 10 shot top-loading internal mag, 5.8 lbs. New 2006.

| MSR $1,100 | $995 | $875 | $775 | $700 | $650 | $600 | $550 |

CARBON-15 MODEL 4 CARBINE – .223 Rem. cal., features carbon composite receiver, collapsible tube stock, 16 in. barrel with compensator, 30 shot mag., semi-auto design styled after the military M4, 5 1/2 lbs. New 2005.

| MSR $1,190 | $1,050 | $925 | $825 | $725 | $625 | $550 | $500 |

CARBON-15 FLAT-TOP CARBINE – .223 Rem. cal., similar to Carbon-15 Model 4 Carbine except has non-extended full-length Picatinny rail with dual aperture flip-up rear sight, 5 1/2 lbs. New 2006.

| MSR $1,190 | $1,050 | $925 | $825 | $725 | $625 | $550 | $500 |

BUSHMASTER .308 SERIES – .308 Win. cal., 16 or 20 in. phosphate coated heavy alloy steel barrel with Izzy compensator, 20 shot mag., solid buttstock or skeletonized stock, available in A2 or A3 style with a variety of configurations, including muzzle brakes, flash suppressors, and sighting options. Mfg. late 2004-2005.

| | $1,495 | $1,250 | $1,050 | $825 | $725 | $625 | $550 | Last MSR was $1,750. |

Add $25 for A3 removable carry handle.
Add $10 for 20 in. barrel.
Add $50 (16 in. barrel) or $60 (20 in. barrel) for skeletonized stock.
Add approx. $100 for free-floating foream.

NOTES

C SECTION

CETME

Previous manufacturer located in Madrid, Spain. CETME is an abbreviation for Centro Estudios Technicos de Materiales Especiales.

MSR	100%	98%	95%	90%	80%	70%	60%

RIFLES: SEMI-AUTO

AUTOLOADING RIFLE – 7.62x51mm NATO cal., 17 3/4 in. barrel, delayed blowback action, utilizing rollers to lock breech, similar to HK-91 in appearance, wood military style stock, aperture rear sight.

	$2,950	$2,650	$2,350	$2,000	$1,725	$1,500	$1,350

The H&K G3 is the next generation of this rifle, and many parts are interchangeable between the CETME and the the G3.

CMMG, INC.

Current rifle manufacturer located in Fayette, MO.

RIFLES: SEMI-AUTO

CMMG, Inc. offers a wide variety of AR-15 tactical style rifles and accessories. All rifles feature hard chrome plated barrels, recessed target crowns, anodized M-4 feed ramps, two 30 shot magazines, cleaning kit, sling, and USMC technical manual. All rifles can be upgraded and customized to specific customer needs, including stocks, grips, triggers, sights, optics, handguards, flash hiders, etc. Base prices for rifles range from $1,075 - $1,125, depending on configuration. Please contact the company directly for current options, delivery time, and pricing (see Trademark Index).

C Z (CESKÁ ZBROJOVKA)

Current manufacturer located in Uhersky Brod, Czech Republic since 1936. Previous manufacture was in Strakonice, Czechoslovakia circa 1923-late 1950s. Newly manufactured CZ firearms are currently imported exclusively by CZ USA located in Kansas City, KS. Previously imported by Magnum Research, Inc. located in Minneapolis, MN until mid-1994. Previously imported before 1994 by Action Arms Ltd. located in Philadelphia, PA. Dealer and distributor sales.

For CZ manufactured airguns, please refer to the *Blue Book of Airguns* by Dr. Robert Beeman and John Allen (now online also).

CZ USA currently has four product lines, which include CZ (pistols, rifles, and shotguns), Safari Classics (best quality bolt action rifles), Dan Wesson (semi-auto pistols) and Brno (combination guns and rifles).

PISTOLS: SEMI-AUTO, RECENT MFG.

CZ P-01 – 9mm Para cal., based on CZ-75 design, but with metallurgical improvements, aluminum alloy frame, hammer forged 3.8 in. barrel, 10 or 13 (new 2005) shot mag., decocker, includes M3 rail on bottom of frame, checkered rubber grips, matte black polycoat finish, 27.2 oz. Importation began 2003.

MSR $672	$550	$500	$450	$400	$350	$300	$275

Add $99 for tactical block with bayonet (new 2006).
Add $67 for Crimson Trace laser grips (mfg. 2007).

CZ P-06 – .40 S&W cal., 10 shot mag., otherwise similar to CZ P-01. Mfg. 2008-2009.

	$575	$495	$450	$400	$350	$325	$295	Last MSR was $695.

CZ P-07 DUTY – 9mm Para. or .40 S&W cal., SA/DA, 3.8 in. barrel, polymer frame, squared off trigger guard, 16 shot mag., fixed sights, decocking lever, Omega trigger system, 27 oz. New 2009.

MSR $579	$495	$425	$365	$320	$280	$260	$240

Add $20 for .40 S&W cal.

CZ-40B/CZ-40P – .40 S&W cal. only, CZ-75B operating mechanism in alloy (CZ-40B) or polymer (CZ-40P) M1911 style frame, single/double action, black polycoat finish, 10 shot double column mag., fixed sights, firing pin block safety. Limited importation 2002 only, reintroduced 2007 only.

	$425	$365	$325	$290	$275	$250	$225	Last MSR was $499.

* **CZ-40 P Compact** – .40 S&W cal., 1,500 imported 2004, reimported 2006.

	$325	$285	$265	$245	$225	$200	$175	Last MSR was $370.

CZ-75, CZ-75 B, CZ-75 BD – 9mm Para. or .40 S&W (disc. 1997, reintroduced 1999) cal., Poldi steel, selective double action, double action only, or single action only, frame safety, 4 3/4 in. barrel, 10 (C/B 1994, standard for .40 S&W cal.) or 15* shot mag., currently available in black polycoat/polymer (standard, DA and SA only), matte

MSR	100%	98%	95%	90%	80%	70%	60%

blue (disc. 1994), high polish (disc. 1994), glossy blue (new 1999), dual tone (new 1998), satin nickel (new 1994), or matte stainless steel (new 2006) finish, black plastic grips, non-suffix early guns did not have a firing pin block safety, reversible mag. release, or ambidextrous safety, and were usually shipped with two mags., B suffix model nomenclature was added 1998, and designated some internal mechanism changes, BD suffix indicates decocker mechanism, 34.3 oz.

MSR $597	$495	$425	$385	$350	$300	$275	$250

Add $18 for .40 S&W cal.
Add $12 for Model CZ-75 BD (decocker).
Add $59 for stainless steel.
Add $20 for glossy blue, dual tone, or satin nickel finish.
Add $412 for CZ Kadet .22 LR adapter (includes .22 LR upper slide assembly and mag., new 1998).
Add $12 for single action only (Model CZ-75 B SA, black polymer frame).
Add $81 for Crimson Trace laser grips (black poly coat finish only, mfg. 2007).

"First Model" variations, mostly imported by Pragotrade of Canada, are identifiable by short slide rails, no half-cock feature, and were mostly available in high polish blue only. These early pistols sell for $1,200 if NIB condition, chrome engraved $1,650 (NIB), factory competition $1,500 (NIB).

* **CZ-75 B Military** – 9mm Para. cal. Importation 2000-2002.

	$365	$315	$270	$250	$225	$210	$195	Last MSR was $429.

* **CZ-75 B Tactical** – similar to CZ-75 B, except has OD green frame and matte black polymer slide, includes CZ knife. Limited importation during 2003.

	$425	$355	$305	$270	$225	$210	$195	Last MSR was $499.

* **CZ-75 SP-01 Series** – 9mm Para. or .40 S&W (Tactical only, mfg. 2009) cal. only, 4 3/4 in. barrel, includes light rail, ambidextrous thumb safety, adj. tritium sights (Tactical), matte black polycoat finish, decocker, checkered black rubber grips, includes two 19 shot mags, 38 oz. New 2006.

MSR $703	$600	$525	$450	$415	$375	$350	$325

Add $117 for .40 S&W cal. (Tactical model only with 10 shot mag., disc. 2009).
Add $61 for tritium sights (Tactical model).
Add $99 for tactical block with bayonet.

* **CZ-75 SP-01 Phantom** – 9mm Para. cal., SA/DA, polymer frame with accessory rail, steel slide, fixed sights, includes two interchangable grip inserts, decocking lever, 19 shot mag. (also fits standard CZ-75 models), black polycoat finish, squared off trigger guard, 28.2 oz. New 2009.

MSR $695	$590	$495	$425	$360	$330	$295	$260

* **CZ-75 Semi-Compact** – 9mm Para. cal. only, 13 shot mag., choice of black polymer, matte, or high polish blue finish. Imported 1994 only.

	$350	$300	$275	$250	$230	$250	$200	Last MSR was $519.

Add $20 for matte blue finish.
Add $40 for high polish blue finish.

* **CZ-75 Compact** – 9mm Para. or .40 S&W (new 2005) cal. only, otherwise similiar to CZ-75, full-size frame, except has 3.9 in. barrel, 10 (C/B 1994) or 13* shot mag., checkered walnut grips, 33 oz. New 1993.

MSR $631	$525	$480	$435	$395	$360	$335	$295

Add $20 for glossy blue (disc. 2006), dual tone, or satin nickel finish.
Add $41 for .40 S&W cal.
Add $99 for tactical block with bayonet (.40 S&W cal. only, new 2006).
Add $412 for CZ Kadet .22 LR adapter (includes .22 LR upper slide assembly and mag., new 1998).

* **CZ-75 D PCR Compact** – 9mm Para. cal., similar to CZ-75 Compact, except has black polymer frame, decocker, 1.7 lbs. Importation began 2000.

MSR $651	$550	$495	$450	$395	$350	$300	$265

* **CZ-75 Kadet** – .22 LR cal., black polymer finish, 10 shot mag, 4.7 in. barrel, 37.9 oz. Mfg. 1999-2004, reintroduced 2006.

MSR $689	$560	$500	$450	$400	$350	$300	$275

CZ-83 – .32 ACP (disc. 1994, reintroduced 1999-2002 and 2006) or .380 ACP (new 1986), or 9mm Makarov (mfg. 1999-2001) cal., modern design, 3-dot sights, 3.8 in. barrel, choice of carry models, blue (disc. 1994), glossy blue (new 1998), satin nickel (new 1999, not available in .32 ACP), or black polymer (disc. 1997) finish, black synthetic grips, 10 (C/B 1994), 12* (.380 ACP) or 15* (.32 ACP) shot mag., 26.2 oz. Mfg. began 1985, but U.S. importation started in 1992.

MSR $495	$395	$325	$275	$235	$200	$175	$160

Add $27 for satin nickel.

MSR	100%	98%	95%	90%	80%	70%	60%

CZ-85, CZ-85 B – 9mm Para. or 9x21mm (imported 1993-94 only) cal., variation of the CZ-75 with ambidextrous controls, new plastic grip design, sight rib, available in black polymer, matte blue (disc. 1994), glossy blue (mfg. 2001 only), or high-gloss blue (9mm Para. only, disc. 1994) finish, includes firing pin block and finger rest trigger, plastic grips, 15 shot mag. new 2005, B suffix model nomenclature was added during 1998, approx. 2.2 lbs.

MSR $628	$525	$450	$400	$365	$330	$295	$275

Add $291 for CZ Kadet .22 LR adapter (includes .22 LR upper slide assembly and mag., mfg. 1998 only).

* **CZ-85 Combat** – similar to CZ-85B, except has fully adj. rear sight, available in black polymer, matte blue (disc. 1994), glossy blue (new 2001), dual-tone, satin nickel, or high-gloss blue finish, walnut (disc. 1994) or black plastic (new 1994) grips, extended mag. release, drop free 15 shot mag. new 2005. Importation began 1992.

MSR $703	$600	$525	$450	$415	$375	$350	$325

Add $30 for glossy blue, satin nickel, or dual-tone finish.
Add $291 for CZ Kadet .22 LR adapter (includes .22 LR upper slide assembly and mag., mfg. 1998 only).

CZ VZ 61 SKORPION – .32 ACP cal., semi-auto copy of VZ 61 Skorpion submachine gun, SA, forward charging knob, steel frame, 4.52 in. barrel, 20 shot mag., hardwood grips, flip up rear sight, lanyard rings, 41 oz. New 2009.

MSR $814	$700	$600	$525	$450	$425	$400	$375

RIFLES: BOLT ACTION, COMMERCIAL MFG.

Ceská Zbrojovka began manufacturing rifles circa 1936. Long gun production was discontinued between 1948-1964, with the exception of the massive military contracts during that time period.

* **CZ 527 M1 American** – .223 Rem. cal., styling similar to U.S. military M1 carbine featuring 3 shot flush detachable mag., walnut or black polymer stock. New 2008.

MSR $685	$575	$475	$425	$365	$335	$295	$250

Add $66 for walnut stock.

* **CZ 550 Magnum H.E.T. (High Energy Tactical)** – .300 Win. Mag., .300 Rem. Ultra Mag., or .338 Lapua cal., 28 in. barrel, flat black finish, Kevlar tactical stock, 4 to 6 shot fixed mag., SST, muzzle brake, oversized bolt handle, 13 lbs. New 2009.

MSR $3,299	$2,850	$2,450	$2,150	$1,850	$1,500	$1,275	$1,050

CZ 700 SNIPER – .308 Win. cal., sniper design features forged billet receiver with permanently attached Weaver rail, 25.6 in. heavy barrel w/o sights, 10 shot detachable mag., laminated thumbhole stock with adj. cheekpiece and buttplate, large bolt handle, fully adj. trigger, 11.9 lbs. Limited importation 2001 only.

	$1,875	$1,575	$1,250	$1,025	$895	$775	$650	Last MSR was $2,097.

CZ 750 SNIPER – .308 Win. cal., sniper design, black synthetic thumbhole stock w/adj. comb, Weaver rail comes installed for scope mounting, 26 in. barrel w/muzzle brake, includes two 10 shot mags., 11.9 lbs. Limited mfg. beginning 2006.

MSR $2,404	$2,100	$1,750	$1,525	$1,225	$1,025	$895	$775

RIFLES: SEMI-AUTO

CZ-M52 (1952) – 7.62x45mm Czech cal., semi-auto, 20 2/3 in. barrel, 10 shot detachable mag., tangent rear sight, this model was also imported briefly by Samco Global Arms, Inc. located in Miami, FL.

	$550	$450	$350	$300	$250	$200	$150

CZ-M52/57 (1957) – 7.62x39mm cal., later variation of the CZ-M52.

	$425	$375	$325	$300	$250	$200	$150

VZ 58 MILITARY/TACTICAL SPORTER – 7.62x39mm cal., gas operated, patterned after the AK-47, milled receiver, 16.14 in. barrel, tilting breech block, choice of Zytel skeletonized (Tactical) or plastic impregnated wood (Military) stock, alloy 30 shot mag., 7.32 lbs. New 2008.

MSR $999	$925	$850	$750	$650	$550	$450	$350

Add $30 for Tactical Sporter model (available with synthetic or folding (new 2010) stock).

CZ (STRAKONICE)

Current manufacturer established in 1919 and located in Strakonice, Czech Republic. No current U.S. importation. Previously imported by Adco Sales, Inc., located in Woburn, MA.

PISTOLS: SEMI-AUTO

Older Strakonice manufacture can be found in the CZ (Ceska Zbrojovka) section.

CZ-TT – 9mm Para., .40 S&W, or .45 ACP cal., single/double action, polymer frame, 3.77 in. ported or unported barrel, matte finish, 10 shot mag., 26.1 oz. Imported 2004-2006.

	$450	$415	$375	$325	$295	$275	$250	Last MSR was $479.

MSR	100%	98%	95%	90%	80%	70%	60%

Add $30 for ported barrel (disc.).
Add $40 for ported barrel and slide serrations (disc.).
Add $399 for conversion kit with one mag.

CZ-T POLYMER COMPACT – similar to CZ-TT, except has shorter barrel. Limited importation 2004 only.

	$475	$425	$375	$325	$295	$275	$225	Last MSR was $559.

CALICO LIGHT WEAPONS SYSTEMS

Current manufacturer established during 1986, and located in Hillsboro, OR. Previously located in Sparks, NV 1998-2001, and in Bakersfield, CA.

CARBINES

Extra magazines are currently priced as follows: $153 for 100 shot 9mm Para. cal., $128 for 50 shot 9mm Para. cal., or $138 for 100 shot .22 LR cal.

LIBERTY I/II & LIBERTY 50-100 – 9mm Para. cal., 16.1 in. barrel, downward ejection, retarded blowback CETME type action, aluminum alloy receiver, synthetic stock with pistol grip (some early post-ban specimens had full wood stocks with thumbhole cutouts), 50 or 100 shot helical feed mag., ambidextrous safety, 7 lbs. Mfg. 1995-2001, reintroduced late 2007.

MSR $875	$775	$700	$650	$600	$500	$450	$400

Add $157 for 100 shot helical feed mag.

M-100 – .22 LR cal., semi-auto carbine, blowback action, tactical design with folding buttstock, 100 shot helical feed mag., alloy frame, aluminum receiver, ambidextrous safety, 16.1 in. shrouded barrel with flash suppressor/muzzle brake, adj. sights, 4.2 lbs. empty. Mfg. 1986-1994, reintroduced late 2007.

MSR $638	$575	$500	$450	$400	$350	$300	$275

* **M-100 FS** – similar to M-100, except has solid stock and barrel does not have flash suppressor. Mfg. 1996-2001, reintroduced late 2007.

MSR $638	$575	$500	$450	$400	$350	$300	$275

M-101 – while advertised, this model never went into production.

M-105 SPORTER – similar to M-100, except has walnut distinctively styled buttstock and forend, 4 3/4 lbs. empty. Mfg. 1989-1994.

	$650	$550	$495	$450	$350	$295	$250	Last MSR was $335.

M-106 – while advertised, this model never went into production.

M-900 – 9mm Para. cal., retarded blowback action, tactical design with wood (disc.) or collapsible buttstock (current mfg.), cast aluminum receiver with stainless steel bolt, static cocking handle, 16 in. barrel, fixed rear sight with adj. post front, 50 (standard) or 100 shot helical feed mag., ambidextrous safety, black polymer pistol grip and forend, appeox. 3.7 lbs. Mfg. 1989-1990, reintroduced 1992-1993, again during 2007.

MSR $875	$775	$700	$650	$600	$500	$450	$400

Add $157 for 100 shot mag.

* **M-900S** – similar to M-900, except has non-collapsible shoulder stock. Disc. 1993.

	$650	$550	$475	$400	$350	$300	$275	Last MSR was $632.

* **M-901 Canada Carbine** – 9mm Para. cal., similar to M-900, except has 18 1/2 in. barrel and sliding stock. Disc. 1992.

	$675	$595	$550	$475	$350	$300	$285	Last MSR was $643.

This model was also available with solid fixed stock (Model 901S).

M-951 TACTICAL CARBINE – 9mm Para. cal., 16.1 in. barrel, similar appearance to M-900 Carbine, except has muzzle brake and extra pistol grip on front of forearm, 4 3/4 lbs. Mfg. 1990-94.

	$750	$700	$675	$650	$600	$475	$450	Last MSR was $556.

* **M-951S** – similar to M-951, except has synthetic buttstock. Mfg. 1991-94.

	$650	$595	$525	$450	$400	$350	$300	Last MSR was $567.

PISTOLS: SEMI-AUTO

M-110 – .22 LR cal., same action as M-100 Carbine, 6 in. barrel with muzzle brake, 100 round helical feed mag., includes notched rear sight and adj. windage front sight, 10 1/2 in. sight radius, ambidextrous safety, pistol grip storage compartment, 2.21 lbs. empty. Mfg. 1989-2001, reintroduced 2007.

MSR $689	$600	$525	$450	$375	$325	$275	$225

MSR	100%	98%	95%	90%	80%	70%	60%

M-950 – 9mm Para. cal., same operating mechanism as the M-900 Carbine, 6 in. barrel, 50 (standard) or 100 shot helical feed mag., 2 1/4 lbs. empty. Mfg. 1989-1994, reintroduced late 2007.

MSR $872	$775	$700	$650	$600	$500	$450	$400

CANIK55

Current trademark of pistols manufactured by Samsun Domestic Defence and Industry Corporation, located in Samsun, Turkey. No current U.S. importation.

PISTOLS: SEMI-AUTO

Canik55 is a line of good quality semi-auto 1911-style pistols, including the Shark Series, Stingray Series, Piranha Series, Standard Series, Light Series, Compact Series, SFC 100 Series, and Dolphin Series. Currently, these models are not imported into the U.S. Please contact the company directly for more information, including pricing and U.S. availability (see Trademark Index).

CARACAL

Current manufacturer of semi-auto pistols established in 2006, and located in the Abu Dhabi, United Arab Emirates. Currently distributed in Italy exclusively by Fratelli Tanfoglio Snc, located in Brescia, Italy. No current U.S. importation.

PISTOLS: SEMI-AUTO

Currently, these guns are not imported into the U.S. Please contact the company directly for more information, including availability and pricing (see Trademark Index).

MODEL C – 9mm Para., 9x21mm, .357 SIG, or .40 S&W cal., modified Browning-type blowback design, double action, 3.54 in. barrel, 14 shot mag., ribbed black polymer frame with interchangable colored inserts and Picatinny rail in front of trigger guard, matte black slide with rear slide serrations and integral sights (fiber optic front sight), Glock style trigger safety, cocking indicator, approx. 25 oz.

U.S. pricing has yet to be established on this model.

MODEL F – similar to Model C, except has 4.1 in. and 18 shot mag., 26 1/2 oz.

U.S. pricing has yet to be established on this model.

MODEL SC – 9mm Para. or 9x21mm cal., similar to Model C, except is compact variation with 13 shot mag. (Model F magazines are interchangable with special grip adapter), approx. 23 oz. New 2009.

U.S. pricing has yet to be established on this model.

CARBON 15

Please refer to Professional Ordnance (discontinued mfg.) and Bushmaster (current mfg.) for more information on this trademark.

CAVALRY ARMS CORPORATION

Current manufacturer located in Gilbert, AZ. Previously located in Mesa, AZ. Consumer and dealer sales.

CARBINES/RIFLES: SEMI-AUTO

Cavalry Arms Corporation manufactures the CAV-15 Series, styled after the AR-15. Cavalry Arms also makes tactical conversions for select slide action shotguns.

CAV-15 SCOUT CARBINE – .223 Rem. cal., 16 in. chrome lined barrel, A2 flash hider, A3 flattop upper receiver, longer sight radius, longer gas system, stand alone rear sight, Black, Green, or Coyote Brown finish, C6 hand guards.

MSR $850	$765	$675	$575	$525	$425	$350	$275

Add $199 for drop in rail system.
Add $259 for free float system.
Add $92 for YHM flip up front or rear sight.

CAV-15 RIFLEMAN – .223 Rem. cal., 20 in. chrome lined Govt. profile barrel, A2 flash hider, A3 flattop upper receiver, stand alone rear sight, Black, Green, or Coyote Brown finish, A2 hand guard.

MSR $850	$765	$675	$575	$525	$425	$350	$275

Add $279 mid-length free float system.
Add $310 for rifle length free float system.
Add $92 for YHM flip up front or rear sight.

CENTURION ORDNANCE, INC.

Previous importer located in Helotes, TX. Centurion Ordnance also imported Aguila ammunition.

MSR	100%	98%	95%	90%	80%	70%	60%

SHOTGUNS: SLIDE ACTION

POSEIDON – 12 ga., 1 3/4 in. chamber (shoots "mini-shells" and slugs), 18 1/4 in. smoothbore barrel, 13 in. LOP, black synthetic stock and forearm, 6 shot mag., adj. rear sight, 5 lbs., 5 oz. Limited importation 2001.

	$285	$250	$225	$200	$185	$170	$155

While prototypes of this model were imported briefly during 2001, this gun never made it into the consumer marketplace.

Mini-shells retailed for $12.60 for a box of 20 (shot sizes include 7, #4 & #1 buckshot).

CENTURY INTERNATIONAL ARMS, INC.

Current importer and distributor with corporate offices located in Delray Beach, FL. Century International Arms, Inc. was previously headquartered in St. Albans, VT until 1997, and Boca Raton, FL from 1997-2004.

Century International Arms, Inc. imports a large variety of used military rifles, shotguns, and pistols. Because inventory changes daily, especially on tactical style rifles, carbines and pistols, please contact the company directly for the most recent offerings and pricing (see Trademark Index).

Additionally, Century International Arms imports a wide range of accessories, including bayonets, holsters, stocks, magazines, grips, mounts, scopes, misc. parts, new and surplus ammunition, etc., and should be contacted directly (see Trademark Index) for a copy of their most recent catalog, or check their web site for current offerings.

RIFLES: SEMI-AUTO

G-3 SPORTER – .308 Win. cal., mfg. from genuine G3 parts, and American made receiver with integrated scope rail, includes 20 shot mag., 19 in. barrel, pistol grip stock, matte black finish, refinished condition only, 9.3 lbs. Imported 1999-2006.

	$785	$685	$590	$535	$430	$355	$275

FAL SPORTER – .308 Win. cal., U.S. mfg., new barrel receiver, synthetic furniture, 20 shot mag. Imported 2004-2006.

	$850	$745	$635	$580	$465	$380	$295

CETME SPORTER – .308 Win. cal., new mfg. Cetme action, 19 1/2 in. barrel, 20 shot mag., choice of blue or Mossy Oak Break-Up camo (disc.) metal finish, wood (disc.) or synthetic stock, pistol grip, and vent. forearm, refinished condition only, 9.7 lbs. New 2002.

No MSR	$625	$550	$475	$400	$350	$300	$275

S.A.R. 1 – 7.62x39mm cal., AK-47 styling, 16 1/2 in. barrel, wood stock and forearm, scope rail mounted on receiver, includes one 10 and two 30 shot double stack mags., 7.08 lbs. Mfg. by Romarm of Romania. Importation disc. 2003.

	$750	$655	$560	$510	$410	$335	$260

S.A.R. 2 – 5.45x39mm cal., AK-47 styling, 16 in. barrel, wood stock and forearm, includes one 10 and one 30 shot double stack mags., 8 lbs. Mfg. by Romarm of Romania. Importation disc. 2003.

	$750	$655	$560	$510	$410	$335	$260

S.A.R. 3 – .223 Rem. cal., AK-47 styling, 16 in. barrel, wood stock and forearm, includes one 10 and one 30 shot double stack mags., 8 lbs. Mfg. by Romarm of Romania. Importation disc. 2003.

	$750	$655	$560	$510	$410	$335	$260

GP WASR-10 LO-CAP – 7.62x39mm cal., AK-47 styling, 16 1/4 in. barrel, wood stock and forearm, includes one 5 and one 10 shot single stack mags., 7 1/2 lbs. Mfg. by Romarm of Romania.

No MSR	$450	$400	$350	$315	$275	$250	$225

GP WASR-10 HIGH-CAP SERIES – 7.62x39mm cal., AK-47 styling, 16 1/4 in. barrel, various configurations, includes two 30 shot double stack mags., 7 1/2 lbs. Mfg. by Romarm of Romania.

No MSR	$550	$495	$450	$395	$350	$300	$275

Add $110 for 100 shot drum mag.

L1A1/R1A1 SPORTER – .308 Win. cal., current mfg. receiver patterned after the British L1A1, includes carrying handle, synthetic furniture, 20 shot mag., 22 1/2 in. barrel, fold over aperture rear sight, 9 1/2 lbs. Mfg. in U.S.

No MSR	$975	$850	$750	$650	$575	$500	$450

Subtract approx. $200 for L1A1 Sporter.

DRAGUNOV – 7.62x54R cal., new CNC milled receiver, Dragunov configuration, thumbhole stock, 26 1/2 in. barrel, supplied with scope and cleaning kit. Mfg. in Romania.

	$975	$855	$730	$665	$535	$440	$340

MSR	100%	98%	95%	90%	80%	70%	60%

GOLANI SPORTER – .223 Rem. cal., 21 in. barrel, 35 shot mag., folding stock, optional bayonet lug, approx. 8 lbs., mfg. in Israel.

No MSR	$750	$675	$585	$530	$430	$350	$275

Add $30 for bayonet lug.

TANTAL SPORTER – 5.45x39mm cal., 18 in. barrel, parkerized finish, side folding wire stock, flash hider, includes extra mag., 8 lbs.

No MSR	$640	$575	$500	$450	$400	$350	$300

GORIUNOV SG43 – 7.62x54R cal., copy of Soviet model, gas operated, 28.3 in. barrel, 250 shot belt-fed, charging handle, spade grips, includes wooden crate, folding carriage, 3 ammo belts, 96 lbs.

No MSR	$5,575	$5,065	$4,340	$3,935	$3,185	$2,605	$2,025

VZ2008 SPORTER – 7.62x39mm cal., copy of the Czech VZ58, 16 1/4 in. barrel, steel receiver, dull matte finish, bead blasted metal parts, wood or plastic buttstock, 7 lbs.

No MSR	$695	$625	$550	$475	$400	$350	$300

M-76 SNIPER MODEL – 8mm Mauser cal., semi-auto version of the Yugoslav M76, new U.S. receiver and 21 1/2 in. barrel, includes original scope, mount, and 10 shot mag., 11.3 lbs.

No MSR	$1,825	$1,650	$1,400	$1,200	$1,000	$875	$750

GP 1975 – 7.62x39mm cal., 16 1/4 in. barrel, black synthetic furniture, new U.S. receiver and barrel, includes two 30 shot mags., approx. 7.4 lbs.

No MSR	$525	$475	$425	$350	$300	$265	$230

Add $200 for collapsible stock.

DEGTYAREV MODEL – top mounted magazine, semi-auto version of the Soviet model, available in three variations.

* **DP 28** – 7.62x54R cal., 23.8 in. barrel, gas operated, 47 shot drum mag., full shoulder stock.

	$3,500	$3,060	$2,625	$2,380	$1,925	$1,575	$1,225

* **DPM 28** – 7.62x54R cal., 23.8 in. barrel, gas operated, 47 shot drum mag., pistol grip stock.

	$3,500	$3,060	$2,625	$2,380	$1,925	$1,575	$1,225

* **DTX Tank Model** – 7.62x54R cal., 23.8 in. barrel, 50 shot drum mag., collapsible stock, approx. 10 lbs.

	$3,500	$3,060	$2,625	$2,380	$1,925	$1,575	$1,225

STERLING SA – 9mm Para. cal., semi-auto version of the Sterling submachine gun, 16 1/4 in. barrel, American made receiver and barrel, original style crinkle painted finish, folding stock, includes two 34 shot mags., available in Type I or Type II.

No MSR	$675	$575	$500	$425	$365	$335	$295

RIFLES: SLIDE ACTION

PAR 1 OR 3 – 7.62x39mm (PAR 1) or .223 Rem. (PAR 3) cal., AK receiver styling, 10 shot mag., accepts double stack AK magazines, wood stock, pistol grip, and forearm, 20.9 in. barrel, 7.6 lbs. Mfg. by PAR, and imported 2002-2009.

	$360	$300	$275	$250	$225	$200	$175

SHOTGUNS

SAS-12 SEMI-AUTO – 12 ga. only, 2 3/4 in. chamber, detachable 3 (Type II) or 5 shot mag., black synthetic stock and forearm, 22 or 23 1/2 in. barrel. Mfg. by PRC in China.

	$225	$195	$170	$155	$125	$100	$80

Add approx. $25 for ghost ring rear with blade front or bead sight.

CHARLES DALY

See Daly, Charles.

CHARTER ARMS

Previously manufactured by Charco, Inc. located in Ansonia, CT 1992-1996. Previously manufactured by Charter Arms located in Stratford, CT 1964-1991.

The company's first model was the Undercover.

PISTOLS: SEMI-AUTO

EXPLORER II & S II PISTOL – .22 LR cal., semi-auto survival pistol, barrel unscrews, 8 shot mag., black, gold

MSR	100%	98%	95%	90%	80%	70%	60%

(disc.), silvertone, or camouflage finish, 6, 8, or 10 in. barrels, simulated walnut grips. Disc. 1986.

| | $90 | $80 | $70 | $60 | $55 | $50 | $45 | Last MSR was $109. |

This model uses a modified AR-7 action.

Manufacture of this model was by Survival Arms located in Cocoa, FL.

RIFLES: SEMI-AUTO

AR-7 EXPLORER RIFLE – .22 LR cal., takedown, barreled action stores in Cycolac synthetic stock, 8 shot mag., adj. sights, 16 in. barrel, black finish on AR-7, silvertone on AR-7S. Camouflage finish new 1986 (AR-7C). Mfg. until 1990.

| | $125 | $100 | $85 | $75 | $65 | $55 | $50 | Last MSR was $146. |

In 1990, the manufacturing of this model was taken over by Survival Arms located in Cocoa, FL. Current mfg. AR-7 rifles will be found under the Henry Repeating Arms Company and AR-7 Industries.

CHEYTAC

Current manufacturer located in Arco, ID. Currently distributed by SPA Defense, located in Ft. Lauderdale, FL, and by Knesek Guns, Inc., located in Van Buren, AR.

RIFLES: BOLT ACTION

Cheytac currently manufactures an advanced 5 shot bolt action design in .375 or .408 Cheyenne Tactical cal. The Intervention Model 200 Military weighs 27 lbs., and includes an advanced ballistic computer to help with accuracy. The M-325 model is also offered. Cheytac also builds an Intervention Model M310 Target Model. Please contact the distributors directly for more information, including pricing and commercial availability (see Trademark Index).

CHRISTENSEN ARMS

Current rifle manufacturer established in 1995, and currently located in Fayette, UT. Previously located in St. George, UT during 1995-99. Direct sales only.

RIFLES: BOLT ACTION

In addition to the models listed below, Christensen Arms also offers the Carbon One Custom barrel installed on a customer action (any caliber) for $995 ($825 if short chambered by competent gunsmith), as well as providing a Carbon Wrap conversion to an existing steel barrel ($650).

Add $1,200 for Remington titanium action, $195 for titanium muzzle brake, $225 for Jewell trigger, $135 for Teflon coated action, $125 for camo stock (Realtree, Mossy Oak, or Natural Gear), and $75 for lightened action on the models listed below.

CARBON RANGER CONQUEST – .50 BMG cal., single shot or repeater (5 shot), McMillan stainless steel bolt action, max barrel length is 32 in. with muzzle brake, Christensen composite stock with bipod, approx. 16 (single shot) - 20 lbs. New 2001.

| MSR $6,000 | $5,350 | $4,600 | $3,800 | $3,200 | $2,625 | $2,200 | $1,900 |

Add $999 for 5-shot repeater.

CARBON RANGER – .50 BMG cal., large diameter graphite barrel casing (up to 36 in. long), no stock or forearm, twin rails extending from frame sides are attached to recoil pad, Omni Wind Runner action, bipod and choice of scope are included, 25-32 lbs. Limited mfg. 1998-2000 only.

| | $9,950 | $8,900 | $8,000 | $7,100 | $6,200 | $5,300 | $4,400 | Last MSR was $10,625. |

CARBON ONE EXTREME – various cals., carbon wrap free floating barrel, Christensen Arms stock, Teflon coated and lightened action, trigger tune, 6-7 lbs. New 2007.

| MSR $2,650 | $2,400 | $2,050 | $1,675 | $1,350 | $1,100 | $925 | $775 |

CITADEL

Current trademark imported beginning 2009 by Legacy Sports International, located in Reno, NV.

PISTOLS: SEMI-AUTO

CITADEL M-1911 FS – .45 ACP cal., full size 1911 style frame, 5 in. barrel, matte black, brushed nickel (new 2010), or polished nickel (new 2010), steel slide, 8 shot, skeletonized hammer and trigger, Novak sights, lowered and flared ejection port, extended ambidextrous safety, checkered wood or Hogue wraparound (available in Black, Green, or Sand, new 2010) grips, includes two magazines and lockable plastic case. New 2009.

| MSR $649 | $550 | $450 | $385 | $325 | $275 | $250 | $225 |

Add $50 for brushed nickel or $101 for polished nickel.
Add $250 for Wounded Warrior Project configuration with matte black finish.

MSR	100%	98%	95%	90%	80%	70%	60%

* ***Citadel M-1911 Compact*** – .45 ACP cal., 3 1/2 in. barrel, 6 shot, similar to Citadel M-1911 FS, except has compact frame, not available in polished nickel. New 2009.

MSR $649	$550	$450	$385	$325	$275	$250	$225

Add $50 for brushed nickel.
Add $50 for Hogue grips.

SHOTGUNS: SLIDE ACTION

CITADEL SLIDE ACTION – 12 ga., 20 in. barrel, 7 shot mag., matte black finish, available in standard, Spec-Ops, or Talon configuration. New 2010.

MSR $459	$385	$335	$285	$240	$210	$180	$150

Add $100 for either Spec-Ops or Talon configuration.

CLARIDGE HI-TEC INC.

Previous manufacturer located in Northridge, CA 1990-1993. In 1990, Claridge Hi-Tec, Inc. was created and took over Goncz Armament, Inc.

All Claridge Hi-Tec firearms utilized match barrels mfg. in-house, which were button-rifled. The Claridge action is an original design and does not copy other actions. Claridge Hi-Tec models can be altered (Law Enforcement Companion Series) to accept Beretta 92F or Sig Model 226 magazines.

PISTOLS

Add $40 for polished stainless steel frame construction.

L-9 PISTOL – 9mm Para., .40 S&W, or .45 ACP cal., semi-auto tactical design, 7 1/2 (new 1992) or 9 1/2 (disc. 1991) in. shrouded barrel, aluminum receiver, choice of black matte, matte silver, or polished silver finish, one-piece grip, safety locks firing pin in place, 10 (disc.), 17, or 30 shot double row mag., adj. sights, 3 3/4 lbs. Mfg. 1991-93.

		$595	$525	$375	$300	$265	$225	$200	Last MSR was $598.

Add $395 for a trigger activated laser sight available in Models M, L, C, and T new mfg.

S-9 PISTOL – similar to L-9, except has 5 in. non-shrouded threaded barrel, 3 lbs. 9 oz. Disc. 1993.

		$695	$625	$550	$475	$350	$280	$250	Last MSR was $535.

T-9 PISTOL – similar to L-9, except has 9 1/2 in. barrel. Mfg. 1992-93.

		$550	$495	$375	$300	$265	$225	$200	Last MSR was $598.

M PISTOL – similar to L Model, except has 7 1/2 in. barrel, 3 lbs. Disc. 1991.

		$575	$515	$375	$300	$265	$225	$200	Last MSR was $720.

RIFLES: CARBINES

C-9 CARBINE – same cals. as L and S Model pistols, 16.1 in. shrouded barrel, choice of composite or uncheckered walnut stock and forearm, 5 lbs. 12 oz. Mfg. 1991-93.

		$650	$595	$525	$450	$395	$350	$300	Last MSR was $675.

Add $74 for black graphite composite stock.
Add $474 for integral laser model (with graphite stock).

This model was available with either gloss walnut, dull walnut, or black graphite composite stock.

LAW ENFORCEMENT COMPANION (LEC) – 9mm Para., .40 S&W, or .45 ACP cal., 16 1/4 in. button rifled barrel, black graphite composition buttstock and foregrip, buttstock also provides space for an extra mag., available in either aluminum or stainless steel frame, matte black finish, available with full integral laser sighting system. Limited mfg. 1992-93.

		$750	$650	$575	$495	$425	$375	$325	Last MSR was $749.

Add $400 for integral laser sighting system.

CLARK CUSTOM GUNS, INC.

Current custom gun maker and gunsmith located in Princeton, LA. Clark Custom Guns, Inc. has been customizing various configurations of handguns, rifles, and shotguns since 1950. It would be impossible to list within the confines of this text the many conversions this company has performed. Please contact the company directly (see Trademark Index) for an up-to-date price sheet and catalog on their extensive line-up of high quality competition pistols and related components. Custom revolvers, rifles, and shotguns are also available in addition to various handgun competition parts, related gunsmithing services, and a firearms training facility called The Shootout.

The legendary James E. Clark, Sr. passed away during 2000. In 1958, he became the first and only full-time civilian to win the National Pistol Championships.

MSR	100%	98%	95%	90%	80%	70%	60%

PISTOLS: SEMI-AUTO

Clark Custom Guns manufactures a wide variety of M1911 style handguns, including the Bullseye Pistols (MSR $1,695-$3,100), the Custom Combat (MSR $1,925-$2,900), the Meltdown (MSR $1,995-$2,295), Millennium Meltdown (damascus slide, only 50 mfg. during 2000 - MSR was $3,795), .460 Rowland Hunter LS (last MSR $2,640), and the Unlimited (last MSR $3,395-$3,790). Clark will also build the above configurations on a customer supplied gun - prices are less. Please contact the company directly regarding more information on its wide variety of pistols, including availability and pricing (see Trademark Index).

CLIFTON ARMS

Previous manufacturer of custom rifles from 1992-1997 located in Medina, TX. Clifton Arms specialized in composite stocks (with or without integral, retractable bipod).

Clifton Arms manufactured composite, hand laminated stocks, which were patterned after the Dakota 76 stock configuration.

RIFLES: BOLT ACTION

CLIFTON SCOUT RIFLE – .243 Win. (disc. 1993), .30-06, .308 Win., .350 Rem. Mag., .35 Whelen, 7mm-08 Rem. (disc. 1993), or .416 Rem. Mag. cal., choice of Dakota 76, pre-64 Winchester Model 70, or Ruger 77 MK II (standard) stainless action with bolt face altered to controlled round feeding, Shilen stainless premium match grade barrel, Clifton synthetic stock with bipod, many other special orders were available. Mfg. 1992-97.

$3,000	$2,350	$1,650	$$1,455	$1,195	$1,010	$835

This model was available as a Standard Scout (.308 Win. cal. with 19 in. barrel), Pseudo Scout (.30-06 cal. with 19 1/2 in. barrel), Super Scout (.35 Whelen or .350 Rem. Mag. with 20 in. barrel), or African Scout (.416 Rem. Mag. with 22 in. barrel).

COBB MANUFACTURING, INC.

Previous rifle manufacturer located in Dallas, GA until 2007.

On Aug. 20, 2007, Cobb Manufacturing was purchased by Bushmaster, and manufacture was moved to Bushmaster's Maine facility. Please refer to the Bushmaster section for current information.

RIFLES: BOLT ACTION

MODEL FA50 (T) – .50 BMG cal., straight pull bolt action, lightweight tactical rifle, standard A2 style stock, ergonomic pistol grip, parkerized finish, Lothar Walther 22 or 30 in. barrel, recoil reducing Armalite muzzle brake, padded Mil-spec sling, includes two 10 shot mags., detachable M60 bipod, watertight case, 29 lbs. Disc. 2007.

$6,275	$5,300	$4,500	$3,900	$2,700	$2,300	$2,100	Last MSR was $6,995.

Add $300 for 22 in. barrel.
Add $1,000 for Ultra Light model with lightweight 22 or 30 in. barrel.
Add $89 for additonal 10 shot mag.

RIFLES: SEMI-AUTO

MCR (MULTI-CALIBER RIFLE) SERIES – available in a variety of calibers from 9mm Para. to .338 Lapua, offered in MCR 100, MCR 200, MCR 300, and MCR 400 configurations, variety of stock, barrel and finish options. Mfg. 2005-2007.

Prices on this series started at $3,000, and went up according to options chosen by customer.

COBRAY INDUSTRIES

See listing under S.W.D. in the S section of this text.

COLT'S MANUFACTURING COMPANY, INC.

Current manufacturer with headquarters located in West Hartford, CT.

Manufactured from 1836-1842 in Paterson, NJ; 1847-1848 in Whitneyville, CT; 1854-1864 in London, England; and from 1848-date in Hartford, CT. Colt Firearms became a division of Colt Industries in 1964. In March 1990, the Colt Firearms Division was sold to C.F. Holding Corp. located in Hartford, CT, and the new company is called Colt's Manufacturing Company, Inc. The original Hartford plant was closed during 1994, the same year the company was sold again to a new investor group headed by Zilkha Co., located in New York, NY. During 1999, Colt Archive Properties LLC, the historical research division, became its own entity. In November 2002, Colt was divided into two separate companies, Colt Defense LLC (rifles) and Colt's Manufacturing Company LLC (handguns).

In late 1999, Colt discontinued many of their consumer revolvers, but reintroduced both the Anaconda and Python Elite through the Custom Shop. Production on both models is now suspended. The semi-auto pistols remaining in production are now referred to as Model "O" Series.

MSR	100%	98%	95%	90%	80%	70%	60%

For more information and current pricing on both new and used Colt airguns, please refer to the *Blue Book of Airguns* by Dr. Robert Beeman & John Allen (also available online). For more information and current pricing on both new and used Colt black powder reproductions and replicas, please refer to the *Blue Book of Modern Black Powder Arms* by John Allen (also available online).

Black Powder Revolvers - Reproductions & Replicas and *Black Powder Long Arms & Pistols - Reproductions & Replicas* by Dennis Adler are also invaluable sources for most black powder reproductions and replicas, and include hundreds of color images on most popular makes/models, provide manufacturer/trademark histories, and up-to-date information on related items/accessories for black powder shooting - www.bluebookinc.com

RIFLES: SEMI-AUTO, CENTERFIRE, AR-15 & VARIATIONS

The AR-15 rifle and variations are the civilian versions of the U.S. armed forces M-16 model, which was initially ordered by the U.S. Army in 1963. Colt's obtained the exclusive manufacturing and marketing rights to the AR-15 from the Armalite division of the Fairchild Engine and Airplane Corporation in 1961.

Factory Colt AR-15 receivers are stamped with the model names only (Sporter II, Government Model, Colt Carbine, Sporter Match H-Bar, Match Target), but are not stamped with the model numbers (R6500, R6550, R6521, MT6430, CR6724). Because of this, if an AR-15 rifle/carbine does not have its original box, the only way to determine whether the gun is pre-ban or not is to look at the serial number and see if the configuration matches the features listed below within the two pre-ban subcategories.

AR-15 production included transition models, which were made up of obsolete and old stock parts. These transition models include: blue label box models having large front takedown pins, no internal sear block, 20 in. barrel models having bayonet lugs, misstamped nomenclature on receivers, or green label bolt assemblies.

Rifling twists on the Colt AR-15 have changed throughout the years, and barrel twists are stamped at the end of the barrel on top. They started with a 1:12 in. twist, changed to a 1:7 in. twist (to match with the new, longer .223 Rem./5.56mm SS109-type bullet), and finally changed to a 1:9 in. twist in combination with 1:7 in. twist models as a compromise for bullets in the 50-68 grain range. Current mfg. AR-15s/Match Targets have rifling twists/turns incorporated into the model descriptions.

Colt's never sold pre-ban lower receivers individually. It only sold completely assembled rifles.

A Colt letter of provenance for the following AR-15 models is $100 per gun.

AR-15, Pre-Ban, 1963-1989 Mfg. w/ Green Label Box

Common features of 1963-1989 mfg. AR-15s are bayonet lug, flash hider, large front takedown pin, no internal sear block, and w/o reinforcement around the magazine release button.

AR-15 boxes during this period of mfg. had a green label with serial number affixed on a white sticker. Box is taped in two places with brown masking tape. NIB consists of the rifle with barrel stick down the barrel, plastic muzzle cap on flash hider, factory tag hanging from front sight post, rifle in plastic bag with ser. no. on white sticker attached to bag, cardboard insert, accessory bag with two 20 round mags., manual, sling, and cleaning brushes. Cleaning rods are in separate bag.

Pre-ban parts rifles are rifles, which are not assembled in their proper factory configuration. Counterfeit pre-ban rifles are rifles using post-ban receivers and assembled into a pre-ban configuration (it is a felony to assemble or alter a post-ban rifle into a pre-ban configuration). Possession of an unstamped L.E. only rifles is a felony; they can be sold only to sworn law enforcement officers.

Add $100 for NIB condition.

Add $300 for early green label box models with reinforced lower receiver.

SP-1 (R6000) – .223 Rem. cal., original Colt tactical configuration without forward bolt assist, 20 in. barrel with 1:12 in. twist, identifiable by the triangular shaped handguards/forearm, no case deflector, A1 sights, finishes included parkerizing and electroless nickel, approx. 6 3/4 lbs. Mfg. 1963-1984.

	$2,100	$1,975	$1,850	$1,725	$1,600	$1,500	$1,200

Early mfg. will command substantial premiums, especially for very low ser. nos. - ser. range is SP00001 (1963)-SP55301 (1976).
Mint original condition models with early two and three digit serial numbers are selling in the $3,250 - $3,500 range.

Pre-ban serialization is ser. no. SP360,200 and lower.

Early SP-1s were packaged differently than later standard green box label guns.

* **SP-1 Carbine (R6001)** – similar to SP-1, except has 16 in. barrel, ribbed handguards, collapsible buttstock, high gloss finish.

	$2,900	$2,700	$2,425	$2,225	$2,075	$1,900	$1,650

Mint original condition models with early two and three digit serial numbers are selling in the $3,250 - $3,500 range.

Pre-ban serialization is ser. no. SP360200 and lower.

Early SP-1s were packaged differently than later standard green box label guns.

SPORTER II (R6500) – .223 Rem. cal., various configurations, receiver stamped "Sporter II", 20 in. barrel, 1:7 twist, A1 sights and forward assist, disc.

	$1,875	$1,650	$1,475	$1,300	$1,175	$1,075	$995

Serial numbers SP360200 and below are pre-ban.

MSR	100%	98%	95%	90%	80%	70%	60%

* **Sporter II Carbine (R6420)** – similar to Sporter II, except has 16 in. barrel, A1 sights and collapsible buttstock.

	$2,225	$2,000	$1,850	$1,675	$1,525	$1,425	$1,275

Serial numbers SP360200 and below are pre-ban.

GOVERNMENT MODEL (R6550) – .223 Rem. cal., receiver is stamped Government Model, 20 in. barrel with 1:7 in. twist and bayonet lug, A2 sights, forward assist and brass deflector, very desirable because this model has the closest configurations to what the U.S. military is currently using.

	$2,250	$2,100	$1,950	$1,800	$1,650	$1,400	$1,200

In 1987, Colt replaced the AR-15A2 Sporter II Rifle with the AR-15A2 Govt. Model. This new model has the 800 meter rear sighting system housed in the receiver's carrying handle (similar to the M-16 A2).

Serial numbers GS008000 and below are pre-ban.

* **Government Model (6550K)** – similar to R6550, except does not have bayonet lug, originally supplied with .22 L.R. cal. conversion kit.

	$2,050	$1,900	$1,750	$1,600	$1,450	$1,250	$1,100

Subtract $300 w/o conversion kit.

Serial numbers GS008000 and below are pre-ban.

* **Government Model (R6550CC)** – similar to R6550, except has Z-Cote tiger striped camo finish, very scarce (watch for cheap imitation paint jobs).

	$3,500	$3,350	$3,100	$2,800	$2,600	$2,400	$2,000

Serial numbers GS008000 and below are pre-ban.

H-BAR MODEL (R6600) – H-Bar model with 20 in heavy barrel, 1:7 twist, forward assist, A2 sights, brass deflector, 8 lbs. New 1986.

	$2,050	$1,900	$1,750	$1,600	$1,400	$1,200	$1,000

Serial numbers SP360200 and below are pre-ban.

* **H-Bar (R6600K)** – similar to R6600, except has no bayonet lug, supplied with .22 LR cal. conversion kit.

	$1,975	$1,825	$1,675	$1,525	$1,375	$1,225	$1,100

Subtract $300 if w/o conversion kit.

Serial numbers SP360200 and below are pre-ban.

* **Delta H-Bar (R6600DH)** – similar to R6600, except has 3-9x rubber armored scope, removable cheekpiece, adj. scope mount, and black leather sling, test range selected for its accuracy, aluminum transport case. Mfg. 1987-1991.

	$2,300	$2,150	$1,925	$1,775	$1,575	$1,375	$1,125	Last MSR was $1,460.

Serial numbers SP360200 and below are pre-ban.

AR-15, Pre-Ban, 1989-Sept. 11, 1994 Mfg. w/Blue Label Box

Common features of 1989-1994 AR-15 production include a small front takedown pin, internal sear block, reinforcement around the mag. release button, flash hider, no bayonet lug on 20 in. models, A2 sights, brass deflector, and forward bolt assist. Models R6430 and 6450 do not have A2 sights, brass deflector, or forward bolt assist.

Blue label boxed AR-15s were mfg. between 1989-Sept. 11, 1994. Please refer to box description under Pre-1989 AR-15 mfg.

Pre-ban parts rifles are rifles which are not assembled in their proper factory configuration. Counterfeit pre-ban rifles are rifles using post-ban receivers and assembled into a pre-ban configuration.

Add $100 for NIB condition.

AR-15A3 TACTICAL CARBINE (R-6721) – .223 Rem. cal., M4 flat-top with 16 in. heavy barrel, 1:9 twist, A2 sights, pre-ban configuration with flash hider, bayonet lug, and 4-position, collapsible stock, removable carry handle, 134 were sold commercially in the U.S., most collectible AR-15. Mfg. 1994 only.

	$2,975	$2,500	$2,275	$2,050	$1,900	$1,775	$1,600

On the R-6721, serial numbers BD000134 and below are pre-ban.

Please note the serial number cutoff on this model, as Colt shipped out a lot of unstamped post-ban law enforcement only "LEO" rifles before finally stamping them as a restricted rifle.

GOVERNMENT CARBINE (R6520) – .223 Rem cal., receiver is stamped Government Carbine, two-position collapsible buttstock, 800 meter adj. rear sight, 16 in. barrel bayonet lug, 1:7 twist, shortened forearm, 5 lbs. 13 oz. Mfg. 1988-94.

	$2,275	$2,125	$2,025	$1,875	$1,750	$1,625	$1,425	Last MSR was $880.

MSR	100%	98%	95%	90%	80%	70%	60%

Add $200 for green label box.

On the R6520, serial numbers GC018500 and below are pre-ban.

Please note the serial number cutoff on this model, as Colt shipped out a lot of unstamped post-ban law enforcement only "LEO" rifles before finally stamping them as a restricted rifle.

This model was manufactured in both green and blue label configurations.

COLT CARBINE (R6521) – receiver is stamped Colt Carbine, similar to R6520, except has no bayonet lug, 16 in. barrel, 1:7 twist. Disc. 1988.

| | $2,150 | $2,000 | $1,850 | $1,700 | $1,625 | $1,475 | $1,300 | Last MSR was $770. |

Serial numbers CC001616 and below are pre-ban.

SPORTER LIGHTWEIGHT (R6530) – .223 Rem. cal., receiver is stamped Sporter Lightweight, 16 in. barrel, 1:7 twist, similar to R6520, except does not have bayonet lug or collapsible stock.

| | $1,650 | $1,500 | $1,350 | $1,100 | $1,000 | $900 | $800 | Last MSR was $740. |

Serial numbers SI027246 and below are pre-ban.

9mm CARBINE (R6430) – 9mm Para. cal., similar to R6450 Carbine, except does not have bayonet lug or collapsible stock. Mfg. 1992-1994.

| | $1,950 | $1,800 | $1,650 | $1,500 | $1,375 | $1,275 | $1,175 | |

Serial numbers NL004800 are pre-ban.

9mm CARBINE (R6450) – 9mm Para. cal., carbine model with 16 in. barrel, 1:10 twist, bayonet lug, w/o forward bolt assist or brass deflector, two-position collapsible stock, 20 shot mag., 6 lbs. 5 oz.

| | $2,250 | $2,100 | $1,950 | $1,800 | $1,725 | $1,575 | $1,400 | Last MSR was $696. |

On the R6450, serial numbers TA010100 are pre-ban.

Please note the serial number cutoff on this model, as Colt shipped out a lot of unstamped post-ban law enforcement only "LEO" rifles before finally stamping them as a restricted rifle.

This model was manufactured with either a green or blue label.

7.62x39mm CARBINE (R6830) – 7.62x39mm cal., 16 in. barrel w/o bayonet lug, 1:12 twist, fixed buttstock. Mfg. 1992-1994.

| | $1,850 | $1,700 | $1,550 | $1,400 | $1,275 | $1,175 | $1,075 | |

Serial numbers LH011326 are pre-ban.

TARGET COMPETITION H-BAR RIFLE (R6700) – .223 Rem. cal., flat-top upper receiver for scope mounting, 20 in. H-Bar barrel (1:9 in. twist), quick detachable carry handle with a 600-meter rear sighting system, dovetailed upper receiver grooved to accept Weaver style scope rings, 8 1/2 lbs.

| | $1,850 | $1,700 | $1,550 | $1,400 | $1,200 | $1,025 | $875 | |

Serial numbers CH019500 and below are pre-ban.

COMPETITION H-BAR CUSTOM SHOP (R6701) – .223 Rem. cal., similar to the R6700, but with detachable scope mount, custom shop enhancements added to trigger and barrel, 2,000 mfg. from Colt Custom Shop.

| | $1,950 | $1,800 | $1,650 | $1,500 | $1,350 | $1,200 | $1,050 | |

MATCH H-BAR (R6601) – heavy 20 in. H-Bar barrel with 1:7 twist, fixed buttstock. 8 lbs.

| | $1,750 | $1,600 | $1,450 | $1,300 | $1,150 | $1,025 | $950 | |

* ***Delta H-Bar (R6601DH)*** – similar to R6601, except has 3-9x rubber armored variable scope, removable cheekpiece, adj. scope mount, black leather sling, test range selected for its accuracy, aluminum transport case. Mfg. 1987-91.

| | $2,450 | $2,300 | $2,150 | $2,000 | $1,850 | $1,700 | $1,550 | Last MSR was $1,460. |

Serial numbers MH086020 and below are pre-ban.

SPORTER TARGET (R6551) – similar to R6601, except had 20 in. barrel with reduced diameter underneath handguard, 7 1/2 lbs.

| | $1,750 | $1,600 | $1,450 | $1,300 | $1,150 | $1,050 | $950 | |

On the R6551, serial numbers ST038100 and below are pre-ban.

AR-15, Post-Ban, Mfg. Sept. 12, 1994-Present

Due to Colt's current military contracts, the commercial availability of AR-15s and variations listed below has been somewhat limited in recent years.

MSR	100%	98%	95%	90%	80%	70%	60%

During 2007, Colt released the M-5 Military Carbine and the LE 10-20, with 11 1/2, 14 1/2, or 16 in. barrel. These guns are only available for military and law enforcement.

Add $368 for Colt Scout C-More Sight on current mfg.
Add $444 for Colt Tactical C-More Sight on current mfg.

MATCH TARGET COMPETITION H-BAR RIFLE (MT6700/MT6700C) – .223 Rem. cal., features flat-top upper receiver for scope mounting, 20 in. barrel (1:9 in. twist), quick detachable carry handle which incorporates a 600-meter rear sighting system, counterbored muzzle, dovetailed upper receiver is grooved to accept Weaver style scope rings, supplied with two 5, 8, or 9 (new 1999) shot mags., cleaning kit, and sling, matte black finish, 8 1/2 lbs. New 1992.

MSR $1,230	$1,100	$925	$850	$750	$650	$575	$525

Add $57 for compensator (MT6700C, new 1999).

TACTICAL ELITE MODEL (TE6700) – .223 Rem. cal., 20 in. heavy barrel, 1:8 in. twist, Hogue finger groove pistol grip, Choate buttstock, fine tuned for accuracy, scope and mount included, approx. 1,000 rifles made by the Custom Shop circa 1996-97.

	$1,650	$1,450	$1,250	$1,025	$900	$800	$700

COLT ACCURIZED RIFLE (CR6724) – .223 Rem. cal., 24 in. stainless match barrel, matte finish, accurized AR-15, 8 (disc. 1998) or 9 (new 1999) shot mag., 9.41 lbs. New 1997.

MSR $1,374	$1,200	$1,050	$875	$795	$725	$650	$575

MATCH TARGET COMPETITION H-BAR II (MT6731) – .223 Rem. cal., flat-top, 16.1 in. barrel (1:9 in.), matte finish, 7.1 lbs. New 1995.

MSR $1,207	$1,075	$925	$850	$725	$625	$575	$525

MATCH TARGET LIGHTWEIGHT (MT6430, MT6530, or MT6830) – .223 Rem. (MT6530, 1:7 in. twist), 7.62x39mm (MT6830, disc. 1996, 1:12 in. twist), or 9mm Para. (MT6430, disc. 1996, 1:10 in. twist) cal., features 16 in. barrel (non-threaded per C/B 1994), initially shorter stock and handguard, rear sight adjustable for windage and elevation, includes two detachable 5, 8, or 9 (new 1999) shot mags., approx. 7 lbs. Mfg. 1991-2002.

	$925	$795	$725	$665	$600	$550	$495	Last MSR was $1,111.

Add $200 for .22 LR conversion kit (disc. 1994).

TARGET GOVT. MODEL RIFLE (MT6551) – .223 Rem. cal., semi-auto version of the M-16 rifle with forward bolt assist, 20 in. barrel (1:7 in.), straight line black nylon stock, aperture rear and post front sight, 5, 8, 9 (new 1999) shot mags., 7 1/2 lbs. Disc. 2002.

	$1,050	$925	$850	$775	$700	$650	$595	Last MSR was $1,144.

Add $200 for .22 LR conversion kit (mfg. 1990-94).

MATCH TARGET M4 CARBINE (MT6400C/MT6400R) – .223 Rem. cal., similar to current U.S. armed forces M4 model, except semi-auto, 10 shot mag., 16.1 in. barrel, 1:7 in. twist, matte black finish, fixed tube buttstock, A3 detachable carrying handle, 7.3 lbs. New 2002.

MSR $1,328	$1,200	$1,075	$950	$850	$750	$650	$550

Add $287 for quad accessory rail (MT6400R).

MATCH TARGET H-BAR RIFLE (MT6601/MT6601C) – .223 Rem. cal., heavy 20 in. H-Bar barrel, 1:7 in. twist, A2 sights, 8 lbs. New 1986.

MSR $1,218	$1,125	$975	$875	$775	$675	$600	$550

Add $200 for .22 LR conversion kit (mfg. 1990-94).
Add $1 for compensator (MT6601C, new 1999).

AR-15 SCOPE (3X/4X) AND MOUNT – initially offered with 3x magnification scope, then switched to 4x. Disc.

	$395	$300	$240	$185	$160	$130	$115	Last MSR was $344.

RIFLES: SEMI-AUTO, RIMFIRE, AR-15 & VARIATIONS

The following models are manufactured by Umarex, located in Arnsberg, Germany, under license from New Colt Holding Corp.

Initial high demand for these models may result in some consumers paying a premium over retail for the following models.

M4 CARBINE – .22 LR cal., 16.2 in. shrouded barrel, flat-top receiver, 10 or 30 shot mag., detachable carry handle, external safety, four position retractable stock, ribbed aluminum handguard, black finish, approx. 6 lbs. New 2009.

MSR $599	$575	$525	$475	$425	$395	$375	$350

* **M4 Ops** – .22 LR cal., 16.2 in. barrel, 10 or 30 shot mag., aluminum upper and lower receiver, black finish, quad tactical rail interface system with elongated Picatinny rail on top of barrel and frame, straight line construction,

MSR	100%	98%	95%	90%	80%	70%	60%

cartridge case deflector, muzzle compensator, detachable rear sight, four position collapsible stock, ejection port cover, approx. 6 1/2 lbs. New 2009.

| MSR $640 | $595 | $550 | $495 | $450 | $425 | $395 | $375 |

M16 – .22 LR cal., 21.2 in. barrel, 10 or 30 shot mag., flat-top receiver with detachable carry handle, fixed stock, elongated ribbed aluminum handguard, removable rear sight, ejection port cover, external safety, black finish, approx. 6 1/4 lbs. New 2009.

| MSR $599 | $575 | $525 | $475 | $425 | $395 | $375 | $350 |

* **M16 SPR (Special Purpose Rifle)** – .22 LR cal., 21.2 in. barrel, 30 shot mag., black finish, fixed stock, aluminum upper and lower receiver, quad tactical rail interface system with Picatinny rail, flip up front and rear sights, straight line construction, cartridge case deflector, muzzle compensator. New 2009.

| MSR $670 | $625 | $575 | $525 | $475 | $450 | $415 | $395 |

COMMANDO ARMS

Previous manufacturer located in Knoxville, TN.

Commando Arms became the new name for Volunteer Enterprises in the late 1970s.

RIFLES: CARBINES

MARK 45 – .45 ACP cal., carbine styled after the Thompson sub-machine gun, 16 1/2 in. barrel.

| | | $495 | $425 | $350 | $315 | $280 | $225 | $195 |

COMPETITIVE EDGE GUNWORKS LLC

Current rifle manufacturer located in Bogard, OR.

RIFLES: BOLT ACTION

Competitive Edge Gunworks LLC builts custom order bolt action rifles based on its patented action. Tactical, Hunting, and Varmint configurations are available. Please contact the company directly for more information, including available options, delivery time and a price quotation (see Trademark Index).

CORE 15

Current trademark of carbines and rifles manufactured by GTO Guns, located in Ocala, FL.

RIFLES: SEMI-AUTO

GTO Guns manufactures a complete line of .223 Rem. cal. Core 15 carbines and rifles patterned after the AR-15. Prices range from $850 - $1,200. All models use the Adams Arms Piston gas system, have Hogue overmolded stocks, and are available in OD Green, Dark Earth, or matte black. Please contact the company directly for availability and pricing (see Trademark Index).

CROSSFIRE LLC

Previous manufacturer located in La Grange, GA 1998-2001.

COMBINATION GUNS

CROSSFIRE MK-I – 12 ga. (3 in. chamber) over .223 Rem. cal., unique slide action O/U design allows stacked shotgun/rifle configuration, 18 3/4 in. shotgun barrel with invector chokes over 16 1/4 in. rifle barrel, detachable 4 (shotgun) and 5 (rifle) shot mags., open sights, Picatinny rail, synthetic stock and forearm, choice of black (MK-I) or RealTree 100% camo (MK-1RT) finish, single trigger with ambidextrous fire control lever, 8.6 lbs. Limited mfg. mid-1998-2001.

| | $1,995 | $1,750 | $1,550 | $1,350 | $1,175 | $995 | $895 | Last MSR was $1,895. |

Add $100 for camo finish.

CZECHPOINT INC.

Current distributor located in Knoxville, TN.

Czechpoint Inc. distributes tactical style semi-auto rifles and pistols manufactured in the Czech Republic by D-Technik. Please contact the company sirectly regarding current model availability and pricing (see Trademark Index).

NOTES

D SECTION

DPMS FIREARMS, LLC

Current manufacturer established in 1986 and located in St. Cloud, MN. Previously located in Becker, MN. Previous company name was DPMS, Inc. (Defense Procurement Manufacturing Services, Inc.) assembles high quality AR-15 style rifles (including a conversion for .22 cal.), in addition to selling related parts and components. Distributor, dealer, and consumer direct sales.

In December 2007, Cerberus Capital Management acquired the assets of DPMS. The new company name is DPMS Firearms, LLC.

MSR	100%	98%	95%	90%	80%	70%	60%

PISTOLS: SEMI-AUTO

PANTHER .22 LR PISTOL – .22 LR cal., 8 1/2 in. heavy chrome-moly steel barrel, 10 shot mag., black aircraft aluminum flat-top upper receiver, black forged aircraft aluminum lower receiver, blowback action, phosphate and hard chrome finished bolt and carrier, aluminum trigger guard, ribbed aluminum tubular hand guard, no sights, 4 1/4 lbs. Limited mfg. 2006-2007.

	100%	98%	95%	90%	80%	70%	60%	
	$775	$700	$625	$550	$475	$425	$375	Last MSR was $850.

PISTOLS: SLIDE ACTION

PANTHER PUMP PISTOL – .223 Rem. cal., slide action tactical design, 10 1/2 in. threaded heavy barrel, aluminum handguard incorporates slide action mechanism, pistol grip only (no stock), carrying handle with sights, 5 lbs. Disc. 2007.

	100%	98%	95%	90%	80%	70%	60%	
	$1,475	$1,200	$1,025	$925	$825	$700	$575	Last MSR was $1,600.

RIFLES: SEMI-AUTO

Each new DPMS rifle/carbine comes equipped with two mags. (high cap where legal), a nylon web sling, and a cleaning kit. Post-crime bill manufactured DPMS rifles may have pre-ban features, including collapsible stocks, high capacity mags, and a flash hider/compensator. Models with these features are not available in certain states.

The Panther AR-15 Series was introduced in 1993 in various configurations, including semi-auto and slide action, and feature a tactical design in various barrel lengths and configurations, with a 10 or 30 shot mag.

PANTHER CLASSIC – 5.56 NATO cal., 16 (disc.) or 20 in. heavy barrel, ribbed barrel shroud, includes carrying handle with sights, 8 lbs.

MSR $849	$795	$675	$575	$475	$425	$375	$335

Add $76 for left-hand variation (Southpaw Panther, disc.)

* ***Panther Classic Bulldog*** – 20 in. stainless fluted bull barrel, flat-top, adj. buttstock, vented free float handguard, 11 lbs. Disc. 1999.

	100%	98%	95%	90%	80%	70%	60%	
	$1,150	$835	$725	$625	$550	$475	$425	Last MSR was $1,219.

PANTHER 7.62x39mm – 7.62x39mm Russian cal., 16 or 20 in. heavy barrel, black Zytel buttstock with trap door assembly, A2 flash hider, A2 pistol grip, 7-9 lbs. New 2000.

MSR $860	$775	$650	$575	$495	$440	$385	$335

Add $10 for 20 in. barrel.

PANTHER DCM – .223 Rem. cal., 20 in. stainless steel heavy barrel, National Match sights, two-stage trigger, black Zytel composition buttstock, 9 lbs. Mfg. 1998-2003, reintroduced 2006.

MSR $1,099	$1,025	$795	$675	$595	$525	$460	$415

PANTHER LITE – 5.56 NATO cal., 16 or 20 (new 2007) in. post-ban chrome-moly barrel, 1:9 in. twist, non-collapsible fiberite CAR stock, choice of forged A1 upper with forward bolt assist, or A3 carry handle, lack Teflon finish, 5 3/4 lbs. New 2002.

MSR $759	$700	$625	$550	$450	$400	$360	$325

Add $30 for 20 in. barrel.

PANTHER LITE 308/338 – .308 Win. or .338 Federal cal., 18 in. free float barrel, no sights, carbon fiber free float hand guard, bipod stud, A3 style flat-top, Picatinny rail, various accessories and options available. New 2009.

MSR $1,499	$1,350	$1,100	$925	$800	$700	$600	$500

PANTHER CLASSIC SIXTEEN – 5.45 NATO cal., 16 in. heavy barrel, adj. sights, black Zytel composition buttstock, 6 1/2 lbs. New 1998.

MSR $829	$775	$650	$550	$475	$425	$375	$335

Add $55 for Panther Free Float Sixteen with free floating barrel and vent. handguard (disc. 2008).

MSR	100%	98%	95%	90%	80%	70%	60%

PANTHER LO-PRO CLASSIC – .223 Rem. cal., 16 in. bull barrel, features flat-top lo-pro upper receiver with push pin. New 2002.

MSR $759	$700	$625	$550	$450	$400	$360	$325

PANTHER TUBER – 5.56 NATO cal., features 16 in. post-ban heavy free float barrel with full length 2 in. dia. aluminum free float handguard, adj. A2 rear sights. Mfg. 2002-2008.

	$675	$625	$565	$485	$435	$375	$335	Last MSR was $754.

PANTHER A2 TACTICAL – 5.56 NATO cal., features 16 in. heavy manganese phosphated barrel, standard A2 handguard, 9 3/4 lbs. New 2004.

MSR $829	$775	$650	$550	$475	$425	$375	$335

PANTHER AP4 CARBINE – 5.56 NATO cal., features 16 in. M4 contour barrel with A2 flash hider, with or w/o attached Miculek compensator, fixed fiberglass reinforced polymer M4 stock, 7 1/4 lbs. New 2004.

MSR $949	$875	$750	$625	$475	$425	$375	$335

Add $40 for Miculek compensator.

* ***Panther AP4 Carbine (Disc.)*** – 6.8x43mm SPC or 5.56x45mm cal., 16 in. barrel, collapsible stock, includes carrying handle, 6 1/2 lbs. Disc.

	$815	$725	$600	$525	$450	$400	$360	Last MSR was $904.

PANTHER AP4 A2 CARBINE – 5.56 NATO cal., 16 in. chrome-moly steel barrel with A2 flash hider, standard A2 front sight assembly, A2 fixed carry handle and adj. rear sight, forged aircraft aluminum upper and lower receiver, hard coat anodized teflon coated black AP4 six position telescoping fiber reinforced polymer stock, 7.1 lbs. New 2006.

MSR $829	$775	$650	$550	$475	$425	$375	$335

PANTHER A2 CARBINE "THE AGENCY" – 5.56 NATO cal., 16 in. chrome-moly steel barrel with A2 flash hider, A3 flat-top forged receiver, two-stage trigger, tactical charging handle, package includes Surefire quad-rail and flashlight, EoTech and "Mangonel" rear sights, Ergo Suregrip forearm and collapsible stock, supplied with two 30-shot mags., 7 lbs. New 2007.

MSR $2,069	$1,850	$1,625	$1,475	$1,350	$1,225	$1,100	$875

PANTHER 6.8mm CARBINE/RIFLE – 6.8x43mm Rem. SPC cal., 16 (new 2007) or 20 in. chrome-moly manganese phosphated steel barrel with A2 flash hider, standard A2 front sight assembly, A3 flat-top upper receiver with detachable carry handle and adj. rear sight, aluminum aircraft alloy lower receiver, black standard A2 Zytel mil spec stock with trap door assembly, A2 handguard, includes two 25 shot mags., approx. 9 lbs. New 2006.

MSR $1,019	$950	$825	$700	$600	$500	$425	$375

Add $10 for 20 in. barrel.

PRAIRIE PANTHER – 20 in. heavy fluted free float barrel, flat-top, vented handguard, 8 3/4 lbs. Disc. 1999.

	$875	$750	$635	$550	$475	$425	$375	Last MSR was $959.

PRAIRIE PANTHER DESERT/BRUSH – .223 Rem. cal., 20 in. stainless steel heavy barrel, target crown, hard anodized finish, carbon fiber free float tube, no sights, choice of King's Desert Shadow (Desert) or Mossy Oak Brush (Brush) camo coverage, A3 Picatinny rail flattop, tactical charging handle assembly, Magpul winter trigger guard, skeletonized black Zytel mil spec stock with trap door assembly, A2 pistol grip, two-stage trigger, approx. 7.1 lbs. New 2010.

MSR $1,249	$1,115	$950	$825	$725	$650	$600	$550

PANTHER BULL – .223 Rem. cal., features 16, 20 (standard), or 24 in. stainless free float bull barrel, flat-top, aluminum forearm, 10 lbs.

MSR $939	$865	$725	$600	$525	$450	$400	$360

Subtract $30 for 16 in. barrel (Panther Bull Sweet Sixteen).
Add $30 for 24 in. barrel (Panther Bull Twenty-Four).

* ***Panther Bull Classic*** – .223 Rem. cal., features 20 in. long, 1 in. bull barrel, adj. sights, 10 lbs. Mfg. 1998-2008.

	$825	$725	$600	$525	$450	$400	$360	Last MSR was $910.

Add $200 for SST lower.

* ***Panther Bull Twenty-Four Special*** – .223 Rem. cal., features 24 in. stainless fluted barrel, adj. A2 buttstock with sniper pistol grip. New 1998.

MSR $1,189	$1,100	$850	$725	$625	$525	$460	$415

* ***Panther Super Bull*** – .223 Rem. cal., 16, 20, or 24 in. extra heavy free float bull barrel, flat-top receiver, handguard; approx. 11 lbs. Mfg. 1997-98, 24 in. model reintroduced during late 2004, disc. 2006.

	$1,075	$835	$725	$600	$525	$460	$415	Last MSR was $1,199.

MSR	100%	98%	95%	90%	80%	70%	60%

* ***Panther Super Bull 24*** – features 24 in. extra heavy stainless steel bull barrel (1 1/8 in. diameter barrel), flat-top, hi-rider upper receiver, skeletonized A2 buttstock, 11 3/4 lbs. Mfg. 1999-2004.

	$1,075	$835	$715	$600	$525	$460	$415	Last MSR was $1,199.

ARCTIC PANTHER – .223 Rem. cal., similar to Panther Bull, except has white powder coat finish on receiver and handguard, 10 lbs. New 1997.

MSR $1,099	$1,025	$795	$675	$595	$525	$460	$415

PANTHER PARDUS – .223 Rem. cal., 16 in. stainless steel free float bull barrel, integrated compensator, titanium nitride plated steel bolt and carrier, three rail extruded upper receiver, aluminum alloy upper and lower receiver, Teflon coated tan or black six position telescoping fiber reinforced polymer stock, curved and serrated buttplate, four-rail aluminum handguard, no sights, includes two 30 shot mags., 8.1 lbs. Mfg. 2006-2008.

	$1,395	$1,150	$950	$800	$675	$575	$525	Last MSR was $1,600.

PANTHER MARK 12 – .223 Rem. cal., 18 in. stainless heavy free float barrel with flash hider, features one-piece four rail tube and six long rail covers, A3 flattop receiver, 5-position collapsible stock with tactical pistol grip, two-stage trigger, two 30 round mags., 8 3/4 lbs. New 2007.

MSR $1,599	$1,375	$1,125	$950	$800	$700	$600	$500

PANTHER SDM-R – .223 Rem. cal., 20 in. heavy stainless free float barrel with A2 flash hider, features four rail aluminum tube, pistol grip stock, National Match front sight, Harris bipod with rail adapter, two 30 shot mags., 8.85 lbs. Mfg. 2007-2008.

	$1,250	$1,075	$925	$825	$725	$650	$575	Last MSR was $1,404.

PANTHER 20TH ANNIVERSARY – .223 Rem. cal., 20 in. stainless steel fluted bull barrel, phosphated steel bolt and carrier, hi-rider forged high polished chrome upper and lower receiver with commemorative engraving, chrome plated charging handle, semi-auto trigger group, aluminum trigger guard and mag. release button, A2 black Zytel mil spec stock with trap door assembly and engraved DPMS logo, no sights, vented aluminum handguard, includes two 30 shot mags., approx. 9 1/2 lbs. Limited mfg. of 100 rifles in 2006.

	$1,995	$1,750	$1,600	$1,475	$1,350	$1,225	$1,100	Last MSR was $1,995.

PANTHER RACE GUN – .223 Rem. cal., 24 in. stainless steel barrel with Hot Rod hand guard, IronStone steel and aluminum stock with rubber buttplate and brass weights, 16 lbs. Mfg. 2001-2008.

	$1,565	$1,250	$1,050	$950	$850	$725	$600	Last MSR was $1,724.

PANTHER SINGLE SHOT – 5.56 NATO cal., 20 in. barrel, A2 black Zytel stock and handguard, single shot only w/o magazine, 9 lbs. Disc. 2008.

	$725	$640	$560	$485	$435	$375	$335	Last MSR was $819.

PANTHER .22 RIFLE – .22 LR cal., AR-15 style receiver, 16 in. bull barrel, black Teflon metal finish, Picatinny rail, black Zytel A2 buttstock, 7.8 lbs. Mfg. 2003-2008.

	$725	$625	$550	$475	$425	$375	$335	Last MSR was $804.

PANTHER DCM .22 LR RIFLE – .22 LR cal., 20 in. fluted stainless steel H-Bar barrel with 1:16 in. twist, A2 upper receiver with National Match sights, black teflon finish, A2 stock and handguards, also available with optional DCM handguard system. Mfg. 2004-2008.

	$875	$775	$650	$550	$475	$425	$375	Last MSR was $994.

PANTHER AP4 .22 LR RIFLE – .22 LR cal., features 16 in. M4 contoured barrel with 1:16 in. twist, M4 handguards and pinned carstock, A3 flat-top upper receiver, detachable carry handle with A2 sights and black teflon finish, 6 1/2 lbs. Mfg. 2004-2008.

	$785	$675	$600	$500	$450	$400	$350	Last MSR was $894.

This model was also available in a pre-ban configuration for law enforcement.

PANTHER LR-.308 – .308 Win. cal., 24 in. free float bull barrel with 1:10 in. twist, ribbed aluminum forearm tube, aircraft alloy upper/lower, A2 buttstock, black Teflon finish. New mid-2003.

MSR $1,169	$1,050	$850	$750	$650	$575	$500	$450

* ***Panther LR-.308B*** – similar features as the Long Range Rifle, except has 18 in. chrome-moly bull barrel and carbine length aluminum handguard. New late 2003.

MSR $1,159	$1,040	$850	$750	$650	$575	$500	$450

* ***Panther LR-.308T*** – similar features as the .308B, except has 16 in. H-Bar barrel. New 2004.

MSR $1,159	$1,040	$850	$750	$650	$575	$500	$450

MSR	100%	98%	95%	90%	80%	70%	60%

* ***Panther LR-.308 AP4*** – similar to Panther .308 Long Range, except has AP4 six position telescoping fiber reinforced polymer stock.

| MSR $1,269 | $1,125 | $950 | $825 | $725 | $650 | $600 | $550 |

* ***Panther LR-308 Classic*** – .308 Win. cal., similar to Panther LR-308, except has 20 in. barrel. New mid-2008.

| MSR $1,099 | $1,025 | $795 | $675 | $595 | $525 | $460 | $415 |

PANTHER LRT-SASS – .308 Win. cal., 18 in. stainless steel contoured barrel with Panther flash hider, A3 style flat-top upper receiver solid alumnium lower receiver, AR-15 trigger group, ambi-selector, JP adj. trigger, black waterproof Vltor Clubfoot carbine 5 position stock, vented handguard and Panther tactical pistol grip. New 2006.

| MSR $2,119 | $1,875 | $1,600 | $1,350 | $1,125 | $950 | $825 | $700 |

PANTHER MINI-SASS – 5.56x45mm cal., 18 in. stainless steel fluted barrel with Panther flash hider, forged A3 flat-top upper receiver, aircraft aluminum alloy lower receiver, aluminum trigger guard, tactical pistol grip, includes Harris bipod, 10 1/4 lbs. New 2008.

| MSR $1,599 | $1,400 | $1,175 | $925 | $800 | $675 | $575 | $525 |

PANTHER LR-30S – .300 RSUM cal., 20 in. stainless steel free float fluted bull barrel, aluminum upper and lower receiver, hard coat anodized teflon coated black skeletonized synthetic stock, integral trigger guard, ribbed aluminum tube handguard, includes two 4 shot mags., nylon web sling and cleaning kit. Mfg. 2004-2008.

| | $1,075 | $925 | $825 | $725 | $650 | $600 | $550 | *Last MSR was $1,255.* |

PANTHER LR-204 – .204 Ruger cal., 24 in. stainless steel bull barrel, no sights, A3 flat-top forged upper and lower receiver, semi-auto trigger group, standard A2 black Zytel mil spec stock with trap door assembly, includes two 30 shot mags., 10 1/4 lbs. New 2006.

| MSR $1,029 | $950 | $825 | $675 | $575 | $475 | $425 | $375 |

PANTHER LR-243 – .243 Win. cal., 20 in. chrome-moly steel heavy or lightweight (Lite Hunter) free float barrel, no sights, raised Picatinny rail, aluminum upper and lower receiver, standard AR-15 trigger group, skeletonized black Zytel mil spec stock with trap door assembly, ribbed aluminum free float handguard, includes two 19 shot mags., 10 3/4 lbs. New 2006.

| MSR $1,199 | $1,075 | $925 | $825 | $725 | $650 | $600 | $550 |

Add $300 for lightweight barrel (Lite Hunter).

PANTHER LR-260/LR-260H/LR-260L – .260 Rem. cal., 18 (new 2007, LR-260L), 20 (LR-260H) or 24 (LR-260) in. stainless steel fluted bull barrel, no sights, raised Picatinny rail, thick walled aluminum upper receiver, solid lower receiver, standard AR-15 trigger goup, integral trigger guard, A2 black Zytel stock with trap door assembly, includes two 19 shot mags., 11.3 lbs. New 2006.

| MSR $1,199 | $1,075 | $925 | $825 | $725 | $650 | $600 | $550 |

Add $300 for 18 in. barrrel (LR-260L) with skeletonized stock, Miculek compensator and JRD trigger.

PANTHER LR-308C – .308 Win. cal., 20 in. heavy steel free float barrel, features A3 flat-top receiver with detachable carrying handle, standard A2 front sight assembly, four rail standard length tube, two 19 shot mags., 11.1 lbs. Mfg. 2007-2008.

| | $1,075 | $925 | $825 | $725 | $650 | $600 | $550 | *Last MSR was $1,254.* |

PANTHER SPORTICAL – .223 Rem. or .308 Win. cal., 16 in. chromemoly heavy or lite contour barrel, single rail gas block, A2 flash hider, various rails and accessories. New mid-2008.

| MSR $715 | $675 | $575 | $550 | $475 | $425 | $375 | $335 |

Add $294 for .308 Win. cal.

PANTHER 6.5 – 6.5 Creedmoor cal., 24 in. stainless steel free float bull barrel, single rail gas block, no sights, ribbed aluminum free float tube handguard, bipod stud, A3 style flat-top, black Teflon coated, standard A2 black Zytel mil spec stock, A2 pistol grip, 11.3 lbs. New 2009.

| MSR $1,199 | $1,075 | $850 | $750 | $650 | $575 | $500 | $450 |

PANTHER REPR – .308 Win. cal., 18 in. fluted chromemoly steel free float barrel, Gem Tech flash hider/suppressor, micro gas block, A3 style flat-top upper receiver, milled aluminum lower receiver, hard coat anodized coyote brown finish, removable hinged trigger guard, Picatinny rail, four rail tube handguard, Magpul Precision Rifle Stock, Hogue rubber grip with finger grooves, 9 1/2 lbs. New 2009.

| MSR $2,519 | $2,250 | $1,925 | $1,650 | $1,350 | $1,125 | $950 | $825 |

PANTHER RAPTR CARBINE – 5.56 NATO cal., 16 in. chrome-moly steel contoured barrel, 30 shot mag., flash hider, A2 front sight, Mangonel flip up rear sight, Ergo Z-Rail two piece four rail handgard, Crimson Trace vertical grip with integrated light and laser combination, A3 Picatinny rail flattop, hard coat anodized black finish, dust cover, aluminum trigger guard, AP4 six position telescoping polymer stock, Ergo Ambi-Sure grip, 8.2 lbs. New 2010.

| MSR $1,649 | $1,400 | $1,140 | $950 | $800 | $700 | $600 | $500 |

MSR	100%	98%	95%	90%	80%	70%	60%

PANTHER CSAT TACTICAL – 5.56 NATO cal., 16 in. chrome-moly steel contoured barrel, 30 shot mag., A2 front sight assembly with A2 front sight popst, detachable rear sight, four rail free float tube, A3 Picatinny rail flattop, aluminum lower receiver, Magpul CTR adj. stock, Magpul MIAD pistol grip, 7.8 lbs. New 2010.

MSR $1,799	$1,550	$1,250	$1,025	$850	$725	$625	$550

PANTHER CSAT PERIMETER – 5.56 NATO cal., similar to Tactical, except has 16 in. heavy barrel, approx. 8 lbs. New 2010.

MSR $1,799	$1,550	$1,250	$1,025	$850	$725	$625	$550

PANTHER 3GI – 5.56 NATO cal., 18 in. stainless heavy barrel, 30 shot mag., Miculek compensator, no sights, VTAC modular handguard, bipod stud, A3 Picatinny rail flattop, black anodized finish, aluminum trigger guard, JP adj. trigger group, Magpul CTR adj. stock, 7 3/4 lbs. New 2010.

MSR $1,199	$1,075	$850	$750	$650	$575	$500	$450

PANTHER MK 12 – .308 Win. cal., 18 in. stainless steel heavy barrel, flash hider, Midwest Industries flip up rear sight, gas block with flip up front sight, A3 Picatinny rail flattop, aluminum lower receiver, integral trigger guard, Magpul CTR adj. stock, Hogue rubber grip with finger grooves, two stage match trigger, hard anodized black finish, four rail free float tube, six rail covers, approx. 9.6 lbs. New 2010.

MSR $1,709	$1,475	$1,200	$975	$825	$725	$625	$550

PANTHER ORACLE – .223 Rem. cal., 16 in. chrome-moly heavy barrel, A2 flash hider, gas block with single rail, no sights, GlacierGuards oval carbine length handguard, A3 Picatinny flattop, hard anodized black finish, integral trigger guard, Pardus six position telescoping stock with cheekpiece, A2 pistol grip, curved and serrated buttplate, multiple sling slots, approx. 8.3 lbs. New 2010.

MSR $1,074	$975	$850	$700	$600	$500	$425	$375

RIFLES: SLIDE ACTION

PANTHER PUMP RIFLE – .223 Rem. cal., tactical design, 20 in. threaded heavy barrel with flash hider, aluminum handguard incorporates slide action mechanism, carrying handle with sights, bayonet lug, designed by Les Branson, 8 1/2 lbs. Disc. 2009.

	$1,525	$1,275	$1,050	$925	$775	$650	$575	Last MSR was $1,700.

DSA INC.

Current manufacturer, importer, and distributor of semi-auto rifles and related components located in Barrington, IL. Previously located in Round Lake and Grayslake, IL.

DSA Inc. is a manufacturer of FAL/SA58 rifles for both civilian and law enforcement purposes (L.E. certificates must be filled out for L.E. purchases). Until recently, DSA, Inc. also imported a sporterized Sig 550 rifle.

RIFLES: BOLT ACTION

DS-MP1 – .308 Win. cal., 22 in. match grade barrel, Rem. 700 action with Badger Ordnance precision ground heavy recoil lug, trued bolt face and lugs, hand lapped stainless steel barrel with recessed target crown, black McMillan A5 pillar bedded stock, Picatinny rail, includes test target guaranteeing 1/2 MOA at 100 yards, black or camo Duracoat finish, 11 1/2 lbs. Mfg. 2004-2009.

	$2,500	$2,150	$1,800	$1,550	$1,250	$1,000	$850	Last MSR was $2,800.

RIFLES: SEMI-AUTO

The SA-58 rifles listed are available in either a standard DuraCoat solid (OD Green or GrayWolf), or optional camo pattern finishes - add $250 for camo. Patterns include: Underbrush, Woodland Prestige, Desert MirageFlage, Urban MirageFlage, Wilderness MirageFlage, OD MirageFlage, Black Forest MirageFlage, Winter Twig, Tiger Stripe, Advanced Tiger Stripe, Vietnam Tiger Stripe, Marsh, AmStripe, Urban Camo, Belgian Camo, ACU, Afghan Camo, Multicolor or Mossy Oak Breakup (disc.). DSA Inc. makes three types of forged steel receivers, and they are distinguished by the machining cuts on Types I and II, and no cuts on Type III.

Add $300-$350 for camo, depending on pattern.

SA58 STANDARD RIFLE/CARBINE – .308 Win. cal., FAL design using high precision CNC machinery, 16 (carbine), 18 (carbine), 19, 21 (standard or bull), or 24 in. (bull only, disc. 2009) steel or stainless steel cyrogenically treated barrel, black synthetic stock, pistol grip (standard 2001) attached to frame, 10 or 20 shot mag., 8.7-11 lbs.

MSR $1,700	$1,600	$1,250	$1,050	$875	$775	$675	$575

Add $250 for stainless steel barrel.
Add $150 for bull barrel.

* **SA58 Standard Rifle Predator** – .243 Win., .260 Rem., or .308 Win. cal., Type 1 or Type 3 receiver, 16 or 19 in.

MSR		100%	98%	95%	90%	80%	70%	60%

barrel with target crown, green fiberglass furniture, Picatinny rail, 5 or 10 shot mag., approx. 9 lbs. New 2003.

MSR $1,750 — $1,625 — $1,250 — $1,050 — $875 — $775 — $675 — $575

* **SA58 Standard Rifle Gray Wolf** – .300 WSM (disc. 2005) or .308 Win. cal., Type 1 or Type 3 receiver, 21 in. bull barrel with target crown, gray aluminum handguard, synthetic stock and adj. pistol grip, Picatinny rail, 5 or 10 shot mag., approx. 13 lbs. New 2003.

MSR $2,295 — $1,975 — $1,750 — $1,450 — $1,250 — $1,050 — $875 — $775

* **SA58 Tactical Carbine** – similar to SA58 Standard Rifle, except has 16 1/4 in. barrel, 8 1/4 lbs. New 1999.

MSR $1,970 — $1,825 — $1,575 — $1,275 — $1,050 — $900 — $800 — $700

Add $200 for SA58 Lightweight Carbine with aluminum receiver components (disc. 2004).
Add $250 for SA58 Stainless Steel Carbine (included scope mount through 2000).
Subtract 5% if w/o fluted barrel (became standard 2009).

* **SA58 Standard Rifle Collectors Series** – .308 Win. cal., configurations includes the Congo ($1,970 - MSR), Para Congo ($2,220 - MSR), and the G1 ($2,000 - MSR). New 2003.

Add $230 for Dura-coat finish.

* **SA58 Standard Rifle T48 Replica** – .308 Win. cal., 10 or 20 shot fixed mag., stripper clip top cover, cryogenically treated barrel, wood furniture, replica Browning flash hider. Imported 2002-2008.

$1,500 — $1,275 — $1,050 — $850 — $725 — $625 — $525 — Last MSR was $1,795.

* **SA58 SPR (Special Purpose Rifle)** – .308 Win. cal., Type I forged receiver, 19 in. fully fluted premium barrel, match grade speed trigger, rail interfaced handguard, extended extreme duty scope mount, SPR side folding adj. stock, SAW pistol grip, Versa-Pod bipod and BUIS included, detachable 10 or 20 shot mag., includes adj. sling., hard case, 13.8 lbs. New 2009.

MSR $4,795 — $4,450 — $3,950 — $3,500 — $3,100 — $2,750 — $2,450 — $2,150

* **SA58 Spartan** – .308 Win. cal., Type 1 non-carry handle cut receiver with Spartan Series logo, aluminum lower receiver, 16 or 18 in. standard weight barrel with Steyr short flash hider or YHM Phantom flashider, DSA custom shop speed trigger, tactical para rear sight, post front sight, standard synthetic buttstock, military grade handguard, black finish or black with OD Green furniture, three detachable 20 shot mags., adj. sling and case. New 2009.

MSR $2,595 — $2,350 — $2,000 — $1,750 — $1,550 — $1,325 — $1,125 — $950

Add $200 for Spartan TAC model with 16 in. medium contour fluted barrel, side folding stock, and A2 flash hider.

STG58 AUSTRIAN FAL – .308 Win. cal., features choice of DSA Type I or Type II upper receiver, carry handle, steel lower receiver, rifle has long flash hider, carbine has Steyr short flash hider, steel handguard with bipod cut, metric FAL buttstock and pistol grip, adj. front and rear sight, 10 or 20 shot detachable mag., 10 - 10.4 lbs. Imported 2006-2008.

$900 — $825 — $750 — $675 — $600 — $550 — $500 — Last MSR was $995.

Add $50 for carbine.
Add $290 for rifle with folding stock.
Add $340 for carbine with folding stock.

DS-S1 – .223 Win. cal., 16, 20, or 24 in. match chamber stainless steel free float bull barrel, A2 buttstock, aluminum handguard, Picatinny gas block sight base, forged lower receiver, NM two-stage trigger, forged flat-top upper receiver, optional fluted barrel, variety of Duracoat solid or camo finishes available, 8-10 lbs. Mfg. 2004-2005.

$850 — $775 — $675 — $600 — $525 — $450 — $400 — Last MSR was $950.

DS-CV1 CARBINE – 5.56 NATO cal., 16 in. chrome-moly D4 barrel with press on mock flash hider, fixed Shorty buttstock, D4 handguard and heatshield, forged front sight base, forged lower receiver, forged flat-top upper receiver, variety of Duracoat solid or camo finishes available, 6 1/4 lbs. Mfg. 2004-2005.

$775 — $700 — $625 — $550 — $500 — $450 — $400 — Last MSR was $850.

DS-LE4 CARBINE – 5.56 NATO cal., 14 1/2 or 16 in. chrome-moly D4 barrel with threaded A2 flash hider, collapsible CAR buttstock, D4 handguard with heatshield, forged lower receiver, forged front sight base with bayonet lug, forged flat-top upper receiver, Duracoat solid or camo finish, 6.15 or 6 1/4 lbs. New 2004.

The 14 1/2 in. model is for law enforcement only. Please contact the factory directly for pricing on this model.

DS-AR SERIES – .223 Rem cal., available in a variety of configurations including carbine and rifle, standard or bull barrels, various options, stock colors and features. Mfg. 2006-2008.

$895 — $800 — $700 — $600 — $525 — $450 — $400 — Last MSR was $1,000.

Add $243 for SOPMOD Carbine. Add $30 for 1R Carbine. Add $150 for 1V Carbine. Add $130 for S1 Bull rifle. Add $500 for DCM rifle. Add $30 for XM Carbine.
Add $1,395 - $1,515 for monolithic rail platform. Add $675 for Z4 GTC Carbine with corrosion resistant operating system.

ZM-4 SERIES – .223 Rem. cal., 16 or 20 in. barrel, forged upper and lower receiver, various configurations, black finish, detachable magazine, hard case. New 2004.

MSR	100%	98%	95%	90%	80%	70%	60%

* ***ZM-4 Standard*** – 20 in. chromemoly heavy barrel with A2 flash hider, mil-spec forged lower receiver and flat-top upper, front sight base with lug, standard handguard with heat shield, fixed A2 buttstock, 9 lbs.

MSR $1,050	**$975**	**$850**	**$725**	**$600**	**$550**	**$495**	**$450**

* ***ZM-4 Mid-Length*** – similar to Standard, except has 16 in. fluted chromemoly barrel and M4 collapsible stock, 6.65 lbs.

MSR $1,050	**$975**	**$850**	**$725**	**$600**	**$550**	**$495**	**$450**

* ***ZM-4 Standard Carbine*** – similar to ZM-4 Mid-Length, except has 16 in. non-fluted barrel, also available in OD Green.

MSR $1,095	**$1,000**	**$850**	**$725**	**$600**	**$550**	**$495**	**$450**

* ***ZM-4 Standard MRP*** – 16 or 18 in. chrome lined (16 in.) or stainless steel free float barrel, mil-spec forged lower receiver, LMT MRP forged upper receiver with 20 1/2 in. full length quad rail, LMT enhanced bolt, dual extractor springs, collapsible CAR stock, detachable 30 shot mag., A2 flash hider.

MSR $2,695	**$2,425**	**$2,050**	**$1,775**	**$1,550**	**$1,325**	**$1,125**	**$950**

Add $100 for stainless steel barrel.

* ***ZM-4 Gas Piston CQB*** – 16 in. chrome lined free floating barrel, Mil-spec forged lower receiver, LMT gas piston CQB forged upper receiver, one piece bolt carrier, quick change barrel system, collapsible CAR stock, detachable 30 shot mag., A2 flash hider.

MSR $2,870	**$2,575**	**$2,150**	**$1,625**	**$1,550**	**$1,325**	**$1,125**	**$950**

* ***ZM-4 Spartan*** – 16 in. fluted chromemoly barrel, Yankee Hill Machine Phantom flash hider, mil-spec forged lower and flat-top upper receiver, mid-length gas system, forged front sight base with lug, M4 collapsible stock, Magpul trigger guard, Robar NP3 bolt, carrier, and charging handle, Hogue pistol grip, 6.65 lbs.

MSR $1,395	**$1,275**	**$1,075**	**$925**	**$800**	**$700**	**$600**	**$500**

Add $500 for LEO model with Chip McCormick match trigger, SOPMOD collapsible stock, and two-piece rail system.

DAEWOO

Current manufacturer located in Korea. No current importation on new manufacture. Previous limited importation by Century International Arms, located in Delray Beach, FL. Previous importation included Kimber of America, Inc. until 1997, Daewoo Precision Industries, Ltd., until mid-1996, located in Southampton, PA, and previously distributed by Nationwide Sports Distributors 1993-96. Previously imported by KBI, Inc. and Firstshot, Inc., both located in Harrisburg, PA, and B-West located in Tucson, AZ.

Daewoo makes a variety of firearms, most of which are not imported into the U.S.

PISTOLS: SEMI-AUTO

DH380 – .380 ACP cal., double action design. Imported 1995-96.

	$330	**$285**	**$260**	**$235**	**$210**	**$185**	**$165**	Last MSR was $375.

DH40 – .40 S&W cal., otherwise similar to DP51, 32 oz. Imported 1995-disc.

	$325	**$270**	**$245**	**$225**	**$200**	**$185**	**$170**

DP51 STANDARD/COMPACT – 9mm Para. cal., "fast action" allows lowering hammer w/o depressing trigger, 3 1/2 (DP51 C or S, disc.) or 4.1 (DP51) in. barrel, 10 (C/B 1994), 12* (.40 S&W), or 13* (9mm Para.) shot mag., 3-dot sights, tri-action mechanism (SA, DA, or fast action), ambidextrous manual safety, alloy receiver, polished or sand-blasted black finish, 28 or 32 oz., includes lockable carrying case with accessories. Recently imported in various configurations circa 1991-2009.

No MSR	**$315**	**$265**	**$240**	**$220**	**$200**	**$185**	**$170**

Add 10% for DP51 Compact (disc.).

DP52 – .22 LR cal., double action, 3.8 in. barrel, alloy receiver, 10 shot mag., blue finish, 23 oz. Imported 1994-96.

	$320	**$275**	**$225**	**$200**	**$180**	**$165**	**$150**	Last MSR was $380.

RIFLES: SEMI-AUTO

MAX II (K2) – .223 Rem. cal., tactical design rifle, 18 in. barrel, gas operated rotating bolt, folding fiberglass stock, interchangeable mags. with the Colt M16, 7 lbs. Importation disc. 1986.

	$950	**$875**	**$800**	**$725**	**$625**	**$550**	**$475**	Last MSR was $609.

MAX I (K1A1) – similar to Max II (K2), except has retractable stock. Importation disc. 1986.

	$1,050	**$925**	**$850**	**$750**	**$650**	**$575**	**$500**	Last MSR was $592.

MSR	100%	98%	95%	90%	80%	70%	60%

DR200 – .223 Rem. cal., tactical configuration with sporterized stock, 10 shot mag. Imported 1995-96.

| | $650 | $550 | $475 | $425 | $395 | $375 | $350 | Last MSR was $535. |

DR300 – 7.62x39mm cal., tactical configuration with or w/o thumbhole stock. Importation disc.

| | $650 | $550 | $475 | $425 | $395 | $375 | $350 | |

DAKOTA ARMS, INC.

Current manufacturer and previous importer established in 1982, located in Sturgis, SD. Dealer and direct sales through manufacturer only. This company is not affiliated with Dakota Single Action Revolvers.

On June 5, 2009, Remington Arms Company purchased Dakota Arms, Inc.

Dakota Arms Inc. also owned the rights to Miller Arms and Nesika actions. Please refer to these individual sections for more information.

Dakota Arms models listed below are also available with many custom options - please contact the factory directly for availability and pricing. Left-hand rifles are also available at no extra charge on all models. Actions (barreled or unbarreled) may also be purchased separately. Please contact the manufacturer directly for individual quotations.

RIFLES: BOLT ACTION

DAKOTA LONGBOW T-76 TACTICAL – .300 Dakota Mag., .300 Win. Mag. (new 2006), .330 Dakota Mag., .308 Win. (new 2006), .338 Lapua Mag., or .338 Dakota Mag. cal., 28 in. stainless barrel, long range tactical design, black synthetic stock with adj. comb, includes Picatinny optical rail, Model 70 style trigger, matte finish metal, controlled round feeding, and deployment kit, 13.7 lbs. Mfg. 1997-2009.

| | $4,300 | $3,760 | $3,225 | $2,925 | $2,365 | $1,935 | $1,505 | Last MSR was $4,795. |

DAKOTA SCIMITAR TACTICAL – .308 Win. or .338 Lapua cal., 24 or 27 in. match grade chromemoly barrel, 2nd generation Longbow with solid top receiver, long and short action, one-piece bolt handle, oversized claw extraction system, true controlled round feed, three postition safety, non-glare matte black finish, synthetic stock, optical rail. Mfg. 2008-2009.

| | $5,850 | $5,120 | $4,385 | $3,980 | $3,215 | $2,630 | $2,045 | Last MSR was $6,295. |

DALY, CHARLES: 1976-2010

Previous manufactured trademark imported late 1996-early 2010 by KBI, Inc. located in Harrisburg, PA. Previously imported by Outdoor Sports Headquarters, Inc. located in Dayton, OH until 1995.

In 1976, Sloan's Sporting Goods sold the Daly division to Outdoor Sports Headquarters, Inc., a sporting goods wholesaler located in Dayton, OH. OSHI continued the importation of high-grade Daly shotguns, primarily from Italy and Spain. By the mid-1980s, the Charles Daly brand was transformed into a broad consumer line of excellent firearms and hunting accessories.

In 1996, OSHI was sold to Jerry's Sports Center, Inc. of Forest City, PA, a major wholesaler of firearms and hunting supplies. Within a few months of Jerry's acquisition of OSHI, K.B.I., Inc. of Harrisburg, PA, purchased the Charles Daly trademark from JSC. As it turned out, Michael Kassnar, president of K.B.I., Inc., had produced almost all of the Charles Daly products for OSHI from 1976-1985 in his capacity of president of Kassnar Imports, Inc. K.B.I., Inc. resurrected the complete line of O/U and SxS shotguns in early 1997.

In 1998, the line expanded to include rimfire rifles and the first pistol produced under the Daly name, a Model 1911-A1 in .45 ACP cal. In 1999, semi-auto and slide action shotguns were also reintroduced. In 2000, the additions included 3 1/2 in. slide actions and semi-autos, Country Squire .410 bore shotguns, bolt action centerfire rifles, and the DDA 10-45, the first double action pistol produced under the Charles Daly name.

During 2004, Charles Daly began importing Bul Transmark pistols from Israel. In 2007, the Little Sharps single shot rifles were introduced.

In 2008, a Charles Daly Defense line was established, which includes AR-15 style semi-auto rifles.

On Jan. 29, 2010, K.B.I. announced it was shutting its doors and discontinued importation of all models.

PISTOLS: SEMI-AUTO

During 2001, the nomenclature on these 1911 models was changed to include a new "E" prefix. The "E" stands for enhanced, and features included extended high-rise beavertail grip safety, combat trigger, combat hammer, beveled magwell, flared and lowered ejection port, dovetailed front and low profile rear sights, and hand checkered double diamond grips. The Enhanced pistols were manufactured by Armscor of the Philipines. M-5 pistols are manufactured by Bul Transmark in Israel.

GOVERNMENT 1911-A2 FIELD EFS HC – .40 S&W or .45 ACP cal., 5 in. barrel, similar to Government 1911 A-1 Field EFS, 13 (.45 ACP cal.), or 15 (.40 S&W cal.) shot mag., blue finish only. Imported 2005-2007.

| | $595 | $520 | $445 | $405 | $325 | $270 | $210 | Last MSR was $725. |

Add $124 for Target Model (.45 ACP cal. only, new 2005).

MODEL DDA 10-45 FS (DOUBLE ACTION) – .40 S&W (disc. 2001) or .45 ACP cal., single or double action, 4 3/8

MSR	100%	98%	95%	90%	80%	70%	60%

in. barrel, polymer frame with checkering, double stack 10 shot mag. with interchangeable base plate (allowing for extra grip length), matte black or two-tone (new 2001) finish, 28 1/2 oz. Imported 2000-2002.

| | $450 | $395 | $340 | $305 | $250 | $205 | $160 | Last MSR was $519. |

Add $40 for two-tone finish.

* ***Model DDA 10-45 CS*** – similar to Model DDA 10-45 FS, except has 3 5/8 in. barrel, 26 oz. Imported 2000-2002.

| | $450 | $395 | $340 | $305 | $250 | $205 | $160 | Last MSR was $519. |

Add approx. $10 for colored frame (yellow, OD green, or fuschia, new 2001) and compensated barrel.

CD9 – 9mm Para. cal., 4.46 in. barrel, black polymer frame and finish, striker fired, adj. sights, trigger safety, forward/lower accessory rail, 10 or 15 shot mag., three grip inserts. Imported 2009 only.

| | $375 | $330 | $280 | $255 | $205 | $170 | $130 | Last MSR was $437. |

G4 1911 SERIES – .45 ACP cal., 5 in. barrel, 7 shot, black finish or stainless steel, beveled mag well, flared and lowered ejection port, beavertail grip safety, internal extractor, Novak sights, three slot aluminum trigger, available in Standard, Target, and Tactical configurations, mfg. in Israel. Imported 2009 only.

| | $750 | $655 | $565 | $510 | $415 | $340 | $265 | Last MSR was $867. |

Add $96 for either Tactical or Target model.
Add $96 for stainless steel.
Add $354 for .22 LR conversion kit.

M-5 FS STANDARD (BUL 1911 GOVERNMENT) – 9mm Para. (new 2010), .40 S&W or .45 ACP cal., single action, 5 in. barrel, polymer double column frame, steel slide, aluminum speed trigger, checkered front and rear grip straps, blue or chrome finished slide, 10, 14, or 17 (9mm Para. cal.) shot staggered mag., 31-33 oz. Mfg. by Bul Transmark in Israel. Imported 2004-2009.

| | $665 | $580 | $500 | $450 | $365 | $300 | $235 | Last MSR was $803. |

* ***M-5 MS Standard Commander*** – .40 S&W or .45 ACP cal., similar to M-5 FS Standard, except has 4 1/3 in. barrel, 29-30 oz. Imported 2004-2009.

| | $665 | $580 | $500 | $450 | $365 | $300 | $235 | Last MSR was $803. |

* ***M-5 Ultra-X*** – 9mm Para. or .45 ACP cal., 10 or 12 (9mm Para. cal. only) shot mag., compact variation with 3.15 in. barrel. Imported 2005-2009.

| | $665 | $580 | $500 | $450 | $365 | $300 | $235 | Last MSR was $803. |

JERICHO SERIES – 9mm Para., .40 S&W, or .45 ACP cal., 3 1/2 (Compact), 3.82 (Mid-Size), or 4.41 (Full Size) in. barrel, DA/SA, 10, 12, 13, or 15 shot mag., polymer or steel frame with black or chrome (Mid-size .45 ACP cal. only) finish, combat style trigger guard, slide mounted thumb decocker, two slot accessory rail (except Compact), ergonomic grips, mfg. by IWI, Ltd. (formerly IMI) in Israel. Limited importation 2009.

| | $595 | $520 | $445 | $405 | $325 | $270 | $210 | Last MSR was $699. |

Add $198 for steel frame and chrome finish (Full or Mid-size only).

RIFLES: SEMI-AUTO

All recently manufactured semi-auto rifles have forged aluminum alloy receivers that are hard coat milspec anodized and Teflon coated, manganese phosphate barrel (except stainless), radiused aluminum magazine release button, aluminum trigger guard, safety selector position on right side of receiver, dust cover, brass deflector, forward assist, and include one magazine and hard plastic carrying case. All recently manufactured rifles were covered by a lifetime repair policy.

DM-4/D-M4P CARBINE – 5.56 NATO cal., 16 in. chrome-moly match barrel with M-203 mounting groove, 10, 20, or 30 shot mag., forged "F" front sight base with bayonet lug and rubber coated sling swivel, A3 detachable carry handle, T-Marked flattop upper, six-position telestock, A2 birdcage flash hider, oval double heat shield M4 forend. Mfg. 2008-2009.

| | $925 | $810 | $695 | $630 | $510 | $415 | $325 | Last MSR was $1,143. |

Add $90 for M4 feed ramp (Model DM-4).

D-M4LE CARBINE – 5.56 NATO cal., similar to D-M4 carbine, except has mil spec diameter receiver extension with "H" buffer. Mfg. 2008-2009.

| | $1,275 | $1,115 | $955 | $865 | $700 | $575 | $445 | Last MSR was $1,373. |

D-M4S CARBINE – similar to D-M4 carbine, except has two Picatinny riser blocks, oval double heat shield M4 forend with QD sling swivel and swivel/bipod stud installed, Magpul enhanced trigger guard. Mfg. 2008-2009.

| | $1,025 | $895 | $770 | $695 | $565 | $460 | $360 | Last MSR was $1,189. |

D-M4LX CARBINE – 5.56 NATO cal., 16 in. chrome-moly H-bar fluted match barrel, M4 feed ramps, T-Marked flattop upper, flip up rear sight, folding front gas block with bayonet lug, aluminum free floating quad rail forend with

MSR	100%	98%	95%	90%	80%	70%	60%	

swiveling sling stud, nine 5-slot low profile ladder style quad rail covers, Ace M4 SOCOM standard length telestock with half buttpad, Phantom flash suppressor, Ergo Ambi AR grip. Mfg. 2008-2009.

| | $1,650 | $1,445 | $1,240 | $1,120 | $910 | $745 | $580 | Last MSR was $1,783. |

D-M4LT CARBINE – 5.56 NATO cal., Milspec diameter receiver extension with "H" buffer, chrome lined lightweight A1 barrel, permanently attached Phantom suppressor, slim carbine type forend, 30 shot Magpul PMAG black mag. Limited mfg. 2009.

| | $1,275 | $1,115 | $955 | $865 | $700 | $575 | $445 | Last MSR was $1,373. |

Add $890 for permanently attached Smith Vortex flash suppressor, Magpul CTR stock with buttpad, and Daniel Defense light rail (Model D-M4LTD, mfg. 2009 only).

Add $1,050 for Vltor Modstock, mid-length gas system, Smith Vortex suppressor, Daniel Defense light rail, and Magpul grip (Model D-M4MG, mfg. 2009 only).

Add $150 for A2 birdcage flash hider, full length hand guard, Troy flip up BUIS (Model D-M4MLL, mfg. 2009 only).

D-MCA4 RIFLE – .223 Rem. cal., 20 in. chrome lined govt. profile barrel, A3 detachable carry handle, A2 buttstock, A2 birdcage flash hider, A2 hand guard, forged front sight base, 30 shot mil spec mag. Limited mfg. 2009.

| | $1,175 | $1,030 | $880 | $800 | $645 | $530 | $410 | Last MSR was $1,317. |

Add $622 for KAC M5 quad rail with KAC panels (Model D-MCA4-M5).

D-M4LED CARBINE – 5.56 NATO cal., 16 in. chrome lined govt. profile barrel, flat Dark Earth finish, Magpul CTR mil spec buttstock, A2 birdcage flash hider, M4 feedramp, Daniel Defense light rail, Magpul MIAD grip, Troy rear BUIS. Limited mfg. 2009.

| | $1,925 | $1,675 | $1,500 | $1,250 | $1,050 | $875 | $725 | Last MSR was $2,209. |

D-MR20 RIFLE – 5.56 NATO cal., 20 in. Wilson Arms stainless steel fluted bull barrel, Magpul PRS II stock, three slot riser blocks, Daniel Defense light rail forearm with Picatinny rail gas block, two-stage match trigger, Phantom suppressor, 20 shot mag. Mfg. 2009.

| | $1,825 | $1,595 | $1,370 | $1,240 | $1,005 | $820 | $640 | Last MSR was $1,979. |

DR-15 TARGET – 5.56 NATO cal., 20 in. chrome-moly match H-bar barrel, A2 upper with carry handle, A2 buttstock, A2 birdcage flash hider, forged front sight tower with bayonet lug and rubber coated sling swivel, fixed position stock. Limited mfg. 2008.

| | $895 | $785 | $670 | $610 | $490 | $405 | $315 | Last MSR was $1,089. |

DV-24 MATCH TARGET/VARMINT – 5.56 NATO cal., 24 in. free float match stainless steel bull barrel, T-Marked flattop upper, two Picatinny half riser blocks, ported aluminum tube forend with swivel/bipod stud installed, Ace skeletonized butt stock, Picatinny rail milled gas block, two-stage match trigger. Mfg. 2008-2009.

| | $1,250 | $1,095 | $940 | $850 | $690 | $565 | $440 | Last MSR was $1,389. |

JR CARBINE – 9mm Para. (JR9), .40 S&W (JR40), or .45 ACP (JR45) cal., 16 1/4 in. triangular contoured barrel, 13 (.45 ACP), 15 (.40 S&W), or 17 (9mm) shot mag., features unique magwell interchangability, allowing the owner to use handgun magazine of choice, matte black synthetic six-position telescoping AR stock, anodized aluminum receiver, Picatinny rail, free float quad rail forearm, ergonomic AR grip, includes two mags., approx. 6 1/2 lbs. Disc. 2009.

| | $875 | $775 | $700 | $625 | $550 | $475 | $400 | Last MSR was $987. |

SHOTGUNS: SEMI-AUTO

The Charles Daly "Novamatic" shotguns were produced in 1968 by Breda in Italy. The Novamatic series was not imported by Outdoor Sport Headquarters, Inc.

TACTICAL – 12 ga., 18 1/2 in. barrel, matte black synthetic pistol grip stock, Picatinny rail, ghost ring sights, extended tactical choke tube. Limited mfg. 2009.

| | $495 | $435 | $370 | $335 | $270 | $225 | $175 | Last MSR was $587. |

Add $80 for 100% A-Tacs camo finish (new 2010).

SHOTGUNS: SLIDE ACTION

TACTICAL – 12 ga. or 20 (new 2009), 3 in. chamber, 18 1/2 in. cyl. bore barrel with front sight, black synthetic stock and forearm or 100% camo coverage (new 2009), matte blue metal or chrome finish, 6 lbs. Imported 2000-2009.

| | $250 | $220 | $190 | $170 | $140 | $115 | $90 | Last MSR was $289. |

Add $24 for Field Tactical AW with chrome finish and adj. sights.

Add $74 for pistol grip stock, ghost ring sights, and MC1 multichoke.

Add $134 for pistol grip stock, ghost ring sights, Picatinny rail, and extended choke tube.

Add $124 for camo with ghost ring and fiber optic sights (new 2009).

DANIEL DEFENSE

Current manufacturer located in Savannah, GA.

MSR	100%	98%	95%	90%	80%	70%	60%

CARBINES: SEMI-AUTO

DDM4 CARBINE SERIES – 5.56 NATO cal., 16 in. chrome lined barrel, A2 birdcage flash hider, 10, 20, or 30 shot mag., mil-spec enhanced mag. well, A4 feed ramp, A1.5 BUIS sight, pinned "F" marked front sight base, Omega X rail hand guard, quad rails, Magpul 5 position extended buttstock, A2 vertical grip, includes plastic case.

MSR $1,537	$1,425	$1,275	$1,075	$900	$775	$650	$525

DD CARBINE SERIES – 5.56 NATO or 6.8mm SPC cal., 16 in. chrome lined barrel, similar to DDM4 Series, except no vertical grip, mil-spec buttstock. New 2010.

MSR $1,300	$1,195	$1,025	$900	$775	$650	$525	$450

Add $68 for DDXV EZ carbine.
Add $129 for DDXVM carbine.

DAUDSONS ARMOURY

Current manufacturer located in Peshawar, Pakistan. No current U.S. importation.

Daudsons Armoury's orgins stretch back over two centuries dealing in the sporting arms and defense firearms trade. The company provides firearms for the armed forces of Pakistan as well as the Defense Ministry.

Daudsons Armoury manufactures the DSA line of 12 ga. shotguns. There are four basic models: DSA Shooter, DSA Commando, DSA Sure Shot, and the DSA Security. All are manufactured from high grade alloy steel, with black synthetic stocks and forearms, and all parts are completely interchangeable. Daudsons also manufactures double barrel rifles and a semi-auto .22 cal. rifle. For more information on these guns, including pricing and U.S. availability, please contact the company directly (see Trademark Index).

DEL-TON INCORPORATED

Current rifle manufacturer located in Elizabethtown, NC. Currently distributed by American Tactical Imports, located in Rochester, NY.

CARBINES/RIFLES: SEMI-AUTO

Many options, accessories, and parts are available. Please contact the company for more information, including current availability and options (see Trademark Index).

All rifles includes a hard case, two mags., and buttstock cleaning kit.

MID-LENGTH CARBINE – .223 Rem. cal., 16 in. mid-length chromemoly barrel, 30 shot mag., black furniture, six postition M4 stock, CAR handguard with single heat shield, A2 flash hider.

MSR $750	$695	$625	$550	$500	$450	$395	$350

MID-LENGTH CARBINE FIXED STOCK – .223 Rem. cal., similar to Mid-Length Carbine, except has A2 fixed stock.

MSR $750	$695	$625	$550	$500	$450	$395	$350

POST-BAN CARBINE – .223 Rem. cal., 16 in. heavy chromemoly barrel with crowned end, 10 shot mag., fixed A2 buttstock, black furniture, CAR handguard with single heat shield, includes sling.

MSR $750	$695	$625	$550	$500	$450	$395	$350

M4 CARBINE – .223 Rem. cal., 16 in. chromemoly barrel, 30 shot mag., black furniture, six position M4 stock, CAR handguard with single heat shield, A2 flash hider, includes sling.

MSR $750	$695	$625	$550	$500	$450	$395	$350

A2 DT-4 CARBINE – .223 Rem. cal., 16 in. chromemoly barrel, six position M4 stock, 30 shot mag., CAR handguard with single heat shield, A2 flash hider, black furniture, includes sling.

MSR $750	$695	$625	$550	$500	$450	$395	$350

A2 CARBINE – .223 Rem. cal., 16 in. heavy chromemoly barrel, fixed A2 stock, CAR handguard with single heat shield, A2 flash hider, black furniture, includes sling.

MSR $750	$695	$625	$550	$500	$450	$395	$350

DTI-4 CARBINE – .223 Rem. cal., 16 in. chromemoly M4 profile barrel, six position M4 stock, 30 shot mag., CAR handguard with single heat shield, A2 flash hider, black furniture, includes sling.

MSR $750	$695	$625	$550	$500	$450	$395	$350

STANDARD RIFLE – .223 Rem. cal., 20 in. chromemoly heavy profile barrel, standard gas system, fixed A2 buttstock, 30 shot mag., standard length handguard with heat shields, A2 flash hider, black furniture, includes sling.

MSR $750	$695	$625	$550	$500	$450	$395	$350

MSR	100%	98%	95%	90%	80%	70%	60%

DEMRO

Previous manufacturer located in Manchester, CT.

RIFLES: SEMI-AUTO

T.A.C. MODEL 1 RIFLE – .45 ACP or 9mm Luger cal., blow back operation, 16 7/8 in. barrel, open bolt firing system, lock-in receiver must be set to fire, also available in carbine model.

	100%	98%	95%	90%	80%	70%	60%
	$650	$595	$525	$475	$425	$395	$360

XF-7 WASP CARBINE – .45 ACP or 9mm Luger cal., blow back operation, 16 7/8 in. barrel.

	100%	98%	95%	90%	80%	70%	60%
	$650	$595	$525	$475	$425	$395	$360

Add $45 for case.

DESERT TACTICAL ARMS

Current rifle manufacturer located in Salt Lake City, UT.

RIFLES: SEMI-AUTO

STEALTH RECON SCOUT – .243 Win., .300 Win. Mag., .308 Win. or .338 Lapua cal., 22 or 26 in. match grade free floating barrel, 5 or 6 shot mag., bullpup designed to be eleven inches shorter than conventional M16A2 rifles, tactical stock with adj. LOP, pistol grip, black or olive drab hard coat anodizing, black, coyote brown, or olive drab finish, full length rail, ambidextrous mag release, 9.4-15.1 lbs.

MSR $3,374	100%	98%	95%	90%	80%	70%	60%
	$3,150	$2,800	$2,500	$2,200	$1,900	$1,600	$1,300

Add $144 for .300 Win. Mag. cal. or $319 for .338 Lapua cal.

DETONICS

Current semi-auto pistol manufacturer established in 2007 and located in Millstadt, IL.

PISTOLS: SEMI-AUTO

Currently, Detonics manufactures a series of 1911 style semi-auto pistols. A wide variety of configurations and options are available. Please contact the company directly for more information, including pricing, options, and availability (see Trademark Index).

DETONICS FIREARMS INDUSTRIES

Previous manufacturer located in Bellevue, WA 1976-1988. Detonics was sold in early 1988 to the New Detonics Manufacturing Corporation, a wholly owned subsidiary of "1045 Investors Group Limited."

Please refer to the New Detonics Manufacturing Corporation in the "N" section of this text for complete model listings of both companies.

DETONICS USA

Previous manufacturer located in Pendergrass, GA circa 2004-mid-2007.

PISTOLS: SEMI-AUTO

MILITARY TACTICAL – .45 ACP cal., black bonded finish, adj. sights, includes rail, forward serrations, checkered front strap, and lanyard ring.

	100%	98%	95%	90%	80%	70%	60%	
	$1,750	$1,525	$1,350	$1,125	$950	$800	$675	Last MSR was $1,975.

DLASK ARMS CORP.

Current manufacturer and distributor located in British Columbia, Canada. Direct sales.

PISTOLS: SEMI-AUTO

Dlask Arms Corp. manufactures custom M-1911 style custom guns for all levels of competition. Current models include the basic Dlask 1911 at $1,250 MSR, Dlask 1911 "Pro" at $1,560 MSR, and the Dlask 1911 "Pro Plus" at $2,500 MSR. Previous models included the TC Tactical Carry at $1,250 last MSR, Gold Team at $2,000 last MSR, Silver Team L/S at $1,700 last MSR, and the Master Class at $3,500 last MSR. In addition, Dlask also manufactures a wide variety of custom parts for the M-1911. For more information, please contact the company directly (see Trademark Index).

RIFLES

Current models include the DAR-701 semi-auto rifle in various configurations (AR-15 style) at $1,560 base MSR. Please contact the company directly for more information, including pricing and availability (see Trademark Index).

MSR	100%	98%	95%	90%	80%	70%	60%

DOMINION ARMS

Current trademark of slide action shotguns manufactured by Rauch Tactical, located in Blaine, WA.

Rauch manufactures 12 ga. tactical style slide action shotguns. Please contact the company for more information, including pricing and availability (see Trademark Index).

DOUBLE STAR CORP.

Current manufacturer located in Winchester, KY. Distributed by JT Distributing. Dealer sales only.

PISTOLS: SEMI-AUTO

DSC STAR-15 PISTOL – .223 Rem. cal., 7 1/2, 10 1/5, or 11 1/2 in. chromemoly match barrel, A2 flash hider, front sight assembly or rail gas block.

MSR $950	$875	$750	$675	$600	$525	$450	$395

1911 COMBAT PISTOL – .45 ACP cal., forged steel frame, stainless steel slide, 1913 Picatinny rail, Novak white dot front and LoMount rear sights, memory groove beavertail grip safety, 8 shot mag., 25 LPI checkering, black finish, 39 oz. New 2010.

MSR $1,350	$1,225	$1,100	$975	$850	$725	$600	$475

RIFLES/CARBINES: SEMI-AUTO

DSC STARCAR CARBINE – .223 Rem. cal., AR-15 design, fixed post-ban CAR type stock, 16 in. barrel, A2 or flattop upper receiver, 7 lbs. Disc.

	$825	$725	$625	$550	$485	$440	$400	Last MSR was $775.

Add $65 for detachable carrying handle.

DSC STAR M4 CARBINE – .223 Rem. cal., AR-15 M4 carbine design, fixed M4 style post-ban buttstock, 16 in. barrel, M4 handguard, 6.76 lbs.

MSR $890	$795	$715	$640	$565	$500	$465	$430

Add $65 for detachable carrying handle.

DSC STAR DISSIPATOR – .223 Rem. cal., AR-15 design, 16 in. dissipator barrel with full length handguard, A2 or CAR buttstock.

MSR $910	$800	$725	$625	$550	$500	$465	$430

Add $65 for detachable carrying handle.

DSC STAR-15 LIGHTWEIGHT TACTICAL – .223 Rem. cal., AR-15 design, 16 in. fluted H-Bar barrel with attached muzzle brake, shorty A2 buttstock, A2 or flattop upper receiver, 6 1/4 lbs. Disc. 2004, reintroduced 2009.

MSR $930	$815	$750	$650	$550	$500	$465	$430

Add $65 for detachable carrying handle.

DSC STAR-15 RIFLE/CARBINE – .223 Rem. or 7.62x39mm cal., AR-15 design, 16 or 20 in. match barrel, ribbed forearm, A2 or flattop upper receiver, 8 lbs.

MSR $860	$795	$700	$625	$550	$500	$450	$395

Add $65 for flattop with detachable carrying handle.
Add $50 for flash hider (Star-15 Commando Carbine).
Add $75 for 7.62x39mm cal.

DSC STAR-15 9MM CARBINE – 9mm Para cal., AR-15 design, 16 in. barrel, ribbed forearm, A2 or flattop upper receiver, 7 1/2 lbs. Mfg. 2004, reintroduced 2009.

MSR $1,080	$975	$825	$725	$650	$575	$500	$450

Add $65 for detachable carry handle.

DSC STAR-15 6.8 SPC RIFLE/CARBINE – 6.8 SPC cal., 16 or 20 in. chromemoly barrel, A2 upper or flattop, A2 (rifle) or six position DS-4 buttstock, 7-8 lbs.

MSR $935	$875	$750	$675	$600	$525	$450	$395

Add $65 for detachable carry handle.

DSC STAR-15 6.8 SPC SUPER MATCH RIFLE – 6.8 SPC cal., 20, 22, or 24 in. free float super match stainless steel bull barrel, Picatinny rail gas block, two-piece NM free floating hand guard.

MSR $1,075	$975	$850	$750	$650	$575	$500	$450

DSC STAR-15 .204 RUGER RIFLE – .204 Ruger cal., 24 in. chromemoly barrel, A2 buttstock, A2 flash hider.

MSR $1,050	$975	$850	$750	$650	$575	$500	$450

DSC STAR-15 6.5 GRENDEL CARBINE/RIFLE – 6.5 Grendel cal., 16 or 20 in. chromemoly barrel, A2 or six

MSR	100%	98%	95%	90%	80%	70%	60%

position (Carbine) buttstock.

MSR $985 $895 $775 $675 $600 $525 $450 $395

Add $65 for detachable carry handle.

DSC STAR-15 6.5 GRENDEL SUPER MATCH RIFLE – 6.5 Grendel cal., 20, 22, or 24 in. free floating match bull barrel, A2 buttstock, Picatinny rail gas block, two-piece NM free floating hand guard.

MSR $1,125 $1,050 $875 $775 $675 $575 $475 $400

DSC CRITTERSLAYER – .223 Rem. cal., AR-15 design, 24 in. fluted Shaw barrel, full length Picatinny rail on receiver and Badger handguard, two-stage match trigger, palmrest, ergonomic pistol grip with finger grooves, includes Harris LMS swivel bipod, flattop or high rise upper receiver, 11 1/2 lbs.

MSR $1,430 $1,300 $1,150 $925 $850 $750 $650 $550

Add $40 for ported barrel.

* *DSC CritterSlayer Jr.* – similar to CritterSlayer, except has 16 in. barrel and fully adj. A2 style buttstock, DSC flattop or high rise upper receiver.

MSR $1,150 $1,050 $875 $775 $675 $575 $475 $400

Add $65 for detachable carrying handle or $35 for removable front sight.
Add $200 for Enhanced CritterSlayer Jr. with 16 in. Expedition barrel, CAR hand guard, and adj. buttstock.

DSC EXPEDITION CARBINE/RIFLE – .223 Rem. cal., AR-15 design, 16 or 20 in. lightweight contour barrel, A2 or flattop upper receiver, 8 lbs.

MSR $900 $825 $750 $650 $550 $475 $425 $375

Add $55 for detachable carry handle.

DSC STAR-15 DCM SERVICE RIFLE – 5.56 NATO cal., AR-15 design, 20 in. free-float match barrel, National Match front and rear sights, two-stage match trigger, DCM handguard, 8 lbs. Disc.

       $895 $825 $725 $650 $550 $485 $440   *Last MSR was $1,000.*

DSC TARGET CARBINE – .223 Rem. cal., AR-15 design, features 16 in. dissipator barrel with full length round one-piece National Match handguard, flip-up sights, Picatinny rail, flattop upper receiver. Disc.

       $1,000 $875 $775 $695 $625 $550 $485   *Last MSR was $1,175.*

DSC SUPER MATCH RIFLE – .223 Rem. cal., AR-15 design, 16, 20, 22, or 24 in. free-float stainless steel Super Match barrel, flattop or high rise upper receiver, includes Picatinny rail and one-piece National Match handguard.

MSR $1,000 $925 $825 $725 $650 $575 $500 $450

DSC MARKSMAN RIFLE – 5.56 NATO cal., 20 in. Wilson Arms stainless steel barrel, Daniel Defense hand guard, Picatinny rail gas block, A2 Phantom flash hider, Magpul PRS buttstock, adj. LOP, approx. 9 lbs.

MSR $1,680 $1,495 $1,275 $1,050 $875 $725 $600 $550

Add $205 for bipod.

DSC PATROL CARBINE – 16 in. chromemoly lightweight barrel, YHM two-piece rail hand guard, flip up rear sight, six position DS-4 buttstock, Hogue overmolded pistol grip, 6 1/2 lbs.

MSR $1,200 $1,075 $950 $825 $700 $600 $500 $450

E SECTION

E.D.M. ARMS

Current manufacturer established in 1997 and located in Hurricane, UT since 2008. Previously located in Redlands, CA 1997-2008. Dealer and consumer direct sales.

MSR	100%	98%	95%	90%	80%	70%	60%

RIFLES: BOLT ACTION

WINDRUNNER MODEL 96 (XM107) – .338 Lapua (new 2002) or .50 BMG cal., takedown repeater action, EDM machined receiver, fully adj. stock, match grade 28 in. barrel that removes within seconds, allowing exact head space every time the barrel is reinstalled, includes two 5 (.50 BMG cal.) or 8 (.338 Lapua) shot mags., Picatinny rail, and bipod, 24 (Lightweight Tactical Takedown) or 36 lbs.

MSR $7,600	$7,600	$6,850	$6,200	$5,500	$5,000	$4,500	$4,000

Add $1,000 for left hand action.

* **Windrunner Model 96 SS99** – similar to Windrunner, except is single shot, w/o mag., includes bipod and sling, 32 lbs. New 2002.

MSR $5,850	$5,850	$5,150	$4,450	$3,850	$3,250	$2,850	$2,450

MODEL 06 MINI-WINDRUNNER – .308 Win. cal., 20 in. barrel, 10 shot mag., Picatinny rail, lightweight, tactical, takedown version of the Windrunner Model 96, 11.2 lbs. New 2007.

MSR $4,250	$4,250	$3,750	$3,300	$2,900	$2,550	$2,175	$1,800

MODEL XM04 CHEYENNE TACTICAL – .408 CheyTac cal., takedown repeater, tactical bolt action configuration, 5 shot mag., 30 in. fluted barrel with suppressor, desert camo finish, retractable stock, effective range is 2,500+ yards, 27 lbs. New 2002.

MSR $7,600	$7,600	$6,850	$6,200	$5,500	$5,000	$4,500	$4,000

Subtract $1,400 for single shot action (disc.).

MODEL 50 – .50 BMG cal., bolt action, single shot, twin rail adj. skeletonized stock, Picatinny rail and bipod. Mfg. 2003.

	$4,250	$3,750	$3,250	$2,850	$2,450	$2,050	$1,650	Last MSR was $4,250.

MODEL 98 – .338 Lapua cal., takedown repeating bolt action, single rail adj. stock, pistol grip, 22 lbs. New 2003.

MSR $7,500	$7,500	$6,850	$6,200	$5,500	$5,000	$4,500	$4,000

510 DTC EUROP – .50 DTC Europ cal. (1 in. shorter than .50 BMG), designed for CA shooters and legal in CA. Mfg. 2007-2008.

	$7,500	$6,850	$6,200	$5,500	$5,000	$4,500	$4,000	Last MSR was $7,500.

RIFLES: SEMI-AUTO

WINDRUNNER .50 CAL. – .50 BMG cal., 28 in. Lilja match grade chromemoly barrel, integrated Picatinny rail, removable black stock with cheekrest and adj. buttpad. New 2006.

MSR $9,250	$8,750	$7,500	$6,750	$6,000	$5,250	$4,500	$3,750

E.M.F. CO., INC.

Current importer and distributor established 1956 and located in Santa Ana, CA. Distributor and dealer sales. E.M.F. stands for Early & Modern Firearms Inc.

For information on Great Western, Dakota Single Action and Hartford revolvers, rifles and carbines imported by E.M.F., please refer to the Great Western, Dakota Single Action Revolvers and Hartford sections. Please refer to the *Blue Book of Modern Black Powder Arms* by John Allen (also online) for more information and prices on E.M.F.'s lineup of modern black powder models.

Black Powder Revolvers - Reproductions & Replicas and *Black Powder Long Arms & Pistols - Reproductions & Replicas* by Dennis Adler are also invaluable sources for most black powder revolver reproductions and replicas, and include hundreds of color images on most popular makes/models, provide manufacturer/trademark histories, and up-to-date information on related items/accessories for black powder shooting - www.bluebookinc.com

PISTOLS: SEMI-AUTO

All current semi-auto pistols are manufactured in the U.S.

1911-A1 – .45 ACP cal., 5 in. barrel, 7 shot mag., patterned after original 1911, parkerized finish, fixed sights, flat or arched mainspring housing, black ergo, brown plastic military, ultra stag, or checkered hardwood grips, includes two mags. New 2009.

MSR $565	$495	$450	$395	$360	$330	$300	$275

MSR	100%	98%	95%	90%	80%	70%	60%

1911 COMBAT MODEL – .45 ACP cal., 7 shot mag., similar to 1911-A1 model, except has choice of fixed Tritium low profile, or adj. sights with Tritium inserts, parkerized, blue, Dura-Coat, or nickel finish, black ergo or checkered hardwood grips, includes two mags, lock, and hard case. New 2009.

MSR $685	$595	$525	$450	$395	$360	$330	$300

1911 CCC MODEL – .45 ACP cal., 4 1/4 in. barrel, 8 shot mag., choice of fixed low profile, Novak style fixed night, or Bo-Mar adj. sights, parkerized, blue, stainless, Dura-Coat, or nickel finishes, includes two mags., lock, and hard case. New 2009.

MSR $1,075	$950	$825	$700	$575	$475	$425	$375

Add $710 for night sights and skip checkered grips.

FMK MODEL 9C1 – 9mm Para. cal., 4 in. barrel, lightweight polymer frame, 10 shot mag., blue steel slide with engraved Bill of Rights, five interchangable front sights, eighteen interchangable rear sights, "Mag Out" safety, striker indicator, and loaded chamber indicator, includes two mags., lock, and case, 23 1/2 oz. New 2009.

MSR $430	$395	$360	$325	$295	$275	$250	$225

RIFLES: SEMI-AUTO, REPRODUCTIONS

These models are authentic shooting reproductions previously mfg. in Italy.

AP 74 – .22 LR or .32 ACP cal., copy of the Colt AR-15, 15 shot mag., 20 in. barrel, 6 3/4 lbs. Importation disc. 1989.

	$350	$295	$250	$200	$175	$155	$145	Last MSR was $295.

Add $25 for .32 cal.

* **AP74 Sporter Carbine** – .22 LR cal. only, wood sporter stock. Importation disc. 1989.

	$375	$325	$275	$225	$195	$175	$160	Last MSR was $320.

* **AP74 Tactical Paratrooper Carbine** – .22 LR cal. only, folding wire or black nylon stock on tactical design model. Importation disc. 1987.

	$395	$350	$300	$260	$215	$175	$165	Last MSR was $325.

Add $10 for wood folding stock.

* **AP74 "Dressed" Military Model** – with Cyclops scope, Colt bayonet, sling, and bipod. Disc. 1986.

	$395	$350	$300	$265	$240	$220	$200	Last MSR was $450.

GALIL – .22 LR cal. only, reproduction of the Israeli Galil. Importation disc. 1989.

	$350	$295	$250	$200	$175	$155	$145	Last MSR was $295.

KALASHNIKOV AK-47 – .22 LR cal. only, reproduction of the Russian AK-47, semi-auto. Importation disc. 1989.

	$350	$295	$250	$200	$175	$155	$145	Last MSR was $295.

FRENCH M.A.S. – .22 LR cal. only, reproduction of the French bullpup combat rifle, with carrying handle, 29 shot mag. Importation disc. 1989.

	$375	$325	$265	$240	$220	$200	$185	Last MSR was $320.

M1 CARBINE – .30 cal. only, copy of the U.S. Military M1 Carbine. Disc. 1985.

	$295	$250	$225	$200	$175	$150	$125	Last MSR was $205.

Add 50% for Paratrooper variation.

EAGLE ARMS, INC.

Previous manufacturer located in Geneseo, IL. Previous division of ArmaLite, Inc. 1995-2002, located in Geneseo, IL. Manufacture of pre-1995 Eagle Arms rifles was in Coal Valley, IL.

During 1995, Eagle Arms, Inc. reintroduced the ArmaLite trademark. The new company was organized under the ArmaLite name. In 2003, Eagle Arms became a separate company, and no longer a division of ArmaLite.

Eagle Arms also made lower receivers only.

RIFLES: SEMI-AUTO, RECENT MFG.

On the following M-15 models manufactured 1995 and earlier, A2 accessories included a collapsible carbine type buttstock (disc. per 1994 C/B) and forward bolt assist mechanism. Accessories are similar, with the addition of National Match sights. The A2 suffix indicates the rifle is supplied with carrying handle, A4 designates a flat-top receiver, some are equipped with a detachable carrying handle.

AR-10 MATCH RIFLE – .308 Win. cal., very similar to the Armalite AR-10 A4 rifle, 20 or 24 (Match rifle) in. chrome-moly barrel, A2 (Service rifle) or A4 style flattop upper receiver (no sights), black stock with pistol grip and forearm,

MSR	100%	98%	95%	90%	80%	70%	60%	

10 shot mag., 9.6 lbs. Mfg. 2001-2005.

	$1,125	**$985**	**$845**	**$765**	**$620**	**$505**	**$395**	Last MSR was $1,000.

Add $65 for Service rifle with A2 front/rear sights.
Add $480 for 24 in. barrel and aluminum free-floating handguard.

MODEL M15 A2/A4 RIFLE (EA-15 E-1) – .223 Rem. or .308 Win. cal., patterned after the Colt AR-15A2, 20 in. barrel, A2 sights or A4 flattop, with (pre 1993) or w/o forward bolt assist, 7 lbs. Mfg. 1990-1993, reintroduced 2002-2005.

	$925	**$810**	**$695**	**$630**	**$510**	**$415**	**$325**	Last MSR was $795.

Add $40 for .223 cal. flattop (Model E15A4B).
Add $205 for .308 Win. cal. flattop.

* **Model M15 A2/A4 Rifle Carbine (EA9025C/EA9027C)** – features collapsible (disc. per C/B 1994) or fixed (new 1994) buttstock and 16 in. barrel, 5 lbs. 14 oz. Mfg. 1990-95, reintroduced 2002-2005.

	$925	**$810**	**$695**	**$630**	**$510**	**$415**	**$325**	Last MSR was $795.

Add $40 for flattop (Model E15A4CB).

1997 retail for the pre-ban models was $1,100 (EA9396).

Beginning 1993, the A2 accessory kit became standard on this model.

* **Model M15 A2 H-BAR Rifle (EA9040C)** – features heavy Target barrel, 8 lbs. 14 oz., includes E-2 accessories. Mfg. 1990-95.

	$1,025	**$895**	**$770**	**$695**	**$565**	**$460**	**$360**	Last MSR was $895.

1997 retail for this pre-ban model was $1,100 (EA9200).

* **Model M15 A4 Rifle Eagle Spirit (EA9055S)** – includes 16 in. premium air gauged National Match barrel, fixed stock, full length tubular aluminum hand guard, designed for IPSC shooting, includes match grade accessories, 8 lbs. 6 oz. Mfg. 1993-95, reintroduced 2002 only.

	$1,025	**$895**	**$770**	**$695**	**$565**	**$460**	**$360**	Last MSR was $850.

The 1995 pre-ban variation of this model retailed at $1,475 (EA9603).

* **Model M15 A2 Rifle Golden Eagle (EA9049S)** – similar to M15 A2 H-BAR, except has National Match accessories and two-stage trigger, 20 in. extra heavy barrel, 12 lbs. 12 oz. Mfg 1991-95, reintroduced 2002 only.

	$1,200	**$1,050**	**$900**	**$815**	**$660**	**$540**	**$420**	Last MSR was $1,125.

The 1997 pre-ban variation of this model retailed at $1,300 (EA9500).

* **Model M15 A4 Rifle Eagle Eye (EA9901)** – includes 24 in. free floating 1 in. dia. barrel with tubular aluminum hand guard, weighted buttstock, designed for silhouette matches, 14 lbs. Mfg. 1993-95.

	$1,525	**$1,335**	**$1,145**	**$1,035**	**$840**	**$685**	**$535**	Last MSR was $1,495.

* **Model M15 Rifle Action Master (EA9052S)** – match rifle, flattop, solid aluminum handguard tube, for free floating 20 in. barrel with compensator, N.M. accessories, fixed stock, 8 lbs. 5 oz. Mfg. 1992-95, reintroduced 2002 only.

	$925	**$810**	**$695**	**$630**	**$510**	**$415**	**$325**	Last MSR was $850.

The 1995 pre-ban variation of this model retailed at $1,475 (EA5600).

* **Model M15 A4 Rifle Special Purpose (EA9042C)** – 20 in. barrel, flattop (A4) or detachable handle receiver. Disc. 1995.

	$1,050	**$920**	**$785**	**$715**	**$575**	**$470**	**$365**	Last MSR was $955.

The 1995 pre-ban variation of this model retailed at $1,165 (EA9204).

* **Model M15 A4 Rifle Predator (EA9902)** – post-ban only, 18 in. barrel, National Match trigger, flattop (A4) or detachable handle receiver. Mfg. 1995 only.

	$1,325	**$1,160**	**$995**	**$900**	**$730**	**$595**	**$465**	Last MSR was $1,350.

EAST RIDGE GUN COMPANY, INC.

Current rifle manufacturer located in Bancroft, WI.

RIFLES: BOLT ACTION, SINGLE SHOT

SHORTY – .50 BMG cal., 30 in. Lothar Walther tapered barrel, muzzle brake, all steel bipod, adj. aluminum tactical stock with removable carry handle, or custom laminated wood stock, scope rail, approx. 31 lbs.

MSR $2,050	**$1,850**	**$1,625**	**$1,385**	**$1,265**	**$1,015**	**$830**	**$650**	

Add $200 for custom laminated wood stock.

MSR	100%	98%	95%	90%	80%	70%	60%

REBEL – .50 BMG cal., 36 in. Lothar Walther bull barrel, muzzle brake, all steel bipod, adj. aluminum tactical stock with removable carrying handle, or custom laminated wood stock, scope rail, AR-15 grip, approx. 38 lbs.

MSR $2,250	$2,050	$1,795	$1,535	$1,395	$1,125	$925	$715

Add $200 for custom laminated wood stock.

BIG BERTHA – .50 BMG cal., 36 in. Lothar Walther premium target bull barrel, muzzle brake, all steel bipod, special tactical or custom laminated wood stock, scope rail, approx. 40 lbs.

MSR $2,750	$2,475	$2,165	$1,850	$1,685	$1,365	$1,115	$865

COMPETITOR 2000 – .50 BMG cal., 30 or 36 in. Lothar Walther fluted bull barrel, extra large muzzle brake, all steel bipod, adj. aluminum stock with military hard coat finish, scope mount, Jewell trigger, pistol grip with palm swell, accuracy guaranteed to be less than 1 minute of angle with custom ammo.

MSR $3,400	$3,075	$2,695	$2,300	$2,095	$1,695	$1,385	$1,075

LIGHT WEIGHT COMPETITOR – .50 BMG cal., 30 in. Lothar Walther fluted bull stainless or chromemoly barrel, reduced weight muzzle brake, adj. skeletonized aluminum stock with black hard coat finish, scope mounting rail, Jewell trigger, sniper type pistol grip with palm swell, optional carrying handle, 28 lbs.

MSR $3,400	$3,075	$2,695	$2,300	$2,095	$1,695	$1,385	$1,075

Add $200 for stainless steel barrel.

TITAN BENCH – .50 BMG cal., 30 in. Lothar Walther stainless steel fluted barrel, muzzle brake, adj. trigger, bench rest style laminated stock in choice of colors, precision ground tapered or flat steel scope base, 26 lbs., 6 oz.

MSR $2,550	$2,295	$2,015	$1,725	$1,560	$1,260	$1,035	$800

ENFIELDS

Previously manufactured by the Royal Small Arms Factory situated on the northern outskirts of London, in Middlesex, England. Various Enfield rifles, carbines and revolvers were produced and/or converted by other British factories (B.S.A., L.S.A., S.S.A., N.R.F., P. Webley & Son, Webley & Scott Ltd., Albion Motors, W.W. Greener, Westley Richards, Vickers (VSM), ROF Fazakerley, ROF Maltby, BSA Shirley (M47C), as well as Australia at Lithgow (from 1913), in Canada at Long Branch (from 1941), the United States by Stevens-Savage (also from 1941), RFI Ishapore, India (from 1905), Nakhu, Pyuthan and Sundrijal in Nepal (from 1911), and at Wah Cantt in Pakistan (from the late 1950s).

The publisher would like to thank Mr. Ian Skennerton for making the following information available.

RIFLES & CARBINES

.303 RIFLE No. 1 Mk III* H.T. SNIPER – factory fitted telescopic sight and heavy barrel, converted at Lithgow, Australia at the end of WWII, special bedding of furniture, some were also fitted with a cheekpiece, British and Lithgow actions.

	$6,500	$5,750	$5,000	$4,500	$4,000	$3,500	$3,000

Buyer beware - check for authentic ser. nos., as there have been some fakes on this model.

.303 No. 3 Mk I* (T) (PATTERN 1914 SNIPER) – converted in England by Periscope Prism Co. (1918) & B.S.A. (1938) from Winchester rifles, the Pattern 1918 telescope on crawfoot mounts was fitted.

	$7,500	$6,500	$5,500	$4,750	$4,500	$3,750	$3,250

.303 No. 3 Mk I* (T) A SNIPER – converted in England by Alex Martin in WWII from Winchester MK I* (F) rifles, Great War Aldis and P.P. Co. telescopes (ex-SMLE snipers) were fitted, original SMLE rifle engraved number is usually visible, usually scope is offset (left) of the bore line.

	$6,500	$5,750	$5,000	$4,250	$3,750	$3,000	$2,750

Add 30% for overhead mount.

.303 No. 5 MK. I JUNGLE CARBINE – 20 1/2 in. barrel with flash hider, lightened action body and shortened furniture. From 1944, for service in the Far East.

	$950	$875	$800	$700	$625	$550	$450

Subtract 20% for Indian service issues that have a transverse wood screw in the forend which is less desirable.

7.62mm L42A1 SNIPER – Enfield conversion and extensive rebuild of the No. 4 Mk I(T) sniper rifle, fitted with an upgraded No. 32 telescopic sight to L1A1, half-stocked furniture, 7.62mm magazine with integral ejector, with heavy target barrel.

	$7,750	$7,000	$6,500	$5,750	$5,000	$4,500	$4,000

Add 20%+ for original green finished chest.
Add 30% for Iraq war issue with 6x Schmidt & Bender scope.

MSR	100%	98%	95%	90%	80%	70%	60%

ENFIELD AMERICA, INC.
Previous manufacturer located in Atlanta, GA.

PISTOLS: SEMI-AUTO

MP-9 – 9mm Para. cal., tactical design, similar to MP-45. Mfg. 1985.

	$550	$475	$425	$350	$295	$260	$240

Add $150 for carbine kit.

MP-45 – .45 ACP cal., tactical design, 4 1/2, 6, 8, 10, or 18 1/2 in. shrouded barrel, parkerized finish, 10, 30, 40, or 50 shot mag., 6 lbs. Mfg. 1985 only.

	$550	$475	$425	$350	$295	$260	$240	Last MSR was $350.

ENTRÉPRISE ARMS INC.
Current manufacturer located in Irwindale, CA, since 1996. Dealer and consumer sales.

PISTOLS: SEMI-AUTO

The models listed are patterned after the Colt M1911, but have "Widebody" frames.

ELITE SERIES – .45 ACP cal., 3 1/4 in. barrel, features steel 1911 Widebody frame, flat mainspring housing, flared ejection port, 10 shot mag., bead blasted black oxide finish, tactical sights, 36 oz. New 1997.

* *Elite Series P325*

MSR $700	$625	$565	$500	$450	$400	$360	$330

* *Elite Series P425* – similar to Elite P325, except has 4 1/4 in. barrel, 38 oz. New 1997.

MSR $700	$625	$565	$500	$450	$400	$360	$330

* *Elite Series P500* – similar to Elite P325, except has 5 in. barrel, 40 oz. New 1997.

MSR $700	$625	$565	$500	$450	$400	$360	$330

TACTICAL SERIES – .45 ACP cal., 3 1/4 in. barrel, features Tactical Widebody with "De-horned" slide and frame allowing snag-free carry, narrow ambidextrous thumb safety, 10 shot mag., low profile Novak or ghost ring sights, squared trigger guard, flat main spring housing, matte black oxide finish, 36 oz. New 1997.

* *Tactical Series P325*

MSR $979	$875	$750	$650	$575	$500	$450	$395

* *Tactical Series P325 Plus* – similar to P325, except has short officer's length slide/barrel fitted onto a full government frame, designed as concealed carry pistol. New 1998.

MSR $979	$875	$750	$650	$575	$500	$450	$395

* *Tactical Series P425* – similar to Tactical P325, except has 4 1/4 in. barrel, 38 oz. New 1997.

MSR $979	$875	$750	$650	$575	$500	$450	$395

* *Tactical Series P500* – similar to Tactical P325, except has 5 in. barrel, 40 oz. New 1997.

MSR $979	$875	$750	$650	$575	$500	$450	$395

CARBINES, SEMI-AUTO

STG58C CARBINE/SCOUT – .308 Win. cal., tactical design, 16 1/2 in. barrel with muzzle brake, synthetic pistol grip stock, last shot bolt hold open, adj. gas system, mil-spec black oxide finish, 20 shot mag., 200-600 meter aperture sights, supplied with black nylon sling, various configurations, approx. 9 lbs. New 2000.

* *STG58C Carbine Scout* – Entreprise Type 03 receiver, integral bipod, includes carry handle. New 2000.

MSR $1,199	$1,075	$875	$750	$625	$575	$500	$450

* *STG58C Carbine* – Entreprise Type 01 receiver, machined aluminum free-floating handguards, carry handle. New 2000.

MSR $1,399	$1,200	$995	$850	$750	$625	$550	$500

RIFLES: SEMI-AUTO

STG58C RIFLE – .308 Win. cal., tactical design, choice of 16 1/2, 21, or 24 in. barrel with muzzle brake, synthetic pistol grip stock, last shot bolt hold open, adj. gas system, mil-spec black oxide finish, 20 shot mag., 200-600 meter aperture sights, supplied with black nylon sling, various configurations, 8 1/2-13 lbs. New 2000.

MSR	100%	98%	95%	90%	80%	70%	60%

* **STG58C Rifle Lightweight Model** – 16 1/2 in. barrel, Entreprise Type 03 receiver, 8 1/2 lbs. New 2000.

| MSR $1,199 | $1,050 | $900 | $800 | $725 | $650 | $600 | $550 |

* **STG58C Rifle Standard Model** – 21 in. barrel, Entreprise Type 03 receiver, integral bipod, 9.8 lbs. New 2000.

| MSR $899 | $795 | $700 | $625 | $525 | $475 | $425 | $375 |

Add $100 for CA configuration.

* **STG58C Rifle Government Model** – 21 in. barrel, Entreprise Type 01 receiver, integral bipod, 9 1/2 lbs. New 2000.

| MSR $1,199 | $1,050 | $900 | $800 | $725 | $650 | $600 | $550 |

* **STG58C Rifle Target Model** – 21 in. free float barrel, Entreprise Type 01 receiver, with aluminum handguard, 11 1/2 lbs. New 2000.

| MSR $1,399 | $1,200 | $995 | $850 | $750 | $625 | $550 | $500 |

* **STG58C Rifle Match Target Model** – 24 in. free-float match heavy barrel, Entreprise Type 01 receiver, with aluminum handguard, 13 lbs. New 2000.

| MSR $1,999 | $1,825 | $1,650 | $1,475 | $1,200 | $1,000 | $850 | $750 |

ERMA SUHL, GmbH

Previous manufacturer located in Suhl, Germany January 1998 - circa 2004. Erma Suhl purchased the remaining assets of Erma-Werke.

RIFLES: BOLT ACTION

SR100 SNIPER RIFLE – .300 Win. Mag., .308 Win., or .338 Lapua Mag. cal., bolt action, tactical rifle featuring brown laminated wood stock with thumbhole, adj. buttplate/cheekpiece, and vent. forend, forged aluminum receiver, 25 1/2 or 29 1/2 in. barrel, muzzle brake, adj. match trigger, approx. 15 lbs. Limited importation 1997-98 only.

| | $6,500 | $5,750 | $5,000 | $4,350 | $3,750 | $3,000 | $2,350 | Last MSR was $8,600. |

This model was imported exclusively by Amtec 2000, Inc., located in Gardner, MA.

Most recent importation was in .300 Win. Mag., and included a Steyr scope mount.

ERMA-WERKE

Previous manufacturer located in Dachau, Germany (Erma-Werke production) until bankruptcy occurred in October of 1997. Pistols were previously imported and distributed by Precision Sales International, Inc. located in Westfield, MA, Nygord Precision Products located in Prescott, AZ, and Mandall's Shooting Supplies, Inc. located in Scottsdale, AZ. Previously distributed by Excam located in Hialeah, FL.

Erma-Werke also manufactured private label handguns for American Arms Inc. (refer to their section for listings).

RIFLES

Models listed were available from Mandall Shooting Supplies, unless otherwise noted.

EM-1 .22 CARBINE – .22 LR cal., M1 copy, 10 or 15 shot mag., 18 in. barrel, rear adj. aperture sight, 5.6 lbs. Mfg. 1966-97.

| | $365 | $295 | $250 | $215 | $190 | $175 | $160 | Last MSR was $400. |

EGM-1 – similar to EM-1 except for unslotted buttstock, 5 shot mag.

| | $260 | $230 | $195 | $175 | $150 | $125 | $100 | Last MSR was $295. |

ESCORT

Current trademark of shotguns manufactured by Hatsan Arms Co., located in Izmir, Turkey, and imported beginning 2002 by Legacy Sports International, located in Reno, NV. Previously located in Alexandria, VA.

SHOTGUNS: SEMI-AUTO

Beginning 2004, all models have a round back receiver with 3/8 in. dovetail milled along top for mounting sights. Beginning in 2009, all Escort semi-auto shotguns use a bottom feed system similar to a Remington 11-87.

ESCORT SERIES - 3 IN. – 12 or 20 (new 2005) ga., 3 in. chamber, gas operated action with 2 position adj. screw (disc. 2003), 20 (disc. 2008), 22 (AS Youth and PS Slug, new 2005), 24 (disc. 2008), 26 (new 2005), or 28 in. VR barrel with 3 multi-chokes, blue finish, vent recoil pad, gold trigger, checkered walnut (Model AS) or polymer (Model PS) black or 100% camo coverage Mossy Oak Break Up (disc. 2004), Mossy Oak Obsession (mfg. 2005-2008), Shadowgrass (disc. 2008), King's Woodland (new 2009), King's Desert (new 2009), or King's Snow (new 2009) camo

MSR	100%	98%	95%	90%	80%	70%	60%

stock and forearm, 6.4-7 lbs. Importation began 2002.

MSR $399	$350	$315	$275	$240	$220	$200	$180

Add $70 for walnut stock and forearm (Model AS).
Add $182 for AS Select Model with select walnut (mfg. 2007-2008).
Add $100 for 100% camo coverage.
Add $74 for HiViz Spark front sight and King's Field metal finish (mfg. 2009).
Add $80 for Model PS Slug with rifled slug barrel and cantilever mount.
Add $175 for Model PS Slug Combo (mfg. 2006-2008).
Add $81 for 24 in. barrel with Model PS TriViz sights and Mossy Oak Break Up camo coverage (disc. 2004).

* *Escort Series - 3 in. - Aimguard* – similar to Escort model, except has black chrome finish, black polymer stock, 18 (new 2006) or 20 (disc. 2005) in. barrel, cylinder bore. Imported 2004-2007.

	$340	$295	$275	$250	$230	$215	$195	Last MSR was $392.

SHOTGUNS: SLIDE ACTION

ESCORT SERIES – 12 or 20 (new 2005) ga., 3 in. chamber, matte blue finish or 100% camo coverage with polymer stock and forearm, 18 (Aimguard or MarineGuard Model), 22 (Field Slug, new 2005), 24 (Turkey, includes extra turkey choke tube and FH TriViz sight combo with Mossy Oak Break Up [disc. 2004] or Obsession camo coverage), 26 (new 2005, Field Hunter), or 28 (Field Hunter) in. barrel, alloy receiver with 3/8 in. milled dovetail for sight mounting, trigger guard safety, 4 or 5 shot mag. with cut off button, two stock adj. shims, 6.4-7 lbs. Importation began 2003.

* *Escort Series Aimguard* – 12 ga., 18 in. barrel with black synthetic stock, fixed cyl. bore choke, 6.4 lbs.

MSR $280	$245	$220	$195	$170	$150	$130	$110

* *Escort Series Marine Guard* – 12 ga., 18 in. barrel with black synthetic stock, nickel receiver, fixed cyl. bore choke, 6.4 lbs.

MSR $320	$275	$240	$210	$185	$160	$140	$120

* *Escort Series Tactical Entry/Special Ops* – 12 ga. only, 18 in. barrel, synthetic stock, available in a variety of configurations. New 2009.

MSR $320	$275	$230	$200	$185	$170	$155	$135

Add $120 for Special Ops model (mfg. 2009).
Add $79 for Tac Stock II (new 2010).

EUROPEAN AMERICAN ARMORY CORP.

Current importer and distributor established in late 1990 and located in Rockledge, FL. Previously located in Sharpes, FL 1990-2006. Distributor and dealer sales.

EAA currently imports its handguns from Tanfoglio, located in Italy, and from H. Weihrauch, located in Germany. All guns are covered by EAA's lifetime limited warranty. EAA has also imported various trademarks of long guns, including Saiga, Weihrauch, and Izhmash. Please refer to those individual sections.

The Zastava Z98 and Z5 bolt actions, in addition to the Sabatti double rifle, are imported by US Sporting Goods Inc.

PISTOLS: SEMI-AUTO

EAA has issued a safety upgrade notice regarding any Witness style semi-auto pistol bearing a serial number between AE00000 - AE700000. Owners are requested to field strip the pistol and send the slide assembly directly to EAA. EAA will replace the firing pin and return it to you. See Trademark Index for contact information.

The following Witness pistols also have a .22 LR conversion kit available for $234.

WITNESS EA 38 SUPER SERIES – .38 Super cal., action patterned after the CZ-75, selective double action, 4 1/2 in. barrel, steel or polymer frame/steel slide (mfg. 1997-2004), 10 (C/B 1994), 18 (new late 2004) or 19* shot mag., choice of Wonder (heat treated grey satin finish, new 1997), stainless steel (disc. 1996), blue (disc.), blue/chrome (disc. 1994), or brushed chrome (disc. 1996) finish, combat sights, black neoprene grips, 33 oz. Importation began 1994.

MSR $542	$450	$400	$365	$315	$280	$230	$185

Subtract $20 for polymer frame.

* *Model EA 38 Compact* – similar to EA 38 Super Series, except has 3 5/8 in. unported or ported barrel, choice of matte blue or Wonder finish, 30 oz. Mfg. 1999-2004.

	$370	$325	$275	$250	$205	$165	$130	Last MSR was $449.

Subtract $20 for polymer frame.
Add $20 for Wonder finish or ported barrel (polymer frame only).

WITNESS EA 9 SERIES – 9mm Para. cal., action patterned after the CZ-75, selective double action, 4 1/2 in. unported or ported (polymer, New Frame only, new 2002) barrel, steel or polymer frame/steel slide (new 1997), 10 (C/B 1994), 16*, or 18 (new late 2004) shot mag., choice of Wonder (new 1997), stainless steel (disc. 1996),

MSR	100%	98%	95%	90%	80%	70%	60%

blue, blue/chrome (disc. 1993), or brushed chrome (disc. 1996) finish, combat sights, black neoprene grips, 33 oz. Importation began late 1990.

MSR $542	**$450**	**$400**	**$365**	**$315**	**$280**	**$230**	**$185**

Subtract $31 for polymer New Frame.

* ***Model EA 9 (L) Compact*** – similar to EA 9, except has 3 5/8 in. unported or ported (polymer frame only, mfg. 2002-2006) barrel and 10 (C/ B 1994), 12 (new late 2004), or 13* shot mag., 27 oz.

MSR $542	**$450**	**$400**	**$365**	**$315**	**$280**	**$230**	**$185**

Subtract $3 for polymer frame.
Add $10-$20 for ported barrel (polymer frame only, disc. 2006).

WITNESS EA 40 SERIES – .40 S&W cal., action patterned after the CZ-75, selective double action, 4 1/2 in. barrel, steel or polymer frame/steel slide (new 1997), 10 (C/B 1994), 12*, or 15 (new late 2004) shot mag., choice of Wonder (new 1997), stainless steel (disc. 1996), blue, blue/chrome (disc.), or brushed chrome (disc. 1996) finish, combat sights, black neoprene grips, 33 oz. Importation began late 1990.

MSR $542	**$450**	**$400**	**$365**	**$315**	**$280**	**$230**	**$185**

Subtract $35 for polymer New Frame.

* ***Model EA 40 (L) Compact*** – similar to EA 40, except has 3 5/8 in. unported or ported barrel, 9 or 12 (new late 2004) shot mag.

MSR $542	**$450**	**$400**	**$365**	**$315**	**$280**	**$230**	**$185**

Subtract $31 for polymer frame.

Add $10-$20 for ported barrel (polymer frame only, disc. 2005).

WITNESS EA 10 SUPER SERIES – 10mm cal., action patterned after the CZ-75, selective double action, 4 1/2 in. barrel, polymer or steel frame, 10, 12*, or 15 (new late 2004) shot mag., choice of stainless steel (disc.), blue, chrome (disc.), or Wonder (new 1999) finish, combat sights, black neoprene grips, 33 oz. Imported 1994 only, and 1999-current.

MSR $542	**$450**	**$400**	**$365**	**$315**	**$280**	**$230**	**$185**

Add $30 for chrome finish (disc.).
Add $65 for stainless steel (disc.).
Subtract $31 for polymer frame.

* ***Model EA 10 Carry Comp*** – similar to EA 10, except has 4 1/2 in. compensated barrel, blue or Wonder (new 2005) finish. Mfg. 1999-2005.

	$415	**$365**	**$310**	**$280**	**$230**	**$185**	**$145**	Last MSR was $489.

Subtract $20 for blue finish.

* ***Model EA 10 Compact*** – similar to EA 10, except has 3 5/8 in. barrel, 8 or 12 (new late 2004) shot mag., 27 oz.

MSR $542	**$450**	**$400**	**$365**	**$315**	**$280**	**$230**	**$185**

Subtract $31 for polymer frame.

WITNESS EA 41 SERIES – .41 Action Express cal., action patterned after the CZ-75, selective double action, 4 1/2 in. barrel, steel frame, 11 shot mag., blue, blue/chrome, or brushed chrome finish, combat sights, black neoprene grips, 33 oz. Importation disc. 1993.

	$450	**$395**	**$335**	**$305**	**$245**	**$200**	**$155**	Last MSR was $595.

Add $40 for blue/chrome or brushed chrome finish.

* ***Model EA 41 Compact*** – similar to EA 41, except has 3 1/2 in. barrel and 8 shot mag.

	$495	**$435**	**$370**	**$335**	**$270**	**$225**	**$175**	Last MSR was $625.

Add $40 for blue/chrome or brushed chrome finish.

WITNESS EA 45 SERIES – .45 ACP cal., action patterned after the CZ-75, selective double action, 4 1/2 in. standard or compensated (mfg. 1998-2005) barrel, steel frame, polymer full size frame (new 2004), or polymer frame/steel slide (new 1997), 10 (C/ B 1994) or 11* shot mag., choice of Wonder (new 1997), stainless steel (disc. 1996), blue, blue/chrome (disc. 1993), or brushed chrome (disc. 1996) finish, combat sights, walnut grips, 35 oz. Importation began late 1990.

MSR $542	**$450**	**$400**	**$365**	**$315**	**$280**	**$230**	**$185**

Add $92 for .45 ACP/.22 LR combo.
Add $40 for ported barrel (steel only, with Wonder finish, disc. 2004).
Subtract $31 for polymer frame or blue finish.

* ***Model EA 45 (L) Compact*** – similar to EA 45, except has 3 5/8 in. unported or ported barrel and 8 shot mag., 26 oz.

MSR $542	**$450**	**$400**	**$365**	**$315**	**$280**	**$230**	**$185**

MSR	100%	98%	95%	90%	80%	70%	60%

Add $30 for ported barrel (polymer frame only, disc. 2004).
Add $50 for single port barrel compensator or carry configuration with compensator (disc.).
Subtract $31 for polymer frame.

WITNESS P CARRY – 9mm Para., 10mm, .40 S&W, or .45 ACP cal., SA/DA, 3.6 in. barrel, 10 (.45 ACP), 15 (10mm or .40 S&W), or 18 (9mm Para.) shot mag., full size polymer frame, compact slide, Commander style, Wonder finish, integral M-1913 rail, 27 oz. New 2006.

MSR $635	$525	$450	$395	$350	$300	$265	$220

WITNESS CARRY COMP GUN – .38 Super (disc. 1997), 9mm Para. (disc. 1997), .40 S&W cal. (disc. 1997), 10mm (disc. 1994, reintroduced 1999), or .45 ACP cal., full size frame with compact slide and 1 in. compensator, 10 (C/B 1994), 12* (.40 S&W), or 16* (9mm Para.) shot mag., Wonder (new 1997), blue, Duo-Tone (disc. 1994) finish. Imported 1992-2004.

	$425	$370	$320	$290	$235	$190	$150	*Last MSR was $479.*

Add $10 for Wonder finish.

WITNESS FCP – .380 ACP, .38 Super, .38 Spl., 9mm Para., .40 S&W, or .45 ACP cal., polymer frame, DAO, blue finish, 6 shot non-detachable mag., 4 in. barrel, fast cycle tube chamber, utitlizes simple reusable tubes that encase each round, no detachable mag., 26 oz. Disc. 2007.

	$185	$160	$140	$125	$100	$85	$65	*Last MSR was $219.*

ZASTAVA EZ – 9mm Para., .40 S&W, or .45 ACP cal., DA/SA, ambidextrous controls, 10 (.45 ACP), 11 (.40 S&W), or 15 (9mm Para.) shot mag., 4 in. barrel, aluminum frame, accessory rail, spur hammer, blue or chrome finish, 33 oz. Importation began 2007.

MSR $573	$495	$435	$375	$335	$285	$250	$215

Add $47 for chrome finish.

* ***Zastava EZ Compact*** – similar to Zastava EZ Model, except is compact frame, 7 (.45 ACP), 8 (.40 S&W), or 12 shot mag., 3 1/2 in. barrel. Importation began 2007.

MSR $573	$495	$435	$375	$335	$285	$250	$215

Add $47 for chrome finish.

ZASTAVA EZ CARRY – 9mm Para. or .40 S&W cal., full size frame, ported barrel, 10 or 14 shot mag. Importation began 2010.

MSR $620	$550	$495	$450	$395	$350	$300	$250

RIFLES

Some EAA rifles were manufactured by Sabatti in Italy (est. 1674), Lu-Mar in Italy, and H. Weihrauch in Germany (see separate listing in the H. Weihrauch section). Imported 1992-96.

ZASTAVA PAP 762 SEMI-AUTO – 7.62x39mm cal., patterned after the AK-47, blond hardwood thumbhole stock and furniture, 10 shot mag., 16 3/4 in. barrel, removable accessory rail, 10 lbs. Importation began 2008.

MSR $464	$425	$365	$335	$295	$265	$240	$220

M-93 BLACK ARROW BOLT ACTION – .50 BMG cal., Mauser action, 36 in. fluted heavy barrel with muzzle brake, adj. folding bipod, iron sights, detachable 5 shot mag., carry handle, detachable scope mount, wood case, 35 lbs. Mfg. by Zastava, importation began 2007.

MSR $6,986	$6,400	$5,800	$5,000	$4,250	$3,500	$2,900	$2,300

SHOTGUNS: SLIDE ACTION

MODEL PM2 – 12 ga. only, slide action, unique 7 shot detachable mag., 20 in. barrel, black wood stock and composite forearm, dual action bars, cross-bolt safety on triggerguard, available in matte blue or chrome finish, 6.81 lbs. Imported 1992 only.

	$550	$480	$410	$375	$300	$245	$190	*Last MSR was $695.*

Add $200 for night sights.
Add $75 for matte chrome finish.

EVOLUTION USA

Current rifle manufacturer located in White Bird, ID since 1984. Distributor and dealer sales.

RIFLES: SEMI-AUTO

GRENADA – .223 Rem. cal., tactical design based on the AR-15 with flat upper receiver, 17 in. stainless steel match barrel with integral muzzle brake, NM trigger. Disc. 2000.

	$985	$825	$675	$600	$525	$465	$400	*Last MSR was $1,195.*

MSR	100%	98%	95%	90%	80%	70%	60%

DESERT STORM – similar to Grenada, except has 21 in. match barrel. Disc. 2003.

| | $975 | $825 | $665 | $560 | $500 | $450 | $400 | Last MSR was $1,189. |

IWO JIMA – features carrying handle incorporating iron sights, 20 in. stainless steel match barrel, A2 HBAR action, tubular handguard. Limited mfg.

| | $1,000 | $875 | $775 | $700 | $600 | $475 | $425 | |

RIFLES : SINGLE SHOT

PHANTOM III SINGLE SHOT – .50 BMG or .700 NE cal., Evolution M-2000 stainless single shot action, 28 in. Lilja match barrel with flutes and muzzle brake, approx. 30 lbs. New 2000.

| MSR $4,700 | $4,700 | $4,300 | $3,850 | $3,500 | $2,950 | $2,400 | $2,250 | |

Add $1,700 for Delta Model (50-80 lbs.) or .700 NE cal. (24-30 lbs.), disc.

EXCAM

Previous importer and distributor located in Hialeah, FL, which went out of business late 1990. Excam distributed Dart, Erma, Tanarmi, Targa, and Warrior exclusively in the U.S. These trademarks will appear under Excam only in this book. All importation of Excam firearms ceased in 1990.

All Targa and Tanarmi pistols were manufactured in Gardone V.T., Italy. All Erma and Warrior pistols and rifles were manufactured in W. Germany. Senator O/U shotguns were manufactured by A. Zoli located in Brescia, Italy.

HANDGUNS: TANARMI MFG.

TA 41 SERIES SEMI-AUTO – .41 Action Express cal., action similar to TA 90 Series, 11 shot mag., matte blue (Model TA 41B) or matte chrome (Model TA 41C) finish, combat sights, black neoprene grips, 38 oz. Imported 1989-90.

| | $450 | $390 | $360 | $330 | $295 | $265 | $240 | Last MSR was $490. |

Add $70 for adj. target sights (Model TA 41BT).

TA 90 SERIES SEMI-AUTO – 9mm Para. cal., double action, copy of the CZ-75, 4 3/4 in. barrel, steel frame, 15 shot mag., matte blue (Model TA 90B) or matte chrome finish (Model TA 90C), combat sights, wood (disc. 1985) or neoprene grips, 38 oz. New 1985.

| | $365 | $300 | $260 | $225 | $205 | $190 | $180 | Last MSR was $415. |

Add $85 for adj. target sights (TA 90BT).

Earlier models featured a polished blue finish and nickel steel alloy frame (35 oz.).

RIFLES: ERMA MFG.

EM 1 CARBINE – .22 LR or .22 Mag. cal., semi-auto, copy of the original M1 carbine, 19 1/2 in. barrel, 15 shot, iron sights, blue only. ESG 22 is .22 Mag. (12 shot). Disc. 1985.

| | $175 | $155 | $140 | $125 | $115 | $100 | $90 | Last MSR was $195. |

Add $100 for ESG 22, .22 Mag.

F SECTION

FEG

Current manufacturer located in Hungary (FEG stands for Fegyver es Gepgyar) since circa 1900. Currently imported beginning 2007 by SSME Deutsche Waffen, Inc., located in Plant City, FL. A few models were imported by Century International Arms located in Delray Beach, FL (see additional information under the Century International Arms in this text). Previously imported and distributed by K.B.I., Inc. located in Harrisburg, PA, and distributed until 1998 by Interarms located in Alexandria, VA.

MSR	100%	98%	95%	90%	80%	70%	60%

RIFLES: SEMI-AUTO

MODEL SA-85M – 7.62x39mm cal., sporter rifle utilizing AKM action, 16.3 in. barrel, 6 shot detachable mag., thumbhole stock, 7 lbs. 10 oz. Imported 1991, banned 1998.

	$550	$480	$410	$375	$300	$245	$190	*Last MSR was $429.*

SA-85 S (SA-2000M) – .223 Rem. (disc. 2000) or 7.62x39mm cal., sporter rifle with skeletonized Choate synthetic stock, 16.3 (new 2007) or 17 3/4 (disc. 2000) in. barrel with muzzle brake, 6, 10, or 30 shot detachable mag. Imported 1999-2000, reimported 2007.

MSR $1,075	$950	$830	$710	$645	$520	$425	$330

F.I.E.

Previous importer (F.I.E. is the acronym for Firearms Import & Export) located in Hialeah, FL until 1990.

F.I.E. filed bankruptcy in November of 1990 and all models were discontinued. Some parts or service for these older firearms may be obtained through Numrich Gun Parts Corp. (see Trademark Index), even though all warranties on F.I.E. guns are void.

PISTOLS: SEMI-AUTO, TITAN SERIES

SPECTRE PISTOL – 9mm Para. or .45 ACP cal., double action, unique triple action blowback system with two piece bolt, 6 in. barrel, military style configuration, adj. sights, 30 or 50 (optional with unique 4 column configuation) shot mag., 4.8 lbs. Mfg. 1989-90 only.

	$675	$600	$525	$480	$440	$400	$360	*Last MSR was $718.*

Add $14 for mag. loading tool.

KG-99 – 9mm Para. cal., tactical design pistol, 36 shot mag. Mini-99 also available with 20 shot mag. and 3 in. barrel. Disc. 1984.

	$550	$475	$440	$400	$365	$330	$300

This model was not manufactured but sold by F.I.E.

RIFLES: SEMI-AUTO

PARA RIFLE – .22 LR cal., tactical designed rifle with tube stock (is also magazine), includes green cloth case with white stenciled letters, takedown, 11 shot mag., matte black receiver finish, approx. 4 lbs. Mfg. by L. Franchi between 1979-84. Imported into the U.S. from 1985-88.

	$325	$275	$225	$195	$155	$130	$110	*Last MSR was $225.*

8,000 of this model were manufactured by L. Franchi. 5,000 went to the Italian Government and were used as training rifles (with German scopes). The remainder were imported by F.I.E. (without scopes).

SPECTRE CARBINE – 9mm Para. cal., same action as Spectre pistol, tactical design carbine, collapsible metal butt stock, 30 or 50 (opt.) shot mag., adj. rear sight, with pistol and forearm grip. Mfg. 1989-disc.

	$550	$450	$375	$300	$275	$250	$225	*Last MSR was $700.*

FNH USA

Current importer established in 1998, and located in McLean, VA. Dealer and distributor sales.

In the U.S., FN (Fabrique Nationale) is represented by two entities - FNH USA, which is responsible for sales, marketing, and business development, and FNM, which stands for FN Manufacturing, which handles manufacturing. FNH USA has two separate divisions - commercial/law enforcement, and military operations. FN Manufacturing is located in Columbia, SC. Design, research and development are conducted under the authority of FN Herstal S.A. Some of the firearms that FNM currently produces for the U.S. government are M16 rifles, M249 light machine guns, and M240 medium machine guns. FNM also produces the FNP line of handguns for the commercial, military, and law enforcement marketplaces. FNM is one of only three small arms manufacturers designated by the U.S. government

MSR	100%	98%	95%	90%	80%	70%	60%

as an industry base for small arms production. In November 2004, the FN model was chosen by the U.S. Special Operations Command (USSOCOM) for the new SCAR tactical rifle.

CARBINES/RIFLES: SEMI-AUTO

PS90 – 5.7x28mm cal., blowback operation, bullpup configuration, 16 in. barrel, 10 or 30 shot box mag. runs horizontally along the top, empty cases are ejected downward, integrated muzzlebrake, olive drab or black finish, configurations include PS90 RD with reflex sight module (mfg. 2009), PS90 USG with non-magnifying black reticle optical sight, and the PS90 TR with three M-1913 rails for optional optics, 6.3 lbs.

MSR $2,199	$1,925	$1,675	$1,450	$1,295	$1,075	$925	$800

* **PS90 Standard** – 5.7x28mm cal., similar to PS90, except no optical sights, only available with 30 shot mag, black or olive drab finish. New 2010.

MSR $1,695	$1,550	$1,325	$1,100	$975	$850	$725	$650

FS2000 TACTICAL – .223 Rem. cal., bullpup configuration, 17.4 in. barrel, gas operated with rotating bolt, 10 or 30 shot AR-15 style mag., empty cases are ejected through a forward port, includes 1.6x optical sighting package, emergency back up folding sights, ambidextrous polymer stock, top mounted M-1913 rail, olive drab (disc.), green, or black finish, 7.6 lbs.

MSR $2,779	$2,425	$2,100	$1,825	$1,675	$1,450	$1,250	$995

SCAR 16S – .223 Rem. cal., semi-auto only version of U.S. SOCOM's newest service rifle, gas operated short stroke piston system, free floating 16 1/4 in. barrel with hard chrome bore, 10 or 30 shot detachable box mag., folding open sights, fully ambidextrous operating controls, three optical rails, side folding polymer stock, fully adj. comb and LOP, black or flat Dark Earth finish on receiver and stock, 7 1/4 lbs. New 2009.

MSR $2,995	$2,695	$2,375	$2,050	$1,850	$1,575	$1,275	$1,050

SCAR 17S – .308 Win. cal., 20 shot mag., otherwise similar to SCAR 16S, 8 lbs. New 2009.

MSR $3,195	$2,850	$2,500	$2,125	$1,875	$1,575	$1,275	$1,050

FNAR STANDARD – .308 Win. cal., 16 (new 2010) or 20 in. light or heavy fluted contoured barrel, 10 or 20 shot detachable box mag., one-piece M-1913 optical rail, three accessory rails attached to forearm, matte black synthetic pistol grip stock with soft cheekpiece, adj. comb, ambidextrous mag. release, 8.8 - 9 lbs. New 2009.

MSR $1,849	$1,675	$1,475	$1,250	$1,100	$950	$800	$650

PISTOLS: SEMI-AUTO

In addition to the models listed, FNH USA also imported the HP-SA ($800 last MSR), and the HP-SFS until 2006.

All FNP guns come standard with three magazines and a lockable hard case.

FIVE-SEVEN USG – 5.7x28mm cal., 4 3/4 in. barrel, USG or standard action, 10 or 20 shot mag., reversible mag. release, textured grip, black, OD Green, or flat Dark Earth finish, polymer frame, MIL-STD mounting, choice of adj., C-More fixed, or C-More fixed night sights, underframe rail, includes three mags., hard case and cleaning kit, 20.8 oz.

MSR $1,299	$1,125	$975	$850	$750	$650	$575	$495

Early mfg. incorporated a larger trigger guard than current mfg.

RIFLES: BOLT ACTION

FNH USA imports a wide range of tactical rifle systems for military and law enforcement only. FNH USA also imported the Patrol Bolt Rifle (PBR) in various configurations (MSRs ranged from $1,209-$1,479). FNH USA also imported a line of modular system rifles, including the Ultima Ratio Intervention, the Ultima Ratio Commando II, and the .338 Lapua Model. Please contact the company directly for more information, including availability and pricing (see Trademark Index).

SPR A3 G (SPECIAL POLICE RIFLE) – .308 Win. cal., 24 in. fluted barrel with hard chromed bore, hinged floorplate, one-piece steel MIL-STD 1913 optical rail, A3 fiberglass tactical stock with adj. comb and LOP, steel sling studs, designed to achieve 1/2 MOA accuracy standard, 14.3 lbs.

MSR $3,395	$3,100	$2,710	$2,325	$2,110	$1,705	$1,395	$1,085

SPR A1/A1a – .308 Win. cal., 20 in. fluted (A1a) or 24 in. non-fluted barrel, 4 shot detachable box mag., pre-'64 Model 70 action, external claw extractor, matte black McMillan fiberglass stock with adj. comb and LOP, textured gripping surfaces, 12.4 lbs.

MSR $2,095	$1,875	$1,625	$1,400	$1,250	$1,025	$825	$725

Add $154 for SPR A1a with 20 in. fluted barrel.

SPR A2 – .308 Win. cal., similar to A1, 20 in. fluted or 24 in. non-fluted barrel, 11.6 or 12.2 lbs. Disc. 2009.

	$2,500	$2,185	$1,875	$1,700	$1,375	$1,125	$875	Last MSR was $2,745.

MSR	100%	98%	95%	90%	80%	70%	60%

SPR A5 M – .308 Win. or .300 WSM cal., 20 in. fluted (.308 Win. cal. only) or 24 in. non-fluted barrel, 3 or 4 shot mag., black synthetic tactical stock, 11.6 or 12.2 lbs.

MSR $2,895	$2,650	$2,325	$1,975	$1,750	$1,475	$1,250	$950

Add $100 for traditional hinged floorplate in .300 WSM cal. or $200 for hinged floorplate .308 Win. cal.

PSR I – .308 Win. cal., 20 in. fluted or 24 in. non-fluted barrel, 3, 4, or 5 shot internal mag., FN tactical sport trigger system, hinged floorplate, matte black McMillan sporter style fiberglass stock, raised comb, recoil pad, steel sling studs, 7.7 or 8.7 lbs. Disc. 2009.

	$2,000	$1,750	$1,500	$1,360	$1,100	$900	$700	*Last MSR was $2,253.*

PSR II/III – .308 Win. or .300 WSM (PSR II) cal., 22 in. fluted or 24 in. non-fluted barrel, 3, 4 (PSR III), or 5 shot internal or detachable box mag., FN tactical sport trigger system, matte olive drab McMillan sporter style fiberglass stock, raised comb, recoil pad, steel sling studs, 8.7 - 9.8 lbs. Disc. 2009.

	$2,000	$1,750	$1,500	$1,360	$1,100	$900	$700	*Last MSR was $2,253.*

TSR XP/XP USA (TACTICAL SPORT RIFLES) – .223 Rem. (XP USA), 7.62x39mm (XP USA, disc. 2009), .300 WSM, or .308 Win. cal., Model 70 short (XP) or ultra short (XP USA) action, 20 in. fluted or 24 in. non-fluted barrel, 3, 4 (detachable box mag., XP Model only), 5, or 6 shot mag., one-piece steel MIL-STD 1913 optical rail, full aluminum bedding block molded into FN/Hogue synthetic stock, olive drab overmolded surface, recoil pad, steel sling studs, 8.7 - 10.1 lbs.

MSR $1,199	$1,050	$925	$800	$700	$600	$500	$400

Add $100 for .300 WSM cal. with floorplate.

SHOTGUNS

FNH USA imported tactical style shotguns, including the FN Police Shotgun ($500 last MSR) and the FN Tactical Police Shotgun (with or w/o fixed stock, $923 last MSR).

FN SLP (SELF LOADING POLICE) – 12 ga., 18 (SLP Standard), or 22 in. standard cantilever Invector choked (Mark I/Tactical) or rifled (Mark I Rifled) barrel, 6 or 8 shot mag., adj. rear sight, black synthetic stock with half or full pistol grip, rail mounted adj. ghost ring rear sight, two gas pistons for heavy and light loads, 7.7 - 8.2 lbs.

MSR $1,199	$1,050	$925	$800	$700	$600	$500	$400

Add $50 for 22 in. rifled barrel (Mark I Rifled) with adj. rear sight.
Add $100 for 18 in. barrel and adj. rifle sights (6 shot mag.).

FABARM, S.p.A.

Current manufacturer established in 1900 and located in Brescia, Italy. No current U.S. importation. Previously imported by Tristar, located in Kansas City, MO circa 2007-2009. Select models retailed by Bill Hanus Birdguns, LLC, located in Newport, OR. Previously imported by SIG Arms during 2005, located in Exeter, NH, and by Heckler & Koch, Inc. 1998-2004. Certain models had limited importation by Ithaca Acquisition Corp. located in King Ferry, NY during 1993-1995. Previously imported and distributed (1988-1990) by St. Lawrence Sales, Inc. located in Lake Orion, MI. Previously imported until 1986 by Beeman Precision Arms, Inc. located in Santa Rosa, CA.

Fabarm currently manufactures approx. 35,000 long guns annually.

Fabarm manufactures a wide variety of shotguns, rifles, and double rifles in assorted configurations, with many options available. Most models, however, are not currently being imported into the U.S. at this time. Please contact the factory directly for more information, including current model availability and pricing (see Trademark Index).

SHOTGUNS: SEMI-AUTO

The following models are gas operated, self compensating, have 4 shot mags., aluminum receivers, twin action bars, blue receiver with photo etched game scene engraving, and checkered walnut stock and forearm.

Add $25 for De Luxe engraving or camouflage wood finish.

TACTICAL SEMI-AUTO – 12 ga. only, 3 in. chamber, 20 in. barrel with TriBore choke system with cylinder choke, tactical configuration with large cocking handle, oversized safety, black polymer stock and forearm, pistol grip stock design new 2003, choice of Picatinny rail with either integral rear or fixed front and ghost ring (new 2003) sight, 5 shot mag., 6.6 lbs. Imported 2001-2004.

	$875	$775	$650	$575	$515	$450	$400	*Last MSR was $1,025.*

SHOTGUNS: SLIDE ACTION

The following models are variations of the same action based on a twin bar slide system, alloy receiver with anti-glare finish (including barrel), rear trigger guard safety, and 2 3/4 or 3 in. shell interchangeability.

Add $25 for camouflage wood finish on the following models.

MODEL S.D.A.S.S. – 12 ga. only, 3 in. chamber, originally designed for police and self defense use, 8 shot tube mag.,

MSR	100%	98%	95%	90%	80%	70%	60%

20 or 24 1/2 in. barrel threaded for external choke tubes, approx. 6 lbs. 6 oz. Imported 1989-90.

| | $325 | $285 | $260 | $230 | $195 | $160 | $140 | Last MSR was $415. |

This model with 24 1/2 in. barrel is threaded for external multi-chokes which can add up to 6 in. to the barrel length - available for a $17 extra charge.

* ***Model S.D.A.S.S. Special Police*** – similar to Model S.D.A.S.S. except has special heavy 20 in. cylinder bored barrel, VR, cooling jacket, 6 shot mag., rubber recoil pad. Imported 1989-90.

| | $340 | $295 | $265 | $230 | $195 | $160 | $140 | Last MSR was $440. |

* ***Model S.D.A.S.S. Martial*** – 12 ga. only, 18, 20, 28, 30, or 35 1/2 (disc. 1989) in. barrel, fixed sights and choke, approx. 6 1/4 lbs. Imported 1989-90.

| | $330 | $290 | $260 | $225 | $190 | $160 | $140 | Last MSR was $424. |

Add $41 for VR.
Add $20 for 35 1/2 (disc. 1989) in. barrel.
Add $33 for multi-choke (plain rib with 1 choke and wrench).
Add $65 for innerchoke (includes 1 choke and wrench - VR barrel only).

FP6 – 12 ga. only, 3 in. chamber, 20 or 28 (new 2001) in. shrouded barrel (non-ported TriBore system became standard 2000) with vent. heat shield, with or w/o Picatinny rail, with (new 2003) or w/o ghost ring rear sight, camo (new 2001), matte, or carbon fiber (new 2000) finished metal, 100% Mossy Oak camo (mfg. 2001-2003) or black synthetic stock and forearm, pistol grip stock design new 2003, various security configurations, includes locking plastic case, 6 1/2-7 lbs. Imported 1998-2005.

| | $460 | $400 | $365 | $325 | $295 | $265 | $240 |

Subtract $30 for 100% Mossy Oak Break-up camo coverage (disc. 2003).

FABRIQUE NATIONALE

Current manufacturer located in Herstal, near Liege, Belgium. The current company name is "Group Herstal", however, the company is better known by "Fabrique Nationale" or "Fabrique Nationale d'Armes de Guerre". FN entered into their first contract with John M. Browning in 1897 for the manufacture of their first pistol, the FN 1899 Model. Additional contracts were signed and the relationship further blossomed with the manufacture of the A-5 shotgun. FN was acquired by GIAT of France in 1992. In late 1997, the company was purchased by the Walloon government of Belgium. Additional production facilities are located in Portugal, Japan, and the U.S.

Also see: Browning Arms under Rifles, Shotguns, and Pistols, and FNH USA for current offerings in the U.S.

The author would like to express his sincere thanks to Anthony Vanderlinden from the Browning Collector's Association for making FN contributions to this edition.

RIFLES: BOLT ACTION

FN SNIPER RIFLE (MODEL 30) – .308 Win. cal., this model was a Mauser actioned Sniper Rifle equipped with 20 in. extra heavy barrel, flash hider, separate removable diopter sights, Hensoldt 4x scope, hardcase, bipod, and sling. 51 complete factory sets were imported into the U.S., with additional surplus rifles that were privately imported.

| | $4,750 | $4,250 | $4,000 | $3,500 | $3,000 | $2,750 | $2,500 |

Subtract 15% if removable diopter sights or bipod is missing.
Subtract 10% if scope is not marked with F.N. logo.

Values assume complete factory outfit with all accessories.

RIFLES: SEMI-AUTO

MODEL 1949 – 7x57mm Mauser, 7.65mm Mauser, 7.92mm Mauser, or .30-06 cal., (.308 Win. cal. for Argentine conversion rifles), gas operated, 10 shot box mag. (20 round detachable mag. for Argentine conversions), 23 in. barrel, military rifle, tangent rear sight.

Columbia	$1,500	$1,300	$1,150	$1,000	$900	$750	$700
Luxemborg	$1,300	$1,100	$1,000	$900	$800	$650	$600
Venezuela	$1,000	$975	$900	$850	$700	$600	$550
Argentina	N/A	$1,025	$975	$900	$800	$700	$600
Egyptian	$1,450	$1,250	$1,100	$995	$895	$725	$675

Add $100 for detachable grenade launcher.
Subtract 30% for U.S. rebuilt, non-matching rifles with reproduction stocks.

FN-49 contract rifles not listed above are very rare in the U.S. and will demand a premium.

Carefully inspect black paint finish for factory originality, as all FN-49s were factory painted.

Original FN-49 sniper rifles are extremely rare and may add $2,000+. Beware of U.S. assembled "sniper" configurations, and Belgian military "ABL" scopes mounted on other contract rifles and sold as original sniper

MSR	100%	98%	95%	90%	80%	70%	60%

configurations.

RIFLES: SEMI-AUTO, FAL/LAR/CAL/FNC SERIES

After tremendous price increases between 1985-88, Fabrique Nationale decided in 1988 to discontinue this series completely. Not only are these rifles not exported to the U.S. any longer, but all production has ceased in Belgium as well. The only way FN will produce these models again is if they are given a large military contract - in which case a "side order" of commercial guns may be built. 1989 Federal legislation regarding this type of tactical design also helped push up prices to their current level. FAL rifles were also mfg. in Israel by I.M.I.

F.N. FAL – semi-auto, French designation for the F.N. L.A.R. (light automatic rifle), otherwise similar to the L.A.R.

	$4,175	$3,950	$3,750	$3,475	$3,150	$3,100	$2,750

* *F.N. FAL G*

	100%	98%	95%	90%	80%	70%	60%
Standard	$4,800	$4,000	$3,500	$2,950	$2,450	$2,150	$2,000
Paratrooper	$5,200	$4,400	$3,900	$3,350	$2,850	$2,550	$2,400
Heavy Barrel	$6,800	$6,250	$4,950	$4,400	$3,750	$3,250	$2,750
Lightweight	$5,200	$4,250	$3,750	$3,100	$2,600	$2,350	$2,100

Values listed assume inclusion of factory bipod.

The Standard G Series was supplied with a wooden stock and wood or nylon forearm. The Heavy Barrel variant had all wood furniture and was supplied with a bipod. The Lightweight Model had an aluminum lower receiver, piston tube and magazine.

G Series FALs were imported between 1959-1962 by Browning Arms Co. This rifle was declared illegal by the GCA of 1968, and was exempted 5 years later. Total numbers exempted are: Standard - 1,822, Heavy Barrel - 21, and Paratrooper - 5.

F.N. L.A.R. COMPETITION (50.00, LIGHT AUTOMATIC RIFLE) – .308 Win. (7.62x51mm) cal., semi-auto, competition rifle with match flash hider, 21 in. barrel, adj. 4 position fire selector on automatic models, wood stock, aperture rear sight adj. from 100-600 meters, 9.4 lbs. Mfg. 1981-83.

	$4,250	$4,025	$3,850	$3,625	$3,450	$3,175	$2,950

This model was designated by the factory as the 50.00 Model.

Mid-1987 retail on this model was $1,258. The last MSR was $3,179 (this price reflected the last exchange rate and special order status of this model).

* *FN L.A.R. Competition Heavy barrel rifle (50.41 & 50.42)* – barrel is twice as heavy as standard L.A.R., includes wood or synthetic stock, short wood forearm, and bipod, 12.2 lbs. Importation disc. 1988.

	$4,495	$4,275	$4,150	$4,000	$3,675	$3,500	$3,250

Add $500 for walnut stock.
Add $350 for match sights.

There were 2 variations of this model. The Model 50.41 had a synthetic buttstock while the Model 50.42 had a wood buttstock with steel buttplate incorporating a top extension used for either shoulder resting or inverted grenade launching.

Mid-1987 retail on this model was $1,497 (Model 50.41) or $1,654 (Model 50.42). The last MSR was $3,776 (this price reflected the last exchange rate and special order status of this model).

* *FN L.A.R. Competition Paratrooper rifle (50.63 & 50.64)* – similar to L.A.R. model, except has folding stock, 8.3 lbs. Mfg. 1950-88.

	$4,275	$3,700	$3,300	$3,000	$2,550	$2,300	$2,150

There were 2 variations of the Paratrooper L.A.R. Model. The Model 50.63 had a stationary aperture rear sight and 18 in. barrel. The Model 50.64 was supplied with a 21 in. barrel and had a rear sight calibrated for either 150 or 200 meters. Both models retailed for the same price.

Mid-1987 retail on this model was $1,310 (both the Model 50.63 and 50.64). The last MSR was $3,239 (this price reflected the last exchange rate and special order status of this model).

CAL – originally imported in 1980, FN's .223 CAL military rifle succeeded the .308 FAL and preceeded the .223 FNC, at first declared illegal but later given amnesty, only 20 imported by Browning.

	$7,800	$7,000	$6,250	$5,500	$4,750	$4,100	$3,600

FNC MODEL – .223 Rem. (5.56mm) cal., lightweight combat carbine, 18 1/2 in. barrel, NATO approved, 30 shot mag., 8.4 lbs. Disc. 1987.

	$2,950	$2,700	$2,550	$2,100	$1,900	$1,650	$1,500

Add $350 for Paratrooper model (16 or 18 1/2 in. barrel).

MSR	100%	98%	95%	90%	80%	70%	60%

While rarer, the 16 in. barrel model incorporated a flash hider that did not perform as well as the flash hider used on the standard 18 1/2 in. barrel.

Mid-1987 retail on this model was $749 (Standard Model) and $782 (Paratrooper Model). The last MSR was $2,204 (Standard Model) and $2,322 (Paratrooper Model) - these prices reflected the last exchange rate and special order status of these models.

FEATHER INDUSTRIES, INC.
Previous manufacturer located in Boulder, CO until 1995.

RIFLES: SEMI-AUTO

AT-22 – .22 LR cal., semi-auto blowback action, 17 in. detachable shrouded barrel, collapsible metal stock, adj. rear sight, with sling and swivels, 20 shot mag., 3 1/4 lbs. Mfg. 1986-95.

	$325	$275	$250	$240	$230	$220	$215	Last MSR was $250.

F2 – similar to AT-22, except is equipped with a fixed polymer buttstock. Mfg. 1992-95.

	$295	$240	$215	$200	$185	$175	$160	Last MSR was $280.

AT-9 – 9mm Para. cal., semi-auto blowback action, 16 in. barrel, tactical design, available with 10 (C/B 1994), 25*, 32 (disc.), or 100 (disc. 1989) shot mag., 5 lbs. Mfg. 1988-95.

	$850	$775	$700	$650	$600	$550	$500	Last MSR was $500.

Add $250 for 100 shot drum mag.

F9 – similar to AT-9, except is equipped with a fixed polymer buttstock. Mfg. 1992-95.

	$725	$675	$600	$550	$485	$450	$375	Last MSR was $535.

SATURN 30 – 7.62x39mm Kalashnikov cal., semi-auto, gas operated, 19 1/2 in. barrel, composite stock with large thumbhole pistol grip, 5 shot detachable mag., drilled and tapped for scope mounts, adj. rear sight, 8 1/2 lbs. Mfg. in 1990 only.

	$800	$700	$625	$575	$525	$450	$425	Last MSR was $695.

KG-9 – 9mm Para. cal., semi-auto blowback action, 25 or 50 shot mag., tactical configuration. Mfg. 1989 only.

	$850	$775	$700	$650	$600	$550	$500	Last MSR was $560.

Add $100 for 50 shot mag.

SAR-180 – .22 LR cal., semi-auto blowback action, 17 1/2 in. barrel, 165 shot drum mag., fully adj. rear sight, walnut stock with combat style pistol grip and forend, 6 1/4 lbs. Mfg. 1989 only.

	$695	$625	$575	$525	$475	$440	$400	Last MSR was $500.

Add $250 for 165 shot drum mag.
Add $200 for retractable stock.
Add $395 for laser sight.

This variation was also manufactured for a limited time by ILARCO (Illinois Arms Company), previously located in Itasca, IL.

KG-22 – .22 LR cal., similar to KG-9, 20 shot mag. Mfg. 1989 only.

	$395	$350	$300	$275	$255	$245	$235	Last MSR was $300.

FEATHER USA/AWI LLC
Current rifle manufacturer established 1996 and located in Eaton, CO.

RIFLES: SEMI-AUTO

Feather USA currently manufactures the following RAV models: .22 LR, 9mm, .45 ACP, 10mm, .40 S&W, .357 SIG, and .460 Rowland. All models except the .22 LR will accept Glock magazines, and many accessories and options are available. Prices range from $450-$950, not including options. Please contact the company directly for more information, including availability (see Trademark Index).

FEDERAL ENGINEERING CORPORATION
Previous manufacturer located in Chicago, IL.

RIFLES: SEMI-AUTO

XC-220 – .22 LR cal., semi-auto tactical design rifle, 16 5/16 in. barrel, 28 shot mag., machined steel action, 7 1/2 lbs. Mfg. 1984-89.

	$495	$450	$400	$350	$320	$295	$275	

MSR	100%	98%	95%	90%	80%	70%	60%

XC-450 – .45 ACP cal. only, semi-auto tactical design carbine, 16 1/2 in. barrel length, 30 shot mag., fires from closed bolt, machined steel receiver, 8 1/2 lbs. Mfg. 1984-89.

	$950	$825	$750	$675	$600	$550	$500

XC-900 – 9mm Para. cal., semi-auto tactical design carbine, 16 1/2 in. barrel length, 32 shot mag., fires from closed bolt, machined receiver action, 8 lbs. Mfg. 1984-89.

	$950	$825	$750	$675	$600	$550	$500

FEDERAL ORDNANCE, INC.

Previous manufacturer, importer, and distributor located in South El Monte, CA from 1966-1992. Briklee Trading Co. bought the remaining assets of Federal Ordnance, Inc. in late 1992, and continued to import various firearms until circa 1998.

Federal Ordnance imported and distributed both foreign and domestic military handguns and rifles until 1992. In addition, they also fabricated firearms using mostly newer parts.

RIFLES/CARBINES

M-14 SEMI-AUTO – .308 Win. cal., legal for private ownership (no selector), 20 shot mag., refinished original M-14 parts, available in either filled fiberglass, G.I. fiberglass, refinished wood, or new walnut stock. Mfg. 1986-91.

	$1,275	$1,075	$995	$940	$865	$800	$750	Last MSR was $700.

Add $50 for filled fiberglass stock.
Add $110 for refinished wood stock.
Add $190 for new walnut stock with handguard.

During the end of production, Chinese parts were used on this model. Values are the same.

TANKER GARAND SEMI-AUTO – .30-06 or .308 Win. cal., original U.S. GI parts, 18 in. barrel, new hardwood stock, parkerized finish. Mfg. began late 1991.

	$975	$900	$850	$800	$750	$700	$625

CHINESE RPK 86S-7 SEMI-AUTO – 7.62x39mm cal., semi-auto version of the Peoples Republic of China RPK light machine gun, 75 shot drum mag., 23 3/4 in. barrel, with bipod. Imported 1989 only.

	$1,450	$1,275	$1,075	$1,000	$825	$775	$650	Last MSR was $500.

Add $100 for 75 shot drum mag.

57 CENTER

Current rifle manufacturer located in Bellevue, WA.

RIFLES: SEMI-AUTO

AR57A1 PDW CARBINE – 5.7x28mm cal., 16 in. barrel, flash suppressor, black matte finish, ergonomic design custom grip with battery and accessory compartment, 50 shot box magazine runs horizontally over barrel and can be inserted from top or side of weapon, mil spec fire control group, M-4 carbine six position stock with forged aluminum stock tube, front and rear upper Picatinny rails between mag., lower accessory rails, includes four 50 shot mags. New 2010.

MSR $1,099	$975	$850	$725	$665	$535	$440	$340

FIREARMS INTERNATIONAL, INC.

Current manufacturer established in 1998, and located in Houston, TX. Dealer sales.

In September, 2004, a new company called Crusader Group Gun Company, Inc. was formed, and is the corporate parent of Firearms International, Inc., High Standard Manufacturing Co., AMT-Auto Mag, and Arsenal Line Products.
While IAI (Israel Arms International) was originally established to market firearms manufactured by Israel Arms, Ltd. through Firearms International, Inc., IAI defaulted on this agreement without any sales being made.

RIFLES: SEMI-AUTO

M1 CARBINE – .30 Carbine cal., 18 in. barrel, parkerized finish, wood stock, adj. rear sight, 10 shot mag., mfg. in the U.S., and patterned after the WWII design, 5 1/2 lbs. Limited mfg. 2001-2003.

	$500	$425	$375	$335	$300	$275	$250	Last MSR was $575.

P50 RIFLE/CARBINE – .50 BMG cal., designed by Robert Pauza, gas operation, 24 or 29 in. barrel, MOA accuracy at 1,000 yards, includes two 5 shot mags. and hard case, 25 (carbine) or 30 lbs. Limited mfg. 2001-2003.

	$7,500	$6,750	$5,750	$5,000	$4,500	$4,000	$3,500	Last MSR was $7,950.

MSR	100%	98%	95%	90%	80%	70%	60%

FIRESTORM

Current trademark of pistols manufactured by Industria Argentina and Fabrinor, S.A.L. Distributed (master distributor) and imported beginning late 2000 by SGS Imports, International Inc., located in Wanamassa, NJ.

PISTOLS: SEMI-AUTO

Beginning 2004, all Firestorm pistols are available with an integral locking system (ILS).

MINI-FIRESTORM – 9mm Para., .40 S&W, or .45 ACP (new 2002) cal., double action, 3 1/2 in. barrel, nickel, matte or duo-tone finish, 7 (.45 ACP cal.), 10, or 13 (9mm Para. only) shot mag., 3 dot sights, polymer grips, safeties include manual, firing pin, and decocking, 24 1/2 - 27 oz. Approx. 5,000 imported 2001-2009.

$365	$315	$275	$230	$195	$180	$165

Last MSR was $425.

Add $10 for duo-tone finish.
Add $20 for nickel finish.

FORT SOE SIA

Current trademark manufactured by the Science Industrial Association Fort of the Ministry of Internal Affairs of Ukraine, located in Vinnitsa, Ukraine. No current U.S. importation.

The Ministry manufactures a line of good quality semi-auto pistols and semi-auto rifles in various tactical configurations with a wide variety of options. Currently, these guns are not imported into the U.S. Please contact the company directly for more information, including pricing and availability (see Trademark Index).

FORT WORTH FIREARMS

Previous manufacturer located in Fort Worth, TX 1995-2000.

SHOTGUNS: SLIDE ACTION

GL 18 – 12 ga. only, security configuration with 18 in. barrel with perforated shroud, thumb operated laser/xenon light built into end of 7 shot mag. tube, ammo storage. Mfg. 1995-96.

$295	$265	$240	$210	$190	$170	$160

Last MSR was $347.

FRANCHI, LUIGI

Current manufacturer established during 1868, and located in Brescia, Italy. This trademark has been imported for approx. the past 50 years. Currently imported exclusively by Benelli USA, located in Accokeek, MD, since 1998. Previously imported and distributed by American Arms, Inc. located in North Kansas City, MO. Some models were previously imported by FIE firearms located in Hialeah, FL.

Also see Sauer/Franchi heading in the S section.

SHOTGUNS: SEMI-AUTO

MODEL 612 DEFENSE – 12 ga. only, 18 1/2 in. barrel with cyl. bore, matte finish metal with black synthetic stock and forearm, 6 1/2 lbs. Imported 2000-2002.

$525	$450	$375	$325	$285	$265	$245

Last MSR was $635.

This model was previously designated the Variopress 612 Defense.

SPAS-12 – 12 ga., 2 3/4 in. chamber, tactical shotgun, pump or semi-auto operation, 5 (new 1991) or 8 (disc.) shot tube mag., alloy receiver, synthetic stock with built-in pistol grip (limited quantities were also mfg. with a folding stock or metal fixed stock), one-button switch to change operating mode, 21 1/2 in. barrel, 8 3/4 lbs. Importation disc. 1994.

$675	$575	$475	$400	$350	$300	$280

Last MSR was $769.

This model was imported exclusively by FIE Firearms located in Hialeah, FL until 1990.

SPAS-15 – 12 ga. only, 2 3/4 in. chamber, tactical shotgun, pump or semi-auto operation, 6 shot detachable box mag., 21 1/2 in. barrel, lateral folding skeleton stock, carrying handle, one button switch to change operating mode, 10 lbs. Limited importation 1989 only.

This model had very limited importation (less than 200) as the BATF disallowed further importation almost immediately. Even though the retail was in the $700 range, demand and rarity have pushed prices past the $2,000 level.

SAS-12 – 12 ga. only, 3 in. chamber, slide action only, synthetic stock with built-in pistol grip, 8 shot tube mag., 21 1/2 in. barrel, 6.8 lbs. Imported 1988-90 only.

$415	$360	$300	$270	$250	$230	$210

Last MSR was $473.

This model was imported exclusively by FIE Firearms located in Hialeah, FL.

MSR	100%	98%	95%	90%	80%	70%	60%

LAW-12 – 12 ga. only, 2 3/4 in. chamber, gas operated semi-auto, synthetic stock with built-in pistol grip, 5 (new 1991) or 8 (disc.) shot tube mag., 21 1/2 in. barrel, 6 3/4 lbs. Imported 1988-94.

$570 $485 $400 $360 $320 $300 $280   Last MSR was $719.

FULTON ARMORY

Current rifle manufacturer and parts supplier located in Savage, MD. Dealer sales.

RIFLES: SEMI-AUTO

Fulton Armory makes a comprehensive array of the four US Gas Operated Service Rifles: M1 Garand, M1 Carbine, M14 and AR-15-type, including corresponding commercial versions and upper receiver assemblies and related parts and components.

Current rifles include: the UPR (Universal Precision Rifle) - $1,798 MSR, the UBR (Universal Battle Rifle) - $1,100 MSR, Predator Varmint Rifle - $1,100 MSR, National Match - $1,375 MSR, M14 - $2,500 MSR, SOPMOD M14 - $3,370 MSR, Titan UPR - $3,370 MSR, and the Titan UPR - $1,100.

Fulton Armory FAR-15 models included: Legacy, a '60s semi-auto M16 replica - $900 last MSR, Classics, mirroring current military M16A2/A4 and M4 models - $775 last MSR, Guardian Carbines - disc., $1,000-$1,100 last MSR, Liberator and Phantom Tactical Carbines and Enhanced Battle Rifles - $1,000-$1,200 last MSR, Mirage NRA/DCM National Match Rifles - $1400-$1,800 last MSR, Accutron NRA Match Rifles - $1,300-$2,200 last MSR, Hornet Lightweight Rifle - $750 MSR, disc. 2003, and the Millennial Lightweight Rifle and Carbine - $750-$850 MSR, disc. 2002.

Current Fulton Armory M14-type rifles using Fulton Armory's semi-auto M14 receiver include: the M14 Service Rifle - $1,800-$2,000 MSR, M14 Competition Rifle (NRA/CMP Service Rifle Match-Legal) - $2,200-$2,500 MSR, M14 JSSW with Sage Stock/Accuracy System - $2,500-$2,900 MSR, and the M14 Peerless Rifle (NRA/CMP Service Rifle Match-Legal) - $2,600-$3,000 MSR.

Additionally, Fulton Armory manufactures U.S. military and enhanced civilian configurations of the M1 Garand and M1 Carbine, using genuine U.S.G.I. receivers. Models include: the M1 Garand Service Rifle - $1,700 MSR, M1 Garand Carbine - $1,200. M1 Garand Competition Rifle (John C. Garand Match-Legal) - $1,600 last MSR, M1 Garand Peerless Rifle (NRA/CMP Service Rifle Match-Legal) - $2,000 last MSR.

Please contact the factory directly for more information, including current availability and pricing (see Trademark Index).

NOTES

G SECTION

GALIL

Current trademark manufactured by Israel Weapon Industries Ltd. (IWI), formerly Israel Military Industries (IMI). No current consumer importation. Recent Galil semi-auto sporterized rifles and variations with thumbhole stocks were banned in April, 1998. Beginning late 1996, Galil rifles and pistols were available in selective fire mode only (law enforcement, military only) and are currently imported by UZI America, Inc., a subsidiary of O.F. Mossberg & Sons, Inc. Previously imported by Action Arms, Ltd. located in Philadelphia, PA until 1994. Previously imported by Springfield Armory located in Geneseo, IL and Magnum Research, Inc., located in Minneapolis, MN.

Magnum Research importation can be denoted by a serial number prefix "MR", while Action Arms imported rifles have either "AA" or "AAL" prefixes.

MSR	100%	98%	95%	90%	80%	70%	60%

RIFLES: SEMI-AUTO

Models 329, 330 (Hadar II), 331, 332, 339 (sniper system with 6x40 mounted Nimrod scope), 361, 372, 386, and 392 all refer to various configurations of the Galil rifle.

MODEL AR – .223 Rem. cal. or .308 Win. cal., semi-auto tactical design rifle, gas operated - rotating bolt, 16.1 in. (.223 Rem. cal. only) or 19 in. (.308 Win. cal. only) barrel, parkerized, folding stock. Flip-up Tritium night sights. 8.6 lbs.

| | $3,150 | $2,650 | $2,475 | $2,150 | $1,925 | $1,750 | $1,625 | Last MSR was $950. |

Add $500 for .308 Win. cal.

MODEL ARM – similar to Model AR, except includes folding bipod, vented hardwood handguard, and carrying handle.

| | $3,450 | $3,100 | $2,850 | $2,600 | $2,300 | $2,100 | $1,900 | Last MSR was $1,050. |

Add $500 for .308 Win. cal.

GALIL SPORTER – similar to above, except has one-piece thumbhole stock, 4 (.308 Win.) or 5 (.223 Rem.) shot mag., choice of wood (disc.) or polymer hand guard, 8 1/2 lbs. Imported 1991-93.

| | $1,650 | $1,525 | $1,375 | $1,200 | $1,100 | $1,000 | $950 | Last MSR was $950. |

Add $400 for .308 Win. cal.

HADAR II – .308 cal., gas operated, tactical type configuration, 1 piece walnut thumbhole stock with pistol grip and forearm, 18 1/2 in. barrel, adj. rear sight, recoil pad, 4 shot (standard) or 25 shot mag., 10.3 lbs. Imported 1989 only.

| | $1,575 | $1,375 | $1,275 | $1,050 | $950 | $825 | $750 | Last MSR was $998. |

SNIPER OUTFIT – .308 Win. cal., semi-auto, limited production, sniper model built to exact I.D.F. specifications for improved accuracy, 20 in. heavy barrel, hardwood folding stock (adj. recoil pad and adj. cheekpiece) and forearm, includes Tritium night sights, bipod, detachable 6x40mm Nimrod scope, two 25 shot mags., carrying/storage case, 14.1 lbs. Imported 1989 only.

| | $6,500 | $5,750 | $5,000 | $4,350 | $3,750 | $3,250 | $2,850 | Last MSR was $3,995. |

GAMBA, RENATO

Current trademark established in 1748, and located in Gardone V.T., Italy. Gamba firearms are currently manufactured by Bre-Mec srl beginning 2007, and imported in limited quantities beginning 2005 by Renato Gamba U.S.A., located in Walnut, CA. The U.S. service center is located in Bernardsville, NJ. Gamba of America, a subsidiary of Firing Line, located in Aurora, CO, was the exclusive importer and distributor for Renato Gamba long guns from 1996-2000. Pistols were previously imported and distributed (until 1990) by Armscorp of America, Inc. located in Baltimore, MD. Shotguns were previously (until 1992) imported by Heckler & Koch, Inc. located in Sterling, VA.

Filli Gamba (Gamba Brothers) was founded in 1946. G. Gamba sold his tooling to his brother, Renato, in 1967 when Renato Gamba left his brothers and S.A.B. was formed. Filli Gamba closed in 1989 and the Zanotti firm was also purchased the same year.

Renato Gamba firearms have had limited importation since 1986. In 1989, several smaller European firearms companies were purchased by R. Gamba and are now part of the Renato Gamba Group - they include Gambarmi and Stefano Zanotti. The importation of R. Gamba guns changed in 1990 to reflect their long term interest in exporting firearms to America. Earlier imported models may be rare but have not enjoyed much collectibility to date.

SHOTGUNS: SLIDE ACTION

MODEL 2100 – 12 ga., 3 in. chamber, 19 1/2 in. barrel, 7 shot mag., law enforcement configuration with matte black metal and wood, 6.62 lbs. Limited importation.

| | $325 | $250 | $225 | $200 | $180 | $160 | $145 | Last MSR was $715. |

MSR	100%	98%	95%	90%	80%	70%	60%

GERMAN SPORT GUNS GmbH

Current firearms and air soft manufacturer and distributor located in Ense-Höingen, Germany. Currently imported by American Tactical Imports, located in Rochester, NY.

CARBINES: SEMI-AUTO

GSG-5 – .22 LR cal., semi-auto design patterned after the H&K MP-5 with forward bolt assist, 16.3 in. barrel with choice of flash hider or faux elongated suppressor, open sights, 10 or 22 shot detachable mag., rail system, black finish, fixed stock with pistol grip, 6.2-6.6 lbs. New 2002, importation began 2008.

MSR $550	$525	$475	$425	$375	$350	$325	$300

KALASHNIKOV – .22 LR cal., patterned after the Kalashnikov action, recoil operated, 10, 15, or 22 shot mag., 16 1/2 in. barrel with protected front sight, available with black synthetic or hardwood pistol grip stock. New 2009.

MSR $550	$525	$475	$425	$375	$350	$325	$300

PISTOLS: SEMI-AUTO

GSG-5P – .22 LR cal., 10 or 22 shot mag., 9 in. barrel with flash suppressor, black finish, patterned after the MP-5 pistol, adj. diopter rear sight with optional Picatinny rail, top lever charging, 5.89 lbs. New 2009.

MSR $500	$450	$400	$365	$335	$300	$275	$250

GSG-5PK – .22 LR cal., 10 or 22 shot mag., 4 5/8 in. barrel flush with top of frame, forward mounted charging lever, operating mechanism similar to GSG-5P, 5.2 lbs. New 2009.

MSR $550	$525	$475	$425	$375	$350	$325	$300

GSG 1911 – .22 LR cal., patterned after the M1911, 5 in. barrel, front and rear slide serrations, checkered diamond walnut grips, skeletonized trigger and hammer, 10 shot mag. New 2009.

MSR $360	$325	$295	$275	$250	$225	$200	$185

GIBBS GUNS, INC.

Previously manufactured by Volunteer Enterprises in Knoxville, TN and previously distributed by Gibbs Guns, Inc. located in Greenback, TN.

CARBINES

MARK 45 CARBINE – .45 ACP cal. only, based on M6 Thompson machine gun, 16 1/2 in. barrel, 5, 15, 30, or 90 shot mag. U.S. mfg. Disc. 1988.

	$750	$625	$525	$450	$375	$330	$300	Last MSR was $279.

Add $200 for 90 shot mag.
Add 10% for nickel plating.

GIBBS RIFLE COMPANY, INC.

Current manufacturer, importer, and distributor located in Martinsburg, WV. Gibbs manufactured rifles with the Gibbs trademark in Martinsburg, WV 1991-1994, in addition to importing Mauser-Werke firearms until 1995. Dealer and distributor sales.

In the past, Gibbs Rifle Company, Inc. imported a variety of older firearms, including British military rifles and handguns (both original and refurbished condition), a good selection of used military contract pistols and rifles, in addition to other shooting products and accessories, including a bipod patterned after the Parker-Hale M-85.

Gibbs Rifle Company, Inc. imported and manufactured military collectibles, historical remakes, and special sporting rifles. All rifles were carefully inspected, commercially cleaned and boxed to ensure their quality, and all had a limited lifetime warranty. Gibbs Rifle Company, Inc. also offered membership in the Gibbs Military Collectors Club, an organization dedicated to military firearms collectors.

RIFLES: BOLT ACTION

ENFIELD NO. 5 JUNGLE CARBINE – .303 British cal., older No. 4 Enfield barreled action with newly manufactured stock, bayonet lug and flash hider have been added, 20 in. barrel, 7 3/4 lbs. Imported 1999-2004, reintroduced 2010 with camo synthetic stock.

	$700	$650	$575	$525	$450	$375	$295

A bayonet and scabbard are also available for this model - please contact the company for pricing.

ENFIELD NO. 7 JUNGLE CARBINE – .308 Win. cal., older 2A action with reconfigured original wood, flash hider and bayonet lug have been added, 20 in. barrel, 8 lbs. Imported 1999-2004.

	$275	$225	$175	$155	$125	$115	$105	Last MSR was $200.

MSR	100%	98%	95%	90%	80%	70%	60%

QUEST EXTREME CARBINE – .303 British cal., updated No. 5 Enfield action with 20 in. barrel with compensator and flash hider, electroless nickel metal finish, new buttstock with survival kit packaged in butt trap, 7 3/4 lbs. Imported 2000-2004.

	$295	$265	$225	$185	$170	$160	$150	Last MSR was $250.

QUEST II – .308 Win. cal., modern 2A Enfield barreled action, mfg. from chrome vanadium steel, 20 in. barrel with compensator/flash-hider and adj. rear sight, front sight protector, pre-fitted see-through scope mount accepts all Weaver based optics and accessories, electroless nickel finish, hardwood stock with survial kit included, 12 shot mag., 8 lbs. Imported 2001-2004.

	$375	$325	$265	$235	$200	$185	$170	Last MSR was $280.

QUEST III – .308 Win. cal., similar to Quest II, except has black syntetic stock, w/o survival kit. Imported 2002-2004.

	$395	$345	$280	$240	$200	$185	$170	Last MSR was $300.

MODEL 85 SNIPER RIFLE – .308 Win. cal., bolt action, 24 in. heavy barrel, 10 shot mag., camo green synthetic McMillan stock with stippling, built in adj. bipod and recoil pad, enlarged contoured bolt, adj. sights, 12 lbs. 6 oz.

	$1,825	$1,450	$1,275	$1,050	$875	$750	$625	Last MSR was $2,050.

M1903A4 SPRINGFIELD SNIPER MODEL – .30-06 cal., replica of original M1903 Springfield, drilled and tapped, Redfield rings, new C stock, barrel marked with modern dates of mfg., includes U.S. issue leather sling and OD Green canvas carrying case. New 2009.

MSR $995	$895	$795	$695	$595	$495	$425	$375	

GIRSAN MACHINE & LIGHT WEAPON INDUSTRY COMPANY

Current handgun manufacturer located in Giresun, Turkey. No current U.S. importation.

Girsan manufactures a complete line of good quality semi-auto pistols in a variety of configurations, calibers, frame sizes, and finishes. Many options are available. Please contact the company directly for more information, including U.S. availability and pricing (see Trademark Index).

GLOCK

Currently manufactured by Glock GmbH in Austria beginning 1983. Glock also opened a production facility for manufacturing its polymer frames in Smyrna, GA during late 2004. Exclusively imported and distributed by Glock, Inc., located in Smyrna, GA. Distributor and dealer sales.

All Glock pistols have a "safe action" operating system (double action only) which includes trigger safety, firing pin safety, and drop safety. Glock pistols have only 35 parts for reliability and simplicity of operation.

PISTOLS: SEMI-AUTO

During 2010, Glock introduced its new 4th Generation of Glocks (Gen4). This enables standard frame Glock pistols to adopt the new short frame technology, which can be almost instantly fitted to any hand size. Features include a rough textured surface finish (RTF), multiple backstrap system (two extra inserts), reversible mag. catch, and long life dual recoil spring assembly.

  Add $18 for adj. rear sight, $22 for steel sight (new 2004), or $47 for Glock night sight (new 2004).
  Add $80 for fixed Meprolight sight or $105 for fixed Trijicon sight (disc. 2003-2004, depending on model.)
  Add $25 for internal locking system (ILS) on most currently manufactured models listed below (new 2004).
  Add $95 for tactical light or $284 for tactical light with laser for most currently manufactured pistols listed below.

MODEL 17/17C SPORT/SERVICE – 9mm Para. cal., double action, polymer frame, mag., trigger and other pistol parts, 4.49 in. steel hexagonal rifled barrel with (Model 17C, new 1999) or w/o ports, steel slide and springs, 10 (C/B 1994), 17* (reintroduced late 2004), or 19* (reintroduced late 2004) shot mag., adj. (Sport Model) or fixed (Service Model) rear sight, includes lockable pistol box, cable lock, cleaning rod, and other accessories, extra mag. and spare rear sight, 24.75 oz. Importation began late 1985.

MSR $599	$475	$425	$395	$365	$335	$295	$250	

  Add $22 for Model 17C with fixed (new 2004) or adj. (disc. 2003) rear sight.
  Add $119 for competition model w/ adj. sights (Model 17CC, mfg. 2000-2003).

* **Model 17L Sport/Service Competition Model** – 9mm Para. cal., competition version of the Model 17, includes internally compensated 6.02 in. barrel, recalibrated trigger pull (3 1/2 lb. pull), adj. rear sight, 26.3 oz. Mfg. 1988-1999.

	$650	$545	$425	$360	$315	$260	$225	Last MSR was $795.

  Add $28 for adj. sight.

Early models with barrel ports matched to relieved slide will command a small premium.

MSR	100%	98%	95%	90%	80%	70%	60%

* ***Model 17 Sport/Service Glock Desert Storm Commemorative*** – 9mm Para. cal., features coalition forces listing on top of barrel, inscription on side of slide "NEW WORLD ORDER". 1,000 mfg. in 1991 only.

	100%	98%	95%	90%	80%	70%	60%	
	$995	$825	$600	N/A	N/A	N/A	N/A	Last MSR was $795.

MODEL 19/19C COMPACT SPORT/SERVICE – 9mm Para. cal., similar to Model 17, except has scaled down dimensions with 4.02 in. ported (Model 19C, new 1999) or unported barrel and serrated grip straps, 10 (C/B 1994), 15* (reintroduced late 2004), or 17* (reintroduced late 2004) shot mag., fixed (Service Model) or adj. (Sport Model) rear sight, 23 1/2 oz. New 1988.

MSR $599	$475	$425	$395	$365	$335	$295	$250

Add $22 for Model 19C with fixed (new 2004) or adj. (disc. 2003) rear sight.
Add $119 for competition model w/ adj. sights (Model 19CC, mfg. 2000-2003).

During 1996, AcuSport Corp. commissioned Glock to make a special production run of matching 9mm Para. cal. sets. Each set consists of a Model 19 and 26 with serialization as follows: Model 19 (ser. range AAA0000-AAA0499) and Model 26 (ser. range AAB0000-AAB0499).

MODEL 20/20C SPORT/SERVICE – 10mm Norma cal., similar action to Model 17, features 4.6 in. ported (Model 20C, new 1999) or unported barrel, 10 (C/B 1994) or 15* (reintroduced late 2004) shot mag., larger slide and receiver, fixed (Service Model) or adj. (Sport Model) rear sight, 30 oz. New 1990.

MSR $637	$500	$440	$410	$375	$350	$325	$295

Add $39 for compensated barrel (Model 20C).
Add $145 for competition model w/ adj. sights (Model 20CC, mfg. 2000-2003).

MODEL 21/21C SPORT/SERVICE – .45 ACP cal., similar to Model 20, except has octagonal profile and rifling, 10 (C/B 1994) or 13* (reintroduced late 2004) shot mag., 29 oz. Introduced May 1991.

MSR $637	$500	$440	$410	$375	$350	$325	$295

Add $39 for compensated barrel (Model 21C).
Add $145 for competition model w/ adj. sights (Model 21CC, mfg. 2000-2003).

MODEL 22/22C SPORT/SERVICE – .40 S&W cal., similar to Model 17, except has locking block pin above trigger guard, 4.49 in. barrel, 10 (C/B 1994) or 15* (reintroduced late 2004) shot mag., 25.5 oz. New 1990.

MSR $599	$475	$425	$395	$365	$335	$295	$250

Add $34 for Model 22C with adj. (disc. 2003) or fixed (new 2004) rear sight.
Add $22 for compensated barrel (Model 22C).
Add $119 for competition model w/ adj. sights (Model 22CC, mfg. 2000-2004).

200 Model 22s were originally shipped with serial numbers beginning with "NY-1." Somehow, they probably were erroneously numbered at the factory (probably thinking that they somehow were part of the New York State Troopers shipment of Model 17s) during 1990. Premiums will occur on this variation.

MODEL 23/23C COMPACT SPORT/SERVICE – .40 S&W cal., compact variation of the Model 22 with 4.02 in. ported (Model 23C, new 1999) or unported barrel and 10 (C/B 1994) or 13* (reintroduced 2004) shot mag., 23 1/2 oz. New 1990.

MSR $599	$475	$425	$395	$365	$335	$295	$250

Add $22 for compensated barrel (Model 23C).
Add $145 for competition model w/ adj. sights (Model 23CC, mfg. 2000-2003).

During 1996, AcuSport Corp. commissioned Glock to make a special production run of matching .40 S&W cal. sets. Each set consists of a Model 23 and 27 with serialization as follows: Model 23 (ser. range AAC0000-AAC1499) and Model 27 (ser. range AAD0000-AAD1499).

MODEL 24/24C – .40 S&W cal., similar to Model 17L Competition, choice of standard or ported (Model 24C) barrel and fixed or adj. rear sight. Mfg. 1994-99.

	$665	$525	$415	$350	$300	$250	$225	Last MSR was $795.

Add $40 for compensated barrel.
Add $28 for adj. rear sight.

MODEL 25 – .380 ACP cal., similar to Model 19 with 4.02 in. barrel, 10 shot mag., 22.5 oz. New 1995.

This model is available for law enforcement only.

MODEL 26 – 9mm Para. cal., sub-compact variation of the Model 19, except has shortened grip, 3 1/2 in. barrel, 10 shot mag., 21 3/4 oz. New 1995.

MSR $599	$475	$425	$395	$365	$335	$295	$250

MODEL 27 – .40 S&W cal., sub-compact variation of the Model 23, except has shortened grip, 3 1/2 in. barrel, 9 shot mag., 21 3/4 oz. New 1995.

MSR $599	$475	$425	$395	$365	$335	$295	$250

MSR	100%	98%	95%	90%	80%	70%	60%

MODEL 28 – .380 ACP cal., similar to Model 26/27/33, except has scaled down dimensions with 3.46 in. barrel, approx. 20 oz. New 1999.

This model is available for law enforcement only.

MODEL 29 – 10mm Norma cal., sub-compact model featuring 3.78 in. barrel, 10 shot mag., 27 oz. New 1997.

MSR $637	$500	$440	$410	$375	$350	$325	$295

MODEL 30 – .45 ACP cal., compact Model 21, 3 3/4 in. barrel, 10 shot mag., features octagonal profile rifling, and extension on mag., 26 1/2 oz. New 1997.

MSR $637	$500	$440	$410	$375	$350	$325	$295

MODEL 31/31C – .357 SIG cal., similar to Model 17, 4.49 in. ported (Model 31C, new 1999) or unported barrel, fixed sights, 10 shot mag., 26 oz. New 1998.

MSR $599	$475	$425	$395	$365	$335	$295	$250

Add $22 for compensated barrel (Model 31C).
Add $119 for competition model w/ adj. sights (Model 31CC, mfg. 2000-2004).

MODEL 32/32C – .357 SIG cal., similar to Model 19, 4.02 in. ported (Model 32C) or unported barrel, 24 oz. New 1998.

MSR $599	$475	$425	$395	$365	$335	$295	$250

Add $22 for compensated barrel (Model 32C).
Add $119 for competition model w/adj. sights (Model 32CC, mfg. 2002-2004).

MODEL 33 – .357 SIG cal., compact variation of Models 31 & 32, features 3 1/2 in. barrel with shortened frame and magazine housing, 10 shot mag., 22 oz. New 1998.

MSR $599	$475	$425	$395	$365	$335	$295	$250

MODEL 34 – 9mm Para. cal., similar construction to Model 17, except has 5.32 in. barrel, extended slide stop lever and magazine catch, fixed sights, target grips with finger grooves, thumbrest, receiver has rails for mounting accessories, 10 shot mag., 25.75 oz. New 1998.

MSR $679	$525	$450	$375	$325	$295	$260	$225

MODEL 35 – .40 S&W cal., 27.5 oz., otherwise similar to Model 34. New 1998.

MSR $679	$525	$450	$375	$325	$295	$260	$225

MODEL 36 – .45 ACP cal., similar to Model 30, except has single column 6 shot mag., 22 1/2 oz. New 1999.

MSR $637	$500	$440	$410	$375	$350	$325	$295

MODEL 37 – .45 G.A.P. (Glock Automatic Pistol) cal., 4.6 in. barrel, similar to Model 21, except has extended slide stop lever, wider and heavier slide, improved locking block and ejector, 10 shot double column mag., 26 oz. New 2003.

MSR $614	$535	$450	$375	$325	$295	$260	$225

MODEL 38 – .45 G.A.P. cal., similar to Model 37, 3.46 in. barrel, double action, compact design, 8 shot double column mag., 19.33 oz.

MSR $614	$535	$450	$375	$325	$295	$260	$225

MODEL 39 – .45 G.A.P. cal., 6 shot single column mag., 3.46 in. barrel, subcompact design, 19.33 oz.

MSR $614	$535	$450	$375	$325	$295	$260	$225

GONCZ ARMAMENT, INC.

Previous manufacturer located in North Hollywood, CA circa 1984-1990.

While advertised, BATF records indicate very few Goncz pistols or carbines were actually produced. All of these guns were prototypes or individually hand-built and none were ever mass produced through normal fabrication techniques.

In 1990, Claridge Hi-Tec, Inc. purchased Goncz Armament, Inc.

GRENDEL, INC.

Previous manufacturer located in Rockledge, FL, circa 1990-1995.

PISTOLS: SEMI-AUTO

MODEL P-31 – .22 Mag. cal., same action as P-30, except has 11 in. barrel, enclosed synthetic barrel shroud and flash hider, 48 oz. Mfg. 1990-95.

	$450	$400	$365	$325	$290	$265	$235	Last MSR was $345.

MSR	100%	98%	95%	90%	80%	70%	60%

RIFLES & CARBINES

MODEL R-31 – similar design to Model P-31, except has 16 in. barrel and telescoping stock, 64 oz. Mfg. 1991-95.

	100%	98%	95%	90%	80%	70%	60%	
	$465	$425	$375	$335	$310	$285	$265	Last MSR was $385.

SRT-20F COMPACT – .243 Win. or .308 Win. cal., bolt action based on the Sako A-2 action, 20 in. match grade finned barrel with muzzle brake, folding synthetic stock, integrated bipod rest, no sights, 9 shot mag., 6.7 lbs. Disc. 1989.

	100%	98%	95%	90%	80%	70%	60%	
	$775	$725	$675	$595	$565	$540	$520	Last MSR was $525.

Grendel previously manufactured the SRT-16F, SRT-20L, and SRT-24 - all were disc. 1988. Values are approx. the same as the SRT-20F.

GUN ROOM CO., LLC

Current rifle manufacturer located in Belgrade, MT.

RIFLES

Gun Room manufactures a complete line of long range precision rifles in .338 Lapua to .50 BMG cal. A wide variety of options, configurations, and accessories are available. Please contact the company directly for more information (see Trademark Index).

GUNCRAFTER INDUSTRIES

Current pistol manufacturer located in Huntsville, AR.

PISTOLS: SEMI-AUTO

MODEL NO. 1 – .45 ACP or .50 GI cal., 1911 style, 7 shot mag., 5 in. heavy match grade barrel, parkerized or hard chrome finish, front strap checkering, Heinie Slant Pro tritium sights, Aluma checkered grips, includes two mags. and cordura case, 41.3 oz.

MSR $2,895	100%	98%	95%	90%	80%	70%	60%
	$2,700	$2,300	$2,000	$1,775	$1,575	$1,350	$1,075

MODEL NO. 2 – .45 ACP or .50 GI cal., 1911 style, 7 shot mag., 5 in. heavy match grade barrel, full profile slide with dust cover frame, integral light rail, parkerized or hard chrome finish, front strap checkering, Heinie Slant Pro tritium sights, Aluma checkered grips, includes two mags. and cordura case, 45.9 oz.

MSR $2,895	100%	98%	95%	90%	80%	70%	60%
	$2,700	$2,300	$2,000	$1,775	$1,575	$1,350	$1,075

H SECTION

H-S PRECISION, INC.

Current custom pistol and rifle manufacturer established 1990 and located in Rapid City, SD. H-S Precision, Inc. also manufactures synthetic stocks and custom machine barrels as well. Dealer and consumer direct sales.

H-S Precision introduced the aluminum bedding block for rifle stocks in 1981, and has been making advanced composite synthetic stocks and custom ballistic test barrels for more than two decades.

In addition to the following models, H-S Precision, Inc. also built rifles using a customer's action (mostly Remington 700 or Winchester Post-'64 Model 70). 2004 MSRs ranged from $1,520-$1,830.

MSR	100%	98%	95%	90%	80%	70%	60%

RIFLES: BOLT ACTION, PRO-SERIES 2000

All H-S Precision rifles feature Kevlar/graphite laminate stocks, cut rifle barrels, and other high tech innovations including a molded aluminum bedding block system. Beginning in 1999, H-S Precision began utilizing their H-S 2000 action, and model nomenclature was changed to begin with Pro-Series 2000.

Add approx. $250 for left-hand action.

PRO-SERIES 2000 LONG RANGE (HEAVY TACTICAL MARKSMAN, HTR) – various cals., stainless fluted barrel standard, Remington BDL (disc. 1999) or Pro-Series 2000 (new 2000) action. New 1990.

MSR $3,070	$2,825	$2,375	$1,925	$1,600	$1,300	$1,100	$950

Add $100 for extended barrel port (Model HTR EP, disc.).

PRO-SERIES 2000 SHORT TACTICAL (STR) – .308 Win. cal., 20 in. fluted barrel, matte Teflon finished action and barrel, 20 in. fluted barrel with standard porting, Pro Series Tactical stock. New 2004.

MSR $3,040	$2,800	$2,375	$1,925	$1,600	$1,300	$1,100	$950

PRO-SERIES 2000 TAKEDOWN TACTICAL LONG RANGE (TTD) – various short and long action cals., stainless steel barrel, Remington BDL takedown action, matte blue finish. Mfg. 1990-2005, reintroduced 2008.

MSR $5,000	$4,650	$4,200	$3,750	$3,250	$2,750	$2,250	$1,650

Add $100 for extended barrel port (Model TTD EP, disc.).
Add $2,500 - $3,000 for extra take-down barrel, depending on cartridge case head size.

PRO SERIES 2000 RAPID DEPLOYMENT RIFLE (RDR) – .308 Win. cal., Pro-Series 2000 stainless steel short action only, 20 in. fluted barrel, black synthetic stock with or w/o thumbhole, black teflon metal finish, approx. 7 1/2 lbs. New 2000.

MSR $2,910	$2,695	$2,300	$1,900	$1,600	$1,300	$1,100	$950

Add $125 for PST60A Long Range stock (disc.).
Add $160 for RDT model (new 2006).

TAKEDOWN LONG RANGE (TACTICAL MARKSMAN) – .223 Rem., .243 Win., .30-06, .308 Win., 7mm Rem. Mag., .300 Win. Mag., or .338 Win. Mag. cal., includes "kwik klip" and stainless fluted barrel. Mfg. 1990-97.

	$2,895	$2,225	$1,675	$1,350	$995	$850	$750	Last MSR was $2,895.

A complete rifle package consisting of 2 calibers (.308 Win. and .300 Win. Mag.), scope and fitted case was available for $5,200 retail.

HAKIM

Trademark of rifle adopted by the Egyptian army during the early 1950s.

RIFLES: SEMI-AUTO

HAKIM – 7.92x57mm or 8x57mm cal., gas operated, 25.1 in. barrel with muzzle brake, cocking the bolt is done by sliding the top cover forword, then pulling it back, manual safety is located in rear of receiver, 10 shot detachable box mag., can also be reloaded using stripper clips, adj. rear sight, hardwood stock, 9.7 lbs. Approx. 70,000 mfg. circa 1950s-1960s, with Swedish machinery.

	$495	$450	$400	$360	$320	$285	$245

A scaled down variation of the Hakim rifle was manufactured later, and called the Rasheed - it was produced in small numbers.

HALO ARMS, LLC

Current rifle manufacturer established in 2003, and located in Phoenixville, PA. Dealer and consumer direct sales.

Halo Arms also manufactures custom alloy stocks.

RIFLES

Halo Arms, LLC manufactures good quality AR-15 style rifles in military, law enforcement, and civilian configurations.

MSR	100%	98%	95%	90%	80%	70%	60%

HA 50 FTR SINGLE SHOT – .50 BMG cal., 22 in. chromemoly barrel, special order only, matte black fnish or optional colors, muzzlebrake, vertical aluminum front grip, bipod, Picatinny rail, flip up front sights, rear iron sights, standard AR trigger, unique bottom load/eject operation.

MSR $4,350	$4,100	$3,850	$3,500	$3,150	$2,700	$2,400	$2,000

Add $300 for deployment package, which includes Storm hard case, cleaning rods, and ammo pouch.

HA 50 LRR SINGLE SHOT – .50 BMG cal., long range rifle. Disc. 2008.

$4,200	$3,900	$3,500	$3,150	$2,700	$2,400	$2,000	Last MSR was $4,500.

HA 308 FTR BOLT ACTION – .308 Win. cal., field tactical rifle, 24 in. heavy contour chromemoly barrel, 5 shot internal mag. with screw removable floorplate, three position safety, matte black finish or optional colors, Picatinny rail, right hand bolt and ejection port, full length vented free float tube with rail attachment points, hand tuned trigger, 11 1/2 lbs. Disc. 2009.

$1,295	$1,100	$925	$800	$675	$575	$475	Last MSR was $1,375.

HARRINGTON & RICHARDSON, INC.

Previous manufacturer located in Gardner, MA - formerly from Worcester, MA. Successors to Wesson & Harrington, manufactured from 1871 until January 24, 1986. H & R 1871, LLC was formed during 1991 (an entirely different company, see listing in the front of this section). H & R 1871, LLC is not responsible for the warranties or safety of older pre-1986 H & R firearms.

A manufacturer of utilitarian firearms for over 115 years, H & R ceased operation on January 24, 1986. Even though new manufacture (under H & R 1871, LLC) is utilizing the H & R trademark, the discontinuance of older models in either NIB or mint condition may command slight asking premiums, but probably will not affect values on those handguns only recently discontinued. Most H & R firearms are still purchased for their shooting value rather than collecting potential.

Please refer to H & R listing in the Serialization section for alphabetical suffix information on how to determine year of manufacture for most H & R firearms between 1940-1982.

The author would like to thank Mr. W.E. "Bill" Goforth and Mr. Jim Hauff for providing pricing and information on many of the H&R models.

RIFLES

MODEL M-4 SURVIVAL – .22 Hornet cal., 5 shot mag., 14 or 16 in. barrel, wire folding stock, mfg. for U.S. military during the 1950s.

$2,000	$1,650	$1,425	$1,125	$965	$855	$750

Add $400 for barrels less than 16 in. (sales restricted).

This model was packaged in survival kits for U.S. pilots, and is usually encounted with a replacement barrel of 16 inches or more.

MODEL M-1 GARAND – .30-06 cal., semi-auto, 8 shot internal mag., some may be arsenal refinished, mfg. for the U.S. military during the 1950s.

$1,650	$1,495	$1,250	$1,050	$875	$750	$625

Subtract 60% if w/o correct parts.

MODEL T-48 FAL/T223 (H&R MFG. FAL) – .308 Win. cal., 20 shot mag., selective fire, approx. 200 mfg. for U.S. military during the 1960s.

Since sales of this rifle are restricted, it is not often encountered in the used marketplace. Recent values are approx. $10,000 for 98% condition.

M-14 RIFLE/GUERILLA GUN – .308 Win. cal., selective fire, 20 shot mag., Guerilla gun mfg. in prototype only, mfg. for the U.S. military during the 1960s.

Since sales of this rifle are restricted, it is not often encountered in the used marketplace. Recent values are approx. $20,000 for 98% condition.

M-16 AUTOMATIC BATTLE RIFLE – 5.56 Nato cal., selective fire, 20 or 30 shot mag., mfg. for the U.S. military during the 1960s-1970s.

Since sales of this rifle are restricted, it is not often encountered in the used marketplace. Recent values are approx. $15,000 for 98% condition.

T-223 (H&R MFG. H&K 93) – .223 Rem. or .308 Win. cal., selective fire, 20 shot mag., approx. 200 mfg. for the U.S. military during the 1960s.

Since sales of this rifle are restricted, it is not often encountered in the used marketplace. Recent values are approx. $15,000 for 98% condition.

HARRIS GUNWORKS

Previous firearms manufacturer located in Phoenix, AZ 1995-March 31, 2000. Previously named Harris-McMillan

MSR	100%	98%	95%	90%	80%	70%	60%

Gunworks and G. McMillan and Co., Inc. (please refer to the M section for more information on these two trademarks).

RIFLES: BOLT ACTION

M-40 SNIPER RIFLE – .308 Win. cal., Remington action with McMillan match grade heavy contour barrel, fiberglass stock with recoil pad, 4 shot mag., 9 lbs. Mfg. 1990-2000.

	$1,825	$1,450	$1,125	$925	$800	$700	$600	Last MSR was $2,000.

M-86 SNIPER RIFLE – .300 Phoenix (disc. 1996), .30-06 (new 1989), .300 Win. Mag., or .308 Win. cal., fiberglass stock, variety of optical sights. Mfg. 1988-2000.

	$2,450	$2,000	$1,675	$1,325	$1,000	$895	$800	Last MSR was $2,700.

Add $300 for .300 Phoenix cal. with Harris action (disc. 1996).
Add $200 for takedown feature (mfg. 1993-96).

M-87 LONG RANGE SNIPER RIFLE – .50 BMG cal., stainless steel bolt action, 29 in. barrel with muzzle brake, single shot, camo synthetic stock, accurate to 1500 meters, 21 lbs. Mfg. 1988-2000.

	$3,450	$2,800	$2,375	$2,000	$1,850	$1,700	$1,575	Last MSR was $3,885.

* ***M-87R Long Range Sniper Rifle*** – similiar specs. as Model 87, except has 5 shot fixed box mag. Mfg. 1990-2000.

	$3,725	$2,950	$2,550	$2,200	$2,000	$1,850	$1,700	Last MSR was $4,000.

M-88 U.S. NAVY – .50 BMG cal., reintroduced U.S. Navy Seal Team shell holder single shot action with thumbhole stock (one-piece or breakdown two-piece), 24 lbs. Mfg. 1997-2000.

	$3,250	$2,600	$2,200	$1,625	$1,250	$1,125	$900	Last MSR was $3,600.

Add $300 for two-piece breakdown stock.

M-89 SNIPER RIFLE – .308 Win. cal., 28 in. barrel with suppressor (also available without), fiberglass stock adj. for length, and recoil pad, 15 1/4 lbs. Mfg. 1990-2000.

	$2,875	$2,525	$2,250	$1,875	$1,650	$1,325	$1,100	Last MSR was $3,200.

Add $425 for muzzle suppressor (disc. 1996).

M-92 BULL PUP – .50 BMG cal., bullpup configuration with shorter barrel. Mfg. 1993-2000.

	$4,300	$3,250	$2,750	$2,300	$2,050	$1,850	$1,700	Last MSR was $4,770.

M-93 – .50 BMG cal., similar to M-87, except has folding stock and detachable 5 or 10 shot box mag. Mfg. 1993-2000.

	$3,800	$3,250	$2,750	$2,300	$2,000	$1,850	$1,700	Last MSR was $4,150.

Add $300 for two-piece folding stock or dovetail combo. quick disassembly fixture.

M-95 TITANIUM/GRAPHITE – .50 BMG cal., features titanium alloy M-87 receiver with graphite barrel and steel liner, single shot or repeater, approx. 18 lbs. Mfg. 1997-2000.

	$4,650	$4,175	$3,475	$2,875	$2,300	$2,050	$1,850	Last MSR was $5,085.

Add $165 for fixed mag.
Add $315 for detachable mag.

M-96 SEMI-AUTO – .50 BMG cal., gas-operated with 5 shot detachable mag., carry handle scope mount, steel receiver, 30 lbs. Mfg. 1997-2000.

	$6,200	$5,625	$5,075	$4,650	$4,175	$3,475	$2,875	Last MSR was $6,800.

HECKLER & KOCH

Current manufacturer established in 1949, and located in Oberndorf/Neckar, Germany. Currently imported and distributed beginning mid-2008 by H & K USA, located in Columbus, GA. Previously imported by Merkel USA, located in Trussville, AL, by Heckler & Koch, Inc. located in Sterling, VA (previously located in Chantilly, VA). During 2004, H & K built a new plant in Columbus, GA, primarily to manufacture guns for American military and law enforcement. In early 1991, H & K was absorbed by Royal Ordnance, a division of British Aerospace (BAE Systems) located in England. During December 2002, BAE Systems sold Heckler & Koch to a group of European investors. Heckler & Koch, Inc. and HKJS GmbH are wholly owned subsidiaries of Suhler Jag und Sportwaffen Holding GmbH and the sole licensees of Heckler & Koch commercial firearms technology.

PISTOLS: SEMI-AUTO, RECENT MFG.

USP and USP Compact (with bobbed hammer) Models are divided into 10 variants. They include: USP Variant 1 (DA/SA with control safety decocking lever on left), USP Variant 2 (DA/SA with control safety decocking lever on right), USP Variant 3 (DA/SA with control safety decocking lever on left), USP Variant 4 (DA/SA with control safety decocking lever on right), USP

MSR	100%	98%	95%	90%	80%	70%	60%

Variant 5 (DAO with control safety decocking lever on left), USP Variant 6 (DAO with control safety decocking lever on right), USP Variant 7 (DAO with no control lever), USP Variant 9 (DA/SA with safety control lever on left), and USP Variant 10 (DA/SA with safety control lever on right). Please contact your H&K dealer for pricing on these variants.

LEM refers to Law Enforcement Modification (enhanced DAO and conventional SA/DA with serrated decocking button on rear of frame).

Add $69 for ambidextrous control lever (safety/decocking lever on right side), and $387 for laser sighting device BA-6 (mfg. 2002-2005) on currently manufactured USP and USP Compact models.

HK-4 – First and Second Variations. Mfg. 1968-1973.

* *HK-4 First Variation* – .22 LR, .25 ACP, .32 ACP, or .380 ACP, DA, blow back action; 8 (.380 ACP), 9 (.32 ACP), or 10 (.22 LR or .25 ACP) shot mag., high polished blue finish on slide, matte black finish, brown checkered plastic grips with HK logo, fixed front sight, adj. rear sight, firing pin block safety mounted on the left side of the slide, 18 oz. Mfg. 1967-1970.

	$485	$435	$360	$300	$265	$220	$195

A four barrel set with in all calibers with recoil springs, 4 mags., .22 cal. ejector, bolt tool and two fitted cases is currently priced in the $650-$850 range.

* *HK-4 Second Variation* – .380 ACP cal., 8 shot mag., DA, blue finish, blowback action, adj. rear sight, 22 LR cal. conversion kit offered as optional 10 round magazine, fixed front sight, adj. rear sight, firing pin block safety mounted on the left side of the slide, 18 oz. Mfg. 1971-1973.

	$475	$425	$355	$300	$260	$220	$195

Add approx. 10%-15% for .22 LR cal. conversion kit.

HK-4 COMMEMORATIVE COMBO – includes one .22 LR cal. and one .380 ACP cal. barrel. Mfg. 1971.

	$650	$565	$485	$425	$360	$310	$265

HK45 – .45 ACP cal., SA/DA and variants (10), 4.53 in. barrel, features black polymer frame with finger groove grips, integrated Picatinny rail, low profile 3-dot sights, interchangable grip panels, twin slide serrations, 10 shot mag., internal mechanical recoil reduction system reduces recoil 30%, 27.7 oz. New 2008.

MSR $1,187	$1,025	$900	$800	$675	$550	$500	$450

* *HK45 Compact* – similar to HK45, except has 8 shot mag. and small grip frame. New 2008.

MSR $1,187	$1,025	$900	$800	$675	$550	$500	$450

P9S – .45 ACP or 9mm Para. cal., double action combat model, 4 in. barrel, phosphate finish, sculptured plastic grips, fixed sights. Although production ceased in 1984, limited quantities were available until 1989.

	$850	$775	$650	$525	$450	$375	$300	Last MSR was $1,299.

Add 25% for .45 ACP.

P9S TARGET – .45 ACP or 9mm Para. cal., 4 in. barrel, phosphate finish, adj. sights and trigger. Although production ceased in 1984, limited quantities were available until 1989.

	$1,000	$800	$600	$540	$500	$465	$430	Last MSR was $1,382.

P9S COMPETITION KIT – 9mm Para. or .45 ACP (rare) cal., similar to P9S Target, except extra 5 1/2 in. barrel and weight, competition walnut grip, 2 slides. Disc. 1984.

	$1,150	$950	$875	$800	$720	$640	$550	Last MSR was $2,250.

P7 PSP – 9mm Para. cal., older variation of the P7 M8, without extended trigger guard, ambidextrous mag. release (European style), or heat shield. Standard production ceased 1986. A reissue of this model was mfg. in 1990, with approx. 150 produced. Limited quantities remained through 1999.

	$850	$750	$650	$550	$460	$410	$390	Last MSR was $1,111.

Add $200 for European Model with larger frame.

P7 M8 – 9mm Para. cal., unique squeeze cocking single action, extended square combat type trigger guard with heat shield, 4.13 in. fixed barrel with polygonal rifling, 8 shot mag., ambidextrous mag. release, fixed 3-dot sighting system, stippled black plastic grips, black phosphate or nickel (mfg. 1992-2000) finish, includes 2 mags., 28 oz. Disc. 2005.

	$1,250	$975	$800	$700	$600	$500	$450	Last MSR was $1,515.

Add $102 for Tritium sights (various colors, new 1993).
Add $566 for .22 LR conversion kit (barrel, slide, and two mags., disc. 1999).

P7 M13 – similar to P7 M8, only with staggered 13 shot mag., 30 oz. Disc. 1994.

	$2,150	$1,825	$1,575	$1,300	$1,075	$875	$725	Last MSR was $1,330.

Add $85 for Tritium sights (various colors, new 1993).
Add 10% for factory wood grips.

MSR	100%	98%	95%	90%	80%	70%	60%

P7 M10 – .40 S&W cal., similar specifications as P7 M13, except has 10 shot mag., 39 oz. Mfg. 1991-94.

| | $1,125 | $950 | $775 | $650 | $550 | $500 | $450 | Last MSR was $1,315. |

Add $85 for Tritium sights (various colors, new 1993).

P7 K3 – .22 LR or .380 ACP cal., uses unique oil-filled buffer to decrease recoil, 3.8 in. barrel, matte black or nickel (less common) finish, 8 shot mag. (includes 2), 26 1/2 oz. Mfg. 1988-94.

| | $1,295 | $850 | $715 | $600 | $525 | $450 | $410 | Last MSR was $1,100. |

Add $525 for .22 LR conversion kit.
Add $228 for .32 ACP conversion kit.
Add $85 for Tritium sights (various colors, new 1993).

P30 – 9mm Para. cal., 3.86 in. barrel, 15 shot mag., 3-dot sights, lower accessory rail, interchangeable backstraps, self decocking DA hammer, six trigger variants, firing pin block safety, loaded chamber indicator, ergonomic grips with interchangeable side panels and backstraps, double slide serrations, internal recoil reduction system, approx. 23 oz. Importation began mid-2007.

| MSR $1,005 | $875 | $750 | $600 | $500 | $425 | $375 | $325 |

* **P30L** – similar to P30, except has 4.5 in. barrel, V3 configuration only. New 2009.

| MSR $1,059 | $925 | $775 | $625 | $525 | $450 | $400 | $350 |

P2000 – 9mm Para., .357 SIG (new 2005), or .40 S&W cal., SA/DA or LEM (Law Enforcement Modification) DAO (w/o control lever), compact design, patterned after USP Compact Model, features pre-cocked hammer system with very short trigger reset distance, lockout safety device, 3-dot sights, 3.62 in. barrel with polygon rifling, 10 or 12 shot mag. with finger extension, or optional 13 shot mag. (new late 2004), with or w/o decocker, interchangeable rear grip panels, black finish, approx. 22 oz.

| MSR $941 | $815 | $700 | $575 | $500 | $450 | $400 | $350 |

Add $18 for 13 shot mag. (9mm Para. or .357 SIG cal. only).

* **P2000 SK SubCompact** – similar to P2000, choice of LEM (Law Enforcement Modification) or regular DA/SA trigger system, 2.48 in. barrel, 9 (.357 SIG or .40 S&W cal.) or 10 (9mm Para.) shot mag., approx. 27 oz. Importation began 2005.

| MSR $983 | $840 | $725 | $600 | $500 | $450 | $400 | $350 |

Add $18 for 9mm Para. or .357 SIG cal.

USP CUSTOM COMBAT – 9mm Para. or .40 S&W cal., DA/SA, Variant 1, Novak combat sight system, includes jet funnel kit and two 16 (.40 S&W cal.) or 18 (9mm Para. cal.) shot mags. Mfg. 2009.

| | $1,150 | $975 | $875 | $775 | $675 | $550 | $450 | Last MSR was $1,295. |

USP COMBAT COMPETITION – 9mm Para. or .40 S&W cal., 4 1/4 in. barrel, includes jet funnel kit with two 16 (.40 S&W) or 18 (9mm Para) mags., Novak combat sight system, LEM trigger became standard mid-2008, lower accessory rail on frame, 26 1/2 oz. Importation began 2007.

| MSR $1,381 | $1,195 | $975 | $850 | $750 | $650 | $550 | $450 |

Subtract approx. $100 if w/o LEM trigger.

USP COMPETITION – similar to USP Combat Competition, except features LEM match trigger system. Imported 2007-2008.

| | $1,125 | $975 | $850 | $750 | $625 | $500 | $450 | Last MSR was $1,279. |

USP 9 – 9mm Para. cal., available in regular DA/SA mode or DA only (10 variants), 4.13 in. barrel with polygonal rifling, Browning-type action with H & K recoil reduction system, polymer frame, all metal surfaces specially treated, can be carried cocked and locked, stippled synthetic grips, bobbed hammer, 3-dot sighting system, multiple safeties, 10 (C/B 1994), 15 (new late 2004), or 16* shot polymer mag., 26.5 oz. New 1993.

| MSR $902 | $785 | $700 | $575 | $525 | $450 | $400 | $350 |

Add $107 for Tritium sights (various colors, new 1993).

* **USP 9 SD** – similar to USP 9, except has target sights and 4.56 in. threaded barrel, approx. 27 oz. Imported 2004-2006.

| | $825 | $700 | $625 | $550 | $500 | $450 | $400 | Last MSR was $939. |

* **USP 9 Stainless** – similar to USP 9, except has satin finished stainless steel slide. Mfg. 1996-2001.

| | $700 | $565 | $475 | $415 | $360 | $300 | $255 | Last MSR was $817. |

USP 9 COMPACT – 9mm Para. cal., compact variation of the USP 9 featuring 3.58 in. barrel, 10 or 13 (new late 2004) shot mag., 25.5 oz. New 1997.

| MSR $941 | $815 | $700 | $575 | $500 | $450 | $400 | $350 |

MSR	100%	98%	95%	90%	80%	70%	60%	

* USP 9 Compact Stainless – similar to USP 9 Compact, except has satin finished stainless steel slide. Mfg. 1997-2004.

| | $735 | $595 | $500 | $430 | $375 | $315 | $270 | Last MSR was $849. |

* USP 9 Compact LEM – LEM designates law enforcement modification, DAO, unique trigger mechanism decreases trigger pull to 7 1/2 - 8 1/2 lbs, blue only, approx. 24 1/2 oz. Imported 2003-2004.

| | $695 | $575 | $495 | $450 | $400 | $350 | $315 | Last MSR was $799. |

USP 9x19 TACTICAL – 9mm Para. cal. enhanced variation of the USP 9, 4.92 in. threaded barrel with rubber o-ring, 10 or 15 shot mag., adj. target type sights and trigger, approx. 28 1/2 oz. New 2007.

| MSR $1,112 | $975 | $850 | $750 | $625 | $525 | $450 | $400 | |

USP 357 – .357 SIG cal., available in 4.25 (Standard, disc. 2004) or 3.58 (Compact) in. barrel, 10 or 12 (optional beginning 2004) shot mag., black finish, approx. 24.5 oz. Imported 2001-2005.

| | $695 | $560 | $500 | $450 | $395 | $350 | $300 | Last MSR was $799. |

Subtract $30 for Standard Model (disc. 2004).

USP 40 – .40 S&W cal., similar to USP 9, 9 variants of DA/SA/DAO, 10 (C/B1994), 13* (reintroduced late 2004), or 16 (optional, new 2005, needs jet funnel modification) shot mag., 27.75 oz. New 1993.

| MSR $902 | $785 | $700 | $575 | $525 | $450 | $400 | $350 | |

Add $107 for Tritium sights (various colors, new 1993).

A desert tan or finish became available during 2005 at no extra charge (includes matching nylon carrying case). Limited mfg. 2005-2006.

* USP 40 Stainless – similar to USP 40, except has satin finished stainless steel slide. Mfg. 1996-2003.

| | $700 | $565 | $470 | $415 | $360 | $300 | $255 | Last MSR was $817. |

USP 40 COMPACT – .40 S&W cal., compact variation of the USP 40 featuring 3.58 in. barrel, 10 or 12 (new late 2004) shot mag., 27 oz. New 1997.

| MSR $941 | $815 | $700 | $575 | $500 | $450 | $400 | $350 | |

A desert tan finish became available during 2005-2006 at no extra charge (includes matching nylon carrying case). Grey was also available in limited quantites during 2005 only.

* USP 40 Compact Stainless – similar to USP 40 Compact, except has satin finished stainless steel slide. Mfg. 1997-2004.

| | $735 | $595 | $500 | $430 | $375 | $315 | $270 | Last MSR was $849. |

* USP 40 Compact LEM – LEM designates law enforcement modification, DAO, unique trigger mechanism decreases trigger pull to 7 1/2 - 8 1/2 lbs, blue only, approx. 24 1/2 oz. Imported 2002-2005.

| | $695 | $575 | $495 | $450 | $400 | $350 | $315 | Last MSR was $799. |

USP 40 TACTICAL – .40 S&W cal., enhanced variation of the USP 40, 4.92 in. threaded barrel with rubber o-ring, 10 (standard) or 13 shot mag., adj. target type sights and trigger, 30 1/2 oz. New 2005.

| MSR $1,262 | $1,125 | $975 | $850 | $750 | $625 | $525 | $450 | |

USP 45 – .45 ACP cal., similar to USP 9, 9 variants of DA/SA/DAO, 10 (C/B 1994), 12 (new late 2004) or 13* shot mag., 27 3/4 oz. New 1995.

| MSR $983 | $825 | $675 | $550 | $475 | $425 | $350 | $315 | |

Add $107 for Tritium sights (various colors, new 1993).

A desert tan or green finish became available during 2005-2006 at no extra charge (includes matching nylon carrying case). Grey was also available in limited quantites during 2005 only.

* USP 45 Stainless – similar to USP 45, except has satin finished stainless steel slide. Mfg. 1996-2003.

| | $760 | $600 | $500 | $430 | $375 | $315 | $270 | Last MSR was $888. |

* USP 45 Match Pistol – .45 ACP cal., features 6.02 in. barrel with polygonal rifling, micrometer adj. high relief and raised rear sight, raised target front sight, 10 shot mag., barrel weight, fluted, and ambidextrous safety, choice of matte black or stainless steel slide, supplied with additional o-rings and setup tools, 38 oz. Mfg. 1997-98.

| | $1,275 | $1,025 | $825 | $750 | $675 | $550 | $500 | Last MSR was $1,369. |

Add $72 for stainless steel slide model.

USP 45 COMPACT – .45 ACP cal., compact variation of the USP 45, featuring 3.8 in. barrel, 8 shot mag., 28 oz. New 1998.

| MSR $1,036 | $885 | $775 | $650 | $550 | $475 | $425 | $375 | |

MSR	100%	98%	95%	90%	80%	70%	60%

* ***USP 45 Compact Stainless*** – similar to USP 45 Compact, except has satin finished stainless steel slide. Mfg. 1998-2004.

| | $775 | $615 | $510 | $440 | $385 | $325 | $275 | Last MSR was $894. |

* ***USP 45 Compact 50th Anniversary*** – commemorates the 50th year of H & K (1950-2000), 1 of 1,000 special edition featuring high polish blue slide with 50th Anniversary logo engraved in gold and silver, supplied with presentation wood case and commemorative coin. Limited mfg. 2000 only.

| | $1,150 | $895 | $795 | N/A | N/A | N/A | N/A | Last MSR was $999. |

USP 45 TACTICAL PISTOL – .45 ACP cal., enhanced variation of the USP 45, 4.92 in. threaded barrel with rubber o-ring, 10 or 12 (optional beginning late 2004) shot mag., adj. target type sights and trigger, limited availability, 36 oz. New 1998.

| MSR $1,301 | $1,125 | $975 | $850 | $750 | $625 | $550 | $495 |

A desert tan finish became available during 2005-2006 at no extra charge (includes matching nylon carrying case).

* ***USP 45 Tactical Pistol Compact*** – .45 ACP cal., compact variation of the USP 45 Tactical, 8 shot mag. Importation began 2006.

| MSR $1,238 | $1,095 | $950 | $850 | $750 | $650 | $550 | $450 |

USP EXPERT – 9mm Para. (mfg. 2003-2005), .40 S&W (new 2002) or .45 ACP cal., features new slide design with 5.2 in. barrel, 10 (standard), 12 (.45 ACP), 13 (.40 S&W), or 15 (9mm Para.) shot mag., match grade SA or DA trigger pull, recoil reduction system, reinforced polymer frame, adj. rear sight, approx. 30 oz. Imported 1999-2009.

| | $1,250 | $1,075 | $925 | $825 | $725 | $625 | $525 | Last MSR was $1,406. |

USP ELITE – 9mm Para. (disc. 2005) or .45 ACP cal, long slide variation of the USP Expert, 6.2 in. barrel, match trigger parts, target sights, ambidextrous control levers, blue finish, includes two 10 shot mags. or 12 (.45 ACP) or 15 (9mm Para.) shot mag. Imported 2003-2009.

| | $1,250 | $1,075 | $925 | $825 | $725 | $625 | $525 | Last MSR was $1,406. |

MARK 23 SPECIAL OPERATIONS PISTOL – .45 ACP cal., 5.87 in. threaded barrel, polymer frame and integral grips, 3-dot sighting, 10 or 12 (optional beginning late 2004) shot mag., squared off trigger guard, 2.6 lbs., limited availability. New 1996.

| MSR $2,310 | $2,000 | $1,750 | $1,500 | $1,250 | $1,000 | $875 | $775 |

The "MK23" is the official military design that is not available to civilians.

A desert tan finish became available during 2005-2006 at no extra charge (includes matching nylon carrying case).

SP 89 – 9mm Para. cal., recoil operated delayed roller-locked bolt system, 4 1/2 in. barrel, 15 shot mag., adj. aperture rear sight (accepts HK claw-lock scope mounts), 4.4 lbs. Mfg. 1990-1993.

| | $4,950 | $4,500 | $4,150 | $4,000 | $3,750 | $3,625 | $3,500 | Last MSR was $1,325. |

VP 70Z – 9mm Para. cal., 18 shot, double action only, 4 1/2 in. barrel, parkerized finish, plastic receiver/grip assembly. Disc. 1984.

| | $750 | $675 | $600 | $550 | $500 | $450 | $400 |

Add 125% if frame cut for shoulder stock (Model VP 70M, NFA Class III).

The majority of pistols that were cut for shoulder stock are the Model VP 70M, and are subject to NFA Class III regulation.

HK-416 – .22 LR cal., 10 or 20 shot mag., blowback action, black finish, 9 in. barrel, steel receiver, fixed front sight, adj. rear sight, external safety, upper and lower rail interface system, approx. 5 lbs, mfg. by Carl Walther in Ulm, Germany. New mid-2009.

| MSR $540 | $495 | $440 | $400 | $375 | $350 | $325 | $300 |

RIFLES: BOLT ACTION

BASR – .22 LR, .22-250 Rem., 6mm PPC, .300 Win. Mag., .30-06, or .308 Win. cal., Kevlar stock, stainless steel barrel, limited production. Special order only. Mfg. 1986 only.

| | $5,750 | $5,000 | $4,500 | $4,000 | $3,650 | $3,300 | $2,600 | Last MSR was $2,199. |

Less than 135 of this variation were manufactured and they are extremely rare. Contractual disputes with the U.S. supplier stopped H & K from receiving any BASR models.

MSR	100%	98%	95%	90%	80%	70%	60%

RIFLES: SEMI-AUTO

Most of the models listed, being of a tactical design, were disc. in 1989 due to Federal legislation. Sporterized variations mfg. after 1994 with thumbhole stocks were banned in April, 1998.

In 1991, the HK-91, HK-93, and HK-94 were discontinued. Last published retail prices (1991) were $999 for fixed stock models and $1,199 for retractable stock models.

In the early '70s, S.A.C.O. importers located in Virginia sold the Models 41 and 43 which were the predecessors to the Model 91 and 93, respectively. Values for these earlier variations will be higher than values listed.

SR-9 – .308 Win. cal., semi-auto sporting rifle, 19.7 in. barrel, Kevlar reinforced fiberglass thumbhole stock and forearm, 5 shot mag., diopter adj. rear sight, accepts H & K claw-lock scope mounts. Mfg. 1990-93.

	$2,075	$1,725	$1,400	$1,225	$1,075	$950	$850	Last MSR was $1,199.

While advertised again during 1998, this model was finally banned in April, 1998.

SR-9T – .308 Win. cal., precision target rifle with adj. MSG 90 buttstock and PSG-1 trigger group, 5 shot mag. Mfg. 1992-93.

	$2,795	$2,375	$2,050	$1,775	$1,375	$1,295	$1,050	Last MSR was $1,725.

While advertised again during 1998, this model was finally banned in April, 1998.

SR-9TC – .308 Win. cal., similar to SR-9T except has PSG-1 adj. buttstock. Mfg. 1993 only.

	$3,350	$2,925	$2,600	$2,275	$1,925	$1,475	$1,250	Last MSR was $1,995.

While advertised again during 1998, this model was finally banned in April, 1998.

PSG-1 – .308 Win. cal. only, high precision marksman's rifle, 5 shot mag., adj. buttstock, includes accessories (Hensholdt illuminated 6x42mm scope) and case, 17.8 lbs. Importation disc. 1998.

	$12,500	$10,950	$9,500	$8,500	$7,500	$7,000	$6,500	Last MSR was $10,811.

MODEL 41 A-2 – .308 Win. cal., predecessor to the Model 91 A-2, originally imported by Golden State Arms.

	$4,150	$3,950	$3,750	$3,500	$3,350	$3,200	$3,000	

MODEL 43 A-2 – predecesor to the Model 93 A-2. Disc.

	$4,350	$4,150	$3,950	$3,750	$3,550	$3,400	$3,200	

MODEL 91 A-2 – .308 Win. cal., tactical design, roller locked delayed blowback action, attenuated recoil, black cycolac stock, 17.7 in. barrel, 20 shot mag., 9.7 lbs. Importation disc. 1989.

* **Model 91 A-2 Fixed stock model**

	$2,650	$2,200	$2,000	$1,750	$1,500	$1,250	$1,000	Last MSR was $999.

Add $200 for desert camo finish.
Add $275 for NATO black finish.

* **Model 91 A-2 SBF (Semi-Beltfed)** – supplied with bipod and M60 link (200 shot with starter tab) and MG42 modified belt (49 shot with fixed starter tab), limited mfg. Disc.

	$10,500	$9,500	$8,500	N/A	N/A	N/A	N/A	

* **Model 91 A-3** – with retractable metal stock.

	$3,100	$2,900	$2,700	$2,500	$2,150	$2,000	$1,895	Last MSR was $1,114.

Add $775 for .22 LR conversion kit.

* **Model 91 A-2 Package** – includes A.R.M.S. mount, B-Square rings, Leupold 3-9x compact scope with matte finish. Importation disc. 1988.

	$3,150	$2,750	$2,400	$2,150	$1,900	$1,700	$1,475	Last MSR was $1,285.

Add 30% for retractable stock.

MODEL 93 A-2 – .223 Rem. cal., smaller version of the H & K 91, 25 shot mag., 16.14 in. barrel, 8 lbs.

* **Model 93 A-2 Fixed stock model**

	$2,750	$2,250	$2,000	$1,750	$1,500	$1,250	$1,000	Last MSR was $946.

Add 10% for desert camo finish.
Add 15% for NATO black finish.

* **Model 93 A-3** – with retractable metal stock.

	$3,400	$3,250	$3,000	$2,800	$2,650	$2,500	$2,250	Last MSR was $1,114.

* **Model 93 A-2 Package** – includes A.R.M.S. mount, B-Square rings, Leupold 3-9x compact scope with matte finish. Importation disc. 1988.

	$3,500	$3,100	$2,850	$2,550	$2,400	$2,100	$1,895	Last MSR was $1,285.

MSR	100%	98%	95%	90%	80%	70%	60%

Add 10% for retractable stock.

MODEL 94 CARBINE A-2 – 9mm Para. cal., semi-auto carbine, 16.54 in. barrel, aperture rear sight, 15 shot mag. New 1983.

* *Model 94 Carbine A-2 Fixed stock model*

	$3,950	$3,750	$3,500	$3,400	$3,000	$2,600	$2,500	Last MSR was $946.

* *Model 94 Carbine A-3* – retractable metal stock.

	$4,150	$3,900	$3,700	$3,550	$3,200	$2,800	$2,700	Last MSR was $1,114.

* *Model 94 Carbine A-2 Package* – includes A.R.M.S. mount, B-Square rings, Leupold 3-9x compact scope with matte finish. Importation disc. 1988.

	$4,300	$3,875	$3,650	$3,300	$3,000	$2,800	$2,500	Last MSR was $1,285.

Add 10% for retractable stock.

* *Model 94 Carbine A-2 SGI* – 9mm Para. cal., target rifle, aluminum alloy bi-pod, Leupold 6X scope, 15 or 30 shot mag. Imported 1986 only.

	$3,950	$3,750	$3,500	$3,000	$2,750	$2,500	$2,150	Last MSR was $1,340.

MODEL 270 – .22 LR cal., sporting rifle, 19.7 in. barrel with standard or polygonal rifling, 5 or 20 shot mag., high luster blue, plain walnut stock, approx. 5.7 lbs. Disc. 1985.

	$975	$895	$725	$675	$525	$400	$350	Last MSR was $200.

MODEL 300 – .22 Mag. cal., 5 or 15 shot, polygonal rifling standard, otherwise similar to H & K 270 with checkered walnut stock. Importation disc. 1989.

	$1,350	$1,050	$925	$775	$700	$600	$550	Last MSR was $608.

Add $350-$400 for factory H & K scope mount system.

* *Model 300 Package* – includes A.R.M.S. mount, B-Square rings, Leupold 3-9x compact scope with matte finish. Importation disc. 1988.

	$1,625	$1,275	$1,075	$900	$800	$700	$650	Last MSR was $689.

MODEL 416 D145RS – .22 LR cal., blowback action, 16.1 in. barrel, fixed front sight, adj. rear sight, external safety, 10 or 20 shot mag., metal receiver, black finish, upper and lower rail interface system, pistol grip with compartment, adj. buttstock, functional dust cover, 6.8 lbs., mfg. by Carl Walther in Ulm, Germany. New late 2009.

MSR $675	$625	$550	$500	$465	$435	$400	$375

MODEL 630 – .223 Rem. cal., roller locked delayed blowback action, 17.7 in. barrel with or w/o muzzle brake (early mfg.), reduced recoil, checkered walnut, 4 or 10 shot mag., 7.04 lbs. Importation disc. 1986.

	$1,650	$1,400	$1,200	$1,100	$1,000	$850	$750	Last MSR was $784.

Add $350-$400 for factory H & K scope mount system.

The .222 Rem. cal. was also available in this model. Most were French contracts.

MODEL 770 – .308 Win. cal., 3 or 10 shot mag., 19.7 in. barrel with or w/o muzzle brake (early mfg.), otherwise similar to Model 630, 7.92 lbs. Importation disc. 1986.

	$2,150	$1,900	$1,650	$1,375	$1,150	$1,000	$900	Last MSR was $797.

Add $350-$400 for factory H & K scope mount system.

Significant price increases stopped the importation of this model.

Approx. 6 Model 770s were imported in .243 Win. cal. during 1984. Values for the .243 Win. cal. will be considerably higher than listed for the .308 Win. cal.

MODEL 911 – .308 Win. cal., earlier importation. Disc.

	$1,900	$1,700	$1,500	$1,275	$1,050	$900	$775	

MODEL 940 – .30-06 cal., 21.6 in. barrel with or w/o muzzle brake (early mfg.), otherwise same as Model 770, 8.62 lbs. Importation disc. 1986.

	$1,950	$1,750	$1,500	$1,250	$995	$875	$750	Last MSR was $917.

Add $350-$400 for factory H & K scope mount system.

Cals. 7x64mm and 9.3x62mm were also available in this model.

Significant price increases stopped the importation of this model.

* *Model 940K* – similar to Model 940, except has 16 in. barrel and higher cheekpiece. Two imported 1984 only.

Rarity precludes accurate price evaluation.

MSR	100%	98%	95%	90%	80%	70%	60%

SLB 2000 – .30-06 or .308 Win. (new 2003) cal. (bolt head dimension allows cartridge interchangeability), short stroke piston actuated gas operating system, alloy receiver with black weather resistant coating, gold accents on receiver, 19.69 in. barrel (interchangeable), checkered walnut stock and specially angled pistol grip, tang mounted safety blocks hammer and trigger, 2, 5, or 10 shot mag., iron sights, 7.28 lbs. Imported 2001-2003.

	100%	98%	95%	90%	80%	70%	60%	
	$1,150	$995	$895	$825	$775	$700	$650	Last MSR was $1,299.

MODELS SL6 & SL7 CARBINE – .223 Rem. or .308 Win. cal., 17.71 in. barrel, roller locked delayed blowback action, reduced recoil, vent. wood hand guard, 3 or 4 shot mag., 8.36 lbs., matte black metal finish, HK-SL6 is .223 Rem. cal., HK-SL7 is .308 Win. cal. Importation disc. in 1986.

	100%	98%	95%	90%	80%	70%	60%
	$1,650	$1,450	$1,250	$1,050	$925	$800	$650

Add $250-$300 for factory H & K scope mount system.
Add $200 for .308 Win. cal.

These models were the last sporter variations H & K imported into the U.S. - no U.S. importation since 1986.

MODEL SL8-1 – .223 Rem. cal., short stroke piston actuated gas operating system, advanced grey carbon fiber polymer construction based on the German Army G36 rifle, thumbhole stock with adj. cheekpiece and buttstock, 10 shot mag., modular and removable Picatinny rail, removable sights, 20.8 in. cold hammer forged heavy barrel, adj. sights, 8.6 lbs. Imported 2000-2003, reimported beginning 2007.

MSR $2,449	100%	98%	95%	90%	80%	70%	60%
MSR $2,449	$1,950	$1,650	$1,500	$1,350	$1,200	$1,000	$900

Add $338 for carrying handle with 1.5X-3x optical sights (disc. 2009).
Add $624 for carrying handle with 1.5X-3x optical sights and red dot reflex sight (disc. 2009).

MODEL SL8-6 – .223 Rem. cal., similar to SL8-1, except has elevated Picatinny rail that doubles as carrying handle. New 2010.

As this edition went to press, U.S. pricing was not available on this model.

MODEL USC .45 ACP CARBINE – .45 ACP cal., similar design/construction as the Model SL8-1, except is blowback action, and has 16 in. barrel and grey skeletonized buttstock, 10 shot mag., 6 lbs. Imported 2000-2003, reimported beginning 2007.

MSR $1,833	100%	98%	95%	90%	80%	70%	60%
MSR $1,833	$1,500	$1,275	$1,050	$925	$825	$725	$625

MR556 CARBINE – 5.56x45mm cal., 16 1/2 in. barrel, gas piston operation, free floating rail system, flip up front and diopter rear sights, black anodized finish, 10 or 30 shot steel mag., upper and lower accessory rails, adj. buttstock with storage compartment, optional pistol grips, limited mfg. in the U.S. New late 2009.

MSR $2,295	100%	98%	95%	90%	80%	70%	60%
MSR $2,295	$2,150	$2,000	$1,800	$1,600	$1,450	$1,300	$1,150

MR762 CARBINE – 7.62x51mm cal., 16 1/2 in. barrel, gas piston operation, free floating rail system, flip up front and diopter rear sights, black anodized finish, 10 or 20 shot polymer mag., upper and lower accessory rails, adj. buttstock with storage compartment, optional pistol grips, limited mfg. in the U.S. New late 2009.

As this edition went to press, U.S. pricing was not available on this model.

MODEL MP5 A5 – .22 LR cal., blowback action, 10 or 25 shot mag., 16.1 in. barrel, black finish, metal receiver, Navy pistol grip, H&K adj. front and rear sights, 3 lug, standard forearm, retractable stock, compensator, external safety, 5.9 lbs., mfg. by Carl Walther in Ulm, Germany. New late 2009.

MSR $525	100%	98%	95%	90%	80%	70%	60%
MSR $525	$475	$430	$395	$375	$350	$325	$300

MODEL MP5 SD – .22 LR cal., blowback action, 10 or 25 shot mag., 16.1 in. barrel, black finish, metal receiver, adj. rear sights, interchangeable front post sight, 3 lug imitation, SD type forearm, Navy pistol grip, retractable stock, compensator, external safety, 5.9 lbs., mfg. by Carl Walther in Ulm, Germany. New late 2009.

MSR $585	100%	98%	95%	90%	80%	70%	60%
MSR $585	$525	$475	$425	$395	$375	$350	$325

SHOTGUNS: SEMI-AUTO

Benelli shotguns previously imported by H&K can be found under Benelli.

MODEL 512 – 12 ga. only, mfg. by Franchi for German military contract, rifle sights, matte finished metal, walnut stock, fixed choke pattern diverter giving rectangular shot pattern. Importation disc. 1991.

	100%	98%	95%	90%	80%	70%	60%
	$1,500	$1,300	$1,100	$925	$800	$700	$600

Last Mfg.'s Wholesale was $1,895.

SLS 2002 – 12 ga. only, 3 in. chamber, IQ-port gas operation (excess gas is vented forward through forearm cap), various barrel lengths, including slug barrel, double slide rails, deluxe checkered walnut stock and forearm, phosphate black finish, prototypes only in Europe, approx. 6 3/4 lbs.

While advertised during 2002, this gun was never manufactured past the prototype stage.

MSR	100%	98%	95%	90%	80%	70%	60%

HEINIE SPECIALTY PRODUCTS

Previous pistol manufacturer established in 1973, and located in Quincy, IL. Heinie currently manufactures sights only.

Heinie manufactured both scratch built personal defense and tactical/carry 1911 packages in a wide variety of chamberings.

HENRY REPEATING ARMS COMPANY

Current rifle manufacturer established during 1997, and located in Bayonne, NJ beginning 2008. Previously located in Brooklyn, NY. Distributor and dealer sales.

RIFLES

HENRY U.S. SURVIVAL .22 SEMI-AUTO – .22 LR cal., patterned after the Armalite AR-7 with improvements, takedown design enables receiver, 2 mags., and barrel to stow in ABS plastic stock, 100% Mossy Oak Break-Up camo (new 2000) or weather resistant silver or black (new 1999) stock/metal finish, two 8 shot mags., adj. sights, 16 1/2 in. long when disassembled and stowed in stock, includes plastic carrying case, approx. 2 1/2 lbs. New 1997.

MSR $245	$200	$175	$155	$135	$120	$110	$100

Add $65 for 100% camo finish (new 2000).

HESSE ARMS

Previous manufacturer located in Inver Grove Heights, MN.

Hesse Arms manufactured very limited quantities of semi-auto pistols, bolt action rifles, and semi-auto rifles. Due to space considerations, this information is available free of charge on www.bluebookinc.com.

HI-POINT FIREARMS

Current trademark marketed by MKS Supply, Inc. located in Dayton, Ohio. Hi-Point firearms have been manufactured since 1988. Dealer and distributor sales.

Prior to 1993, trademarks sold by MKS Supply, Inc. (including Beemiller, Haskell Manufacturing, Inc., Iberia Firearms, Inc., and Stallard Arms, Inc.) had their own separate manufacturers' markings. Beginning in 1993, Hi-Point Firearms eliminated these individualized markings and chose instead to have currently manufactured guns labeled "Hi-Point Firearms". All injection molding for Hi-Point Firearms is done in Mansfield, OH.

CARBINES

MODEL 995/4095 – 9mm Para. or .40 S&W (Model 4095, mfg. late 2003-2008) cal., 16 1/2 or 17 1/2 (.40 S&W cal. only) in. barrel, one-piece camo or black polymer stock features pistol grip, 10 shot mag., aperture rear sight, parkerized or chrome (disc. 2007) finish. New 1996.

MSR $220	$180	$140	$120	$100	$85	$75	$70

Add $22 for .40 S&W cal.
Add $10 for chrome finish (disc. 2007).
Add $15 for camo stock (new 2002).
Add $85 for detachable compensator, laser, and mount (new 1999).
Add $25 for 4x scope or $55 for red dot scope.

This model is manufactured by Beemiller, located in Mansfield, OH.

HIGH STANDARD

Previous manufacturer located in New Haven, Hamden, and East Hartford, CT. High Standard Mfg. Co. was founded in 1926. They entered the firearms business when they purchased Hartford Arms and Equipment Co. in 1932. The original plant was located in New Haven, CT. During WWII High Standard operated plants in New Haven and Hamden. After the war, the operations were consolidated in Hamden. In 1968, the company was sold to the Leisure Group, Inc. A final move was made to East Hartford, CT in 1977 where they remained until the doors were closed in late 1984. In early 1978, the Leisure Group sold the company to the management and the company became High Standard, Inc.

Many collectors have realized the rarity and quality factors this trademark has earned. 13 different variations (Models C, A, D, E, H-D, H-E, H-A, H-B First Model, G-380, GB, GD, GE, and Olympic, commonly called the GO) had a total production of less than 48,000 pistols. For these reasons, top condition High Standard pistols are getting more difficult to find each year.

As a final note on High Standard pistols, they are listed under the following category names: Letter Series, Letter Series w/ Hammer, Lever Letter Series, Lever Name Series, 100 Series, 101 Series, 102 Series, 103 Series, 104 Series, 105 Series, 106 Series - Military Models, 107 Series, Conversion Kits, and SH Series.

Note: catalog numbers were not always consistent with design series, and in 1966-1967 changed with accessories offered, but not design series.

The approx. ser. number cut-off for New Haven, CT marked guns is 442,XXX.

The approx. ser. number range for Hamden, CT marked guns is 431,XXX-2,500,811, G 1,001-G 13,757 (Shipped)

MSR	100%	98%	95%	90%	80%	70%	60%

or G15,650 (Packed) or ML 1,001-ML 23,065. One exception is a 9211 Victor serial number 3,000,000 shipped 1 March, 1974.

The first gun shipped 16 June, 1977 from E. Hartford was a Victor 9217 serial number EH0001.

The approx. ser. number ranges for E. Hartford, CT manufacture is ML 25,000-ML 86,641 and SH 10,001-SH 34,034. One exception is a single gun numbered ML90,000.

Original factory boxes have become very desirable. Prices can range from $50-$100 for a good condition Model 106 or 107 factory box to over $150 for an older box of a desirable model.

SHOTGUNS: DEFENSE & LAW ENFORCEMENT

SEMI AUTOMATIC MODEL – 12 ga., 20 in. cylinder bore barrel, 4 shot mag., recoil pad walnut stock and forearm.

	100%	98%	95%	90%	80%	70%	60%
	$250	$205	$180	$160	$130	$110	$100

C-1200, 12 ga., 20 in. barrel, cylinder bore, Riot 20-5, catalog #8294, mfg. 1969.

C-1200, 12 ga., 20 in. barrel, cylinder bore, rifle sights, Riot 20-5, catalog #8295, mfg. 1969.

MODELS 10A/10B SEMI-AUTO – 12 ga., combat model, 18 in. barrel, semi-auto, unique bullpup design incorporates raked pistol grip in front of receiver and metal shoulder pad attached directly to rear of receiver, black cycolac plastic shroud and pistol grip, very compact size (28 in. overall). Disc. - 12 ga., folding carrying handle, provisions made for attaching a Kel-lite flashlight to receiver top, extended blade front sight, 4 shot mag., carrying case.

* ***Model 10-A Semi-Auto*** – 4 shot mag., fixed carrying handle and integral flashlight.

	100%	98%	95%	90%	80%	70%	60%
	$775	$725	$665	$600	$475	$400	$350

12 ga., 18 in. barrel, cylinder bore, catalog #8290, mfg. 1967-69.

* ***Model 10-B Semi-Auto***

	100%	98%	95%	90%	80%	70%	60%
	$700	$655	$600	$575	$450	$375	$325

Add 15% for flashlight.

Cat. No. 50284 optional carrying case and attachable flashlight; Cat. No. 50285 sold optionally.

12 ga., 18.13 in. barrel, cylinder bore, catalog #8291, mfg. 1970-77.

SLIDE ACTION RIOT SHOTGUN – 12 ga. only on the Flite King Action, 18 or 20 in. barrel, police riot gun, available with or w/o rifle sights, plain pistol grip oiled walnut stock & forearm forearm, changed to walnut stained and lacquered birch in the mid-1970s.

	100%	98%	95%	90%	80%	70%	60%
	$230	$200	$175	$150	$125	$115	$105

Catalog #8111/#8113 magazine capacity 6. # 8104/#8129 magazine capacity 5. A 1963 flyer mentions the #8105 Flite King Brush 20 in. and the #8107 Flite King Deluxe 20 in. as riot guns. The data on the #8105 and #8107 is listed under the Flite King Brush.

K-101, K-120, K-1200, 12 ga., 20 in. barrel, cylinder bore, Riot 20-6, catalog #8104, mfg. 1963-1977.

K-120, K-1200, 12 ga., 18 1/8 in. barrel, cylinder bore, Riot 18-7, catalog #8111, mfg. 1964-1978.

K-120, K-1200,12 ga., 18 in. barrel, cylinder bore, rifle sights, Riot 18-7, catalog #8113, mfg. 1965-1978.

K-120, 12 ga., 18 1/8 in. barrel, cylinder bore, rifle sights, Riot 18-6, catalog #8118, mfg. 1968.

12 ga., 20 in. barrel, cylinder bore, rifle sights, catalog #8129, mfg. 1976-77.

K-102, 12 ga., 20 in. barrel, cylinder bore, catalog #8112, 1964-65.

12 ga., 18 in. barrel, cylinder bore, rifle sights, catalog #8128, mfg. 1976-77.

HIGH STANDARD MANUFACTURING CO.

High Standard is a current trademark of firearms manufactured by Firearms International Inc., established in 1993 and located in Houston, TX.

This company was formed during 1993, utilizing many of the same employees and original material vendors which the original High Standard company used during their period of manufacture (1926-1984). During 2004, Crusader Group Gun Company, Inc. was formed, and this new company includes the assets of High Standard Manufacturing Co, Firearms International Inc., AMT-Auto Mag, Interarms, and Arsenal Line Products.

RIFLES/CARBINES: SEMI-AUTO

HSA-15 – .223 Rem. cal., 20 in. barrel, with or w/o adj. sights.

MSR $905	100%	98%	95%	90%	80%	70%	60%
	$850	$775	$700	$625	$550	$500	$450

Add $40 for adj. sights.

HSA-15 NATIONAL MATCH – .223 Rem. cal., available with either 20 in. (National Match) or 24 in. (Long Range Rifle, disc. 2008) fluted barrel, includes Knight's military two-stage trigger. New 2006.

MSR $1,250	100%	98%	95%	90%	80%	70%	60%
	$1,125	$950	$850	$750	$650	$550	$495

MSR	100%	98%	95%	90%	80%	70%	60%

M-4 CARBINE – .223 Rem. or 9mm Para. cal., 16 in. barrel, fixed A2 (.223 Rem. cal. only, new 2010) or six position adj. stock, fixed or adj. sights. New 2009.

MSR $895	$825	$750	$650	$550	$500	$450	$395

Add $50 or $90 for six position adj. stock, depending on caliber.
Add $50 for adj. sight.

Add $450 for chrome lined barrel, free floating quad rails, flip up sights, flash hider and two-stage match trigger (.223 Rem. cal. only, disc. 2009).

HOLLOWAY ARMS CO.
Previous manufacturer located in Fort Worth, TX.

Holloway made very few rifles or carbines before operations ceased and existing specimens are scarce.

RIFLES: SEMI-AUTO

HAC MODEL 7 RIFLE – .308 Win. cal., gas operated semi-auto tactical design rifle, 20 in. barrel, adj. front and rear sights, 20 shot mag., side folding stock, right or left-hand action. Mfg. 1984-85 only.

	$3,750	$3,350	$3,100	$2,800	$2,650	$2,350	$2,000	Last MSR was $675.

* **HAC Model 7C Rifle Carbine** – 16 in. carbine, same general specifications as Model 7. Disc. 1985.

	$3,750	$3,350	$3,100	$2,800	$2,650	$2,350	$2,000	Last MSR was $675.

Also available from the manufacturer were the Models 7S and 7M (Sniper and Match models).

HOLMES FIREARMS
Previous manufacturer located in Wheeler, AR. Previously distributed by D.B. Distributing, Fayetteville, AR.

PISTOLS: SEMI-AUTO

These pistols were mfg. in very limited numbers, most were in prototype configuration and exhibit changes from gun to gun. These models were open bolt and subject to 1988 federal legislation regulations.

MP-83 – 9mm Para. or .45 ACP cal., tactical design pistol, 6 in. barrel, walnut stock and forearm, blue finish, 3 1/2 lbs.

	$700	$600	$500	$450	$400	$375	$350	Last MSR was $450.

Add 10% for deluxe package.
Add 40% for conversion kit (mfg. 1985 only).

MP-22 – .22 LR cal., 2 1/2 lbs., steel and aluminum construction, 6 in. barrel, similar appearance to MP-83. Mfg. 1985 only.

	$395	$360	$320	$285	$250	$230	$210	Last MSR was $400.

SHOTGUNS

COMBAT 12 – 12 ga., riot configuration, cylinder bore barrel. Disc. 1983.

	$795	$720	$650	$595	$550	$500	$450	Last MSR was $750.

HOWA
Current manufacturer established in 1967, and located in Tokyo, Japan. Howa sporting rifles are currently imported beginning Oct., 1999 by Legacy Sports International, LLC, located in Reno, NV. Previously located in Alexandria, VA. Previously imported until 1999 by Interarms/Howa, located in Alexandria, VA, Weatherby (Vanguard Series only), Smith & Wesson (pre-1985), and Mossberg (1986-1987).

RIFLES: BOLT ACTION

Howa also manufactures barreled actions in various configurations. MSRs range from $389-$525.

MODEL 1500 PCS – .308 Win. cal., police counter sniper rifle featuring 24 in. barrel, choice of blue metal or stainless steel, black synthetic or checkered walnut stock, no sights, approx. 9.3 lbs. Imported 1999-2000.

	$385	$335	$290	$260	$210	$175	$135	Last MSR was $465.

Add $20 for wood stock.
Add $60 for stainless steel.

NOTES

NOTES

I SECTION

IAI INC. - AMERICAN LEGEND

Previous manufacturer, importer, and distributor located in Houston, TX. Firearms were manufactured by Israel Arms International, Inc., located in Houston, TX. IAI designates Israel Arms International, and should not be confused with Irwindale Arms, Inc. (also IAI).

The models listed were part of an American Legend Series that are patterned after famous American and Belgian military carbines/rifles and semi-auto pistols.

MSR	100%	98%	95%	90%	80%	70%	60%

CARBINES/RIFLES

MODEL 888 M1 CARBINE – .22 LR or .30 Carbine cal., 18 in. barrel, mfg. from new original M1 parts and stock by IAI (barrel bolt and receiver) and unused GI parts, 10 shot mag., choice of birch or walnut stock, parkerized finish, metal or wood handguard, 5 1/2 lbs. Mfg. by IAI in Houston, TX 1998-2004.

	100%	98%	95%	90%	80%	70%	60%	
	$675	$595	$565	$435	$395	$315	$295	*Last MSR was $556.*

Add $11 for .22 LR cal.
Add $31 for walnut/metal forearm or $47 for walnut/wood forearm.

MODEL 333 M1 GARAND – .30-06 cal., patterned after the WWII M1 Garand, 24 in. barrel, internal magazine, 8 shot en-bloc clip., parkerized finish, 9 1/2 lbs. Mfg. 2003-2004.

	100%	98%	95%	90%	80%	70%	60%	
	$950	$875	$775	$625	$525	$400	$350	*Last MSR was $972.*

PISTOLS: SEMI-AUTO

MODEL 2000 – .45 ACP cal., patterned after the Colt Govt. 1911, 5 or 4 1/4 (Commander configuration, Model 2000-C) in. barrel, parkerized finish, plastic or rubber finger groove grips, 36-38 oz. Mfg. in South Africa 2002-2004.

	100%	98%	95%	90%	80%	70%	60%	
	$415	$365	$325	$295	$275	$250	$225	*Last MSR was $465.*

I.O., INC.

Current importer located in Monroe, NC.

I.O. Inc. imports a wide variety of rifles and handguns, mostly from former Soviet bloc countries. Also refer to the Russian Service Pistols and Rifles section for current information and values on recently imported Tokarev pistols and Mosin-Nagant rifles.

RIFLES: SEMI-AUTO

I.O. currently imports the following AK-47 style semi-auto rifles in 7.62x39mm cal.: STG2000-C with fixed, folding, or collapsible stock (MSR $685-$770), the AK47-C with fixed, folding, collapsible or polymer stock (Galil-type forearm), synthetic or wood stock (MSR $500-$670), an AK-22 rifle for $500 MSR, STG-22 rifle for $500 MSR, and a CASAR AK series of rifles ($693 MSR). Please contact the company directly for availability and more information (see Trademark Index).

ISSC HANDELSGESELLSCHAFT

Current manufacturer of semi-auto pistols located in Ried, Austria.

PISTOLS: SEMI-AUTO

M22 – .22 LR cal., 4 in. barrel, SA, 10 shot mag., black polymer frame with contoured grip, adj. rear sight, tactical rail, black or two-tone finish, 21 oz., mfg. by ISSC in Austria. New 2009.

MSR $400	100%	98%	95%	90%	80%	70%	60%
	$350	$310	$280	$250	$225	$200	$185

INGRAM

Previously manufactured until late 1982 by Military Armament Corp. (MAC) located in Atlanta, GA.

PISTOLS: SEMI-AUTO

MAC 10 – .45 ACP or 9mm Para. cal., open bolt, semi-auto version of the sub machine gun, 10 (.45 ACP cal.), 16 (9mm Para cal.), 30 (.45 ACP cal.), or 32 (9mm Para cal.) shot mag., compact all metal welded construction, rear aperture and front blade sight. Disc. 1982.

	100%	98%	95%	90%	80%	70%	60%
	$950	$875	$800	$700	$650	$575	$525

Add approx. $160 for accessories (barrel extension, case, and extra mag.).

MAC 10A1 – similar to MAC 10 except fires from a closed bolt.

	100%	98%	95%	90%	80%	70%	60%
	$395	$375	$350	$280	$265	$225	$210

MSR	100%	98%	95%	90%	80%	70%	60%

MAC 11 – similar to MAC 10 except in .380 ACP cal.

	$750	$695	$650	$575	$550	$535	$485

INTERARMS ARSENAL

Current trademark of firearms imported and distributed by High Standard Manufacturing Company, located in Houston, TX.

RIFLES: SEMI-AUTO

POLISH MODEL WZ.88 TANTAL – 5.45x39mm cal., choice of side folding stock with wood forend furniture or fixed stock, chrome lined barrel, mfg. in U.S.

MSR $895	$795	$700	$625	$550	$475	$425	$350

HUNGARIAN ADM 65 STYLE AKM – 7.62x39mm cal., side folding stock.

MSR $895	$795	$700	$625	$550	$475	$425	$350

AKM SERIES – 7.62x38mm cal., black polymer stock, Russian, Polish, Hungarian, or Bulgarian configurations.

MSR $895	$795	$700	$625	$550	$475	$425	$350

INTERCONTINENTAL ARMS INC.

Previous importer located in Los Angeles, CA circa 1970s.

Intercontinental Arms Inc. imported a variety of SA revolvers, an AR-15 type semi-auto rifle, a derringer, a rolling block single shot rifle, and a line of black powder pistol reproductions and replicas. While these firearms were good, utilitarian shooters, they have limited desirability in today's marketplace. The single action revolvers manufactured by Hämmerli are typically priced in the $200-$395 range, the derringer is priced in the $115-$175 range, the AR-15 copy is priced in the $425-$675 range, and the single shot rolling block rifle is priced in the $150-$200 range, depending on original condition.

INTERDYNAMIC OF AMERICA, INC.

Previous distributor located in Miami, FL 1981-84.

PISTOLS: SEMI-AUTO

KG-9 – 9mm Para. cal., 3 in. barrel, open bolt, tactical design pistol. Disc. approx. 1982.

	$850	$800	$700	$675	$650	$600	$575

KG-99 – 9mm Para. cal., 3 in. barrel, semi-auto tactical design pistol, closed bolt, 36 shot mag., 5 in. vent. shroud barrel, blue only, a stainless steel version of the KG-9. Mfg. by Interdynamic 1984 only.

	$425	$375	$325	$275	$250	$225	$195

* **KG-99M Mini Pistol**

	$495	$450	$400	$325	$275	$250	$225

INTERSTATE ARMS CORP.

Current importer located in Billerica, MA.

Interstate Arms Corp. imports a variety of Chinese made cowboy action shotguns and reproductions, as well as pistols from Turkey.

SHOTGUNS: SLIDE ACTION

MODEL 97T WWI TRENCH GUN – 12 ga. only, authentic reproduction of the original Winchester WWI Trench Gun, complete with shrouded barrel, proper markings, finish, and wood. Imported mid-2002-2006, reintroduced 2010. Mfg. by Sun City Machinery Ltd.

MSR $425	$345	$295	$265	$225	$195	$175	$160

MODEL 372 – 12 ga., 3 in. chamber, 18 1/2 in. barrel with heat shield and ghost ring sights, bottom ejection port, cylinder choke, black synthetic stock and forearm. Limited importation 2007-2009.

While advertised, this model had limited mfg. with no established pricing.

MODEL 982T (981) – 12 ga. only, 3 in. chamber, defense configuration with 18 1/2 in. cylinder bore barrel with fixed choke, black synthetic stock and forearm, matte black metal finish, current mfg. uses ghost ring sights. Importation began 2001.

MSR $230	$195	$170	$150	$125	$115	$95	$85

MSR	100%	98%	95%	90%	80%	70%	60%

INTRAC ARMS INTERNATIONAL INC.

Previous importer located in Knoxville, TN. Intrac imported trademarks manufactured by Arsenal Bulgaria, and by IM Metal Production facility in Croatia late 2000-2004. Previously imported by HS America, located in Knoxville, TN.

RIFLES: SEMI-AUTO

ROMAK 1 & 2 – 7.62x39mm (Romak 1) or 5.45x39mm (Romak 2) cal., AK-47 copy with 16 1/2 in. barrel and scope mount on left side of receiver, wood thumbhole stock, includes 5 and 10 shot mags., and accessories. Imported 2002-2004.

	$595	$550	$525	$475	$450	$400	$350	Last MSR was $329.

SLR-101 – similar to Romak, except has 17 1/4 in. cold hammer forged barrel and black polymer stock and forearm, includes 2 mags. and accessories. Imported 2002-2004.

	$650	$575	$500	$450	$425	$350	$325	Last MSR was $359.

ROMAK 3 – 7.62x54R cal., based on current issue PSL/FPK sniper configuration, 5 or 10 shot mag., last shot bolt hold open, 26 1/2 in. barrel with muzzle brake, mil-spec scope with range finder, bullet drop compensator and illuminated recticle. Imported 2002-2004.

	$900	$825	$750	$650	$575	$525	$475	Last MSR was $899.

INTRATEC

Previous manufacturer circa 1985-2000 located in Miami, FL.

PISTOLS: SEMI-AUTO

PROTEC-25 – .25 ACP. cal., double action only, 2 1/2 in. barrel, 8 shot mag., 13 oz. Disc. 2000.

	$110	$80	$65	$45	$35	$30	$25	Last MSR was $137.

Add $5 for Tec-Kote finish or black slide/frame finish (disc.).

TEC-DC9 – 9mm Para. cal., tactical design pistol, 5 in. shrouded barrel, matte black finish, 10 (C/B 1994) or 32* shot mag. Mfg. 1985-94.

	$475	$425	$375	$300	$275	$225	$200	Last MSR was $269.

* **TEC-9DCK** – similar to TEC-9, except has new durable Tec-Kote finish with better protection than hard chrome. Mfg. 1991-94.

	$495	$465	$425	$375	$325	$295	$260	Last MSR was $297.

* **TEC-DC9S** – matte stainless version of the TEC-9. Disc. 1994.

	$550	$500	$450	$400	$350	$300	$250	Last MSR was $362.

Add $203 for TEC-9 with accessory package (deluxe case, 3-32 shot mags., tactical design grip, and recoil compensator).

TEC-DC9M – mini version of the Model TEC-9, including 3 in. barrel and 20 shot mag. Disc. 1994.

	$495	$465	$425	$375	$325	$295	$260	Last MSR was $245.

* **TEC-DC9MK** – similar to TEC-9M, except has Tec-Kote rust resistant finish. Mfg. 1991-94.

	$525	$450	$400	$350	$300	$250	$200	Last MSR was $277.

* **TEC-DC9MS** – matte stainless version of the TEC-9M. Disc. 1994.

	$575	$500	$450	$400	$350	$300	$275	Last MSR was $339.

TEC-22 "SCORPION" – .22 LR cal., tactical design, 4 in. barrel, ambidextrous safety, military matte finish, or electroless nickel, 30 shot mag., adj. sights, 30 oz. Mfg. 1988-94.

	$375	$325	$275	$225	$200	$175	$160	Last MSR was $202.

Add $20 for TEC-Kote finish.

* **TEC-22N** – similar to TEC-22, except has nickel finish. Mfg. 1990 only.

	$395	$345	$300	$275	$250	$230	$220	Last MSR was $226.

Add $16 for threaded barrel (Model TEC-22TN).

TEC-22T – threaded barrel variation of the TEC-22 "Scorpion." Mfg 1991-94.

	$395	$350	$300	$250	$225	$195	$175	Last MSR was $161.

Add $23 for Tec-Kote finish.

SPORT-22 – .22 LR cal., 4 in. non-threaded barrel, 10 shot Ruger styled rotary mag., matte finish, adj. rear sight, 29 1/2 oz. New 1995.

	$195	$175	$150	$125	$100	$85	$75	Last MSR was $170.

Add $15 for stainless steel barrel.

MSR	100%	98%	95%	90%	80%	70%	60%

CAT-9, CAT-45, CAT-380 – .380 ACP (new 1995), 9mm Para., or .45 ACP (new 1995) cal., double action only, black finish, polymer frame, sight channel, in slide, only 27 parts, blowback action on 9mm Para., locked breech on .45 ACP, 6 (.45 ACP cal.) or 7 (.380 ACP or 9mm Para.) shot mag., 3 or 3 1/4 (.45 ACP only) in. barrel, 18-21 oz. Mfg. 1993-2000.

| | $235 | $200 | $175 | $150 | $125 | $100 | $90 | Last MSR was $260. |

Subtract $25 for .380 ACP cal.
Add $20 for .45 ACP cal.
Add $15 for Fire Sights.

This series was designed by N. Sirkis of Israel.

AB-10 – 9mm Para. cal., design similar to Luger, 2 3/4 in. non-threaded barrel, choice of 32* (limited supply) or 10 shot mag., black synthetic frame, firing pin safety block, black or stainless steel finish, 45 oz. Mfg. 1997-2000.

| | $325 | $275 | $235 | $200 | $180 | $160 | $150 | Last MSR was $225. |

Add $20 for stainless steel (new 2000).
Add $100 for 32 shot mag.

INTRATEC U.S.A., INC.
Previous manufacturer located in Miami, FL.

CARBINES

TEC-9C – 9mm Para. cal., carbine variation with 16 1/2 in. barrel, 36 shot mag.

Only 1 gun mfg. 1987 - extreme rarity precludes pricing.

PISTOLS: SEMI-AUTO

TEC-9 – 9mm Para. cal., tactical design, 5 in. shrouded barrel, 32 shot mag. Disc.

| | $550 | $495 | $450 | $395 | $350 | $295 | $250 | |

ISRAEL ARMS INTERNATIONAL, INC.
Previous importer (please refer to IAI listing) and manufacturer located in Houston, TX, 1997-2004.

ISRAEL ARMS LTD.
Previous manufacturer located in Kfar Saba, Israel. Imported and distributed exclusively by Israel Arms International, Inc. located in Houston, TX 1997-2001.

RIFLES

MODEL 333 M1 GARAND – .30-06 cal., 24 in. barrel, parts remanufactured to meet GI and mil specs, parkerized finish, 8 shot en-bloc clip, 9 1/2 lbs. Mfg. 2000-2001.

| | $895 | $850 | $800 | $700 | $600 | $500 | $400 | Last MSR was $852. |

MODEL 444 FAL – .308 Win. cal., patterned after the FN FAL model. Mfg. by Imbel, located in Brazil, 2000-2001.

| | $925 | $850 | $795 | $725 | $675 | $595 | $550 | Last MSR was $897. |

ISRAEL MILITARY INDUSTRIES (IMI)
Current manufacturer established during 1933, and located in Israel. Limited importation currently.

IMI manufactured guns (both new and disc. models) include Galil, Jericho, Magnum Research, Timberwolf, Uzi, and others, and can be located in their respective sections.

ITHACA GUN COMPANY
Current manufacturer established in 2006 and located in Upper Sandusky, OH.

During December of 2007, Ithaca Gun Company bought out the remaining assets and equipment of Ithaca Gun Company LLC and moved production to Upper Sandusky, OH.

Please contact the company directly for more information, including price and options on available models (see Trademark Index).

SHOTGUNS

Ithaca offers O/U and slide action shotguns in 12, 16, 20 and 28 ga. (2 3/4 or 3 in. chambers). Prices begin at $499 and go up according to options.

M37 SERIES – 12, 16, 20 (2 3/4 and 3 in. chamber), or 28 ga. (2 3/4 in. chamber), 26, 28, or 30 in. barrel, 5 or 8 shot, wood, synthetic, or laminated stock, vent. rib or field barrel, brass bead front sight, fixed scope mount

MSR	100%	98%	95%	90%	80%	70%	60%

(DeerSlayer only), or Marble Arms rear sight (Featherweight Upland), bottom ejection action, Pachmayr recoil pad, high luster, matte blue or Perma-Guard finish, over 30 configurations - DeerSlayer/DeerSlayer II (fixed barrel), DeerSlayer III (fixed tapered, fluted, heavy wall barrel), Defense (18 1/2 or 20 in. barrel), TurkeySlayer (24 in. fixed barrel, rifle sights and Weaver scope base), and Law Enforcement (Class III only).

Prices for this model range from $499-$3,499.

ITHACA GUN COMPANY LLC

Previous manufacturer located in Ithaca, NY from 1883-1986, King Ferry, NY circa 1989-2005, and Auburn, NY right before it closed in June, 2005.

Ithaca Gun Company, LLC had resumed production on the Model 37 slide action shotgun and variations during 1989, and then relocated to King Ferry, NY shortly thereafter. In the past, Ithaca also absorbed companies including Syracuse Arms Co., Lefever Arms Co., Union Fire Arms Co., Wilkes-Barre Gun Co., as well as others.

SHOTGUNS: SLIDE ACTION

In 1987, Ithaca Acquisition Corp. reintroduced the Model 37 as the Model 87. Recently manufactured Model 87s are listed in addition to both new and older Model 37s

(produced pre-1986). During late 1996, Ithaca Gun Co., LLC resumed manufacture of the Model 37, while discontinuing the Model 87.

Over 2 million Model 37s have been produced.

Model 37s with ser. nos. above 855,000 will accept both 2 3/4 and 3 in. chambered barrels interchangeably. Earlier guns have incompatible threading for the magnum barrels.

MODEL 37 DS POLICE SPECIAL – 12 ga. only, 18 1/2 in. barrel with rifle sights, Parkerized finish on metal, oil finished stock, typically subcontracted by police departments or law enforcement agencies, with or without unit code markings.

	$325	$275	$235	$200	$185	$170	$160

MODEL 37 PROTECTION SERIES – 12 ga. only, 18.5 or 20 in. smoothbore barrel w/o chokes, 5 or 8 shot tube mag., approx. 6 3/4 lbs. Limited mfg. 2005.

	$425	$375	$325	$275	$250	$225	$195	Last MSR was $482.

Add $27 for 20 in. barrel.

MODEL 87 MILITARY & POLICE – 12 (3 in.) or 20 (new 1989) ga., short barrel Model 37 w/ normal stock or pistol grip only, 18 1/2, 20, or 24 3/4 (scarce) in. barrel, choice of front bead or rifle sights, front blade was usually a flourescent orange plastic, 5, 8, or 10 shot. Originally disc. 1983, reintroduced 1989-95.

	$265	$230	$200	$180	$170	$160	$150	Last MSR was $323.

Add $104 for nickel finish (mfg. 1991-92 only).

IVER JOHNSON ARMS, INC. (NEW MFG.)

Current manufacturer established during 2004 and located in Rockledge, FL.

The new Iver Johnson Arms, Inc. company was formed during 2004, and currently manfactures the Model 1911A1 Series in both .22 LR and .45 ACP cal. (MSR $567), the Eagle Series (MSR $675-$709), the Trojan Series (MSR $574), and the Hawk Series (MSR $641-$675). Iver Johnson previously manufactured the Raven Series in both .22 LR and .45 ACP cals. until 2009, and the last MSR was $532. Also discontinued during 2009 was the Frontier Four Derringer and the Model PM 30G M1 Carbine.

Please contact the company directly for more information, including availability and pricing (see Trademark Index).

IVER JOHNSON ARMS & CYCLE WORKS

Previously located in Worchester, MA, 1883-1890, Fitchburg, MA, 1890-1975, Middlesex, NJ 1975-1983 (name changed to Iver Johnson Arms Inc.) and Jacksonville, AR 1984-1993. Formerly Johnson Bye & Co. 1871-1883. Renamed Iver Johnson's Arms & Cycle Works mid-year 1894-1975 (incorporated as Iver Johnson's Arms & Cycle Works Inc. in 1915). Renamed Iver Johnson's Arms & Cycle Works in 1891 with manufacturing moving to Fitchburg, MA. In 1975 the name changed to Iver Johnson's Arms, Inc., and two years later, company facilities were moved to Middlesex, NJ. In 1982, production was moved to Jacksonville, AR under the trade name Iver Johnson Arms, Inc. In 1983, Universal Firearms, Inc. was acquired by Iver Johnson Arms, Inc.

PISTOLS: SEMI-AUTO

I.J. SUPER ENFORCER (M1 CARBINE) – .30 Carbine cal., gas operated pistol version of the M1 Carbine, 5, 10, or 15 shot mag., walnut stock, fires from closed bolt, 9 1/2 in. barrel, 4 lbs. Mfg. 1978-1993.

	$850	$745	$640	$580	$470	$385	$300

MSR	100%	98%	95%	90%	80%	70%	60%

UNIVERSAL ENFORCER (M1 CARBINE) – .30 Carbine cal., gas operated, blue finish, single action, pistol version of the M1 carbine, 5, 10, or 15 shot mag., 9 1/2 in. barrel, hard wood stock, fires from close bolt, trigger block safety, 4 lbs. Mfg. 1986.

	$850	$745	$640	$580	$470	$385	$300

RIFLES

Iver Johnson's first rifle was manufactured in 1928 and remained the only rifle manufactured entirely within the Iver Johnson factory in Fitchburg. The later .22 cal. rifles were all imported from either Canada or Germany, except the Lil Champ Model, which was manufactured in Jacksonville, AR. The M1 Carbine models were manufactured in either Middlesex, NJ or Jacksonville, AR.

I.J. PLAINSFIELD SEMI-AUTO CARBINE – .30 Carbine, 9mm Para. (new 1986), or 5.7mm (disc. 1986) cal., gas operated, copy of WWII U.S. Military Carbine, 5, 10, 15, or 30 shot detachable mag., stainless steel or blue finish, 18 in. barrel, American walnut or hardwood stock, model names and numbers changed several times, M2 full auto model available during the 1980s, 6 1/2 lbs. Mfg. 1978-1993.

	$450	$395	$335	$285	$245	$210	$180

Add 10% for walnut stock.
Add 20% for stainless steel.
Add 35% for 5.7mm cal. (Spitfire Model) or 9mm Para. cal.

I.J. PARATROOPER SEMI-AUTO CARBINE – .30 Carbine cal., gas operated, copy of WWII U.S. Military Carbine, 5, 10, 15, or 30 shot detachable mag., stainless steel or blue finish, 18 in. barrel, American walnut or hardwood stock, with collapsible stock extension model names and numbered changed several times, M2 full auto model available with 12 in. barrel, 4 1/2 lbs. Mfg. 1978-1989.

	$595	$550	$500	$460	$430	$395	$360

Add 10% for walnut stock.
Add 20% for stainless steel.

I.J. SURVIVAL CARBINE SEMI-AUTO – .30 Carbine or 5.7mm cal., gas operated, copy of WWII military carbine, 5, 10, 15, or 30 shot detachable mag., stainless steel or blue finish, Zytel black plastic pistol grip stock, 6 1/2 lbs.

	$450	$395	$335	$285	$245	$210	$180

Add 20% for stainless steel.
Add 35% for 5.7mm cal. (Spitfire Model).

* ***I.J. Survival Carbine Semi-Auto w/Folding Stock*** – .30 Carbine or 5.7mm cal., similar to Survival Carbine, except has folding stock. Mfg. 1983-1989.

	$585	$500	$425	$375	$325	$275	$235

Add 20% for stainless steel.
Add 35% for 5.7mm cal. (Spitfire Model).

I.J. UNIVERSAL CARBINE SEMI-AUTO – .30 Carbine or .256 Win. Mag. cal., gas operated, GI military type carbine, 5 or 10 shot detachable mag., 18 in. barrel, stainless steel or blue finish, walnut stained hardwood, sling swivel, drilled and tapped, known as Model 1003 (.30 Carbine) or Model 1256 (.256 Win. Mag., 5 shot only). Mfg. 1986.

	$450	$395	$335	$285	$245	$210	$180

Iver Johnson marked models are rare.

I.J. UNIVERSAL PARATROOPER SEMI-AUTO CARBINE – 30 Carbine cal., similar to Universal Carbine model, except has Schmeisser-type hardwood folding stock, 5 or 10 shot detachable mag., drilled and tapped. Mfg. 1986.

	$550	$475	$415	$360	$315	$265	$230

Iver Johnson marked models are rare.

MODEL 5100 BOLT ACTION SNIPER – .338 Win., .416 Win., or .50 BMG cal., single shot, free floating 29 in. barrel, no sights, drilled and tapped, marketed with Leupold Ultra M1 20X scope, adj. composite stock, adj. trigger, two different model numbers, ltd. mfg., 36 lbs. Mfg. 1985-1993.

	$4,550	$3,775	$3,375	$3,000	$2,600	$2,300	$2,000

J SECTION

J.L.D. ENTERPRISES, INC.

Previous rifle manufacturer located in Farmington, CT. In 2006, the company name was changed to PTR 91, Inc.
Please refer to PTR 91, Inc. listing for current information.

JMC FABRICATION & MACHINE, INC.

Previous manufacturer located in Rockledge, FL 1997-99.

MSR	100%	98%	95%	90%	80%	70%	60%

RIFLES: BOLT ACTION

MODEL 2000 M/P – .50 BMG cal., rapid takedown, 30 in. barrel, matte black finish, cast aluminum stock with Pachmayr pad, fully adj. bipod, 10 shot staggered mag., two-stage trigger, includes 24X U.S. Optics scope, prices assume all options included, 29 1/2 lbs. Limited mfg. 1998-99.

	100%	98%	95%	90%	80%	70%	60%	
	$7,950	$7,400	$6,800	$6,150	$5,500	$4,900	$4,200	Last MSR was $8,500.

Subtract $2,800 if w/o options.

JP ENTERPRISES, INC.

Current manufacturer and customizer established in 1978, and located in White Bear Lake, MN since 2000, Vadnais Heights, MN 1998-2000, and in Shoreview, MN 1995-98. Distributor, dealer, and consumer sales.

JP Enterprises is a distributor for Infinity pistols, and also customizes Remington shotgun models 11-87, 1100, and 870, the Remington bolt action Model 700 series, Glock pistols, and the Armalite AR-10 series. Please contact the company directly or refer to their website (www.jprifles.com) for more information regarding these customizing services.

RIFLES: BOLT ACTION

MODEL MOR-07 – .260 Rem., 7mm WSM (new 2009), or .308 Win. cal., 24 in. stainless steel cryo-treated bull barrel, benchrest quality bolt action, Picatinny rail, JP Tactical Chassis system, Timney trigger, benchrest or tactical style forend, Precision grip system, matte black hard coat anodizing, 10 shot detachable, includes hard case.

MSR $4,499	$4,250	$3,850	$3,350	$2,925	$2,500	$2,000	$1,600

RIFLES: SEMI-AUTO

A-2 MATCH – .223 Rem. cal., JP-15 lower receiver with JP fire control system, 20 in. JP Supermatch cryo-treated stainless barrel, standard A-2 stock and pistol grip, DCM type free float forend, Mil-Spec A-2 upper assembly with Smith National Match rear sight. Mfg. 1995-2003.

	$1,525	$1,300	$1,100	$925	$825	$700	$600	Last MSR was $1,695.

JP15 (GRADE I A-3 FLAT TOP) – .223 Rem. cal., features Eagle Arms (disc. 1999), DPMS (disc. 1999) or JP15 lower assembly with JP fire control system, Mil Spec A-3 type upper receiver with 18 or 24 in. JP Supermatch cryo-treated stainless barrel, synthetic modified thumbhole or laminated wood thumbhole (disc. 2002) stock, JP vent. two-piece free float forend, JP adj. gas system and recoil eliminator. New 1995.

MSR $1,999	$1,775	$1,475	$1,175	$925	$825	$700	$600

Add $400 for NRA Hi-Power version with 24 in. bull barrel and sight package (disc. 2002).
Add $200 for laminated wood thumbhole stock (disc. 2002).

* **JP15 Grade I IPSC Limited Class** – similar to Grade I, except has quick detachable match grade iron sights, Versa-pod bipod. Mfg. 1999-2004.

	$1,675	$1,400	$1,150	$995	$775	$625	$550	Last MSR was $1,795.

* **JP15 Grade I Tactical/SOF** – similar to Grade I, all matte black non-glare finish, 18, 20, or 24 in. Supermatch barrel. Mfg. 1999-2003.

	$1,425	$1,225	$1,050	$925	$800	$700	$600	Last MSR was $1,595.

Add $798 for Trijicon A-COG sight with A-3 adapter.

GRADE III (THE EDGE) – .223 Rem. cal., RND machined match upper/lower receiver system, 2-piece free f¹ forend, standard or laminated thumbhole wood stock, 18 to 24 in. barrel (cryo treated beginning 1998) w¹ eliminator, includes Harris bipod, top-of-the-line model, includes hard case. Mfg. 1996-2002.

	$2,550	$2,125	$1,750	$1,450	$1,150	$875	$750	Last MS⌐

Add $250 for laminated thumbhole stock.

MODEL AR-10T – .243 Win. or .308 Win. cal., features Armalite receiver system with JP fire cont. vent. free floating forend, 24 in. cryo treated stainless barrel, black finish. Mfg. 1998-2004.

	$2,175	$1,825	$1,600	$1,450	$1,150	$875	$750	Last MS⌐

MSR	100%	98%	95%	90%	80%	70%	60%

Add $150 for anodized upper assembly in custom color.
Add $350 for laminated wood thumbhole stock.

* **Model AR-10LW** – lightweight variation of the Model AR-10T, includes 16-20 in. cryo treated stainless barrel, composite fiber forend, black finish only, 7-8 lbs. Mfg. 1998-2004.

| | $2,175 | $1,825 | $1,600 | $1,450 | $1,150 | $875 | $750 | Last MSR was $2,399. |

Add $200 for detachable sights.

CTR-02 COMPETITION TACTICAL RIFLE – .223 Rem. cal., state-of-the-art advanced AR design with many improvements, integral ACOG interface, mag well, various stock configurations, available with two different types of operating systems, depending on use, JP recoil eliminator and fire control system, 1/4 MOA possible. New 2002.

| MSR $2,599 | $2,325 | $1,850 | $1,375 | $1,050 | $825 | $750 | $650 |

Add $599 for presentation grade finish.

MODEL LRP-07 – .260 Rem. or .308 Win. cal., 18 or 22 in. stainless steel cryo-treated barrel, left side charging system (new 2009), tactical compensator, various stocks and pistol grip options, JP adj. gas system, matte black hard coat anodizing, aluminum components, 19 shot mag.

| MSR $3,299 | $3,050 | $2,725 | $2,275 | $1,900 | $1,500 | $1,250 | $1,000 |

JACKSON RIFLES

Previous rifle manufacturer located in Castle Douglas, Scotland. Currently, the company manufactures and distributes parts for custom rifles.

Jackson Rifles manufactured high quality long-range competition rifles, including the J5-P (single shot) and the J5-T (bolt action repeater), available in both right and left-hand actions.

JARRETT RIFLES, INC.

Current manufacturer established in 1979, and located in Jackson, SC. Direct custom order sales only.

RIFLES: BOLT ACTION

Jarrett Rifles, Inc. is justifiably famous for its well-known Beanfield rifles (refers to shooting over a beanfield at long range targets). A Jarrett innovation is the Tri-Lock receiver, which has 3 locking lugs, and a semi-integral recoil lug. Jarrett blueprints every action for proper dimensioning and rigid tolerances, and this explains why their rifles have set rigid accuracy standards.

A wide variety of options are available for Jarrett custom rifles (holders of 16 world records in rifle accuracy). The factory should be contacted directly (see Trademark Index) for pricing and availability regarding these special order options. Custom gunsmithing services for Jarrett rifles are also available and the manufacturer should be contacted directly for gunsmith quotations.

Jarrett also offers a Custom Short Jarrett action rifle for $6,847.

BENCHREST/YOUTH/TACTICAL – various cals., various configurations depending on application. New 1999.

| | $4,625 | $4,150 | $3,650 | $3,150 | $2,750 | $2,150 | $1,750 | Last MSR was $4,625. |

ORIGINAL BEANFIELD RIFLE – built on customer supplied action, choice of caliber, stock style, color, barrel length and finish, with or w/o muzzle brake, supplied with 20 rounds of ammo and test target. New 2005.

| MSR $5,380 | $5,380 | $4,850 | $4,250 | $3,825 | $3,400 | $3,000 | $2,600 |

.50 CAL. – .50 BMG cal., McMillan custom receiver, choice of repeater or single shot, 30 or 34 in. barrel with muzzle brake, 28-45 lbs. Mfg. 1999-2003.

| | $8,050 | $6,500 | $5,300 | $4,350 | $3,650 | $3,000 | $2,500 | Last MSR was $8,050. |

Add $300 for repeater action.

JERICHO

Previous trademark of Israel Military Industries (I.M.I.). Previously imported by K.B.I., Inc. located in Harrisburg, PA.

PISTOLS: SEMI-AUTO

JERICHO 941 – 9mm Para. cal. or .41 Action Express (by conversion only) cal., semi-auto double action or single action, 4.72 in. barrel with polygonal rifling, all steel fabrication, 3 dot Tritium sights, 11 or 16 (9mm Para.) shot mag., ambidextrous safety, polymer grips, decocking lever, 38 1/2 oz. Imported 1990-92.

| | $625 | $550 | $475 | $425 | $375 | $325 | $295 | Last MSR was $649. |

Add $299 for .41 AE conversion kit.

Industrial hard chrome or nickel finishes were also available for all Jericho pistols.

Jericho 941 Pistol Package – includes 9mm Para. and .41 AE conversion kit, cased with accessories. Mfg. 1990-91 only.

| | $850 | $775 | $700 | $625 | $575 | $495 | $450 | Last MSR was $775. |

MSR	100%	98%	95%	90%	80%	70%	60%

JOHNSON AUTOMATICS, INC.

Previous manufacturer located in Providence, RI. Johnson Automatics, Inc. moved many times during its history, often with slight name changes. M.M. Johnson, Jr. died in 1965, and the company continued production at 104 Audubon Street in New Haven, CT as Johnson Arms, Inc. mostly specializing in sporter semi-auto rifles with Monte Carlo stocks in .270 Win. or 30-06 cal.

RIFLES: SEMI-AUTO

MODEL 1941 – .30-06 or 7x57mm cal., 22 in. removable air cooled barrel, recoil operated, perforated metal handguard, aperture sight, military stock. Most were made for Dutch military, some used by U.S. Marine Paratroopers, during WWII all .30-06 and 7x57mm were ordered by South American governments.

$7,350	**$6,750**	**$6,000**	**$5,250**	**$4,500**	**$3,950**	**$3,250**

MilTech offers a restored version of this model. Inspect this model carefully for originality before considering a possible purchase. Values are somewhat lower for restored guns.

NOTES

K SECTION

K.B.I., INC.

Previous importer and distributor located in Harrisburg, PA until Jan. 29, 2010. Distributor sales.

K.B.I., Inc. imported Charles Daly semi-auto pistols, Bul Transmark semi-auto pistols, SA revolvers, AR-15 style rifles, and shotguns in many configurations, including O/U, SxS, semi-auto, lever action, and slide action. K.B.I. also imported Armscor (Arms Corp. of the Philippines), FEG pistols, and Liberty revolvers and SxS coach shotguns. These models may be found within their respective alphabetical sections. K.B.I. previously imported the Jericho pistol manufactured by I.M.I. from Israel. Older imported Jericho pistols may be found under its own heading in this text, and more recently imported pistols are listed under the Charles Daly listing.

MSR	100%	98%	95%	90%	80%	70%	60%	

RIFLES: BOLT ACTION

KASSNAR GRADE I – available in 9 cals., thumb safety that locks trigger, with or w/o deluxe sights, 22 in. barrel, 3 or 4 shot mag., includes swivel posts and oil finished standard grade European walnut with recoil pad, 7 1/2 lbs. Imported 1989-93.

	100%	98%	95%	90%	80%	70%	60%	
	$445	$385	$325	$275	$225	$195	$175	Last MSR was $499.

NYLON 66 – .22 LR cal., patterned after the Remington Nylon 66. Imported until 1990 from C.B.C. in Brazil, South America.

	$125	$110	$95	$85	$75	$70	$65	Last MSR was $134.

MODEL 122 – .22 LR cal., bolt action design with mag. Imported from South America until 1990.

	$125	$110	$95	$85	$75	$70	$65	Last MSR was $136.

MODEL 522 – .22 LR cal., bolt action design with tube mag. Imported from South America until 1990.

	$130	$115	$100	$85	$75	$70	$65	Last MSR was $142.

BANTAM SINGLE SHOT – .22 LR cal., youth dimensions. Imported 1989-90 only.

	$110	$90	$85	$75	$70	$65	$60	Last MSR was $120.

SHOTGUNS

GRADE I O/U – 12, 20, 28 ga., or .410 bore, gold plated SST, extractors, vent. rib, checkered walnut stock and forearm. Imported 1989-93.

	$525	$425	$350	$295	$265	$240	$220	Last MSR was $599.

Add $70 for 28 ga. or .410 bore.
Add $50 for choke tubes (12 and 20 ga. only).
Add $150 for automatic ejectors (with choke tubes only).

GRADE II SxS – 10, 12, 16, 20, 28 ga., or .410 bore, boxlock action, case hardened receiver, English style checkered European walnut stock with splinter forearm, chrome barrels with concave rib, extractors, double hinged triggers. Imported 1989-90 only.

	$515	$435	$375	$325	$275	$250	$225	Last MSR was $575.

Add $95 for 28 ga. or .410 bore.
Add $85 for 10 ga.

KDF, INC.

Previous rifle manufacturer until circa 2007 and current custom riflesmith specializing in restocking and installing muzzle brakes, in addition to supplying specialized rifle parts. Located in Seguin, TX. KDF utilized Mauser K-15 actions imported from Oberndorf, Germany for many rifle models. Previously, KDF rifles were manufactured by Voere (until 1987) in Vöhrenbach, W. Germany.

Older KDF rifles were private labeled by Voere and marked KDF. Since Voere was absorbed by Mauser-Werke in 1987, model designations changed. Mauser-Werke does not private label (i.e. newer guns are marked Mauser-Werke), and these rifles can be found under the Mauser-Werke heading in this text.

RIFLES: OLDER VOERE MFG. (PRE-1988)

* **K-15 Swat Rifle** – .308 Win. cal. standard, 24 or 26 in. barrel, parkerized metal, oil finished target walnut stock, 3 or 4 shot detachable mag., 10 lbs. Importation disc. 1988.

	$1,475	$1,250	$1,000	$850	$725	$650	$575	Last MSR was $1,725.

KSN INDUSTRIES LTD.

Previous distributor (1952-1996) located in Houston, TX. Previously imported until 1996 exclusively by J.O. Arms, Inc. located in Houston, TX. Currently mfg. Israel Arms, Ltd. pistols may be found under their individual listing.

MSR	100%	98%	95%	90%	80%	70%	60%

PISTOLS: SEMI-AUTO

The pistols listed below were mfg. by Israel Arms, Ltd.

KAREEN MK II – 9mm Para. or .40 S&W (new late 1994) cal., single action, 4.64 in. barrel, two-tone finish, rubberized grips, regular or Meprolite sights, 10 (C/B 1994), 13*, or 15* shot mag., 33 oz. Imported 1993-96.

	$360	$305	$255	$225	$200	$185	$170	Last MSR was $411.

Add approx. $160 for two-tone finish with Meprolite sights.

* Kareen Mk II Compact – compact variation with 3.85 in. barrel. Imported 1993-96.

	$415	$360	$315	$255	$225	$200	$185	Last MSR was $497.

KAHR ARMS

Current manufacturer established 1993, with headquarters located in Blauvelt, NY, and manufacturing in Worchester, MA. Distributor and dealer sales.

PISTOLS: SEMI-AUTO

All Kahr pistols are supplied with two mags (except CW Series), hard polymer case, trigger lock, and lifetime warranty. Except for the CW Series, all pistols feature Lothar Walther polygonal rifled match grade barrels.

K9 COMPACT – 9mm Para. cal., trigger cocking, double action only with passive striker block, locked breech with Browning type recoil lug, steel construction, 3 1/2 in. barrel with polygonal rifling, 7 shot mag., wraparound black polymer grips, matte black, black titanium (Black-T, mfg. 1997-98), or electroless nickel (mfg. 1996-99) finish, 25 oz. Mfg. 1993-2003.

	$560	$485	$435	$385	$340	$315	$285	Last MSR was $648.

Add $74 for electroless nickel finish (disc.).
Add $126 for black titanium finish (Black-T, disc.).
Add $103 for tritium night sights (new 1996).

* K9 Compact Stainless – similar to K9 Compact, except is matte finished stainless steel, NYCPD specs became standard 2006 (trigger LOP is 1/2 in. compared to 3/8 in.). New 1998.

MSR $855	$750	$665	$550	$450	$385	$335	$280

Add $130 for tritium night sights.
Add $36 for matte black finish (new 2004).

P9 POLYMER COMPACT – 9mm Para cal., similar to K9 Compact, except has 3.6 in. barrel, lightweight polymer frame, 7 shot mag., matte stainless slide, 17.9 oz. New 1999.

MSR $739	$630	$525	$450	$375	$325	$285	$250

Add $118 for tritium night sights (new 2000).
Add $47 for matte black stainless slide (new 2004).

* MK9 Micro Series Elite 2000 Stainless – similar to MK9 Elite 98 Stainless, except features black stainless frame and slide, black Roguard finish. Mfg. 2001-2002.

	$575	$485	$425	$360	$315	$260	$225	Last MSR was $694.

PM9 MICRO POLYMER COMPACT – 9mm Para cal., 3 in. barrel with polygonal rifling, black polymer frame, trigger cocking DAO, blackened stainless steel slide, 6 or 7 (with mag. grip extension, disc.) shot mag., 16 oz. New 2003.

MSR $786	$665	$550	$460	$400	$350	$300	$275

Add $122 for tritium night sights.
Add $51 for matte black stainless slide (new 2004).
Add $138 for external safety and loaded chamber indicator (new 2010).
Add $205 for stainless slide with Crimson Trace triggerguard laser (new 2010).

K40 COMPACT – .40 S&W cal., similar to K9, except has 6 shot mag., matte black or electroless nickel finish (disc. 1999), 26 oz. Mfg. 1997-2003.

	$560	$485	$435	$385	$340	$315	$285	Last MSR was $648.

Add $103 for tritium night sights (new 1997).
Add $74 for electroless nickel finish (disc. 1999).
Add $126 for black titanium finish (Black-T, disc. 1998).

* K40 Compact Stainless – similar to K40 Compact, except is stainless steel. New 1997.

MSR $855	$695	$575	$475	$375	$325	$260	$225

Add $130 for tritium night sights.
Add $36 for matte black stainless steel (new 2004).

P40 COMPACT POLYMER – .40 S&W cal., similar to P9 Compact, 6 shot mag., 18.9 oz. New 2001.

MSR $739	$630	$525	$450	$375	$325	$285	$250

Add $118 for tritium night sights.
Add $47 for matte black stainless slide (new 2004).

MSR	100%	98%	95%	90%	80%	70%	60%

PM40 COMPACT POLYMER – .40 S&W cal., black polymer frame, 3 in. barrel, supplied with one 5 shot and one 6 shot (with grip extension) mag., matte finished stainless slide, 17 oz. New 2004.

MSR $786	$665	$550	$460	$400	$350	$300	$275

Add $122 for tritium night sights.
Add $51 for matte black stainless slide (new 2005).
Add $205 for stainless slide and Crimson Trace trigger guard laser (new 2010).

P45 POLYMER – .45 ACP cal., DAO, black polymer frame with matte or black stainless steel slide, 3.54 in. barrel, 6 shot mag., ribbed grip straps, low profile white dot combat sights, 18 1/2 oz. New 2005.

MSR $805	$685	$560	$460	$410	$340	$290	$250

Add $116 for Novak night sights.
Add $50 for black stainless slide (new 2006).

PM45 POLYMER – similar to TP45, except has 3.14 in. barrel and 5 shot mag., approx. 19 oz. New 2007.

MSR $855	$750	$665	$550	$450	$385	$335	$280

Add $119 for Novak night sights.
Add $48 for black stainless steel slide (new late 2008).

KEL-TEC CNC INDUSTRIES, INC.

Current manufacturer established in 1991, and located in Cocoa, FL. Dealer sales.

CARBINES/RIFLES: SEMI-AUTO

RFB CARBINE – .308 Win. cal., bullpup configuration with pistol grip and rear detachable mag., 18 (Carbine), 24 (Sporter), or 32 (Target) in. barrel with muzzle brake, Picatinny rail, front ejection from tube located above barrel, 10 or 20 shot mag., accepts FAL type mags., tilting breech block design, ambidextrous controls, black synthetic lower, adj. trigger, 8.1-11.3 lbs. New 2009.

MSR $1,880	$1,775	$1,550	$1,375	$1,150	$900	$800	$700

SUB-9/SUB-40 CARBINE – 9mm Para. or .40 S&W cal., unique pivoting 16.1 in. barrel rotates upwards and back, allowing overall size reduction and portability (16 in. x 7 in.), interchangable grip assembly will accept most popular double column high capacity handgun mags., including Glock, S&W, Beretta, SIG, or Kel-Tec, tube stock with polymer buttplate, matte black finish, 4.6 lbs. Mfg. 1997-2000.

	$365	$335	$300	$265	$235	$200	$180	Last MSR was $700.

Add $25 for .40 S&W cal.

SUB-2000 CARBINE – 9mm Para or .40 S&W (new 2004) cal., similar to Sub-9/Sub-40, choice of blue, parkerized or hard chrome, 4 lbs. New 2001.

MSR $406	$365	$335	$300	$265	$235	$200	$180

Add $31 for parkerized finish or $40 for hard chrome finish (disc. 2006, reintroduced 2008).

SU-16 RIFLE/CARBINE – .223 Rem. cal., unique downward folding stock, forearm folds down to become a bipod, 16 (new 2005) or 18 1/2 in. barrel, Picatinny receiver rail, M16 breech locking and feeding system, black synthetic stock (stores extra mags.) and forearm, approx. 4.7 lbs. New 2003.

MSR $665	$625	$550	$500	$450	$400	$350	$300

Add $53 for lightweight variation.
Add $105 for carbine.

SU-22 RIFLE SERIES – similar to SU-16, except is .22 LR cal., parkerized finish, Picatinny rail on top of receiver and bottom of aluminum quad forearm, open sights, 27 shot mag., 4 lbs. New 2008.

MSR $440	$395	$350	$315	$285	$266	$245	$225

Add $10 for under folding stock with $15 shot mag. (SU-22C).
Add $50 for pistol grip style AR stock (SU-22E).

PISTOLS: SEMI-AUTO

PLR-16 – .223 Rem. cal., M16 type gas operation, 9.2 in. threaded barrel, upper frame has integrated Picatinny rail, 10 shot detachable mag., black composite frame, 3.2 lbs. New 2006.

MSR $665	$590	$510	$430	$375	$325	$295	$275

PLR-22 – similar to PLR-16, except is .22 LR cal., 26 shot mag., 2.8 lbs. New 2008.

MSR $390	$335	$280	$250	$215	$195	$180	$150

PF-9 – 9mm Para. cal., similar operating system as P-11, 3.1 in. barrel, single stack 7 shot mag., includes lower accessory rail, black finish, 12.7 oz. Limited mfg. 2006, reintroduced 2008.

MSR $333	$275	$220	$185	$165	$150	$135	$125

Add $44 for parkerized finish.
Add $57 for hard chrome finish.

MSR	100%	98%	95%	90%	80%	70%	60%

KEPPELER - TECHNISCHE ENTWICKLUNGEN GmbH

Current rifle manufacturer located in Fichtenberg, Germany. No current U.S. importation.

Keppeler manufactures a wide variety of top quality rifles, in many target configurations (including UIT-CISM, Prone, Free, and Sniper Bullpup). Both metric and domestic calibers are available as well as a variety of special order options. Keppeler also manufactures precision caliber conversion tubes for the shotgun barrel(s) on combination guns and drillings. Please contact the factory directly for more information and current pricing (see Trademark Index).

KIMBER

Current trademark manufactured by Kimber Mfg., Inc., established during 1997, with company headquarters and manufacturing located in Yonkers, NY. Previous rifle manufacture was by Kimber of America, Inc., located in Clackamas, OR circa 1993-97. Dealer sales.

PISTOLS: SEMI-AUTO

Kimber pistols, including the very early models marked "Clackamas, Oregon", have all been manufactured in the current plant in Yonkers, NY. Prior to the 1998 production year, the "Classic" model pistols were alternately roll-scrolled "Classic", "Classic Custom" or "Custom Classic". During 1997-98, the "Classic" moniker was dropped from Kimber pistol nomenclature as a specific model.

All Kimber pistols are shipped with lockable high impact synthetic case with cable lock and one mag., beginning 1999.

Beginning in 2001, the "Series II" pistol, incorporating the Kimber Firing Pin Safety System, was, again, phased into almost all centerfire models. All pistols incorporating the firing pin block have the Roman Numeral "II" following the name of the pistol presented on the slide directly under the ejection port. This conversion was completed by February, 2002, and almost all subsequent Kimber centerfire pistols were Series II. There was no "Series I" pistol per se, but pre-series II models are often referred to in that manner.

During 2003, external extractors were phased into almost all .45 ACP models. Due to consumer demand, most models were phased back to traditional (internal) extractors during 2006.

All three changes (disuse of the term "Classic" for pistols, Series II safety system, and external extractor) were "phased in" throughout normal production cycles. Therefore, no distinctive cut-off dates or serial numbering series were established to identify specific product runs or identify when these features were incorporated.

Add $330 for .22 LR cal. or $344-$379 for .17 Mach 2 cal. (mfg. 2005-2006) conversion kit for all mil-spec 1911 pistols (includes complete upper assembly, lightweight aluminum slide, premium bull barrel, and 10 shot mag.). Available in satin black and satin silver. Kimber began manufacture of these kits in early 2003. Prior to that, they were mfg. by a vendor.

CUSTOM II – .45 ACP cal., patterned after the Colt Government Model 1911, 5 in. barrel, various finishes, 7 shot mag., forged steel frame, match grade barrel, bushing and trigger group, dovetail mounted sights, frame machined from steel forging, high ride beavertail grip safety, choice of rubber, laminated wood (disc.), walnut or rosewood (disc.) grips, 38 oz. New 1995.

MSR $828	$675	$590	$505	$460	$370	$305	$235

Add $44 for walnut or rosewood (disc.) grips.
Add $128 for night sights.
Add $185 for Royal II finish (polished blue and checkered rosewood grips).

This series' nomenclature added the Roman numeral "II" during 2001.

* **Custom Target II** – .45 ACP cal., similar to Custom II, except features Kimber adj. rear sight. New 1998.

MSR $942	$795	$695	$595	$540	$435	$360	$280

* **Stainless II** – .38 Super (advertised in 1999, mfg. late 2005-2008), 9mm Para (advertised in 1999, new 2008), .40 S&W (mfg. 1999-2007), or .45 ACP cal., similar to Custom II, except has stainless steel slide and frame.

MSR $964	$800	$700	$600	$545	$440	$360	$280

Add $128 for night sights.
Add $19 for 9mm Para. or $11 for .40 S&W (disc. 2007) cal.
Add $143 for high polish stainless in .38 Super cal. only (mfg. late 2005-2008).
Subtract $27 for Stainless Limited Edition marked "Stainless LE" (disc. 1998).

* **Stainless Target II** – similar to Stainless II, except is available in .38 Super (new 2002), 9mm Para., or 10mm (new 2003) cal., features Kimber adj. rear sight. New 1998.

MSR $1,068	$885	$775	$665	$600	$485	$400	$310

Add $30 for .40 S&W cal. (disc. 2002).
Add $41 for .38 Super cal. or $72 for 10mm or 9mm Para. cal.
Add $130 for high polish stainless in .38 Super cal. only (mfg. late 2005-2008).

GOLD MATCH II – .45 ACP cal., features Kimber adj. sight, stainless steel match barrel and bushing, premium aluminum match grade trigger, ambidextrous thumb safety became standard in 1998, 8 shot mag., fancy checkered

MSR	100%	98%	95%	90%	80%	70%	60%

rosewood grips in double diamond pattern, high polish blue, hand fitted barrel by Kimber Custom Shop, 38 oz.

| MSR $1,345 | $1,195 | $1,045 | $895 | $810 | $655 | $540 | $420 |

This series' nomenclature added the Roman numeral "II" during 2001.

* ***Gold Match Stainless II*** – .38 Super (advertised in 1999, never mfg.), 9mm Para (advertised in 1999, new 2008), .40 S&W (mfg. 1999-2007), or .45 ACP cal., similar to Gold Match, except is stainless steel, 38 oz.

| MSR $1,519 | $1,275 | $1,115 | $955 | $865 | $700 | $575 | $445 |

Add $44 for 9mm Para. or .40 S&W cal.

TEAM MATCH II – 9mm Para. (new 2009), .45 ACP, or .38 Super (limited mfg. 2003-2004, reintroduced 2006) cal., same pistol developed for USA Shooting Team (2004 Olympics Rapid Fire Pistol Team) competition, satin finish stainless steel frame and slide, 5 in. match grade barrel, 30 LPI front strap checkering, match grade trigger, Tactical Extractor system (disc.) or internal extractor, extended magazine well, 8 shot mag., laminated red/white/blue grips, 38 oz. New 2003.

| MSR $1,535 | $1,295 | $1,135 | $970 | $880 | $710 | $585 | $455 |

Add $48 for .38 Super cal.
Add $11 for 9mm Para. cal.

A donation is made to the U.S.A. Shooting Team for every Team Match II sold.

GOLD COMBAT II – .45 ACP cal. only, 5 in. barrel (bushingless bull became standard 2008), full size carry pistol based on the Gold Match, steel frame and slide, stainless steel match grade barrel and bushing, matte black KimPro finish, rear night sight, serrated flattops and scalloped French shoulders also became standard 2008, tritium night sights, checkered walnut (disc. 2008) or 24 LPI herringbone pattern micarta grips, ambidextrous thumb safety, extended and beveled mag. well, full length guide rod, 38 oz, mfg. by Custom Shop. Mfg. 1994-2008.

| | $1,925 | $1,685 | $1,445 | $1,310 | $1,060 | $865 | $675 | Last MSR was $2,224. |

This series' nomenclature added the Roman numeral "II" during 2001.

* ***Gold Combat Stainless II*** – similar to Gold Combat, except is all steel. Mfg. 1994-2008.

| | $1,895 | $1,660 | $1,420 | $1,290 | $1,040 | $855 | $665 | Last MSR was $2,172. |

* ***Gold Combat RL II*** – similar to Gold Combat, except is has Picatinny rail machined into the lower forward frame to accept optics and other tactical accessories. Mfg. 1994-2008.

| | $1,995 | $1,745 | $1,495 | $1,355 | $1,095 | $900 | $700 | Last MSR was $2,319. |

SUPER MATCH II – .45 ACP cal. only, 5 in. barrel, top-of-the-line model, two-tone stainless steel construction, KimPro finish on slide, match grade trigger, custom shop markings, 38 oz. New 1999.

| MSR $2,225 | $1,925 | $1,685 | $1,445 | $1,310 | $1,060 | $865 | $675 |

This series' nomenclature added the Roman numeral "II" during 2001.

LTP II – .45 ACP cal., designed for Limited Ten competition, Tactical Extractor, steel frame and slide, KimPro finish, 20 LPI front strap checkering, 30 LPI checkering under trigger guard, tungsten guide rod, flattop serrated slide, beveled mag. well, ambidextrous thumb safety, adj. rear sight. Mfg. by Custom Shop 2002-2006.

| | $1,850 | $1,620 | $1,385 | $1,260 | $1,015 | $830 | $645 | Last MSR was $2,106. |

RIMFIRE TARGET – .17 Mach 2 (mfg. 2004-2005) or .22 LR cal., aluminum frame in silver or black anodized finish (disc. 2006), black oxide steel or satin stainless slide (.17 Mach 2 cal. only), 5 in. barrel, black synthetic grips, Kimber adj. rear sight, 28 oz. New 2003.

| MSR $834 | $725 | $635 | $545 | $495 | $400 | $325 | $255 |

Add $39 for .17 Mach 2 cal.

* ***Rimfire Target Super*** – .22 LR cal., similar to Rimfire Target, except has flattop slide with aggressive fluting on upper sides, premium aluminum trigger, ambidextrous safety, rosewood grips with logo inserts, guaranteed to fire a sub-1.5 in. 5 shot group at 25 yards, test target included, 23 oz., mfg. by Kimber Custom Shop. New 2004.

| MSR $1,172 | $1,000 | $875 | $750 | $680 | $550 | $450 | $350 |

POLYMER MODEL – .45 ACP cal., features widened black polymer frame offering larger mag. capacity, choice of fixed (Polymer Model) or adj. Kimber target (Polymer Target Model, disc. 1999) rear sight, matte black slide, 10 shot mag., 34 oz. Mfg. 1997-2001.

| | $675 | $590 | $505 | $460 | $370 | $305 | $235 | Last MSR was $795. |

Add $88 for Polymer Target Model.

All Polymer Models were disc. in 2002 in favor of the new "Ten" Series with improved Kimber made frame. Magazines are interchangeable.

* ***Polymer Model Stainless*** – .38 Super (advertised in 1999, never mfg.), 9mm Para (advertised in 1999, never

MSR	100%	98%	95%	90%	80%	70%	60%

mfg.), .40 S&W (mfg. 1999 only), or .45 ACP cal., similar to Polymer Model, except has satin finish stainless steel slide. Mfg. 1998-2001.

| | $745 | $650 | $560 | $505 | $410 | $335 | $260 | Last MSR was $856. |

Add $88 for Polymer Stainless Target Model (disc. 1999).

* ***Polymer Model Gold Match*** – .45 ACP cal. only, similar to Gold Match, except has polymer frame, supplied with 10 shot double stack mag., 34 oz. Mfg. 1999-2001.

| | $925 | $810 | $695 | $630 | $510 | $415 | $325 | Last MSR was $1,041. |

»**Polymer Model Gold Match Stainless** – similar to Gold Match, except has polymer frame and stainless steel slide, 34 oz. Mfg. 1999-2001.

| | $1,025 | $895 | $770 | $695 | $565 | $460 | $360 | Last MSR was $1,177. |

* ***Polymer Model Pro Carry*** – .45 ACP cal. only, 4 in. bushingless bull barrel, steel slide, 32 oz. Mfg. 1999-2001.

| | $725 | $635 | $545 | $495 | $400 | $325 | $255 | Last MSR was $814. |

»**Polymer Model Pro Carry Stainless** – similar to Polymer Pro Carry, except has stainless steel slide. Mfg. 1999-2001.

| | $755 | $660 | $565 | $515 | $415 | $340 | $265 | Last MSR was $874. |

* ***Polymer Model Ultra Ten*** – .45 ACP cal., black polymer frame with aluminum frame insert, stainless slide, 3 in. barrel, 10 shot staggered mag., low profile sights, lighter version of the Polymer Series frame, Kimber Firing Pin Safety, 24 oz.

While advertised during 2001 with an MSR of $896, this model never went into production.

COMPACT II – .45 ACP cal., features 4 in. barrel, .4 in. shorter aluminum or steel frame, 7 shot mag., Commander style hammer, single recoil spring, low profile combat sights, checkered black synthetic grips, 28 (aluminum) or 34 (steel) oz. Mfg. 1998-2001.

| | $635 | $555 | $475 | $430 | $350 | $285 | $220 | Last MSR was $764. |

* ***Compact Stainless II*** – .40 S&W (mfg. 1999-2001) or .45 ACP cal., features stainless steel slide, 4 in. bull barrel, 4 in. shorter aluminum (disc., reintroduced 2009) or stainless (mfg. 2002-2008) frame, 7 shot mag., Commander style hammer, single recoil spring, low profile combat sights, black synthetic grips, 34 oz. New 1998.

| MSR $1,009 | $875 | $765 | $655 | $595 | $480 | $395 | $305 |

Add $32 for .40 S&W cal. (disc. 2001).

This model's nomenclature added the Roman numeral "II" during 2001.

COMBAT CARRY – .40 S&W or .45 ACP cal., 4 in. barrel, carry model featuring aluminum frame and trigger, stainless steel slide, tritium night sights, and ambidextrous thumb safety, 28 oz. Limited mfg. 1999 only.

| | $940 | $820 | $705 | $640 | $515 | $425 | $330 | Last MSR was $1,044. |

Add $30 for .40 S&W cal.

PRO CARRY II – 9mm Para. (new mid-2005), .40 S&W (disc. 2001) or .45 ACP cal., 4 in. barrel, features full length grip similar to Custom Model, aluminum frame, steel slide, 7 or 8 shot mag., 28 oz. New 1999.

| MSR $888 | $775 | $680 | $580 | $525 | $425 | $350 | $270 |

Add $35 for .40 S&W cal. (disc.).
Add $109 for night sights (.45 ACP cal. only).
Add $41 for 9mm Para. cal.

This series' nomenclature added the Roman numeral "II" during 2001.

* ***Stainless Pro Carry II*** – similar to Pro Carry, except has stainless steel slide, not available in 9mm Para. cal. New 1999.

| MSR $979 | $850 | $745 | $635 | $580 | $465 | $380 | $295 |

Add $41 for 9mm Para (new 2008) or $38 for .40 S&W (disc. 2007) cal.
Add $109 for night sights (.45 ACP cal. only).
Add $295 for Crimson Trace grips (.45 ACP cal. only, disc. 2009).

* ***Pro Carry II HD*** – .38 Super (new 2002) or .45 ACP cal., similar to Pro Carry Stainless, except has heavier stainless steel frame, 35 oz. New 2001.

| MSR $1,008 | $925 | $810 | $695 | $630 | $510 | $415 | $325 |

Add $41 for .38 Super cal.

ULTRA CARRY II – .40 S&W (disc. 2001) or .45 ACP cal., 3 in. barrel, aluminum frame, 7 shot mag., 25 oz. New 1999.

| MSR $888 | $775 | $680 | $580 | $525 | $425 | $350 | $270 |

Add $39 for .40 S&W cal. (disc. 2001).

MSR	100%	98%	95%	90%	80%	70%	60%

Add $108 for night sights.
Add $375 for Crimson Trace grips (disc. 2009).

This series' nomenclature added the Roman numeral "II" during 2001.

* ***Stainless Ultra Carry II*** – 9mm Para. (new 2008), .40 S&W (disc. 2007), and .45 ACP cal., similar to Ultra Carry, except has stainless steel slide. New 1999.

MSR $980	$850	$745	$635	$580	$465	$380	$295

Add $41 for 9mm Para. (new 2008) or $45 for .40 S&W cal. (disc. 2007).
Add $109 for night sights (.45 ACP cal. only, disc. 2009).

SUPER CARRY SERIES – .45 ACP cal., 3 (Ultra), 4 (Pro), or 5 (Custom) in. barrel, stainless steel slide, aluminum frame, KimPro II finish, night sights, rounded edges, checkered double diamond wood grips, recessed slide stop pin with surrounding bevel, rear slide serrations. New 2010.

MSR $1,530	$1,295	$1,135	$970	$880	$710	$585	$455

ECLIPSE II SERIES – 10mm (Eclipse Custom II, new 2004) or .45 ACP cal., stainless steel slide and frame, black matte finish with brush polished flat surfaces for elegant two-tone finish, Tritium night sights, target models have adj. bar/dot sights, silver/grey laminated double diamond grips, black small parts, 30 LPI front strap checkering, include Eclipse Ultra II (3 in. barrel, short grip), Eclipse Pro II and Eclipse Pro-Target II (4 in. barrel, standard grip), Eclipse Custom II, and Eclipse Target II (full size). New 2002.

MSR $1,236	$1,125	$985	$845	$765	$620	$505	$395

Add $14 for Eclipse Custom II.
Add $109 for Eclipse Target II or Eclipse Pro-Target II.
Add $55 for Eclipse Custom II in 10mm cal.

The initial Custom Shop version of these pistols was mfg. during late 2001, featuring an ambidextrous thumb safety, and "Custom Shop" markings on left side of slide, 7,931 were mfg.

CUSTOM TLE II SERIES – .45 ACP cal., tactical law enforcement pistol with exactly the same features as the Kimber pistols carried by LAPD SWAT, black oxide coated frame and slide, same features as Custom II, except has 30 LPI front strap checkering and night sights. New 2003.

MSR $1,044	$925	$810	$695	$630	$510	$415	$325

Add $274 for Crimson Trace laser grips.

* ***Stainless TLE II*** – similar to Custom TLE II, except has stainless steel slide and frame. New 2004.

MSR $1,177	$1,050	$920	$785	$715	$575	$470	$365

* ***Custom TLE/RL II Series*** – similar to Custom TLE II, except has Picatinny rail machined into the frame to accept optics and other tactical accessories. New 2003.

MSR $1,139	$1,025	$895	$770	$695	$565	$460	$360

* ***Stainless Custom TLE/RL II*** – similar to Custom TLE/RL II, except is stainless. New 2004.

MSR $1,272	$1,100	$960	$825	$750	$605	$495	$385

* ***Pro Custom TLE/RL II*** – similar to Custom TLE/RL II, except has 4 in. bushingless barrel. New 2004.

MSR $1,197	$1,050	$920	$785	$715	$575	$470	$365

* ***Pro TLE II (LG)*** – similar to Custom TLE/RL II, except has 4 in. bushingless barrel and Crimson Trace laser grips. Mfg. 2006-2008.

	$975	$855	$730	$665	$535	$440	$340	Last MSR was $1,102.

Subtract $240 if w/o Crimson Trace laser grips (new 2008).

* ***Stainless Pro Custom TLE/RL II*** – similar to Stainless TLE/RL II, except has 4 in. bushingless barrel. New 2004.

MSR $1,322	$1,175	$1,030	$880	$800	$645	$530	$410

ULTRA TLE II – .45 ACP cal., 3 in. barrel, 7 shot mag., dovetail mounted night sights, matte black finish, aluminum frame. New 2010.

MSR $1,102	$915	$800	$700	$600	$485	$400	$310

Add $244 for Crimson Trace laser grips.

* ***Stainless Ultra TLE II*** – .45 ACP cal., similar to Ultra TLE II, except is stainless steel. New 2010.

MSR $1,210	$1,050	$950	$825	$725	$625	$525	$425

Add $252 for Crimson Trace laser grips.

TACTICAL II SERIES – 9mm Para (Tactical Pro II, new 2004) or .45 ACP cal., lightweight tactical pistol, grey anodized (disc. 2008) or Gray KimProII finished frame with black carbon steel slide, fixed tritium Meprolight 3-dot night sights, extended magazine well, 30 LPI front strap checkering, black/grey laminated logo grips, 7 shot mag. with bumper

MSR	100%	98%	95%	90%	80%	70%	60%

pad, available in Tactical Ultra II (3 in. barrel, short grip, 25 oz.), Tactical Pro II (4 in. barrel, standard grip, 28 oz.), Tactical Custom II (5 in. barrel, standard grip, 31 oz.). Tactical Custom HD II (.45 ACP only, new 2009), or Tactical Entry II (.45 ACP only, includes integral rail and night sights). New 2003.

MSR $1,250	$1,095	$960	$820	$745	$600	$495	$385

Add $41 for Tactical Pro II in 9mm Para. cal.
Add $83 for Tactical Custom HD II.
Add $178 for Tactical Entry II.

A Custom Shop version of the Pro Tactical II was manufactured in 2002, but w/o checkering and night sights.

STAINLESS TEN II SERIES – .45 ACP cal., high capacity polymer frame, stainless steel slide with satin finish, impressed front grip strap checkering and serrations under trigger guard, textured finish, polymer grip safety and mainspring housing, 10 or 13 (new 2005) round double stack mag., includes Ultra Ten II (3 in. barrel, short grip, disc. 2003), Pro Carry Ten II (4 in. barrel, standard grip), Stainless Ten II (full size), and Gold Match Ten II (stainless steel barrel, polished stainless steel slide flats, hand fitted barrel/bushing to slide, adj. sight), 14 (pre-ban) round mags. also available, accepts magazines from older Kimber mfg. polymer pistols. Mfg. 2002-2007.

	$715	$625	$535	$485	$395	$320	$250	Last MSR was $812.

Add $9 for Pro-Carry Ten II, $35 for Ultra Ten II (disc. 2003), or $294 for Gold Match Ten II.

* **BP Ten II** – similar to Stainless Ten II, except has black oxide carbon steel slide, and aluminum frame for lighter weight. Mfg. 2003-2007.

	$570	$500	$425	$385	$315	$255	$200	Last MSR was $652.

* **Pro BP Ten II** – similar to Pro Carry Ten II, except has black oxide carbon steel slide, and aluminum frame for lighter weight. Mfg. 2003-2007.

	$570	$500	$425	$385	$315	$255	$200	Last MSR was $666.

CDP II (CUSTOM DEFENSE PACKAGE) – 9mm Para. (new 2008), .40 S&W (disc. 2007), or .45 ACP cal., Custom Shop pistol featuring tritium night sights, stainless steel slide with black anodized aluminum frame, 3 in. (Ultra CDP II, 25 oz.), 4 in. (Pro CDP II and Compact CDP II, 28 oz.), or 5 in. (Custom CDP II, 31 oz.) barrel, carry bevel treatment, ambidextrous thumb safety, double diamond pattern checkered rosewood grips, 30 LPI checkered front strap and under trigger guard (new 2003), two-tone finish. New 2000.

MSR $1,318	$1,150	$1,005	$860	$780	$630	$515	$400

Add $40 for .40 S&W cal., available in either Ultra CDP II or Pro CDP II configuration.
Add $41 for 9mm Para cal. (new 2008).
Add $285 for Crimson Trace laser grips (new 2010).

The Pro CDP II has a full length grip frame.

This series' nomenclature added the Roman numeral "II" during 2001.

ULTRA TEN II CDP – .45 ACP cal., tritium night sights, stainless steel slide with black polymer frame, 3 in. barrel, carry bevel treatment, standard manual safety, 10 shot mag., 24 oz. Mfg. 2003 only.

	$825	$720	$620	$560	$455	$370	$290	Last MSR was $926.

RAPTOR II – .45 ACP cal., full size carbon steel or stainless steel (new 2008) frame with "scales" on front strap, continuing on slide in lieu of standard serrations, flats on frame and slide polished, black oxide finish, back cut flattop, 5 in. stainless barrel with engraved "Raptor II" and "Custom Shop", black anodized trigger, ambidextrous safety, scaled Zebra wood grip panels with Kimber logo, fixed slant night sights, 38 oz. New mid-2004.

MSR $1,379	$1,175	$1,030	$880	$800	$645	$530	$410

Add $131 for stainless steel frame (new 2008).

PRO RAPTOR II – .45 ACP cal., full size stainless steel frame with "scales" on front strap, continuing on carbon steel slide in lieu of standard serrations, flats on frame and slide polished, black oxide finish, back cut flattop, 4 in. stainless barrel with engraved "Pro Raptor II" and "Custom Shop", black anodized trigger, ambidextrous safety, scaled Zebra wood grip panels with Kimber logo, fixed slant night sights, 38 oz. New mid-2004.

MSR $1,247	$1,075	$940	$805	$730	$590	$485	$375

Add $112 for Stainless Pro Rapter II (new 2009).

ULTRA RAPTOR II – .45 ACP cal., all-matte black finish, 3 in. ramped bushingless barrel, lightweight aluminum frame, lizard scale serrations on flat-top slide and frontstrap, feathered logo wood grips, flats on frame and slide polished, night sights, mfg. by Custom Shop. New 2006.

MSR $1,247	$1,075	$940	$805	$730	$590	$485	$375

Add $112 for Stainless Ultra Raptor II.

GRAND RAPTOR II – .45 ACP cal., full-size stainless steel frame, blued slide, flats on frame and slide polished, two-tone finish, lizard scale rosewood grips with Kimber logo, extended ambidextrous thumb safety, bumped beavertail grip safety, night sights, mfg. by Custom Shop. New 2006.

MSR $1,587	$1,375	$1,205	$1,030	$935	$755	$620	$480

MSR	100%	98%	95%	90%	80%	70%	60%

WARRIOR – .45 ACP cal., production began following adoption of this pistol by the Marine Expeditionary Unit (MEU) Special Operations Capable (SOC), Detachment 1 (Det. 1), civilian version with 5 in. barrel, Series I (no firing pin block), carbon steel slide and frame, integral Picatinny light rail, internal extractor, lanyard loop, bumped grip safety, G-10 material grip (coyote brown), wedge night sights, ambidextrous safety, GI length guide rod finished in black KimPro, 38 oz. New mid-2004.

MSR $1,441	$1,275	$1,115	$955	$865	$700	$575	$445

DESERT WARRIOR – similar to Warrior, except has Dark Earth metal finish and light tan G-10 grips. New mid-2005.

MSR $1,458	$1,275	$1,115	$955	$865	$700	$575	$445

COVERT SERIES – .45 ACP cal., 3 (Ultra Covert II) or 4 (Pro Covert II) in. bushingless barrel, Custom Covert II has Kimber logo and digital camo pattern, carry bevel treatment, 30 LPI front strap checkering, night sights, Desert Tan finish, matte black oxide slide, approx. 25-30 oz. New 2007.

MSR $1,603	$1,375	$1,205	$1,030	$935	$755	$620	$480

KPD – while advertised during 2006-2007, this model never went into production.

SIS SERIES – .45 ACP cal., stainless steel slide, frame, and serrated mainspring housing, 7 or 8 shot mag., 3 (Ultra), 4 (Pro), or 5 (Custom or Custom RL) in. barrel, SIS Night Sight, cocking shoulder for one-hand cocking, lightweight hammer, solid trigger, slide serrations, grey KimPro II finish, beavertail grip safety, stippled black laminate logo grips, ambidextrous thumb safety, choice of rounded frame and mainspring housing (SIS Ultra), Picatinny rail (SIS Pro & Custom RL), standard length guide rod (Custom & Custom RL), 31-39 oz. Mfg. 2008-2009.

MSR	100%	98%	95%	90%	80%	70%	60%
	$1,250	$1,095	$935	$850	$685	$560	$435

Last MSR was $1,427.

Add $95 for SIS Custom RL model with standard length guide rod and Picatinny rail.

AEGIS II SERIES – 9mm Para. cal., 3 (Ultra), 4 (Pro), or 5 (Custom) in. barrel, 8 or 9 shot mag., compact aluminum frame w/satin silver premium KimPro II finish, matte black slide, thin rosewood grips, 30 LPI front strap checkering, high relief cut under triggerguard, tactical Wedge night sights, bumped and grooved grip safety, hammer, thumb safety and mag. release button are bobbed, carry melt treatment on both frame and slide, 25 oz. New 2006.

MSR $1,277	$1,100	$960	$825	$750	$605	$495	$385

ULTRA RCP II – .45 ACP cal., refined carry pistol, black annodized frame, carry melt treatment, matte black slide with premium KimPro II finish, no sights, bobbed mag. release, hammer, beavertail grip safety and thumb safety, round mainspring housing and rear of frame, thin black micarta grip panels, older mfg. had distinctive "hook" on hammer, new mfg. has straight hammer, 25 oz. Mfg. 2003-2005 by Custom Shop, reintroduced 2007.

MSR $1,299	$1,125	$975	$850	$750	$605	$495	$385

CRIMSON CARRY II – .45 ACP cal., satin silver aluminum frame, 3 (Ultra), 4 (Pro), or 5 (Custom) in. barrel, matte black slide with black sights, shortened slide stop pin, beveled frame, rosewood Crimson Trace laser grips. New mid-2008.

MSR $1,156	$1,025	$875	$750	$675	$545	$450	$350

Pistols: Kimber Non-Cataloged Models

Kimber has over the past several years, manufactured a number of pistols that did not appear in their catalog. To help identify non-cataloged models, pistols are listed in two categories: Custom Shop/Special Edition Pistols and Limited Edition Pistols.

Pistols: Kimber Custom Shop/Special Editions

Beginning in 1998, the Kimber Custom Shop began producing special edition pistols. Special edition models have been issued in either fixed numbers, or time limited. Where available, time limited models show the actual number produced. All models are .45 ACP caliber unless otherwise specified.

ROYAL CARRY – compact aluminum frame, 4 in. bushingless barrel, highly polished blue, night sights, ambidextrous safety, hand checkered rosewood grips, 28 oz. 600 mfg. 1998.

Last MSR was $903.

GOLD GUARDIAN – highly polished stainless steel slide and frame, hand fitted 5 in. match barrel and bushing, tritium night sights, ambidextrous safety, extended magazine well, skeletonized match trigger, hand checkered rosewood grips, 38 oz. 300 mfg. 1998.

Last MSR was $1,350.

ELITE CARRY – black anodized compact aluminum frame, stainless slide, 4 in. barrel, meltdown treatment on slide and frame, tritium night sights, 20 LPI checkered front strap, ambidextrous safety, aluminum match trigger, hand checkered rosewood grips, 28 oz. 1,200 mfg. 1998.

Last MSR was $1,019.

MSR	100%	98%	95%	90%	80%	70%	60%

STAINLESS COVERT – meltdown stainless slide and frame finished in silver KimPro, 4 in. barrel, 30 LPI front strap checkering, 3-dot tritium night sights, hand checkered rosewood grips, 34 oz. 1,000 mfg. 1999.

Last MSR was $1,135.

PRO ELITE – aluminum frame with silver KimPro finish, stainless slide with black KimPro finish, full meltdown treatment on slide and frame, 4 in. barrel, 30 LPI front strap checkering, 3-dot tritium night sights, hand checkered rosewood grips, 28 oz. 2,500 mfg. 1999.

Last MSR was $1,140.

ULTRA ELITE – aluminum frame with black KimPro finish, satin stainless slide, full meltdown treatment on slide and frame, 3 in. barrel, 30 LPI front strap checkering, 3-dot tritium night sights, hand checkered rosewood grips, 25 oz. 2,750 mfg. 1999.

Last MSR was $1,085.

HERITAGE EDITION – black oxide steel frame and slide, 30 LPI front strap checkering,ambidextrous safety, premium aluminum trigger, NSSF Heritage medallion and special markings on slide, ser. no. begins with KHE, 38 oz. 1,041 mfg. 2000.

Last MSR was $1,065.

STAINLESS GOLD MATCH SE II – .38 Super or .45 ACP cal., stainless steel frame and slide, 5 in. barrel, serrated flat-top slide, 30 LPI front strap checkering, hand checkered rosewood grips, ambidextrous safety, polished flats, ser. no. begins with KSO, 38 oz. 260 (.38 Super) and 294 (.45 ACP) mfg. 2001.

Last MSR was $1,487.

Add $88 for .38 Super cal.

ULTRA SHADOW II – black steel slide and anodized aluminum frame, 3 in. barrel, fixed tritium night sights, 30 LPI front strap checkering, grey laminate grips, silver grip and thumb safeties and mainspring housing, ser. no. begins with KUSLE, 25 oz.

Last MSR was $949.

PRO SHADOW II – black steel slide and anodized aluminum frame, 4 in. barrel, fixed tritium night sights, 30 LPI front strap checkering, grey laminate grips, silver grip and thumb safeties and mainspring housing, ser. no. begins with KPSLE, 28 oz.

Last MSR was $949.

ULTRA CDP ELITE II – .45 ACP cal., first Kimber .45 pistols with ramped match grade barrels, black anodized aluminum frame, black oxide carbon steel slide, 3 in. barrel, carry melt treatment for rounded and blended edges, Meprolight 3-dot tritium night sights, 30 LPI checkering on front strap and under trigger guard, ambidextrous thumb safety and charcoal/ruby laminated logo grips, 25 oz. Mfg. 2002-Jan., 2003.

Last MSR was $1,216.

ULTRA CDP ELITE STS II – .45 ACP cal., first Kimber .45 pistols with ramped match grade barrels, silver anodized aluminum frame, satin stainless steel slide, 3 in. barrel, carry melt treatment for rounded and blended edges, Meprolight 3-dot tritium night sights, 30 LPI checkering on front strap and under trigger guard, ambidextrous thumb safety and charcoal/ruby laminated logo grips, 25 oz. Mfg. 2002-Jan., 2003.

Last MSR was $1,155.

ULTRA RCP II – .45 ACP cal., refined carry pistol, black annodized frame, meltdown treatment with bobbed heel, 3 line ball milled front strap and bobbed grip safety, Kimpro finished, melted 3 in. trench cut slide (no sights), carbon steel barrel, bobbed spur hammer, black micarta ball milled slim grips, bobbed magazine catch, 25 oz. Mfg. 2003-2005.

MSR	100%	98%	95%	90%	80%	70%	60%
	$1,075	$950	$825	$750	$675	$600	$525

Last MSR was $1,228.

* ***Ultra SP II*** – special anodized frame colors (black/blue, black/red, and black/silver) with black oxide slide, 7 shot mag., 3 in. bushingless barrel, 3-dot sights, carry melt, ball milled micarta grips, standard fixed sights, 25 oz. Mfg. 2003-2005.

	$1,025	$900	$800	$725	$625	$575	$495

Last MSR was $1,175.

25th ANNIVERSARY CUSTOM LIMITED EDITION – .45 ACP cal., black oxide frame and slide, 5 in. barrel, premium aluminum trigger, fancy walnut anniversary logo grips, "1979-2004" engraving on slide, Series I safeties and traditional extractor, ser. no. range is KAPC0001-KAPC1911. Limited production of 1,911 during 2004-2005.

	$825	$725	$650	$575	$500	$425	$350

Last MSR was $923.

* ***25th Anniversary Custom Limited Edition Gold Match*** – blued frame and slide, deep polish on flats, 5 in. stainless barrel, premium aluminum trigger, ambidextrous safety, adj. sights, fancy walnut anniversary logo grips, "1979-2004" engraving in slide, Series I safeties and traditional extractor, ser. no. range KAPG0001-KAPG0500, 38 oz. Limited production of 500 during 2004-2005.

	$1,175	$995	$875	$775	$700	$625	$550

Last MSR was $1,357.

* ***25th Anniversary Custom Limited Edition Pistol Set*** – includes one Custom (ser. no. range KMSC0001-KMSC250) and one Gold Match (ser. no. range KMSG0001 - KMSG250), matched ser. nos., wood presentation case. Limited production of 250 during 2004-2005.

	$2,250	$2,000	$1,775	$1,525	$1,300	$1,100	$900

Last MSR was $2,620.

MSR	100%	98%	95%	90%	80%	70%	60%

CENTENNIAL EDITION – .45 ACP cal., steel frame with finish by Turnbull Restoration, ivory grips, adj. target sights, light scroll engraving, aluminum trigger, includes presentation case, Limited mfg. of 250 beginning 2010.

MSR $4,352	$3,995	$3,650	$3,275	N/A	N/A	N/A	N/A

Pistols: Kimber Limited Editions

Kimber has produced limited runs of pistols for dealer groups, NRA Events, sporting goods stores, law enforcement agencies, special requests, etc. Limited run pistols can be as small as 25 mfg.

PRO CARRY SLE – all stainless steel slide and frame, 4 in. barrel, identical to Stainless Pro Carry Model, except has stainless frame, mfg. for Kimber Master Dealers, cataloged in 2001, later production known as Pro Carry HD II, 1,329 mfg. during 2000.

Last MSR was $815.

PRO COMBAT – black oxide stainless steel frame and slide, 4 in. barrel, ambidextrous safety, tritium 3-dot night sights, match grade aluminum trigger, 30 LPI front strap checkering, hand checkered rosewood grips, 35 oz. Marketed by RGuns. 52 mfg. 2000.

Last MSR was $860.

TARGET ELITE II – two-tone stainless frame and slide, black oxide coating on frame, slide natural stainless, adj. rear sight, rosewood double diamond grips, sold through stores affiliated with Sports Inc. buying group, 38 oz. 220 mfg. 2001.

Last MSR was $950.

CUSTOM DEFENDER II – two-tone stainless frame and slide, black oxide coating on frame, slide natural stainless, fixed low profile rear sight, double diamond rosewood grips, sold only through stores affiliated with National Buying Service, 38 oz. 290 mfg. 2001.

Last MSR was $839.

CUSTOM ECLIPSE II – stainless slide and frame, 5 in. barrel, black oxide finish brush polished on the flats, 30 LPI front strap checkering, adj. night sights, laminated grey grips, ser. no. begins with KEL, 38 oz. 4,522 mfg. 2001.

Last MSR was $1,121.

PRO ECLIPSE II – stainless steel frame and slide, 4 in. barrel, black oxide finish brush polished on the flats, 30 LPI front strap checkering, fixed 3-dot night sights, laminated grey grips, ambidextrous safety, ser. no. begins with KRE, 35 oz. 2,207 mfg. 2001.

Last MSR was $1,065.

ULTRA ECLIPSE II – stainless steel frame and slide, 3 in. barrel, black oxide finish brush polished on the flats, 30 LPI front strap checkering, fixed 3-dot night sights, laminated grey grips, ambidextrous safety, 34 oz. 1,202 mfg. 2001.

Last MSR was $1,054.

STRYKER TEN II – Ultra Ten II with black polymer frame and frame insert and small parts, natural stainless slide, 25 oz. 200 mfg. 2002.

Last MSR was $850.

LAPD SWAT – black oxide coated stainless frame and slide, 5 in. barrel, low profile Meprolight 3-dot night sights, 30 LPI front strap checkering, black rubber double diamond grips, 38 oz. 300 mfg. 2002.

Following extensive testing to select a duty pistol, LAPD SWAT chose a Kimber Stainless Custom II and had it enhanced to their specifications. This model was made strictly for law enforcement and not sold to the public. A civilian version called the Tactical law Enforcement (TLE) Series went into production in 2003.

NRA EPOCH II – stainless slide and frame, 5 in. barrel, black oxide finish brush polished on flats, 30 LPI front strap checkering, standard safety, fixed tritium night sights, laminated grey grips, ser. no. begins with KNRAE, Friends of NRA pistol available only at NRA banquets, 38 oz. 58 mfg. 2002.

This model had no established MSR.

THE BOSS II – limited edition to commemorate Blythe Sports 50th anniversary, stainless steel slide and frame, carry melt treatment, fixed white dot sights, premium aluminum 2 hole trigger, 5 in. barrel, engraved "The BOSS II" on ejection port side, and "SPECIAL EDITION", black and sliver laminate grips with Blythe 50th anniversary logo in center on white insert, ser. no. KBSS000-KBSS024, 25 mfg.

This model had no established MSR.

ECLIPSE CLE II – 5 in. barrel, Eclipse Custom II finish on slide with black over stainless frame (no front strap checkering), charcoal/ruby Kimber logo grips, sold only through stores affiliated with National Buying Service, 38 oz. 271 mfg. 2003.

Last MSR was $917.

* **Eclipse PLE II** – similar to Eclipse CLE II, except has 4 in. bushingless barrel, sold only through stores affiliated with Sports Inc. buying group, 35 oz. 232 mfg. 2003.

Last MSR was $877.

* **Eclipse ULE II** – Eclipse Ultra II finish on slide with black over stainless frame (no front strap checkering), 3 in. bushingless barrel, charcoal/ruby Kimber logo grips, sold only through stores affiliated with National Buying Service, 34 oz. 227 mfg. 2003.

Last MSR was $890.

MSR	100%	98%	95%	90%	80%	70%	60%

TEAM MATCH II 38 SUPER – .38 Super cal., identical to original Team Match II, with .38 Super ramped barrel, match grade chamber, bushing and trigger group, special Team Match features, including 30 LPI checkered front strap, adj. sight, extended magazine well, premium aluminum trigger and red, white, and blue USA Shooting Team logo grips, 38 oz. Mfg. 2003-2004.

| | $1,150 | $995 | $875 | $775 | $675 | $575 | $475 | Last MSR was $1,352. |

MCSOCOM ICQB (2004) – .45 ACP cal., at the request of the Marine Corps Special Operations Command (MCSOCOM) Detachment 1 (Det. 1), Kimber produced Interim Close Quarters Battle (ICQB) 1911 patterned pistols in accordance with very high specific requirements: steel frame and slide finished in matte black, internal extractor, GI length guide rod and plug, light rail, bumped grip safety and ambidextrous manual safety, lanyard loop, Simonich G-10 "Gunner" grips, and Novak Lo-Mount night sights.

There was no MSR on this model, as it was not available for sale to the general public. The civilian version of this pistol is called the Warrior.

TARGET MATCH – .45 ACP cal., oversized 5 in. stainless steel barrel, matte black frame and slide with brush polished flats, high relief cut under triggerguard, wide cocking serrations, solid match trigger, engraved bullseye inlaid burl walnut logo grips, 30 LPI checkering on froont strap and under trigger guard, special ser. no. starting with "KTM", 38 oz. 1,000 mfg. 2006-2009.

| | $1,215 | $1,025 | $875 | $775 | $700 | $600 | $500 | Last MSR was $1,427. |

CLASSIC TARGET II – .45 ACP cal., two-tone stainless steel frame, matte black oxide slide, no cocking serrations, adj. sights, premium match grade trigger, smooth/stippled logo grips, match grade chamber, barrel, and barrel bushing, 38 oz. Sold exclusively through Gander Mountain. Mfg. 2006-2008.

| | $825 | $675 | $555 | $460 | $395 | $350 | $300 | Last MSR was $999. |

FRANKLIN CUSTOM II – similar to Custom II, silver finished slide stop, bushing, mag. release, grip safety and mainspring housing, red, white and blue laminate grips with Franklin's Gun Shop logo, commemorates 44th anniversary of Franklin's Gun Shop, ser. no. KFGS01 - KFGS50, 50 mfg. 2006.

This model had no established MSR.

RIFLES: BOLT ACTION

Rimfire Models, Repeating and Single Shot

A three position Win. Model 70 type safety became a standard feature on all Kimber .22 LR and .17 Mach 2 cal. rifles in early 2004.

HUNTER – .17 Mach 2 (new 2007) or .22 LR cal., similar to Classic, except has grade A walnut, clear stock finish, straight barrel contour, 6.7 lbs. Mfg. 2002-2007.

| | $715 | $595 | $515 | $455 | $400 | $350 | $300 | Last MSR was $863. |

Add $40 for .17 Mach 2 cal.

YOUTH – .22 LR cal., similar to Hunter, except has 12 1/4 in. LOP.

While this model was cataloged during 2002-2003 with an MSR of $746, it never went into production.

CLASSIC – .22 LR cal., Mauser claw extractor with 2 position Model 70 type safety, unique eccentric bolt that allows a "centerfire-type" firing pin for faster lock time and greater strength, AA walnut sporter stock with 20 LPI 4-point panel checkering and hand rubbed oil finish, 22 in. match grade sporter barrel with match chamber and Custom Sporter contour, 5 shot mag., steel grip cap, pillar bedding, bead blasted blue finish, adj. trigger, approx. 6 1/2 lbs. Mfg. 1999-2007.

| | $1,025 | $875 | $765 | $655 | $550 | $450 | $350 | Last MSR was $1,223. |

Through 2002, all Kimber .22 cal. Classic rifles had an A grade claro walnut stock, 2-point checkering pattern, urethane finish, and straight barrel taper contour.

* **Classic Varmint** – .17 Mach 2 (new mid-2004) or .22 LR cal., similar to Classic, except has A walnut and 20 in. stainless fluted barrel in a heavy sporter contour. Mfg. 2003-2007.

| | $975 | $825 | $725 | $600 | $500 | $425 | $375 | Last MSR was $1,125. |

* **Classic Pro Varmint** – .17 Mach 2 (new mid-2004) or .22 LR cal., similar to Classic Varmint, except has grey laminate uncheckered stock, brush polished stainless 20 in. barrel with black flutes. Mfg. 2004-2007.

| | $995 | $850 | $760 | $655 | $550 | $450 | $350 | Last MSR was $1,182. |

Add $46 for .17 Mach 2 cal.

* **Custom Classic** – .22 LR cal., similar to Classic, except has 24 LPI wrap checkering, ebony forend tip and AAA walnut stock, 6 1/2 lbs. Mfg. 2003-2007.

| | $1,375 | $1,150 | $900 | $765 | $650 | $550 | $475 | Last MSR was $1,607. |

MSR	100%	98%	95%	90%	80%	70%	60%	

SUPERAMERICA MODEL – .22 LR cal., top-of-the-line model with AAA claro walnut with 24 LPI full wrap checkering, highly polished blue finish, hand rubbed oil finish, Custom Sporter barrel contour, ebony forend tip, cheekpiece and black recoil pad, 5 shot mag., 6 1/2 lbs. Limited mfg. 2001-2007.

| | $1,675 | $1,375 | $1,100 | $925 | $825 | $700 | $600 | Last MSR was $1,988. |

Through 2001, all Superamerica rifles had urethane finish and straight taper barrel contour.

* ***SuperAmerica Model Custom Match 25th Anniversary Ltd. Ed.*** – .22 LR cal., similar to SuperAmerica model, except has AAA French walnut stock, black oxide matte finish barrel and receiver, steel buttplate, engraved grip cap, specially marked barrel and jeweled bolt. Limited production of 300 sequentially numbered rifles during 2004-2005.

| | $2,325 | $2,000 | $1,700 | $1,400 | $1,100 | $900 | $750 | Last MSR was $2,852. |

SVT (SHORT VARMINT/TARGET) MODEL – .17 Mach 2 (new mid-2004) or .22 LR cal., 18 in. fluted stainless steel bull barrel, uncheckered grey laminate wood stock with high comb target design, matte blue action and satin stainless steel barrel, 5 shot mag., no sights, 7 1/2 lbs. Mfg. 1999-2007.

| | $945 | $800 | $700 | $575 | $475 | $375 | $300 | Last MSR was $1,073. |

Add $52 for .17 Mach 2 cal.

HS (HUNTER SILHOUETTE) MODEL – .22 LR cal., features 24 in. half-fluted medium sporter match grade barrel w/o sights, checkered walnut high comb Monte Carlo stock with clear stock finish, adj. trigger, matte blue finish, 7 lbs. Mfg. 1999-2007.

| | $850 | $700 | $585 | $515 | $425 | $350 | $275 | Last MSR was $976. |

Through 2001, all HS Models had urethane finish.

MODEL 82C CLASSIC – .22 LR cal., 22 in. drilled and tapped receiver, repeater with 4 shot mag., checkered A claro walnut stock, polished and blue metal, 6 1/2 lbs. Mfg. 1995-99.

| | $775 | $625 | $550 | $475 | $400 | $360 | $330 | Last MSR was $917. |

The C suffix on this model designates manufacture by Kimber of America.

* ***Model 82C Classic Stainless*** – .22 LR cal., features stainless steel barrel with matte blue action. Approx. 600 mfg. 1997-98.

| | $800 | $650 | $565 | $470 | $400 | $345 | $295 | Last MSR was $968. |

* ***Model 82C Classic Stainless Varmint*** – .22 LR cal., features 20 in. fluted stainless steel barrel, A claro walnut with 18 LPI side panel checkering. Approx. 1,000 mfg. 1995-98.

| | $825 | $675 | $575 | $500 | $425 | $350 | $275 | Last MSR was $1,002. |

MODEL 82C SVT – .22 LR cal., single shot, features 18 in. fluted heavy stainless barrel with uncheckered high comb target style walnut stock, matte blue action, 7 1/2 lbs. Mfg. 1997 only.

| | $675 | $550 | $495 | $425 | $375 | $315 | $270 | Last MSR was $825. |

SVT designates Short Varmint/Target.

MODEL 82C HS – while advertised during 1997, this model never went into production.

MODEL 82C SUPERAMERICA – .22 LR cal., 22 in. drilled and tapped barrel, 4 shot mag., AAA claro checkered walnut stock with steel pistol grip cap, polished and blue metal, 6 1/2 lbs. Mfg. 1993-99.

| | $1,275 | $995 | $875 | $750 | $650 | $575 | $400 | Last MSR was $1,488. |

MODEL 82C CUSTOM MATCH – .22 LR cal., features AA French walnut with 22 LPI wraparound checkering, steel Neidner-style buttplate, matte rust blue finish. Mfg. 1995-99.

| | $1,900 | $1,525 | $1,225 | $975 | $775 | $650 | $525 | Last MSR was $2,158. |

MODEL 82C SUPER CLASSIC – .22 LR cal., features AAA claro walnut with 18 LPI side panel checkering, polished and blue metal. Mfg. 1995-96.

| | $975 | $875 | $775 | $675 | $600 | $550 | $450 | Last MSR was $1,090. |

Centerfire Models

The models below feature a Mauser style action with controlled round feeding and extraction.

MODEL 84C SINGLE SHOT CLASSIC – while advertised during 1996-97, this model never went into production.

MODEL 84C SINGLE SHOT SUPERAMERICA – while advertised during 1996-97, this model never went into production.

MODEL 84C SINGLE SHOT VARMINT STAINLESS – while advertised during 1997, this model never went into production.

MSR	100%	98%	95%	90%	80%	70%	60%

MODEL 84C SINGLE SHOT VARMINT – .17 Rem. or .223 Rem. cal., features 24 (first 200 rifles only), or 25 in. stainless match grade fluted barrel with recessed crown, matte blue receiver finish, checkered A claro walnut stock with beavertail forend, 7 1/2 lbs. Mfg. 1997-99.

	$895	$785	$670	$610	$490	$405	$315	Last MSR was $1,032.

Add $150 for .17 Rem. cal. (less than 100 mfg.).

MODEL 84M – .22-250 Rem., .204 Ruger (new 2004), .223 Rem. (new 2004), .243 Win. (new 2004), .260 Rem., .308 Win., or 7mm-08 Rem. cal., true Mauser action, much improved version of the Model 84C, longer and stronger receiver, 2 position Model 70 type safety, 22 in. light sporter (Classic), 24 in. heavy stainless steel fluted (.308 Win. cal., LongMaster Classic, new 2002), 26 in. heavy stainless steel fluted sporter (Varmint), or 26 in. stainless bull (.22-250 Rem. cal., LongMaster VT) match grade barrel, match grade trigger, 5 shot mag. with sculpted steel floorplate), grey/black laminate target stock with high comb and extended pistol grip (LongMaster VT) or checkered walnut stock and forend, 5 lbs., 10 oz. (Sporter), 7 lbs., 5 oz. (Varmint and LongMaster Classic), or 10 lbs (LongMaster VT). New 2001.

A three position Win. Model 70 type safety became a standard feature on all Kimber 84M rifles in early 2004.

* ***Model 84M Classic*** – .22-250 Rem., .223 Rem. (new 2009), .243 Win., .25-06 Rem. (Select Grade only), .257 Roberts (Select Grade only), .260 Rem. (disc. 2009), .270 Win. (new 2010, Model 84L only), .30-06 (Model 84L only), .308 Win., 7mm-08 Rem., or .338 Federal (new 2007) cal.

MSR $1,172	$1,000	$875	$750	$650	$550	$450	$395

Add $187 for Classic Select Grade with Claro walnut (new 2006).
Add $164 for Classic Select Grade with French walnut (mfg. 2006-2007).
Add $51 for stainless steel action and barrel (new 2009, .243 Win., .308 Win., or 7mm-08 Rem. cal. only).

Beginning in 2010, this model is also available with a left-hand action (Model 84L Classic, available in .270 Win., .30-06, .25-06 Rem. cals. only) at no extra charge.

* ***Model 84M Longmaster Classic*** – .223 Rem., .243 Win. (disc. 2007), or .308 Win. cal.

MSR $1,255	$1,100	$975	$850	$750	$650	$550	$425

* ***Model 84M Longmaster VT*** – .22-250 Rem. cal. only.

MSR $1,391	$1,150	$975	$850	$725	$600	$500	$450

* ***Model 84M SVT*** – .223 Rem cal., short barrel variation of the Model 84M Longmaster VT.

MSR $1,391	$1,150	$975	$850	$725	$600	$500	$450

* ***Model 84M Varmint*** – .204 Ruger or .22-250 Rem. cal., features 26 in. heavy stainless steel fluted barrel.

MSR $1,255	$1,095	$950	$825	$725	$600	$500	$400

* ***Model 84M Pro Varmint*** – .204 Ruger, .22-250 Rem., or .223 Rem. cal., grey laminate uncheckered stock, brush polished 24 in. stainless steel barrel with black flutes. New 2004.

MSR $1,391	$1,150	$975	$850	$725	$600	$500	$450

MODEL 84M SUPERAMERICA – .223 Rem. (disc. 2009), .243 Win. (disc. 2009), .260 Rem. (disc. 2009), 7mm-08 Rem., .308 Win., or .338 Federal (disc. 2009) cal., similar to Model 84M Repeater, except has 24 LPI wrap checkering, ebony forend tip, AAA walnut, highly polished blue action and barrel. New 2003.

MSR $2,240	$1,925	$1,700	$1,450	$1,275	$1,025	$875	$750

MODEL 84M MONTANA – .204 Ruger (new 2009), .223 Rem. (new 2009), .243 Win., .257 Roberts (new 2008), .260 Rem. (disc. 2009), 7mm-08 Rem., .308 Win., or .338 Federal (new 2007) cal., synthetic stock and satin stainless steel barreled action, 5 lbs. 2 oz. New 2003.

MSR $1,312	$1,150	$995	$875	$775	$675	$575	$450

Add $248 for Montana Black KimPro in .308 Win. cal. only (disc.).

MODEL 84M LONGMASTER PRO – .22-250 Rem. or .308 Win. cal., similar to Longmaster VT, except has synthetic stock, 24 (.308 Win. cal.) or 26 (.22-250 Rem. cal.) in. brush polished stainless bull barrel with black flutes.

While this model was cataloged during 2003 with an MSR of $1,189, it never went into production.

MODEL 84M LPT (LIGHT POLICE TACTICAL) – .223 Rem. or .308 Win. cal., 24 in. matte blue heavy sporter contour fluted barrel, 5 shot mag., black laminate stock with panel stippling, Picatinny rail, oversize bolt handle, sling swivels, recoil pad, full length Mauser claw extractor, 3-position Model 70 style safety, adj. trigger, 8 lbs., 7 oz. New 2008.

MSR $1,476	$1,275	$1,075	$925	$800	$700	$600	$500

MODEL 84M LIMITED EDITION – .257 Roberts or .308 Win. cal., Classic Select Grade French walnut stock and forearm, limited mfg. New 2010.

MSR $1,767	$1,575	$1,375	$1,175	N/A	N/A	N/A	N/A

MODEL 8400 CLASSIC – .25-06 Rem. (mfg. 2006-2009), .270 WSM, .270 Win. (mfg. 2006-2009), 7mm Rem. Mag. (new 2009), 7mm WSM (disc. 2009), .300 WSM, .300 Win. Mag. (new 2006), .30-06 (mfg. 2006-2009), .325 WSM

MSR	100%	98%	95%	90%	80%	70%	60%

(new 2005), or .338 Win. Mag. (new 2006) cal., A walnut stock, 20 LPI panel checkering, 3-position Model 70 type safety, 24 in. sporter match grade blue barrel, match grade adj. trigger. New 2003.

MSR $1,172	$1,000	$875	$750	$650	$550	$450	$395

Add $187 for Classic Select Grade with Claro walnut (new 2006, .270 WSM, .300 WSM, or .325 WSM cals. only).
Add $171 for Classic Select Grade with French walnut (mfg. 2006-2007, .270 WSM, .300 WSM, or .325 WSM cals. only).
Add $51 for stainless.

While a left-hand version of this model was cataloged during 2003, they were never produced.

MODEL 8400 SUPERAMERICA – .270 Win. (mfg. 2009), .30-06 (mfg. 2009), .270 WSM, 7mm WSM (disc. 2009), .300 WSM, .300 Win. Mag. (new 2006), .325 WSM (mfg. 2005-2009), or .338 Win. Mag. (new 2006) cal., similar to Model 8400 Classic, except has AAA walnut stock, 24 LPI panel checkering, ebony forend tip, highly polished blue action, and 24 in. custom sporter barrel. New 2003.

MSR $2,240	$1,925	$1,700	$1,450	$1,275	$1,025	$875	$750

MODEL 8400 MONTANA – .25-06 Rem. (mfg. 2006-2009), .270 Win. (mfg. 2006-2009), .270 WSM, .280 Ackley Improved (disc. 2009), 7mm WSM (disc. 2009), .300 WSM, .300 Win. Mag. (new 2006), .30-06 (mfg. 2006-2009), .325 WSM (new 2005) or .338 Win. Mag. (new 2006) cal., similar to Model 8400 Classic, except has synthetic stock and 24 in. satin stainless steel custom sporter barrel, 6 lbs., 2 oz. New 2003.

MSR $1,312	$1,150	$995	$875	$775	$675	$575	$450

MODEL 8400 TACTICAL SERIES – .300 Win. Mag. or .308 Win. cal., matte blue (Tactical) or KimPro II Dark Earth (Advanced Tactical) finish, grey (Tactical) or Desert Camo (Advanced Tactical) McMillan synthetic stock, 24 in. fluted bull barrel, 5 shot mag., 9 lbs., 4 oz. New 2007.

MSR $1,937	$1,650	$1,445	$1,235	$1,120	$905	$740	$575

Add $697 for Advanced Tactical.

MODEL 8400 CAPRIVI – .375 H&H, .416 Rem. Mag. (new 2010), or .458 Lott cal., 24 in, contoured blue barrel, 4 shot mag., Mauser claw extractor, 3-position Model 70 style safety, adj. trigger, oil finished checkered pistol grip stock, pancake cheekpiece, ebony forend tip, swivel studs, three leaf express sight, double cross bolts, recoil pad, 8 lbs., 7 oz. New 2008.

MSR $3,196	$2,775	$2,400	$2,100	$1,800	$1,500	$1,275	$1,075

MODEL 8400 TALKEETNA – .375 H&H cal., stainless barrel with single leaf express sight, Kevlar/carbon fiber pistol grip stock, 7 3/4 lbs. New 2008.

MSR $2,108	$1,775	$1,555	$1,330	$1,205	$975	$800	$620

MODEL 8400 SONORA – .25-06 Rem., .30-06 (disc. 2009), .300 Win. Mag., 7mm Rem. Mag., or .308 Win. (disc. 2009) cal., brown laminate stock, fluted stainless steel match grade barrel w/o sights, approx. 9 1/2 lbs. New 2008.

MSR $1,359	$1,100	$960	$825	$750	$605	$495	$385

MODEL K770 CLASSIC – while advertised during 1997, this model never went into production. Prototypes only.

MODEL K770 SUPER AMERICA – while advertised during 1997, this model never went into production. Prototypes only.

MODEL 8400 PATROL/POLICE TACTICAL – .300 Win. Mag. or .308 Win. (new 2010) cal., features 20 (Patrol), 24, or 26 in. match grade barrel, chamber, and trigger, trued bolt face, custom McMillan glass bedded stock, fixed Picatinny rail, enlarged bolt handle and knob, 8 3/4 lbs. New 2009.

MSR $1,476	$1,325	$1,160	$995	$900	$730	$595	$465

Mauser 96 Sporters

MODEL 96 SPORTER – .308 Win. cal., features M-96 action with stainless steel fluted heavy barrel. Mfg. 1995-97.

	$450	$415	$365	$300	$260	$225	$200	Last MSR was $520.

During 1995-96, Kimber began sporterizing the Swedish Mauser Model 96 military surplus rifles. They featured stainless steel fluted barrels and a black synthetic Ramline stock, receivers were drilled and tapped to accept Weaver scope mounts, bead blasted bluing, and original reprofiled military bolt. The Sporter configuration included .243 Win., 6.5x55mm, or .308 Win. cal., while the heavy fluted barrel models were available in .22-250 Rem. or .308 Win. (Varmint or Heavy Barrel). Retail prices ranged from $340-$415 for the Standard Sporter, while the Varmint/Heavy barrel variation was priced at approx. $510. Sporter variations were also available as a combo package with scope and hardshell case - add approx. $30.

Mauser 98 Sporters

MODEL 98 SPORTER – .220 Swift (100 mfg.), .257 Roberts (100 mfg.), .270 Win., .280 Rem. (100 mfg.), .30-06, .300 Win. Mag., .338 Win. Mag., or 7mm Rem. Mag. cal., features Mauser M-98 action with stainless match grade

MSR	100%	98%	95%	90%	80%	70%	60%	

fluted barrel, choice of synthetic or claro walnut stock, and Warne bases, matte black finish receiver. Mfg. 1996-98.

| | $465 | $425 | $375 | $315 | $270 | $230 | N/A | Last MSR was $535. |

Add $25 for Mag. cals.
Add $100 for Claro walnut stock.

* ***Mauser 98 Sporter Matte*** – .300 Win. Mag., .338 Win. Mag., or 7mm Rem. Mag. cal., features 25 in. non-fluted sporter barrel, synthetic stock, and Weaver style bases. Disc. 1998.

| | $275 | $250 | $225 | $200 | $185 | $170 | $155 | Last MSR was $339. |

SHOTGUNS: O/U

AUGUSTA SERIES – 12 ga., 2 3/4 (Trap & Skeet) or 3 (Sporting & Field) in. chambers, Boss type boxlock action with shallow frame, blue (Trap & Skeet) or polished metal (Field & Sporting) frame, ejectors, SST, tang safety with ejector, 26-34 in. vent. barrel lengths with VR backbored to .736 in., available in Field, Sporting, Skeet, and Trap variations, beavertail or Schnabel forend, Pachmayr Decelerator recoil pad, 7 lbs., 2 oz-7 lbs., 13 oz. Mfg. in Italy by Investarm 2002-2005, limited delivery 2003-2005.

| | $4,750 | $4,250 | $3,750 | $3,250 | $2,750 | $2,250 | $1,850 | Last MSR was $5,676. |

MARIAS SERIES – 12 or 20 ga., 3 in. chambers, 26, 28, or 30 in. VR barrels with 5 choke tubes, ejectors, charcoal case colored detachable sidelock action with engraving, deluxe checkered walnut English or pistol grip stock and forearm, available in Grade I with Grade III Turkish walnut or Grade II with Grade IV Turkish walnut, imported from Turkey. Imported 2006-2008.

| | $4,995 | $4,375 | $3,750 | $3,250 | $2,700 | $2,200 | $1,825 | Last MSR was $5,799. |

SHOTGUNS: SxS

VALIER SERIES – 16 (new 2006) or 20 ga., 26 or 28 in. barrels, hand engraved sidelock action with seven pins, hand checkered Turkish walnut straight grip English stock, DT, fixed chokes, hand engraved blue (20 ga. only), case colored, or optional bone charcoal case colored action, extractors, approx. 6 1/2 lbs., mfg. in Turkey 2005-2007.

| | $3,525 | $3,050 | $2,675 | $2,200 | $1,850 | $1,450 | $1,100 | Last MSR was $3,999. |

* ***Valier Grade II*** – similar to Grade I, except has ejectors, with or w/o (disc. 2007) charcoal case colored frame, mfg. in Turkey. Imported 2005-2008.

| | $4,495 | $3,995 | $3,050 | $2,675 | $2,200 | $1,850 | $1,450 | Last MSR was $4,999. |

Subtract approx. $600 if w/o bone charcoal case colors.

KIMEL INDUSTRIES, INC.

Previously manufactured until late 1994 by A.A. Arms located in Monroe, NC. Previously distributed by Kimel Industries, Inc. located in Matthews, NC.

CARBINES

AR-9 CARBINE – 9mm Para. cal., carbine variation of the AP-9 with 16 1/2 in. barrel, 20 shot mag., and steel rod folding stock. Mfg. 1991-94.

| | $625 | $550 | $475 | $425 | $365 | $315 | $275 | Last MSR was $384. |

PISTOLS: SEMI-AUTO

AP-9 PISTOL – 9mm Para. cal., tactical design, blowback action with bolt knob on left side of receiver, 5 in. barrel with vent. shroud, front mounted 10 (C/B 1994) or 20* shot detachable mag., black matte finish, adj. front sight, 3 lbs. 7 oz. Mfg. 1989-94.

| | $475 | $425 | $375 | $325 | $300 | $275 | $250 | Last MSR was $279. |

* ***AP-9 Pistol Mini*** – compact variation of the AP-9 Model with 3 in. barrel, blue or nickel finish. Mfg. 1991-94.

| | $550 | $500 | $425 | $375 | $325 | $300 | $275 | Last MSR was $273. |

* ***AP-9 Pistol Target*** – target variation of the AP-9 with 12 in. match barrel with shroud, blue finish only. Mfg. 1991-94.

| | $600 | $550 | $475 | $425 | $375 | $350 | $325 | Last MSR was $294. |

* ***P-95 Pistol*** – similar to AP-9, except without barrel shroud and is supplied with 5 shot mag., parts are interchangeable with AP-9. Mfg. 1990-91 only.

| | $395 | $350 | $300 | $250 | $200 | $175 | $150 | Last MSR was $250. |

KINTREK, INC.

Previous rifle manufacturer located in Owensboro, KY.

MSR	100%	98%	95%	90%	80%	70%	60%

RIFLES: SEMI-AUTO

BULLPUP MODEL – .22 LR cal., bullpup configuration, hinged dust cover, clear Ram-Line type coil spring mag., black synthetic thumbhole stock, A-2 type front/rear sight. Disc.

$350	$300	$250	$225	$200	$175	$150

KNIGHT'S MANUFACTURING COMPANY

Current manufacturer established in 1983, and located in Titusville, FL. Previously located in Vero Beach, FL. Dealer and consumer direct sales.

RIFLES: SEMI-AUTO

Some of the models listed below were also available in pre-ban configurations. SR-25 Enhanced Match model has 10 or 20 shot mag. Some of the following models, while discontinued for civilian use, may still be available for military/law enforcement.

STONER SR-15 M-5 RIFLE – .223 Rem. cal., 20 in. standard weight barrel, flip-up low profile rear sight, two-stage target trigger, 7.6 lbs. Mfg. 1997-2008.

	100%	98%	95%	90%	80%	70%	
	$1,675	$1,475	$1,225	$1,025	$900	$825	$725

Last MSR was $1,837.

* **Stoner SR-15 M-4 Carbine** – similar to SR-15 rifle, except has 16 in. barrel, choice of fixed synthetic or non-collapsible buttstock. Mfg. 1997-2005.

$1,400	$1,175	$950	$850	$775	$700	$650

Last MSR was $1,575.

Add $100 for non-collapsible buttstock (SR-15 M-4 K-Carbine, disc. 2001).

* **Stoner SR-15 URX E3 Carbine** – features 16 in. free floating barrel with URX forearm, E3 type rounded lug improved bolt. New 2004.

MSR $2,207	$1,975	$1,700	$1,325	$1,075	$900	$775	$675

STONER SR-15 MATCH RIFLE – .223 Rem. cal., features flattop upper receiver with 20 in. match grade stainless steel free floating barrel with RAS forend, two-stage match trigger, 7.9 lbs. Mfg. 1997-2008.

$1,795	$1,525	$1,200	$975	$850	$750	$700

Last MSR was $1,972.

STONER SR-25 SPORTER – .308 Win. cal., 20 in. lightweight barrel, AR-15 configuration with carrying handle, 5, 10, or 20 (disc. per C/B 1994) shot detachable mag., less than 2 MOA guaranteed, non-glare finish, 8.8 lbs. Mfg. 1993-97.

$2,650	$2,250	$1,900	$1,600	$1,300	$1,000	$850

Last MSR was $2,995.

* **Stoner RAS Sporter Carbine (SR-25 Carbine)** – 16 in. free floating barrel, grooved non-slip handguard, removable carrying handle, 7 3/4 lbs. Mfg. 1995-2005.

$3,025	$2,550	$2,125	$1,750	$1,500	$1,250	$1,000

Last MSR was $3,495.

Subtract 15% if w/o RAS.

In 2003, the Rail Adapter System (RAS) became standard on this model.

SR-25 STANDARD MATCH – .308 Win. cal., free-floating 24 in. match barrel, fiberglass stock, inlcudes commercial gun case and 10 shot mag. Disc. 2008.

$3,600	$3,300	$2,950	$2,600	$2,300	$2,000	$1,600

Last MSR was $3,918.

SR-25 RAS MATCH – similar to SR-25 Standard, except has 24 in. free floating match barrel and flat-top receiver, less than 1 MOA guaranteed, RAS became standard 2004, 10 3/4 lbs. Mfg. 1993-2008.

$3,350	$2,800	$2,300	$1,800	$1,500	$1,250	$1,000

Last MSR was $3,789.

Subtract approx. 15% if w/o Rail Adapter System (RAS).

Over 3,000 SR-25s have been made to date.

* **SR-25 RAS Match Lightweight** – features 20 in. medium contour free floating barrel, 9 1/2 lbs. Mfg. 1995-2004.

$2,875	$2,450	$2,125	$1,750	$1,500	$1,250	$1,000

Last MSR was $3,244.

Add approx. 15% for Rail Adapter System.

SR-25 ENHANCED MATCH RIFLE/CARBINE – .308 Win. cal., 16 or 20 in. barrel, 10 or 20 shot mag., URX rail system, two-stage trigger, ambidextrous mag. release, integrated adj. folding front sight, micro adj. folding rear sight, EM gas block, combat trigger guard, chrome plated multi-lug bolt and bolt carrier, fixed or nine position adj. stock, black anodized finish, flash hider (carbine only), approx. 8 1/2 lbs.

MSR $4,994	$4,750	$4,250	$3,750	$3,250	$2,750	$2,250	$1,875

Add $625 for 16 in. carbine.

SR-25 MK11 MOD O CIVILIAN DELUXE SYSTEM PACKAGE – .308 Win. cal., consumer variation of the Navy Model Mark Eleven, Mod O, w/o sound suppressor, includes Leupold 3.5-10X scope, 20 in. military grade match barrel, backup sights, cell-foam case and other accessories. Mfg. 2003-2008.

$7,950	$7,250	$6,350	$5,850	$5,100	$4,500	$4,000

Last MSR was $8,534.

MSR	100%	98%	95%	90%	80%	70%	60%	

SR-25 MK11 MATCH RIFLE – .308 Win. cal., includes MK11 Mod O features and 20 in. heavy barrel. Mfg. 2004-2008.

	$5,675	$5,200	$4,775	$4,400	$3,750	$3,150	$2,700	Last MSR was $6,325.

SR-25 MK11 CARBINE – .308 Win. cal., includes MK11 Mod O features and 16 in. match grade stainless steel barrel with muzzle brake, URX 4x4 rail forend, 4-position buttstock. New 2005.

MSR $6,636	$6,000	$5,500	$4,950	$4,550	$3,875	$3,250	$2,800	

SR-25 BR CARBINE – .308 Win. cal., similar to SR-25 MK11 Carbine, except has chrome lined steel barrel. Mfg. 2005-2008.

	$5,675	$5,200	$4,775	$4,400	$3,750	$3,150	$2,700	Last MSR was $6,307.

SR-M110 SASS – 7.62x51mm cal., 20 in. military match grade barrel, full RAS treatment on barrel, civilian variation of the Army's semi-auto sniper rifle system, includes Leupold long-range tactical scope, 600 meter back up iron sights, system case and other accessories. Mfg. 2006-2009.

	$13,000	$11,000	$9,500	$8,000	$7,000	$6,000	$5,000	Last MSR was $14,436.

"DAVID TUBB" COMPETITION MATCH RIFLE – .260 Rem. or .308 Win. cal., incorporates refinements by David Tubb, top-of-the-line competition match rifle, including adj. and rotating buttstock pad. Mfg. 1998 only.

	$5,200	$4,000	$3,600	$3,150	$2,700	$2,300	$1,995	Last MSR was $5,995.

STONER SR-50 – .50 BMG cal., features high strength materials and lightweight design, fully locked breech and two lug rotary breech bolt, horizontal 5 shot box mag., tubular receiver supports a removable barrel, approx. 31 lbs. Limited mfg. 2000, non-commercial sales only.   **Last MSR was $6,995.**

KORRIPHILA

Previous trademark manufacturered until 2004 by Intertex, located in Eislingen, Germany. Previously imported 1999-2004 by Korriphila, Inc., located in Pineville, NC., and by Osborne's located in Cheboygan, MI until 1988.

PISTOLS: SEMI-AUTO

Less than 30 Korriphila pistols were made annually.

HSP 701 – 7.65 Luger (disc.), .38 Spl. (disc.), 9mm Para., 9mm Police (disc.), 9mm Steyr (disc.), .45 ACP, or 10mm Norma (disc.) cal., double action, Budischowsky delayed roller block locking system assists in recoil reduction, 40% stainless steel parts, 4 or 5 in. barrel, blue or satin finish, walnut grips, 7 or 9 shot mag., approx. 2.6 lbs, very limited production.

	$6,500	$5,500	$3,750	$2,950	$2,150	$1,850	$1,675	

KRICO

Current trademark manufactured by Kriegeskorte Handels GmbH, located in Pyrbaum, Germany. Currently imported exclusively beginning mid-2005 by Northeast Arms LLC, located in Fort Fairfield, ME. Previously distributed by Precision Sales, Int'l, located in Westfield, MA 1999-2002. Previously manufactured in Vohburg-Irsching, Germany 1996-1999, and in Fürth-Stadeln, Germany by Sportwaffenfabrik Kriegeskorte GmbH pre-1996.

During 2000, Krico was purchased by Marocchi. Krico has been imported/distributed by over ten U.S. companies/individuals. Krico manufactures high quality rifles, and to date, has mostly sold their guns in Europe. Many of the discontinued models listed below may still be current within the European marketplace. Please contact the importer directly for more information, including availability and pricing (see Trademark Index).

The Krico name is an abridgement of the family name Kriegeskorte.

RIFLES: BOLT ACTION

Values and information below reflect the most current information available to the publisher. Please contact the importer or factory directly for current pricing and model availability (see Trademark Index).

MODEL 640 DELUXE/SUPER SNIPER – .223 Rem. or .308 Win. cal., 23 in. barrel, select walnut stock has stippled hand grip, adj. cheekpiece and vent. forearm, engine turned bolt assembly, 3 shot mag., match trigger, 10 lbs. Importation disc. 1988.

	$1,795	$1,650	$1,475	$1,325	$1,200	$1,100	$995	Last MSR was $1,725.

This model was known as the 650 Sniper/Match until 1986.

KRISS

Please refer to Transformational Defense Industries, Inc. listing.

L SECTION

L.A.R. MANUFACTURING, INC.

Current rifle manufacturer located in West Jordan, UT. Dealer sales.

In addition to its .50 cal. bolt action rifles, L.A.R. also makes upper receiver assemblies in the AR-15 configuration. Please contact the factory directly for both up-to-date information and pricing (see Trademark Index).

MSR	100%	98%	95%	90%	80%	70%	60%

RIFLES: BOLT ACTION

GRIZZLY BIG BOAR COMPETITOR RIFLE – .50 BMG cal., single shot, bolt action design in bullpup configuration, alloy steel receiver and bolt, 36 in. heavy barrel with compensator, thumb safety, match or field grade, includes bipod, scope mount, leather cheek pad and hard carry case, 30.4 lbs. New 1994.

MSR $2,350	$2,150	$1,725	$1,575	$1,375	$1,175	$1,050	$950

Add $100 for parkerizing.
Add $250 for nickel trigger housing finish.
Add $350 for full nickel frame.
Add $250 for stainless steel Lothar Walther barrel.
Add $522 for redesigned (2002) tripod and pintle mount.

A Big Bore Hunter Package is also available on this model, and includes: Nightforce scope and rings, cleaning kit, tripod with pintle mount, drag bag, and hard carry case. MSR is $4,890.

GRIZZLY T-50 – .50 BMG cal., single shot, 32-36 in. barrel with muzzle brake, extended barrel shroud with top and bottom Picatinny rails, black parkerized finish, cheek saddle on frame, carry handle in front of triggerguard, extended bolt handle, 30 1/2 - 32 lbs. New 2009.

MSR $3,200	$3,000	$2,800	$2,600	$2,400	$2,200	$2,000	$1,800

A T-50 Tactical Package is available on this model and includes: Nightforce scope and rings, cleaning kit, heavy duty bipod, carry handle, Accu-Shot monopod, drag bag, and hard carry case. MSR is $5,653.

RIFLES: SEMI-AUTO

GRIZZLY 15 – .223 Rem. cal., patterned after the AR-15, available in either A2 or A3 configuration, limited mfg. 2004-2005.

	$825	$725	$650	$575	$525	$475	$425	Last MSR was $795.

Add $85 for detachable carry handle.

L E S INCORPORATED

Previous manufacturer located in Morton Grove, IL.

PISTOLS: SEMI-AUTO

P-18 ROGAK – 7.65mm Para. (limited mfg.) or 9mm Para. cal., double action, 18 shot, 5 1/2 in. barrel, stainless steel, black plastic grips with partial thumb rest. Disc.

	$450	$395	$350	$325	$295	$275	$250
High Polish Finish	$525	$450	$395	$375	$325	$295	$275

Add 25% for 7.65mm Para. cal.

This pistol was patterned after the Steyr Model GB. Approx. 2,300 P-18s were mfg. before being disc.

LRB ARMS

Current manufacturer located in Floral Park, NY. Currently distributed by LRB of Long Island, NY.

RIFLES: SEMI-AUTO

Additionally, LRB also manufactures AR-15, M-14, and M-25 receivers and barreled actions. Please contact the company directly for more information (see Trademark Index).

GOVERNMENT ISSUE/TANKER MODEL – .308 Win. cal., new M14 receiver with USGI parts, 18 1/2 (Tanker) or 20 (Government) in. Criterion National Match standard weight barrel, choice of birch or walnut original GI stock, 10 shot mag., includes sling and field manual.

MSR $2,680	$2,495	$2,200	$1,925	$1,750	$1,575	$1,375	$1,075

LWRC INTERNATIONAL, INC.

Current rifle manufacturer located in Cambridge, MD. Dealer and distributor sales.

MSR	100%	98%	95%	90%	80%	70%	60%

PISTOLS: SEMI-AUTO

LWRC manufactures a M6A2 PSD (Personal Security Detail) semi-auto pistol in 5.56 NATO and 6.8mm SPC cal, with an 8 in. barrel and permanently attached flash hider and 30 shot mag. Please contact the company directly for more information, including pricing and availability (see Trademark Index).

RIFLES: SEMI-AUTO

LWRC manufactures a complete line of short-stroke, gas-piston operated, AR-15, M-16, and M-4 semi-auto rifles. Civilian models include: The M6 (MSR $1,668-$1,778), M6A1 (MSR $1,975-$2,085), M6A2 (MSR $2,217-$2,327), M6A3 (MSR $2,675-$3,175), M6A4-IAR (MSR $2,775-$2,895), REPR (MSR N/A), and SABR (MSR $2,875-$3,125). These models have a wide variety of sights, accessories, and related hardware available. Please contact the company directly for more information, including current retail pricing (see Trademark Index).

LABANU INCORPORATED

Labanu, Inc. SKSs were manufactured by Norinco in China, and imported exclusively until 1998 by Labanu, Inc., located in Ronkonkoma, NY.

RIFLES: SEMI-AUTO

MAK 90 SKS SPORTER RIFLE – 7.62x39mm cal., sporterized variation of the SKS with thumbhole stock, 16 1/2 in. barrel, includes accessories, 5 lbs. Importation began 1995, banned 1998.

| | $625 | $550 | $475 | $425 | $375 | $325 | $295 | Last MSR was $189. |

LAKESIDE MACHINE LLC

Current manufacturer located in Horseshoe Bend, AR. Previously located in Pound, WI.

RIFLES: SEMI-AUTO

Lakeside manufactures half-scale, semi-auto, belt fed replicas of many of America's famous machine guns, including the 1919 A4 ($3,495 MSR), 1919 M37 ($3,895 MSR), 1917A1 ($3,995 MSR), M2 HB ($4,495 MSR), M2 WC ($4,995 MSR), and a dual mount M2 HB (POR). Calibers include: .22 LR, .17 Mach 2 (optional), and .22 Mag. Additionally, Lakeside also manufactures a semi-auto, closed bolt, belt fed .22 LR cal. Model Vindicator BF1 with 16 1/4 in. shrouded barrel ($2,695 MSR).

LARUE TACTICAL

Current manufacturer located in Leander, TX.

RIFLES: SEMI-AUTO

OBR (OPTIMIZED BATTLE RIFLE) – .308 Win. cal., 16.1, 18, or 20 in. stainless steel barrel, adj. gas block, 20 shot box mag., flared magwell, A2 fixed stock, black anodized finish, Mil-Std 1913 one piece upper rail, Troy front and optional BUIS rear sight, A2 flash hider, detachable side rails, approx. 10 lbs.

| MSR $2,995 | | $2,750 | $2,500 | $2,250 | $2,000 | $1,750 | $1,500 | $1,250 |

A variety of accessories are available on this model for additional cost.

LASERAIM ARMS, INC.

Previous distributor located in Little Rock, AR. Previously manufactured until 1999 in Thermopolis, WY. Laseraim Arms, Inc. was a division of Emerging Technologies, Inc.

PISTOLS: SEMI-AUTO

SERIES I – .40 S&W, .400 Cor-Bon (new 1998), .45 ACP, or 10mm cal., single action, 3 3/8 (Compact Model), 5, or 6 in. barrel with compensator, ambidextrous safety, all stainless steel metal parts are Teflon coated, beveled mag. well, integral accessory mounts, 7 (.45 ACP) or 8 (10mm or .40 S&W) shot mag., 46 or 52 oz. Mfg. 1993-99.

| | $325 | $295 | $265 | $215 | $185 | $150 | $125 | Last MSR was $349. |

Add $120 for wireless laser combo (new 1997).

* *Series I Compact* – .40 S&W or .45 ACP cal., features 3 3/8 in. non-ported slide and fixed sights. Mfg. 1993-99.

| | $325 | $295 | $265 | $215 | $185 | $150 | $125 | Last MSR was $349. |

Series I Illusion and Dream Team variations were made during 1993-94. Retail prices respectively were $650 and $695.

SERIES II – .40 S&W (disc. 1994), .45 ACP, or 10mm cal., similar technical specs. as the Series I, except has non-reflective stainless steel finish, fixed or adj. sights, and 3 3/8 (Compact Model, .45 ACP only), 5, or 7 (.45 ACP only)

MSR	100%	98%	95%	90%	80%	70%	60%

in. non-compensated barrel, 37 or 43 oz. Mfg. 1993-96.

| | $485 | $385 | $300 | $240 | $210 | $180 | $155 | Last MSR was $550. |

Series II Illusion and Dream Team variations were made during 1993-94. Retail prices respectively were $500 and $545.

SERIES III – .45 ACP cal., 5 in. ported barrel, serrated slide, Hogue grips. Mfg. 1994-disc.

| | $595 | $465 | $415 | $375 | $345 | $310 | $275 | Last MSR was $675. |

SERIES IV – .45 ACP cal., 3 3/8 (Compact Model) or 5 in. ported barrel, serrated slide, diamond checkered wood grips. Mfg. 1994-disc.

| | $550 | $450 | $400 | $360 | $330 | $300 | $265 | Last MSR was $625. |

LAW ENFORCEMENT ORDNANCE CORPORATION

Previous manufacturer located in Ridgway, PA until 1990.

SHOTGUNS: SEMI-AUTO

STRIKER-12 – 12 ga. Mag., tactical design shotgun featuring 12 shot rotary mag., 18 1/4 in. barrel, semi-auto, alloy shrouded barrel with PG extension, folding or fixed tactical design stock, 9.2 lbs., limited mfg. 1986-90.

| | $1,000 | $875 | $750 | $675 | $600 | $550 | $500 | Last MSR was $725. |

Add $200 for folding stock.
Add $100 for Marine variation ("Metal Life" finish).

Earlier variations were imported and available to law enforcement agencies only. In 1987, manufacture was started in PA and these firearms could be sold to individuals (18 in. barrel only). This design was originally developed in South Rhodesia.

LEGACY SPORTS INTERNATIONAL

Current importer located in Reno, NV. Previously located in Alexandria, VA.

Legacy Sports International imports a wide variety of firearms trademarks in various configurations, including pistols, rifles, and shotguns. Trademarks include: Citadel, Escort, Howa, Puma, and Verona. Please refer to these individual listings.

LEITNER-WISE DEFENSE, INC.

Current rifle manufacturer located in Alexandria, VA.

RIFLES: SEMI-AUTO

M.U.L.E. MOD. 1 (MODULAR URBAN LIGHT ENGAGEMENT CARBINE) – 5.56 NATO cal., 16 in. steel barrel standard, other lengths optional, op-rod operating system, single stage trigger, Magpul ACS buttstock, MOE pistol grip, black finish, upper and lower rails, 30 shot mag., flared magwell, E sights, includes one mag., manual, and cleaning kit, 7.9 lbs.

| MSR $1,680 | $1,550 | $1,375 | $1,175 | $1,000 | $850 | $700 | $575 |

Add $100 for precision trigger.

M.U.L.E. MOD. 2 (MODULAR URBAN LIGHT ENGAGEMENT CARBINE) – .308 Win. cal., 16 or 20 in. steel barrel, similar to Mod. 1, except has heavier barrel, 8 1/2 lbs.

| MSR $2,100 | $1,895 | $1,700 | $1,500 | $1,300 | $1,100 | $900 | $700 |

Add $100 for 20 in. barrel.

LEITNER-WISE RIFLE CO. INC.

Previous manufacturer located in Springfield, VA circa 2006. Previously located in Alexandria, VA 1999-2005.

RIFLES: SEMI-AUTO

LW 15.22 – .22 LR or .22 Mag. cal., tactical configuration patterned after the AR-15, forged upper and lower receivers, choice of carry handle or flattop upper receiver, forward bolt assist, last shot hold open, 16 1/2 or 20 in. barrel, 10 or 25 shot mag. Mfg. 2000-2005.

| | $775 | $675 | $600 | $550 | $500 | $450 | $425 | Last MSR was $850. |

Add $50 for A2 carrying handle.

LW 15.499 – .499 (12.5x40mm) cal., receiver and action patterned after the AR-15, mil spec standards, 16 1/2 in. steel or stainless steel barrel, flattop receiver, 5 (disc.), 10, or 14 (new 2006) shot mag., approx. 6 1/2 lbs. Mfg. 2000-2005.

| | $1,350 | $1,150 | $995 | $875 | $750 | $675 | $600 |

Add $92 for stainless steel barrel.

MSR	100%	98%	95%	90%	80%	70%	60%

LW 6.8/5.56 S.R.T. – 5.56x45mm NATO or 6.8x43mm SPC cal., 16.1 in. barrel, hard chrome lined bore, gas operated, locking bolt, Troy front and rear sights, forged T7075 aluminum flattop upper receiver, six position collapsible stock, Picatinny rail, removable carry handle, A2 flash hider, LW forged lower receiver, 28 or 30 shot mag., 5.38 lbs. Ltd. mfg. 2006.

	$2,050	$1,800	$1,600	$1,400	$1,200	$1,000	$850

Add $100 for 6.8x43mm SPC cal.

LES BAER CUSTOM, INC.

Current manufacturer and customizer established in 1993, and located in LeClaire, IA since 2008. Previously located in Hillsdale, IL until 2008. Dealer sales only.

PISTOLS: SEMI-AUTO

Les Baer has been customizing and manufacturing M1911 type pistols for decades. Currently, Les Baer is offering the following models: Ultimate Master Combat Series (MSR $2,670-$2,940), National Match Hardball (MSR $1,890), Bullseye Wadcutter Series (MSR $1,890-$1,980), PPC Series (MSR $1,999-$2,340), Premier II Series (MSR $1,790-$2,590), Custom Carry Series (MSR $1,830-$2,120), Ultimate Recon Series (MSR $2,290-$2,590), Thunder Ranch Series (MSR $1,990-$6,590), SRP Series (MSR $2,490), Monolith Series (MSR $1,870-$2,290), Stinger Series (MSR $1,890-$1,995), Concept Series (MSR $1,690-$1,940), Baer/Emerson CQC (MSR $3,123), Limited Ed. Presentation Grade (MSR $6,590-$6,690), and the Custom 25th Anniversary (MSR $6,995).

The company should be contacted directly (see Trademark Index) for an up-to-date price sheet and catalog on their extensive line-up of high quality competition/combat pistols. A wide range of competition parts and related gunsmithing services are also available. Early guns with low ser. nos. have become collectible.

RIFLES: BOLT ACTION

TACTICAL RECON/VARMINT CLASSIC RIFLE – .243 Win., .260 Rem., or .308 Win. cal., 24 in. match grade barrel, Still Tac 30 action and thick lug, Timney match trigger, front and back of action are glass bedded and lug is bedded into Bell & Carlson adj. stock, fitted Wyatts precision floorplate with box mag., Picatinny one piece rail, Dupont S coated finish, with (Tactical) or w/o (Varmint Classic) Harris bipod. New 2010.

MSR $3,410		$3,250	$2,850	$2,450	$2,000	$1,650	$1,375	$1,125

Add $150 for Tactical model with Harris bipod.

RIFLES: SEMI-AUTO

CUSTOM ULTIMATE AR MODEL – .204 Ruger (new 2004), .223 Rem., or 6.5 Grendel (mfg. 2007-2009) cal., individual rifles are custom built with no expense spared, everything made in-house ensuring top quality and tolerances, all models are guaranteed to shoot 1/2-3/4 MOA groups, various configurations include Varmint Model (disc.), Super Varmint Model, NRA Match Rifle, Super Match Model (new 2002), M4 Flattop Model, and IPSC Action Model. New 2001.

MSR $2,240		$2,100	$1,900	$1,700	$1,500	$1,300	$1,100	$900

Add $950-$1,305 for Super Varmint scope packages (includes Leupold Vari-X III 4.5-14x40mm scope).
Add $140 for Super Match model.
Add $90 for M4 flattop model.
Add $320 for IPSC action model.
Add $349 for Thunder Ranch rifle.
Add $849 for CMP competition rifle.
Add $240 for NRA match rifle w/o sights.
Add $245 for Super Varmint model (.204 Ruger cal.)
Add $210 for 6.5 Grendel cal. with M4 style barrel.

.264 LBC-AR – .264 LBC-AR cal., available in Ultimate Super Varmint, Ultimate Super Match, and Ultimate M4 Flattop configurations, fixed stock, black finish, 14 shot mag., features similar to Ultimate Model in .223 cal. New 2010.

MSR $2,240		$2,100	$1,900	$1,700	$1,500	$1,300	$1,100	$900

Add $50 for Super Varmint model.
Add $150 for Super Match model.

6x45 ULTIMATE AR – 6x45mm cal., available in Super Varmint, Super Match, and M4 Flattop configurations, black finish, fixed stock, similar to Ultimate AR in .223 configuration. New 2010.

MSR $2,240		$2,100	$1,900	$1,700	$1,500	$1,300	$1,100	$900

Add $50 for Super Varmint model.
Add $150 for Super Match model.

CUSTOM AR STYLE PISTON RIFLE – .223 Rem., .264 LBC-AR, or 6x45mm cal., 16 in. precision button rifled steel barrel, 14 or 30 shot mag., removable carry handle with rear sight, Picatinny flattop upper rail, National Match chromed carrier, flip up front sight, six position ATI collapsible stock with adj. cheekpiece and grip, Picatinny four-way handguard, A2 flash hider, Timney match trigger group, lockable sling swivel mounted on stud on four-way

MSR	100%	98%	95%	90%	80%	70%	60%

handguard, includes two mags. New 2010.

| MSR $1,690 | $1,550 | $1,375 | $1,125 | $995 | $875 | $750 | $625 |

LEWIS MACHINE & TOOL COMPANY (LMT)

Current tactical rifle and accessories manufacturer established in 1980, and located in Milan, IL.

RIFLES: SEMI-AUTO

CQB SERIES – .223 Rem. cal., gas piston operating system, 16 in. chrome lined barrel, 30 shot mag., standard trigger, SOPMOD stock, monolithic rail platform, tactical charging handle assembly, includes sling, manual, tactical adj. front and rear sights, torque wrench/driver, and three rail panels, 6.8 lbs.

| MSR $1,829 | $1,725 | $1,575 | $1,375 | $1,175 | $975 | $825 | $675 |

* **CQB16 6.8** – 6.8 SPC cal., similar to CQB16 Standard, except has 25 shot mag. New 2010.

| MSR $2,030 | $1,900 | $1,700 | $1,500 | $1,300 | $1,100 | $900 | $700 |

* **CQBPS16** – .223 Rem. cal., 16 in. barrel, gas piston operating system, tactical charging handle assembly, Defender lower with SOPMOD buttstock, 30 shot mag., standard trigger group, includes sling, tactical front and rear sights, torque wrench/driver, and three rail panels. New 2010.

| MSR $2,055 | $1,925 | $1,700 | $1,500 | $1,300 | $1,100 | $900 | $700 |

* **CompCQB16** – .223 Rem. cal., similar to CQB16 Standard model, except has 10 shot mag.

| MSR $1,829 | $1,725 | $1,575 | $1,375 | $1,175 | $975 | $825 | $675 |

COMP16 – .223 Rem. cal., 16 in. chrome lined barrel, standard flattop upper receiver, 10 shot mag., tactical charging handle assembly, Defender lower with fixed SOPMOD buttstock, standard trigger group, includes sling, tactical adj. rear sight.

| MSR $1,326 | $1,225 | $1,075 | $950 | $825 | $700 | $575 | $475 |

STD16 – .223 Rem. cal., 16 in. chrome lined barrel, standard trigger and bolt, choice of SOPMOD or Gen. 2 collapsible stock, 5.9 - 6.2 lbs.

| MSR $1,288 | $1,175 | $1,000 | $875 | $750 | $625 | $500 | $450 |

SPM16 – .223 Rem. cal., similar to STD16, except has Generation 2 buttstock. New 2010.

| MSR $1,273 | $1,175 | $1,000 | $875 | $750 | $625 | $500 | $450 |

LM308MWS – .308 Win. cal., 16 in. barrel, 20 shot mag., monolithic rail platform, gas piston operating system, Defender lower with SOPMOD stock, two stage trigger, includes sling, manual, tactical front and rea sights, torque wrench/driver, and three rail panels. New 2010.

| MSR $2,500 | $2,295 | $2,050 | $1,825 | $1,650 | $1,450 | $1,250 | $995 |

LIBERTY ARMS INTERNATIONAL LLC

Current importer located in Albion, NY.

Liberty Arms imports a variety of firearms, including AK, AR-15, and Moisin-Nagant style rifles and 1911A1 style pistols. Please contact the company directly for more information, including pricing and model availability (see Trademark Index).

LIBERTY ARMS WORKS, INC.

Previous manufacturer located in West Chester, PA circa 1991-1996.

PISTOLS: SEMI-AUTO

L.A.W. ENFORCER – .22 LR, 9mm Para., 10mm, .40 S&W (new 1994), or .45 ACP cal., patterned after the Ingram MAC 10, single action, 6 1/4 in. threaded barrel, closed bolt operation, manual safety, 10 (C/B 1994) or 30* shot mag., 5 lbs. 1 oz. Mfg. 1991-96.

| | $575 | $500 | $450 | $415 | $385 | $335 | $295 | Last MSR was $545. |

LJUNGMAN

Previously manufactured by Carl Gustaf, located in Eskilstuna, Sweden.

RIFLES: SEMI-AUTO

AG 42 – 6.5x55mm Swedish cal., 10 shot mag., wood stock, tangent rear and hooded front, bayonet lug, designed in 1941.

| | $850 | $700 | $600 | $495 | $450 | $400 | $365 |

This was the first mass produced, direct gas operated rifle. This weapon was also used by the Egyptian armed forces and was known as the Hakim, and chambered in 8x57mm Mauser.

LONE STAR ARMAMENT, INC.

Previous pistol manufacturer circa 1970-2004, and located in Stephenville, TX. During 2003, Lone Star Armament was absorbed by STI, located in Georgetown, TX.

PISTOLS: SEMI-AUTO

Lone Star Armament manufactured a lineup of M1911 style pistols. Models included: Ranger Match ($1,595 last MSR), Lawman Match ($1,595 last MSR), Lawman Series ($1,475 last MSR), Ranger Series ($1,475 last MSR), and the Guardian Series ($895 last MSR).

LUSA USA

Current manufacturer located in Hooksett, NH. Dealer and distributor sales.

CARBINES

Lusa USA manufactures a 9mm Para. cal. carbine with a 16 in. barrel in three configurations - the 94 SA (A2 Standard, MSR $999), the 94 PDW (side folding stock, MSR $1,099), and the 94 AWB (fixed stock, MSR $999). Please contact the company directly for more information, including options and availability (see Trademark Index).

M SECTION

MG ARMS INCORPORATED

Current manufacturer established in 1980, and located in Spring, TX. MG Arms Incoroporated was previously named Match Grade Arms & Ammunition. Consumer direct sales.

MSR	100%	98%	95%	90%	80%	70%	60%

RIFLES: SEMI-AUTO

K-YOTE VARMINT SYSTEM – various cals. from .17 Rem. - .458 Lott, target trigger, stainless match grade free floating barrel, standard or camo finish four rail aluminum hand guard, adj. stock, A3 flattop upper receiver, machined lower receiver, scope rail. New 2009.

MSR $3,695	$3,450	$3,100	$2,850	$2,550	$2,300	$2,250	$1,995

MGI

Current rifle manufacturer located in Bangor, ME.

RIFLES: SEMI-AUTO

The MARCK-15 (Hydra) is a completely modular tactical style rifle, consisting of a quick change barrel upper receiver and a modular lower with interchangeable magazine wells, capably of firing calibers from .22 LR up to .50 Beowulf (using unmodified magazines). No tools are required, and it utilizes standard barrels. Retail on the base systems starts at $1,995. A wide variety of configurations are available. Please contact the company directly for more information, including available options and pricing (see Trademark Index).

M-K SPECIALTIES INC.

Previous rifle manufacturer circa 2000-2002 located in Grafton, WV.

RIFLES: SEMI-AUTO

M-14 A1 – .308 Win. cal., forged M-14 steel receiver using CNC machinery to original government specifications, available as Rack Grade, Premier Match, or Tanker Model, variety of National Match upgrades were available at extra cost, base price is for Rack Grade. Mfg. 2000-2002.

	$1,475	$1,275	$995	$875	$750	$625	$500	Last MSR was $1,595.

National Match upgrades ranged from $345-$955.

MK ARMS INC.

Previous manufacturer located in Irvine, CA circa 1992.

CARBINES

MK 760 – 9mm Para. cal., tactical design carbine configuration, steel frame, 16 in. shrouded barrel, fires from closed bolt, 14, 24, or 36 shot mag., parkerized finish, folding metal stock, fixed sights. Mfg. 1983-approx. 1992.

	$725	$650	$575	$525	$475	$415	$375	Last MSR was $575.

MAADI-GRIFFIN CO.

Previous rifle manufacturer located in Mesa, AZ until 2003. Consumer direct sales.

RIFLES: SEMI-AUTO

MODEL MG-6 – .50 BMG cal., gas operated, bullpup configuration, one piece cast lower receiver, 5, 10, or 15 shot side mounted mag., 26-30 in. barrel, includes bipod, hard carrying case, and 3 mags. 23 lbs. Mfg. 2000-2003.

	$5,500	$4,750	$3,850	$3,250	$2,600	$2,200	$1,800	Last MSR was $5,950.

Add $450 for MK-IV tripod.

RIFLES: SINGLE SHOT

MODEL 89 – .50 BMG cal., one piece cast lower receiver, 36 in. barrel, felt recoil is less than 12 ga., tig-welded interlocking assembly, no screws, tripod optional, 22 lbs. Mfg. 1990-2003.

	$3,100	$2,750	$2,400	$2,050	$1,775	$1,500	$1,250	Last MSR was $3,150.

Add $600 for stainless steel.

MODEL 92 CARBINE – .50 BMG cal., 20 in. barrel, 5 lbs. trigger pull, 18 1/2 lbs. Mfg. 1990-2003.

	$2,950	$2,550	$2,225	$1,875	$1,650	$1,400	$1,200	Last MSR was $2,990.

Add $650 for stainless steel.

MSR	100%	98%	95%	90%	80%	70%	60%

MODEL 99 – .50 BMG cal., similar to Model 89, except has 44 in. barrel, 28 lbs. Mfg. 1999-2003.

| | $3,150 | $2,725 | $2,450 | $2,050 | $1,775 | $1,500 | $1,250 | Last MSR was $3,350. |

Add $650 for stainless steel.

MAGNUM RESEARCH, INC.

Current trademark of pistols and rifles with company headquarters located in Minneapolis, MN. Pistols are currently manufactured in Pillager, MN beginning 2009. Desert Eagle Series was manufactured 1998-2008 by IMI, located in Israel. Previously manufactured by Saco Defense located in Saco, ME during 1995-1998, and by TAAS/IMI (Israeli Military Industries) 1986-1995. .22 Rimfire semi-auto pistols (Mountain Eagle) were previously manufactured by Ram-Line. Single shot pistols (Lone Eagle) were manufactured by Magnum Research sub-contractors. Distributed by Magnum Research, Inc., in Minneapolis, MN. Dealer and distributor sales.

PISTOLS: SEMI-AUTO, CENTERFIRE

IMI SP-21 – 9mm Para., .40 S&W, or .45 ACP cal., DA or SA, traditional Browning operating system, polymer frame with ergonomic design, 3.9 in. barrel with polygonal rifling, 10 shot mag., finger groove grips, 3 dot adj. sights, reversible mag. release, multiple safeties, matte black finish, decocking feature, approx. 29 oz. Limited importation from IMI late 2002-2005.

| | $425 | $375 | $335 | $300 | $280 | $260 | $240 | Last MSR was $499. |

The IMI SP-21 uses the same magazines as the Baby Eagle pistols. This model is referred to the Barak SP-21 in Israel.

PISTOLS: SEMI-AUTO, CENTERFIRE - EAGLE SERIES

Magnum Research also offers a Collector's Edition Presentation Series. Special models include a Gold Edition (serial numbered 1-100), a Silver Edition (serial numbered 101-500), and a Bronze Edition (serial numbered 501-1,000). Each pistol from this series is supplied with a walnut presentation case, 2 sided medallion, and certificate of authenticity. Prices are available upon request by contacting Magnum Research directly.

Alloy frames on the Desert Eagle Series of pistols were discontinued in 1992. However, if sufficient demand warrants, these models will once again be available to consumers at the same price as the steel frames.

Beginning late 1995, the Desert Eagle frame assembly for the .357 Mag., .44 Mag., and .50 AE cals. is based on the .50 caliber frame. Externally, all three pistols are now identical in size. This new platform, called the Desert Eagle Pistol Mark XIX Component System, enables .44 Mag. and .50 AE conversions to consist of simply a barrel and a magazine - conversions to or from the .357 Mag. also include a bolt.

The slide assembly on the Mark I and Mark VII is physically smaller than the one on a Mark XIX. Also, the barrel dovetail on top is 3/8 in. on a Mark I or Mark VII, while on a Mark XIX, it is 7/8 in., and includes cross slots for scopes.

Individual Desert Eagle Mark XIX 6 in. barrels are $389-$564, depending on finish, and 10 in. barrels are $459-$634, depending on finish. Add $129 for Trijicon night sights (new 2006). Add $49-$89 for Hogue Pau Ferro wooden grips (new 2007) or $49 for Hogue soft rubber grips with finger grooves (disc. 2008).

MARK I DESERT EAGLE .357 MAG – .357 Mag. cal., similar to Mark VII, except has standard trigger and safety lever is teardrop shaped, and slide catch release has single serration. Disc.

| | $925 | $825 | $725 | $625 | $525 | $450 | $400 | |

MARK XIX .357 MAG. DESERT EAGLE – features .50 cal. frame and slide, standard black finish, 6 or 10 in. barrel, full Picatinny top rail with fixed sights became standard late 2009 (U.S. mfg.), 4 lbs., 6 oz. Mfg. by Saco 1995-98, by IMI 1998-2009, and domestically beginning 2010.

| MSR $1,563 | $1,350 | $1,125 | $875 | $775 | $650 | $550 | $475 | |

Add $87 for 10 in. barrel.

MARK VII .357 MAG. DESERT EAGLE – .357 Mag. cal., gas operated, 6 (standard barrel length), 10, or 14 in. barrel length with 3/8 in. dovetail rib, steel (58.3 oz.) or alloy (47.8 oz.) frame, adj. trigger, safety lever is hook shaped, slide catch/release lever has three steps, adaptable to .44 Mag. with optional kit, 9 shot mag. (8 for .44 Mag.). Mfg. 1983-95, limited quantities were made available again during 1998 and 2001.

| | $995 | $875 | $750 | $650 | $550 | $475 | $425 | Last MSR was $929. |

Add approx. $150 for 10 or 14 in. barrel (disc. 1995).
Add $495 for .357 Mag. to .41 Mag./.44 Mag. conversion kit (6 in. barrel). Disc. 1995.
Add approx. $685 for .357 Mag. to .44 Mag. conversion kit (10 or 14 in. barrel). Disc. 1995.

* *Mark VII .357 Mag. Desert Eagle Stainless Steel* – similar to .357 Mag. Desert Eagle, except has stainless steel frame, 58.3 oz. Mfg. 1987-95.

| | $750 | $650 | $550 | $460 | $395 | $335 | $285 | Last MSR was $839. |

Add approx. $150 for 10 or 14 in. barrel.

MSR	100%	98%	95%	90%	80%	70%	60%

MARK VII .41 MAG. DESERT EAGLE – .41 Mag. cal., similar to .357 Desert Eagle, 6 in. barrel only, 8 shot mag., steel (62.8 oz.) or alloy (52.3 oz.) frame. Mfg. 1988-95, limited quantities available during 2001.

| | $785 | $675 | $565 | $500 | $465 | $420 | $390 | Last MSR was $899. |

Add $395 for .41 Mag. to .44 Mag. conversion kit (6 in. barrel only).

* **Mark VII .41 Mag. Desert Eagle Stainless Steel** – similar to .41 Mag. Desert Eagle, except has stainless steel frame, 58.3 oz. Mfg. 1988-95.

| | $825 | $700 | $550 | $460 | $395 | $335 | $285 | Last MSR was $949. |

MARK I DESERT EAGLE .44 MAG – .44 Mag. cal., similar to Mark VII, except has standard trigger and safety lever is teardrop shaped, and slide catch release has single serration. Disc.

| | $975 | $850 | $750 | $650 | $550 | $475 | $425 | |

MARK XIX .44 MAG. DESERT EAGLE – features .50 cal. frame and slide, standard black finish, 6 or 10 in. barrel, full Picatinny top rail with fixed sights became standard late 2009 (U.S. mfg.), 4 lbs., 6 oz. Mfg. by Saco 1995-98, by IMI 1998-2009, and domestically beginning 2009.

| MSR $1,563 | $1,350 | $1,125 | $875 | $775 | $650 | $550 | $475 | |

Add $87 for 10 in. barrel.
Add $199 for black muzzle brake (new 2010).

MARK VII .44 MAG. DESERT EAGLE – .44 Mag. cal., similar to .357 Desert Eagle, 8 shot mag., steel (62.8 oz.) or alloy (52.3 oz.) frame. Originally mfg. 1986-95, re-released 1998-2000.

| | $975 | $850 | $750 | $650 | $550 | $475 | $425 | Last MSR was $1,049. |

Add $100 for 10 (current) or 14 (disc. 1995) in. barrel.
Add $475 for .44 Mag. to .357 Mag. conversion kit (6 in. barrel). Disc. 1995.
Add $675 for .44 Mag. to .357 Mag. conversion kit (10 or 14 in. barrel). Disc. 1995.
Add $395 for .44 Mag. to .41 Mag. conversion kit (6 in. barrel). Disc. 1995.

* **Mark VII .44 Mag. Desert Eagle Stainless Steel** – similar to .44 Mag. Desert Eagle, except has stainless steel frame, 58.3 oz. Mfg. 1987-95.

| | $900 | $800 | $700 | $600 | $500 | $450 | $400 | Last MSR was $949. |

Add approx. $210 for 10 or 14 in. barrel.

MARK VII .50 MAG. DESERT EAGLE – .50 AE cal., 6 in. barrel with 7/8 in. rib with cross slots for Weaver style rings, steel only, black standard finish, frame slightly taller than the Mark VII .357 Mag./.44 Mag., 7 shot mag., 72.4 oz. Mfg. 1991-95 by IMI, limited quantities were made available again during 1998 only.

| | $1,175 | $950 | $825 | $700 | $575 | $500 | $450 | Last MSR was $1,099. |

This cartridge utilized the same rim dimensions as the .44 Mag. and was available with a 300 grain bullet. The .50 Action Express cal. has 60% more stopping power than the .44 Mag., with a minimal increase in felt recoil.

MARK XIX CUSTOM 440 – .440 Cor-Bon cal., similar to Mark XIX .44 Mag. Desert Eagle, 6 or 10 in. barrel, standard black finish, rechambered by MRI Custom Shop, limited mfg. 1999-2001.

| | $1,175 | $995 | $850 | $725 | $575 | $500 | $450 | Last MSR was $1,389. |

Add $40 for 10 in. barrel.

MARK XIX .50 MAG. DESERT EAGLE – features .50 AE cal., larger frame, standard black finish, 6 or 10 in. barrel, full Picatinny top rail with fixed sights became standard late 2009 (U.S. mfg.), 4 lbs., 6 oz. Mfg. by Saco 1995-98, and by IMI again beginning 1998.

| MSR $1,563 | $1,350 | $1,125 | $875 | $775 | $650 | $550 | $475 | |

Add $87 for 10 in. barrel.
Add $199 for black muzzle brake (new 2010).

MARK XIX 3 CAL. COMPONENT SYSTEM – includes Mark XIX .44 Mag. Desert Eagle and 5 barrels including .357 Mag. (6 and 10 in.), .44 Mag., and .50 AE (6 and 10 in.) cals., .357 bolt assembly and ICC aluminum carrying case. Also available in custom finishes at extra charge. New 1998.

| MSR $4,402 | $3,900 | $3,450 | $2,800 | $2,400 | $2,000 | $1,750 | $1,500 | |

* **Mark XIX 3 Cal. Component System (6 or 10 in. Barrel)** – includes component Mark XIX system in 6 or 10 in. barrel only. New 1998.

| MSR $2,910 | $2,550 | $2,225 | $1,775 | $1,500 | $1,250 | $1,000 | $850 | |

Add $262 for 10 in. barrel.

RIFLES: BOLT-ACTION

MOUNTAIN EAGLE TACTICAL RIFLE – .223 Rem. (new 2002), .22-250 Rem. (new 2002), .308 Win., .300 Win. Mag., or .300 WSM (new 2002) cal., accurized Rem. M-700 action, 26 in. Magnum Lite barrel, H-S Precision tactical

MSR	100%	98%	95%	90%	80%	70%	60%

stock, adj. stock and trigger, 9 lbs., 4 oz. New 2001.

| MSR $2,379 | $2,075 | $1,750 | $1,425 | $1,125 | $850 | $700 | $575 |

Add $96 for any cal. other than .300 WSM.

MAJESTIC ARMS, LTD.

Current manufacturer established during 2000, and located on Staten Island, NY. Dealer sales only.

SHOTGUNS: SLIDE ACTION

BASE-TAC – 12 or 20 ga., 3 in. chamber, based on M870 Remington action, approx. 18 in. barrel with ghost ring sights, black synthetic (12 ga.) or hardwood stock and forearm, extended 6 shot tube mag., 6-7 lbs. New 2004.

| MSR $759 | $675 | $575 | $500 | $450 | $400 | $350 | $300 |

Add $30 for 20 ga.

MARLIN FIREARMS COMPANY

Current manufacturer located in North Haven, CT. Marlin has been manufacturing firearms since 1870. Recent manufacture (1969-present) is in North Haven, CT. Previously, Marlin was manufactured (1870-1969) in New Haven, CT. Distributor sales only.

On Nov. 10th, 2000, Marlin Firearms Company purchased H&R 1871, Inc. This includes the brand names Harrington & Richardson, New England Firearms, and Wesson & Harrington (please refer to individual sections in this text).

During 2005, Marlin Firearms Company once again started manufacturing a L.C. Smith line of both SxS and O/U shotguns.

In late Jan. of 2008, Remington acquired the Marlin Firearms Company, including the H&R, New England Firearms (NEF), and L.C. Smith brands, and plans to continue with production of these trademarks.

Marlin Firearms Company had been a family-owned and operated business since 1921 until 2007.

SHOTGUNS: BOLT ACTION

* **Model 512DL Slugmaster** – similar to Model 512 Slugmaster, except has black Rynite stock, Fire Sights (with red fiberoptic inserts) became standard 1998. Disc. 1998.

| | $310 | $230 | $200 | $180 | $160 | $145 | $130 | Last MSR was $372. |

* **Model 512P Slugmaster** – 12 ga., 3 in. chamber, features 21 in. ported fully rifled barrel with front and rear Fire Sights (high visibility red and green fiberoptic inserts), 2 shot detachable box mag., black fiberglass synthetic stock with molded-in checkering, receiver is drilled and tapped, 8 lbs. Mfg. 1999-2001.

| | $315 | $235 | $200 | $180 | $165 | $155 | $145 | Last MSR was $388. |

MASTERPIECE ARMS

Current pistol and rifle manufacturer located in Braselton, GA. Dealer sales only.

CARBINES: SEMI-AUTO

MPA manufactures a line of tactical style semi-auto carbines patterned after the MAC Series with 30 shot mags. (interchangable with its pistols).

SIDE COCKING CARBINE – 9mm Para. (MPA20ST-A) or .45 ACP (MPA1ST-A) cal., 16 in. threaded barrel, 30 shot stick mag., black skeletonized stock, with or w/o scope mount.

| MSR $600 | $525 | $450 | $400 | $365 | $335 | $300 | $275 |

Add $259 for scope mount, Intrafuse handguard, holosight, flashlight and muzzle brake.
Subtract $20 for 9mm Para. cal.
Subtract $50-$70 if w/o side cocker.

TOP COCKING CARBINE – 9mm Para. (MPA20T-A) or .45 ACP (MPA1T-A) cal., 16 in. threaded barrel, black skeletonized stock, 30 shot stick mag.

| MSR $530 | $480 | $425 | $360 | $325 | $265 | $215 | $170 |

Add $30 for .45 ACP cal.

MPA460 CARBINE – .460 Rowland cal., 16 in. threaded barrel, 30 shot mag., side cocking, muzzle brake, black finish, with or w/o .45 ACP upper. New 2010.

| MSR $800 | $725 | $650 | $575 | $500 | $425 | $375 | $325 |

Add $54 for scope mount, hand guard, and Mark III tactical scope.

PISTOLS: SEMI-AUTO

MPA manufactures a line of tactical style pistols patterned after the original MAC Series from Ingram.

MSR	100%	98%	95%	90%	80%	70%	60%

SIDE COCKING MODEL – 9mm Para. (MPA30ST-A) or .45 ACP (MPA10ST-A) cal., tactical style pistol patterned after the original MAC Series from Ingram, 30 shot mag., 6 or 10 in. threaded barrels.

MSR $450	$325	$295	$235	$195	$150	$125	$115

Add $50 for scope mount.
Add $30 for 9mm Para. cal.
Add $180 for holosight, flashlight, upper Picatinny rail, and safety extension with 6 in. barrel or $254 if w/ 10 in. barrel.
Subtract $30-$80 if w/o side charger.

TOP COCKING MODEL – 9mm Para. (MPA30T-A) or .45 ACP (MPA10T-A) cal., similar to side cocking model, except is top cocking.

MSR $430	$395	$350	$295	$275	$215	$180	$140

Add $20 for .45 ACP cal.
Add $80 for 10 in. barrel and AR-15 hand guard.

MPA22T MINI PISTOL – .22 LR cal., 4 in. threaded barrel, 27 shot mag., top cocker (MPA22T-A) or side cocker with scope mount (MPA22SST-A), black finish. New 2010.

MSR $405	$365	$335	$300	$275	$250	$225	$195

Add $50 for side cocker with scope mount.

MPA930 MINI PISTOL – 9mm Para. cal., 4 in. threaded barrel, 30 shot mag., optional scope mount (MPA930SST-A), black finish.

MSR $450	$325	$295	$235	$195	$150	$125	$115

Add $50 for scope mount.
Add $180 for holosight, flashlight, pressure switch, upper Picatinny rail, and safety extension.

MPA460 PISTOL – .460 Rowland cal., 6 or 10 in. threaded barrel, 30 shot mag., side cocker, scope mount, muzzle brake, black finish. New 2009.

MSR $580	$495	$450	$395	$365	$335	$300	$275

Add $90 for .45 ASP upper.
Add $96 for 10 in. barrel.

MAUNZ

Previous manufacturer located in Maumee, OH until 1987.

RIFLES: SEMI-AUTO

MATCH SERVICE RIFLE – .308 Win. cal., 22 in. barrel, M1A configuration with M1 and M14 G.I. parts, fiberglass stock, NM sights, M1 trigger assembly, 10 lbs., approx. 200 mfg.

	$2,500	$2,250	$2,000	$1,800	$1,500	$1,250	$1,050

MODEL 87 – various cals., 26 in. medium weight barrel, synthetic stock, G.I. parts with TRW bolts, satin black finish, open sights, ser. nos. 00001-03030, 11 lbs. Mfg. 1985-89.

	$2,300	$2,100	$1,800	$1,500	$1,250	$1,050	$925

MAUSER JAGDWAFFEN GmbH

Current trademark established during 1871, and currently owned by SIG Arms AG beginning late 2000. Mauser Model 98 Magnum bolt action rifles are currently manufactured by Mauser Jagdwaffen GmbH, located in Isny, Germany. Currently imported beginning 2009 by Mauser USA, lcoated in San Antonio, TX.

In late 2000, SIG Arms AG, the firearms portion of SIG, was purchased by two Germans named Michael Lüke and Thomas Ortmeier, who have a background in textiles. Today the Lüke & Ortmeier group includes independently operational companies such as Blaser Jadgwaffen GmbH, Mauser Jagdwaffen GmbH, J.P. Sauer & Sohn GmbH, SIG-Sauer Inc., SIG-Sauer GmbH and SAN Swiss Arms AG.

From late March, 2006-2009, Models 98 and 03 were distributed exclusively by Briley Manufacturing, located in Houston, TX. The former transistion name was Mauser Jagd-und Sportwaffen GmbH. On January 1, 1999, Mauser transferred all production and distribution rights of both hunting and sporting weapons to SIG-Blaser. Mauser-Werke Oberndorf Waffensysteme GmbH continues to manufacture military defense contracts (including making small bore barrel liners for tanks), in addition to other industrial machinery.

Previously imported exclusively by Brolin Arms, located in Pomona, CA during 1997-98 only. During 1998, the company name was changed from Mauser-Werke Oberndorf Waffensysteme GmbH. During 1994, the name was changed from Mauser-Werke to Mauser-Werke Oberndorf Waffensysteme GmbH. Previously imported by GSI located in Trussville, AL, until 1997, Gibb's Rifle Co., Inc. until 1995, Precision Imports, Inc. located in San Antonio, TX until 1993, and KDF located in Seguin, TX (1987-89).

MSR	100%	98%	95%	90%	80%	70%	60%

PISTOLS: SEMI-AUTO, RECENT IMPORTATION

M-2 – .357 SIG (disc. 2001), .40 S&W, or .45 ACP cal., short recoil operation, striker fired operating system, rotating 3.54 in. barrel lockup, manual safety, 8 (.45 ACP) or 10 shot, DAO, hammerless, aluminum alloy frame with nickel chromium steel slide, black finish, includes case and trigger lock, approx. 29 or 32 1/2 oz. Mfg. by SIG in Europe, limited importation 2000-04.

	$450	$400	$350	$300	$275	$250	$225

MAVERICK ARMS, INC.

Currently manufactured by Maverick Arms, Inc. located in Eagle Pass, TX. Administrative offices are at O.F. Mossberg & Sons, located in North Haven, CT. Distributor sales only.

SHOTGUNS

Beginning 1992, all Maverick slide action shotguns incorporate twin slide rails in the operating mechanism.

* **Model 88 Field Slide Action Combat** – 12 ga. only, combat design featuring pistol grip stock and forearm, black synthetic stock is extension of receiver, 18 1/2 in. cyl. bore barrel with vented shroud with built-in carrying handle, open sights. Mfg. 1990-92.

	$375	$330	$280	$255	$205	$170	$130	Last MSR was $282.

McCANN INDUSTRIES

Current rifle and accessories manufacturer located in Spanaway, WA.

McCann Industries manufactures new Garand semi-auto rifles with design improvements that utilize a .338 or .458 Mag cal. cartridge (not Win. Mag.), in addition to a .300 Win. Mag. bolt action pistol. For more information, including pricing and availability, contact the company directly (see Trademark Index).

McMILLAN BROS. RIFLE CO.

Previous division of McMillan Group International, located in Phoenix, AZ. Dealer and consumer direct sales. During 1998, the company name changed from McBros Rifles to McMillan Bros. Rifle Co. The company name changed again during 2007 to McMillian Firearms Manufacturing. Please refer to McMillian Firearms Manufacturing LLC listing.

RIFLES: BOLT ACTION

MCR TACTICAL – .308 Win. or .300 Win. Mag. cal. Mfg. 1993-2007.

	$2,950	$2,400	$1,900	$1,500	$1,250	$1,050	$925	Last MSR was $3,300.

This model was formerly designated the MCR Sniper Model.

* **MCRT Tactical** – .300 Win. Mag. or .338 Lapua (new 1998), similar to MCR Tactical. Mfg. 1993-2007.

	$3,050	$2,550	$2,100	$1,825	$1,550	$1,375	$1,100	Last MSR was $3,500.

Add $500 for .338 Lapua Mag (muzzle brake is standard).

This model was formerly designated the MCRT Sniper Model.

BIG MAC/BOOMER – .50 BMG cal., available as either single shot sporter, repeater sporter, light benchrest, or heavy benchrest variation. Mfg. 1993-2007.

	$4,450	$3,850	$3,250	$2,700	$2,225	$1,825	$1,525	Last MSR was $4,900.

Add $300 for repeating action.
Add $500 for Tactical 50 variation.
Add $100 for Tactical single shot.
Add $100 for heavy benchrest variation.

McMILLAN FIREARMS MANUFACTURING, LLC

Current manufacturer located in Phoenix, AZ beginning 2007.

McMillan Group International is a group of McMillan family companies: McMillan Fiberglass Stocks, McMillan Firearms Manufacturing, and McMillan Machine Company.

RIFLES: TACTICAL

Current models include the TAC bolt action series in various centerfire calibers: .300, .308, and .338. MSRs range from $4,999-5,499. A TAC 50 in .50 BMG cal. is also available with a current MSR of $7,599. McMillan also has a M1A Series patterned after the popular M1A rifle, with either a folding or collapsible stock. MSRs are currently $3,099-$3,299.

Please contact the company directly for more information (see Trademark Index).

MSR	100%	98%	95%	90%	80%	70%	60%

McMILLAN, G. & CO., INC.

Previous trademark established circa 1988, located in Phoenix, AZ.

G. McMillan & Co., Inc. had various barrel markings from 1988-1995 including G. McMillan, Harris - McMillan, and Harris Gunworks.

RIFLES: BOLT ACTION

The models listed were also available with custom wood stocks at varying prices. McMillan also manufactured a custom rifle from a supplied action. Features included new barreling, a fiberglass stock, matte black finish, and range testing to guarantee 3/4 M.O.A. Prices started at $1,400.

Add $150 for stainless steel receiver on most models.

M-40 SNIPER RIFLE – .308 Win. cal., Remington action with McMillan match grade heavy contour barrel, fiberglass stock with recoil pad, 4 shot mag., 9 lbs. Mfg. 1990-95.

$1,775	$1,475	$1,150	$925	$825	$725	$625	Last MSR was $1,800.

M-86 SNIPER RIFLE – .300 Phoenix, .30-06 (new 1989), .300 Win. Mag. or .308 Win. cal., fiberglass stock, variety of optical sights. Mfg. 1988-95.

$1,825	$1,500	$1,150	$975	$85	$775	$675	Last MSR was $1,900.

Add $550 for .300 Phoenix cal.
Add $200 for takedown feature (new 1993).

* ***M-86 Sniper Rifle System*** – includes Model 86 Sniper Rifle, bipod, Ultra scope, rings, and bases. Cased. Mfg. 1988-92.

$2,460	$2,050	$1,825	$1,600	$1,350	$1,100	$950	Last MSR was $2,665.

M-87 LONG RANGE SNIPER RIFLE – .50 BMG cal., stainless steel bolt action, 29 in. barrel with muzzle brake, single shot, camo synthetic stock, accurate to 1500 meters, 21 lbs. Mfg. 1988-95.

$3,650	$2,950	$2,500	$2,150	$1,900	$1,700	$1,575	Last MSR was $3,735.

* ***M-87 Long Range Sniper Rifle System*** – includes Model 87 Sniper Rifle, bipod, 20X Ultra scope, rings, and bases. Cased. Mfg. 1988-92.

$4,200	$3,400	$2,875	$2,550	$2,250	$2,100	$1,800	Last MSR was $4,200.

* ***M-87R Long Range Sniper Rifle*** – same specs. as Model 87, except has 5 shot fixed box mag. Mfg. 1990-95.

$3,995	$3,300	$2,700	$2,300	$2,000	$1,850	$1,700	Last MSR was $4,000.

Add $300 for Combo option.

M-89 SNIPER RIFLE – .308 Win. cal., 28 in. barrel with suppressor (also available without), fiberglass stock adj. for length and recoil pad, 15 1/4 lbs. Mfg. 1990-95.

$2,200	$1,825	$1,575	$1,250	$1,050	$875	$750	Last MSR was $2,300.

Add $425 for muzzle suppressor.

M-92 BULLPUP – .50 BMG cal., bullpup configuration with shorter barrel. Mfg. 1993-95.

$3,750	$2,950	$2,550	$2,200	$2,000	$1,850	$1,700	Last MSR was $4,000.

M-93SN – .50 BMG cal., similar to M-87, except has folding stock and detachable 5 or 10 shot box mag. Mfg. 1993-95.

$3,950	$3,250	$2,750	$2,300	$2,000	$1,850	$1,700	Last MSR was $4,300.

.300 PHOENIX LONG RANGE RIFLE – .300 Phoenix cal., special fiberglass stock featuring adj. cheekpieces to accommodate night vision optics, adj. buttplate, 29 in. barrel, conventional box mag., 12 1/2 lbs. Mfg. 1992 only.

$2,700	$2,195	$1,850	$1,450	$1,100	$925	$825	Last MSR was $3,000.

.300 Phoenix was a cartridge developed to function at ranges in excess of 800 yards. It produced muzzle velocities of 3100 ft. per second with a 250 grain bullet.

MICROTECH SMALL ARMS RESEARCH, INC. (MSAR)

Current rifle manufacturer located in Bradford, PA.

CARBINES/RIFLES: SEMI-AUTO

MSAR manufactures American-made semi-auto bullpup carbines and rifles, patterned after the Steyr AUG.

STG-556 – .223 Rem. cal., 16 or 20 in. chrome lined barrel, gas operated rotating bolt, short piston drive, 10, 20, 30, or 42 shot mag., black, tan, or OD Green finish, with or w/o 9 inch Picatinny rail, right or left hand, synthetic stock, 7.2 lbs.

MSR $1,839							
	$1,725	$1,575	$1,395	$1,275	$1,150	$995	$825

Add $156 for 1.5x Optic.

MSR	100%	98%	95%	90%	80%	70%	60%

* **STG-556 Gebirgsjager Limited Edition** – similar to STG-556, engraved Edelweiss flower insignia, except includes all OD Green finish, 1.5x CQB optical sight, 6 in. Picatinny side rail, three 30 shot mags., OD Green Currahee knife with nylon sheath, Giles sling with Uncle Mike's sling swivels, custom Pelican 1700 green case, and certificate of authenticity.

	$3,495	$3,100	$2,750	$2,525	$2,300	$2,100	$1,875

STG-680 – 6.8mm Rem. cal., 16 or 20 in. chrome lined barrel, 10, 20, 30, or 42 shot mag., black , tan, or OD Green synthetic stock, with or w/o 9 inch Picatinny rail, right or left hand action, 7.2 lbs.

	$1,725	$1,575	$1,395	$1,275	$1,150	$995	$825

Add $156 for 1.5x Optic.

MITCHELL ARMS, INC.

Previous manufacturer, importer, and distributor located in Fountain Valley, CA.

RIFLES: DISC.

LW22 SEMI-AUTO – .22 LR cal., 10 shot mag., composite or skeleton stock, patterned after Feather Industries semi-auto. Limited mfg. 1996-97.

	$300	$265	$240	$220	$195	$175	$160	Last MSR was $275.

Add $30 for composite stock.

LW9 SEMI-AUTO – 9mm Para. cal., semi-auto, blowback action, composite or skeleton stock, patterned after Feather Industries 9mm Para. semi-auto. Limited mfg. 1996-97.

	$550	$495	$450	$395	$365	$335	$295	Last MSR was $500.

Add $35 for composite stock.

M-16A3 – .22 LR, .22 Mag. (disc. 1987), or .32 ACP cal., patterned after Colt's AR-15. Mfg. 1987-94.

	$450	$395	$350	$300	$275	$250	$225	Last MSR was $266.

Add 20% for .22 Mag. cal. or .32 ACP (disc. 1988).

CAR-15/22 – .22 LR cal., carbine variation of M-16 with shorter barrel and collapsible stock. Mfg. 1990-94.

	$495	$450	$395	$350	$300	$275	$250	Last MSR was $266.

GALIL – .22 LR or .22 Mag. cal., patterned after Galil semi-auto tactical design rifle, choice of wood stock or folding stock (new 1992). Mfg. 1987-93.

	$395	$350	$295	$265	$230	$200	$185	Last MSR was $359.

MAS – .22 LR or .22 Mag. cal., patterned after French MAS rifle. Mfg. 1987-93.

	$395	$350	$295	$265	$230	$200	$185	Last MSR was $359.

Add $75 for .22 Mag. cal. (disc. 1988).

PPS-30/50 – .22 LR cal., patterned after the Russian WWII PPS military rifle, full length barrel shroud, 20 shot banana mag., adj. rear sight, walnut stock. Mfg. 1989-94.

	$325	$275	$250	$225	$200	$185	$170	Last MSR was $266.

Add $150 for 50 shot drum magazine.

AK-22 – .22 LR or .22 Mag. (new 1988) cal., copy of the famous Russian AK-47, fully adj. sights, built-in cleaning rod, high quality European walnut or folding stock, 20 shot mag. Mfg. 1985-94.

	$325	$275	$250	$225	$200	$185	$170	Last MSR was $266.

Add $40 for folding stock.

AK-47 – 7.62x39mm cal., copy of the original Kalashnikov AK-47, semi-auto, teak stock and forend, 30 shot steel mag., last shot hold open. Mfg. in Yugoslavia. Imported 1986-89.

	$1,895	$1,700	$1,550	$1,400	$1,300	$1,200	$1,100	Last MSR was $675.

Add $100 for steel folding buttstock.
Add $200 for 75 shot steel drum mag.

.308 WIN. NATO AK-47 (M77B1) – .308 Win. cal., milled receiver, adj. gas port, otherwise similar to AK-47 except has scope rail, day/night Tritium sights, and 20 shot mag. Imported 1989 only.

	$1,895	$1,700	$1,550	$1,400	$1,300	$1,200	$1,100	Last MSR was $775.

Add $600 for military issue sniper scope and rings.

M76 – 7.92mm cal., similar to AK-47, except has longer barrel and frame set up for scope mount, counter sniper design, 10 shot mag., mfg. to mil. specs. Imported 1986-1989.

	$2,000	$1,875	$1,650	$1,475	$1,200	$950	$850	Last MSR was $1,995.

MSR	100%	98%	95%	90%	80%	70%	60%	

SKS-M59 – 7.62x39mm cal., copy of the SKS-M59 standard rifle, full walnut stock, fully adj. sights, gas operated. Mfg. in Yugoslavia. Imported 1986-1989.

	$775	$675	$550	$450	$400	$350	$300	Last MSR was $699.

R.P.K. – 7.62x39mm or .308 Win. cal., forged heavy barrel with cooling fins, teak stock, detachable bipod, mil. specs. Importation disc. 1992.

	$1,300	$1,100	$975	$850	$750	$650	$550	Last MSR was $1,150.

Add $845 for .308 Win. cal.

MODEL M-90 – 7.62x39mm or .308 Win. cal., AK-47 type action, in various configurations (heavy barrel, folding or fixed stock, finned barrel, etc.), plastic thumbhole stock, 5 shot mag., limited importation from Yugoslavia 1991-92.

	$1,100	$900	$800	$700	$650	$600	$550	Last MSR was $829.

Add 20% for folding stock.
Add 10% for .308 Win. cal. (wood stock only).

This model was subjected to modification due to ATF regulations after arrival in the U.S.

SHOTGUNS: SLIDE ACTION

MODEL 9108/9109 – 12 ga. only, all-purpose self-defense model featuring 20 in. barrel with 7 shot mag., choice of military green (special order), brown walnut, or black regular or pistol grip stock and forearm. Mfg. 1994-96.

	$240	$195	$175	$160	$145	$130	$120	Last MSR was $279.

Add $20 for adj. rear rifle sight (Model 9109).
Add $20 for interchangeable choke tube (Model 9108 only).

MODEL 9111/9113 – 12 ga. only, 18 1/2 in. barrel with bead sights, 6 shot mag., choice of brown or green synthetic (special order), brown walnut or black regular or pistol grip stock and forearm. Mfg. 1994-96.

	$240	$195	$175	$160	$145	$130	$120	Last MSR was $279.

Add $20 for adj. rear rifle sight (Model 9113).
Add $20 for interchangeable choke tube (Model 9111 only).

MODEL 9114 – 12 ga. only, designed for police and riot control, choice of synthetic pistol grip or top folding (disc. 1994) buttstock, 20 in. barrel with iron sights, 6 shot mag. Mfg. 1994-96.

	$295	$255	$210	$180	$160	$145	$130	Last MSR was $349.

MODEL 9115 – 12 ga. only, design based on Special Air Services riot gun, 18 1/2 in. barrel with vent. heat shield, parkerized finish, 6 shot mag., stealth grey stock featuring 4 shell storage. Mfg. 1994-96.

	$295	$255	$210	$180	$160	$145	$130	Last MSR was $349.

Add $20 for interchangeable choke tube.

MITCHELL'S MAUSERS

Current importer located in Fountain Valley, CA.

Additionally, Mitchell's Mausers imports centerfire ammunition, including the .50 BMG cal. Please refer to the Escalade and Sabre sections for currently imported semi-auto and slide action shotguns.

RIFLES: BOLT ACTION

Beginning 1999, Mitchell's Mausers imported a sizeable quantity of WWII Mauser 98Ks manufactured in Yugoslavia during/ after WWII. These guns are basically in new condition, having been only test fired over the past 50 years. They are supplied with bayonet and scabbard, military leather sling, original field cleaning kit, and leather ammo pouch. Caliber is 8mm Mauser (7.9x57mm), and all parts numbers match on these rifles. Basic retail on the Standard Grade is $225, w/o accessories. Additionally, a Collector Grade is $395, and a premium grade rifle is available for $495 (both include accessories).

MODEL M48 – 8mm Mauser cal., original Mauser 98K rifle manufactured with German technology in Serbia, various grades, matching serial numbers on all parts. Limited importation 2006.

	$450	$395	$375	$345	$295	$265	$235	Last MSR was $499.

The above price is for the Premium grade rifle without accessories. A special Museum Grade with bayonet, scabbard, belt hanger, and other accessories for $1,000. The Collector Grade was also available for $299 MSR.

TANKER MAUSER M63 (MODEL M48) – .243 Win., .270 Win., .30-06, 8mm Mauser, or .308 Win. cal., similar to Model 48, except the barrel length is 17.4 in., 5 shot internal mag., 1400m adj. rear sight, hardwood stock with semi-gloss finish, 7.4 lbs. Importation began 2006.

MSR $495	$450	$395	$375	$345	$295	$265	$235	

MODEL K98 – 8mm Mauser cal., original WWII Mauser mfg., all matching parts, various configurations available, including Collector Grade and Premium Grade.

MSR $499	$450	$395	$375	$345	$295	$265	$235	

MSR	100%	98%	95%	90%	80%	70%	60%

BLACK ARROW – 50 BMG cal., Mauser action, 5 shot detachable box mag., fluted and compensated barrel, includes bipod and quick detachable scope mount, shock absorbing buttstock. Imported 2003-2006.

$5,750 $4,950 $4,275 $3,600 $3,000 $2,400 $2,150   Last MSR was $6,500.

SOVIET MOSIN-NAGANT – various cals., original gun dated 1942 to commemorate the battle of Stalingrad. Limited importation 2009.

U.S. pricing was not available on this model.

MOSSBERG, O.F. & SONS, INC.

Current manufacturer located in North Haven, CT, 1962-present and New Haven, CT, 1919-1962.

Oscar Mossberg developed an early reputation as a designer and inventor for the Iver Johnson, Marlin-Rockwell, Stevens, and Shattuck Arms companies. In 1915, he began producing a 4-shot, .22 LR cal. palm pistol known as the "Novelty," with revolving firing pin. After producing approx. 600 of these pistols, he sold the patent to C.S. Shattuck, which continued to manufacture guns under the name "Unique." The first 600 had no markings except serial numbers, and were destined for export to South America. Very few of these original "Novelty" pistols survived in this country, and they are extremely rare specimens.

Mossberg acquired Advanced Ordnance Corp. during 1996, a high quality manufacturer utilizing state-of-the-art CNC machinery.

SHOTGUNS: SEMI-AUTO & SLIDE ACTION, RECENT PRODUCTION

In 1985, Mossberg purchased the parts inventory and manufacturing rights for the shotguns that Smith & Wesson discontinued in 1984. These 1000 and 3000 Series models (manufactured in Japan) are identical to those models which S&W discontinued. Parts and warranties are not interchangeable.

Beginning 1989, all Mossbergs sold in the U.S. and Canada have been provided with a Cablelock which goes through the ejection port, making the gun's action inoperable.

To celebrate its 75th anniversary, Mossberg released a new Crown Grade variation within most models during 1994, including the slide action 500 and 835 Series. These can be differentiated from previous manufacture by cut checkering, redesigned walnut or American hardwood stocks and forearms, screw-in choke tubes, and 4 different camo patterns. The Crown Grade was discontinued in 2000.

MODEL 500 CAMPER – 12, 20 ga., or .410 bore only, 18 1/2 in. barrel, synthetic pistol grip (no stock), camo carrying case optional, blued finish. Mfg. 1986-90 only.

$250 $220 $185 $170 $135 $110 $85   Last MSR was $276.

Add $25 for .410 bore.
Add $30 for camo case.

MODEL 500 BULLPUP – 12 ga., 18 1/2 (6 shot) or 20 (9 shot) in. barrel, bullpup configuration, 6 or 9 shot mag., includes shrouded barrel, carrying handle, ejection port in stock, employs high impact materials. Mfg. 1986-90.

$650 $525 $450 $415 $325 $275 $215   Last MSR was $425.

Add $15 for 8 shot mag. (disc.).

MODEL 500 HOME SECURITY – 20 (1996 only) ga. or .410 bore, 3 in. chamber, 18 1/2 in. barrel with spreader choke, Model 500 slide-action, 5 shot mag., blue metal finish, synthetic field stock with pistol grip forearm, 6 1/4 lbs. New 1990.

MSR $416 $340 $300 $250 $225 $185 $150 $115

* **Model 500 Home Security Laser .410** – includes laser sighting device in right front of forearm. Mfg. 1990-93.

$400 $350 $300 $270 $220 $180 $140   Last MSR was $451.

MODEL 500 PERSUADER – 12 or 20 (new 1995) ga., 6 or 8 shot, 18 1/2 in. plain barrel, cyl. bore or Accu-chokes (new 1995), optional rifle (12 ga./20 in. cyl. bore barrel only) or ghost ring (new 1999) sights, blue, matte (new 2006, 12 ga. only), or parkerized (12 ga. with ghost ring sights only) finish, Speedfeed stock was disc. 1990, optional bayonet lug, plain pistol grip wood (disc. 2004) or synthetic stock, approx. 6 3/4 lbs.

MSR $406 $350 $305 $260 $240 $190 $155 $120

Add $14 for pistol grip.
Add $41 for 20 ga. with 18 1/2 in. stand off barrel (new 2009).
Add $127 for parkerized finish and ghost ring sights (disc. 2004).
Add $40 for combo with pistol grip (disc.).
Add $23 for rifle sights (disc., 12 ga. only).

* **Model 500 Persuader Night Special Edition** – 12 ga. only, includes synthetic stock and factory installed Mepro-Light night sight bead sight, only 300 mfg. for Lew Horton Distributing in 1990 only.

$350 $260 $225 $200 $160 $135 $115   Last MSR was $296.

MSR	100%	98%	95%	90%	80%	70%	60%

MODEL 500 TACTICAL – 12 ga. only, 3 in. chamber, 18 1/2 in. cylinder bore barrel, 6 shot, adj. tactical synthetic stock, choice of matte blue or Marinecoate finish, approx. 6 3/4 lbs. New 2006.

MSR $524	$455	$395	$335	$300	$245	$200	$155

Add $134 for Marinecote finish.

MODEL 500 SPX SPECIAL PURPOSE – 12 ga. only, 18 1/2 in. ported barrel with M16 style front sight, LPA ghost ring rear sight, Picatinny rail, adj. tactical black synthetic stock with pistol grip, 6 3/4 lbs. New 2009.

Retail pricing has yet to be established on this model.

MODEL 500 SPECIAL PURPOSE ROAD BLOCKER – 12 ga. only, features pistol grip (no stock), 18 1/2 in. barrel with heat shield and large muzzle brake, 6 lbs. New 2009.

Retail pricing has yet to be established on this model.

MODEL 500 SPECIAL PURPOSE – 12 ga. only, 18 in. cylinder bored barrel, choice of blue or parkerized finish, synthetic stock with or without Speedfeed. Disc. 1996.

	$350	$295	$250	$225	$200	$175	$160	Last MSR was $378.

Add $21 for Speedfeed stock.
Add $76 for ghost ring sight (parkerized finish only).

MODEL 500 CRUISER – 12, 20, or .410 (new 1993) ga., 14 (12 ga. only, Law Enforcement Model, disc. 1995), 18 1/2, 20, or 21 (20 ga. only - mfg. 1995-2002) in. cylinder bore barrel, shroud is available in 12 ga. only, 6 or 8 (12 ga. only) shot mag., pistol grip forearm only, 5 3/4 - 7 lbs. New 1989.

MSR $406	$350	$300	$255	$230	$185	$155	$120

Add $14 for heat shield around barrel (12 ga. only).
Add $41 for tactical Cruiser with matte blue metal finish, bead sight, and pistol grip stock.
Add $96 for 14 in. barrel (disc.).
Add approx. $34 for camper case (1993-1996).
Add $14 for 8 shot (20 in. barrel, 12 ga. only).
Add $79 for Rolling Thunder model with heat shield and large barrel stabilizer (new 2009).

* **Model 500 Cruiser Mil-Spec** – 12 ga. only, 20 in. cylinder bored barrel with bead sights, built to Mil-Specs., parkerized finish. Mfg. 1997 only.

	$395	$345	$295	$270	$215	$180	$140	Last MSR was $478.

MODEL 500 GHOST RING SIGHT – 12 ga. only, 3 in. chamber, 18 1/2 or 20 in. cyl. bore or Accu-choke (20 in. only - new 1995) barrel, 6 or 9 shot tube mag., blue or parkerized finish, synthetic field stock, includes ghost ring sighting device. Mfg. 1990-97.

	$270	$235	$200	$185	$150	$120	$95	Last MSR was $332.

Add $53 for parkerized finish.
Add $49 for 9 shot mag. (20 in. barrel only).
Add $123 for Accu-choke barrel (parkerized finish only).
Add $134 for Speedfeed stock (new 1994 - 9 shot, 20 in. barrel only).

MODEL 500 MARINER – 12 ga. only, 3 in. chamber, 18 1/2 or 20 in. cyl. bore barrel, 6 or 9 (disc. 2008) shot, Marinecote finish on all metal parts (more rust-resistant than stainless steel), pistol grip black synthetic stock and forearm, fixed or ghost ring (mfg. 1995-99) sights, approx. 6 3/4 lbs.

MSR $555	$465	$400	$345	$305	$245	$200	$155

Add $51 for 9 shot model with 20 in. barrel (disc. 2008).
Add $68 for ghost ring rear sight (disc. 1999).
Add $23 for Speedfeed stock (mini-combo only - disc.).

MODEL 500 J.I.C. (JUST IN CASE) – 12 ga., 3 in. chamber, 18 in. cyl. bore barrel, comes with pistol grip, impact resistant tube and strap, available in three configurations: Crusier (survival kit in a can, blue metal, OD Green tube), Mariner (multi-tool and knife, Orange tube, Marinecote finish), or Sandstorm (Desert camo tube and finish), 5 1/2 lbs. New 2007.

MSR $435	$375	$325	$275	$250	$200	$160	$125

Add $53 for Sandstorm or $128 for Marinecote finish.

MODEL 500/590 INTIMIDATOR LASER – 12 ga. only, 3 in. chamber, 18 1/2 (Model 500) or 20 (Model 590) in. cyl. bore barrel, 6 (Model 500) or 9 (Model 590) shot tube mag., blue or parkerized finish, synthetic field stock, includes laser sighting device. Mfg. 1990-93.

* **Model 500 Intimidator**

	$500	$385	$340	$300	$265	$230	$195	Last MSR was $505.

Add $22 for parkerized finish.

* **Model 590 Intimidator**

	$550	$495	$440	$375	$340	$295	$260	Last MSR was $556.

Add $45 for parkerized finish.

MSR	100%	98%	95%	90%	80%	70%	60%

MODEL 590 SPECIAL PURPOSE SLIDE ACTION – 12 ga., 3 in. chamber, similar to Model 500, except has 9 shot mag., 20 in. cyl. bore barrel with or w/o 3/4 shroud, and bayonet lug, blue or parkerized finish, regular black synthetic stock, with or w/o Speedfeed, 7 1/4 lbs. New 1987.

MSR $485	$425	$375	$310	$280	$230	$185	$145

Add $36 for parkerized finish.
Add $74 for heavy barrel with ghost ring sights, metal triggerguard and safety.
Add $74 for ghost ring sights.
Add $33 for Speedfeed (blue, disc. 1999) or $83 for Speedfeed (parkerized) stock.

* *Model 590 Special Purpose Slide Action Mariner* – similar to Model 500 Mariner except is 9 shot and has 20 in. barrel, 7 lbs. Mfg. 1989-1993, reintroduced 2009.

MSR $609	$505	$440	$370	$335	$270	$225	$175

Add 5% for Speedfeed stock (disc. 1990).
Subtract 10% if w/o pistol grip adapter (disc.)

* *Model 590 Special Purpose Slide Action Bullpup* – similar to Model 500 Bullpup except is 9 shot and has 20 in. barrel. Mfg. 1989-90 only.

	$650	$525	$450	$410	$325	$275	$210	Last MSR was $497.

* *Model 590A1 Special Purpose Slide Action (Disc.)* – 12 ga., marked 590A1 on receiver, parkerized, ghost ring rear sight, synthetic stock and forend, ramp front sight. Disc. 1997.

	$550	$480	$410	$375	$300	$245	$190	

* *Model 590 Special Purpose Slide Action Double Action* – 12 ga. only, 3 in. chamber, world's first double action shotgun (long trigger pull), 18 1/2 or 20 in. barrel, 6 or 9 shot, bead or ghost ring sights, black synthetic stock and forearm, top tang safety, parkerized metal finish, 7-7 1/4 lbs. Mfg. 2000-2003.

	$450	$395	$335	$305	$245	$200	$155	Last MSR was $510.

Add $31 for 9 shot capacity.
Add $48 for ghost ring sights.
Add $124 for Speedfeed stock (20 in. barrel with ghost ring sights only).

* *Model 590 Special Purpose Slide Action Line Launcher* – special purpose Marine and rescue shotgun with blaze orange synthetic stock, line dispensing canister, floating and distance heads, nylon and spectra line refills, includes case and two boxes of launching loads.

	$850	$745	$635	$580	$465	$380	$295	Last MSR was $927.

MODEL 590A1 SLIDE ACTION – 12 ga., 3 in. chamber, 6 or 9 shot mag., 18 1/2 in. cylinder bore heavy barrel, parkerized finish, metal trigger guard and top safety, black synthetic stock, optional Speedfeed stock, choice of 3-dot, bead, or ghost ring sights, approx. 7 1/2 lbs. New 2009.

MSR $527	$475	$410	$350	$315	$255	$210	$165

Add $35 for ghost ring sights.
Add $47 for Speedfeed stock.
Add $81 for choice of 3-dot or ghost rings sights with Speedfeed stock.
Add $78 for Bantam Model with shortened LOP and ghost ring sights (6 shot only, limited mfg.).
Add $63 for 9 shot model.

* *Model 590A1 Adj. Stock Slide Action* – 12 ga. only, similar to Model 590A1, except has six position adj. aluminum stock with pistol grip, 9 shot model has 20 in. barrel, 3 dot (6 shot) or ghost ring (9 shot) sights, 7 1/2 lbs. New 2009.

MSR $714	$615	$535	$450	$410	$330	$270	$210

Add $47 for 6 shot model with 3 dot sights.

* *Model 590A1 Mariner Slide Action* – 12 ga. only, 18 1/2 in. cyl. bore barrel with bead sights, Marinecote finish, black synthetic stock and forearm, 6 shot only, 6 3/4 lbs. New 2009.

MSR $661	$565	$490	$410	$375	$300	$245	$190

* *Model 590A1 SPX Slide Action* – 12 ga. only, 20 in. cyl. bore barrel with ghost ring sights, parkerized finish, black synthetic stock and forearm, 9 shot, includes M9 bayonet and scabbard, receiver Picatinny rail, fiber optic front sight, 7 1/4 lbs. New 2009.

Prices have yet to be established on this model.

MODEL 590A1 SLIDE ACTION CLASS III RESTRICTED – 12 ga. only, law enforcement/military use only with 14 in. barrel, 6 shot, seven different configurations, plus X12 model designed to use Taser International products.

Retail pricing is not available on these models.

* *Model 930 Semi-Auto Special Purpose Home Security* – 12 ga., 3 in. chamber, 18 1/2 cylinder bore barrel, bead sights, blue finish, black synthetic stock, 7 1/2 lbs. New 2007.

MSR $561	$480	$410	$350	$315	$255	$210	$165

MSR	100%	98%	95%	90%	80%	70%	60%

Add $44 for tactical barrel in matte blue finish.
Add $61 for Field/Security combo (new 2010).

* ***Model 930 Semi-Auto Special Purpose Roadblocker*** – similar to Home Security Model, except has 18 1/2 in. barrel with large muzzlebrake, 5 shot, 7 3/4 lbs. New 2009.

MSR $638	$565	$490	$410	$375	$300	$245	$190

* ***Model 930 Semi-Auto Special Purpose SPX*** – 12 ga., 3 in. chamber, features 8 shot mag., Picatinny rail, LPA ghost ring rear sight, and winged fiber optic front sight, with or w/o pistol grip stock, 7 3/4 lbs. New 2008.

MSR $721	$640	$555	$470	$425	$345	$280	$220

Add $86 for pistol grip stock.

* ***Model 3000 Slide Action Law Enforcement*** – 12 or 20 ga. only, 18 1/2 or 20 in. cylinder bore only, rifle or bead sights. Mfg. 1986-87 only.

	$325	$285	$245	$220	$180	$145	$115	Last MSR was $362.

Add $25 for rifle sights.
Add $33 for black speedfeed stock.

* ***Model 9200 Crown Semi-Auto Jungle Gun*** – 12 ga. only, 18 1/2 in. plain barrel with cyl. bore, parkerized metal, synthetic stock. Mfg. 1998-2001.

	$610	$535	$455	$415	$335	$275	$215	Last MSR was $704.

NOTES

N SECTION

NAVY ARMS COMPANY

Current importer established during 1958, and located in Martinsburg, WV beginning 2005. Previously located in Union City, NJ, 2001-2005, in Ridgefield, NJ. Navy Arms imports are fabricated by various manufacturers including the Italian companies Davide Pedersoli & Co., Pietta & Co., and A. Uberti & C. Navy Arms also owns Old Western Scrounger ammo, which markets obsolete and hard-to-find ammo. Distributor and dealer sales.

Navy Arms has also sold a wide variety of original military firearms classified as curios and replics. Handguns included the Mauser Broomhandle, Japanese Nambu, Colt 1911 Government Model, Tokarev, Browning Hi-Power, S&W Model 1917, and others. Rifles included Mauser contract models, Japanese Type 38s, Enfields, FNs, Nagants, M1 Carbines, M1 Garands, Chinese SKSs, Egyptian Rashids, French MAS Model 1936s, among others. Most of these firearms are priced in the $75-$500 price range depending on desirability of model and condition.

For more information and up-to-date pricing regarding recent Navy Arms black powder models, please refer to *Blackpowder Revolvers - Reproductions and Replicas* and *Blackpowder Long Arms & Pistols - Reproductions and Replicas* by Dennis Adler and the *Blue Book of Modern Black Powder Arms* by John Allen (also online). These books feature hundreds of color photographs and support text of the most recent black powder models available, as well as complete pricing and a reference guide.

MSR	100%	98%	95%	90%	80%	70%	60%

RIFLES: MODERN PRODUCTION

In addition to the models listed, Navy Arms in late 1990 purchased the manufacturing rights of the English firm Parker-Hale. In 1991, Navy Arms built a manufacturing facility, Gibbs Rifle Co., located in Martinsburg, WV and produced these rifles domestically 1991-1994 (see Gibbs Rifle Co. listing for more info on models the company currently imports).

RPKS-74 – .223 Rem. or 7.62x39mm (new 1989) cal., semi-auto version of the Chinese RPK Squad Automatic Weapon, Kalashnikov action, 19 in. barrel, integral folding bipod, 9 1/2 lbs. Imported 1988-89 only.

	100%	98%	95%	90%	80%	70%	60%	
	$525	$445	$350	$250	$195	$175	$150	Last MSR was $649.

MODEL 1 CARBINE/RIFLE – .45-70 Govt. cal., action is sporterized No. 1 MKIII Enfield, choice of 18 (carbine) or 22 (rifle) in. barrel with iron sights, black Zytel Monte Carlo (rifle) or straight grip walnut (carbine) stock, 7 (carbine) or 8 1/2 (rifle) lbs. Limited importation 1999 only.

	100%	98%	95%	90%	80%	70%	60%	
	$325	$255	$200	$175	$160	$145	$130	Last MSR was $375.

MODEL 4 CARBINE/RIFLE – .45-70 Govt. cal., action is sporterized No. 4 MKI Enfield, choice of 18 (carbine) or 22 (rifle) in. barrel, blue metal, choice of checkered walnut Monte Carlo (rifle) or uncheckered straight grip (carbine, disc. 1999) stock, 7 or 8 lbs. Mfg. 1999-2001.

	100%	98%	95%	90%	80%	70%	60%	
	$325	$255	$200	$175	$160	$145	$130	Last MSR was $375.

NEMESIS ARMS

Current rifle manufacturer located in Calimesa, CA.

RIFLES: BOLT ACTION

WINDRUNNER – .260 Rem., .243 Win., .308 Win., or .338 Lapua cal., 20 in. chromemoly steel heavy fluted barrel, steel alloy upper, steel lower, adj. stock, 5 shot mag., Weaver rail, Versapod bipod, 11 lbs.

MSR $3,850	100%	98%	95%	90%	80%	70%	60%
	$3,500	$3,150	$2,725	$2,400	$2,125	$1,775	$1,300

NESIKA

Current trademark of rifles and actions manufactured by Nesika Bay Precision, Inc., located in Sturgis, SD. Actions are currently distributed by Dakota Arms. Previously located in Poulsbo, WA until 2003. Dealer and consumer sales.

On June 5, 2009, Remington Arms Company purchased Dakota Arms, Inc., including the rights to Nesika.

RIFLES: BOLT ACTION

Nesika also sells its proprietary rifle actions in Classic ($1,275 - $1,475 MSR), Round ($1,000 - $1,350 MSR), Hunter ($1,050 - $1,450 MSR), and Tactical ($1,400 - $1,700 MSR) configurations and in a variety of cals. A Model NXP bolt action single shot pistol model was also available. Last MSR was $1,100 circa 2008.

URBAN TACTICAL – various tactical cals., heavy duty receiver with Picatinny rail and fluted 24 or 28 in. barrel, detachable box mag., black synthetic stock with adj. recoil pad. Mfg. 2004-2005.

	100%	98%	95%	90%	80%	70%	60%	
	$4,500	$4,000	$3,500	$3,000	$2,500	$2,000	$1,650	Last MSR was $5,040.

Add $160 for heavy .308 Win. cal. or $520 for Lapua or Lazzeroni Warbird or Patriot cals.

MSR	100%	98%	95%	90%	80%	70%	60%

NEW DETONICS MANUFACTURING CORPORATION

Previous manufacturer located in Phoenix, AZ 1989-1992. Formerly named Detonics Firearms Industries (previous manufacturer located in Bellevue, WA 1976-1988). Detonics was sold in early 1988 to the New Detonics Manufacturing Corporation, a wholly owned subsidiary of "1045 Investors Group Limited."

PISTOLS: SEMI-AUTO, STAINLESS

MARK I – .45 ACP cal., matte blue. Disc. 1981.

$550	$450	$395	$335	$290	$245	$215

COMBATMASTER MC1 (FORMERLY MARK I) – .45 ACP, 9mm Para., or .38 Super cal., 3 1/2 in. barrel, two-tone (slide is non-glare blue and frame is matte stainless) finish, 6 shot mag., fixed sights, 28 oz. Disc. 1992.

$775	$575	$450	$385	$335	$280	$235	Last MSR was $920.

Add $15 for OM-3 model (polished slide - disc. 1983).
Add $100 for 9mm Para. or .38 Super cal. (disc. 1990).

This model was originally the MC1, then changed to the Mark I, then changed back to the MC1.

COMBATMASTER MARK V – .45 ACP, 9mm Para., or .38 Super cal., matte stainless finish, fixed sights, 6 shot mag. in .45 ACP, 7 shot in 9mm Para. and .38 Super, 3 1/2 in. barrel, 29 oz. empty. This model was disc. 1985.

$620	$550	$495	$430	$375	$315	$270	Last MSR was $689.

Add $100 for 9mm Para. or .38 Super cal.

MILITARY COMBAT MC2 – .45 ACP, 9mm Para., or .38 Super cal., dull, non-glare combat finish, fixed sights. Comes with camouflaged pile-lined wallet, and Pachmayr grips. Disc. 1984.

$621	$560	$500	$430	$375	$315	$270

Add $55 for 9mm Para. or .38 Super.

SERVICEMASTER – .45 ACP cal. only, shortened version of the Scoremaster, non-glare combat finish, 4 1/4 in. barrel, coned barrel system, 8 shot mag., interchangeable front and adj. rear sights, 39 oz. Disc. 1986.

$825	$675	$575	$480	$410	$350	$295	Last MSR was $686.

NEW ENGLAND FIREARMS

Current trademark established during 1987, located and previously manufactured in Gardner, MA until Nov. 1, 2007. Beginning Nov. 1, 2007, the NEF trademark applies to imported guns only. Distributor sales.

During late Jan. of 2008, Remington acquired the Marlin Firearms Company, which had purchased the H&R, New England Firearms (NEF), and L.C. Smith brands during 2000. On May 31st, 2007, Remington Arms Co. was acquired by Cerberus Capital.

During 2000, Marlin Firearms Co. purchased the assets of H&R 1871, Inc., and the name was changed to H&R 1871, LLC. Brand names include Harrington & Richardson, New England Firearms, and Wesson & Harrington.

All NEF firearms utilize a transfer bar safety system and have a $10 service plan which guarantees lifetime warranty. New England Firearms should not be confused with New England Arms Corp.

RIFLES: SINGLE SHOT

Beginning Nov. 1, 2007, H&R 1871 decided that all products built in the USA will carry the H&R brand name, and all imported products will be sold under the NEF brand name. The Handi-Rifle, Super Light Handi-Rifle, Sportster, and Survivor are now under the H&R brand name.

SURVIVOR – .223 Rem., .308 Win. (new 1999), .357 Mag. (disc. 1998) or .410/45 LC (new 2007) cal., similar in design to the Survivor Series shotgun, removable forearm with ammo storage, thumbhole stock with storage compartment, no iron sights, 20 (.410/45 LC cal. only) or 22 in. barrel, blue or nickel finish, .357 Mag. cal. has open sights, .223 Rem. and .308 Win. cal. have heavy barrels and scope mount rail, 6 lbs. Mfg. 1996-2008.

$230	$180	$145	$110	$80	$70	$60	Last MSR was $281.

Add approx. $15 for nickel finish (disc. 1998, reintroduced 2007 for .410/45 LC cal. only).
Subtract $76 for .410/45 LC cal. (new 2007).

SHOTGUNS: SINGLE SHOT

Beginning Nov. 1, 2007, H&R 1871 decided that all products built in the USA will carry the H&R brand name, and all imported products will be sold under the NEF brand name. The Pardner Series and Tracker Slug are now under the H&R brand name.

SURVIVOR SERIES – 12 (disc. 2003), 20 ga. (disc. 2003), or .410/.45 LC (new 1995) bore, 3 in. chamber, 20 (.410/.45 LC) or 22 in. barrel with Mod. choke, blue or electroless nickel finish, synthetic thumbhole designed hollow stock with pistol grip, removable forend holds additional ammo, sling swivels, and black nylon sling, 13 1/4 in. LOP, 6 lbs. Mfg. 1992-93, reintroduced 1995-2006.

$175	$150	$120	$100	$85	$75	$65	Last MSR was $219.

MSR	100%	98%	95%	90%	80%	70%	60%

Add $18 for electroless nickel finish.
Subtract 20% for 12 or 20 ga.

SHOTGUNS: SLIDE ACTION

* ***Pardner Pump Protector*** – .12 ga., black synthetic stock, 18 1/2 in. barrel, bead front sight, matte finished metal, swivel studs, vent. recoil pad, 5 shot tube mag., crossbolt safety. Mfg. 2006-2007.

	$155	$135	$115	$100	$85	$75	$65	Last MSR was $186.

* ***Pardner Pump Slug*** – 12 or 20 ga., take-down action, 21 (20 ga.) or 22 (12 ga.) in. rifled barrel, matte metal finish, black synthetic (12 ga.) or walnut (20 ga.) pistol grip stock with fluted comb, swivel studs, vent. recoil pad, ramp front sight, adj. rear sight, drilled and tapped, 5 shot mag., crossbolt safety, approx. 6 1/2 lbs. New 2006.

MSR $298	$250	$215	$190	$160	$140	$115	$100

Add $33 for full cantilever scope mount (new 2009).
Add $44 for walnut stock and forearm.

NEXT GENERATION ARMS

Current rifle manufacturer located in Toledo, OR.

RIFLES: SEMI-AUTO

Next Generation Arms manufactures a AR-15 style 14 1/2 in. barreled rifle for military/law enforcement, designed for extreme conditions - the MP168 Special Purpose Carbine. Please contact the company directly for more information (see Trademark Index).

NIGHTHAWK CUSTOM

Current manufacturer located in Berryville, AR. since 2004. Consumer custom order sales.

PISTOLS: SEMI-AUTO

Nighthawk Custom offers a complete line of high quality 1911 style semi-auto pistols. Please contact the company directly for more information on custom pistols, a wide variety of options, gunsmithing services and availability.

Add $200 for Crimson Trace laser grips on any applicable model (not bobtail).
Add $150 for Ed Brown bobtail.
Add $65 for ambidextrous safety.

GRP (GLOBAL RESPONSE PISTOL) – .45 ACP cal., black Perma Kote ceramic based finish, 5 in. match grade barrel, 8 shot mag., match grade trigger, front and rear cocking serrations, Heinie or Novak Extreme Duty adj. night sights, Gator Back (disc.) or Green Linen (new 2009) grips, 41 oz.

MSR $2,350	$2,125	$1,825	$1,575	$1,275	$1,000	$850	$725

Add $100 for GRP II with 4 1/4 in. barrel.
Add $200 for GRP Recon Model with integrated lower rail with Surefire X300 weapon light.
Add $200 Crimson Trace laser grips.

TALON – 9mm Para., .40 S&W, 10mm, or .45 ACP cal., blue finish, 4 1/4 (Talon II) or 5 in. match grade or bull barrel, lightweight aluminum match trigger, hand checkering on rear of slide with serrated top slide, Novak night sights, double diamond cocobolo, walnut, or black cristobal grips, tactical mag. release, 31-39 oz.

MSR $2,550	$2,300	$2,000	$1,625	$1,300	$1,050	$875	$750

Add $55 for Talon II with green lower frame.
Add $105 for Talon III with 4 1/4 in. barrel.

* ***Talon IV*** – similar to Talon, except compact model with 3.6 in. barrel, gray frame and black slide, rear slide serrations, and black grips.

MSR $2,425	$2,225	$1,950	$1,600	$1,300	$1,050	$875	$750

PREDATOR – .45 ACP cal., 4 1/4 or 5 in. barrel, grey finish with black slide, double diamond cocobolo, walnut, or black cristobal checkered grips, Heinie Slant Pro Staight Eight or Novak low mount night sights, unique one piece precision fit barrel designed to reduce muzzle flip and felt recoil, one inch at 25 yards guaranteed accuracy, top-of-the-line model, 32-34 oz.

MSR $2,824	$2,575	$2,175	$1,850	$1,525	$1,200	$1,000	$850

Add $51 for Predator II with 4 1/4 in. barrel.
Add $101 for Predator III model with Officer frame and 4 1/4 in. barrel.

DOMINATOR – .45 ACP cal., 5 in. match grade barrel hard chrome frame with black PermaKote slide, 8 shot, front and rear slide serrations, 25 LPI checkering on front strap, cocobolo double diamond grips with laser engraved Nighthawk Custom logo, adj. sights, 40 oz.

MSR $2,775	$2,550	$2,150	$1,850	$1,525	$1,200	$1,000	$850

MSR	100%	98%	95%	90%	80%	70%	60%

HEINIE TACTICAL CARRY – .45 ACP cal., 5 in. Heinie match grade barrel, choice of PermaKote, hard chrome, or Diamond black finish, double diamond cocobolo or aluminum grips with Heinie logo, Heinie Slant Pro Straight Eight night sights, Heinie trigger, complete carry dehorned, Heinie magwell, flat slide top with 40 LPI serrations, 40 oz. New 2009.

| MSR $3,895 | $3,600 | $3,250 | $2,850 | $2,450 | $2,000 | $1,600 | $1,200 |

HEINIE PDP – .45 ACP cal., 4 1/2 in. Heinie match grade barrel, cocbolo wood grips with Heinie logo, fixed sights, scalloped front strap and mainspring housing, extended combat safety, contoured for carry mag. well, wider ejection port, Heinie match hammer, sear, and disconnector, serrated rear of slide, slide top, Heinie aluminum trigger, tactical mag release, 38 oz. New 2009.

| MSR $2,895 | $2,600 | $2,300 | $1,900 | $1,550 | $1,275 | $1,000 | $875 |

T3 – .40 S&W or .45 ACP cal., 4 1/4 in. match grade stainless steel fully crowned barrel, black Perma Kote finish, extended mag. well, flush forged slide stop with chamfered frame, tactical mag. release, horizontally serrated no-snag mainspring housing and rear of slide, skeletonized aluminum match trigger, 30 oz. New 2009.

| MSR $2,700 | $2,495 | $2,100 | $1,800 | $1,500 | $1,175 | $975 | $825 |

Add $200 for stainless steel frame.

LADY HAWK – 9mm Para. cal., 4 1/4 in. crowned match grade barrel, ultra thin aluminum grips, Heinie Slant Pro Straight Eight sights, modified chain link front strap and mainspring housing, titanium blue Perma Kote finish with hard chromed controls, 36 oz. New 2009.

| MSR $2,895 | $2,600 | $2,300 | $1,900 | $1,550 | $1,275 | $1,000 | $875 |

10-8 – .45 ACP cal., 5 in. barrel, green or black linen micarta grips, black Perma Kote finish, 8 shot, Hilton Yam/10-8 performance designed U-notched rear and serrated front sights with tritium inserts, low profile Dawson light speed rail, front/rear cocking serrations, long solid trigger with hidden fixed over travel stop, strong side only safety, 42 oz. New 2009.

| MSR $2,595 | $2,350 | $2,025 | $1,650 | $1,325 | $1,175 | $900 | $775 |

ENFORCER – .45 ACP cal., 5 in. barrel, Novak low mount tritium or Heinie Slant Pro night sights, extended tactical mag. catch, Perma Kote finish in black, Sniper Gray, Desert Tan, Titanium Blue, hard chrome, or Diamond black finish, 39 oz. New 2009.

| MSR $2,895 | $2,600 | $2,300 | $1,900 | $1,550 | $1,275 | $1,000 | $875 |

RIFLES: BOLT ACTION

BOLT ACTION RIFLE – various cals., bolt action, available in Hunting, Varmint, and Bench Rest configurations, Broughton barrel, synthetic stock.

| MSR $3,295 | $2,950 | $2,600 | $2,300 | $1,950 | $1,650 | $1,375 | $1,125 |

TACTICAL RIFLE – .308 Win., 7mm Rem. Mag., .300 Rem. Mag., or .338 Lapua cal., with or w/o Surgeon action, with or w/o bolt on Picatinny rail with choice of 0 or 20 MOA elevation built in, Jewell trigger, PermaKote finish in choice of Desert Sand, OD Green, Sniper Gray, Desert camo, Woodland camo, or Urban camo finish, tactical synthetic stock with adj. comb. New 2009.

| MSR $3,650 | $3,325 | $2,995 | $2,600 | $2,250 | $1,825 | $1,500 | $1,225 |

Add $300 for integral rail (also available with Surgeon action).
Add $550 for short Surgeon action.
Add $625 for Magnum Surgeon action.
Add $650 for long Surgeon action.
Add $875 for XL action in .338 Lapua cal.

SHOTGUNS

TACTICAL SLIDE ACTION – 12 ga., collapsible stock with Hogue pistol grip and quick disconnect sling swivel, receiver mounted Picatinny rail, forend Picatinny rail and barrel clamp, Surefire Z2 combat light, tritium night sight, 2 in. extended breaching device, choice of camo or other color finishes.

| MSR $1,100 | $995 | $875 | $750 | $625 | $500 | $450 | $375 |

Add $165 for 5-position stock.

TACTICAL SEMI-AUTO – 12 ga., Rem. 870 style, 3 in. chamber, 18 in. barrel, Hogue overmolded buttstock with pistol grip and 12 or 14 in. LOP, hand tuned action, ceramic Perma Kote finish in Sniper Gray, OD Green, Desert Tan, or black color, ghost ring rear sight, red fiber optic front sight, choice of 4 or 6 shot aluminum shell carrier.

| MSR $1,695 | $1,495 | $1,300 | $1,075 | $925 | $800 | $675 | $550 |

NORINCO

Current Chinese conglomerate (China North Industries Corp.) located in China which manufactures small arms and military firearms. Previously imported and distributed exclusively by Interstate Arms Corp., located in Billerica, MA.

MSR	100%	98%	95%	90%	80%	70%	60%

Previous importers have included: Norinco Sports U.S.A., located in Diamond Bar, CA, Century International Arms, Inc. located in St. Albans, VT; China Sports, Inc. located in Ontario, CA; Interarms located in Alexandria, VA; KBI, Inc. located in Harrisburg, PA; and others. Dealer and distributor sales only.

Norinco pistols, rifles, and shotguns are manufactured in the People's Republic of China by China North Industries Corp. (Norinco has over 100 factories). Currently, due to the 1994 Crime bill and recent presidential orders, Norinco cannot legally sell weapons in the U.S.

RIFLES: SEMI-AUTO

TYPE 84S AKS RIFLE – .223 Rem. cal., semi-auto Kalashnikov action, 16.34 in. barrel, hardwood stock and pistol grip, 30 shot mag., 1,000 meter adj. rear sight, includes bayonet and sheath, 8.87 lbs. Imported 1988-89 only.

| | $1,450 | $1,250 | $1,150 | $1,000 | $925 | $875 | $795 | Last MSR was $350. |

* *Type 84S-1 AKS Rifle* – similar to Type 84S AKS except has under-folding metal stock. Imported 1989 only.

| | $1,600 | $1,500 | $1,400 | $1,250 | $1,100 | $1,000 | $900 | Last MSR was $350. |

* *Type 84S-3 AKS Rifle* – similar to Type 84S AKS except has composite fiber stock (1 1/2 in. longer than wood stock). Imported 1989 only.

| | $1,295 | $1,100 | $1,000 | $950 | $900 | $800 | $750 | Last MSR was $365. |

* *Type 84S-5 AKS Rifle* – similar to Type 84S AKS except has side-folding metal stock. Imported 1989 only.

| | $1,600 | $1,500 | $1,450 | $1,350 | $1,200 | $1,100 | $1,000 | Last MSR was $350. |

NHM-90/91 (AK-47 THUMBHOLE) – .223 Rem. or 7.62x39mm cal., features new thumbhole stock for legalized import, 5 shot mag. Imported 1991-1993, configuration was restyled and renamed NHM-90/91 in 1994.

| | $750 | $675 | $575 | $500 | $450 | $350 | $300 | Last MSR was $375. |

NHM-90/91 SPORT – 7.62x39mm cal., choice of 16.34 (NHM-90) or 23.27 (NHM-91) in. barrel, hardwood thumbhole stock, NHM-91 has bipod, 5 shot mag., 9-11 lbs. Imported 1994-95.

| | $550 | $500 | $450 | $425 | $385 | $350 | $325 | |

The .223 Rem. cal. was also available for the Model NHM-90. Each Model NHM-90/91 was supplied with three 5 shot mags., sling, and cleaning kit.

MODEL B THUMBHOLE – 9mm Para. cal., patterned after the Uzi, features sporterized thumbhole wood stock, 10 shot mag. Importation 1995 only.

| | $795 | $695 | $600 | $550 | $500 | $450 | $400 | Last MSR was $625. |

R.P.K. RIFLE – 7.62x39mm cal., includes bipod. Importation disc. 1993.

| | $1,200 | $1,000 | $900 | $800 | $725 | $650 | $600 | Last MSR was $600. |

TYPE SKS – .223 Rem. or 7.62x39mm cal., SKS action, 20.47 in. barrel, 10 (C/B 1994) or 30* shot mag., 1,000 meter adj. rear sight, hardwood stock, new design accepts standard AK mag., with or w/o folding bayonet, 8.8 lbs. Imported 1988-1989, reintroduced 1992-95 with Sporter configuration stock.

| | $475 | $400 | $350 | $325 | $300 | $250 | $225 | Last MSR was $150. |

Add $100 for synthetic stock and bayonet.
Subtract 15% if refinished.

TYPE 81S AKS RIFLE – 7.62x39mm cal., semi-auto Kalashnikov action, 17 1/2 in. barrel, 5, 30, or 40 shot mag., 500 meter adj. rear sight, fixed wood stock, hold open device after last shot, 8 lbs. Imported 1988-1989.

| | $1,200 | $1,000 | $900 | $800 | $725 | $650 | $600 | Last MSR was $385. |

* *Type 81S-1 AKS Rifle* – similar to Type 81S AKS except has under-folding metal stock. Imported 1988-89.

| | $1,300 | $1,075 | $950 | $850 | $750 | $625 | $575 | Last MSR was $385. |

TYPE 56S-2 – 7.62x39mm cal., older Kalashnikov design with side-folding metal stock. Importation disc. 1989.

| | $1,500 | $1,350 | $1,200 | $1,100 | $1,000 | $900 | $800 | Last MSR was $350. |

TYPE 86S-7 RPK RIFLE – 7.62x39mm cal., AK action, 23.27 in. heavy barrel with built-in bipod, in-line buttstock, 11.02 lbs. Imported 1988-1989.

| | $1,500 | $1,275 | $1,075 | $950 | $850 | $750 | $650 | Last MSR was $425. |

TYPE 86S BULLPUP RIFLE – 7.62x39mm cal., bullpup configuration with AK action, under-folding metal stock, 17 1/4 in. barrel, ambidextrous cocking design, folding front handle, 7 lbs. Imported 1989 only.

| | $1,850 | $1,650 | $1,500 | $1,250 | $1,100 | $1,000 | $900 | Last MSR was $400. |

DRAGUNOV (MODEL 350 NDM-86) – 7.62x54mm Russian, sniper variation of the AK-47, features 24 in. barrel

MSR	100%	98%	95%	90%	80%	70%	60%

with muzzle brake, special laminated skeletonized wood stock with vent. forearm, detachable 10 shot mag., 8 lbs. 9 oz. Importation disc. 1995.

| | $2,950 | $2,650 | $2,400 | $2,250 | $2,000 | $1,850 | $1,650 | Last MSR was $3,080. |

This model was also imported by Gibbs Rifle Co. located in Martinsburg, WV.

* ***Dragunov Carbine*** – similar to Dragunov rifle, except shorter barrel, various accessories including a lighted scope were also offered, plastic furniture.

| | $1,200 | $1,000 | $875 | $775 | $675 | $600 | $550 |

OFFICERS NINE – 9mm Para. cal., 16.1 in. barrel, action patterned after the IMI Uzi, 32 shot mag., black military finish, 8.4 lbs. Limited 1988-89.

| | $1,100 | $995 | $850 | $725 | $650 | $575 | $500 | Last MSR was $450. |

SHOTGUNS: SEMI-AUTO

* ***Model 2000 Field Defense*** – 12 ga. only, 2 3/4 in. chamber, 18 1/2 in. barrel with cyl. choke tube and choice of bead, rifle, or ghost ring sights, matte black metal finish, black synthetic stock and forearm with recoil pad. Limited importation 1999 only.

| | $245 | $225 | $190 | $175 | $160 | $155 | $145 | Last MSR was $282. |

Add $5 for rifle sights.
Add $17 for ghost ring sights.

SHOTGUNS: SLIDE ACTION

* ***Model 98 Field Defense*** – 12 ga. only, 3 in. chamber, 18 1/2 in. barrel with cyl. choke tube and choice of bead, rifle, or ghost ring sights, matte black metal finish, black synthetic stock and forearm with recoil pad. Limited importation 1999 only.

| | $170 | $150 | $130 | $115 | $100 | $90 | $80 | Last MSR was $190. |

Add $15 for ghost ring sights.

NOWLIN MFG., INC.

Current custom handgun and components manufacturer established in 1982, and located in Claremore, OK. Dealer or consumer direct sales.

PISTOLS: SEMI-AUTO

Nowlin Mfg., Inc. manufactures a complete line of high quality M1911 A1 styled competition and defense pistols, available in 9mm Para., 9x23mm, .38 Super, .40 S&W, or .45 ACP cal. Various frame types are available, including a variety of Nowlin choices. Recent models (available in blue or nickel finish) include the NRA Bianchi Cup (approx. 1997 retail was $2,750 - disc.), 007 Compact ($1,395 - disc.), Compact X2 ($1,436 - disc.), Match Classic ($1,695), Crusader ($1,999), Avenger w/ STI frame ($2,279), Challenger ($2,049), World Cup PPC ($2,219), STI High Cap. Frame ($1,595 - disc. 1999), Mickey Fowler Signature Series ($2,187), Compact Carry ($1,695 - disc. 1999), Compact 4 1/4 in. ($1,750, .45 ACP, disc. 2002), Gladiator ($1,447 in .45 ACP cal., disc. 2002), Match Master ($2,795), Bianchi Cup Master Grade ($5,019 MSR, .38 Super cal.) and the Custom Shop Excaliber Series ($3,029). Please contact the factory directly for more information, including specific pricing (see Trademark Index).

O SECTION

OBERLAND ARMS

Current manufacturer of tactical style firearms located in Huglfing, Germany. Previously located in Habach, Germany. No current U.S. importation.

Oberland Arms manufactures a wide variety of high quality tactical style rifles, including an OA-15 series based on the AR-15 design. Oberland Arms also used to manufacture pistols. Many rifle options and configurations are available. Please contact the company directly for more information, including pricing, options, and U.S. availability (see Trademark Index).

MSR	100%	98%	95%	90%	80%	70%	60%

OHIO ORDNANCE WORKS, INC.

Current rifle manufacturer established in 1981, and located in Chardon, OH.

RIFLES: SEMI-AUTO

MODEL BAR 1918A3 – .30-06 cal., patterned after the original Browning BAR (M1918A2) used during WWI, all steel construction utilizing original parts except for lower receiver, 24 in. barrel, original folding type rear sight, includes two 20 shot mags., matte metal and wood finish, Bakelite or American walnut stock and forearm, carrying handle, web sling, bipod, flash hider, bolt open hold device, 20 lbs.

MSR $3,500	$3,500	$3,150	$2,600	$2,350	$1,975	$1,650	$1,425

Add $300 for American black walnut stock and forearm.

MODEL BAR A1918 SLR – .30-06 cal., similar to Model BAR 1918A3, except does not have A3 carry handle, mfg. by Ohio Ordnance Works, Inc. 2005-2007.

	$3,100	$2,800	$2,450	$2,100	$1,800	$1,575	$1,300	Last MSR was $3,350.

Add $200 for walnut stock.

MODEL 1928 BROWNING – .30-06, 7.65mm, .308 Win., or 8mm (disc.) cal., semi-auto action patterned after the 1928 Browning watercooled machine gun, blue (disc.) or parkerized finish, includes tripod, water hose, ammo can, 3 belts, and belt loader. Limited production late 2001-2007.

	$3,750	$3,400	$3,000	$2,650	$2,300	$2,100	$1,900	Last MSR was $4,000.

Add $200 for .308 Win. or 8mm (disc.) cal.
Add approx. $2,000 for blue finish (limited mfg.).

MODEL M-240 SLR – 7.62mm cal., belt fed, gas operated, air cooled, fires from closed bolt, sling, cleaning kit, ruptured case extractor, gas regulator cleaning tool, disassembly tools, 2500 M-13 links, custom fit hard case. New 2007.

MSR $13,500	$13,500	$11,750	$9,750	$8,250	$7,500	$6,750	$6,000

MODEL VZ2000/VZ2000 SBR – 7.62x39mm cal., Czech VZ 58 copy, new milled receiver, original barrels, bakelite stocks, heat cured paint finish (matches original Czech finish), folding stock, includes four 30 shot mags., pouch, sling, cleaning kit, original bayonet.

MSR $1,125	$1,125	$950	$825	$700	$600	$500	$400

Add $125 for VZ2000 SBR.

OLYMPIC ARMS, INC.

Current manufacturer established during 1976, and located in Olympia, WA. Dealer direct sales.

In late 1987, Olympic Arms, Inc. acquired Safari Arms of Phoenix, AZ. As of Jan. 2004, the Safari Arms product name was discontinued, and all 1911 style products are now being manufactured in the Olympic Arms facility in Olympia, WA. Schuetzen Pistol Works is the in-house custom shop of Olympic Arms.

PISTOLS: SEMI-AUTO

Please refer to the Safari Arms section for previously manufactured pistols made under the Safari Arms trademark.

ENFORCER – .45 ACP cal., 3.8 (disc.) or 4 in. bushingless bull barrel, 6 shot mag., shortened grip, available with max hard finish aluminum frame, parkerized, electroless nickel, or lightweight (disc.) anodized finishes, Triplex counterwound self-contained spring recoil system, flat or arched mainspring housing, adj. sights, ambidextrous safety, neoprene or checkered walnut grips, 27 (lightweight model) or 35 oz.

MSR $1,034	$925	$825	$675	$575	$475	$400	$350

This model was originally called the Black Widow. After Safari Arms became Schuetzen Pistol Works, this model was changed extensively to include stainless construction, beavertail grip safety, and combat style hammer.

MSR	100%	98%	95%	90%	80%	70%	60%

MATCHMASTER – similar to the Enforcer, except has 5 or 6 in. barrel and 7 shot mag. rounded (R/S) or squared off trigger guard, finer slide serrations, approx. 40 oz.

MSR $904	$775	$675	$575	$475	$425	$395	$375

Add $71 for 6 in. barrel.

BLAK-TAC MATCHMASTER – .45 ACP cal., 5 in. National Match barrel, 7 shot mag., widened and lowered ejection port, Blak-Tac treated frame and slide, low profile combat sights, adj. trigger, approx. 40 oz. Mfg. 2003-2008.

	$875	$775	$675	$575	$500	$450	$400	Last MSR was $995.

BIG DEUCE – .45 ACP cal., 6 in. longslide version of the MatchMaster, matte black slide with satin stainless steel frame, smooth walnut grips, 40.3 oz. Mfg. 1995-2004, reintroduced 2006.

MSR $1,034	$925	$825	$675	$575	$475	$400	$350

COHORT – .45 ACP cal., features Enforcer slide and MatchMaster frame, 3.8 in. stainless steel barrel, beavertail grip safety, extended thumb safety and slide release, commander style hammer, smooth walnut grips with laser etched Black Widow logo, 37 oz. New 1995.

MSR $974	$850	$750	$650	$550	$450	$400	$350

K23P – .223 Rem. cal., 6 1/2 in. steel barrel, A2 upper w/aluminum handguard, flash supressor, recoil buffer in back of frame. New 2007.

MSR $974	$895	$825	$725	$625	$525	$450	$400

Add $95 for A3 upper receiver or $144 for A3 upper w/Picatinny rail and Firsh handguard.

OA-93 PISTOL – .223 Rem. (most common, current mfg.) or 7.62x39mm (very limited mfg., disc.) cal., gas operated without buffer tube stock, or charging handle, 6 (most common, disc.), 6 1/2 (new 2005), 9 (disc.), or 14 (disc.) in. free-floated match threaded barrel with flash suppressor, upper receiver utilizes integral scope mount base, 30 shot mag., 4 lbs. 3 oz., approx. 500 mfg. 1993-94 before Crime Bill discontinued production, reintroduced late 2004.

MSR $1,203	$1,095	$995	$875	$800	$750	$700	$650	Last MSR in 1994 was $2,700.

Add 100% for 7.62x39mm cal.

OA-96 AR PISTOL – .223 Rem. cal., 6 in. barrel only, similar to OA-93 Pistol, except has pinned (fixed) 30 shot mag. and rear takedown button for rapid reloading, 5 lbs. Mfg. 1996-2000.

	$860	$775	$650	$575	$495	$450	$395	Last MSR was $860.

OA-98 PISTOL – .223 Rem. cal., skeletonized, lightweight version of the OA-93/OA-96, 6 1/2 in. non-threaded barrel, 10 shot fixed (disc.) or detachable (new 2006) mag., denoted by perforated appearance, 3 lbs. Mfg. 1998-2003, reintroduced 2005-2007.

	$995	$875	$800	$750	$700	$650	$600	Last MSR was $1,080.

RIFLES: BOLT ACTION

In 1993, Olympic Arms purchased the rights, jigs, fixtures, and machining templates for the Bauska Big Bore Magnum Mauser action. Please contact Olympic Arms (see Trademark Index) for more information regarding Bauska actions both with or without fluted barrels.

ULTRA CSR TACTICAL RIFLE – .308 Win. cal., Sako action, 26 in. broach cut heavy barrel, Bell & Carlson black or synthetic stock with aluminum bedding, Harris bipod, carrying case. Mfg. 1996-2000.

	$1,450	$1,250	$1,100	$1,000	$800	$700	$600	Last MSR was $1,140.

COUNTER SNIPER RIFLE – .308 Win. cal., bolt action utilizing M-14 mags., 26 in. heavy barrel, camo-fiberglass stock, 10 1/2 lbs. Disc. 1987.

	$1,300	$1,100	$975	$895	$750	$650	$600	Last MSR was $1,225.

SURVIVOR I CONVERSION UNIT – .223 Rem. or .45 ACP cal., converts M1911 variations into carbine, bolt action, collapsible stock, 16 1/4 in. barrel, 5 lbs.

	$275	$225	$195	$150	$125	$110	$95

This kit was also available for S&W and Browning Hi-Power models.

RIFLES: SEMI-AUTO

Olympic Arms is currently shipping high capacity mags. with its rifles/carbines to those states where legal.

The PCR (Politically Correct Rifle) variations listed below refer to those guns manufactured after the Crime Bill was implemented in September 1994 through 2004. PCR rifles have smooth barrels (no flash suppressor), a 10 shot mag., and fixed stocks. Named models refer to the original, pre-ban model nomenclature.

Add $20 for Coyote Brown furniture on models with carbine length handguards, pistol grip, and collapsible buttstock (new 2010).

MSR	100%	98%	95%	90%	80%	70%	60%

COMPETITOR RIFLE – .22 LR cal., Ruger 10/22 action with 20 in. barrel featuring button cut rifling, Bell & Carlson thumbhole fiberglass stock, black finish and matte stainless fluted barrel, includes bipod, 6.9 lbs. Mfg. 1996-99.

	$575	$500	$450	$400	$360	$330	$300	Last MSR was $575.

ULTRAMATCH/PCR-1 – .223 Rem. cal., AR-15 action with modifications, 20 or 24 in. match stainless steel barrel, Picatinny flattop upper receiver, Williams set trigger optional, scope mounts, 10 lbs. 3 oz. New 1985.

* *Ultramatch PCR-1* – disc. 2004.

	$950	$850	$750	$675	$625	$575	$525	Last MSR was $1,074.

* *Ultramatch PCR-1P* – .223 Rem. cal., premium grade ultramatch rifle with many shooting enhancements, including Maxhard treated upper and lower receiver, 20 or 24 in. broach cut Ultramatch bull barrel, 1x10 in. or 1x8 in. rate of twist. Mfg. 2001-2004.

	$1,175	$1,050	$925	$825	$725	$625	$550	Last MSR was $1,299.

* *Ultramatch UM-1* – 20 in. stainless Ultramatch barrel with non-chromed bore, approx. 8 1/2 lbs. Disc. 1994, reintroduced late 2004.

MSR $1,329	$1,250	$1,075	$950	$825	$750	$675	$600	
								Last MSR in 1994 was $1,515.

* *Ultramatch UM-1P* – similar to UM-1 Ultramatch, except has 20 (disc. 2006) or 24 in. Ultramatch bull barrel, premium grade ultramatch rifle with many shooting enhancements, 9 1/2 lbs. New 2005.

MSR $1,624	$1,495	$1,325	$1,100	$975	$825	$775	$700

INTERCONTINENTAL – .223 Rem. cal., features synthetic wood-grained thumbhole buttstock and aluminum handguard, 20 in. Ultramatch barrel (free floating). Mfg. 1992-1993.

	$1,650	$1,350	$1,050	$875	$750	$600	$550	Last MSR was $1,371.

INTERNATIONAL MATCH – .223 Rem. cal., similar to Ultramatch, except has custom aperture sights. Mfg. 1991-93.

	$1,475	$1,150	$950	$800	$675	$575	$525	Last MSR was $1,240.

SERVICE MATCH/PCR SERVICE MATCH – .223 Rem. cal., AR-15 action with modifications, 20 in. SS Ultramatch barrel, carrying handle, standard trigger, choice of A1 or A2 flash suppressor (Service Match only), 8 3/4 lbs.

* *Service Match SM-1* – 9.7 lbs., disc. 1994, reintroduced late 2004.

MSR $1,273	$1,095	$995	$875	$775	$700	$625	$550	
								Last MSR in 1994 was $1,200.

* *Service Match SM-1P Premium Grade* – .223 Rem. cal., Maxhard upper and lower receiver, 20 in. broach cut Ultramatch super heavy threaded barrel (1 turn in 8 in. is standard), flash suppressor, 2-stage CMP trigger, Blak-Tak Armour bolt carrier assembly, Bob Jones NM interchangable rear sight system, AC4 pneumatic recoil buffer, Turner Saddlery competition sling, GI style pistol grip. New 2005.

MSR $1,728	$1,575	$1,350	$1,200	$1,025	$900	$800	$725

* *Service Match PCR* – disc. late 2004.

	$825	$750	$675	$625	$550	$500	$450	Last MSR was $1,062.

* *Service Match PCR-SMP Premium Grade* – .223 Rem. cal., Maxhard upper and lower receiver, 20 in. broach cut Ultramatch super heavy barrel (1 turn in 8 in. is standard), 2-stage CMP trigger, Blak-Tak Armour bolt carrier assembly, Bob Jones NM interchangable rear sight system, AC4 pneumatic recoil buffer, Turner Saddlery competition sling, GI style pistol grip. Mfg. 2004 only.

	$1,100	$950	$800	$700	$600	$550	$475	Last MSR was $1,613.

MULTIMATCH ML-1/PCR-2 – .223 Rem. cal., tactical short range rifle, 16 in. Ultramatch barrel with A2 upper receiver, aluminum collapsible (Multimatch ML-1) or fixed (PCR-2) stock, carrying handle, stealth Vortex flash suppressor (Multimatch ML-1 only). New 1991.

* *Multimatch ML-1* – 7.35 lbs.

MSR $1,188	$1,050	$950	$850	$750	$675	$600	$525	
								Last MSR in 1994 was $1,200.

* *Multimatch PCR-2* – disc. late 2004.

	$750	$675	$600	$525	$450	$425	$400	Last MSR was $958.

MULTIMATCH ML-2/PCR-3 – .223 Rem. cal., features Picatinny flattop upper receiver with stainless steel 16 in. Ultramatch bull (new 2005) barrel, carrying handle (disc.), 5 lbs. 14 oz. New 1991.

* *Multimatch ML-2* – 7 1/2 lbs., disc. 1994, reintroduced late 2004.

MSR $1,188	$1,050	$950	$850	$750	$675	$600	$525	
								Last MSR in 1994 was $1,200.

MSR	100%	98%	95%	90%	80%	70%	60%	

* Multimatch PCR-3 – disc. late 2004.

	$850	$750	$650	$550	$500	$450	$350	Last MSR was $958.

AR-15 MATCH/PCR-4 – .223 Rem. cal., patterned after the AR-15 with 20 in. barrel and solid synthetic stock, 8 lbs. 5 oz. Mfg. 1975-2004.

* PCR-4

	$850	$750	$650	$575	$525	$475	$425	Last MSR was $803.

* AR-15 Match

	$1,095	$995	$875	$775	$650	$575	$495	Last MSR was $1,075.

CAR-15/PCR-5 – modified AR-15 with choice of 11 1/2 (disc. 1993) or 16 in. barrel, stow-away pistol grip and collapsible stock (CAR-15 only), 7 lbs. Mfg. 1975-1998, PCR-5 reintroduced 2000-2004.

* PCR-5 – .223 Rem., 9mm Para. (new 1996), .40 S&W (new 1996), or .45 ACP (new 1996) cal. Disc. 1998, reintroduced 2000-2004.

	$950	$850	$800	$725	$650	$600	$550	Last MSR was $755.

Add $45 for 9mm Para., .40 S&W, or .45 ACP cal.

* CAR-15 – .223 Rem., 9mm Para., .40 S&W, .45 ACP, or 7.62x39mm cal.

	$1,050	$950	$850	$775	$650	$575	$495	Last MSR was $1,030.

Add $170 for pistol cals.

PCR-6 – 7.62x39mm cal., 16 in. barrel, post-ban only, A-2 stowaway stock, carrying handle, 7 lbs. Mfg. 1995-2002.

	$895	$795	$725	$650	$500	$475	$425	Last MSR was $870.

PCR-7 ELIMINATOR – .223 Rem. cal., similar to PCR-4, except has 16 in. barrel, 7 lbs. 10 oz. Mfg. 1999-2004.

	$850	$750	$675	$625	$585	$540	$510	Last MSR was $844.

PCR-8 – .223 Rem. cal., same configuration as the PCR-1, except has standard 20 in. stainless steel heavy bull barrel with button rifling. Mfg. 2001-2004.

	$825	$725	$675	$640	$600	$550	$525	Last MSR was $834.

* PCR-8 Mag. – .223 WSSM or .243 WSSM cal., otherwise similar to PCR-8. Mfg. 2004.

	$925	$825	$750	$675	$600	$550	$500	Last MSR was $1,074.

This model was also scheduled to be available in .308 Olympic Mag. and 7mm Olympic Mag. cals.

PCR-9/10/40/45 – 9mm Para., 10mm, .40 S&W, or .45 ACP cal., similar to PCR-5 Carbine except for pistol cal., A2 upper standard, 16 in. barrel, A2 buttstock, mil spec lower receiver. Mfg. 2001-2004.

	$875	$775	$675	$600	$550	$495	$450	Last MSR was $835.

PCR-16 – .223 Rem. cal., 16 in. match grade bull barrel, two-piece aluminum free-floating handguard, Picatinny receiver rail, 7 1/2 lbs. Mfg. 2003-2004.

	$825	$750	$650	$600	$565	$535	$500	Last MSR was $714.

PCR-30 – .30 Carbine cal., forged aluminum receiver with matte black anodizing, parkerized steel parts, A-2 adj. rear sight, accepts standard GI M1 .30 Carbine mags., 16 in. barrel with 1 turn in 12 in. twist, 7.15 lbs. Mfg. 2004.

	$875	$825	$750	$700	$650	$600	$575	Last MSR was $899.

PLINKER – .223 Rem. cal., similar to PCR-5, except has 16 in. button rifled barrel standard, A1 sights, cast upper/lower receiver, 100% standard mil spec parts, 7 lbs. Mfg. 2001-2004.

	$650	$595	$550	$500	$495	$450	$425	Last MSR was $598.

PLINKER PLUS – .223 Rem. cal., similar to Plinker, except has 16 (disc. 2009) or 20 in. button rifled threaded barrel with flash suppressor, A1 sights, cast upper/lower receiver, 100% standard mil spec parts, 7-8.4 lbs. New 2005.

MSR $844	$775	$675	$625	$550	$500	$475	$450	

Subtract approx. 10% for 16 in. barrel.

CAR-97 – .223 Rem., 9mm Para., 10mm, .40 S&W, or .45 ACP cal., similar to PCR-5, except has 16 in. button rifled barrel, A2 sights, fixed CAR stock, post-ban muzzle brake, approx. 7 lbs. Mfg. 1997-2004.

	$795	$750	$675	$600	$550	$500	$450	Last MSR was $780.

Add approx. $65 for 9mm Para., .40 S&W, or .45 ACP cal.

* CAR-97 M4 – .223 Rem. cal., M4 configuration with contoured barrel, fixed carbine tube stock, factory installed muzzle brake, oversized shortened handguard. Mfg. 2003-2004.

	$800	$750	$675	$600	$550	$500	$450	Last MSR was $839.

MSR	100%	98%	95%	90%	80%	70%	60%	

Add $95 for detachable carrying handle (new 2004).

FAR-15 – .223 Rem. cal., featherweight model with lightweight 16 in. barrel, fixed collapsible stock, A1 contour lightweight button rifled barrel, 9.92 lbs. Mfg. 2001-2004.

	$775	$700	$650	$600	$550	$500	$450	Last MSR was $822.

GI-16 – .223 Rem. cal., forged aluminum receiver with black matte finish, A1 type upper receiver, parkerized steel parts, A1 adj. rear sights, 16 in. button rifled match grade barrel, collapsible stock, 6.6 - 7 lbs. Mfg. 2004, reintroduced 2006.

MSR $857	$800	$750	$700	$625	$575	$525	$475	

GI-20 – .223 Rem. cal., similar to GI-16, except has 20 in. heavy barrel and A-2 lower receiver, 8.4 lbs. Mfg. 2004.

	$725	$650	$595	$550	$495	$450	$425	Last MSR was $749.

OA-93 CARBINE – .223 Rem. cal., 16 in. threaded barrel, design based on OA-93 pistol, aluminum side folding stock, flattop receiver, round aluminum handguard, Vortex flash suppressor, 7 1/2 lbs. Mfg. 1995 - civilian sales disc. 1998, reintroduced 2004-2007.

	$1,250	$1,050	$925	$825	$750	$675	$625	

Last MSR in 1998 was $1,550.
Last MSR in 2007 was $1,074.

* **OA-93PT Carbine** – .223 Rem. cal., aluminum forged receiver, black matte hard anodized finish, no sights, integral flattop upper receiver rail system, match grade 16 in. chromemoly steel barrel with removable muzzle brake, push button removable stock, vertical pistol grip, 7.6 lbs. Mfg. 2004 only, reintroduced 2006-2007.

	$985	$875	$825	$750	$675	$600	$550	Last MSR was $1,074.

LTF/LT-MIL4 LIGHTWEIGHT TACTICAL RIFLE – .223 Rem. cal., available in LTF (fluted) or LT-MIL4 (disc. 2009) configuration, black matte anodized receiver, Firsh type forearms with Picatinny rails, parkerized steel parts, adj. flip-up sight system, 16 in. non-chromed fluted or MIL4 threaded barrel with flash suppressor, tube style Ace FX buttstock, 6.4 lbs. New 2005.

MSR $1,240	$1,125	$975	$850	$775	$700	$650	$600	

Subtract approx. 10% if w/o fluted barrel.

K3B CARBINE – .223 Rem. cal., 16 in. match grade chromemoly steel threaded barrel with flash suppressor, adj. A2 rear sight, A2 buttstock, adj. front post sight, optional A3 flattop receiver.

MSR $941	$875	$775	$675	$575	$525	$475	$425	

Add $30 for A3 flattop receiver.

* **K3B-CAR Carbine** – similar to K3B Carbine, except has carbine length handguard and collapsible stock, approx. 6 lbs. New 2005.

MSR $969	$895	$795	$695	$595	$550	$500	$450	

Add $95 for A3 upper receiver.

* **K3B-FAR Carbine** – similar to K3B Carbine, except has smaller barrel diameter and is lightweight, 5.8 lbs. New 2005.

MSR $1,006	$925	$825	$700	$600	$550	$500	$450	

Add $95 for A3 upper receiver.

* **K3B-M4 Carbine** – similar to K3B Carbine, except has M4 handguard, collapsible stock, and M4 barrel, 6.3 lbs. New 2005.

MSR $1,039	$950	$850	$725	$625	$575	$525	$475	

Add $154 for A3 upper receiver.

* **K3B-M4-A3-TC Carbine** – similar to K3B-M4, except is tactical carbine version with Firsh handguard, flattop upper receiver and Picatinny rail, 6.7 lbs. New 2005.

MSR $1,247	$1,150	$1,025	$925	$825	$775	$700	$650	

K4B/K4B68 – .223 Rem. or 6.8 SPC (new 2010) cal., 20 in. match grade chromemoly steel button rifled threaded barrel with flash suppressor, adj. A2 rear sight, A2 buttstock, adj. front post sight, A2 upper receiver and handguard, 8 1/2 lbs.

MSR $969	$895	$795	$695	$595	$550	$500	$450	

Add $95 for Picatinny flattop receiver and A3 detachable carry handle.

K4B-A4 – .223 Rem. cal., features 20 in. barrel with A2 flash suppressor, elevation adj. post front sight, bayonet lug, Firsh rifle length handguard with Picatinny rails, flattop receiver, 9 lbs. Mfg. 2006-2008.

	$850	$760	$675	$600	$550	$500	$450	Last MSR was $941.

K7 ELIMINATOR – .223 Rem. cal., 16 in. stainless steel threaded barrel with flash suppressor, adj. A2 rear sight, A2 buttstock, adj. front post sight, 7.8 lbs. New 2005.

MSR $974	$895	$795	$695	$595	$550	$500	$450	

Add $141 for A3 upper flattop receiver and detachable carry handle.

MSR	100%	98%	95%	90%	80%	70%	60%

K8 – .223 Rem. cal., 20 in stainless steel button rifled bull barrel, A2 buttstock, Picatinny flattop upper receiver, 8 1/2 lbs. New 2005.

MSR $909	$850	$775	$700	$625	$550	$500	$450

This model is marked "Target Match" on mag. well.

* ***K8-MAG*** – similar to K8, except available in .223 WSSM, .243 WSSM, .25 WSSM, or .300 WSM (mfg. 2006) cals., and has 24 in. barrel, 9.4 lbs. New 2005.

MSR $1,364	$1,250	$1,125	$995	$900	$800	$700	$600

K9/K10/K40/K45 – 9mm Para. (K9), 10mm Norma (K10), .40 S&W (K40), or .45 ACP (K45) cal., blow back action, adj. A2 rear sight, 10 shot converted Uzi (10mm, .40 S&W or .45 ACP cal.) or 32 (9mm Para.) shot converted Sten detachable mag., 16 in. threaded barrel with flash suppressor, collapsible buttstock, bayonet lug, 6.7 lbs. New 2005.

MSR $1,006	$925	$825	$700	$600	$550	$500	$450

* ***K9GL/K40GL*** – similar to K9 Series, except available only in 9mm Para. or .40 S&W cal., lower receiver designed to accept Glock magazines, 16 in. barrel with flash suppressor, collapsible stock, does not include magazine. New 2005.

MSR $1,092	$1,025	$950	$850	$75-	$650	$575	$500

Add $95 for A3 upper receiver.

K16 – .223 Rem. cal., 16 in. free floating button rifled barrel, A2 buttstock, Picatinny flattop upper receiver, 7 1/2 lbs. New 2005.

MSR $831	$775	$725	$650	$600	$550	$500	$450

K30 – .30 Carbine cal., similar to K16, except has A2 upper receiver, collapsible stock, and threaded barrel with flash suppressor, 6.6 lbs. Mfg. 2005-2006.

	$825	$700	$625	$550	$500	$450	$400	*Last MSR was $905.*

Add $95 for A3 upper receiver.

K30R – 7.62x39mm cal., 16 in. stainless steel barrel, M4 six-point collapsible stock, A2 flash suppressor, pistol grip, matte black anodized receiver, parkerized steel parts, A2 upper with adj. rear sight, 7.9 lbs. New 2007.

MSR $974	$895	$795	$695	$595	$550	$500	$450

Add $95 for A3 upper receiver.

K68 – 6.8 Rem. SPC cal., 16 in. stainless steel barrel, M4 six-position collapsible stock, A2 upper with adj. rear sight, matte black anodized receiver, parkerized steel parts, pistol grip, A2 flash suppressor, 6.62 lbs. New 2007.

MSR $1,039	$950	$850	$725	$625	$575	$525	$475

Add $95 for A3 upper receiver.

K74 – 5.45x39mm cal., 16 in. button rifled barrel, A2 upper with adj. front sight, A2 flash suppressor, M4 type six-position collapsible stock, 6 3/4 lbs. New 2009.

MSR $917	$875	$825	$750	$675	$600	$550	$495

GAMESTALKER – .243 WSSM, .25 WSSM, or .300 WSSM cal., 22 in. stainless steel barrel, flattop upper receiver, free floating aluminum handguard, ACE skeleton stock with ERGO Sure Grip, 100% camo coverage, approx. 7 1/2 lbs. New 2010.

MSR $1,359	$1,250	$1,125	$995	$900	$800	$700	$600

OMEGA WEAPONS SYSTEMS INC.

Previous shotgun manufacturer established circa 1998, and located in Tucson, AZ. Previously distributed by Defense Technology, Inc., located in Lake Forest, CA.

SHOTGUNS: SEMI-AUTO

OMEGA SPS-12 – 12 ga. only, 2 3/4 in. chamber, features gas operation and 5 shot detachable mag., 20 in. barrel, protected ghost ring rear and front sight, synthetic stock (with or w/o pistol grip) and forearm, 9 lbs. Mfg. 1998-2005.

	$195	$180	$165	$150	$135	$125	$115	*Last MSR was $225.*

OMNI

Previous manufacturer located in Riverside, CA 1992-1998. During 1998, Omni changed its name to E.D.M. Arms. Previously distributed by First Defense International located in CA.

RIFLES: BOLT ACTION

LONG ACTION SINGLE SHOT – .50 BMG cal., competition single shot, chromemoly black finished receiver, 32-34 in. steel or stainless steel barrel with round muzzle brake, benchrest fiberglass stock, designed for FCSA competition

MSR	100%	98%	95%	90%	80%	70%	60%

shooting, 32 lbs. Mfg. 1996-98.

	$3,600	$3,200	$2,800	$2,500	$2,150	$1,800	$1,500	Last MSR was $3,500.

Add $400 for painted stock (disc. 1996).

SHELL HOLDER SINGLE SHOT – similar to Long Action Single Shot, except has fiberglass field stock with bipod, 28 lbs. Mfg. 1997-98.

	$2,975	$2,750	$2,525	$2,150	$1,800	$1,500	$1,250	Last MSR was $2,750.

MODEL WINDRUNNER – .50 BMG cal., long action, single shot or 3 shot mag., 1-piece I-beam, chrome-moly black finished receiver, 36 in. barrel with round muzzle brake, fiberglass tactical stock, 35 lbs. Mfg. 1997-1998.

	$6,950	$6,425	$5,875	$5,325	$4,750	$4,175	$3,500	Last MSR was $7,500.

Add $750 for 3 shot repeater.

MODEL WARLOCK – .50 BMG or 20mm cal., single, 3 (20mm), or 5 (.50 BMG) shot fixed mag., fiberglass field stock, massive design chrome-moly black finished receiver, muzzle brake, 50 lbs. Mfg. 1997-1998.

	$10,750	$8,950	$7,750	$6,750	$5,500	$4,750	$3,950	Last MSR was $12,000.

E.D.M. ARMS MODEL 97 – available in most cals. up to .308 Win., single shot or repeater (cals. .17 Rem. through .223 Rem. only), wire-cut one-piece receiver, black tactical stock with pillar-bedded chromemoly barrel, black finished receiver, unique trigger with safety, 9 lbs. Mfg. 1997-98.

	$2,525	$2,150	$1,800	$1,500	$1,250	$1,100	$925	Last MSR was $2,750.

E.D.M. ARMS WINDRUNNER WR50 – .50 BMG cal., sniper rifle, 5 shot mag., removable tactical adj. stock, takedown action with removable barrel, wire-cut one-piece receiver, titanium muzzle brake, blackened chromemoly barrel, approx. 29 lbs. Mfg. 1998 only.

	$11,750	$10,250	$9,500	$8,250	$7,000	$5,750	$4,500	Last MSR was $12,900.

NOTES

P/Q SECTIONS

P.A.W.S., INC.

Previous manufacturer located in Salem, OR. Distributor and dealer sales. Previously distributed by Sile Distributors, Inc. located in New York, NY.

MSR	100%	98%	95%	90%	80%	70%	60%

CARBINES

ZX6/ZX8 CARBINE – 9mm Para. or .45 ACP cal., semi-auto tactical design carbine, 16 in. barrel, 10 or 32* shot mag., folding metal stock, matte black finish, aperture rear sight, partial barrel shroud, 7 1/2 lbs. Mfg. 1989-2004.

	$715	$635	$550	$475	$375	$300	$250

The ZX6 is chambered for 9mm Para., while the ZX8 is chambered for .45 ACP.

PGW DEFENCE TECHNOLOGIES, INC.

Current manufacturer established in 1992, and located in Winnipeg, Manitoba, Canada. Previous company name was Prairie Gun Works until 2003. Currently imported by Leroy's Big Valley Gun Works, located in Glasgow, MT.

RIFLES: BOLT ACTION

PGW manufactures approx. 50-60 guns annually. They also sell their actions separately for $400-$2,300, depending on caliber and configuration.

LRT-3 (PGW/GIBBS) – .50 BMG cal., single shot action, Big Mac stock. Mfg. 1999-2009.

	$4,150	$3,700	$3,400	$3,100	$2,800	$2,500	$2,250

PTR 91, INC.

Current rifle manufacturer located in Farmington, CT. Represented by Vincent A. Pestilli & Associates, located in Brownfield, ME. Previous company name was J.L.D. Enterprises.

RIFLES: SEMI-AUTO

MODEL PTR-91F – .308 Win. cal., CNC machined scope mounts, H&K style hooded front blade and four position diopter rear sight, 18 in. barrel with 1:12 twist, black furniture, pre-ban H&K flash hider, or welded muzzle brake (PTR-91C), H&K Navy type polymer trigger group, 20 shot mag., one piece forged cocking handle, parkerized finish, matte black coated.

MSR $1,295	$1,200	$1,025	$900	$800	$700	$600	$550

Add $200 for tactical handguard, side folding stock, and pre-ban flash hider (PTR-91R, disc. 2008).
Add $200 for tactical handguard, side folding stock, and muzzle brake (PTR-91 RC, disc. 2008).

* **Model PTR-91T** – .308 Win. cal., similar to Model PTR-91, except has green furniture and original H&K flash hider. Limited mfg. 2005.

	$895	$800	$700	$600	$500	$450	$400	Last MSR was $995.

MODEL PTR-91 AI – .308 Win. cal., match grade rifle with polymer trigger group, match grade barrel, H&K style hooded front blade and four position diopter rear sight, 20 shot mag., steel bipod, steel handguard with bipod recesses, pre-band H&K flash hider, with (PTR-91 AI C) or w/o (PTR-91 AI F) muzzle brake with match grade barrel. Mfg. 2005-2008.

	$1,150	$925	$825	$725	$600	$500	$425	Last MSR was $1,295.

MODEL PTR-91 KC – .308 Win. cal., "Kurz" law enforcement carbine with 16 in. barrel, H&K style hooded front blade and four position diopter rear sight, 20 shot mag., tropical green (disc.) or black furniture, wide handguard with bipod recesses, pre-ban H&K flash hider or welded muzzle compensator (PTR-91KC). New 2005.

MSR $1,295	$1,195	$1,050	$900	$800	$700	$600	$550

Add $100 for PTR-91 KFO with side folding stock and pre-ban flash hider (disc. 2006).

MODEL PTR-91 KFM4 – .308 Win. cal., "Kurz" paratrooper carbine, 16 in. barrel, H&K style hooded front blade and four position diopter rear sight, 20 shot mag., tropical green (disc.) or black furniture, wide handguard with bipod recesses and three complete rails, H&K Navy type polymer trigger group, M4 type 6 position telescoping stock and flash hider. New 2005.

MSR $1,435	$1,295	$1,095	$975	$850	$725	$600	$500

MODEL PTR-91 KF – .308 Win. cal., 16 in. barrel, 20 shot mag., black furniture with tactical handguard, pre-ban H&K flash hider, H&K Navy polymer trigger group.

MSR $1,295	$1,200	$1,025	$900	$800	$700	$600	$550

MSR	100%	98%	95%	90%	80%	70%	60%

MODEL PTR-91 KPF GERMAN PARATROOPER – .308 Win. cal., 16 in. barrel, 20 shot mag., black furniture, three rails, pre-ban H&K flash hider, H&K Navy polymer trigger group, original German telescoping stock.

MSR $1,915	$1,775	$1,575	$1,375	$1,150	$925	$800	$675

MODEL PTR-MSG 91 SNIPER – .308 Win. cal., 18 in. fluted target barrel, black furniture, tactical aluminum handguard, welded Picatinny accessory rail, Harris bipod, adj. Magpul stock with cheekpiece, pre-ban H&K flash hider, with (Model PTR-MSG 91 C) or w/o (PTR-MSG 91) welded muzzle compensator.

MSR $2,125	$1,975	$1,775	$1,575	$1,375	$1,150	$900	$750

PTR-MSG 91 SS SUPER SNIPER – .308 Win. cal., 20 in. fluted free floating match barrel, 10 shot mag., black furniture with tactical super sniper handguard, welded Picatinny accessory rail, Harris bipod, no sights, adj. Magpul stock.

MSR $2,770	$2,495	$2,250	$1,975	$1,750	$1,500	$1,225	$975

MODEL PTR-91 SC SQUAD CARBINE – .308 Win. cal., 16 in. fluted barrel, H&K style hooded front blade and four position diopter rear sight, black furniture, tactical aluminum handguard with three rails, welded Picatinny accessory rail, standard stock, pre-ban H&K flash hider, with or w/o welded compensator (compliant model).

MSR $1,580	$1,425	$1,250	$1,050	$925	$800	$675	$550

PTR-32 KF – .7.62x39mm cal., 16 in. barrel, H&K style hooded front blade and four position diopter rear sight, 30 shot mag., black furniture, tactical aluminum handguard, pre-ban H&K flash hider, H&K Navy type polymer trigger group, standard stock.

MSR $1,365	$1,250	$1,025	$900	$800	$700	$600	$500

PTR-32 KF C – .7.62x39mm cal., 16 in. barrel, H&K style hooded front blade and four position diopter rear sight, 10 shot mag., black furniture, tactical aluminum handguard, H&K Navy type polymer trigger group, welded muzzle compensator.

MSR $1,365	$1,250	$1,025	$900	$800	$700	$600	$500

PTR-32 KFM4 – .7.62x39mm cal., 16 in. barrel, H&K style hooded front blade and four position diopter rear sight, 30 shot mag., black furniture, tactical aluminum handguard with three rails, pre-ban H&K flash hider, H&K Navy type polymer trigger group, M4 six position telescoping stock.

MSR $1,485	$1,325	$1,100	$975	$850	$725	$600	$500

PTR-32 KCM4 – .7.62x39mm cal., 16 in. barrel, H&K style hooded front blade and four position diopter rear sight, 10 shot mag., black furniture, tactical aluminum handguard with three rails, H&K Navy type polymer trigger group, M4 style fixed stock, welded compensator.

MSR $1,485	$1,325	$1,100	$975	$850	$725	$600	$500

PARA USA, INC.

Current manufacturer established in 1988, and located in Pineville, NC. Previous company name was Para-Ordnance Mfg. Inc., and was located in Scarborough, Ontario, Canada until June 2009. Previously located in Ft. Lauderdale, FL. Dealer and distributor sales.

PISTOLS: SEMI-AUTO

In 1999, Para-Ordnance introduced their LDA trigger system, originally standing for Lightning Double Action. During 2002, all alloy frame pistols were discontinued, and the abbreviation LDA became Light Double Action. Beginning 2003, all Para-Ordnance models were shipped with two magazines. Beginning Jan. 1, 2004, all Para-Ordnance models were replaced for the general market (except California) with the introduction of the new Power Extractor (PXT) models. The Griptor system, featuring front grip strap grasping grooves, became available during 2005, and the accessory mounting rail option became available during 2006.

Previous Para-Ordnance model nomenclature typically listed the alphabetical letter of the series, followed by a one or two digit number indicating magazine capacity, followed by the number(s) of the caliber. Hence, a Model P14.45 is a P Series model with a 14 shot mag. in .45 ACP cal., and a 7.45LDA indicates a .45 ACP cal. in Light Double Action with a 7 shot mag.

Current Para-Ordnance nomenclature typically features the configuration type on the left side of the slide. The model designation is located on the right side of the slide and underneath it on the frame the product code (new 2006)/order number (changed to product code during 2006), which is alpha-numeric, may also appear. For current product codes for the various Para-Ordnance models, please visit www.paraord.com.

Para-Ordnance offers the following finishes on its pistols: Regal (black slide, black frame w/stainless fire controls), Midnight Blue (blue slide, blue frame w/blue fire controls), Coyote Brown, Covert Black (black slide, black frame, and black fire controls), Black Watch (black slide, green frame, green (double stack) or black (single stack) fire controls), Spec Ops (green slide, green

MSR	100%	98%	95%	90%	80%	70%	60%

frame w/black fire controls), or Sterling (all stainless, black slide w/polished sides), in addition to stainless steel construction.

6.45 LDA/LLDA – Models 6.45 LDA (changed to Para-Companion, marked Para-Companion on left side of slide and C7.45LDA on right side of slide) and 6.45 LLDA were advertised in the 2001 Para-Ordnance catalog (became the Para-Carry, marked Para-Carry on left side of slide and 6.45 LLDA on right side of frame), the 6.46 LLDA was never mfg., prototype only. Mfg. 2001-2003.

C SERIES MODELS – .45 ACP cal., DAO, 3 (Carry), 3 1/2 (Companion or Companion Carry), 4 1/2 (CCW or Tac-Four), or 5 in. barrel, stainless steel only, single or double (Tac-Four only) stack mag., 6 (Carry), 7, or 10 (Tac-Four only) shot mag., approx. 30-34 oz. Mfg. 2003.

	$775	$680	$580	$525	$425	$350	$270	Last MSR was $939.

Add $70 for Companion Carry Model.

D SERIES MODELS – 9mm Para., .40 S&W, or .45 ACP cal., DAO, 3 1/2 or 5 in. barrel, 7 or 10 shot single stack mag., steel receiver, matte black finish or stainless steel. Mfg. 2003.

	$715	$625	$535	$485	$395	$320	$250	Last MSR was $859.

Add $80 for stainless steel.

P SERIES MODELS – 9mm Para. or .45 ACP cal., single action, 3 1/2, 4 1/4, or 5 in. barrel, 10 shot mag., matte black (5 in. barrel only) or stainless steel finish.

* ***P Series Model P13*** – .40 S&W (disc. 2000) or .45 ACP cal., similar to P14, except has 10 (C/B 1994) or 12* shot mag., 4 1/4 in. barrel, 35 oz. with steel frame (disc. 2002) or 25 oz. with alloy frame (disc. 2002), stainless steel became standard 2003 (duo-tone stainless was disc. 2000). Mfg. 1993-2003.

	$750	$655	$560	$510	$410	$335	$260	Last MSR was $899.

* ***P Series Model P14*** – .40 S&W (mfg. 1996-2000) or .45 ACP cal., patterned after the Colt Model 1911A1 except has choice of alloy (matte black, disc. 2002), steel (matte black), or stainless steel (stainless or duo-tone finish) frame that has been widened slightly for extra shot capacity (13* shot), 10 shot (C/B 1994) mag., single action, 3-dot sight system, rounded combat hammer, 5 in. ramped barrel, 38 oz. with steel frame or 28 oz. with alloy frame (disc. 2002), duo-tone stainless steel was disc. 2000. Mfg. 1990-2003.

	$685	$600	$515	$465	$375	$310	$240	Last MSR was $829.

Add $70 for stainless steel.

PXT 1911 SINGLE STACK SERIES – .38 Super or .45 ACP cal., features new power extractor design with larger claw (PXT), left slide is marked "Para 1911", right side marked with individual model names, various configurations, barrel lengths, and finishes, single action, single stack mag., spurred or spurless (light rail models only) hammer. New 2004.

* ***Slim Hawg*** – .45 ACP cal. only, 3 in. barrel, 6 shot mag., 3-dot sights, choice of stainless steel or Covert Black (new 2006) finish, 24 or 30 (stainless) oz.

MSR $989	$875	$765	$655	$595	$480	$395	$305	

Add $140 for stainless steel.

* ***GI Expert*** – .45 ACP cal., 5 in. barrel, 8 shot mag., 3 dot sights, steel frame, black finish. New 2009.

MSR $599	$550	$480	$410	$375	$300	$245	$190	

* ***1911 OPS*** – .45 ACP cal. only, 3 1/2 in. barrel, 7 shot mag., 3-dot sights, stainless steel construction, 32 oz. Disc. 2008.

	$975	$855	$730	$665	$535	$440	$340	Last MSR was $1,099.

* ***1911 LTC*** – 9mm Para. (new 2008) or .45 ACP cal., 4 1/4 in. barrel, 8 or 9 (9mm Para) shot mag., 3-dot sights, steel alloy or stainless steel construction, Covert black (9mm Para.) or Regal finish, 28 (alloy) or 35 oz.

MSR $959	$875	$765	$655	$595	$480	$395	$305	

Add $20 for steel, or $150 for stainless steel.

* ***1911 SSP Series*** – .38 Super or .45 ACP cal., 5 in. barrel, 8 or 9 (.38 Super cal. only) shot mag., 3-dot or Novak adj. (Tactical Duty Model only) sights, steel or stainless steel (new 2006) construction, Black Covert (new 2008) or Regal finish, stainless, or bright stainless (.38 Super cal. only), checkered wood or pearl (.38 Super cal.) grips, 39 oz. Disc. 2008.

	$775	$680	$580	$525	$425	$350	$270	Last MSR was $899.

Add $230 for stainless steel.
Add $250 for .38 Super cal., or $280 for .38 Super with pearl grips.
Add $250 for Tactical Duty SSP with Novak adj. sights (disc. 2008).

* ***1911 Nite-Tac*** – .45 ACP cal. only, 5 in. barrel, 8 shot mag., 3-dot sights, stainless steel construction, Covert Black finish or stainless, features light rail on frame, flush spurless hammer, 40 oz. Disc. 2008.

	$1,025	$875	$750	$650	$550	$450	$375	Last MSR was $1,149.

MSR	100%	98%	95%	90%	80%	70%	60%

PXT HIGH CAPACITY SERIES – 9mm Para., 40 S&W, or .45 ACP cal., single action, 10 shot or high capacity mag., various barrel lengths, construction, and finishes.

* **Hawg 9** – 9mm Para. cal., compact frame, 12 shot mag., 3 in. ramped barrel with guide rod, dovetailed, low mount, 3-dot fixed sights, alloy receiver, steel slide, spurred competition hammer, match grade trigger, balck polymer grips, Regal black finish, three safeties, 24 oz. New 2005.

MSR $959	$875	$765	$655	$595	$480	$395	$305

* **Lite Hawg 9** – similar to Hawg 9, except is steel and has light rail, flush spurless hammer, Covert Black finish. Disc. 2008.

	$990	$865	$740	$675	$545	$445	$345	Last MSR was $1,099.

* **Lite Hawg .45** – .45 ACP cal., similar to Lite Hawg 9, except has 10 shot mag., flush spurless hammer, Covert Black finish. Disc. 2008.

	$990	$865	$740	$675	$545	$445	$345	Last MSR was $1,099.

* **Warthog** – .45 ACP cal., lightweight, compact design, 3 in. ramped barrel, alloy or stainless frame, 10 shot mag., tritium night (disc.) or 3-dot sights, spur competition hammer, match grade trigger, extended slide lock, beavertail grip and firing pin safeties, black polymer grips, Covert Black (Para-Kote, disc.), or Regal finish, or stainless steel construction, 24 or 31 oz. New 2004.

MSR $959	$875	$765	$655	$595	$480	$395	$305

Add $110 for stainless steel.

* **Nite Hawg** – .45 ACP cal., 3 in. barrel, 10 shot mag., tritium night sights, compact alloy frame, Covert Black finish, black plastic grips, 24 oz.

MSR $1,099	$995	$870	$745	$675	$545	$450	$350

* **Big Hawg** – .45 ACP cal., 5 in. barrel, 14 shot mag., 3-dot sights, alloy frame, Regal finish with chrome accents, black plastic grips, 28 oz.

MSR $959	$875	$765	$655	$595	$480	$395	$305

* **P14.45** – .45 ACP cal., 5 in. barrel, 14 shot mag., 3-dot sights, Covert Black finish steel (new 2008) or stainless steel construction, black synthetic grips, brushed stainless steel, 40 oz.

MSR $919	$850	$745	$635	$580	$465	$380	$295

Add $230 for stainless steel.

* **S14.45 Limited (PXT High Capacity Limited)** – .45 ACP cal., single action, 10 (disc.) or 14 shot mag., adj. sights, 3 1/2 (stainless steel, disc. 2005), 4 1/4 (stainless steel, disc. 2005), or 5 (steel, disc. 2005, or stainless steel) in. barrel, Covert (disc. 2005) or Sterling finish, black synthetic grips, 40 oz.

MSR $1,259	$1,125	$985	$845	$765	$620	$505	$395

Add $75 for 3 1/2 or 4 1/4 in. barrel or stainless steel (disc. 2006).

* **S16.40 Limited (PXT High Capacity Limited)** – .40 S&W cal., single action, 10 (disc.) or 16 shot mag., adj. sights, 3 1/2 (stainless steel, disc. 2005), 4 1/4 (stainless steel, disc. 2005), or 5 (steel, disc. 2005, or stainless steel) in. barrel, Covert (disc. 2005) or Sterling finish, black synthetic grips, 40 oz.

MSR $1,259	$1,125	$985	$845	$765	$620	$505	$395

Add $75 for 3 1/2 or 4 1/4 in. barrel or stainless steel (disc. 2006).

PXT LDA SINGLE STACK (CARRY OPTION SERIES) – 9mm Para. (new mid-2006), .45 GAP (new mid-2006) or .45 ACP cal., DAO, single stack mag., various barrel lengths and finishes, features Griptor grips (grooved front grip strap), spurless flush hammer and rounded grip safety.

* **Carry Gap** – .45 GAP cal., 3 in. barrel, 6 shot mag., 3-dot sights, steel frame, Covert Black finish, 30 oz. Disc. 2008.

	$975	$855	$730	$665	$535	$440	$340	Last MSR was $1,079.

* **CCO Gap** – similar to Carry Gap, except has 7 shot mag. and 3 1/2 in. barrel, 31 oz. Mfg. 2006-2008.

	$975	$855	$730	$665	$535	$440	$340	Last MSR was $1,079.

* **Covert Black Carry** – .45 ACP cal., 6 shot mag., 3 in. barrel, Novak adj. sights, stainless steel construction, Covert Black finish, 30 oz.

MSR $1,149	$1,025	$895	$770	$695	$565	$460	$360

* **Carry** – similar to Covert Black Carry, except has 3-dot sights and is brushed stainless steel.

MSR $1,149	$1,025	$895	$770	$695	$565	$460	$360

MSR	100%	98%	95%	90%	80%	70%	60%

* ***Carry 9*** – 9mm Para. cal., 8 shot mag., 3 in. barrel, 3-dot sights, alloy frame, Covert Black finish, 24 oz. New mid-2006.

MSR $999	$900	$785	$675	$610	$495	$405	$315

* ***PDA*** – 9mm Para cal., 3 in. barrel with fiber optic front and two-dot rear sights, alloy frame with Sterling/Covert Black finish. New 2008.

MSR $1,219	$1,100	$960	$825	$750	$605	$495	$385

* ***PDA .45*** – .45 ACP cal., 3 in. barrel with three dot sights, 6 shot mag., alloy frame with stainless/Covert Black finish. New 2008.

MSR $1,269	$1,125	$985	$845	$765	$620	$505	$395

* ***CCO*** – .45 ACP cal., 7 shot mag., 3 1/2 in. barrel, 3-dot sights, stainless steel construction, brushed stainless finish, 32 oz. Disc. 2008.

	$1,000	$875	$750	$680	$550	$450	$350	Last MSR was $1,129.

* ***CCW*** – similar to CCO model, except has 4 1/4 in. barrel, 34 oz. Disc. 2008.

	$1,000	$875	$750	$680	$550	$450	$350	Last MSR was $1,129.

PXT LDA SINGLE STACK – .45 ACP cal., DAO, non-carry option models, spurless flush hammer, various configurations and barrel lengths.

* ***CCO Companion Black Watch*** – .45 ACP cal., 7 shot mag., 3 1/2 in. barrel, 3-dot sights, stainless steel construction, Black Watch finish, 32 oz.

	$975	$855	$730	$665	$535	$440	$340	Last MSR was $1,099.

* ***Tac-S*** – .45 ACP cal., 8 shot mag., 4 1/4 in. barrel, 3-dot sights, steel frame, Spec Ops finish, 35 oz.

	$865	$755	$650	$590	$475	$390	$305	Last MSR was $999.

* ***Covert Black Nite-Tac SS*** – .45 ACP cal., 8 shot mag., 5 in. barrel, 3-dot sights, stainless steel construction, Covert Black finish, includes light rail, checkered wood grips, 40 oz. Mfg. 2006-2007.

	$1,000	$875	$750	$650	$550	$450	$375	Last MSR was $1,125.

* ***Nite-Tac SS*** – .45 ACP cal., 8 shot mag., 5 in. barrel, 3-dot sights, stainless steel construction, brushed stainless finish, includes light rail, checkered wood grips, 40 oz. Mfg. 2006-2007.

	$1,000	$875	$750	$650	$550	$450	$375	Last MSR was $1,125.

PXT LDA HIGH CAPACITY (CARRY OPTION SERIES) – 9mm Para., .40 S&W, or .45 ACP cal., spurless flush hammer, rounded grip safety, various options, barrel lengths and magazine capacity.

* ***Carry 12*** – .45 ACP cal., 12 shot mag., 3 1/2 in. barrel, low mount 3-dot tritium night sights, stainless steel construction, black synthetic grips, brushed stainless finish, 34 oz.

	$1,050	$920	$785	$715	$575	$470	$365	Last MSR was $1,199.

* ***Tac-Four*** – .45 ACP cal., 13 shot mag., 4 1/4 in. barrel, 3-dot sights, stainless steel construction, black synthetic grips, brushed stainless finish, 36 oz.

	$960	$840	$735	$625	$525	$425	$350	Last MSR was $1,099.

* ***Tac-Forty*** – .40 S&W cal., 15 shot mag., 4 1/4 in. barrel, 3-dot sights, stainless steel construction, black synthetic grips, brushed stainless finish, 36 oz. Mfg. 2007.

	$925	$825	$725	$625	$525	$425	$350	Last MSR was $1,049.

* ***Tac-Five*** – 9mm Para cal., 18 shot mag., 5 in. barrel, Novak adj. sights, stainless steel construction, black synthetic grips, Covert Black finish, 37 1/2 oz. Mfg. 2007.

	$1,050	$920	$785	$715	$575	$470	$365	Last MSR was $1,185.

PXT LDA HIGH CAPACITY SERIES – .45 ACP cal., DAO, 14 shot mag., 5 in. barrel, 3-dot sights, steel or stainless steel construction, spurless flush hammer, Covert Black finish or stainless steel.

* ***Covert Black Hi-Cap .45*** – steel frame, Covert Black finish. Disc. 2008.

	$950	$830	$710	$645	$520	$425	$330	Last MSR was $1,099.

* ***Hi-Cap .45*** – stainless steel construction, brushed stainless finish. Disc. 2008.

	$955	$840	$730	$625	$525	$425	$350	Last MSR was $1,099.

* ***Covert Black Nite-Tac .45*** – steel frame, Covert Black finish, includes light rail. Mfg. 2006-2008.

	$955	$840	$730	$625	$525	$425	$350	Last MSR was $1,099.

MSR	100%	98%	95%	90%	80%	70%	60%	

* **Coyote Brown Nite-Tac .45** – .45 ACP cal., similar to Covert Black Nite-Tac, except has adj. fiber optic sights and Coyote Brown finish.

	$1,175	$1,030	$880	$800	$645	$530	$410	Last MSR was $1,349.

* **Nite-Tac .45** – stainless steel construction, brushed stainless finish, includes light rail. Mfg. 2006-2008.

	$1,025	$900	$775	$650	$550	$450	$350	Last MSR was $1,199.

* **Colonel** – .45 ACP cal., 4 1/4 in. ramped barrel, low mount white 3-dot fixed sights, steel frame, 10 or 14 shot mag., spur competition hammer, LDA trigger, black polymer grips with medallions, green spec. ops. finish, 37 oz. Mfg. 2005-2006.

	$795	$695	$595	$540	$435	$360	$280	Last MSR was $899.

PXT LTC HIGH CAPACITY – .45 ACP cal., 4 1/4 in. barrel, 10 or 14 shot mag., 3-dot fixed sights, stainless steel frame, match grade trigger, black polymer grips with medallions, green spec. ops. finish, three safeties, 37 oz. Mfg. 2005-2006.

	$750	$655	$560	$510	$410	$335	$260	Last MSR was $855.

S SERIES MODELS – .40 S&W or .45 ACP cal., single action, 3 1/2, 4 1/4, or 5 in. barrel, 10 shot mag., matte black (5 in. barrel only) or stainless steel finish.

* **S Series Model S10 Limited** – similar to P10, except has competition shooting features, including beavertail grip safety, competition hammer, tuned trigger, match grade barrel, front slide serrations, choice of steel or alloy frame with matte black finish or stainless steel, 40 oz. Mfg. 1999-2002.

	$765	$670	$575	$520	$420	$345	$270	Last MSR was $865.

Add $10 for steel receiver.
Add $24 for stainless steel.

* **S Series Model S12 Limited** – .40 S&W (disc. 2002) or .45 ACP cal., similar to P12, except has competition shooting features, including beavertail grip safety, competition hammer, tuned trigger, match grade barrel, front slide serrations, choice of steel or alloy (disc. 2002) frame, matte black (disc. 2002) or stainless steel finish, 40 oz. Mfg. 1999-2003.

	$895	$785	$670	$610	$490	$405	$315	Last MSR was $1,049.

Subtract 10% for steel frame (disc. 2002).

* **S Series Model S13 Limited** – .40 S&W (disc. 2002) or .45 ACP cal., similar to P13, except has competition shooting features, including beavertail grip safety, competition hammer, tuned trigger, match grade barrel, front slide serrations, choice of steel or alloy (disc. 2002) frame, matte black (disc. 2002) or stainless steel finish, 40 oz. Mfg. 1999-2003.

	$895	$785	$670	$610	$490	$405	$315	Last MSR was $1,049.

* **S Series Model S14 Limited** – .40 S&W (disc. 2002) or .45 ACP cal., similar to P14, except has competition shooting features, including beavertail grip safety, competition hammer, tuned trigger, match grade barrel, front slide serrations, matte black or stainless steel, 40 oz. Mfg. 1998-2003.

	$850	$745	$635	$580	$465	$380	$295	Last MSR was $989.

Add $60 for stainless steel.

* **S Series Model S16 Limited** – .40 S&W cal., similar to P16, except has 5 in. barrel and competition shooting features, including beavertail grip safety, competition hammer, tuned trigger, match grade barrel, front slide serrations, matte black steel or stainless steel, 40 oz. Mfg. 1998-2003.

	$850	$745	$635	$580	$465	$380	$295	Last MSR was $989.

Add $60 for stainless steel.

T SERIES MODELS – 9mm Para., .40 S&W (stainless steel only), or .45 ACP cal., DAO, 5 in. barrel, 7 (.45 ACP cal. only, single stack mag.) or 10 shot mag., steel or stainless steel, matte black finish or stainless steel. Mfg. 2003.

	$825	$720	$620	$560	$455	$370	$290	Last MSR was $1,009.

Add $80 for stainless steel.

RIFLES: SEMI-AUTO

TTR SERIES – .223 Rem. cal., tactical design, 16 1/2 in. chrome lined barrel, DIGS (delayed impingement gas system) operation, 30 shot mag., flip up front sight and adj. flip up rear sight, flattop receiver with full length Picatinny rail, black finish, single stage trigger, available in Short Rail with fixed stock (TTR-XASF), or 5 position folding stock with Short Rail (TTR-XAS), Long Rail (TTR-XA), and Nylatron (TTR-XN) forearm configurations. New 2009.

MSR $2,297	$1,995	$1,775	$1,550	$1,350	$1,150	$975	$825	

Add $100 for 5 position folding stock.
Add $100 for Nylatron forearm.

MSR	100%	98%	95%	90%	80%	70%	60%

PARKER-HALE LIMITED

Previous gun manufacturer located in Birmingham, England. Rifles were manufactured in England until 1991 when Navy Arms purchased the manufacturing rights and built a plant in West Virginia for fabrication. This new company was called Gibbs Rifle Company, Inc. and they manufactured models very similar to older Parker-Hale rifles during 1992-94. Shotguns were manufactured in Spain and imported by Precision Sports, a division of Cortland Line Company, Inc. located in Cortland, NY until 1993.

Parker was the previous trade name of the A.G. Parker Company, located in Birmingham, England, which was formed from a gun making business founded in 1890 by Alfred Gray Parker. The company became the Parker-Hale company in 1936. The company was purchased by John Rothery Wholesale circa 2000.

Parker-Hale Ltd. continues to make a wide variety of high quality firearms cleaning accessories for both rifles and shotguns, including their famous bipod.

RIFLES: BOLT ACTION

All Parker-Hale rifle importation was discontinued in 1991. Parker-Hale bolt action rifles utilize the Mauser K-98 action and were offered in a variety of configurations. A single set trigger option was introduced in 1984 on most models, which allows either "hair trigger" or conventional single stage operation - add $85.

MODEL 85 SNIPER RIFLE – .308 Win. cal., bolt action, extended heavy barrel, 10 shot mag., camo green synthetic stock with stippling, built in adj. bipod, enlarged contoured bolt, adj. recoil pad. Importation began 1989.

$2,650	$2,250	$1,700	$1,475	$1,250	$1,050	$875

Last MSR was $1,975.

PATRIOT ORDNANCE FACTORY (POF)

Current rifle manufacturer located in Glendale, AZ.

CARBINES/RIFLES: SEMI-AUTO

Patriot Ordnance Factory manufactures AR-15 style tactical rifles and carbines, as well as upper and lower receivers and various parts. The semi-auto carbines and rifles use a unique gas piston operating system that requires no lubrication. A wide variety of options are available for each model. Please contact the company directly for more information, including option pricing (see Trademark Index).

Due to current high demand and market speculation, consumers may pay a premium over values listed below.

P308 RIFLE/CARBINE – .308 Win. cal., 16 1/2 or 20 in. heavy contour fluted barrel, gas piston operated, FMP-A3 muzzle device, corrosion resistant operating system, chrome plated mil spec bolt, nickel plated A3 flattop upper receiver and charging handle, fixed removable hooded front sight, optional Troy flip up rear sight, aircraft aluminum alloy modular railed receiver, nickel and black hard coat anodized Teflon finish, oversized trigger guard, Ergo pistol grip, Magpul CTR six position (carbine) or PRS adj. (rifle) buttstock, Ergo ladder rail cover handguard, approx. 9 lbs.

MSR $2,600	$2,375	$1,975	$1,700	$1,525	$1,225	$1,050	$875

P415 SPECIAL PURPOSE RIFLE – .223 Rem. cal., 18 in. heavy contour chrome lined fluted barrel, gas piston operated, A3 muzzle device, corrosion resistant operating system, nickel plated A3 flattop uppper receiver and charging handle, M4 feed ramp, nickel and black hard coat anodized Teflon finish, fixed removable hooded front sight, optional Troy flip up sight, single stage trigger, Magpul PRS or six position adj. buttstock, tactical rail handguard, approx. 9 lbs.

MSR $1,975	$1,800	$1,650	$1,425	$1,295	$1,050	$875	$675

P415 RECON CARBINE – .223 Rem. cal., 16 in. heavy contour chrome lined fluted barrel, gas piston operated, A3 muzzle device, corrosion resistant operating system, nickel plated A3 flattop uppper receiver and charging handle, M4 feed ramp, nickel and black hard coat anodized Teflon finish, fixed removable hooded front sight, optional Troy flip up sight, single stage trigger, oversized trigger guard, Magpul PRS or six position adj. buttstock, tactical rail handguard, approx. 8 lbs.

MSR $1,975	$1,800	$1,650	$1,425	$1,295	$1,050	$875	$675

P415 CARBINE – .223 Rem. cal., 16 in. heavy contour chrome lined fluted barrel, gas piston operated, A3 muzzle device, corrosion resistant operating system, nickel plated A3 flattop uppper receiver and charging handle, M4 feed ramp, nickel and black hard coat anodized Teflon finish, fixed removable hooded front sight, optional Troy flip up sight, single stage trigger, oversized trigger guard, Magpul CTR retractable six position buttstock, M4 plastic handguard or Predator P-9 tactical rail system, sling/bipod mount, approx. 7-7.4 lbs.

MSR $1,975	$1,800	$1,650	$1,425	$1,295	$1,050	$875	$675

Add $300 for Predator P-9 tactical rail system.

MSR		100%	98%	95%	90%	80%	70%	60%

PAUZA SPECIALTIES

Previously manufactured by Pauza Specialties circa 1991-96, and located in Baytown, TX. Previously distributed by U.S. General Technologies, Inc. located in South San Francisco, CA.

Pauza currently manufactures the P50 semi-auto rifle for Firearms International, Inc. - please refer to that section for current information.

RIFLES

P50 SEMI-AUTO – .50 BMG cal., semi-auto, 24 (carbine) or 29 (rifle) in. match grade barrel, 5 shot detachable mag., one-piece receiver, 3-stage gas system, takedown action, all exterior parts Teflon coated, with aluminum bipod, 25 or 30 lbs. Mfg. 1992-96.

		$5,950	$5,250	$4,600	$4,100	$3,650	$3,200	$2,800	Last MSR was $6,495.

PEACE RIVER CLASSICS

Previous manufacturer located in Bartow, FL until 2001. Peace River Classics was a division of Tim's Guns.

RIFLES: SEMI-AUTO

PEACE RIVER CLASSICS SEMI-AUTO – .223 Rem. or .308 Win. (new 1998) cal., available in 3 configurations including the Shadowood, the Glenwood, and the Royale, hand-built utilizing Armalite action, patterned after the AR-15, match grade parts throughout, special serialization, laminate thumbhole stock. Mfg. 1997-2001.

		$2,575	$2,275	$2,000	$1,775	$1,525	$1,250	$995	Last MSR was $2,695.

Add $300 for .308 Win. cal.

PETERS STAHL GmbH

Current pistol manufacturer located in Paderborn, Germany. Previously imported until 2009 by Euro-Imports, located in Yoakum, TX. Previously distributed by Swiss Trading GmbH, located in Bozeman, MT. Previously imported 1998-1999 by Peters Stahl, U.S.A. located in Delta, UT, and by Franzen International Inc. located in Oakland, NJ until 1998. Dealer direct sales only.

PISTOLS: SEMI-AUTO

Peters Stahl manufactures high quality semi-auto pistols based on the Model 1911 design, but to date, has had limited U.S. importation. Current models include the Multicaliber, 92-Sport, O7-Sport, HC-Champion and variations, 1911-Tactical/Classic, PLS, and a .22 LR. Peters-Stahl also manufactures multicaliber conversion kits of the highest quality. Recent models previously imported (until 2000) included the Model Millennium (MSR was $2,195), Match 22 LR (MSR was $1,995), Trophy Master (MSR was $1,995), Omega Match (MSR was $1,995), High Capacity Trophy Master (MSR was $1,695), O7 Multicaliber (MSR was $1,995), and the 92 Multicaliber (MSR was $2,610-$2,720). In the past, Peters Stahl has manufactured guns for Federal Ordnance, Omega, Schuetzen Pistol Works, and Springfield Armory. The company should be contacted directly (see Trademark Index) for current model information, U.S. availability, and pricing.

POLY TECHNOLOGIES, INC.

Previously distributed by PTK International, Inc. located in Atlanta, GA. Previously imported by Keng's Firearms Specialty, Inc., located in Riverdale, GA. Manufactured in China by Poly Technologies, Inc.

Poly Technologies commercial firearms are made to Chinese military specifications and have excellent quality control. These models were banned from domestic importation due to 1989 Federal legislation.

RIFLES: SEMI-AUTO

Add 10% for NIB.

POLY TECH AKS-762 – 7.62x39mm or .223 Rem. cal., 16 1/4 in. barrel, semi-auto version of the Chinese AKM (Type 56) tactical design rifle, 8.4 lbs., wood stock. Imported 1988-89.

		$1,495	$1,325	$1,100	$975	$875	$795	$750	Last MSR was $400.

Add $100 for side-fold plastic stock.

This model was also available with a downward folding stock at no extra charge.

CHINESE SKS – 7.62x39mm cal., 20 9/20 in. barrel, full wood stock, machined steel parts to Chinese military specifications, 7.9 lbs. Imported 1988-89.

		$550	$475	$400	$350	$300	$275	$250	Last MSR was $200.

RUSSIAN AK-47/S (LEGEND) – 7.62x39mm cal., 16 3/8 in. barrel, semi-auto configuration of the original AK-47, fixed, side-folding, or under-folding stock, with or w/o spike bayonet, 8.2 lbs. Imported 1988-89.

		$2,000	$1,800	$1,600	$1,350	$1,200	$1,000	$925	Last MSR was $550.

Add 10% for folding stock.

MSR	100%	98%	95%	90%	80%	70%	60%

The "S" suffix in this variation designates third model specifications.

* ***Russian AK-47/S National Match Legend*** – utilizes match parts in fabrication.

	$1,950	$1,750	$1,550	$1,275	$1,050	$975	$900

RPK – 7.62x39mm cal. Disc.

	$1,475	$1,300	$1,150	$1,025	$925	$850	$775

U.S. M-14/S – .308 Win. cal., 22 in. barrel, forged receiver, patterned after the famous M-14, 9.2 lbs. Imported 1988-89.

	$1,100	$950	$850	$775	$725	$650	$575	Last MSR was $700.

PROFESSIONAL ORDNANCE, INC.

Previous manufacturer located in Lake Havasu City, AZ 1998-2003. Previously manufactured in Ontario, CA circa 1996-1997. Distributor sales only.

During 2003, Bushmaster bought Professional Ordnance and the Carbon 15 trademark. Please refer to the Bushmaster section for currently manufactured Carbon 15 rifles and pistols (still manufactured in Lake Havasu City).

PISTOLS: SEMI-AUTO

CARBON-15 TYPE 20 – .223 Rem. cal., Stoner type operating system with recoil reducing buffer assembly, carbon fiber upper and lower receiver, hard chromed bolt carrier, 7 1/4 in. unfluted stainless steel barrel with ghost ring sights, 30 shot mag. (supplies were limited), also accepts AR-15 type mags., 40 oz. Mfg. 1999-2000.

	$950	$800	$725	$650	$575	$525	$475	Last MSR was $1,500.

CARBON-15 TYPE 21 – .223 Rem cal., ultra lightweight carbon fiber upper and lower receivers, 7 1/4 in. "Profile" stainless steel barrel, quick detachable muzzle compensator, ghost ring sights, 10 shot mag., also accepts AR-15 type mags., Stoner type operating sytem, tool steel bolt, extractor and carrier, 40 oz. Mfg. 2001-2003.

	$850	$750	$675	$600	$550	$500	$450	Last MSR was $899.

CARBON-15 TYPE 97 – similar to Carbon 15 Type 20, except has fluted barrel and quick detachable compensator, 46 oz. Mfg. 1996-2003.

	$925	$800	$725	$625	$575	$525	$475	Last MSR was $964.

RIFLES: SEMI-AUTO

CARBON-15 TYPE 20 – .223 Rem. cal., same operating system as the Carbon-15 pistol, 16 in. unfluted stainless steel barrel, carbon fiber buttstock and forearm, includes mil spec optics mounting base, 3.9 lbs. Mfg. 1998-2000.

	$975	$850	$795	$725	$650	$550	$475	Last MSR was $1,550.

CARBON-15 TYPE 21 – .223 Rem. cal., ultra light weight carbon fiber upper and lower receivers, 16 in. "Profile" stainless steel barrel, quick detachable muzzle compensator, Stoner type operating system, tool steel bolt, extractor and carrier, optics mounting base, quick detachable stock, 10 shot mag., also accepts AR-15 type mags., 3.9 lbs. Mfg. 2001-2003.

	$975	$850	$795	$725	$650	$550	$475	Last MSR was $988.

CARBON-15 TYPE 97/97S – .223 Rem. cal., ultra lighweight carbon fiber upper and lower receivers, Stoner type operating system, hard chromed tool steel bolt, extractor and carrier, 16 in. fluted stainless steel barrel, quick detachable muzzle compensator, optics mounting base, quick detachable stock, 30 shot mag., also accepts AR-15 type mags., 3.9 lbs. Mfg. 2001-2003.

	$1,075	$900	$825	$750	$675	$600	$550	Last MSR was $1,120.

Add $165 for Model 97S (includes Picatinny rail and "Scout" extension, double walled heat shield forearm, ambidextrous safety, and multipoint silent carry).

QUALITY PARTS CO./BUSHMASTER

Quality Parts Co. was a division of Bushmaster Firearms, Inc. located in Windham, ME that manufactured AR-15 type tactical rifles and various components and accessories for Bushmaster. Please refer to the Bushmaster section in this text for current model listings and values.

NOTES

R SECTION

RND MANUFACTURING

Current manufacturer located in Longmont, CO. Previously distributed by Mesa Sportsmen's Association, L.L.C. located in Delta, CO. Dealer or consumer direct sales.

MSR	100%	98%	95%	90%	80%	70%	60%

RIFLES: SEMI-AUTO

RND EDGE SERIES – .223 Rem. (RND 400), .300 WSM (RND 1000, new 2003), .300 RSM (RND 2100, new 2003), .338 Lapua Mag. (RND 2000, new 1999), .375 Super Mag. (RND 2600), .408 Cheytac (RND 2500), 7.62x39mm (disc.), or .50 BMG (RND 3000) cal., patterned after the AR-15, CNC machined, 18, 20, or 24 in. barrel, choice of synthetic (Grade I), built to individual custom order, handmade laminated thumbhole (Grade II, disc. 1998), or custom laminated thumbhole stock with fluted barrel (Grade III, disc. 1998), vented aluminum shroud, many options and accessories available, approx. 11 1/2-16 lbs., custom order only, values represent base model. New 1996.

MSR N/A	$2,195	$1,950	$1,725	$1,300	$1,050	$850	$725

Add $355 for Grade II.
Add $605 for Grade III or .308 Win. cal.
Add $1,855 for .338 Lapua Mag. cal.

RPA INTERNATIONAL LTD.

Current rifle manufacturer located in Kent, England. No current U.S. importation.

RIFLES

RPA International Ltd. manufactures high quality bolt action rifles, including a tactical long range sniper model, the Rangemaster 7.62 STBY (£6,074 MSR), Rangemaster 7.62 (£5,834 MSR), Rangemaster 338 (£6,500 MSR), and the Rangemaster 50 (£7,000 MSR). The Rangemaster Series includes a folding stock, stainless steel barrel and muzzle brake, Picatinny rails and tactical bipod. The Interceptor is available in a single shot (£2,042 MSR) and a repeater (£2,427 MSR) version. The Hunter rifle comes with or w/o a thumbhole stock (£2,064 base MSR). The Target Rifle Series includes the Elite Single Shot (£2,978 MSR), and the Ranger (£2,459 MSR). Additionally, the company makes custom rifles and actions. Please contact the company directly for pricing, U.S. availability and options (see Trademark Index).

RPB INDUSTRIES

Previous company located in Avondale, GA. RPB Industries' guns were made by Masterpiece Arms.

CARBINES: SEMI-AUTO

RPB CARBINE – .45 ACP cal., closed bolt blowback action, 16 1/4 in. barrel, fixed skeletonized stock and forearm pistol grip, accepts M-3 military submachine gun mags., black finish, 9 1/2 lbs. Mfg. 2000-2004.

	$450	$375	$325	$285	$260	$235	$210

Add $75 for Deluxe Model with EZ cocker and installed scope mount.

RAMO DEFENSE SYSTEMS

Previous rifle manufacturer 1999-2003 and located in Nashville, TN.

RIFLES: BOLT ACTION

TACTICAL .308 – .308 Win. cal., Rem. M-700 long action, match grade stainless steel barrel, skeletonized black synthetic stock with cheekpad, matte black metal finish, 4 shot mag., 16 lbs. Mfg. 1999-2003.

	$2,495	$2,100	$1,850	$1,600	$1,400	$1,200	$995	Last MSR was $2,495.

M91/M91A2 – .308 Win. or .300 Win. Mag. cal., Rem. M-700 long action, black Kevlar and fiberglass stock, matte black metal finish, 4 shot mag., 14 lbs. Mfg. 1999-2003.

	$2,695	$2,250	$1,950	$1,675	$1,475	$1,250	$995	Last MSR was $2,695.

Add $200 for .300 Win. Mag. cal.

M600 SINGLE SHOT – .50 BMG cal., single shot, twin tube skeletonized stock with pistol grip and cheekpiece, 32 in. barrel with fins at breech and muzzle brake, 23 lbs. Mfg. 1999-2003.

	$4,195	$3,700	$3,200	$2,750	$2,250	$1,950	$1,675	Last MSR was $4,195.

M650 REPEATER – .50 BMG cal., repeater action with 6 shot detachable rotary mag., stock and barrel (30 in.) similar to M600, approx. 30 lbs. Mfg. 1999-2003.

	$6,395	$5,750	$5,150	$4,500	$3,750	$3,000	$2,250	Last MSR was $6,395.

MSR		100%	98%	95%	90%	80%	70%	60%

RASHEED (RASHID)

Previous Egyptian military rifle mfg. circa mid-1960s.

RIFLES: SEMI-AUTO

RASHEED – 7.62x39mm cal., gas operated mechanism with tilting bolt, 20 1/2 in. barrel with folding bayonet, bolt cocking is by separate bolt handle installed on right side of receiver, detachable 10 shot mag., open type sights, hardwood stock with vent. forend, approx. 8,000 mfg. circa mid-1960s.

		$650	$575	$475	$425	$350	$275	$200

RED ROCK ARMS

Current manufacturer established April 2003 and located in Mesa, AZ. During late 2006, the company name was changed from Bobcat Weapons, Inc. to Red Rock Arms.

PISTOLS: SEMI-AUTO

BWA5 FSA – 9mm Para cal., tactical design, delayed blowback, 8.9 in. stainless steel barrel, black duracoat finished stock, pistol grip, and forearm, 10, 30, or 40 shot mag., approx. 5.3 lbs. Mfg. 2007-2008.

		$1,525	$1,350	$1,125	$900	$775	$650	$550	Last MSR was $1,700.

RIFLES: SEMI-AUTO

BW-5 FSA – 9mm Para cal., tactical design, stamped steel lower receiver, roller lock bolt system with delayed blowback, 16 1/2 in. stainless steel barrel (3-lug barrel and 9 in. fake supressor), black duracoat finished stock, pistol grip, and forearm, 10, 30, or 40 shot mag., approx. 6.7 lbs. Mfg. 2006-2008.

		$1,525	$1,350	$1,125	$900	$775	$650	$550	Last MSR was $1,700.

ATR-1 CARBINE – .223 Rem. cal., 16 1/4 in. barrel, adj. front and rear sight, black furniture, 30 shot AR-15 style mag., available with or w/o flash suppressor, 8 lbs. New 2007.

MSR $1,400		$1,250	$1,075	$925	$825	$750	$650	$575

GARY REEDER CUSTOM GUNS

Current custom manufacturer located in Flagstaff, AZ. Consumer direct sales.

For over 30 years, Gary Reeder has specialized in customizing revolvers from various manufacturers, and is now building several series of custom revolvers on his own frames. Gary's son Kase also manufacturers several series of Model 1911 style pistols built to customers specifications in .45 ACP and 10mm. Reeder currently produces well over 60 different series of custom hunting handguns, cowboy guns, custom 1911s, and large caliber hunting rifles. For more information on his extensive range of custom guns, please contact the factory directly (see Trademark Index).

REMINGTON ARMS COMPANY, INC.

Current manufacturer and trademark established in 1816, with factories currently located in Ilion, NY, and Mayfield, KY.

Founded by Eliphalet Remington II and originally located in Litchfield, Herkimer County, NY circa 1816-1828. Remington established a factory in Ilion, NY next to the Erie Canal in 1828, and together with his sons Philo, Samuel, and Eliphalet III pioneered many improvements in firearms manufacture. Corporate offices were moved to Madison, NC in 1996. DuPont owned a controlling interest in Remington from 1933-1993, when the company was sold to Clayton, Dubilier & Rice, a New York City based finance company. The Mayfield, KY plant opened in 1997. On May 31st, 2007, a controlling interest in the company was sold to Cerberus Capital. Currently, Remington employs 2,500 workers in the U.S., including 1,000 in its Ilion, NY plant alone.

For current information on long guns imported by Spartan Gun Works, a Remington subsidiary, please refer to the Spartan Gun Works section in this text.

RIFLES: SEMI-AUTO - CENTERFIRE

The models have been listed in numerical sequence for quick reference.

* ***Model 7400 SP (Special Purpose)*** – .270 Win. or .30-06 cal., similar to Model 7400, except has non-reflective matte finish on both wood and metalwork. Mfg. 1993-94.

		$435	$370	$300	$255	$230	$210	$185	Last MSR was $524.

* ***Model 7400 Synthetic*** – same cals. as Model 7400, features black fiberglass reinforced synthetic stock and forend, matte black metal finish, 22 in. barrel only. Mfg. 1998-2006.

		$465	$385	$330	$285	$265	$240	$220	Last MSR was $589.

MSR	100%	98%	95%	90%	80%	70%	60%

»Model 7400 Synthetic Carbine – .30-06 cal., similar to Model 7400 Synthetic, except has 18 1/2 in. barrel. 7 1/4 lbs. Mfg. 1998-2006.

	$465	$385	$330	$285	$265	$240	$220	Last MSR was $589.

R-15 VTR (VARMINT TARGET RIFLE) PREDATOR – .204 Ruger or .223 Rem. cal., 18 (carbine, .204 Ruger disc. 2009) or 22 in. free floating chromemoly fluted barrel, fixed or telestock (Carbine CS) with pistol grip, 5 shot detachable mag. (compatible with AR-15 style mags.), R-15 marked on magwell, single stage trigger, flattop receiver with Picatinny rail, no sights, round vent. forearm, 100% Advantage Max-1 HD camo coverage, includes lockable hard case, mfg. by Bushmaster. New 2008.

MSR $1,276	$1,125	$995	$895	$775	$700	$625	$550

* **R-15 VTR Stainless** – .223 Rem. cal., similar to Predator, except has 24 in. stainless triangular barrel, OD Green camo pistol grip fixed stock. New 2009.

MSR $1,470	$1,275	$1,125	$1,000	$900	$775	$700	$625

* **R-15 VTR Thumbhole** – .223 Rem. cal., similar to VTR Stainless, except has 24 in. fluted barrel, OD Green camo thumbhole stock. New 2009.

MSR $1,470	$1,275	$1,125	$1,000	$900	$800	$700	$625

* **R-15 VTR Hunter** – .30 Rem. AR cal., 22 in. fluted barrel, camo pistol grip fixed stock, Picatinny rail, 4 shot detachable mag. New 2009.

MSR $1,276	$1,125	$1,000	$900	$800	$700	$625	$550

MODEL R-25 – .243 Win., 7mm-08 Rem., or .308 Win. cal., 20 in. free floating fluted chromemoly barrel, single-stage trigger, ergonomic pistol grip fixed stock with Mossy Oak Treestand camo finish, front and rear sling swivels, 4 shot detachable mag., R-25 marked on magwell, includes hard case, 8 3/4 lbs. New 2009.

MSR $1,631	$1,425	$1,200	$1,075	$950	$850	$750	$650

RIFLES: SLIDE ACTION, CENTERFIRE

* **Model 7600P Patrol Rifle** – .308 Win. cal., 16 1/2 in. barrel, synthetic stock, parkerized finish, Wilson Combat ghost ring sights, designed for police/law enforcement only.

Remington does not publish consumer retail pricing for this police/law enforcement model. Secondary prices for this model will be slightly higher than for current pricing on the Model 7600 Synthetic.

* **Model 7600 Synthetic** – same cals. as Model 7600, features black fiberglass reinforced synthetic stock and forend, matte black metal finish, 22 in. barrel only, 7 1/2 lbs. New 1998.

MSR $693	$540	$435	$365	$310	$265	$240	$225

During 2007, Grice offered 500 Model 7600 QWAC (Quick Woods Action Carbine) in .308 Win. cal. with 18 1/2 in. barrels, Realtree AP camo synthetic stocks and fiber optic front and rear sights.

»Model 7600 Synthetic Carbine – .30-06 cal., similar to Model 7600 Synthetic, except has 18 1/2 in. barrel. 7 1/4 lbs. New 1998.

MSR $693	$540	$435	$365	$310	$265	$240	$225

MODEL 7615 – .223 Rem., 10 shot AR-15 compatible detachable box mag., accepts AR-15 and M16 style magazines, 16 1/2 (tactical model with pistol grip and non-collapsible tube stock and Knoxx Special Ops NRS recoil suppressor), 18 1/2 (ranch rifle, walnut stock and forearm), or 22 (camo hunter, 100% Mossy Oak Brush camo coverage) in. barrel w/o sights, synthetic or walnut (ranch carbine) stock and forearm, drilled and tapped, approx. 7 lbs. Mfg. 2007-2008, mfg. in Ilion, NY.

	$790	$685	$575	$500	$450	$400	$350	Last MSR was $955.

Add $54 for Camo Hunter with 100% camo coverage.

MODEL 7615P PATROL RIFLE – .223 Rem. cal., 16 1/2 in. barrel, 10 shot or extended mag., synthetic stock, parkerized finish, accepts AR-15 and M16 style magazines, Wilson Combat ghost ring sights, designed for police/law enforcement, 7 lbs.

Remington does not publish consumer retail pricing for this police/law enforcement model. Secondary prices for this model will be slightly higher than for current pricing on the Model 7600 Carbine.

MODEL 7615 SPS – .223 Rem. cal., 16 1/2 in. blue barrel, Picatinny rail, action, slide release and safety based on the Model 870, 10 shot mag., accepts AR-15 and M16 style mags., black pistol grip synthetic stock. Mfg. 2008.

	$695	$625	$550	$500	$450	$400	$350	Last MSR was $805.

This model was available through Remington Premier dealers only.

MSR	100%	98%	95%	90%	80%	70%	60%

RIFLES: BOLT ACTION, MODEL 700 & VARIATIONS

MODEL 700 TACTICAL – 6.8mm SPC cal., 20 in. parkerized barrel, synthetic stock, approx. 9 lbs. Limited availability 2005-2006.

	$795	$625	$500	$375	$335	$300	$275	Last MSR was $990.

MODEL 700 TARGET TACTICAL – .308 Win. cal., 26 in. triangular contour barrel with 5-R tactical rifling, steel trigger guard and floorplate, X-MARK PRO adj. trigger, Bell & Carlson Medalist adj. stock. New 2009.

MSR $2,053	$1,775	$1,575	$1,350	$1,150	$950	$825	$700

MODEL 700P & VARIATIONS – various cals., long or short action, various barrel lengths, designed for police/law enforcement and military, current configurations include: 700P, 700P TWS (Tactical Weapons System, includes scope, bipod and case), 700P LTR (Light Tactical Rifle), 700P LTR TWS (Light Tactical Rifle/Tactical Weapons System, includes scope, bipod, and case), 700P USR (Urban Sniper Rifle), and the Model M24/M24A2/M24A3 Sniper Weapon System (combination of Model 700 and Model 40-XB design, with scope, case, and bipod).

Remington does not publish consumer retail pricing for these police/law enforcement models. Secondary prices for base models w/o scopes and other options will be slightly higher than for current pricing on the Model 700BDL Custom Deluxe. Prices for rifles with scopes and other features will be determined by how much the individual options and accessories add to the base value.

MODEL 700 XCR TACTICAL – .223 Rem., .308 Win. or .300 Win. Mag. cal., 3-5 shot mag., features 26 in. stainless steel receiver/barrel with black TriNyte PVD coating, tactical Bell & Carlson OD Green stock with full length aluminum bedding, X-MARK PRO trigger, 9 1/8 lbs. New 2007.

MSR $1,465	$1,225	$1,050	$925	$825	$725	$625	$500

* **Model 700 XCR Compact Tactical** – .223 Rem. or .308 Win. cal., similar to Model 700 XCR, except has 20 in. fluted varmint contour barrel, compact dimensions, 7 1/2 lbs. New 2008.

MSR $1,465	$1,225	$1,050	$925	$825	$725	$625	$500

RIFLES: BOLT ACTION, MODEL 40X & VARIATIONS

MODEL 40-XB TACTICAL – .308 Win. cal., repeater action with adj. 40-X trigger, aluminum bedding block, 27 1/4 in. button rifled fluted stainless barrel, Teflon coated metal, matte black H-S Precision synthetic tactical stock with vertical pistol grip, 10 1/4 lbs. New 2004.

MSR $2,992	$2,550	$2,200	$1,800	$1,450	$1,200	$925	$800

MODEL 40-XB TDR/TIR (TARGET DEPLOYMENT/INTERDICTION RIFLE) – .308 Win. cal., super match stainless steel hand lapped barrel, BCS 1000 (TDR) or H-S PST25 tactical/vertical pistol grip stock (TIR), custom tuned match trigger, one-piece heavy duty steel trigger guard, heavy stainless recoil lug, integral mounting system with #8 screws, Picatinny rail, double pinned bolt handle, muzzle brake, MOA accuracy guarateed to 600 yards, includes hard carrying case, mfg. by custom shop.

These models are POR.

MODEL 40-XS TACTICAL – .308 Win. or .338 Lapua cal., stainless steel action and barrel, adj. trigger, non-reflective black polymer coating, titanium bedded McMillan A5 adj. stock, AR type extractor, detachable mag., muzzle brake (.338 Lapua cal.), steel trigger guard and floorplate, mfg. by custom shop.

MSR $4,400	$3,675	$3,050	$2,500	$2,000	$1,650	$1,350	$1,175

Add $550 for .338 Lapua cal.
Add $2,731 for Model 40-XS Tactical Weapons System with Harris bipod, Picatinny rail, Leupold Mark IV 3.5-10x40mm long range M1 scope, Turner AWS tactical sling, and military grade hard case (.308 Win. cal. only).

MODEL XM3 TACTICAL – .308 Win. cal., match grade 18 1/2 in. stainless threaded barrel, Model 40-X action, custom bedded McMillan stock with adjustable LOP, Harris bipod, steel trigger guard, Nightfore NXS 3.5-15x50mm mil dot scope, guaranteed MOA accuracy to 1,000 yards, Hardigg Storm case with all tools and maintenance equipment, mfg. by Custom Shop. New 2009.

This model is currently POR.

SHOTGUNS: SEMI-AUTO, DISC.

MODEL 48A RIOT GUN – 12 ga. only, 20 in. plain barrel.

	$275	$220	$195	$165	$150	$140	$110

Shotguns: Semi-Auto, Model 1100 & Variations

3 in. shells (12 or 20 ga.) may be shot in Magnum receivers only, regardless of what the barrel markings may indicate (the ejection port is larger in these Magnum models with "M" suffix serialization).

MSR	100%	98%	95%	90%	80%	70%	60%

Model 1100 serial numbers on the receiver started with the number 1001. All but the early guns also have a prefix letter. All Model 1100 Remington shotguns were serial numbered in blocks of numbers. Each serial number has a suffix and the following indicates the meaning: V = 12 ga. standard, M = 12 ga. Mag., W = 16 ga., X = 20 ga., N = 20 ga. Mag., K = 20 ga. lightweight, U = 20 ga. lightweight Mag., J = 28 ga., H = .410 bore.

Add $877 for custom shop Etchen stock and forearm installed on new Model 1100s (new 2000).

MODEL 1100 TACTICAL – 12 ga. only, 3 in. chamber, choice of Speedfeed IV pistol grip or black synthetic stock and forearm, 6 (Speedfeed IV) or 8 (22 in. barrel only) shot mag., 18 (Speedfeed IV with fixed IC choke) or 22 (synthetic with Rem Chokes and HiViz sights) in. VR barrel, OD Green metal finish, R3 recoil pad, approx. 7 1/2 lbs. Disc. 2006.

	$640	$575	$515	$450	$400	$350	$295	Last MSR was $759.

Add $40 for 22 in. barrel.

MODEL 1100 TAC-2/TAC-4 – 12 ga., 2 3/4 in. chamber, 18 or 22 in. barrel, Hi-Viz sights, bead blasted black oxide metal finish, black synthetic stock with (Tac-2) or w/o (Tac-4) pistol grip, fixed (18 in.) or Rem Chokes, 6 or 8 shot mag., sling swivels, R3 recoil pad, 7 1/2 - 7 3/4 lbs. New 2007.

MSR $915	$775	$650	$550	$500	$450	$400	$350

Add $70 for Tac-4 with 4 shot mag. and 22 in. barrel.

<hr>

Shotguns: Semi-Auto, Model 11-87 & Variations

Model 11-87 barrels will not fit the Model 1100 or Model 11-87 Super Magnum models.

Remington MSRs on extra barrels (3 in. chamber standard) for the following currently manufactured models range from $239-$363 per barrel, depending on configuration.

Many options are available from the custom shop, and are POR.

MODEL 11-87 P (POLICE) – 12 ga. only, 18 in. barrel, improved cylinder choke, synthetic stock, parkerized finish, choice of bead or rifle sights, 7 shot extended mag., designed for police/law enforcement.

Remington does not publish consumer retail pricing for this police/law enforcement model. Secondary prices for this model will be slightly higher than for current pricing on the Model 11-87 SPS.

MODEL 11-87 SPS (SPECIAL PURPOSE SYNTHETIC) – see individual sub-models listed below.

* ***Model 11-87 SPS 3 in. Magnum*** – similar to Model 11-87 SP 3 in. Mag., except is supplied with black synthetic stock and forearm. Disc. 2004.

	$610	$475	$400	$360	$315	$275	$250	Last MSR was $791.

* ***Model 11-87 SPS-BG Camo (Special Purpose Synthetic Big Game)*** – 12 ga. only, 21 in. plain barrel with rifle sights and Rem Choke. Mfg. 1994 only.

	$555	$425	$350	$290	$250	$225	$200	Last MSR was $692.

* ***Model 11-87 SP/SPS (Special Purpose Deer Gun)*** – 12 ga. only, 3 in. chamber, 21 in. IC or Rem Choke (Model SP, mfg. 1989-2003) or fully rifled (new 1993, became standard 2004) barrel with rifle sights, parkerized metal with matte finished wood or black synthetic (Model SPS, new 1993) stock and forearm, vent. recoil pad, includes camouflaged nylon sling, 7 1/4 lbs. Mfg. 1987-2005.

	$695	$525	$450	$395	$350	$300	$250	Last MSR was $908.

Subtract 10% for fixed choke barrel or if w/o cantilever (became standard 2005) scope mount.

Rem Chokes were standard on this model between 1989-1992.

<hr>

SHOTGUNS: SLIDE ACTION, DISC.

MODEL 17R – 20 ga. only, security configuration, 20 in. cylinder bore barrel, 4 shot mag. Mfg. circa 1920s.

	$325	$265	$235	$200	$150	$120	$100

MODEL 29R – 12 ga. only, security configuration, 20 in. cylinder bore barrel, 5 shot mag. Mfg. circa 1920s.

	$375	$325	$265	$235	$200	$150	$120

MODEL 31R "RIOT" GRADE – features shortened barrel.

	$425	$365	$325	$295	$270	$230	$190

<hr>

SHOTGUNS: SLIDE ACTION, MODEL 870 & RECENT VARIATIONS

3 in. shells (12 or 20 ga.) may be shot in Magnum receivers only regardless of what the barrel markings may indicate (the ejection port is larger in these Magnum models with M suffix serialization).

Remington has manufactured many limited production runs for various distributors and wholesalers over the years. These shotguns are usually built to a specific configuration (gauge, stock, barrel length, finish, etc.), and are usually available until supplies run out. While these models are not included in this section, pricing in most cases will be similar to the base models from which they were derived.

MSR	100%	98%	95%	90%	80%	70%	60%

Many custom shop options are available, all are POR.

Add 25%-35% for 16 ga. on older mfg., if original condition is 95%+.

Remington MSRs on extra barrels (3 in. chamber is standard, except for Skeet barrel) for the following currently manufactured models range from $124-$327 per barrel, depending on configuration.

* Model 870 Express Synthetic Tactical (HD, Home Defense) – 12 or 20 (new 2007, 7 shot mag. only) ga., 18 in. cyl. choked barrel with bead front sight, black synthetic stock and forend. New 1991.

MSR $387	$300	$255	$225	$200	$175	$150	$125

Add $28 for 12 ga. 7 shot tube mag. or $36 for 20 ga. 7 shot tube mag.

Add $125 for Knoxx Special Ops stock with 7 shot mag., 20 ga. only.

* Model 870 Express Tactical – 12 ga., 18 1/2 in. barrel with RemChoke, black synthetic stock, with or w/o grey powder coat finish, with or w/o XS ghost ring sights, drilled and tapped, 2 shot mag. extension. New 2009.

MSR $513	$425	$365	$315	$275	$240	$210	$180

Add $42 for ghost ring sights.

»Model 870 Express Tactical Camo – 12 ga., 6 shot mag. with 2 shot mag. extension, 18 1/2 in. barrel, XS Ghost Ring Sight Rail and XSR Ghost Ring sights, synthetic stock with A-Tacs camo coverage, 7 1/2 lbs. New 2010.

MSR $665	$550	$475	$425	$375	$325	$275	$225

* Model 870 Express Specialty – 12 or 20 ga., 18 in. cylinder bore or Rem Choke barrel, folding or Knoxx Spec-Ops pistol grip stock, 2 or 7 shot mag extension. Mfg. 2008.

	$365	$315	$270	$235	$200	$180	$160	Last MSR was $452.

Add $27 for 2 shot mag. extension with Knoxx Spec-Ops stock.

Add $53 for synthetic folding stock with 7 shot mag extension.

This model was available through Remington Premier dealers only.

MODEL 870 SPECIAL PURPOSE MARINE MAGNUM – 12 ga. only, 3 in. chamber, 18 in. plain barrel bored cyl., features electroless nickel plating on all metal parts, supplied with 7 shot mag., R3 recoil pad became standard during 2004, sling swivels and Cordura sling, 7 1/2 lbs.

MSR $804	$650	$550	$450	$400	$350	$300	$250

Add $117 for XCS Marine Model with black TriNyte metal coating (mfg. 2007-2008).

MODEL 870 POLICE – 12 ga. only, 18 or 20 in. plain barrel, choice of blue or parkerized finish, bead or rifle (disc. 1995, 20 in. barrel only) sights, Police cylinder (disc.) or IC choke. Mfg. 1994-2006 (last year of civilan sales).

	$385	$315	$250	$200	$175	$160	$145	Last MSR was $492.

Add $13 for parkerized finish.

Add $44 for rifle sights (disc. 1995).

Remington also offers a Model 870P, 870P MAX ,870MCS, and 870P Synthetic for police/law enforcement, featuring extended capacity magazines, improved cylinder chokes, collapsible stocks, with some models having shorter than 18 in. barrels. While Remington does not publish consumer retail pricing for these police/law enforcement models, secondary prices for these guns will be slightly higher than for current pricing on the Model 870 Police.

MODEL 870 TACTICAL – 12 ga. only, 3 in. chamber, 18 or 20 in. fixed IC choke barrel, 6 or 7 (20 in. barrel only) shot mag., OD Green metal finish, black synthetic tactical or Knoxx SpecOps adj. recoil absorbing stock with pistol grip, open sights, approx. 7 1/2 lbs. Mfg. 2006.

	$515	$465	$425	$385	$350	$320	$290	Last MSR was $599.

Add $26 for SpecOps adj. stock.

MODEL 870 TAC-2/TAC-3 – 12 ga., 3 in. chamber, 18 or 20 in. barrel with fixed cylinder choke, black oxide metal finish, black synthetic stock and forearm, pistol grip with choice of Knoxx Special Ops folding stock (Tac-2 FS), Knoxx Special Ops tube stock or regular synthetic (disc. 2008) stock, 6 (Tac-2 w/18 in. barrel) or 8 (Tac-3 w/20 in. barrel, disc. 2008) shot mag., bead sights, R3 recoil pad on fixed stock, approx. 7 lbs. New 2007.

MSR $721	$595	$525	$465	$415	$380	$340	$300

Add $7 for Knoxx Special Ops folding stock and blasted black oxide finish (new 2010).

MODEL 870 TACTICAL DESERT RECON – 12 ga., 18 or 20 in. barrel, Digital Tiger TSP Desert Camo stock and forend, special ported tactical extended Rem Choke tube, Speedfeed stock with 2 or 3 shot carrier. Mfg. 2008-2009.

	$575	$500	$450	$400	$365	$335	$295	Last MSR was $692.

Add $67 for 20 in. barrel.

MODEL 870 RIOT – 12 ga. only, 18 or 20 in. barrel, choice of blue or parkerized metal finish. Disc. 1991.

	$295	$265	$225	$200	$170	$150	$130	Last MSR was $355.

Add $40 for police rifle sights (20 in. barrel only).

MODEL 887 NITRO MAG TACTICAL – 12 ga., 18 1/2 in. barrel with Rem Choke, black synthetic stock and forearm, 4 shot mag. with 2 shot mag. extension, Picatinny rail, Hi-Viz sights, ArmorLokt coated metal finish, 6 7/8 lbs. New 2010.

MSR $498	$400	$360	$330	$295	$260	$230	$195

MSR	100%	98%	95%	90%	80%	70%	60%

REPUBLIC ARMS, INC.

Previous manufacturer 1997-2001, and located in Chino, CA.

PISTOLS: SEMI-AUTO

THE PATRIOT – .45 ACP cal., double action only, ultra compact with 3 in. barrel, 6 shot mag., ultra compact black polymer frame and stainless steel slide (either brushed or with black Melonite coating, new 2000), locked breech action, checkered grips, 20 oz. New 1997.

	100%	98%	95%	90%	80%	70%	60%	
	$265	$230	$210	$185	$175	$165	$155	Last MSR $299.

REPUBLIC ARMS OF SOUTH AFRICA

Previous manufacturer located in Jeppestown, Union of South Africa. Previously imported until 2002 by TSF Ltd., located in Fairfax, VA.

PISTOLS: SEMI-AUTO

RAP 401 – 9mm Para. cal., 8 shot mag., otherwise similar to Rap-440. Importation 1999-circa 2002.

	100%	98%	95%	90%	80%	70%	60%
	$495	$425	$375	$350	$325	$300	$275

RAP-440 – .40 S&W cal., compact double action, 3 1/2 in. barrel with high contrast 3-dot sights, last shot hold open, hammer drop safety/decocking lever, firing pin block safety, 7-shot mag., all steel construction, 31 1/2 oz., includes case, spare magazine, and lock. Imported 1998-circa 2002.

	100%	98%	95%	90%	80%	70%	60%
	$545	$475	$425	$395	$375	$330	$300

Add $50 for Trilux tritium night sights.

SHOTGUNS: SLIDE ACTION

MUSLER MODEL – 12 ga., lightweight shotgun, polymer reinforced stock and forearm, action opening release lever, action locks open after the last round. Imported 1998-circa 2002.

	100%	98%	95%	90%	80%	70%	60%
	$549	$475	$425	$395	$375	$330	$300

RHINO ARMS

Current rifle manufacturer located in Washington, MO.

RIFLES: SEMI-AUTO

RA-4B SERIES – .223 Rem. cal., 16 or 20 (RA-4BV only) in. chromemoly heavy barrel, aluminum lower receiver, flattop upper, A2 flash hider, choice of A2 buttstock (RA-4B or RA-4BV) or M4 buttstock (RA-4BG or RA-4BT), 10 or 30 shot mag., anti-walk receiver retaining pins.

MSR $978	100%	98%	95%	90%	80%	70%	60%
	$895	$825	$750	$675	$595	$550	$495

Add $44 for RA-4BG model with rail gas block and M4 buttstock.
Add $248 for RA-BT model with four rail handguard and M4 buttstock.
Add $119 for RA-4BV model with 20 in. barrel, free float tube and A2 buttstock.

RA-4P SERIES – .223 Rem. cal., 16 or 20 (RA-4PV) in. chromemoly steel barrel, flattop upper, aluminum lower, A2 or Rhino flash hider, 10 or 30 shot mag., ERGO grip, Magpul CTR or PRS buttstock, anti-walk receiver retaining pins.

MSR $1,243	100%	98%	95%	90%	80%	70%	60%
	$1,150	$1,000	$875	$750	$625	$550	$500

Add $35 for RA-4PG model with four rail gas block, CAR handguard, and CTR buttstock.
Add $185 for RA-4PT model with four rail gas block, four rail handguard, and CTR buttstock.
Add $247 for RA-PV model with four rail gas block, free float tube, and PRS buttstock.

RA-5D – .308 Win. cal., 18 in. chromemolly heavy barrel, aluminum upper and lower receiver, rail gas block, 10 or 20 shot mag., Rhino flash hider, free float tube, Magpul UBR stock, ERGO grip, anti-walk receiver retaining pins.

As this edition went to press, pricing was not yet available on this model.

RIB MOUNTAIN ARMS, INC.

Previous rifle manufacturer circa 1992-2000, and located in Beresford and Sturgis, SD.

RIFLES: BOLT ACTION

MODEL 92 – .50 BMG cal., match grade barrel with muzzle brake, long action, walnut thumbhole stock, Timney trigger, approx. 28 lbs. Mfg. 1997-2000.

	100%	98%	95%	90%	80%	70%	60%	
	$3,175	$2,725	$2,275	$2,000	$1,750	$1,575	$1,300	Last MSR was $3,475.

MODEL 93 – similar to Model 92, except has short action with removable shell holder bolt, approx. 25 lbs. Mfg. 1997-2000.

	100%	98%	95%	90%	80%	70%	60%	
	$3,175	$2,725	$2,275	$2,000	$1,750	$1,575	$1,300	Last MSR was $3,475.

MSR	100%	98%	95%	90%	80%	70%	60%

THE ROBAR COMPANIES, INC.

Current customizer established during 1986, and located in Phoenix, AZ.

Robar is a leader in custom metal finishing, including combination finishes. These include the Roguard black finish, NP3 surface treatment, and additional finishes including bluing, electroless nickel, Polymax camoflauge, and Polymax finish. Please contact Robar directly (see Trademark Index) for more information, including current prices on their lineup of firearms, custom metal and wood finishes, and customizing services, including shotguns.

PISTOLS: SEMI-AUTO

Robar offers customizing services on new Colt-style semi-auto .45 ACP pistols. These guns are built up from other makers including Springfield, Glock, and Browning to provide the configuration/modifications necessary. Current variations include the Springfield Alloy Xtreme Pistol in either 9mm Para. or .40 S&W cal. MSR is $1,449, or $1,749 with detail finishing. Previous configurations included the Super Deluxe Pistol Package, Robar Combat Master, or Basic Carry.

ROBERT HISSERICH COMPANY

Previous gunsmith and previous custom rifle manufacturer located in Mesa, AZ. Previous company name was Stockworks.

RIFLES: BOLT ACTION

ROBERT HISSERICH BOLT GUN – various cals., features Weatherby Vanguard action, Pac-Nor stainless steel barrel, Pachmayr decelerator pad, hinged floor plate, black synthetic stock. Mfg. 2003 - disc.

	$1,795	$1,500	$1,250	$1,050	$875	$750	$625

LIGHTWEIGHT RIFLES SLR – various cals., Rem. long or short action, Kevlar/fiberglass MPI stock, match grade Pac-Nor barrel, straight flutes in bolt body, Timney trigger, straight line muzzle brake, pillar bedded action, free floating barrel, "window" cuts in action for lightening, black oxide finish on carbon or stainless steel, English or Claro walnut deluxe checkered stock, custom order only - allow 3-4 months. Approx. 4 3/4-5 lbs.

	$2,600	$2,300	$2,000	$1,800	$1,600	$1,400	$1,200

Add $200 for stainless steel.

SHARPSHOOTER – various cals., Win. Model 70 action with controlled feeding, precision long range hunting rifle with Schnieder stainless steel fluted barrel, laminated stock with ebony forend tip, titanium firing pin, pillar glass bedded with free floating barrel, includes Leupold 6.5-20x40mm scope, custom order only.

	$5,950	$5,100	$4,500	$3,900	$3,400	$2,850	$2,150

ROBINSON ARMAMENT CO.

Current rifle manufacturer located in Salt Lake City, UT. Currently distributed by ZDF Import/Export, Inc., located in Salt Lake City, UT. Dealer and consumer direct sales.

PISTOLS: SEMI-AUTO

XCR-L MICRO PISTOL – 5.56 NATO, 6.8 SPC, or 7.62x39mm cal., 7 or 7 1/2 in. chrome lined barrel, upper, side, and lower rails, two stage trigger, accepts M-16 magazines, left side charging handle, various sight options, approx. 5 lbs. New 2010.

MSR $1,500	$1,395	$1,200	$1,000	$800	$725	$600	$500

RIFLES: SEMI-AUTO

M96 EXPEDITIONARY RIFLE/CARBINE – .223 Rem. cal., tactical modular design, unique action allows accessory kit (new 2000) to convert loading from bottom to top of receiver, 16.2 (Recon Model, new 2001), 17 1/4 (carbine, new 2000) or 20 1/4 in. barrel with muzzle brake, stainless steel receiver and barrel, matte black finish metal, black synthetic stock and forearm, adj. sights, gas operated with adjustment knob, last shot hold open, rotating bolt assembly, 8 1/2 lbs. Mfg. 1999-2006.

	$1,495	$1,300	$1,100	$925	$850	$775	$700

Add $750 for rifle/carbine with top feed.

XCR-L MODEL – .223 Rem., 6.8mm SPC, or .308 Win. (new 2008) cal., tactical design, 16 in. full floating barrel, handguard with 8 in. side and bottom Picatinny rails, open sights, quick change barrel system, bolt hold open, side folding stock standard until 2008, stock configuration optional beginning 2009, two-stage trigger, uses M16 mags., 7 1/2 lbs. New 2006.

MSR $1,500	$1,395	$1,200	$1,000	$850	$725	$600	$500

Add $500-$550 for conversion kit, depending on caliber (includes barrel, bolt, and 25 shot mag.).
Add $200 for 6.8mm SPC or .308 Win. cal.

MSR	100%	98%	95%	90%	80%	70%	60%

Add $150-$250 for stock option, depending on configuration.
Add $50 for 16 in. heavy barrel or $75 for 18 in. heavy barrel.

The model nomenclature was changed from XCR to XCR-L (lightweight) during 2008.

ROCK RIVER ARMS, INC.
Current handgun and rifle manufacturer located in Colona, IL beginning 2004. Previously located in Cleveland, IL until 2003. Dealer and consumer direct sales.

PISTOLS: SEMI-AUTO

Rock River Arms makes a variety of high quality M-1911 based semi-autos. They specialize in manufacturing their own National Match frames and slides. Previous models included: the Standard Match (disc. 2003, last MSR was $1,150), Ultimate Match Achiever (disc. 2003, last MSR was $2,255), Matchmaster Steel (disc. 2001, last MSR was $2,355), Elite Commando (disc. 2005, last MSR was $1,725), Hi-Cap Basic Limited (disc. 2003, last MSR was $1,895), and the Doug Koenig Signature Series (disc. 2003, last MSR was $5,000, .38 Super cal.). Rock River Arms also offers additional options and parts.

BASIC LIMITED MATCH – 9mm Para., .38 Super, .40 S&W, or .45 ACP cal., blue, hard chrome, black "T", or black/green "T" duotone finish, 4 1/4, 5, or 6 in. barrel, National Match frame and slide with low mount Bo-Mar hidden leaf rear sight, beveled mag well and choice of 20, 25, or 30 LPI checkered front strap, match Commander hammer and match sear, tuned and polished extractor and extended ejector, lowered and flared ejection port, beavertail grip safety, aluminum speed trigger, two piece recoil guide road and polished feed ramp, RRA dovetail front sight, serrated slide stop and ambidextrous safety, deluxe checkered grips.

MSR $1,840	$1,675	$1,465	$1,255	$1,140	$920	$755	$585

LIMITED MATCH – 9mm Para., .38 Super, .40 S&W, or .45 ACP cal., blue, hard chrome, black "T" or black/green duotone finish, National match frame with beveled mag well and choice of 20, 25, or 30 LPI checkered front and rear strap, 4 1/4, 5, or 6 in. barrel with double slide serrations and RRA borders, low mount Bo-Mar hidden leaf rear sight, RRA dovetail front sight, 40 LPI checkering under trigger guard, Match Commander hammer and match sear, aluminum speed trigger, beavertail grip safety with raised pad, extended mag. release button, tuned and polished feed ramp, deluxe checkered grips, two-piece recoil guide rod.

MSR $2,185	$1,975	$1,700	$1,500	$1,300	$1,100	$900	$750

NATIONAL MATCH HARDBALL – 9mm Para., .38 Super, .40 S&W, or .45 ACP cal., blue, hard chrome, black "T" or black/green "T" duotone finish, forged National Match frame with 4 1/4, 5, or 6 in. barrel, beveled mag well, choice of 20, 25, or 30 LPI checkered front strap, choice of rear or double slide serrations, aluminum speed trigger, milled in Bo-Mar rear sight with hidden rear leaf, lowered and flared ejection port, polished feed ramp, tuned and polished extrator and extended ejector, checkered rosewood grips.

MSR $1,550	$1,400	$1,225	$1,050	$950	$770	$630	$490

BULLSEYE WADCUTTER – 9mm Para., .38 Super, .40 S&W, or .45 ACP cal., blue, hard chrome, black "T" or black/green "T" duotone finish, 7 shot mag., 4 1/4, 5, or 6 in. barrel, National Match frame with choice of RRR Slide mount, Bo-Mar rib, Caspian frame mount sights, or Weigand 3rd Gen. frame mount, double slide serrations, choice of 20, 25, or 30 LPI checkered front strap, beavertail grip safety with raised pad, lowered and flared ejection port, Commander hammer and match sear, aluminum speed trigger, checkered rosewood grips.

MSR $1,715	$1,550	$1,355	$1,160	$1,055	$850	$695	$540

Add $35 for Caspian frame mount or Bo-Mar rib.

TACTICAL PISTOL – 9mm Para., .38 Super, .40 S&W, .45 ACP cal., blue, hard chrome, black "T" or black/green "T" duotone finish, 5 in. barrel with double slide serrations, RRA bar stock frame with integral light rail, choice of 20, 25, or 30 LPI checkered front strap, lowered and flared ejection port, RRA dovetail front sight with tritium inserts, Heinie rear sight with tritium inserts, optional Novak rear sight, aluminum speed trigger, tuned and polished extractor, extended ejector, beavertail grip safety, tactical mag. catch and safety, standard recoil system, completely dehorned for carry, checkered rosewood grips, optional ambidextrous safety, optional Smith & Alexander magwell.

MSR $2,040	$1,850	$1,620	$1,385	$1,260	$1,015	$830	$645

BASIC CARRY – .45 ACP cal., 5 in. National Match barrel with double slide serrations, parkerized finish, checkered rosewood grips, RRA forged National Match frame, choice of 20, 25, or 30 LPI checkered front strap, lowered and flared ejection port, RRA dovetail front sight, Heinie rear sight, Match Commander hammer and match sear, aluminum speed trigger, beavertail grip safety, standard mag. catch, safety, and standard recoil system.

MSR $1,600	$1,450	$1,270	$1,085	$985	$795	$650	$505

RRA PRO CARRY – 9mm Para., .38 Super, .40 S&W, or .45 ACP cal., 4 1/4, 5, or 6 in. barrel with slide serrations, RRA National Match frame with choice of 20, 25, or 30 LPI checkered front strap, lowered and flared ejection port, RRA dovetail front sight with tritium inserts, Match Commander hammer, aluminum speed trigger, tuned and polished extractor, extended ejector, deluxe rosewood grips, choice of Heinie or Novak rear sight with tritium inserts,

MSR	100%	98%	95%	90%	80%	70%	60%

beavertail grip safety.

| MSR $1,920 | $1,675 | $1,465 | $1,255 | $1,140 | $920 | $755 | $585 |

RRA SERVICE AUTO – 9mm Para. cal., similar to RRA Pro Carry, except with 5 in. barrel and double slide serrations. New 2009.

| MSR $1,790 | $1,575 | $1,380 | $1,180 | $1,070 | $865 | $710 | $550 |

LIMITED POLICE COMPETITION – 9mm Para. cal., 5 in. National Match barrel, blue, hard chrome, black "T", or black/green "T" duotone finish, RRA forged National Match frame with beveled mag well with choice of 20, 25, or 30 LPI checkered front strap, double slide serrations, 3-position rear sight, choice of wide or narrow blade, RRA dovetail front sight, tall, thinned, and relieved for PPC, Smith & Alexander flared mag well, lowered and flared ejection port, Match Commander hammer and match sear, tuned and polished extractor and extended ejector, beavertail grip safety and flat checkered mainspring housing, deluxe checkered grips, ambidextrous safety, tuned and polished feed ramp, two-piece recoil spring guide rod.

| MSR $2,375 | $2,095 | $1,825 | $1,600 | $1,375 | $1,250 | $1,000 | $775 |

UNLIMITED POLICE COMPETITION – 9mm Para. cal., forged 6 in. National Match barrel, RRA forged National Match frame with beveled mag well, choice of 20, 25, or 30 LPI checkered front strap, double slide serrations, similar configuration as Limited Police Competition.

| MSR $2,375 | $2,095 | $1,825 | $1,600 | $1,375 | $1,250 | $1,000 | $775 |

LAR-15 – .223 Rem. cal., 7 or 10 1/2 in. barrel, A2 or A4 configuration, A2 flash hider, single stage trigger, Hogue rubber pistol grip, approx. 5 lbs.

| MSR $945 | $850 | $740 | $625 | $560 | $455 | $370 | $290 |

Add $10 for aluminum free floating forearm or $45 for gas block sight base.

LAR-9 – similar to LAR-15, except is 9mm Para. cal., A1 flash hider, 4.8 - 5.2 lbs.

| MSR $1,080 | $995 | $865 | $750 | $650 | $550 | $450 | $350 |

Add $10 for A4 handguard, $60 for aluminum free floating forearm with A2 front sight, or $70 for aluminum free floating handguard with gas block sight base.

LAR-40 – .40 S&W cal., 7 or 10 1/2 in. barrel, forged lower receiver with integral magwell, A2 or A4 upper, single stage trigger, Hogue rubber pistol grip, approx. 5 lbs. New 2010.

| MSR $1,120 | $1,050 | $900 | $800 | $700 | $600 | $500 | $400 |

Add $45 for 7 in. barrel and free float tube handguard.
Add $10-$15 for gas block sight base.

PPS PISTOL (PERFORMANCE PISTON SYSTEM) – .223 Rem. cal., 8 in. barrel, features full length upper and partial lower Picatinny rails, and performance piston system with adj. gas piston, Hogue rubber pistol grip, ribbed forend, single stage trigger, flanged handguard, folding ambidextrous non-reciprocating charging handles, two-position regulator, approx. 5 lbs. New 2010.

| MSR $1,335 | $1,225 | $1,100 | $950 | $875 | $800 | $725 | $650 |

RIFLES: SEMI-AUTO

Rock River Arms makes a variety of tactical style rifles/carbines patterned after the AR-15 in .223 Rem. cal. Previous models include the CAR UTE (disc. 2004, last MSR was $850), Tactical Carbine A2, M4 Entry (disc. 2003, last MSR was $875), and NM A2-DCM Legal (disc. 2005, last MSR was $1,265).

Beginning 2006, Rock River Arms released a series of tactical style rifles in 9mm Para. cal. Also during 2006, the company released a series of tactical style rifles in .308 Win. cal.

A wide variety of options are available for each rifle. Base model assumes black furniture.

STANDARD A2 – .223 Rem. cal., forged A2 upper receiver, 20 in. Wilson chromemoly barrel, A2 flash hider, two-stage match trigger, A2 pistol grip, handguard, and buttstock, 8.6 lbs.

| MSR $980 | $900 | $775 | $655 | $595 | $480 | $395 | $305 |

STANDARD A4 – similar to Standard A2 model, except has forged A4 upper receiver, 8.2 lbs.

| MSR $940 | $850 | $715 | $600 | $525 | $465 | $395 | $295 |

NATIONAL MATCH A2 – .223 Rem. cal., forged A2 upper receiver, 20 in. Wilson heavy match stainless barrel, 20 shot mag., two-stage match trigger, A2 flash hider, A2 pistol grip and buttstock, free floating handguard, 9.7 lbs.

| MSR $1,215 | $1,075 | $925 | $775 | $675 | $575 | $500 | $415 |

NATIONAL MATCH A4 – .223 Rem. cal., similar to National Match A2 model, except has forged A4 upper receiver with NM carry handle, 9.7 lbs.

| MSR $1,310 | $1,175 | $1,000 | $850 | $750 | $600 | $495 | $385 |

MSR	100%	98%	95%	90%	80%	70%	60%

CAR A2 – .223 Rem. cal., forged A2 upper receiver, 16 in. Wilson chromemoly barrel, A2 flash hider, two-stage match trigger, CAR length handguard, A2 pistol grip and buttstock, 7 1/2 lbs.

MSR $960	$875	$750	$635	$580	$465	$380	$295

Add $15 for six-position tactical stock.

CAR A4 – .223 Rem. cal., similar to CAR A2, except has forged A4 upper receiver, 7.1 lbs.

MSR $925	$850	$715	$600	$525	$465	$395	$295

Add $15 for six-position tactical stock.

MID-LENGTH A2 – .223 Rem. cal., forged A2 upper receiver, 16 in. Wilson chromemoly barrel, two-stage match trigger, mid-length handguard, A2 pistol grips and buttstock, 7 1/2 lbs.

MSR $960	$875	$750	$635	$580	$465	$380	$295

Add $15 for six-position tactical stock.

MID-LENGTH A4 – .223 Rem. cal., similar to Mid-Length A2 model, except has forged A4 upper receiver, 7.1 lbs.

MSR $925	$850	$715	$600	$525	$465	$395	$295

Add $15 for six-position tactical stock.

TACTICAL CAR A4 – .223 Rem. cal., forged A4 upper receiver, detachable tactical carry handle, 16 in. Wilson chromemoly barrel, A2 flash hider, two-stage match trigger, Hogue rubber pistol grip, R-4 handguard, six-position tactical CAR stock, 7 1/2 lbs.

MSR $995	$925	$810	$695	$630	$510	$415	$325

Add $40 for chrome lined barrel.

ELITE CAR A4 – .223 Rem. cal., similar to Tactical CAR A4, except has mid-length handguard, 7.7 lbs.

MSR $995	$925	$810	$695	$630	$510	$415	$325

Subtract $80 if w/o carry handle/mount.
Add $40 for chrome lined barrel.

ELITE COMP – .223 Rem. cal., 16 in. barrel with tactical muzzle brake, MagPul CTR stock, features free floating half-round, half-quad handguard, Pads flip up rear sight, pistol grip, 8.4 lbs. New 2008.

MSR $1,450	$1,375	$1,205	$1,030	$935	$755	$620	$480

TACTICAL CAR UTE2 – .223 Rem. cal., forged Universal Tactical Entry 2 upper receiver, 16 in. Wilson chromemoly barrel, A2 flash hider, two-stage match trigger, Hogue rubber pistol grip, R-4 handguard, six-position tactical CAR stock, 7 1/2 lbs.

MSR $1,060	$965	$825	$700	$630	$510	$415	$325

ELITE CAR UTE2 – .223 Rem. cal., similar to Tactical CAR UTE2, except has mid-length handguard, 7.7 lbs.

MSR $1,060	$965	$825	$700	$630	$510	$415	$325

ENTRY TACTICAL – .223 Rem. cal., forged A4 upper receiver, 16 in. Wilson chromemoly R-4 heavy barrel, detachable tactical carry handle, A2 flash hider, two-stage match trigger, Hogue rubber pistol grip, R-4 handguard with double heat shields, six-position tactical CAR stock, 7 1/2 lbs.

MSR $995	$925	$810	$695	$630	$510	$415	$325

Subtract $80 if w/o carry handle/mount.
Add $40 for chrome lined barrel.

TASC RIFLE – .223 Rem. cal., forged A2 upper receiver with lockable windage and elevation adj. rear sight, 16 in. Wilson chromemoly barrel, A2 flash hider, two-stage match trigger, Hogue rubber pistol grip, A2 buttstock or six-position CAR tactical buttstock, choice of R-4 or mid-length handguard, approx. 7 1/2 lbs. Disc. 2009.

	$875	$765	$655	$595	$480	$395	$305	Last MSR was $950.

Add $15 for six-position collapsible stock.

PRO-SERIES GOVERNMENT – .223 Rem. cal., forged A4 upper receiver, 16 in. chrome lined Wilson chromemoly barrel, A2 flash hider, two-stage match trigger, flip-up rear sight, Hogue rubber pistol grip, six-position tactical CAR stock, Surefire M73 quad rail handguard, Surefire M951 WeaponLight light system, EOTech 552 Holosight red-dot optical sight, side mount sling swivel, 8.2 lbs.

MSR $2,350	$2,125	$1,850	$1,575	$1,430	$1,155	$945	$735

PRO-SERIES TASC – .223 Rem. cal., forged A2 upper reciever, chrome lined 16 in. Wilson chromemoly barrel, Smith Vortex flash hider, two-stage match trigger, oversize winter trigger guard, A2 rear sight with lockable windage and elevation, Hogue rubber pistol grip, six-position tactical CAR stock, Surefire M85 mid-length quad rail, graphite fore grip, EOTech 511 Holosight, Midwest Industries A2 adj. cantilever sight mount, 8.7 lbs. Disc. 2009.

	$1,850	$1,600	$1,400	$1,200	$1,000	$800	$675	Last MSR was $2,000.

PRO-SERIES ELITE – .223 Rem. cal., forged A4 upper receiver, chrome lined 16 in. Wilson chromemoly barrel, RRA

MSR	100%	98%	95%	90%	80%	70%	60%

tactical muzzle brake, flip front sight and gas block assembly, two-stage match trigger, Winter trigger guard, Badger tactical charging handle latch, A.R.M.S. #40L low profile flip-up rear sight, ERGO sure-grip pistol grip, six-position tactical CAR stock, MWI front sling adapter, MWI CAR stock end plate adapter loop rear sling mount, Daniel Defense 12.0 FSPM quad rail handguard, SureFire M910A-WH vertical foregrip weaponlight, Aimpoint Comp M2 red dot optical sight and QRP mount with spacer, 9 1/2 lbs.

| MSR $2,950 | $2,725 | $2,535 | $2,170 | $1,970 | $1,590 | $1,305 | $1,015 |

VARMINT EOP (ELEVATED OPTICAL PLATFORM) – .223 Rem. cal., forged EOP upper receiver, 16, 18, 20, or 24 in. Wilson air gauged stainless steel bull barrel, Weaver style light varmint gas block with sight rail, two-stage match trigger, Winter trigger guard, knurled and fluted free floating aluminum tube handguard, Hogue rubber pistol grip, A2 buttstock, approx. 8.2 - 10 lbs.

| MSR $1,140 | $1,025 | $875 | $730 | $665 | $535 | $440 | $340 |

Add $10 for 18, $20 for 20, or $30 for 24 in. barrel.

VARMINT A4 – .223 Rem. or .308 Win. (new 2010) cal., similar to Varmint EOP, except has forged A4 upper receiver., 7.9 - 11.6 lbs.

| MSR $1,105 | $995 | $850 | $725 | $655 | $530 | $435 | $340 |

Add $10 for 18, $20 for 20, or $30 for 24 in. barrel.
Add $395 for .308 Win. cal. (new 2010).

PREDATOR PURSUIT RIFLE – .223 Rem. cal., similar to Varmint A4, except has 20 in. Wilson heavy match stainless steel barrel, 8.1 lbs.

| MSR $1,125 | $1,000 | $875 | $730 | $665 | $535 | $440 | $340 |

COYOTE – .223 Rem. or 6.8 SPC (new 2010) cal., forged A4 upper receiver, 16 or 20 in. Wilson chromemoly HBar barrel, Smith Vortex flash hider, Weaver style light varmint gas block with sight rail, two-stage match trigger, Winter trigger guard, Hogue rubber pistol grip, Hogue overmolded free float tube handguard, ACE ARFX skeleton stock, 8.4 lbs.

| MSR $1,190 | $1,065 | $925 | $775 | $695 | $565 | $460 | $360 |

Add $15 for 20 in. barrel.

LAR-6.8 A2/A4 – .6.8mm Rem. SPC cal., forged A2 or A4 upper receiver, 16 in. Wilson chromemoly barrel, A2 flash hider, two-stage match trigger, A2 pistol grip and buttstock, choice of CAR length or mid-length handguard, 7 1/2 lbs.

| MSR $950 | $860 | $725 | $625 | $525 | $465 | $395 | $295 |

Add $15 for A4 with six-position stock.
Add $35 for A2 buttstock.

LAR-458 CAR A4 – .458 SOCOM cal., forged A4 upper receiver, 16 in. Wilson chromemoly bull barrel, A2 flash hider, Weaver style varmint gas block with sight rail, two-stage match trigger, knurled and fluted free floating aluminum tube handguard, A2 buttstock and pistol grip, 7.6 lbs.

| MSR $1,150 | $1,025 | $875 | $750 | $675 | $550 | $440 | $340 |

Add $270 for Operator model with half quad free float with full length top rail and CAR stock (new 2010).

LAR-458 MID-LENGTH A4 – .458 SOCOM cal., forged A4 upper receiver, 16 in. chromemoly bull barrel, A2 flash hider, gas block with sight rail, two-stage match trigger, knurled and fluted free floating aluminum tube handguard, A2 buttstock and pistol grip, 7.8 lbs. New 2010.

| MSR $1,150 | $1,025 | $875 | $750 | $675 | $550 | $440 | $340 |

Add $295 for Operator model with half quad free float with full length top rail, Vortex flash hider and CAR stock (new 2010).

LAR-10 VARMINT A4 – .308 Win. cal., forged A4 upper reciever with forward assist and port door, 26 in. Wilson stainless steel bull barrel, Weaver type sight base gas block, two-stage match trigger, knurled and fluted free floating aluminum tube handguard, Hogue pistol grip, A2 buttstock, 11.6 lbs.

| MSR $1,350 | $1,225 | $1,070 | $920 | $835 | $675 | $550 | $430 |

LAR-10 STANDARD A2/A4 – .308 Win. cal., forged A2 or A4 upper receiver, with forward assist and port door, 20 in. Wilson chromemoly barrel, A2 flash hider, A2 front sight or A4 gas block sight base, two-stage match trigger, A2 handguard, Hogue rubber pistol grip, A2 buttstock, 9.3 lbs. Disc. 2009.

| | $1,000 | $875 | $750 | $680 | $550 | $450 | $350 | Last MSR was $1,100. |

Add $45 for A2 sights.

LAR-10 MID-LENGTH A2/A4 – .308 Win. cal., forged A2 or A4 upper receiver with forward assist and ejection port door, 16 in. Wilson chrome-moly barrel, A2 flash hider, A2 front sight or A4 gas block with sight base, two-stage match trigger, mid-length handguard, Hogue rubber pistol grip, six-position tactical CAR stock, approx. 8 lbs. Disc. 2009.

| | $1,000 | $875 | $750 | $680 | $550 | $450 | $350 | Last MSR was $1,100. |

Add $50 for A2 sights.

MSR	100%	98%	95%	90%	80%	70%	60%

LAR-9 CAR A2/A4 – 9mm Para. cal., forged A2 or A4 upper receiver, 16 in. Wilson chromemoly barrel, A1 flash hider, standard single stage trigger, CAR length handguard, A2 pistol grip, six-position tactical CAR stock, approx. 7 lbs.

MSR $1,085	$995	$875	$750	$675	$535	$440	$340

Add $25 for A2 buttstock.

LAR-8 MID LENGTH A4 – .308 Win. cal. 16 in. barrel, CAR buttstock, A2 flash hider, gas block sight base, Hogue rubber grip, two stage trigger, forged A4 upper receiver, mid-length handguard, approx. 8 lbs. New 2010.

MSR $1,265	$1,125	$975	$825	$750	$600	$495	$385

LAR-8 ELITE OPERATOR – .308 Win. cal. 16 in. barrel, similar to Mid-length A4, except has advanced half quad rail, flip front sight, gas block sight base, Operator stock and Smith Vortex flash hider. New 2010.

MSR $1,655	$1,500	$1,300	$1,100	$900	$700	$600	$550

LAR-8 STANDARD A4 – .308 Win. cal., forged lower and upper receiver, 20 in. chromemoly barrel, A2 flash hider, gas block sight base, two stage trigger, A2 buttstock, A2 handguard, Hogue rubber pistol grip, approx. 9 lbs. New 2010.

MSR $1,300	$1,150	$975	$825	$750	$600	$495	$385

LAR-8 STANDARD OPERATOR – .308 Win. cal. 16 in. barrel, similar to LAR-8 Standard A4, except has advanced half quad rail, flip front sight, gas block sight base, Operator stock and Smith Vortex flash hider. New 2010.

MSR $1,705	$1,525	$1,300	$1,100	$900	$700	$600	$550

LAR-8 PREDATOR HP – .308 Win. cal., forged lower and upper receiver, 20 in. bead blasted lightweight stainless steel barrel, gas block sight base, two stage trigger, A2 buttstock, free float tube handguard, Hogue rubber pistol grip, approx. 8.6 lbs. New 2010.

MSR $1,535	$1,425	$1,225	$1,030	$935	$755	$620	$480

LAR-40 CAR A2/A4 – .40 S&W cal., forged A2 or A4 upper receiver, 16 in. chromemoly barrel, A2 flash hider, single stage trigger, R-4 handguard, six-position tactical CAR stock with Hogue pistol grip, approx. 7 lbs.

MSR $1,125	$1,000	$875	$730	$665	$535	$440	$340

Add $25 for A2 buttstock.

LAR-40 MID-LENGTH A2/A4 – .40 S&W cal., forged A2 upper, 16 in. chrome-moly barrel, A2 flash hider, two-stage match trigger, mid-length handguard, Hogue rubber pistol grip, six-position tactical CAR stock, approx. 7 lbs. New 2010.

MSR $1,125	$1,000	$875	$730	$665	$535	$440	$340

Add $15 for A2 configuration.

ROCKY MOUNTAIN ARMS, INC.

Current firearms manufacturer located in Longmont, CO since 1991.

Rocky Mountain Arms is a quality specialty manufacturer of rifles and pistols. All firearms are finished in a Dupont Teflon-S industrial coating called "Bear Coat".

PISTOLS: SEMI-AUTO

BAP (BOLT ACTION PISTOL) – .308 Win., 7.62x39mm, or 10mm Rocky Mountain Thunderer (10x51mm) cal., features 14 in. heavy fluted Douglas Match barrel, Kevlar/graphite pistol grip stock, supplied with Harris bipod and black nylon case. Mfg. 1993 only.

	$1,425	$1,275	$1,100	$950	$825	$700	$575	Last MSR was $1,595.

22K PISTOLS – .22 LR cal., AR style pistols featuring 7 in. barrel, choice of matte black or NATO Green Teflon-S finish, will use Colt conversion kit, choice of carrying handle or flattop upper receiver, 10 or 30 shot mag., includes black nylon case. Mfg. 1993 only.

	$475	$425	$375	$350	$325	$295	$275	Last MSR was $525.

Add $50 for flattop receiver with Weaver style bases.

PATRIOT PISTOL – .223 Rem. cal., AR style pistol featuring 7 in. match barrel with integral Max Dynamic muzzle brake, 21 in. overall, available with either carrying handle upper receiver and fixed sights or flattop receiver with Weaver style bases, fluted upper receiver became an option in 1994, accepts standard AR-15 mags, 5 lbs. Mfg. 1993-94 (per C/B), reintroduced 2005.

MSR $3,000	$2,850	$2,500	$2,250	$2,000	$1,750	$1,500	$1,250

KOMRADE – 7.62x39mm cal., includes carrying handle upper receiver with fixed sights, floating 7 in. barrel, Teflon red or black finish, 5 lbs., 5 shot mag. Mfg. 1994-95.

	$1,825	$1,650	$1,425	$1,200	$975	$850	$775	Last MSR was $1,995.

MSR	100%	98%	95%	90%	80%	70%	60%	

RIFLES: BOLT ACTION

PROFESSIONAL SERIES – .223 Rem., .30-06, .308 Win., or .300 Win. Mag. cal., bolt action rifle utilizing modified Mauser action, fluted 26 in. Douglas premium heavy match barrel with integral muzzle brake, custom Kevlar-Graphite stock with off-set thumbhole, test target. Mfg. 1991-95.

	$2,050	$1,650	$1,275	$995	$850	$725	$600	Last MSR was $2,200.

Add $100 for .300 Win. Mag. cal.
Add $300 for left-hand action.

PRAIRIE STALKER – .223 Rem., .22-250 Rem., .30-06, .308 Win., or .300 Win. Mag. cal., choice of Remington, Savage, or Winchester barreled action, includes Choate ultimate sniper stock, lapped bolt and match crown, "Bear Coat" all-weather finish, includes factory test target. Limited mfg. 1998 only.

	$1,595	$1,350	$1,150	$950	$875	$775	$675	Last MSR was $1,795.

* ***Prairie Stalker Ultimate*** – similar to Prairie Stalker, except custom barrel and caliber specifications are customer's choice. Limited mfg. 1998 only.

	$2,200	$1,875	$1,625	$1,400	$1,200	$1,000	$895	Last MSR was $2,495.

PRO-VARMINT – .22-250 Rem., or .223 Rem. cal., RMA action, 22 in. heavy match barrel with recessed crown, "Bear Coat" metal finish, Choate stock with aluminum bedding. Mfg. 1999-2002.

	$995	$875	$800	$725	$650	$575	$450	Last MSR was $1,095.

POLICE MARKSMAN – .308 Win. or .300 Win. Mag. cal., similar to Professional Series, except has 40X-C stock featuring adj. cheekpiece and buttplate, target rail, Buehler micro-dial scope mounting system. Mfg. 1991-95.

	$2,325	$1,995	$1,650	$1,325	$1,100	$900	$700	Last MSR was $2,500.

Add $100 for .300 Win. Mag. cal.
Add $400 for left-hand action.
Add $400 for illuminated dot scope (4-12x56mm).

* ***Police Marksman II*** – .308 Win. cal., RMA action, 22 in. heavy match barrel with recessed crown, "Bear Coat" metal finish, Choate stock with aluminum bedding. Mfg. 1999-2002.

	$995	$875	$800	$725	$650	$575	$450	Last MSR was $1,095.

PRO-GUIDE – .280 Rem., .35 Whelen, .308 Win., 7x57mm Mauser, or 7mm-08 Rem. cal., Scout Rifle design with 17 in. Shilen barrel, "Bear Coat" finish, approx. 7 lbs. Mfg. 1999-2002.

	$2,025	$1,800	$1,600	$1,425	$1,200	$1,000	$825	Last MSR was $2,295.

NINJA SCOUT RIFLE – .22 Mag. cal., takedown rifle based on Marlin action, black stock, 16 1/2 in. match grade crowned barrel, forward mounted Weaver style scope base, adj. rear sight, 7 shot mag. Mfg. 1991-95.

	$640	$575	$525	$460	$430	$390	$360	Last MSR was $695.

Add $200 for illuminated dot scope (1.5-4X) w/extended eye relief.

SCOUT SEMI-AUTO – .22 Mag. cal., patterned after Marlin action. Mfg. 1993-95.

	$650	$575	$495	$395	$350	$295	$260	Last MSR was $725.

Add $200 for illuminated dot scope (1.5-4X) w/extended eye relief.

RIFLES: SEMI-AUTO

M-SHORTEEN – .308 Win. cal., compact highly modified M1-A featuring 17" match crowned barrel, custom front sight, mod. gas system, hand honed action and trigger, custom muzzle brake. Mfg. 1991-94.

	$1,650	$1,425	$1,175	$995	$850	$725	$600	Last MSR was $1,895.

Add $200 for Woodland/Desert camo.

VARMINTER – .223 Rem. cal. only, AR-15 style rifle with 20 in. fluted heavy match barrel, flattop receiver with Weaver style bases, round metal National Match hand guard, free float barrel, choice of NATO green or matte black Teflon-S finish, supplied with case and factory test target (sub-MOA accuracy). Mfg. 1993-94.

	$2,195	$1,800	$1,600	$1,400	$1,200	$1,000	$875	Last MSR was $2,495.

PATRIOT MATCH RIFLE – .223 Rem. cal., 20 in. Bull Match barrel, regular or milled upper and lower receivers, two-piece machined aluminum hand guard, choice of DuPont Teflon finish in black or NATO green, 1/2 MOA accuracy, hard case. Mfg. 1995-97, reintroduced 2005.

MSR $2,500	$2,350	$2,050	$1,700	$1,425	$1,200	$1,000	$895	

SHOTGUNS: SLIDE ACTION

870 COMPETITOR – 12 ga., 3 in. chamber, security configuration with synthetic stock, hand-honed action, ghost ring adj. sights, "Bear Coat" finish, high visibility follower. Mfg. 1996-97.

	$695	$625	$550	$500	$450	$400	$360	Last MSR was $795.

MSR	100%	98%	95%	90%	80%	70%	60%

ROHRBAUGH FIREARMS CORP.

Current manufacturer located in Deer Park, NY.

PISTOLS: SEMI-AUTO

R-9 – 9mm Para or .380 ACP (new 2007) cal., DAO, 2.9 in. barrel, free bored to reduce felt recoil, frame is 7075-T651 aluminum, stainless steel or black Stealth slide, 6 shot mag., parts cut from solid billets, all internal parts are stainless, short recoil locked breech with cam operated tilting barrel locking system, recessed hammer, carbon fiber (disc.) or G10 grips, no sights, 12.8 (carbon fiber grips) or 13 1/2 (G10 grips) oz. New 2003.

MSR $1,150	$1,000	$875	$750	$680	$550	$450	$350

Add $45 for black Stealth slide.

* **R9S Model** – similar to Model R-9, except has fixed open sights. New 2004.

MSR $1,150	$1,000	$875	$750	$680	$550	$450	$350

Add $45 for black Stealth slide.
Add $45 for Elite Custom Model (Model R9SE, disc.).

ROHRBAUGH ROBAR R9 SERIES – similar to original R9, except frame, barrel, slide and trigger are treated with Robar Industries NP3 coating (corrosion resistant and self lubricating), polished stainless steel, limited lifetime warranty. New 2010.

MSR $1,795	$1,500	$1,315	$1,125	$1,020	$825	$675	$525

RUSSIAN AMERICAN ARMORY COMPANY

Current importer located in Scottsburg, IN.

RIFLES AND SHOTGUNS

Russian American Armory Company is an import company for both Izhmash and Molot, located in Russia. Current product/model lines include Saiga semi-auto rifles and shotguns, Vepr. rifles, in addition to a line of bolt action rifles, including the LOS/BAR Series, CM-2 Target rifle, Korshun, and Sobol hunting model. Please check individual listing. For current U.S. availability and pricing, please contact the company for more information (see Trademark Index).

RUSSIAN SERVICE PISTOLS AND RIFLES

Previously manufactured at various Russian military arsenals (including Tula).

RIFLES

Original Soviet Mosin-Nagant bolt action rifles/carbines include: M1891 rifle, M1891 Dragoon, M1891/30 Rifle, M1891/30 Sniper Model, M1910 Carbine, M1938 Carbine, and the M1944 Carbine. Values for these older original military configurations will approximate values listed for the original mfg. Mosin-Nagant.

TOKAREV M1938 & M1940 (SVT) SEMI-AUTO – 7.62x54R cal., SVT M40 is the more common variation, while the SVT M38 sniper is very rare, 10 shot mag., first Russian military semi-auto, large quantities manufactured beginning 1938, but original surviving specimens in excellent condition are now very scarce.

	100%	98%	95%	90%	80%	70%	60%
SVT M38	$2,950	$2,600	$2,400	$1,900	$1,600	$1,400	$1,200
SVT M40	$1,200	$1,000	$800	$700	$600	$500	$425

RPD SEMI-AUTO – 7.62x39mm cal., converted from belt fed to semi-auto only, fired from closed bolt, milled receiver, includes 50 shot mag., recent importation.

	$3,795	$3,495	$2,950	$2,600	$2,300	$2,000	$1,750

NOTES

S SECTION

SKS

SKS designates a semi-auto rifle design originally developed by the Russian military, and manufactured in Russia by both Tula Arsenal (1949-1956) and by Izhevsk Arsenal from 1953-1954. Currently manufactured in Russia, China, and many other countries. Previously manufactured in Russia, China (largest quantity), N. Korea, East Germany, Romania, Albania, Yugoslavia, and North Vietnam.

SKS DEVELOPMENT & HISTORY

SKS (Samozaryadnyi Karabin Simonova) - developed by Sergei Gavrilovich Simonov in the late 1940s to use the 7.62 cartridge of 1943 (7.62x39mm). The SKS is actually based on an earlier design developed by Simonov in 1936 as a prototype self-loading military rifle. The SKS was adopted by the Soviet military in 1949, two years after the AK-47, and was originally intended as a complement to the AK-47s select-fire capability. It served in this role until the mid-to-late 1950s, when it was withdrawn from active issue and sent to reserve units and Soviet Youth "Pioneer" programs. It was also released for use in military assistance programs to Soviet Bloc countries and other "friendly" governments. Much of the original SKS manufacturing equipment was shipped to Communist China prior to 1960. Since then, most of the SKS carbines produced, including those used by the Viet Cong in Vietnam, have come from China.

Like the AK-47, the Simonov carbine is a robust military rifle. It, too, was designed to be used by troops with very little formal education or training. It will operate reliably in the harshest climatic conditions, from the Russian arctic to the steamy jungles of Southeast Asia. Its chrome-lined bore is impervious to the corrosive effects of fulminate of mercury primers and the action is easily disassembled for cleaning and maintenance.

The SKS and a modified sporter called the OP-SKS (OP stands for Okhotnichnyi Patron) are the standard hunting rifles for a majority of Russian hunters. It is routinely used to take everything from the Russian saiga antelope up to and including moose, boar, and brown bear. The main difference between the regular SKS and the OP variant is in the chamber dimensions and the rate of rifling. The OP starts as a regular SKS, then has the barrel removed and replaced with one designed to specifically handle a slightly longer and heavier bullet.

Prior to the "assault weapons" ban, hundreds of thousands of SKS carbines were imported into the U.S. The SKS was rapidly becoming one of the favorites of American hunters and shooters. Its low cost and durability made it a popular "truck gun" for those shooters who spend a lot of time in the woods, whether they are ranchers, farmers, or plinkers. While the Russian made SKS is a bonafide curio and relic firearm and legal for importation, the Clinton administration suspended all import permits for firearms having a rifled bore and ammunition from the former Soviet Union in early 1994. In order to get the ban lifted, the Russian government signed a trade agreement, wherein they agreed to deny export licenses to any American company seeking SKS rifles and a variety of other firearms and ammunition deemed politically incorrect by Clinton & Gore. The BATF then used this agreement as a reason to deny import licenses for any SKS from any country.

Most of the SKS carbines imported into the U.S. came from the Peoples Republic of China. They were a mix of refurbished military issue, straight military surplus, and even some new manufacture. Quality was rather poor. Compared to the SKS Chinese carbines, only a few Russian made SKSs ever made it into the U.S. All are from military stockpiles and were refurbished at the Tula Arms Works, probably the oldest continuously operating armory in the world. Recently, more SKS carbines have been imported from the former Yugoslavia by Century International Arms. These carbines carry the former Soviet Bloc designation of "Type 58" and feature milled receivers. Quality is generally good, and values are comparable to other Russian/European SKS imports. Values for unmodified Russian and Eastern European made SKS carbines (those with the original magazines and stock) are higher than the Chinese copies.

The most collectible SKS is East German mfg., and SKS rifles mfg. in N. Korea and N. Vietnam are also quite rare in the U.S. Over 600 million SKS carbines have been manufactured in China alone, by over 45 different manufacturers, in addition to the millions manufactured in other former Soviet Bloc countries. The Simonov carbine was the best selling semi-auto rifle in America (and other countries) during 1993-94, and remains a popular choice for plinking, hunting, and protection in the new millennium.

RIFLES: SEMI-AUTO

SKS – 7.62x39mm Russian cal., Soviet designed, original Soviet mfg. as well as copies mfg. in China, Russia, Yugoslavia, and many other countries, gas operated weapon, 10 shot fixed mag., wood stock (thumbhole design on newer mfg.), with or w/o (newer mfg.) permanently attached folding bayonet, tangent rear and hooded front sight, no current importation from China, Russia, or the former Yugoslavia.

Please refer to individual importers for other SKS listings, including Norinco, Poly-Technologies, and Mitchell Arms.

* SKS Mfg. in Russia, Yugoslavia, Romania

$395	$365	$325	$295	$275	$235	$195

MSR	100%	98%	95%	90%	80%	70%	60%

* SKS Chinese Recent Mfg. w/Thumbhole Stock

	$295	$275	$250	$225	$200	$185	$165

SOG ARMORY

Current rifle manufacturer located in Houston, TX.

CARBINES: SEMI-AUTO

All rifles come standard with one magazine, manual, sling, and hard case.

SOG GUARDIAN – .223 Rem. cal., 16 in. chrome lined steel barrel, 30 shot mag., Mil Spec hard coat anodized upper and lower, black phosphate finish, enhanced mag well and trigger guard, M16 bolt and carrier, flash hider, ERGO pistol grip, M4 six position tactical stock, M4 stock pad, charging handle, CAR M4 handguard with double heat shield and detachable carry handle.

MSR $1,500	$1,350	$1,125	$950	$825	$700	$600	$495

SOG ENFORCER – .223 Rem. cal., 16 in. chrome lined steel barrel, 30 shot mag., Mil Spec hard coat anodized upper and lower, black phosphate finish, enhanced mag well and trigger guard, M16 bolt and carrier, flash hider, ERGO pistol grip, M4 six position tactical stock, M4 stock pad, charging handle, CAR M4 handguard with double heat shield, SOG/Troy rear slip up sight.

MSR $1,600	$1,425	$1,175	$975	$825	$700	$600	$495

SOG DEFENDER – .223 Rem. cal., 16 in. chrome lined steel barrel, 30 shot mag., Mil Spec hard coat anodized upper and lower, black, tan, or OD green phosphate finish, enhanced mag well and trigger guard, M16 bolt and carrier, flash hider, ERGO pistol grip, M4 six position tactical stock, M4 stock pad, charging handle, SOG/Troy four rail handguard, detachable carry handle.

MSR $1,700	$1,500	$1,225	$1,000	$850	$725	$650	$550

SOG CRUSADER – .223 Rem. cal., 16 in. chrome lined steel barrel, 30 shot mag., Mil Spec hard coat anodized upper and lower, black, tan, or OD green phosphate finish, enhanced mag well and trigger guard, M16 bolt and carrier, flash hider, ERGO pistol grip, M4 six position tactical stock, M4 stock pad, charging handle, SOG/Troy four rail handguard, SOG/Troy rear flip up sight.

MSR $1,800	$1,575	$1,275	$1,025	$875	$750	$725	$675

SOG WARRIOR – .223 Rem. cal., 16 in. chrome lined steel barrel, 30 shot mag., Mil Spec hard coat anodized upper and lower, black or tan phosphate finish, enhanced mag well and trigger guard, M16 bolt and carrier, flash hider, ERGO pistol grip, VLTOR EMOD stock, M4 stock pad, charging handle, SOG/Troy Extreme free float handguard with rails, SOG/Troy flip front and rear sights.

MSR $1,900	$1,725	$1,500	$1,250	$1,000	$850	$750	$675

SOG OPERATOR – .223 Rem. cal., 16 in. chrome lined steel barrel, 30 shot mag., Mil Spec hard coat anodized upper and lower, black, tan, or OD green phosphate finish, enhanced mag well, M16 bolt and carrier, flash hider, ERGO pistol grip, six position tactical stock, M4 stock pad, charging handle, SOG/Troy four rail handguard, SOG/Troy flip up sight, Magpul Winter trigger guard, Wolf Eye's 260 Lumens tactical light, SOG mount, graphite vertical grip.

MSR $2,300	$2,100	$1,850	$1,625	$1,425	$1,200	$825	$750

STI INTERNATIONAL

Current manufacturer established during 1993, and located in Georgetown, TX. Distributor and dealer sales.

In addition to manufacturing the pistols listed, STi International also makes frame kits in steel, stainless steel, aluminum, or titanium - prices range between $204-$600.

PISTOLS: SEMI-AUTO

The beginning numerals on all STi pistols designate the barrel length, and most of the following models are listed in numerical sequence.

2.5 NEMESIS – 7mm Penna cal., 2 1/2 in. barrel. New 2010.

MSR $870	$840	$725	$625	$525	$450	$400	$350

3.0 SHADOW – 9mm Para., .40 S&W, or .45 ACP cal., 3 in. bull barrel, matte black KG coated finish, forged aluminum frame, undercut trigger guard, stippled front strap, ultra thin G-10 grips with STI logo, rear cocking serrations, curved trigger, beavertail grip safety, fixed tritium 2 dot sights, 23.4 oz. New 2010.

MSR $1,370	$1,195	$1,000	$875	$725	$625	$525	$450

MSR	100%	98%	95%	90%	80%	70%	60%

3.0 ELEKTRA – 9mm Para., .40 S&W, or .45 ACP cal., forged aluminum frame, 3 in. bull barrel, stainless steel slide, rear cocking serrations, beavertail grip safety, fixed tritium 2 dot sights. New 2010.

MSR $1,370	$1,195	$1,000	$875	$725	$625	$525	$450

3.0 ROGUE – 9mm Para. cal., 3 in. bull barrel, forged aluminum compact frame, STI stippled front strap, undercut trigger guard, blued slide with Duracoated frame, intergral sights, 21 oz. Mfg. 2009.

	$925	$825	$725	$650	$575	$500	$425	Last MSR was $1,024.

3.0 ESCORT – 9mm Para. or .45 ACP cal., 3 in. bull barrel, checkered cocobolo grips, round top slide with rear cocking serrations, adj. 3-dot sights, blue slide with Duracoated frame, stippled front strap, 22.8 oz. New 2009.

MSR $1,155	$1,025	$925	$825	$725	$650	$575	$500

3.0 OFF DUTY – 9mm Para. or .45 ACP cal., compact frame, blued or hard chrome matte finish, 3 in. barrel with blue slide, checkered cocobolo grips, stippled front strap, competition front sight, tactical rear sight, 31.3 oz. New 2009.

MSR $1,231	$1,075	$950	$825	$700	$600	$525	$450

3.25 GP5 – 9mm Para. cal., 3 1/4 in. barrel, DAO, blue finish, chromemoly steel frame with integral tactical rail, textured polymer grips, double slide serrations, ambidextrous safety, internal extractor, adj. sights, 24.2 oz. New 2010.

MSR $663	$595	$550	$500	$450	$400	$375	$350

3.4 BLS9/BLS40 – 9mm Para. or .40 S&W cal., blue finish, Govt. length grips, Heinie low mounted sights, single stack mag., 30 oz. Mfg. 1999-2005.

	$765	$650	$565	$460	$400	$360	$330	Last MSR was $889.

3.4 LS9/LS40 – 9mm Para. or .40 S&W (disc. 2008) cal., blue finish, Commander length grips, single stack mag., Heinie low mounted sights, 28 oz. New 1999.

MSR $992	$925	$750	$625	$525	$450	$400	$350

3.4 ESCORT – 9mm Para. or .45 ACP cal., 1911 forged aluminum Commander style frame, 3.4 in. ramped bull barrel, slide with rear cocking serrations, Duracoat finish with blue slide, undercut trigger guard, stippled front strap, rosewood grips, STi hi-ride beavertail grip safety, fixed Novak style 3-dot sights, 22.8 oz. Mfg. 2007-2008.

	$925	$825	$725	$650	$575	$500	$425	Last MSR was $1,024.

3.9 FALCON – .38 Super, .40 S&W, or .45 ACP cal., STi standard frame, 3.9 in. barrel, size is comparable to Officers Model, adj. rear sight. Limited mfg. 1993-98.

	$1,875	$1,375	$1,175	$925	$850	$775	$675	Last MSR was $2,136.

3.9 STINGER – 9mm Para. or .38 Super cal., black frame, designed for IPSC and USPSA competition, 38 oz. Mfg. 2005-2008.

	$2,500	$2,225	$1,975	$1,750	$1,575	$1,375	$1,150	Last MSR was $2,773.

3.9 V.I.P. – 9mm Para. (new 2009), .40 S&W (new 2009), or .45 ACP cal. only, aluminum frame, STi modular polymer frame, stainless steel slide, 3.9 in. barrel with STi Recoilmaster muzzle brake, 10 shot double stack mag., STi fixed sights, 25 oz. Mfg. 2001-2006, reintroduced 2009.

MSR $1,646	$1,425	$1,275	$1,025	$950	$850	$750	$650

3.9 GUARDIAN – 9mm Para. (new 2009) or .45 ACP cal., 1911 Commander style blue frame, 3.9 in. ramped bull barrel, stainless slide with polished sides, stippled front strap, undercut trigger guard, rosewood grips, fixed 3-dot sights, 32.4 oz. New 2007.

MSR $1,110	$995	$850	$750	$650	$575	$500	$425

4.15 TACTICAL – 9mm Para., .40 S&W, or .45 ACP cal., blue steel, fixed sights, short trigger, ambidextrous safety, 34 1/2 oz. New 2004.

MSR $1,999	$1,750	$1,500	$1,250	$1,000	$875	$800	$675

4.15 RANGER II (3.9 RANGER) – 9mm Para. (new 2009), .40 S&W (new 2009), or .45 ACP cal. only, Officer's Model with 3.9 (Ranger, disc. 2004) or 4.15 (Ranger II, new 2005) in. barrel and 1/2 in. shortened grip frame, 6 shot mag., blue steel frame with stainless steel slide, single stack mag., low mount STI/Heinie sights, 29 oz. New 2001.

MSR $1,110	$995	$850	$750	$650	$575	$500	$425

Add $200 for Ranger III configuration (new 2010).

4.15 DUTY CT – 9mm Para., .40 S&W or .45 ACP cal., 5 in. bull barrel, matte blue finish, integral tactical rail, flattop slide with rear cocking serrations, ramped front sight, fixed rear sight, 36.6 oz. Mfg. 2006-2008.

	$1,100	$950	$825	$700	$600	$525	$450	Last MSR was $1,286.

MSR	100%	98%	95%	90%	80%	70%	60%

4.15 STEELMASTER – 9mm Para. cal., 4.15 in. Trubore barrel, blue finish with polished classic slide, sabertooth cocking serrations, C-More red dot scope with blast shield and thumbrest, black glass filled nylon polymer grips with aluminum magwell, 38.9 oz. New 2009.

MSR $2,864	$2,475	$2,050	$1,750	$1,450	$1,200	$995	$875

4.15 MATCHMASTER – .38 Super cal., 4.15 in. Trubore barrel, blue finished with polished classic slide, sabertooth front and rear cocking serrations, black glass filled nylon polymer grips with aluminum magwell, drilled and tapped, C-More red dot scope with blast shield and thumb rest, 38.9 oz. New 2009.

MSR $2,999	$2,600	$2,200	$1,850	$1,500	$1,250	$995	$875

4.25 GP6 – 9mm Para. cal., 4 1/4 in. barrel, DA/SA, blue finish, chromemoly steel frame with integral tactical rail, textured polymer grips, double slide serrations, ambidextrous safety, internal extractor, adj. sights, 26.1 oz. New 2009.

MSR $663	$595	$550	$500	$450	$400	$375	$350

Add $164 for GP6-C model with fiber optic front sight and adj. rear sight (new 2010).

4.3 HAWK – various cals., 4.3 in. barrel, STi standard frame (choice of steel or aluminum), 27 or 31 oz. Mfg. 1993-1999.

	$1,725	$1,275	$1,075	$875	$800	$700	$600	*Last MSR was $1,975.*

4.3 NIGHT HAWK – .45 ACP cal., 4.3 in. barrel, STi wide extended frame, blue finish, 33 oz. Limited mfg. 1997-99.

	$1,875	$1,375	$1,175	$925	$850	$775	$675	*Last MSR was $2,136.*

5.0 G.I. – .45 ACP cal., 5 in. barrel. New 2010.

MSR $822	$765	$700	$625	$550	$500	$450	$395

5.0 FB7 – 7mm Penna or 9mm Para. cal., 5 in. barrel. New 2010.

MSR $1,940	$1,750	$1,500	$1,250	$1,000	$875	$800	$675

5.0 SPARROW – .22 LR cal. only, unlocked blowback action, STi standard extended frame, 5.1 in. ramped bull barrel, fixed sights, blue finish, 30 oz. Limited mfg. 1998-1999 only.

	$1,025	$900	$800	$700	$600	$500	$400	*Last MSR was $1,090.*

5.0 EDGE – 9mm Para., 10mm Norma (disc. 2008), .40 S&W, or .45 ACP cal., designed for limited/standard IPSC competition, STi wide extended frame, wide body with staggered stack mag., blue finish, 39 oz. New 1998.

MSR $1,994	$1,750	$1,500	$1,250	$1,000	$875	$800	$675

5.0 DUTY ONE – 9mm Para., .40 S&W, or .45 ACP cal., ramped bull barrel, checkered wood grips, 38 oz. New 2005.

MSR $1,299	$1,125	$950	$825	$700	$600	$525	$450

5.0 SENTRY – 9mm Para., .40 S&W, or .45 ACP cal., 5 in. ramped barrel with bushing, classic polished flattop slide with front and rear cocking serrations, checkered cocbolo grips, blue finish, competition front and adj. rear sights, 35.3 oz. New 2009.

MSR $1,598	$1,375	$1,150	$1,000	$875	$750	$625	$500

5.0 APEIRO – 9mm Para., .40 S&W, or .45 ACP cal., 5 in. Schuemann Island style barrel, long wide steel frame, stainless steel slide, blue finish, black glass filled nylon polymer grips, stainless magwell, Dawson fiber optic front and adj. rear sights, 38 oz. New 2010.

MSR $2,690	$2,325	$1,950	$1,725	$1,450	$1,200	$1,000	$900

5.0 EXECUTIVE – .40 S&W cal. only, STi long/wide frame, 10 shot double stack mag., stainless construction, grey nylon polymer grips and square triggerguard, hard chrome finish with black inlays, fiberoptic front and STi adj. rear sights, approved for IPSC standard and USPSA limited edition, 38 oz. New 2001.

MSR $2,464	$2,150	$1,825	$1,525	$1,300	$1,050	$900	$800

* **5.0 Executive IPSC 30th Commemorative** – 9mm Para., .40 S&W, or .45 ACP cal., ramped bull barrel, two-tone hard chrome finish, special engraved slide with "IPSC 30th Anniversary" on side, 39 oz. Mfg. 2005-2006.

	$2,500	$2,225	$1,975	N/A	N/A	N/A	N/A	*Last MSR was $2,775.*

* **5.0 Executive Special Edition** – 9mm Para., .40 S&W, or .45 ACP cal., ramped bull barrel, 24Kt. gold on all steel surfaces, checkered black grips, "Special Edition" engraved on slide, 39 oz. Mfg. 2005-2006.

	$2,625	$2,325	$2,000	N/A	N/A	N/A	N/A	*Last MSR was $2,930.*

5.0 STI 20TH ANNIVERSARY – 9mm Para., .40 S&W, or .45 ACP cal., 5 in. bull barrel, steel frame, PVD and TIN

MSR	100%	98%	95%	90%	80%	70%	60%

(titanium nitride) finish, black glass filled nylon polymer filled grips, TIN coated magwell, beavertail grip safety, Dawson fiber optic front and STi adj. rear sight, 38 oz. Limited edition of 200 beginning 2010.

MSR $3,623	$3,300	$2,950	$2,600	N/A	N/A	N/A	N/A

5.0 TROJAN – 9mm Para., .40 S&W, .38 Super, or .45 ACP, standard Govt. length grips, single stack mag., stainless steel available 2006, 36 oz. New 1999.

MSR $1,110	$995	$850	$750	$650	$575	$500	$425

Add $288 for .38 Super with .45 ACP conversion kit.
Add $412 for stainless steel.

5.0 SPARTAN – .45 ACP cal., 1911 Govt. steel frame, parkerized finish, bald front strap, hand checkered double diamond wood grips, front and rear slide serrations, STi long curved trigger, 5 in. chrome ramped bushing barrel, STi high ride beavertail grip safety, fiber optic front sights, adj. rear sights, 35.3 oz. New 2007.

MSR $699	$650	$575	$500	$450	$400	$375	$350

5.0 USPSA SINGLE STACK – 9mm Para., .40 S&W, or .45 ACP cal., 5 in. stainless steel barrel, tri-top two-tone slide with sabertooth cocking serrations, blue frame, 30 LPI front strap checkering, checkered steel D&T mainspring housing and magwell, competition front and adj. rear sight, 38.3 oz. New 2009.

MSR $1,796	$1,525	$1,225	$950	$800	$675	$550	$475

5.0 USPSA DOUBLE STACK – 9mm Para., .40 S&W, or .45 ACP cal., 5 in. stainless steel barrel, tri-top two-tone slide with sabertooth cocking serrations, blue frame, 30 LPI front strap checkering, checkered steel D&T mainspring housing and magwell, competition front and adj. rear sight, 38.3 oz. New 2009.

MSR $2,790	$2,400	$2,000	$1,750	$1,450	$1,200	$1,000	$900

5.0 IPSC DOUBLE STACK – 9mm Para., .40 S&W, or .45 ACP cal., 5 in. bull barrel, blue frame, two-tone hard chrome slide with sabertooth cocking serrations, Dawson fiber optic front and adj. rear sights, black glass filled nylon polymer grips with stainless steel magwell, 38 oz. New 2009.

MSR $2,790	$2,400	$2,000	$1,750	$1,450	$1,200	$1,000	$900

5.0 RANGEMASTER – 9mm Para. or .45 ACP cal., black frame, ramped bull barrel, STI Recoilmaster guide rod, 38 oz. New 2005.

MSR $1,521	$1,350	$1,100	$900	$775	$625	$525	$475

5.0 RANGEMASTER II – similar to 5.0 Rangemaster, except does not have extended frame dust cover. Mfg. 2006.

	$1,175	$965	$850	$725	$625	$525	$475	Last MSR was $1,344.

5.0 EAGLE – various cals., 5.1 in. barrel, STi standard frame (choice of steel or aluminum) govt. model full-size, wide body with staggered stack mag., adj. rear sight, 31 or 35 oz.

MSR $1,944	$1,750	$1,500	$1,250	$1,000	$875	$800	$675

Add $266 for .38 Super with .45 ACP conversion kit.

5.0 TACTICAL – 9mm Para., .40 S&W, or .45 ACP cal., blue steel, fixed sights, short trigger, ambidextrous safety, 39 oz. New 2004.

MSR $1,999	$1,750	$1,500	$1,250	$1,000	$875	$800	$675

* **5.0 Tactical Lite** – similar to 5.0 Tactical, except stainless slide, alloy frame, fixed sights, 34 1/2 oz. Mfg. 2004-2005.

	$1,800	$1,525	$1,300	$1,050	$900	$825	$700	Last MSR was $2,002.

5.0 TRUSIGHT – 9mm Para., .40 S&W, or .45 ACP (disc. 2008) cal., 5 in. ramped bull barrel with expansion chamber, black glass filled nylon polymer grip with aluminum magwell, Dawson fiber optic front sight, adj. rear sight, blue finish with polished slide, 39 oz. Mfg. 2006-2009.

	$1,795	$1,525	$1,275	$1,050	$900	$825	$700	Last MSR was $1,985.

5.0 LEGEND – 9mm Para., .40 S&W, or .45 ACP cal., STi modular steel long wide frame, Tri-top forged slide with sabertooth cocking serrations and hard chrome with black inlay and polished sides, blue frame, black glass filled nylon polymer grips with hard chrome magwell, Dawson fiber optic front sights, adj. rear sight, 38 oz. New 2007.

MSR $2,670	$2,300	$1,950	$1,725	$1,450	$1,200	$1,000	$900

LEGACY MODEL – 45 ACP cal., 5 in. ramped STI bushing barrel, PVD finish, polished flat top black slide, rear cocking serrations, front strap checkering, custom cocobolo grips, ambidextrous thumb safety, ramped front sight, 36 oz. Mfg. 2006-2008.

	$1,750	$1,500	$1,250	$1,000	$900	$825	$700	Last MSR was $1,929.

5.0 (LSA) LAWMAN – .45 ACP cal., 1911 Govt. style, 5 in. barrel, hammer forged carbon steel frame, designed for

MSR	100%	98%	95%	90%	80%	70%	60%

IPSC, USPSA, and IDPA competition, 36 oz. New 2005.

| MSR $1,420 | $1,225 | $995 | $850 | $725 | $575 | $500 | $450 |

5.0 SENTINEL – 9mm Para., .40 S&W, or .45 ACP cal., 1911 Govt. forged frame, 5 in. barrel, flattop slide with rear cocking serrations, matte blue finish, front strap 30 LPI checkering, checkered steel D&T mainspring housing and flared magwell, STi competition front sights, adj. rear sight, thick rosewood grips, 38.3 oz. Mfg. 2007-2008.

| | $1,395 | $1,200 | $1,025 | $875 | $750 | $625 | $550 | Last MSR was $1,598. |

5.0 SENTINEL PREMIER – .45 ACP cal., 1911 Govt. forged frame, 5 in. barrel with bushing, polished slide with rear cocking serrations, hard chrome finish, front strap 30 LPI checkering, checkered steel D&T mainspring housing and flared magwell, tritium sights, 36.7 oz. New 2009.

| MSR $1,944 | $1,700 | $1,575 | $1,225 | $1,000 | $875 | $800 | $675 |

5.1 LIMITED – while advertised during 1998, this model never went into production.   Last MSR was $1,699.

5.5 EAGLE – various cals., features STi standard frame, 5 1/2 in. compensated barrel, 44 oz. Limited mfg. 1994-98.

| | $2,100 | $1,750 | $1,475 | $1,200 | $995 | $895 | $775 | Last MSR was $2,399. |

5.5 TRUBOR COMPETITOR (COMPETITOR) – 9mm Para. or .38 Super cal. only, standard frame, classic slide with front and rear serrations, square hammer, compensator, double stack mag., match sear, STi "Alchin" style blast deflector mount, TruBore compensator became standard 2005, C-More rail scope, wide ambidextrous and grip safeties, 41.3 oz. New 1999.

| MSR $2,864 | $2,475 | $2,050 | $1,750 | $1,450 | $1,200 | $995 | $875 |

5.5 GM – 9mm Para. or .38 Super cal., 5 in. TruBore bull barrel, hard chrome finish with blue color inlays, classic flattop slide, sabertooth cocking serrations, blue glass filled nylon polymer grips with stainless steel magwell, drilled and tapped, C-More gray scope, 44.6 oz. New 2009.

| MSR $3,655 | $3,350 | $3,000 | $2,700 | $2,250 | $1,800 | $1,400 | $1,175 |

5.5 GRANDMASTER – .38 Super cal. standard, custom order gun with any variety of options available, double stack mag., 42 oz. Mfg. 2001-2008.

| | $3,075 | $2,650 | $2,275 | $1,900 | $1,650 | $1,425 | $1,200 | Last MSR was $3,371. |

6.0 HUNTER – 10mm cal. only, 6 in. barrel, STi super extended heavy frame with single stack mag., blue finish, 51 oz. Only 2 mfg. 1998, disc. 2000.

| | $2,250 | $1,875 | $1,650 | $1,425 | $1,200 | $995 | $895 | Last MSR was $2,485. |

Add $350 for Leupold 2X scope with terminator mount.

6.0 EAGLE – various competition cals., features STi super extended heavy frame, 6 in. barrel, blue finish, wide body with staggered stack mag., 42 oz. New 1998.

| MSR $2,050 | $1,775 | $1,500 | $1,300 | $1,050 | $875 | $800 | $725 |

Add $267 for .38 Super with .45 ACP conversion kit (disc. 2008).

6.0 TROJAN – similar to 5.0 Trojan, except has 6 in. barrel and single stack mag., 36 oz. New 2000.

| MSR $1,420 | $1,225 | $995 | $850 | $725 | $575 | $500 | $450 |

Add $143 for .38 Super with .45 ACP conversion kit (disc. 2008).

6.0 PERFECT 10 – 10mm Norma cal., 6 in. bull barrel, blue finish with polished classic flattop slide, front and rear cocking serrations, ramped front and Heinie fixed rear sights, 6 inch integral tactical rail, black glass filled nylon polymer grips with aluminum magwell, 37 1/2 oz. New 2009.

| MSR $2,458 | $2,150 | $1,825 | $1,525 | $1,300 | $1,050 | $900 | $800 |

6.0 TARGETMASTER – 9mm Para. or .45 ACP cal., black frame, ramped bull barrel, two piece steel guide rod, 40 oz. New 2005.

| MSR $1,695 | $1,450 | $1,175 | $925 | $800 | $675 | $550 | $475 |

6.0 .450 XCALIBER – .450 cal., single stack mag., V-10 barrel and slide porting, stainless grip and thumb safeties, adj. rear sight. Limited mfg. 2000-2002.

| | $1,000 | $850 | $750 | $650 | $525 | $450 | $395 | Last MSR was $1,122. |

6.0 .450+ XCALIBER – .450+ cal., otherwise similar to 6.0 .450 Xcaliber, except has 6 in. frame with patented polymer grip and staggered stack mag. Limited mfg. 2000-2002.

| | $1,775 | $1,575 | $1,350 | $1,175 | $995 | $875 | $775 | Last MSR was $1,998. |

RIFLES/CARBINES: SEMI-AUTO

STI SPORTING/TACTICAL CARBINE – .223 Rem. cal., 16 in. stainless steel barrel, JP trigger group, gas block,

MSR	100%	98%	95%	90%	80%	70%	60%

Valkyrie handguard, tactical compensator, black Teflon coating, JP trigger group, fixed A2 or collapsible buttstock, optional rails, approx. 7 lbs. New 2010.

MSR $1,329	$1,200	$1,075	$925	$800	$675	$550	$475

S.W.D., INC.

Previous manufacturer located in Atlanta, GA.

Similar models have previously been manufactured by R.P.B. Industries, Inc. (1979-82), and met with BATF disapproval because of convertibility into fully automatic operation. "Cobray" is a trademark for the M11/9 semiautomatic pistol.

CARBINES

SEMI-AUTO CARBINE – 9mm Para. cal., same mechanism as M11, 16 1/4 in. shrouded barrel, telescoping stock.

	$550	$495	$450	$400	$325	$275	$235

PISTOLS: SEMI-AUTO

COBRAY M-11/NINE mm – 9mm Para. cal., fires from closed bolt, 3rd generation design, stamped steel frame, 32 shot mag., parkerized finish, similar in appearance to Ingram Mac 10.

	$475	$395	$350	$300	$295	$275	$250

This model was also available in a fully-auto variation, Class III transferable only.

REVOLVERS

LADIES HOME COMPANION – .45-70 Govt. cal., double action design utilizing spring wound 12 shot rotary mag., 12 in. barrel, steel barrel and frame, 9 lbs. 6 oz. Mfg. 1990-94.

	$650	$525	$400	$360	$335	$310	$290

SHOTGUNS: SINGLE SHOT

TERMINATOR – 12 or 20 ga., tactical design shotgun with 18 in. cylinder bore barrel, parkerized finish, ejector. Mfg. 1986-88 only.

	$150	$125	$95	$80	$70	$60	$55	Last MSR was $110.

SWS 2000

Current rifle manufacturer located in Krefeld, Germany. Previously imported until 2009 by Euro-Imports, located in Yoakum, TX.

RIFLES

SWS 2000 manufactures a variety of sporting and tactical style rifles in a variety of configurations. Prices range from €2,600-€3,759 for sporting and hunting models, and €6,162-€7,910 for tactical rifles. Please contact the company directly for more information, including U.S. availability (see Trademark Index).

SABRE

Current trademark of shotguns previously imported by Mitchell's Mausers, located in Fountain Valley, CA.

SHOTGUNS: SEMI-AUTO

SABRE – 12 ga. only, gas operated, 18 1/2 (w/o VR), 22, or 28 in. VR barrel with choke tubes, choice of black fiberglass or checkered walnut stock and forearm, configurations include Hunting, Turkey, Deer Hunter, and Police, mfg. in Turkey. Importation disc. 2007.

	$435	$375	$325	$275	$235	$210	$190	Last MSR was $495.

Add $50 for Police model.

SABRE DEFENCE INDUSTRIES LLC.

Current manufacturer established in 2002, with production headquarters located in Nashville, TN, and sales offices located in Middlesex, U.K. This company was previously known as Ramo, which was founded in 1977. Sabre Defence was also the U.S. distributor for Sphinx pistols until 2009.

CARBINES/RIFLES: SEMI-AUTO

Sabre Defence Industries manufactures many variations of the XR15 line of tactical design carbines and rifles for civilians, law enforcement, and military.

Please contact the U.S. office directly about options and availability (see Trademark Index).

MSR	100%	98%	95%	90%	80%	70%	60%

XR15A3 COMPETITION EXTREME – .223 Rem. cal., 16, 18, or 20 in. stainless steel fluted barrel, 30 shot mag., A3 upper and matched lower, black anodized finish, CTR six position retractable stock, free float handguard, Ergo grip, match trigger, flip up sights, mid-length barrel assembly, M4 feed ramp, includes two mags., cleaning kit, and tactical case.

MSR $2,189	$1,950	$1,700	$1,450	$1,275	$1,025	$850	$750

XR15A3 COMPETITION SPECIAL – .223 Rem. or 6.5 Grendel cal., 16 (.223 Rem. cal. only), 18, or 20 in. stainless steel fluted barrel, 30 shot mag., A3 upper and matched lower, black anodized finish, A2 fixed stock, tubular free float handguard, Ergo grip, match trigger, mid-length barrel assembly, M4 feed ramp, includes two mags., cleaning kit, and tactical case.

MSR $1,899	$1,700	$1,475	$1,250	$1,125	$895	$725	$575

Add $200 for 6.5 Grendel cal.

XR15A3 COMPETITION DELUXE – .223 Rem. or 6.5 Grendel cal., 16, 18, or 20 in. stainless or vanadium steel fluted barrel, 25 (6.5 Grendel cal.) or 30 shot mag., A3 upper and matched lower, black anodized finish, five position retractable stock, tactical handguard, Ergo grip, match trigger, flip up sights, competition Gill-brake, fluted mid-length barrel assembly, M4 feed ramp, includes two mags., cleaning kit, and tactical case.

MSR $2,299	$2,075	$1,815	$1,555	$1,415	$1,150	$950	$725

Add $200 for 6.5 Grendel cal.
Add $300 for piston system upgrade (Competition Deluxe Piston, new 2010).

XR15A3 SPR – .223 Rem. or 6.5 Grendel cal., 16, 18, or 20 in. stainless or vanadium steel fluted barrel, 25 (6.5 Grendel cal.) or 30 shot mag., A3 upper and matched lower, black anodized finish, five position retractable stock, tactical handguard, Ergo grip, match trigger, flip up sights, bipod, fluted mid-length barrel assembly, M4 feed ramp, includes two mags., cleaning kit, and tactical case, 8.7 lbs.

MSR $2,499	$2,250	$1,975	$1,695	$1,525	$1,225	$1,015	$785

Add $200 for 6.5 Grendel cal.

XR15A3 M4 FLAT TOP – .223 Rem., 6.5 Grendel, or 7.62x39mm (disc. 2009) cal., 16 in. vanadium contoured barrel, 25 (6.5 Grendel cal. only) or 30 shot mag., A3 upper and matched lower, M4 oval handguard, flip up sights, black anodized finish, A2 grip, single stage trigger, six position collapsible stock, M4 feed ramp, A2 flash hider, includes two mags., cleaning kit, and tactical case, 6.4 lbs.

MSR $1,507	$1,350	$1,150	$995	$875	$750	$650	$525

Add $70 for 7.62x39mm cal. (disc. 2009).
Add $34 for chrome lined barrel.
Add $193 for 6.5 Grendel cal.

XR15A3 M5 FLAT TOP – .223 Rem. or 6.5 Grendel cal., 16 in. vanadium contoured mid-length barrel, 25 (6.5 Grendel cal. only) or 30 shot mag., black anodized finish, A3 upper and matched lower, flip up sights, single stage trigger, six position collapsible stock, M4 feed ramp, A2 flash hider, mid-length handguard, Ergo grip, includes two mags., cleaning kit, and tactical case, 6 1/2 lbs.

MSR $1,504	$1,350	$1,150	$995	$875	$750	$650	$525

Add $195 for 6.5 Grendel cal.
Add $33 for chrome lined barrel.

XR15A3 M4 CARBINE – .223 Rem., 6.5 Grendel, or 7.62x39mm (disc. 2009) cal., 16 in. vanadium contoured alloy barrel, 25 (6.5 Grendel cal. only) or 30 shot mag., black anodized finish, A3 upper and matched lower, M4 oval handguard, forged front sight, no rear sight, A2 grip, single stage trigger, six position collapsible stock, M4 feed ramp, A2 flash hider, includes two mags., cleaning kit, and tactical case, 6.3 lbs.

MSR $1,344	$1,195	$1,050	$875	$775	$650	$550	$450

Add $100 for 7.62x39mm cal. (disc. 2009).
Add $33 for chrome lined barrel.
Add $205 for 6.5 Grendel cal.

XR15A3 PRECISION MARKSMAN RIFLE – .223 Rem. or 6.5 Grendel cal., 20 or 24 in. stainless steel barrel, 25 (6.5 Grendel cal.) or 30 shot mag., A3 upper and match lower, mid-length gas system, rail handguards, Ergo tactical deluxe grip with palm rest, match trigger, fluted mid-length barrel assembly, black anodized finish, M4 feed ramp, Magpul PRS adj. stock, includes Leupold 6.5-20x50 Mark IV scope (standard through 2009), two mags., cleaning kit and tactical case, approx. 10 lbs.

MSR $2,415	$2,200	$1,950	$1,700	$1,475	$1,225	$1,000	$800

Add $126 for 6.5 Grendel cal.
Add $1,185 for Leupold scope.

XR15A3 M4 TACTICAL – .223 Rem., 6.5 Grendel, or 7.62x39mm (disc. 2009) cal., 16 in. vanadium chrome lined contoured barrel, 25 (6.5 Grendel cal. only) or 30 shot mag., A3 upper and matched lower, multi-rail handguards, flip up sights, black anodized finish, Ergo grip, single stage trigger, six position collapsible stock, M4 feed ramp, A2 flash hider, tactical Gill-brake, includes two mags., cleaning kit, and tactical case, approx. 7 lbs.

MSR $1,993	$1,825	$1,625	$1,400	$1,225	$975	$800	$650

MSR	100%	98%	95%	90%	80%	70%	60%

Add $40 for 7.62x39mm cal. (disc. 2009).
Add $176 for 6.5 Grendel cal.

* **M4 Tactical Piston Carbine** – .223 Rem. cal., 16 in. chromemoly steel barrel, 30 shot mag., similar to M4 Tactical, except has mid-length gas piston system, 7 lbs. New 2010.

MSR $2,499	$2,250	$1,975	$1,695	$1,525	$1,225	$1,015	$785

XR15A3 M5 CARBINE – .223 Rem., 6.5 Grendel, or 7.62x39mm (disc. 2009) cal., 16 in. vanadium contoured barrel, 25 (6.5 Grendel cal. only) or 30 shot mag., A3 upper and matched lower, mid-length handguards, black anodized finish, forged front sight, Ergo grip, single stage trigger, six position collapsible stock, M4 feed ramp, A2 flash hider, includes two mags., cleaning kit, and tactical case, 6.4 lbs.

MSR $1,341	$1,195	$1,050	$875	$775	$650	$550	$450

Add $30 for 7.62x39mm cal. (disc. 2009).
Add $33 for chrome lined barrel.
Add $208 for 6.5 Grendel cal.

M5 TACTICAL CARBINE – .223 Rem. or 6.5 Grendel cal., 16 in. chromemoly chrome lined barrel, 25 or 30 shot mag., mid-length gas system, free float quadrail handguards, flip up front and rear sights, collapsible buttstock, single stage Mil Spec trigger, ergonomic pistol grip, trigger lock, sling, cleaning kit, and case, approx. 7 lbs. New 2009.

MSR $2,117	$1,925	$1,700	$1,475	$1,250	$1,025	$875	$725

Add $235 for 6.5 Grendel cal.

* **M5 Tactical Piston Carbine** – .223 Rem. cal., 16 in. chromemoly steel barrel, 30 shot mag., similar to M5 Tactical, except has mid-length gas piston system, 7.3 lbs. New 2010.

MSR $2,499	$2,250	$1,975	$1,695	$1,525	$1,225	$1,015	$785

XR15A3 A4 RIFLE – .223 Rem. cal., 20 in. vanadium govt. contour barrel, 30 shot mag., black anodized finish, A3 upper and matched lower, A2 round handguard, forged front sight, A2 grip, single stage trigger, fixed A2 stock, M4 feed ramp, A2 flash hider, includes two mags., approx. 7.2 lbs.

MSR $1,384	$1,215	$1,075	$895	$775	$650	$550	$450

Add $34 for chrome lined barrel.

XR15A3 A2 NATIONAL MATCH – .223 Rem. cal., 20 in. stainless steel matte finished H-Bar barrel, 30 shot mag., black anodized finish, A3 upper and matched lower, NM handguards, forged front sights, NM rear sight, A2 grip, two-stage trigger, fixed A2 stock, M4 feed ramp, A2 flash hider, includes two mags. Disc. 2009.

	$1,525	$1,335	$1,150	$1,050	$850	$695	$550	Last MSR was $1,699.

XR15A3 FLAT TOP CARBINE – .223 Rem. cal., 16 in. vanadium barrel, 30 shot mag., A3 upper and matched lower, black anodized finish, CAR round handguards, flip up sights, Ergo grip, single stage trigger, six position collapsible stock, M4 feed ramp, A2 flash hider, includes two mags. Disc. 2009.

	$1,200	$1,050	$895	$825	$675	$550	$425	Last MSR was $1,319.

Add $40 for chrome lined barrel.

XR15A3 HEAVY BENCH TARGET – .204 Ruger, .223 Rem., or 6.5 Grendel cal., 24 in. fluted match grade stainless steel heavy barrel, 4 (6.5 Grendel, disc. 2009), 10, or 25 (6.5 Grendel) shot mag., black anodized finish, A3 upper and matched lower, tubular free float handguards, flip up sights, Ergo grip, single stage adj. trigger, fixed A2 stock, sling swivel stud and bipod, includes two mags., cleaning kit, and tactical case, 9.3 lbs.

MSR $1,889	$1,700	$1,475	$1,275	$1,125	$900	$750	$600

Add $200 for 6.5 Grendel cal.

XR15A3 VARMINT – .223 Rem. cal., 20 in. fluted match grade stainless steel heavy barrel, 10 shot mag., A3 upper and matched lower, black anodized finish, tubular free float handguards, Ergo grip, match trigger, fixed A2 stock, sling swivel stud, includes two mags., cleaning kit, and tactical case. Disc. 2009.

	$1,550	$1,350	$1,175	$1,050	$850	$695	$550	Last MSR was $1,709.

LIGHT SABRE – .223 Rem. cal., 16 in. chromemoly barrel, 30 shot mag., mid-length gas system, M5 carbine upper, forged front sight, one piece polymer lower assembly, single stage Mil Spec trigger, 5.9 lbs. New 2009.

MSR $1,229	$1,100	$1,075	$925	$800	$675	$550	$425

SACO DEFENSE INC.

Previous firearms manufacturer located in Saco, ME. Saco Defense was purchased by General Dynamics in July of 2000, and continues to produce guns for military defense contracts. This company was previously owned by Colt's Manufacturing Company, Inc. during late 1998-2000.

In the past, Saco Defense utilized their high-tech manufacturing facility to produce guns for Magnum Research, Weatherby (contract ended Sept., 2001), and others.

MSR	100%	98%	95%	90%	80%	70%	60%

SAFARI ARMS

Previous trademark manufactured in Olympia, WA. M-S Safari Arms, located in Phoenix, AZ, was started in 1978 as a division of M-S Safari Outfitters. In 1987, Safari Arms was absorbed by Olympic Arms. Safari Arms manufactured 1911 style pistols since the acquisition of M-S Safari Arms in 1987. In Jan. 2004, the Safari Arms name was discontinued and all 1911 style pistols are now being manufactured by Olympic Arms. Please refer to the Olympic Arms section for currently manufactured models.

Safari Arms previously made the Phoenix, Special Forces, Camp Perry, and Royal Order of Jesters commemoratives in various configurations and quantities. Prices average in the $1,500 range except for the Royal Order of Jesters ($2,000).

SCHUETZEN PISTOL WORKS

Schuetzen Pistol Works is the current custom shop of Olympic Arms. Some of the pistols made by Safari Arms had the "Schuetzen Pistol Works" name on them (c. 1994-96). Until Jan. 2004, all pistols were are marked with the Safari Arms slide marking. All pistols, however, have been marked "Safari Arms" on the frame. The pistols formerly in this section have been moved to the PISTOLS: SEMI-AUTO category.

PISTOLS: SEMI-AUTO

Safari Arms manufactured mostly single action, semi-auto pistols derived from the Browning M1911 design with modifications. Please refer to Olympic Arms listing for currently manufactured pistols.

GI SAFARI – .45 ACP cal., patterned after the Colt Model 1911, Safari frame, beavertail grip safety and commander hammer, parkerized matte black finish, 39.9 oz. Mfg. 1991-2000.

	100%	98%	95%	90%	80%	70%	60%	
	$500	$455	$395	$350	$295	$275	$250	Last MSR was $550.

CARRYCOMP – similar to MatchMaster, except utilizes W. Schuemann designed hybrid compensator system, 5 in. barrel, available in stainless steel or steel, 38 oz. Mfg. 1993-99.

	100%	98%	95%	90%	80%	70%	60%	
	$1,030	$875	$750	$600	$500	$425	$375	Last MSR was $1,160.

* **CarryComp Enforcer** – similar to Enforcer, except utilizes W. Schuemann designed hybrid compensator system, available in stainless steel or steel, 36 oz. Mfg. 1993-96.

	100%	98%	95%	90%	80%	70%	60%	
	$1,175	$1,025	$875	$750	$600	$500	$425	Last MSR was $1,300.

CARRIER – .45 ACP cal. only, reproduction of the original Detonics ScoreMaster, except has upgraded sights, custom made by Richard Niemer from the Custom Shop. New 1999-2001.

	100%	98%	95%	90%	80%	70%	60%	
	$750	$625	$575	$500	$450	$400	$350	Last MSR was $750.

RENEGADE – .45 ACP cal., left-hand action (port on left side), 4 1/2 (4-star, disc. 1996) or 5 (new 1994) in. barrel, 6 shot mag., adj. sights, stainless steel construction, 36-39 oz. Mfg. 1993-98.

	100%	98%	95%	90%	80%	70%	60%	
	$955	$800	$700	$600	$525	$450	$395	Last MSR was $1,085.

Add $50 for 4-star (4 1/2 in. barrel, disc.).

RELIABLE – similar to Renegade, except has right-hand action. Mfg. 1993-98.

	100%	98%	95%	90%	80%	70%	60%	
	$730	$620	$525	$450	$425	$400	$375	Last MSR was $825.

Add $60 for 4-star (4 1/2 in. barrel, disc.).

GRIFFON PISTOL – .45 ACP cal., 5 in. stainless steel barrel, 10 shot mag., standard govt. size with beavertail grip safety, full-length recoil spring guide, commander style hammer, smooth walnut grips, 40 1/2 oz. Disc. 1998.

	100%	98%	95%	90%	80%	70%	60%	
	$855	$725	$650	$575	$500	$450	$395	Last MSR was $920.

BLACK WIDOW – .45 ACP cal., 3.9 in. barrel, hand contoured front gripstrap, schrimshawed ivory Micarta grips with Black Widow emblem, 6 shot mag., 27 oz. Inventory was depleted 1988.

	100%	98%	95%	90%	80%	70%	60%	
	$565	$510	$460	$430	$400	$375	$350	Last MSR was $595.

SAFETY HARBOR FIREARMS, INC.

Current manufacturer located in Safety Harbor, FL.

RIFLES: BOLT ACTION

SHF R50 – .50 BMG cal., 18, 22, or 29 in. barrel, side mounted 3 (disc. 2009) or 5 shot mag., black reinforced fixed tube stock with vent. recoil pad, partially shrouded barrel with muzzle brake, Picatinny rails, 17 1/2 lbs.

	100%	98%	95%	90%	80%	70%	60%
MSR $2,450	$2,450	$2,150	$1,825	$1,675	$1,350	$1,100	$850

SHF S50 – .50 BMG cal., single shot, 18, 22, or 29 in. barrel, similar stock and handguard as the SHF R50. New mid-2009.

	100%	98%	95%	90%	80%	70%	60%
MSR $1,950	$1,950	$1,700	$1,460	$1,325	$1,075	$875	$680

MSR	100%	98%	95%	90%	80%	70%	60%

SAIGA

Current trademark manufactured by Izhmash, located in Izhevsk, Russia. Currently imported by Russian American Armory Company, located in Scottsburg, IN. Previously imported by European American Armory Corp., located in Sharpes, FL.

RIFLES: SEMI-AUTO

For current pricing information and availability on Saiga semi-auto rifles, including the Saiga .223 Rem., Saiga 7.62mm, Saiga 100 Series, Saiga 9 and Saiga .308, please contact the importer directly.

SAIGA RIFLE – .223 Rem. or .308 Win. cal., Kalashnikov type action, black synthetic or hardwood (new 2003, only available in .308 Win. cal.) stock and forearm, 16.3-22 in. barrel length, matte black metal, 7-8 1/2 lbs. Imported 2002-2004, reintroduced 2006.

MSR N/A	$550	$495	$450	$400	$375	$350	$325

Add approx. 20% for .308 Win. cal.

* **Saiga Rifle 7.62x39mm Cal.** – 7.62x39mm cal., 16.3 or 20 1/2 in barrel, otherwise similar to Saiga Rifle. Imported 2002-2004, reintroduced 2006.

MSR N/A	$550	$495	$450	$400	$375	$350	$325

SAIGA 100 – .223 Rem., .30-06, .308 Win., or 7.62x39mm cal., hunting configuration with black synthetic stock, 3 or 10 shot mag., 22 in. barrel with open sights, 7.7 lbs. Importation began 2006.

MSR N/A	$650	$595	$550	$495	$450	$400	$350

Add 15% for .308 Win. cal.

SHOTGUNS: SEMI-AUTO

SAIGA SHOTGUN – 12 or 20 ga., 3 in. chamber, 5 shot detachable box mag., Kalashnikov type action, black synthetic stock and forearm, 19-22 in. barrel length, matte black metal, 6.7-7.8 lbs. Imported 2002-2004, reintroduced 2006.

MSR N/A	$475	$425	$375	$325	$295	$275	$250

Add 10% for choke tubes (12 ga. only).

* **Saiga Shotgun .410 Bore** – .410 bore, 19 or 21 in barrel, 4 shot detachable box mag., otherwise similar to Saiga Shotgun, approx. 6.6 lbs. Imported 2002-2004, reintroduced 2006.

MSR N/A	$375	$335	$300	$275	$250	$225	$200

SAKO, LTD.

Current rifle manufacturer established circa 1921 and located in Riihimäki, Finland. Current models are presently being imported by Beretta USA, located in Accokeek, MD. Previously imported by Stoeger Industries, Inc. located in Wayne, NJ, Garcia, and Rymac.

During 2000, Sako, Ltd. was purchased by Beretta Holding of Italy. All currently produced Sakos are imported by Beretta USA Corp. located in Accokeek, MD.

Beginning 2000, most Sako rifles (except the Action I in .223 Rem. cal.) are shipped with a Key Concept locking device. This patented system uses a separate key to activate an almost invisible lock which totally blocks the firing pin and prevents bolt movement.

RIFLES: BOLT ACTION, RECENT PRODUCTION

Beginning late 2001, Sako established a custom shop, which allows the consumer to select from a wide variety of finishes, options, and special orders, including individual stock dimensions. Please contact Beretta USA for more information regarding the Sako custom shop.

All Sako left-handed models are available in medium or long action only.

Some older model TRG rifles (Models TRG-S, TRG-22, and TRG-42) have experienced firing pin breakage. Ser. no. ranges on these U.S. distributed rifles are 202238 - 275255 and 973815 - 998594. Please contact Beretta USA directly (str@berettausa.com or 800-803-8869) for a replacement firing pin assembly if you have a rifle within these serial number ranges.

MODEL TRG-21 – .308 Win. cal., bolt action, 25 3/4 in. barrel, new design features modular synthetic stock construction with adj. cheekpiece and buttplate, stainless steel barrel, cold hammer forged receiver, and resistance free bolt, 10 shot detachable mag., 10 1/2 lbs. Imported 1993-99.

	$2,300	$2,000	$1,800	$1,600	$1,400	$1,200	$975	Last MSR was $2,699.

MODEL TRG-22 – .308 Win. cal., bolt action, 20 or 26 in. barrel, updated TRG-21 design featuring adj. modular synthetic stock (green, desert tan, or all black) construction with adj. cheekpiece and buttplate, competition trigger,

MSR	100%	98%	95%	90%	80%	70%	60%

choice of blue (disc. 2002) or phosphate (new 2002) metal finish, stainless steel barrel, cold hammer forged receiver, and resistance free bolt, 10 shot detachable mag., approx. 10 1/4 lbs. Importation began 2000.

MSR $2,850	$2,375	$1,950	$1,750	$1,500	$1,250	$1,000	$875

Add $2,975 for folding stock.
Add $505 for Picatinny rail (desert tan stock only).
Add $1,710 for folding stock in green finish.

MODEL TRG-41 – .338 Lapua Mag. cal., similar to Model TRG-21, except has long action and 27 1/8 in. barrel, 7 3/4 lbs. Imported 1994-99.

	$2,700	$2,425	$2,150	$1,850	$1,625	$1,400	$1,200	Last MSR was $3,099.

MODEL TRG-42 – .300 Win. Mag. (disc. 2008) or .338 Lapua Mag. cal., updated TRG-41 design featuring long action and 27 1/8 in. barrel, choice of black composite/blue finish, desert tan, or green composite/phosphate (new 2002) finish, 5 shot mag., 11 1/4 lbs. Importation began 2000.

MSR $3,500	$3,150	$2,775	$2,325	$1,925	$1,750	$1,500	$1,250

Add $3,250 for folding stock with Picatinny rail (desert tan stock only).
Add $775 for Picatinny rail (desert tan stock only).

MODEL TRG-S – available in medium action (disc. 1993) in .243 Win. or 7mm-08 cal., or long action in .25-06 Rem. (Mfg. 1994-98), .270 Win. (disc. 2000), 6.5x55mm Swedish (disc. 1998), .30-06 (disc.), .308 Win. (disc. 1995), .270 Wby. Mag. (disc. 1998), 7mm Wby. Mag. (Mfg. 1998), 7mm Rem. Mag. (disc.), .300 Win. Mag. (disc.), .300 Wby. Mag. (mfg. 1994-99), .30-378 Wby. Mag. (new 1998, 26 in. barrel only), .338 Win. Mag. (disc. 1999), .338 Lapua Mag. (new 1994), .340 Wby. Mag. (disc. 1998), 7mm STW (26 in. barrel only, disc. 1999), .375 H&H (disc. 1998), or .416 Rem. Mag. (disc. 1998) cal., black synthetic stock, Sporter variation derived from the Model TRG - 21, 22 (disc.), 24 (Mag. cals. only, disc.), or 26 in. barrel, 3 or 5 shot detachable mag., fully adj. trigger, 60 degree bolt lift, matte finish, 8 1/8 lbs. Imported 1993-2004.

	$775	$650	$525	$475	$440	$415	$380	Last MSR was $896.

SAMCO GLOBAL ARMS, INC.

Current importer and distributor located in Miami, FL. Dealer sales.

Samco Global Arms currently imports a variety of foreign and domestic surplus military rifles, including various contract Mausers, Loewe, Steyr, Czech, Lee Enfield, Mosin-Nagant, etc. Most of these guns offer excellent values to both shooters and collectors. Please contact the company directly for current availability and pricing, as its inventory changes weekly (see Trademark Index).

SAN SWISS ARMS AG

Current company established during late 2000, with headquarters located in Neuhausen, Switzerland.

In late 2000, SIG Arms AG, the firearms portion of SIG, was purchased by two Germans named Michael Lüke and Thomas Ortmeier, who have a background in textiles. Today the Lüke & Ortmeier group includes independently operational companies such as Blaser Jadgwaffen GmbH, Mauser Jagdwaffen GmbH, J.P. Sauer & Sohn GmbH, SIG-Sauer Inc., SIG-Sauer GmbH and SAN Swiss Arms AG. Please refer to individual listings.

SARCO, INC.

Current importer and wholesaler located in Stirling, NJ.

Sarco Inc. imports a wide variety of foreign and domestic surplus military style rifles and shotguns that offer excellent values for the shooter. Please contact the company directly, as inventory changes constantly (see Trademark Index).

SARSILMAZ

Current manufacturer established during 1880, and located in Istanbul, Turkey. Pistols currently imported by Armalite, Inc., located in Geneseo, IL. Previously distributed 2000-2003 by PMC, located in Boulder City, NV. Previously imported and distributed until 2000 by Armsport, Inc. located in Miami, FL.

PISTOLS: SEMI-AUTO

Sarsilmaz manufactures a wide variety of semi-auto pistols in many configurations. Current models include the K2, K10, K12, Kilinc 2000, B6, V8, CM9, P6, P8 Series, and the ST10. These models/series are not currently imported into the U.S. Please refer to the Armalite section for current importation.

Please contact Sarsilmaz directly for more information, including pricing on its line of non-imported semi-auto pistols (see Trademark Index).

SHOTGUNS

Sarsilmaz manufactures a variety of shotguns in O/U, semi-auto, and slide action configurations. Some of these models have

MSR	100%	98%	95%	90%	80%	70%	60%

been imported in the past in limited quantities. Currently, Sarsilmaz is manufacturing some models for Bernardelli. Please contact the factory directly for more information regarding U.S. availability and pricing (see Trademark Index).

SAUER, J.P., & SOHN

Current manufacturer located in Eckernförde, Germany since 1751 (originally Prussia). Currently imported by Blaser USA, located in San Antonio, TX. Previously manufactured in Suhl pre-WWII. Previously imported and warehoused 1995-2007 by SIG Arms, located in Exeter, NH. Rifles were previously imported until 1995 by the Paul Company Inc. located in Wellsville, KS and until 1994 by G.U., Inc. located in Omaha, NE.

In 1972, J.P. Sauer & Sohn entered into a cooperative agreement with SIG. During 2000, SAN Swiss Arms AG purchased SIG Arms AG, including the J.P. Sauer & Sohn trademark. Production remains in Eckernförde, Germany.

RIFLES: BOLT ACTION

SSE 3000 PRECISION RIFLE – .308 Win. cal., very accurate, law enforcement counter Sniper Rifle, built to customer specifications.

	$4,845	$3,655	$3,200	$2,850	$2,500	$2,275	$2,000

SSG 2000 – available in .223 Rem., 7.5mm Swiss, .300 Wby. Mag., or .308 Win. (standard) cal., bolt action, 4 shot mag., no sights, deluxe sniper rifle featuring thumbhole style walnut stock with stippling and thumbwheel adj. cheekpiece, 13 lbs. Importation disc. 1986.

	$2,480	$2,260	$1,950	$1,700	$1,500	$1,300	$1,100	Last MSR was $2,850.

This model was available in .223 Rem., .300 Wby. Mag., or 7.5mm cal. by special order only.

SSG 3000 – .223 Rem., 22 1/2 in. barrel, Parker-Hale bipod, 2-stage match trigger, includes 2 1/2-10x52mm Zeiss scope, 200 mfg. for Swiss police.

	$12,000	$10,000	$8,500	$7,000	$6,750	$5,500	$4,250

SAVAGE ARMS, INC.

Current manufacturer located in Westfield, MA since 1959, with sales offices located in Suffield, CT. Previously manufactured in Utica, NY - later manufacture was in Chicopee Falls, MA. Dealer and distributor sales.

This company originally started in Utica, NY in 1894. The Model 1895 was initially manufactured by Marlin between 1895-1899. The company was renamed Savage Arms Co. in 1899. After WWI, the name was again changed to the Savage Arms Corporation. Savage moved to Chicopee Falls, MA circa 1946 (to its Stevens Arms Co. plants). In the mid-1960s the company became The Savage Arms Division of American Hardware Corp., which later became The Emhart Corporation. This division was sold in September 1981, and became Savage Industries, Inc. located in Westfield, MA (since the move in 1960). On November 1, 1989, Savage Arms Inc. acquired the majority of assets of Savage Industries, Inc.

Savage Arms, Inc. will offer service and parts on their current line of firearms only (those manufactured after Nov. 1, 1995). These models include the 24, 99, and 110 plus the imported Model 312. Warranty and repair claims for products not acquired by Savage Arms, Inc. will remain the responsibility of Savage Industries, Inc. For information regarding the repair and/or parts of Savage Industries, Inc. firearms, please refer to the Trademark Index in the back of this text. Parts for pre-1989 Savage Industries, Inc. firearms may be obtained by contacting the Gun Parts Corporation located in West Hurley, NY (listed in Trademark Index). Savage Arms, Inc. has older records/info. on pistols, the Model 24, older mfg. Model 99s, and Model 110 only. A factory letter authenticating the configuration of a particular specimen may be obtained by contacting Mr. John Callahan (see Trademark Index for listings and address). The charge for this service is $30.00 per gun, and $25.00 per gun for Models 1895, 1899, and 99 rifles. Please allow 6 weeks for an adequate response.

For more Savage model information, please refer to the Serialization section in the back of this text.

Please refer to the *Blue Book of Modern Black Powder Arms* by John Allen (also online) for more information and prices on Savage's lineup of modern black powder models. For more information and current pricing on both new and used Savage airguns, please refer to the *Blue Book of Airguns* by Dr. Robert Beeman & John Allen (also online).

Black Powder Long Arms and Pistols - Reproductions & Replicas by Dennis Adler is also an invaluable source for most black powder reproductions and replicas, and includes hundreds of color images on most popular makes/models, provides manufacturer/trademark histories, and up-to-date information on related items/accessories for black powder shooting - www.bluebookinc.com

COMBINATION GUNS

All Model 24s are under the domain of Savage Arms, Inc.

Add 20% for .22 Mag. cal. on models listed below, where applicable.

MODEL 24F (PREDATOR) – choice of .17 HMR (new 2004), .22 Hornet, .222 Rem. (disc. 1989), .223 Rem., or .30-30 Win. (12 ga. only) cal., over 12, 20 ga., or .410 bore (mfg. 1998-2000), 3 in. chamber, 24 in. barrels, 12 ga. barrel is available either with fixed choke or choke tube, wood (disc.) or matte black Dupont Rynite synthetic stock,

MSR	100%	98%	95%	90%	80%	70%	60%

hammer block safety, DTs, approx. 8 lbs. Mfg. 1989-2007.

| | $585 | $450 | $345 | $290 | $235 | $200 | $180 | Last MSR was $698. |

Add $31 for 12 ga.
Add $55 for .410 bore adaptor (12 ga. only, disc. 2000).
Add $14 for Camo Rynite stock (disc., Model 24F-T, Turkey Model-12 ga./.22 Hornet or .223 Rem. cal. only).

MODEL 24V – similar to Model 24, in .22 Hornet (disc. 1984), .222 Rem. (new 1967), .223 Rem., .30-30 Win., .357 Max., or .357 Mag.(disc.), 20 ga., 3 in. chamber, 24 in. barrels, single trigger, 7 lbs. Mfg. 1967-1989.

| | $495 | $425 | $375 | $325 | $275 | $250 | $225 |

Action was changed to under lever opening in front of trigger guard circa 1980.

MODEL 24 VS – similar to Model 24CS, only .357 Mag. over 20 ga., nickel finish, accessory pistol grip stock is included.

| | $595 | $550 | $475 | $400 | $350 | $275 | $225 |

MODEL 2400 O/U – 12 ga. full choke barrel over .222 Rem. or .308 Win. rifle barrel, 23 1/2 in. barrels, folding leaf sight, solid rib, dovetailed for scope mount, checkered Monte Carlo stock. Mfg. by Valmet 1975-1980.

| | $695 | $625 | $575 | $525 | $495 | $440 | $415 |

MODEL 389 – 12 ga. with 3 in. chamber over choice of .308 Win. or .222 Rem., choke tubes standard, hammerless, double triggers, checkered walnut stock and forearm with recoil pad. Mfg. 1988-90 only.

| | $850 | $775 | $675 | $550 | $450 | $375 | $325 | Last MSR was $919. |

RIFLES: CENTERFIRE, CURRENT/RECENT PRODUCTION

The 110 Series was first produced in 1958. Beginning in 1992, Savage Arms, Inc. began supplying this model with a master trigger lock, earmuffs, shooting glasses (disc. 1992), and test target.

Beginning 1994, all Savage rifles employ a laser etched bolt featuring the Savage logo. During 1996, Savage began using pillar bedded stocks for many of their rifles.

Recent Savage nomenclature usually involves alphabetical suffixes which mean the following: B - laminated wood stock, BT - laminated thumbhole stock, C - detachable box mag., F - composite/synthetic stock, G - hardwood stock, H - hinged floorplate, K - AccuStock or standard muzzle brake, AK - adj. muzzle brake with fluted barrel, L - left-hand, LE - Law Enforcement, NS - no sights, P - police (tactical) rifle, SB - smooth bore, SE - safari express, SS - stainless steel, SS-S - stainless steel single shot, T - Target (aperture rear sight), U - high luster blue, blue metal finish and/or stock finish, V - Long Range (Varmint w/ heavy barrel), XP - package gun (scope, sling, and rings/base), Y - Youth/Ladies Model. A 2 digit model number (10) designates new short action. A 3 digit model number (110) indicates long action.

Hence, the Model 111FCNS designates a 111 Series firearm with synthetic stock, detachable magazine, and no sights. Likewise, a Model 11FYCXP3 indicates a Model 11 Series with synthetic stock, youth dimensions, detachable magazine, is a packaged gun which includes scope. The Model 116FHSAK indicates a long action rifle with hinged floorplate, synthetic stock, stainless steel action/barrel with adj. muzzlebrake.

During 2003, Savage released its new patented AccuTrigger, which allows the consumer to adjust the trigger pull from the outside of the rifle from 1 1/2 lbs. - 6 lbs. using a proprietary tool. The AccuTrigger also has almost no trigger creep and is infinitely adjustable. Initially, it was released in all Varmint, LE, and heavy barrel long range rifles, and during 2004, the AccuTrigger became standard on nearly all Savage centerfire rifles, except the Model 11 and 11FCXP3 and 10/110G Package guns. During 2007, Savage began offering target actions with AccuTrigger, right bolt, and choice of left or right port ejection with .223 Rem. bolt head - MSR is $560-$595.

During 2008, Savage Arms introduced a new personal anti-recoil device (P.A.D.), which is installed in many Savage bolt action centerfire rifles. The P.A.D. reduces recoil by 45% from OEM solid and vented pads.

During 2009, Savage introduced varmint short actions, along with both long and short sporter actions. Sporter actions have a current MSR of $481, while the varmint short actions' MSR is $505. A dual port receiver, allowing left loading and right ejection was also released in 2009 - MSR is $595.

Whenever possible, the models within this category have been listed in numerical sequence.

Subtract approx. 10% on models listed below w/o AccuTrigger (became standard on all centerfire rifles in 2004).

MODEL 10 LAW ENFORCEMENT SERIES – .223 Rem., .260 Rem. (mfg. 1999-2001), .308 Win., or 7mm-08 (mfg. 1999-2001) cal., short action, tactical/law enforcement model, checkered black synthetic stock, features 20 (new 2006) or 24 in. heavy barrel w/o sights, AccuTrigger became standard 2003, 8 lbs. Mfg. 1998-2007.

| | $505 | $395 | $320 | $275 | $230 | $190 | $165 | Last MSR was $621. |

* **Model 10FP** – .223 Rem. or .308 Win. cal., short action, 20 or 24 in. heavy free floating and button rifled barrel, 4 shot box mag., black McMillan synthetic sporter style stock, drilled and tapped, swivel stud, oversized bolt handle,

MSR	100%	98%	95%	90%	80%	70%	60%

6 1/4 or 7 1/4 lbs. New 1998.

MSR $740	$595	$465	$365	$310	$250	$200	$165

This model is also available in left-hand action (Model 10FLP, 24 in. barrel only, disc. 2009).

* ***Model10FP Duty*** – similar to Model 10FP, except has open iron sights. Mfg. 2002 only.

	$435	$355	$290	$250	$215	$180	$165	Last MSR was $525.

* ***Model10FP 20 In. (LE1/LE1A)*** – .223 Rem. (LE1A only, disc. 2007) or .308 Win. cal., similar to Model 10FP, except has 20 in. heavy barrel with no sights, choice of standard (LE1, disc. 2005) or Choate (LE1A) stock (folding only, new 2006). New 2002.

MSR $1,034	$865	$695	$565	$475	$425	$350	$300

Subtract 20% for standard stock (LE1).

* ***Model10FP 26 In. (LE2/LE2A)*** – .223 (LE2A only) or .308 Win. cal., similar to Model 10FP-LE1/LE1A, except has 26 in. heavy barrel and choice of standard (LE2, disc. 2005) or Choate stock (LE2A). Mfg. 2002-2006.

	$625	$500	$400	$360	$330	$300	$275	Last MSR was $754.

Subtract 20% for standard stock.

* ***Model10FP McMillan (LE2B)*** – .308 Win. cal., short action, features McMillan tactical fiberglass stock with stippled grip areas, 4 shot mag., 26 in. heavy barrel. Mfg. 2003-2006.

	$860	$725	$625	$525	$425	$325	$265	Last MSR was $1,033.

* ***Model 10FP H-S Precision*** – .308 Win. cal., 24 in. barrel, features H-S Precision stock. Mfg. 2006 only.

	$720	$585	$475	$425	$350	$300	$275	Last MSR was $864.

* ***Model 10FPCPXP/10FPXP (LE/LEA)*** – .308 Win. cal. only, short action, features skeletonized synthetic stock, 24 (new 2006) or 26 (disc. 2005) in. barrel w/o sights, H-S Precision stock became standard 2006, LEA has Choate stock, LE has standard stock (disc. 2005), includes Burris (disc.) or Leupold (new 2004) 3.5-10x50mm scope with flip covers and sling, 4 shot internal (FPXP, disc. 2006) or detachable (FPCPXP, new 2007) mag., Harris bipod, aluminum case, 10 1/2 lbs. Mfg. 2002-2009.

	$2,275	$1,850	$1,550	$1,300	$1,100	$900	$750	Last MSR was $2,715.

Subtract 20% LE standard stock or 10% for Choate stock (Model 10FPXP-LEA package).

* ***Model 10FCP H-S Precision*** – .308 Win. cal., 24 in. barrel, features H-S Precision stock, detachable box mag. New 2007.

MSR $1,124	$995	$850	$750	$650	$550	$450	$350

* ***Model 10FCP Choate*** – .308 Win. cal., 24 in. barrel, features Choate stock, detachable box mag. Mfg. 2007 only.

	$700	$575	$475	$425	$350	$300	$275	Last MSR was $833.

* ***Model 10FCP McMillan*** – .308 Win. cal., 24 in. barrel, features McMillan stock, detachable box mag. New 2007.

MSR $1,360	$1,175	$925	$795	$650	$550	$450	$350

* ***Model 10 FCP-K AccuStock*** – .223 Rem. or .308 Win. cal., short action, 24 in. heavy blue barrel with muzzle brake, 4 shot detachable box mag., drilled and tapped, black synthetic AccuStock with aluminum spine and 3-D bedding cradle, swivel stud for bipod, oversized bolt handle, 8.9 lbs. New 2009.

MSR $893	$750	$625	$525	$425	$375	$350	$300

This model is also available in left-hand action at no extra charge (Model 10 FLCP-K).

MODEL 10 PRECISION CARBINE – .223 Rem. or .308 Win. cal., 20 in. matte blue free floating button rifled barrel, 4 shot detachable box mag., swivel stud, oversized bolt handle, green camo Accustock with aluminum spine and 3-D bedding cradle, 7 lbs. New 2009.

MSR $854	$715	$565	$460	$375	$325	$275	$250

MODEL 10BAS-K – .308 Win. cal., 24 in. barrel with muzzle brake, short action, 10 shot detachable box mag., black synthetic telescoping stock with handguard, bipod, Picatinny rail, oversize bolt handle. New 2009.

MSR $1,907	$1,625	$1,400	$1,100	$925	$800	$700	$600

* ***Model 10BAT/S-K*** – .308 Win. cal., 24 in. barrel with muzzle brake, short action, 10 shot detachable box mag., similar to Model 10BAS-K, except has tactical stock with adj. buttpad. New 2009.

MSR $2,071	$1,750	$1,450	$1,125	$925	$800	$700	$600

MODEL 110-FP LAW ENFORCEMENT (TACTICAL POLICE) – .223 Rem. (disc. 1998), .25-06 Rem. (new 1995),

MSR	100%	98%	95%	90%	80%	70%	60%

.300 Win. Mag. (new 1995), .30-06 (mfg. 1996-2006), .308 Win. (disc. 1998), or 7mm Rem. Mag. (mfg. 1995-2007) cal., long action, 24 in. heavy barrel pillar bedded tactical rifle, all metal parts are non-reflective, 4 shot internal mag., black Dupont Rynite stock, right- or left-hand (new 1996) action, drilled and tapped for scope mounts, AccuTrigger became standard 2003, 8 1/2 lbs. Mfg. 1990-2001, reintroduced 2003-2008.

| | $575 | $465 | $360 | $310 | $265 | $240 | $210 | Last MSR was $678. |

Also available in left-hand action at no additional charge (mfg. 1996-2001, Model 110-FLP).

* **Model 110FCP** – .25-06 Rem. or .300 Win. Mag. cal., 24 in. heavy barrel with Savage muzzlebrake, 4 shot detachable box mag., black synthetic AccuStock with aluminum spine and 3-D bedding cradle, drilled and tapped, swivel stud for bipod, oversized bolt handle, 9 lbs. Mfg. 2009.

| | $725 | $600 | $500 | $425 | $375 | $350 | $300 | Last MSR was $866. |

MODEL 110BAS – .300 Win. Mag. or .338 Lapua cal., 26 in. fluted carbon steel barrel, 5 or 6 shot detachable box mag., drilled and tapped, open sights, includes Picatinny top rail, muzzle brake, matte black aluminum tactical AccuStock with handguard, AccuTrigger, 15 3/4 lbs. New 2010.

| MSR $2,267 | $1,895 | $1,750 | $1,525 | $1,300 | $1,100 | $900 | $725 | |

SCATTERGUN TECHNOLOGIES INC. (S.G.T.)

Current manufacturer located in Berryville, AR since 1999. Previously located in Nashville, TN 1991-1999. Distributor, dealer, and consumer sales.

During 1999, Wilson Combat purchased Scattergun Technologies. S.G.T. manufactures practical defense, tactical, and hunting shotguns in 12 ga. only, utilizing Remington Models 870 and 11-87 (disc.) actions in various configurations as listed. All shotguns feature 3 in. chamber capacity and parkerized finish.

SHOTGUNS: SEMI-AUTO

Add $15 for short stock on models listed.
Add $125 for Armor-Tuff finish on models listed.

K-9 MODEL – 12 ga., 18 in. barrel, adj. ghost ring sight, 7 shot mag., side saddle, synthetic buttstock and forearm. Disc. 2003.

| | $1,100 | $875 | $775 | $665 | $560 | $465 | $410 | Last MSR was $1,325. |

SWAT MODEL – 12 ga., similar to K-9 Model, except has 14 in. barrel and forearm with 11,000 CP flashlight. Disc. 2003.

| | $1,400 | $1,150 | $895 | $785 | $655 | $550 | $465 | Last MSR was $1,750. |

This model was available for military and law enforcement only.

URBAN SNIPER MODEL – 12 ga., 18 in. rifled barrel, scout optics, 7 shot mag., side saddle, synthetic buttstock, forearm and bipod. Disc. 1999.

| | $1,225 | $1,075 | $950 | $835 | $685 | $585 | $485 | Last MSR was $1,390. |

SHOTGUNS: SLIDE ACTION

On the following models, Armor-Tuff finish became standard during 2003.

Add $15 for short stock on models listed.
Subtract approx. $100 if w/o Armor Tuff finish.

STANDARD MODEL – 12 or 20 ga., 18 in. barrel, adj. ghost ring sight, 7 shot mag., side saddle, synthetic buttstock and forearm with 11,000 CP flashlight.

| MSR $1,325 | $1,100 | $975 | $875 | $650 | $550 | $450 | $400 | |

PROFESSIONAL MODEL – 12 ga., similar to Standard Model, except has 14 in. barrel and 6 shot mag.

This model is available for military and law enforcement only.

EXPERT MODEL – 12 ga., 18 in. barrel with mod. choke, nickel/Teflon finished receiver, adj. ghost ring sight, forearm incorporates 11,000 CP flashlight. Mfg. 1997-2000.

| | $1,200 | $995 | $775 | $665 | $560 | $465 | $410 | Last MSR was $1,350. |

ENTRY MODEL – 12 ga., 12 1/2 in. barrel with mod. choke, adj. ghost ring sights, 5 shot mag., side saddle, synthetic buttstock with 5,000 CP flashlight and nylon loop strap. Disc.

| | $995 | $800 | $600 | $495 | $430 | $365 | $315 | Last MSR was $1,125. |

This model was available for military and law enforcement only.

COMPACT MODEL – 12 1/2 in. barrel with mod. choke, adj. ghost ring sight, 5 shot mag., synthetic buttstock and forearm. Mfg. 1994-99.

| | $575 | $510 | $420 | $360 | $315 | $260 | $225 | Last MSR was $635. |

This model was available for military and law enforcement only.

MSR	100%	98%	95%	90%	80%	70%	60%

PRACTICAL TURKEY MODEL – 20 in. barrel with extra full choke, adj. ghost ring sight, 5 shot mag. for 3 in. shells, synthetic buttstock and forearm. Mfg. 1995-99.

| | $545 | $500 | $465 | $405 | $350 | $290 | $250 | Last MSR was $595. |

LOUIS AWERBUCK SIGNATURE MODEL – 18 in. barrel with fixed choke, adj. ghost ring sight, 5 shot mag., side saddle, wood buttstock with recoil reducer and forearm. Mfg. 1994-99.

| | $625 | $490 | $385 | $325 | $275 | $230 | $200 | Last MSR was $705. |

F.B.I. MODEL – similar to Standard Model, except has 5 shot mag. Disc. 1999.

| | $715 | $625 | $490 | $420 | $370 | $305 | $265 | Last MSR was $770. |

MILITARY MODEL – 18 in. barrel with vent. handguard and M-9 bayonet lug, adj. ghost ring rear sight, 7 shot mag., synthetic stock and grooved corncob forearm. Mfg. 1997-98.

| | $625 | $490 | $385 | $325 | $275 | $230 | $200 | Last MSR was $690. |

PATROL MODEL – 18 in. barrel, adj. ghost ring sight, 5 shot mag., synthetic buttstock and forearm. Disc. 1999.

| | $545 | $500 | $465 | $405 | $350 | $290 | $250 | Last MSR was $595. |

BORDER PATROL MODEL 20 – 12 or 20 ga., similar to Patrol Model, except has 7 shot mag., black synthetic stock and forearm, choice of 18 or 20 in. barrel.

| MSR $1,050 | $925 | $850 | $750 | $650 | $550 | $460 | $395 | |

Add $35 for 20 ga.

BORDER PATROL MODEL 21 – similar to Border Patrol Model 20, except has 14 in. barrel and 6 shot mag.

| MSR $1,075 | $950 | $875 | $775 | $675 | $550 | $460 | $395 | |

This model is available for military and law enforcement only.

CONCEALMENT MODEL 00 – 12 1/2 in. barrel with fixed choke, 5 shot mag., bead sight, grooved wood forearm and pistol grip. Disc. 1998.

| | $490 | $395 | $280 | $230 | $200 | $170 | $145 | Last MSR was $550. |

This model was available for military and law enforcement only.

CONCEALMENT MODEL 01 – similar to Concealment Model 00, except has synthetic finger-grooved combat forearm and pistol grip. Disc. 1993.

| | $475 | $395 | $295 | $235 | $205 | $175 | $150 | Last MSR was $525. |

This model was available for military and law enforcement only.

CONCEALMENT MODEL 02 – similar to Concealment Model 00, except has Pachmayr forearm and pistol grip. Disc. 1993.

| | $495 | $415 | $315 | $255 | $225 | $190 | $165 | Last MSR was $555. |

This model was available for military and law enforcement only.

CONCEALMENT MODEL 03 – similar to Concealment Model 01, except has synthetic nylon strap assisted forearm with 5,000 CP flashlight. Disc. 1993.

| | $550 | $455 | $350 | $285 | $250 | $215 | $185 | Last MSR was $625. |

This model was available for military and law enforcement only.

BREACHING MODEL – similar to Concealment Model 00, except has standoff device. Disc. 1998.

| | $450 | $390 | $340 | $275 | $240 | $200 | $175 | Last MSR was $500. |

This model was available for military and law enforcement only.

SCHUETZEN PISTOL WORKS

Schuetzen Pistol Works is the in-house custom shop of Olympic Arms. Schuetzen Pistol Works has been customizing Safari Arms and Olympic Arms 1911 style pistols since 1997. For currently manufactured pistols, please refer to the Olympic Arms listing. For discontinued models, please refer to the Safari Arms listing.

SCHWABEN ARMS GMBH

Current manufacturer located in Rottweil, Germany.

Schwaben Arms GmbH manufactures 600-800 guns annually. Production includes an extensive lineup of quality tactical rifles and carbines, primarily patterned after H&K models and other historically significant military rifles/carbines, including a .308 Win. cal. semi-auto MP5. Both commercial and military/law enforcement models are available. Please contact the factory directly for U.S. availability and pricing (see Trademark Index).

MSR	100%	98%	95%	90%	80%	70%	60%

SERBU FIREARMS, INC.

Current manufacturer located in Tampa, FL.

RIFLES: BOLT ACTION

BFG-50 RIFLE/CARBINE – .50 BMG cal., single shot bolt action, 22 (carbine) or 29 (rifle) in. match grade barrel with muzzle brake, AR-15 style trigger and safety, Picatinny rail, parkerized finish, 17-22 lbs.

MSR $2,195	$2,195	$1,850	$1,650	$1,450	$1,250	$1,175	$975

Add $25 for "Have a Nice Day" engraving on Shark muzzle brake.
Add $120 for bi-pod.

BFG-50A – .50 BMG cal., gas operated, 26 in. barrel with 8 port Shark Brake muzzle brake, 10 shot mag., 3-lug bolt, sliding plate extrator, dual plunger ejectors, removeable barrel extension and handguard. New 2008.

MSR $6,700	$6,250	$5,500	$4,950	$4,000	$3,650	$3,350	$2,995

SHOOTERS ARMS MANUFACTURING INCORPORATED

Current manufacturer established in 1992, and located in Cebu, the Philippines. Currently imported by Century International Arms, located in Delray Beach, FL. Previously imported by Pacific Arms Corp. in Modesto, CA.

Shooter Arms Manufacturing Inc. makes semi-auto pistols, including the Elite, Commodore, Military, GI, Desert Storm, Seahawk, 1911A1, Eagle, Hawk, and the Trojan. Previous models have included the React, React-2, Military Enhanced, GI Enhanced, Elite Sport, Chief, Scout, Falcon, Raven, Omega, and Alpha. Shooters Arms Manufacuring Inc. also manufactures a revolver, the Protector, and a 12 ga. shotgun called the SAS 12. Please contact the importer directly for more information, including pricing and U.S. availability (see Trademark Index).

SIDEWINDER

Previous trademark manufactured by D-Max, Inc. located in Bagley, MN circa 1993-96. Dealer or consumer sales.

REVOLVERS

SIDEWINDER – .45 LC or 2 1/2/3 in. .410 bore shotshells/slugs, 6 shot, stainless steel construction, 6 1/2 or 7 1/2 in. bull barrel (muzzle end bored for removable choke), Pachmayr grips, transfer bar safety, adj. rear sight, unique design permits one cylinder to shoot above listed loads, cased with choke tube, 3.8 lbs. Mfg. 1993-1996.

	$695	$575	$475	$415	$360	$300	$255	Last MSR was $775.

SIG ARMS AG

Current Swiss company (SIG) established during 1860 in Neuhausen, Switzerland. P 210 pistols are currently imported and distributed by Sig Sauer (formerly SIG Arms, Inc.), established in 1985, located in Exeter, NH. Previously located in Herndon, VA and Tysons Corner, VA.

In late 2000, SIG Arms AG, the firearms portion of SIG, was purchased by two Germans named Michael Lüke and Thomas Ortmeier, who have a background in textiles. Today the Lüke & Ortmeier group includes independently operational companies such as Blaser Jadgwaffen GmbH, Mauser Jagdwaffen GmbH, J.P. Sauer & Sohn GmbH, SIG-Sauer Inc., SIG-Sauer GmbH and SAN Swiss Arms AG. Please refer to individual listings.

PISTOLS: SEMI-AUTO

SIG Custom Shop variations of the P 210 were also available in three configurations - United We Stand ($8,990 last MSR) and two variations of the 50 Year Jubilee ($4,995 or $5,999 last MSR).

Add $1,473 for .22 LR conversion kit on the following models (not available on the P 210-8).

P 210 – 9mm Para. or 7.65mm Para. (disc.) cal., single action, 4 3/4 in. barrel, 8 shot mag., standard weapon of the Swiss Army, 2 lbs.

Originally mfg. in 1947, this pistol was first designated the SP 47/8 and became the standard military pistol of the Swiss Army in 1949. Later designated the P 210, this handgun has been mfg. continuously for over 55 years.

* **P 210 Danish Army M49** – Danish Army version of the Model P 210, approx. 25,000 mfg.

	$2,750	$2,200	$1,750	$1,500	$1,350	$1,100	$1,000

* **P 210-1** – polished finish, walnut grips, special hammer, fixed sights. Importation disc. 1986.

	$2,500	$2,000	$1,500	$1,250	$1,000	$900	$750	Last MSR was $1,861.

* **P 210-2** – matte finish, field or combat (recent mfg.) sights, plastic (disc.) or wood grips. Limited importation 1987-2002.

	$1,675	$1,375	$1,050	$900	$750	$625	$550	Last MSR $1,680.

Add 20% for high polish Swiss Army pistols with "A" prefix.

MSR	100%	98%	95%	90%	80%	70%	60%

Add 20% for West German Police Contract models with unique loaded chamber indicator on slide. Approx. 5,000 mfg. in "D" prefix serial range.

* **P 210-5** – matte finish, heavy frame, micrometer target sights, 150mm or 180mm (disc.) extended barrel, hard rubber (disc.) or wood (current mfg.) grips, bottom (EU) or push-button side mounted (U.S.) mag. release, very limited mfg. Limited importation 1997-2007.

	$2,250	$2,150	$1,675	$1,350	$1,125	$1,000	$895

Add $124 for side mounted mag. release.

* **P 210-6** – matte blue finish, fixed (current importation) or micrometer sights, 120mm barrel, checkered walnut grips, bottom (EU) or push-button side mounted (U.S.) mag. release.

	$1,850	$1,700	$1,500	$1,300	$1,125	$1,000	$895

* **P 210-7** – .22 LR or 9mm Para. cal., regular or target long barrel, limited importation. Disc.

	$3,500	$3,000	$2,700	$2,350	$2,000	$1,750	$1,500

* **P 210-8** – features heavy frame, target sights, and wood grips. Special order only. Limited importation 2001-2003.

	$3,750	$3,250	$2,650	$2,300	$1,950	$1,600	$1,275	Last MSR was $4,289.

RIFLES: BOLT ACTION

SHR 970 – .25-06 Rem., .270 Win., .280 Rem., .30-06, .308 Win., .300 Win. Mag., or 7mm Rem. Mag. cal., steel receiver, standard model featuring easy take-down (requires single tool) and quick change 22 or 24 (Mag. cals. only) in. barrel, detachable 3 or 4 shot mag., 65 degree short throw bolt, 3 position safety, standard medium gloss walnut stock with checkering, ultra-fast lock time, nitrided bore, no sights, includes hard carry case, approx. 7.3 lbs. Mfg. 1998-2002.

	$475	$395	$350	$325	$295	$275	$250	Last MSR was $550.

Add $395 for extra barrel.

* **SHR 970 Synthetic** – similar to SHR 970, except has checkered black synthetic stock with stippled grip. Mfg. 1999-2002.

	$445	$375	$325	$295	$275	$250	$230	Last MSR was $499.

STR 970 LONG RANGE – .308 Win. or .300 Win. Mag. cal., inlcudes stippled black McMillan composite stock with precision bedding blocks, 24 in. fluted heavy barrel with integral muzzle brake and non-reflective Ilaflon metal coating, cased, 11.6 lbs. Mfg. 2000-2002.

	$875	$795	$675	$575	$525	$475	$425	Last MSR was $899.

RIFLES: SEMI-AUTO

PE-57 – 7.5 Swiss cal. only, semi-auto version of the Swiss military rifle, 24 in. barrel, includes 24 shot mag., leather sling, bipod and maintenance kit. Importation disc. 1988.

	$6,500	$5,500	$4,500	$4,000	$3,500	$3,000	$2,500	Last MSR was $1,745.

The PE-57 was previously distributed in limited quantities by Osborne's located in Cheboygan, MI.

SIG-AMT RIFLE – .308 Win. cal., semi-auto version of SG510-4 auto tactical design rifle, roller delayed blowback action, 5, 10, or 20 shot mag., 18 3/4 in. barrel, wood stock, folding bipod. Mfg. 1960-1988.

	$4,750	$4,250	$3,750	$3,250	$2,750	$2,250	$1,750	Last MSR was $1,795.

SG 550/551 – .223 Rem. cal. with heavier bullet, Swiss Army's semi-auto version of newest tactical design rifle (SIG 90), 20.8 (SG 550) or 16 in. (SG 551 Carbine) barrel, some synthetics used to save weight, 20 shot mag., diopter night sights, built-in folding bipod, 7.7 or 9 lbs.

	100%	98%	95%	90%	80%	70%	60%	
Sig 550 (Rifle)	$8,500	$7,750	$7,000	$6,250	$5,500	$4,950	$4,500	
Sig 551 (Carbine)	$10,500	$9,500	$8,875	$8,000	$7,250	$6,500	$5,600	Last MSR was $1,950.

This model had very limited domestic importation before 1989 Federal legislation banned its configuration.

SIG 556 – Please refer to the Sig Sauer section.

SIG SAUER

Current firearms trademark manufactured by SIG Arms AG (Schweizerische Industrie-Gesellschaft) located in Neuhausen, Switzerland. Currently imported, manufactured (some models), and distributed by Sig Sauer, Inc., established in 2007, and located in Exeter, NH. Previously imported and distributed from 1985-2006 by Sigarms, Inc. located in Exeter, NH. Previously located in Herndon, VA and Tysons Corner, VA.

MSR	100%	98%	95%	90%	80%	70%	60%

In late 2000, SIG Arms AG, the firearms portion of SIG, was purchased by two Germans named Michael Lüke and Thomas Ortmeier, who have a background in textiles. Today the Lüke & Ortmeier group includes independently operational companies such as Blaser Jadgwaffen GmbH, Mauser Jagdwaffen GmbH, J.P. Sauer & Sohn GmbH, SIG-Sauer Inc., SIG-Sauer GmbH and SAN Swiss Arms AG. Please refer to individual listings.

On Oct. 1, 2007, SIG Arms changed its corporate name to Sig Sauer.

PISTOLS: SEMI-AUTO

Beginning 2001, add approx. $20 for all handguns that are MA compliant (which requires a loaded chamber indicator). Pistols which are NY compliant (includes empty shell casing) are priced the same as the models listed.

The Sigarms Custom Shop, located in Exeter, NH, has recently been established, and offers a wide variety of custom shop services, including action enhancement, full servicing, DA/SA conversions, trigger and hammer modifications, barrel replacement, and many refinishing options. Please contact Sigarms Custom Shop directly for more information and current pricing on these services.

During 2005, the Sigarms Custom Shop produced 12 limited editions, including the P229 Rail (January), P245 w/nickel accents and Meprolight night sights (February), P220 .45 ACP Rail (March), P239 Satin Nickel w/Hogue rubber grips (April), GSR 1911 Reverse Two-Tone (May), P229 Satin Nickel Reverse Two-Tone (June), P232 Rainbow Titanium (July), P226 Rail (August), P220 Sport Stock (September), P239 w/ extra .357 SIG cal. barrel (October), P228 Two-Tone (November), and the P226 package w/ Oakley glasses (December).

Early SIG Sauer pistols can be marked either with the Herndon or Tysons Corner, VA barrel address, and can also be marked "W. Germany" or "Germany". Earlier mfg. had three proofmarks on the bottom front of the slide, with a fourth on the frame in front of the serial number. Early guns with these barrel markings will command a slight premium over prices listed below, if condition is 98%+. Current mfg. has Exeter, NH barrel address.

Add $376 - $422 for caliber X-Change kit on current models.

P 210 – please refer to listing under SIG ARMS AG heading.

MOSQUITO – .22 LR cal., compact design similar to P226, 3.98 in. barrel, polymer frame, 10 shot mag., SA/DA, decocker, ambidextrous manual safety, Picatinny rail on bottom of frame, internal locking device, adj. rear sight, molded composite grips, black, nickel (mfg. 2007-2008), blue, pink (new 2009), desert digital camo (new 2009), or reverse two-tone (new 2007) finish, 24.6 oz. New 2005.

MSR $390	$340	$295	$260	$220	$190	$170	$155

Add $15 for nickel or reverse two-tone finish.
Add $15 for hot pink frame.
Add $112 for camo finish with threaded barrel or $142 for camo finish, threaded barrel, and tactical trainer package (disc. 2009).
Add $45 for threaded barrel.
Add $75 for long slide with barrel weight (black finish only, new 2007, Sporter model).

MODEL P220 – .22 LR (disc.), .38 Super (disc.), 7.65mm (disc.), 9mm Para. (disc 1991), or .45 ACP cal., 7 (.45 ACP, disc.) or 8 shot mag., full size, SAO, regular double action or double action only (.45 ACP cal. only), 4.4 in. barrel, decocking lever, choice of matte blue (disc. 2006), black nitron (new 2007), stainless steel (mfg. 2001-2007), K-Kote (disc. 1999), electroless nickel (disc. 1991), two-tone with nickel finished slide, or Ilaflon (mfg. 2000 only) finish, lightweight alloy frame, black plastic grips, optional DAK trigger system (DAO with 6 1/2 lb. trigger pull) available during 2005 only, tactical rail became standard 2004 at no extra charge (blue or stainless only), approx. 30.4 or 41.8 (stainless steel) oz. New 1976.

MSR $976	$875	$725	$625	$525	$450	$400	$350

Add $40 for DAK trigger system (limited mfg. 2005).
Add $74 for Siglite night sights.
Add $100 for P220 SAO Model (single action only, disc. 2009).
Add $306 for Crimson Trace laser grips w/night sights (disc. 2009).
Add $134 for two-tone (nickel slide) finish.
Add $95 for stainless steel frame & slide (mfg. 2001-2007).
Add $40 for Ilaflon finish (disc. 2000).
Add $45 for factory K-Kote finish (disc. 1999).
Add $70 for electroless nickel finish (disc. 1991).
Add $376 for .22 LR conversion kit (current mfg.) or $680 for older mfg. .22 LR conversion kit.
Subtract 10% for "European" Model (bottom mag. release - includes 9mm Para. and .38 Super cals.).

Values are for .45 ACP cal. and assume American side mag. release (standard 1986).

This model was also available as a Custom Shop Limited Edition during July, 2004 (MSR was $800 and November, 2004 (MSR was $861).

* **Model P220 Combat** – features flat Dark Earth finish, alloy frame, Nitron stainless slide, corrosion resistant parts, 8 shot mag., M1913 Picatinny rail, Siglite night sights, with (Combat TB) or w/o (Combat) threaded barrel. New 2007.

MSR $1,200	$1,050	$925	$825	$725	$625	$525	$425

Add $150 for Combat TB Model with threaded barrel.

MSR	100%	98%	95%	90%	80%	70%	60%

* **Model P220 Elite** – .45 ACP cal., similar to P220, except has short reset trigger, DA/SA or SAO, two-tone (limited mfg.), black Nitron finish, or stainless steel, 8 shot mag., ergonomic beavertail, Picatinny rail, front cocking serrations, custom shop wood grips, black aluminum (Elite Dark), or checkered aluminum (platinum Elite) grips. New 2007.

MSR $1,200	$1,050	$925	$825	$725	$625	$525	$425

Add $150 for stainless steel.
Add $205 for platinum Elite with aluminum grips (stainless only).
Add $106 for Elite Dark with threaded barrel.

* **Model P220 Carry Elite** – .45 ACP cal., similar to P220 Elite, except is compact model, stainless or black Nitron finish (new 2009). New 2007.

MSR $1,200	$1,050	$925	$825	$725	$625	$525	$425

Add $150 for stainless steel.

* **Model P220 Carry** – .45 ACP cal., compact model w/full size frame, 3.9 in. barrel, 8 shot single stack mag., DA/SA, DAK, or SAO, black Nitron or two-tone (only available in Carry SAS beginning 2010) finish, Siglite night sights, Picatinny rail, black polymer or custom shop brown (Carry SAS) wood grips. New 2007.

MSR $976	$875	$725	$625	$525	$450	$400	$350

Add $75 for Siglite night sights.
Add $150 for two-tone finish (Carry SAS only).
Add $100 for SAO trigger (disc. 2008).
Add $73 for P220 Carry SAS model (Generation II features became standard 2008).

* **Model P220 Carry Equinox** – similar to P220 Carry, except has two-tone accented slide with nitron finish, Truglo TFO front sight, Siglite rear sight, black wood grips w/custom shop logo. New 2007.

MSR $1,200	$1,050	$925	$825	$725	$625	$525	$425

* **Model P220 Compact** – .45 ACP cal., compact beavertail frame, 3.9 in. barrel, 6 shot mag., DA/SA or SAO, black Nitron or two-tone finish, Siglite night sights, black polymer or custom shop wood (Compact SAS) grips. New 2007.

MSR $1,050	$920	$800	$700	$600	$500	$400	$350

Add $75 for two-tone finish.
Add $45 for P220 Compact SAS model (Generation II features became standard 2009).

* **Model P220 Equinox** – similar to P220, except has two-tone accented slide with nitron finish, Truglo TFO front sight, Siglite rear sight, black wood grips w/custom shop logo. New 2007.

MSR $1,200	$1,050	$925	$825	$725	$625	$525	$425

* **Model P220 Match** – .45 ACP cal., similar to P220, except has 5 in. cold hammer forged barrel, DA/SA or SAO, ambidextrous safety, two-tone finish, adj. sights, black polymer or custom shop wood (Super Match) grips, Elite Match became standard during 2010. New 2007.

MSR $1,350	$1,175	$975	$850	$725	$625	$550	$450

Add $106 for Super Match model.
Subtract approx. $200 for Match (disc. 2009, last MSR was $1,170).

* **Model P220 NRALE** – .45 ACP cal., features NRA Law Enforcement logo and the words "NRA Law Enforcement" engraved in 24Kt. gold, cocobolo grips with NRA medallions, gold trigger and appointments. Limited production of 1,000, including P226 NRALE 2002-2003.

	$850	$650	$495	N/A	N/A	N/A	N/A	Last MSR was $911.

* **Model P220 Sport** – .45 ACP cal., features 4.8 in. heavy compensated barrel, stainless steel frame and slide, 10 shot mag., target sights, improved trigger pull, single or double action, 46.1 oz. Imported 1999-2000, reintroduced 2003-2005.

	$1,375	$975	$800	$695	$585	$485	$415	Last MSR was $1,600.

* **Model P220R .22 LR** – .22 LR cal., 4.4 in. barrel, 10 shot mag., DA/SA, matte black anodized finish, adj. sights, otherwise similar to standard P220. New 2009.

MSR $609	$550	$495	$450	$395	$350	$300	$275

MODEL P225 – 9mm Para. cal., regular double action or double action only, similar to P220, shorter dimensions, 3.85 in. barrel, 8 shot, thumb actuated button release mag., fully adj. sights, 28.8 oz. Disc. 1998.

	$595	$525	$450	$425	$395	$350	$310	Last MSR was $725.

Add $45 for factory K-Kote finish.
Add $105 for Siglite night sights.
Add $45 for nickel finished slide (new 1992).
Add $70 for electroless nickel finish (disc. 1991).

This model was also available as a Custom Shop Limited Edition during March, 2004. MSR was $803.

MSR	100%	98%	95%	90%	80%	70%	60%

MODEL P226 – .357 SIG (new 1995), 9mm Para. (disc. 1997, reintroduced 1999), or .40 S&W (new 1998) cal., full size, choice of double action or double action only (new 1992) operation, 10 (C/B 1994), 12 (new mid-2005, .357 SIG or .40 S&W cal.) or 15* (9mm Para. cal. only) shot mag., 4.4 in. barrel, alloy frame, currently available in blackened stainless steel (Nitron finish became standard 2000), two-tone, or nickel (disc. 2002) finish (stainless slide only), tactical rail became standard 2004, choice of traditional DA or DAK trigger system (DAO with 6 1/2 lb. trigger pull, not available in all stainless) available beginning 2005, high contrast sights, automatic firing pin block safety, 31.7 or 34 oz. New 1983.

MSR $976	$875	$725	$625	$525	$450	$400	$350

Add $74 for Siglite night sights.
Add $376 for .22 LR cal. conversion kit.
Add $74 for .357 SIG cal. (includes night sights, black Nitron finish only).
Add $306 for Crimson Trace laser grips w/Siglite night sights (mfg. 2007).
Add $95 for stainless steel frame and slide (mfg. 2004-2005).
Add $134 for two-tone finish (nickel finished stainless steel slide) w/night sights.
Add $45 for K-Kote (Polymer) finish (mfg. 1992-97, 9mm Para. only).
Add $70 for electroless nickel finish (disc. 1991).

This model is also available in double action only (all finishes) at no extra charge.

This model was also available as a Custom Shop Limited Edition during Feb., 2004 (MSR was $1,085). A limited edition P226 America with blue titanium and gold finishes was also available from SIG's Custom Shop (MSR was $7,995).

This model is also available as the P226R Tactical, sold exclusively by Ellett Bros distribtors - no pricing information is available.

* **Model P226 Jubilee** – 9mm Para. cal., limited edition commemorating SIG's 125th anniversary, features gold-plated small parts, carved select walnut grips, special slide markings, cased. Mfg. 1985 only.

	$1,495	$1,175	$950	$835	$685	$585	$485	Last MSR was $2,000.

* **Model P226 NRALE** – .40 S&W cal., features NRA Law Enforcement logo and the words "NRA Law Enforcement" engraved in 24Kt. gold, cocobolo grips with NRA medallions, gold trigger and appointments. Limited production of 1,000, including P220 NRALE, 2002-2003.

	$850	$650	$495	N/A	N/A	N/A	N/A	Last MSR was $911.

* **Model P226 Sport** – 9mm Para. cal., features 5.6 in. match or heavy compensated barrel, stainless steel frame and slide, 10 shot mag., target sights, improved trigger pull, single or double action, rubber grips, 48.8 oz. Mfg. 2003-2005.

	$1,375	$975	$800	$695	$585	$485	$415	Last MSR was $1,600.

* **Model P226 Elite** – .45 ACP cal., similar to P226, except has short reset trigger, DA/SA or SAO, two-tone (disc.), black Nitron finish, or stainless steel, 8 shot mag., ergonomic beavertail, Picatinny rail, front cocking serrations, custom shop wood grips. New 2007.

MSR $1,200	$1,050	$925	$825	$725	$625	$525	$425

Add $150 for stainless steel.
Add $76 for platinum Elite with aluminum grips.
Add $106 for TB Model with threaded barrel.

* **Model P226 Combat** – 9mm Para. cal., DA/SA, 4.4 in. barrel, 10 or 15 shot mag., Siglite night sights, flat dark earth frame and grips, black Nitron slide, Picatinny rail, 34 oz. New 2008.

MSR $1,199	$1,050	$925	$825	$725	$625	$525	$425

Add $150 for TB model with threaded barrel.

* **Model P226 Tactical/Blackwater Tactical** – similar to P226, black Nitron finish, Picatinny rail, threaded barrel, post and dot contrast Siglite night sights, available in standard (disc. 2009) and Blackwater configuration (black Nitron finish, Siglite night sights, and wood grips). New 2007.

MSR $1,300	$1,150	$975	$850	$750	$650	$550	$450

Subtract approx. $50 for standard tactical - (disc. 2009, last MSR was $1,245).

* **Model P226 Super Cap Tactical** – .40 S&W cal., similar to P226 Tactical, black Nitron finish, TruGlo front sight, Siglite rear sight, includes four 15 shot mags. New 2009.

MSR $1,156	$1,025	$925	$825	$725	$625	$525	$425

* **Model P226 ST** – 9mm Para., .40 S&W, or .357 Mag. cal., 4.4 in. barrel, white stainless slide and frame, blue barrel, Picatinny rail, 10 shot mag., 38.8 oz.

While advertised during 2006, this model never went into production - prototypes only.

* **Model P226 USPSA** – 9mm Para. cal., short reset trigger, 4.4 in. barrel, 15 shot mag., Dawson fiber optic front sight, Warren rear sight, polymer grips, aluminum frame with stainless steel slide, black Nitron finish, USPSA engraving, includes three mags. New 2009.

MSR $1,246	$1,095	$950	$825	$725	$625	$525	$400

MSR	100%	98%	95%	90%	80%	70%	60%

* **Model P226 E2** – 9mm Para. cal., 15 shot mag., black Nitron finish, ergonomic slim profile one piece grips, Siglite night sights, short reset trigger, integral accessory rail, includes three mags. New 2010.

MSR $1,149	$1,000	$895	$775	$675	$575	$525	$450

* **Model P226R** – .22 LR cal., Nitron finish, adj. sights, DA/SA or SAO, 10 shot mag., with or w/o beavertail grip. New 2009.

MSR $609	$550	$495	$450	$395	$350	$300	$275

* **Model P226 Equinox** – .40 S&W cal., 4.4 in. barrel, two-tone Nitron stainless steel slide, lightweight black anodized alloy frame, nickel accents, 10 or 12 shot mag., Truglo tritium front sight, rear Siglite night sight, Picatinny rail, grey laminated wood grips, 34 oz., mfg. by the Custom Shop. New 2006.

MSR $1,200	$1,050	$925	$825	$725	$625	$525	$425

* **Model P226 Special Editions** – 9mm Para. or .40 S&W (Cops Commemorative only, disc. 2008) cal., engraved, variations include Navy (black Nitron finish, phosphate components and anchor engraving), or Cops Commemorative (Siglite night sights and wood grips, disc. 2008).

MSR $1,020	$895	$775	$675	$575	$475	$400	$350

MODEL P226 X-FIVE – 9mm Para. or .40 S&W cal., SA, adj. trigger, 5 in. stainless steel barrel and slide, ambidextrous thumb safety, all stainless construction with magwell, low profile adj. sights, 14 (.40 S&W) or 19 (9mm Para.) shot mag., available in blue, two-tone, stainless or black Nitron finish, checkered walnut grips, includes 25 meter test target, checkered front grip strap, 47.2 oz. New mid-2005.

MSR $2,926	$2,575	$2,200	$1,775	$1,475	$1,250	$1,000	$850

* **Model P226 X-Five Competition** – 9mm Para. or .40 S&W cal., similar to X-Five, except has black polymer grips. New 2007.

MSR $2,100	$1,850	$1,525	$1,275	$1,050	$875	$700	$650

* **Model P226 X-Five All Around** – 9mm Para. or .40 S&W cal., adj. sights, ergonomic beavertail grip, DA/SA, stainless slide and frame, black polymer grips. New 2007.

MSR $1,800	$1,575	$1,275	$995	$875	$775	$675	$550

* **Model P226 X-Five Tactical** – 9mm Para. cal., black Nitron finish, contrast sights, lightweight alloy frame, Picatinny rail, single action trigger, ergonomic beavertail grips. New 2007.

MSR $1,800	$1,575	$1,275	$995	$875	$775	$675	$550

MODEL P228 – 9mm Para., choice of double action or double action only (new 1992) operation, compact design, 3.86 in. (compact) barrel, 10 (C/B 1994) or 13* (reintroduced 2004) shot mag., automatic firing pin block safety, high contrast sights, alloy frame, choice of blue, Nitron (new 2004), nickel (mfg. 1991-97), or stainless steel (new 2004) slide, or K-Kote (disc. 1997) finish, 29.3 oz. Mfg. 1990-97, reintroduced 2004-2006.

	$700	$600	$500	$450	$400	$350	$310	Last MSR was $840.

Add $50 for Siglite night sights.
Add $376 for .22 LR cal. conversion kit.
Add $45 for K-Kote (Polymer) finish (disc. 1997).
Add $45 for nickel finished slide (1991-97).
Add $70 for electroless nickel finish (disc. 1991).

This model was also available in double action only (all finishes) at no extra charge.

This model was also available as a Custom Shop Limited Edition during April, 2004 (MSR was $800).

MODEL P229 – .357 SIG (new 1995), 9mm Para. (mfg. 1994-96, reintroduced 1999), or .40 S&W cal., compact size, 3.9 in. barrel, similar to Model P228, except has blackened Nitron or satin nickel (disc.) finished stainless steel slide with aluminum alloy frame, 10 (C/B 1994), 12* (.357 SIG or .40 S&W cal. only), or 13 (9mm Para. cal. only, new 2005) shot mag., choice of traditional DA or DAK trigger system (DAO with 6 1/2 lb. trigger pull) available beginning 2005, tactical rail became standard in 2004 (Nitron finish only), includes lockable carrying case, 31.1 or 32.4 oz. New 1991.

MSR $976	$875	$725	$625	$525	$450	$400	$350

Add $74 for .357 SIG cal. - includes Siglite night sights.
Add $74 for Siglite night sights.
Add $306 for Crimson Trace laser grips w/Siglite night sights (mfg. 2007-2008).
Add $180 for black Nitron finish with TruGlo TFO front and Siglite rear sights with four hi-cap mags. (Super Cap Tactical model, not available in .357 SIG cal.).
Add $134 for two-tone finish (nickel finished stainless steel slide) with night sights.
Add $376 for .22 LR cal. conversion kit.

This model was also available in double action only at no extra charge.

This model was also available as a Custom Shop Limited Edition during June, 2004 (MSR was $873), during August, 2004 (MSR was $916) and during Dec., 2004 (MSR was $844).

MSR	100%	98%	95%	90%	80%	70%	60%

* **Model P229 Elite** – .45 ACP cal., similar to P229, except has short reset trigger, DA/SA or SAO, two-tone (disc.), dark (new 2009) or black Nitron finish, or stainless steel, 8 shot mag., ergonomic beavertail, Picatinny rail, front cocking serrations, custom shop wood or aluminum grips. New 2007.

MSR $1,200	$1,050	$925	$825	$725	$625	$525	$425

Add $76 for platinum Elite with aluminum grips.
Add $150 for stainless steel.
Add $106 for TB model with threaded barrel.

* **Model P229 Equinox** – .40 S&W cal., 4.4 in. barrel, two-tone Nitron stainless steel slide, lightweight black anodized alloy frame, nickel accents, 10 or 12 shot mag., Truglo tritium front sight, rear Siglite night sight, Picatinny rail, grey laminated wood grips, 34 oz., mfg. by the Custom Shop. New 2007.

MSR $1,200	$1,050	$925	$825	$725	$625	$525	$425

* **Model P229 Sport** – .357 SIG or .40 S&W (new 2003) cal., features 4.8 in. match or heavy (disc. 2000) compensated barrel, stainless steel frame and slide, target sights, improved trigger pull, single or double action, 43.6 oz. Mfg. 1998-2000, reintroduced 2003-2005.

	$1,375	$975	$800	$695	$585	$485	$415	Last MSR was $1,600.

* **Model P229 SAS** – 9mm Para., .357 SIG, or .40 S&W cal., 3.86 in. barrel, 12 shot mag., DAK trigger, smooth dehorned stainless steel slide, two-tone or black Nitron (new 2009) finish, Siglite night sights, contrast rear sight, light-weight black hard anodized frame, rounded trigger guard, checkered wood grips, designed for snag-free profile for concealed carry, Generation II features became standard 2009, 32 oz. Mfg. by Custom Shop. New 2005.

MSR $1,096	$975	$850	$725	$625	$525	$475	$425

Add $30 for two-tone finish.

* **Model P229 E2** – 9mm Para. cal., 15 shot mag., black Nitron finish, ergonomic slim profile one piece grips, Siglite night sights, short reset trigger, integral accessory rail, includes three mags. New 2010.

MSR $1,149	$1,000	$895	$775	$675	$575	$525	$450

* **Model P229 HF (Heritage Fund)** – .40 S&W cal., 10 shot, 3.9 in. barrel, slide marked "10th Anniversary P229", frame marked "1992-2002", gold engraving and accents, brushed stainless steel, gold trigger, cocobolo Hogue grips with NSSF Heritage Fund medallion, includes wood display case. Limited mfg. late 2001-2004.

	$1,195	$750	$600	N/A	N/A	N/A	N/A	Last MSR was $1,299.

* **Model P229R .22 LR** – .22 LR cal., 4.4 in. barrel, 10 shot mag., DA/SA, matte black anodized finish, adj. sights, otherwise similar to standard P229. New 2009.

MSR $609	$550	$495	$450	$395	$350	$300	$275

MODEL P230 – .22 LR (disc.)-10 shot, .32 ACP-8 shot, .380 ACP-7 shot, or 9mm Ultra (disc.) cal., 7 shot, 3.6 in. barrel, regular double action or double action only, blue, composite grips, 17.6 oz. Mfg. 1976-96.

	$425	$375	$300	$270	$240	$215	$190	Last MSR was $510.

Add $35 for stainless slide (.380 ACP only).

* **Model P230 SL Stainless** – similar to Model P230, except stainless steel construction, 22.4 oz. Disc. 1996.

	$480	$400	$375	$315	$270	$230	$200	Last MSR was $595.

MODEL P232 – .380 ACP cal., choice of double action or double action only, 3.6 in. barrel, 7 shot mag., aluminum alloy frame, compact personal size, blue or two-tone stainless slide, automatic firing pin block safety, composite grips, 17.6 oz. New 1997.

MSR $720	$640	$575	$495	$410	$360	$310	$260

Add $60 for Siglite night sights (mfg. 2001-2006) or $106 for two-tone finish (new 2007).
Subtract $60 if w/o night sights (became standard 2010).

* **Model P232 Stainless** – similar to Model P232, except stainless steel construction, natural finish, 22.4 oz. New 1997.

MSR $900	$795	$650	$500	$425	$350	$300	$275

Subtract $75 if w/o Siglite night sights and Hogue grips (standard beginning 2007).

MODEL P238 – .380 ACP cal., black Nitron or two-tone finish, fixed or Siglite night sights, 15.2 oz. New 2009.

MSR $629	$525	$450	$400	$365	$330	$300	$275

Subtract $40 if w/o Siglite night sights (standard beginning 2010).
Add $14 for two-tone finish.
Add $70 for rosewood grips (new 2010), two-tone finish with black wood grips (new 2010), or rainbow titanium finish and wood grips (new 2010).
Add $120 for two-tone finish, two-tone alloy grips, and tactical laser sight (new 2010).

* **Model P238 Equinox** – similar to Model P238, except has two-tone nitron finish, TruGlo TFO front sight, Siglite

MSR	100%	98%	95%	90%	80%	70%	60%

rear sight, black wood grips, approx. 16 oz. New 2010.

MSR $699   **$625**   **$550**   **$465**   **$425**   **$385**   **$325**   **$275**

* ***Model P238 Stainless*** – similar to P238, except has stainless steel frame and slide, Siglite night sights, G10 grips, approx. 20 oz. New 2010.

MSR $719   **$650**   **$575**   **$500**   **$450**   **$395**   **$350**   **$295**

MODEL P239 – .357 SIG, 9mm Para., or .40 S&W (new 1998) cal., compact personal size, double action or double action only, black Nitron or two-tone stainless steel slide and aluminum alloy frame, firing pin block safety, 3.6 in. barrel, 7 or 8 (9mm Para. only) shot mag., fixed sights, approx. 29 oz. New 1996.

MSR $840   **$735**   **$625**   **$525**   **$450**   **$375**   **$325**   **$295**

Add $76 for Siglite night sights.
Add $305 for Crimson Trace laser grips and night sights (mfg. 2007).
Add $135 for two-tone stainless slide with night sights (disc. 2009).
Add $76 for .357 SIG cal. with night sights.

This model was also available as a Custom Shop Limited Edition during May, 2004 (MSR was $673).

* ***Model P239 SAS*** – 9mm Para. (new 2008), .357 SIG, or .40 S&W cal., 3.6 in. barrel, 7 shot mag., DAK trigger, smooth dehorned stainless steel slide, Siglite night sights, contrast rear sight, light-weight black hard anodized frame, black Nitron or two-tone finish, rounded trigger guard, checkered/carved wood grips, designed for snag-free profile for concealed carry, Generation II features became standard 2009, 29 1/2 oz. Mfg. by Custom Shop beginning June, 2005.

MSR $1,006   **$885**   **$750**   **$625**   **$550**   **$475**   **$425**   **$350**

Add $44 for two-tone finish.

MODEL P245 – .45 ACP cal., compact model featuring 3.9 in. barrel, traditional double action, includes 6 and 8 shot mag., blue, two-tone (disc. 2005), Ilaflon (mfg. 2000 only), or K-Kote (disc. 1999) finish, approx. 30 oz. Mfg. 1999-2006.

   $695   **$585**   **$495**   **$440**   **$400**   **$350**   **$310**   Last MSR was $840.

Add $75 for Siglite night sights.
Add $56 for two-tone or K-Kote finish (disc.).
Add $50 for Ilaflon finish (mfg. 2000 only).

MODEL P250 – 9mm Para., .357 SIG, .40 S&W, or .45 ACP cal., DAO, choice of 4.7 (full size), 3.9 (Compact), or 3.1 (Subcompact) in. barrel, steel frame with black polymer grip shell (three different sizes), features modular synthetic frame with removable fire control assembly, 10 (.45 ACP), 17 (.357 SIG or .40 S&W) or 20 (9mm Para.) shot mag., ambidextrous slide release lever, black Nitron or two-tone finish, night sights, integrated accessory rail, converts into various calibers by changing slides, grip modules, and magazine, 27.6 oz. New mid-2008.

MSR $640   **$575**   **$500**   **$450**   **$400**   **$365**   **$325**   **$275**

Add $72 for .45 ACP cal. or $15 for two-tone finish (not available in .45 ACP cal.).

* ***Model P250 Compact*** – similar to P250 Full Size, except has 3.9 in. barrel, 8 (.45 ACP), 13 (.357 SIG or .40 S&W) or 16 (9mm Para.) shot mag., 24.6 oz. New mid-2008.

MSR $640   **$575**   **$500**   **$450**   **$400**   **$365**   **$325**   **$275**

Add $72 for .45 ACP cal. or $15 for two-tone finish.
Add $215 for desert digital camo finish (9mm Para. cal. only), includes Siglite night sights, medium grips, and DAO (new 2009).

* ***Model P250 Subcompact*** – similar to P250 Compact, except has 3.1 in. barrel, 6 (.45 ACP), 9 (.357 SIG or .40 S&W) or 12 (9mm Para.) shot mag., 22.6 oz. New mid-2008.

MSR $640   **$575**   **$500**   **$450**   **$400**   **$365**   **$325**   **$275**

Add $74 for .45 ACP cal. or $15 for two-tone finish (9mm Para. or .40 S&W cal.).
Add $375 for desert digital camo finish (9mm Para. cal. only), includes Siglite night sights, medium grips, and DAO (mfg. 2009).

1911 (GSR REVOLUTION) – .45 ACP cal., single action, 5 in. match grade barrel, choice of white (disc.), standard blue, two-tone, reverse two-tone (new 2007), XO Black (new 2007), or black Nitron finished stainless steel, includes two 8 shot mags., with or w/o under frame Picatinny rail, firing pin safety, front and rear strap checkering, Novak sights, checkered wood (all stainless) or synthetic (blued stainless) grips, approx. 41 oz. Mfg. in Exeter, NH. New 2004.

MSR $1,170   **$1,025**   **$895**   **$775**   **$675**   **$575**   **$525**   **$450**

Add $30 for black Nitron finish.
Add $30 for Target Model with adj. target night sights (new 2007).
Add $120 for TTT Model with two-tone finish, black controls, and adj. combat night sights (disc. 2009).
Add $286 for STX Model with two-tone finish, flattop, adj. combat night sights and magwell.
Add $106 for platinum Elite with aluminum grips (new 2008).
Add $120 for Blackwater model (new 2009).
Subtract $40 for reverse two-tone finish (mfg. 2007).
Subtract $164 for XO Model with black finish, Novak contrast sights, and black ergo-grips (new 2007).

The abbreviation GSR on this model stands for Granite Series Revolution.

MSR	100%	98%	95%	90%	80%	70%	60%

1911 CARRY (REVOLUTION) – similar to GSR, except is carry configuration with short stainless slide, 4 in. barrel, stainless steel frame or black Nitron finish, Novak night sights, 8 shot mag., custom wood grips. New 2007.

| MSR $1,170 | $1,025 | $895 | $775 | $675 | $575 | $525 | $450 |

Add $30 for black Nitron finish.

1911 COMPACT (REVOLUTION) – .45 ACP cal., short slide and compact frame, 6 shot, stainless or black Nitron finish, 4 in. barrel, available in three variations, Compact (disc. 2009), Compact C3 (black hard coat anodized alloy frame, stainless slide and rosewood grips), or Compact RCS (dehorning and anti-snag treatment, black Nitron or two-tone finish and rosewood custom shop grips). New 2007.

| MSR $1,306 | $1,125 | $975 | $825 | $700 | $600 | $550 | $450 |

Add $57 for two-tone finish.
Subtract $106 for C3 Model.
Subtract approx. $130 for Compact model (disc. 2009, last MSR was $1,170).

MODEL P522 – .22 LR cal., blowback action, 10.6 in. barrel, aluminum flattop upper receiver, choice of polymer or quad rail (P522 SWAT) forend, flash suppressor, 10 or 25 shot polymer mag., amidextrous safety selector, sling attachments, approx. 6 1/2 lbs. New 2010.

| MSR $572 | $525 | $465 | $415 | $365 | $335 | $300 | $275 |

Add $71 for P522 SWAT model with quad rail forend.

MODEL P556 – 5.56 NATO cal., action similar to SIG 556 carbine, 10 in. cold hammer forged barrel with A2 type flash suppressor, Picatinny top rail, pistol grip only, ribbed and vented black polymer forearm, black Nitron finish, mini red dot front sight, aluminum alloy two-stage trigger, ambidextrous safety, 30 shot mag (accepts standard AR-15 style mags.), 6.3 lbs. New 2009.

| MSR $1,876 | $1,825 | $1,650 | $1,450 | $1,300 | $1,200 | $1,100 | $1,000 |

Add $147 for P556 SWAT model with quad rail forend.

* **Model P556 Lightweight** – similar to Model P556, except has lightweight polymer lower unit and forend. New 2010.

| MSR $1,356 | $1,250 | $1,075 | $950 | $825 | $725 | $625 | $525 |

Add $172 for quad rail forend.

MODEL SIG PRO SP2009 – 9mm Para. cal., otherwise identical to SP2340, 28 oz. Mfg. 1999-2005.

| | $510 | $450 | $355 | $290 | $260 | $220 | $195 | Last MSR was $640. |

Add $60 for Siglite night sights.
Add $31 for two-tone finish.

MODEL SIG PRO SP2022 – 9mm Para., .357 SIG, or .40 S&W cal., 10, 12 or 15 (9mm Para. cal. only) shot mag., 3.85 in. barrel, polymer frame, Picatinny rail, Nitron, blue, or two-tone (disc. 2005) stainless steel slide, black Nitron finish, convertible DA/SA to DAO, optional interchangeable grips, 26.8 (9mm Para.) or 30 oz. Mfg. 2004-2007.

| | $495 | $440 | $355 | $290 | $260 | $220 | $195 | Last MSR was $613. |

Subtract 10% if w/o Siglite night sights (became standard 2007).

MODEL SIG PRO SP2340 – .357 SIG, or .40 S&W cal., features polymer frame and one-piece Nitron finished stainless steel or two-tone (new 2001) finished slide, 3.86 in. barrel, includes two interchangeable grips, 10 shot mag., approx. 30.2 oz. Mfg. 1999-2005.

| | $510 | $450 | $355 | $290 | $260 | $220 | $195 | Last MSR was $640. |

Add $60 for Siglite night sights.
Add $31 for two-tone finish.

RIFLES: BOLT ACTION

Please refer to listing in J.P. Sauer & Sohn section for previously manufactured SSG 3000 rifles.

SSG 3000 PRECISION TACTICAL RIFLE – .308 Win. cal., modular design, ambidextrous McMillan tactical stock with adj. comb, 23.4 in. barrel with muzzle brake, 5 shot detachable mag., supplied in 3 different levels, Level I does not have bipod or scope, cased, 12 lbs. New 2000.

| MSR $4,199 | $3,650 | $3,200 | $2,700 | $2,275 | $1,850 | $1,500 | $1,325 |

Add $1,500 for Level II (includes Leupold Vari-X III 3.5-10x40mm duplex reticle scope and Harris bipod, disc.).
Add $2,300 for Level III (includes Leupold Mark 4 M1 10x40mm Mil-Dot reticle scope and Harris bipod, disc.).
Add $1,500 for .22 LR cal. conversion kit (disc.).

RIFLES: SEMI-AUTO

SIG 522 – .22 LR cal., 16 in. barrel, blowback action, adj. folding stock, 10 or 25 shot, black polymer frame, folding collapsible or non-folding Swiss style stock, Picatinny rail, polymer or quad rail (522 SWAT) forend, flash suppressor, approx. 6 1/2 lbs. New 2009.

| MSR $572 | $525 | $465 | $415 | $365 | $335 | $300 | $275 |

MSR	100%	98%	95%	90%	80%	70%	60%

Add $114 for SWAT model with quad rail.
Add $222 for rotary front sight (disc. 2009).
Add $57 for non-folding stock.
Add $375 for mini red dot sight.
Add $210 for Harris bipod.

SIG 556 – 5.56 NATO cal., gas operated w/rotary bolt, tactical design, 16 in. barrel with muzzle brake, polymer forearm, alloy trigger housing, choice of SIG quad-rail (SWAT Model) or tri-rail, integrated Picatinny rails, two-stage trigger, collapsible or collapsible/folding tube stock, Magpul CTR Carbine stock type (SWAT) or M4 style stock (556ER or 556 Holo), 30 shot AR-15 type mag., 7.8-8.7 lbs. New 2007.

MSR $2,250	$2,100	$1,850	$1,575	$1,250	$1,050	$925	$825

Add $150 for quad-rail system (SWAT Model).
Add $45 for Holo model with holographic sight (disc. 2009).
Add $150 for collapsible stock with GLR and Stoplite (disc. 2009).
Add $306 for Classic 16 with adj. folding stock and red dot sight (disc. 2009).
Add $456 for Classic 17 with adj. folding stock and rotary sight (disc. 2009).
Add $300 for 16 in. barrel with GLR and Stoplite (disc. 2009).
Subtract $200 if w/o iron sights (became standard 2008).

* **SIG 556 Patrol** – similar to SIG 556, 16 in. barrel, 30 shot mag., steel upper receiver, choice of polymer (Patrol) or alloy quad rail (Patrol SWAT) forend, black anodized finish, A2 flash suppressor, folding collapsible Swiss style stock, rotary diopter sight, 7 1/2 lbs. New 2010.

MSR $2,000	$1,875	$1,675	$1,450	$1,225	$1,050	$900	$775

Add $143 for SWAT model with quad rail forend.

SIG 556 DMR – similar to Model 556, except has 24 in. heavy barrel w/o sights, adj. Magpul PRS stock, vented synthetic forearm, Picatinny rail on bottom of forearm and top of receiver, includes tactical bipod, 12 lbs. New 2008.

MSR $2,400	$2,100	$1,825	$1,600	$1,425	$1,200	$1,000	$900

SIG SCM – 5.56 NATO cal., 16 in. barrel, 10 shot mag., steel upper receiver, polymer forend with lower accessory rail, Holo sight, aluminum lower, target crowned muzzle, A2 fixed stock, Picatinny top rail, approx. 8 lbs. New 2010.

MSR $1,839	$1,800	$1,625	$1,450	$1,300	$1,200	$1,100	$1,000

SIRKIS INDUSTRIES, LTD.

Previous manufacturer located in Ramat-Gan, Israel. Previously imported and distributed by Armscorp of America, Inc. located in Baltimore, MD.

PISTOLS: SEMI-AUTO

S.D. 9 – 9mm Para. cal., double action mechanism, frame is constructed mostly of heavy gauge sheet metal stampings, 3.07 in. barrel, parkerized finish, loaded chamber indicator, 7 shot mag., plastic grips, 24 1/2 oz. Imported under the Sirkis and Sardius trademarks between 1986-90.

	$375	$295	$250	$200	$190	$180	$170	Last MSR was $350.

RIFLES

MODEL 35 MATCH RIFLE – .22 LR cal. only, single shot bolt action, 26 in. full floating barrel, select walnut, match trigger, micrometer sights. Disc. 1985.

	$650	$625	$595	$550	$510	$460	$420	Last MSR was $690.

MODEL 36 SNIPER RIFLE – .308 Win. cal. only, gas operated action, carbon fiber stock, 22 in. barrel, flash suppressor, free range sights. Disc. 1985.

	$670	$580	$520	$475	$430	$390	$350	Last MSR was $760.

SMITH & WESSON

Current manufacturer located in Springfield, MA, 1857 to date. Partnership with H. Smith & D.B. Wesson 1856-1874. Family owned by Wesson 1874-1965. S&W became a subsidiary of Bangor-Punta from 1965-1983. Between 1983-1987, Smith & Wesson was owned by the Lear Siegler Co. On May 22, 1987, Smith & Wesson was sold to Tomkins, an English holding company. During 2001, Tomkins sold Smith & Wesson to Saf-T-Hammer, an Arizona-based safety and security company.

Smith & Wessons have been classified under the following category names - PISTOLS: LEVER ACTION, ANTIQUE, TIP-UPS, TOP-BREAKS, SINGLE SHOTS, EARLY HAND EJECTORS (Named Models), NUMBERED MODEL REVOLVERS (Modern Hand Ejectors), SEMI-AUTOS, RIFLES, and SHOTGUNS.

Each category is fairly self-explanatory. Among the early revolvers, Tip-ups have barrels that tip up so the cylinder

MSR	100%	98%	95%	90%	80%	70%	60%

can be removed for loading or unloading, whereas Top-breaks have barrels & cylinders that tip down with automatic ejection.

Hand Ejectors are the modern type revolvers with swing out cylinders. In 1958, S&W began a system of numbering all models they made. Accordingly, the Hand Ejectors have been divided into two sections - the Early Hand Ejectors include the named models introduced prior to 1958. The Numbered Model Revolvers are the models introduced or continued after that date, and are easily identified by the model number stamped on the side of the frame, visible when the cylinder is open. The author wishes to express his thanks to Mr. Sal Raimondi, Jim Supica, Rick Nahas, and Roy Jinks, the S&W Historian, for their updates and valuable contributions.

Factory special orders, such as ivory or pearl grips, special finishes, engraving, and other production rarities will add premiums to the values listed. After 1893, all ivory and pearl grips had the metal S&W logo medallions inserted on top.

FACTORY LETTER OF AUTHENTICITY - S&W charges $30 for a formal letter of authenticity. A form is available for downloading on their website: www.smith-wesson.com for this service. Turnaround time is usually 8-12 weeks.

For more information and current pricing on both new and used Smith & Wesson airguns, please refer to the *Blue Book of Airguns* by Dr. Robert Beeman & John Allen (also online).

NUMBERED MODEL REVOLVERS (MODERN HAND EJECTORS)

Smith & Wesson handguns manufactured after 1958 are stamped with a model number on the frame under the cylinder yoke. The number is visible when the cylinder is open. All revolvers manufactured by S&W from 1946-1958 were produced without model numbers.

To locate a particular revolver in the following section, simply swing the cylinder out to the loading position and read the model number inside the yoke. The designation Mod. and a two- or three-digit number followed by a dash and another number designates which engineering change was underway when the gun was manufactured. Hence, a Mod. 15-7 is a Model 15 in its 7th engineering change (and should be indicated as such when ordering parts). Usually, earlier variations are the most desirable to collectors unless a particular improvement is rare. The same rule applies to semi-auto pistols, and the model designation is usually marked on the outside of the gun.

Beginning 1994, S&W started providing synthetic grips and a drilled/tapped receiver for scope mounting on certain models.

S&W revolvers are generally categorized by frame size. Frame sizes are as follows: J-frame (small), K-frame (medium), L-frame (medium), N-frame (large), and X-frame (extra large). All currently manufactured S&W revolvers chambered for .38 S&W Spl. cal. will also accept +P rated ammunition.

Current S&W abbreviations for revolver feature codes used on its price sheets and literature are as follows: Grips: CTG - Crimson Trace laser grips, RG - rubber grips, WG - wood grips, GF - finger groove grips. Sights: ADJ - adj., BB - black blade front, DWD - dovetail white dot, SC - interchangeable front, FIX - fixed, GB - gold bead front, SH - Hi-Viz, INTCH - integral front, PAT - Patridge front, NS - front night, RR - red ramp front, WB - white bead, and WO - white outline. Frame Material: AL - alloy, SS - stainless, CS - carbon. Frame Sizes: SM - Small/Compact, MD - Medium, LG - Large, XL - Extra Large. Finishes: ZB - Blue/Black, ZC - Clear Cote, ZG - Grey, ZM - Matte, ZS - Satin. Cylinder: CA - alloy, CC - carbon, CS - stainless, CT - titanium. Barrel: BF - full lug, BO - one piece, BP - PowerPort, BT - traditional, B2 - two piece. Action: AD - double action only, A2 - single action/double action.

Pre-2010 S&W abbreviations for revolver feature codes used on its price sheets and literature are as follows: Grips: GC - Crimson Trace laser grips, GR - rubber grips, GW - wood grips, GF - finger groove grips. Sights: SA - adj., SB - black blade front, SC - interchangeable front, SF - fixed, SG - gold bead front, SH - Hi-Viz, SI - integral front, SP - Patridge front, SN - front night, SR - red ramp front, SW - white outline adj. rear. Frame Material: FA - alloy, FS - stainless, FC - carbon.

Add 10%-15% for those models listed that are pinned and recessed (pre-1981 mfg.), if in 90% or better condition.

Earlier mfg. on the following models with lower engineering change numbered suffixes are more desirable than later mfg. (i.e., a Model 10-1 is more desirable than a Model 10-14).

Factory error stamped revolvers generally bring a small premium (5%-10%, if in 95%+ original condition) over a non-error gun, if the right collector is found.

MODEL 310 NIGHTGUARD – 10mm or .40 S&W (mfg. 2009) cal., 2 3/4 (mfg. 2009) or 2 1/2 (new 2010) in. barrel, matte black finish, large Scandium alloy frame with stainless steel cylinder, 6 shot, SA/DA, XS 24/7 standard dot tritium (mfg. 2009) or night (new 2010) front sight, fixed rear sight, Pachmayr grips, 28 oz. New 2009.

MSR $1,185	$895	$685	$530	$425	$350	$300	$275

MODEL 315 NIGHTGUARD – .38 Spl. + P cal., 2 1/2 in. barrel, K-frame, blue/black finish, 6 shot, rubber grips, front night sight, fixed rear sight, alloy frame with stainless cylinder. Mfg. 2009.

	$740	$550	$460	$385	$335	$295	$250	Last MSR was $995.

MODEL 325 PD-AIRLITE Sc – .45 ACP cal., 2 1/2 (disc. 2006) or 4 in. barrel, otherwise similar to Model 329 PD, approx. 21 1/2 - 25 oz. Mfg. 2004-2007.

	$800	$625	$485	$400	$335	$300	$275	Last MSR was $1,067.

MSR	100%	98%	95%	90%	80%	70%	60%

MODEL 325 NIGHTGUARD – .45 ACP cal., two-piece 2 1/2 in. barrel, alloy frame with stainless steel cylinder, black alloy finish, 6 shot, N-frame, SA/DA, rubber grips, fixed rear sight with front night sight, 28 oz. New 2008.

MSR $1,185	$895	$685	$530	$425	$350	$300	$275

MODEL 327 PD-AIRLITE Sc – .357 Mag., 8 shot, N-frame, 4 in. two-piece barrel, wood grips, Scandium frame with titanium cylinder, matte black finish, 26 1/2 oz. Mfg. 2008-2009.

	$950	$725	$550	$450	$350	$315	$285	*Last MSR was $1,264.*

MODEL 327 NIGHTGUARD – .357 Mag. cal., two-piece 2 1/2 in. barrel, alloy frame with stainless steel cylinder, black alloy finish, 8 shot, N-frame, SA/DA, rubber grips, fixed rear sight with front night sight, 27.6 oz. New 2008.

MSR $1,185	$895	$685	$530	$425	$350	$300	$275

MODEL 329 PD-AIRLITE Sc – .44 Mag. cal., 4 in barrel, N-frame, 6 shot, Scandium frame and titanium cylinder with matte black metal finish, wood Ahrends grips with finger grooves, and Hogue rubber mongrip, Hi-Viz front sight, approx. 26 oz. New 2003.

MSR $1,304	$995	$750	$575	$450	$375	$325	$300

MODEL 329 NIGHTGUARD – .44 Mag. cal., two-piece 2 1/2 in. barrel, alloy frame with stainless steel cylinder, black alloy finish, 6 shot, N-frame, SA/DA, rubber grips, fixed rear sight with front night sight, 29.3 oz. New 2008.

MSR $1,185	$895	$685	$530	$425	$350	$300	$275

MODEL 337 AIRLITE Ti CHIEFS SPECIAL – .38 S&W Spl.+P cal., J-frame, 5 shot, 1 7/8 in. barrel, similar design as the Model 331, 11.9 oz. Mfg. 1999-2003.

	$565	$435	$375	$335	$310	$280	$250	*Last MSR was $716.*

Add $24 for Dymondwood Boot grips (mfg. 1999 only).

MODEL 340 AIRLITE Sc CENTENNIAL – .357 Mag. cal., J-frame, 5 shot, 1 7/8 in. barrel only, Scandium alloy frame, barrel shroud, and yoke, titanium cylinder, two-tone matte stainless/grey finish, hammerless, Hogue Bantam grips, 12 oz. Mfg. 2001-2008.

	$775	$575	$475	$400	$340	$295	$250	*Last MSR was $1,019.*

MODEL 340 PD AIRLITE Sc CENTENNIAL – similar to Model 340 Airlite Sc, except has black/grey finish, Hi-Viz sight became standard 2009, 12 oz. New 2000.

MSR $1,153	$865	$635	$510	$400	$340	$295	$250

MODEL 340 M & P CENTENNIAL – .357 Mag. cal., 5 shot, J-frame, DAO, concealed hammer, 1 7/8 in. barrel, includes XS sights (24/7 tritium night and integral U-notch), Scandium alloy frame with stainless steel cylinder, matte black finish, synthetic or Crimson Trace laser grips, 13.3 oz. New 2007.

MSR $980	$660	$530	$395	$325	$275	$250	$225

Add $292 for Crimson Trace laser grips.

MODEL 342 AIRLITE Ti CENTENNIAL – .38 S&W Spl.+P cal., similar to Model 337, except is hammerless and double action only, matte stainless/grey finish, Uncle Mike's Boot grips, 12 oz. Mfg. 1999-2003.

	$575	$445	$390	$345	$310	$280	$250	*Last MSR was $734.*

Add $24 for Dymondwood Boot grips (mfg. 1999 only).

MODEL 342 PD AIRLITE Ti CENTENNIAL – .38 S&W Spl.+P cal., J-frame, 5 shot, double action only, aluminum alloy frame with titanium cylinder and stainless steel 1 7/8 in. barrel, hammerless, black/grey finish, Hogue Bantam grips, 10.8 oz. Mfg. 2000-2003.

	$595	$460	$390	$340	$310	$280	$250	*Last MSR was $758.*

MODEL 351 PD AIRLITE Sc CHIEFS SPECIAL (CENTENNIAL) – .22 Mag. cal., J-frame, 1 7/8 in. barrel, 7 shot, black finish, aluminum (new 2007) or Scandium (disc. 2006) alloy frame and cylinder, wood grips, 10.6 oz. New 2004.

MSR $853	$565	$410	$310	$255	$220	$200	$180

MODEL 357 PD – .41 Rem. Mag. cal., 6 shot, 4 in. barrel, N frame, Scandium alloy frame with titanium cylinder, matte black finish, uncheckered wood grips with finger grooves, Hi-Viz front sight, adj. V-notch rear sight, 27 1/2 oz. Mfg. mid-2005-2007.

	$815	$575	$475	$400	$340	$300	$275	*Last MSR was $1,067.*

MODEL 357 NIGHTGUARD – .41 Mag. cal., 2 1/2 in. barrel, N-frame, blue/black finish, 6 shot, rubber grips, alloy frame with stainless steel cylinder, fixed rear sight, front night sight. New 2009.

MSR $1,185	$895	$685	$530	$425	$350	$300	$275

MSR	100%	98%	95%	90%	80%	70%	60%

MODEL 360 AIRLITE Sc CHIEFS SPECIAL – .357 Mag. cal., J-frame, 5 shot, 1 7/8 in. barrel, Scandium alloy frame with titanium cylinder, matte stainless/grey finish, Hogue Bantam grips, fixed sights, 12 oz. Mfg. 2001-2007.

	$775	$575	$475	$400	$340	$295	$250	Last MSR was $1,019.

MODEL 360 PD AIRLITE Sc CHIEFS SPECIAL – similar to Model 360 Airlite Sc Chiefs Special, except has matte stainless/grey finish, Hi-Viz sight became standard 2009, 12 oz. New 2002.

MSR $1,153	$865	$635	$510	$400	$340	$295	$250

MODEL 360 M & P CHIEFS SPECIAL – .357 Mag. cal., 5 shot, J-frame, SA/DA, 1 7/8 in. barrel, includes XS sights (24/7 tritium night and intergral U-notch), Scandium alloy frame with stainless steel cylinder, matte black finish, synthetic grips, 13.3 oz. New 2007.

MSR $980	$660	$530	$395	$325	$275	$250	$225

MODEL 386 AIRLITE Sc MOUNTAIN LITE – .357 Mag. cal., L-frame, 7 shot, 2 1/2 (new 2007) or 3 1/8 (disc. 2006) in. stainless steel barrel with Hi-Viz front sight, Scandium alloy frame with titanium cylinder, two-tone matte stainless/grey finish, Hogue Bantam grips, 18 1/2 oz. Mfg. 2001-2007.

	$650	$510	$420	$365	$325	$295	$265	Last MSR was $869.

MODEL 386 PD AIRLITE Sc – .357 Mag. cal., L-frame, 7 shot, 2 1/2 in. stainless barrel with adj. black rear sight, Scandium alloy frame with titanium cylinder, black/grey finish, Hogue Bantam grips, 17 1/2 oz. Mfg. 2001-2005.

	$665	$500	$415	$355	$315	$285	$250	Last MSR was $872.

Add $22 for Hi-Viz front sight (disc. 2005).

MODEL 386 Sc/S – .357 Mag., 7 shot, 2 1/2 in. barrel, L-frame, synthetic finger groove grips, matte black finish, Scandium alloy frame with stainless steel cylinder, red ramp front sight, adj. rear sight, 21.2 oz. Mfg. mid-2007-2008.

	$695	$550	$440	$375	$330	$295	$265	Last MSR was $948.

MODEL 386 NIGHTGUARD – .357 Mag. cal., two-piece 2 1/2 in. barrel, alloy frame with stainless cylinder, black alloy finish, 7 shot, L-frame, SA/DA, rubber grips, fixed rear sight with front night sight, 24 1/2 oz. New 2008.

MSR $1,106	$840	$660	$550	$475	$425	$375	$335

MODEL 396 AIRLITE Ti MOUNTAIN LITE – .44 S&W Spl. cal., L-frame, 5 shot, 3 1/8 in. barrel with stainless liner and Hi-Viz front sight, aluminum alloy frame with titanium cylinder, matte stainless/grey finish, Hogue Bantam grips, 18 oz. Mfg. 2001-2004.

	$625	$475	$400	$355	$315	$285	$250	Last MSR was $812.

There has been one engineering change to this model.

MODEL 396 NIGHTGUARD – .44 Spl. cal., two-piece 2 1/2 in. barrel, alloy frame with stainless steel cylinder, black alloy finish, 5 shot, L-frame, SA/DA, rubber grips, fixed sight with front night sight, 24.2 oz. Mfg. 2008-2009.

	$825	$650	$550	$475	$425	$375	$335	Last MSR was $1,074.

MODEL 681 DISTINGUISHED SERVICE MAGNUM – .357 Mag. cal., stainless steel, 4 in. barrel, L-Frame. Mfg. 1980-1992.

	$425	$350	$275	$225	$175	$140	$125	Last MSR was $412.

1991 mfg. includes square butt.

MODEL 686 DISTINGUISHED COMBAT MAGNUM – .357 Mag./.38 S&W Spl.+P cal., L-Frame, similar to Model 586, except 2 1/2 (new 1990), 4, 6 (with or w/o PowerPort), or 8 3/8 (disc. 2002) in. barrel, fixed (disc.) or adj. sights, blue, stainless, Midnight Black (ltd. ed. 1989 only) finish, current production uses Hogue rubber grips, 35-51 oz. New 1980.

MSR $932	$615	$485	$360	$275	$225	$195	$165

* **Model 686 Distinguished Combat Magnum Plus** – .357 Mag./.38 S&W Spl.+P cal., L-frame, 7 shot, 2 1/2, 3 (new 2007), 4, or 6 in. barrel, synthetic or Hogue rubber grips, stainless steel, round (2 1/2 in. barrel only) or square butt, white outline rear sight on 4 or 6 in. barrel, 34 1/2 - 43 oz. New 1996.

MSR $964	$650	$515	$375	$300	$225	$195	$165

MODEL 686SSR PRO SERIES – .357 Mag. cal., 6 shot, L-frame, 4 in. barrel, SA/DA, interchangeable front sight, adj. rear sight, satin stainless finish, checkered wood grips, stainless steel frame and cylinder, forged hammer and trigger, custom barrel with recessed crown, bossed mainspring, and tuned action, 38.3 oz. New 2007.

MSR $1,090	$795	$610	$480	$400	$350	$325	$275

Subtract $31 for full moon clips (new 2010).

MSR	100%	98%	95%	90%	80%	70%	60%

PISTOLS: SEMI-AUTO

Listed in order of model number (except .32 and .35 Automatic Pistols). Alphabetical models will appear at the end of this section.

To understand S&W 3rd generation model nomenclature, the following rules apply. The first two digits (of the four digit model number) specify caliber. Numbers 39, 59, and 69 refer to 9mm Para. cal. The third digit refers to the model type. 0 means standard model, 1 is for compact, 2 is for standard model with decocking lever, 3 is for compact variation with decocking lever, 4 is for standard with double action only, 5 designates a compact model in double action only, 6 indicates a non-standard barrel length, 7 is a non-standard barrel length with decocking lever, and 8 refers to non-standard barrel length in double action only. The fourth digit refers to the material(s) used in the fabrication of the pistol. 3 refers to an aluminum alloy frame with stainless steel slide, 4 designates an aluminum alloy frame with carbon steel slide, 5 is for carbon steel frame and slide, 6 is a stainless steel frame and slide, and 7 refers to a stainless steel frame and carbon steel slide. Hence, a Model 4053 refers to a pistol in .40 S&W cal. configured in compact version with double action only and fabricated with an aluminum alloy frame and stainless steel slide. This model nomenclature does not apply to 2 or 3 digit model numbers (i.e., Rimfire Models and the Model 52).

Current S&W abbreviations for pistol feature codes used on its price sheets and literature are as follows: Grips: CTG - Crimson Trace laser grips, PG - plastic grips, RG - rubber grips, WG - wood grips. Sights: ADJ - adjustable, ADJFO - adj. fiber optic, FIXEDB - fixed black, LMC - low mount carry, WD - white dot, BB - black blade, BP - black post, FO - fiber optic, GB - gold bead - INTCH - interchangeable, NS - night sights, PAT - Patridge, RR - red ramp, WB - white bead, WD - white dot. Frames: AL - alloy, SS - stainless steel, CS - carbon steel, SM - stainless melonite, POLY - polymer. Safeties: AMBI - ambidextrous, MS - magazine, NMS - no magazine, IL - internal lock. Action: DA - double action only, SA - single action only, SA/DA - single action/double action, SF - striker fire.

Pre-2010 S&W abbreviations are as follows: Grips: GC - Crimson Trace laser grips, GR - rubber grips, GW - wood grips, GF - finger groove grips, GP - plastic grips. Sights: SA - adj., SB - black blade front, SC - interchangeable front, SD - dot front, SF - fixed, SG - gold bead front, SH - Hi-Viz, SL - Lo Mount Carry, SP - Patridge front, SR - red ramp front, SV - black post, S1 - front night. Frame Material: FA - alloy, FS - stainless, FC - carbon, FM - stainless Melonite, FP - polymer. Frame Sizes: SM - Small/Compact, MD - Medium, LG - Large, XL - Extra Large. Finishes: ZB - Blue/Black, ZC - Clear Cote, ZG - Grey, ZL - Melonite, ZM - Matte, ZS - Satin Stainless, ZT - Two-Tone, ZW - Camo. Barrel: BC - carbon, BL - light, BO - one piece, BS - stainless, BT - traditional, BX - heavy, B2 - two piece. Action: AD - double action only, AF - striker fire, AS - single action only, AT - traditional double action. Slide: DS - stainless steel, DC - carbon, DM - stainless Melonite.

When applicable, early variations of some of the older semi-auto models listed in this category will be more desirable than later mfg.

MODEL 39-2 ALLOY FRAME (LATER PRODUCTION) – 7.65mm (.30 Luger) or 9mm Para. cal., double action, 8 shot mag., 4 in. barrel, checkered walnut grips, adj. sight, alloy frame, approx. 1971, the 39-2 was introduced as an improved version. Mfg. 1970-82.

	100%	98%	95%	90%	80%	70%	60%
9mm Para. cal.	$395	$365	$325	$260	$240	$220	$200
7.65mm cal.	$1,375	$1,250	$1,100	$950	$825	$700	$625

Add 10% for nickel finish.

The .30 Luger cal. (7.65mm) was mfg. for the European marketplace only. Very hard to find in the U.S.

MODEL 59 – similar to Model 39, except has 14 shot mag., black nylon grips. Disc. 1981.

	100%	98%	95%	90%	80%	70%	60%
	$475	$400	$350	$275	$250	$225	$215

Add $35 for nickel finish.
Add $150 for smooth (ungrooved) grip frame.

MODEL 410 – .40 S&W cal., traditional double action, steel slide with alloy frame, blue finish, 4 in. barrel, 10 or 11 shot mag., single side safety, 3-dot sights, straight backstrap with synthetic grips, 28 1/2 oz. Mfg. 1996-2007.

	100%	98%	95%	90%	80%	70%	60%	
	$525	$370	$275	$230	$195	$175	$165	Last MSR was $687.

Add $21 for Hi-Viz front sight (disc. 2003).

MODEL 411 – .40 S&W cal., 4 in. barrel, 11 shot mag., fixed sights, blue finish, aluminum alloy frame, manual safety. Mfg. 1993-95.

	100%	98%	95%	90%	80%	70%	60%	
	$475	$400	$350	$325	$295	$280	$265	Last MSR was $525.

MODEL 439 – 9mm Para. cal., double action, 4 in. barrel, blue or nickel finish, alloy frame, 8 shot mag., checkered walnut grips, 30 oz. Disc. 1988.

	100%	98%	95%	90%	80%	70%	60%	
	$475	$35	$325	$275	$240	$225	$210	Last MSR was $472.

Add $34 for nickel finish (disc. 1986).
Add $26 for adj. sights.

MODEL 457 COMPACT – .45 ACP cal., traditional double action, alloy frame and steel slide, 3 3/4 in. barrel, single side safety, 3-dot sights, 7 shot mag., straight backstrap, blue finish only, black synthetic grips, 29 oz. Mfg. 1996-2006.

	100%	98%	95%	90%	80%	70%	60%	
	$525	$365	$270	$225	$195	$175	$165	Last MSR was $681.

MSR	100%	98%	95%	90%	80%	70%	60%	

MODEL 459 – 9mm Para. cal., 14 shot version of Model 439, checkered nylon stocks, limited mfg. with squared-off triggerguard with serrations. Disc. 1988.

| | $450 | $400 | $350 | $300 | $275 | $255 | $240 | *Last MSR was $501.* |

Add $26 for adj. sights.
Add $44 for nickel finish (disc. 1986).

MODEL 469 "MINI" – 9mm Para. cal., double action, alloy frame, 12 shot finger extension mag., short frame, bobbed hammer, 3 1/2 in. barrel, sandblast blue or satin nickel finish, ambidextrous safety standard (1986), molded Delrin black Grips, 26 oz. Disc. 1988.

| | $475 | $35 | $325 | $275 | $240 | $225 | $210 | *Last MSR was $478.* |

MODEL 539 – 9mm Para. cal., double action, steel frame, 8 shot, 4 in. barrel, blue or nickel. Approx. 8,300 mfg. Disc. 1983.

| | $550 | $475 | $415 | $375 | $350 | $325 | $300 | |

Add $35 for nickel finish.
Add $30 for adj. rear sight.

MODEL 559 – 9mm Para. cal., double action, steel frame, 14 shot mag., 4 in. barrel, blue or nickel. Approx. 1,700 mfg. Disc. 1983.

| | $600 | $525 | $450 | $375 | $275 | $250 | $225 | |

Add $35 for nickel finish.
Add $30 for adj. rear sight.

MODEL 639 STAINLESS – 9mm Para. cal., similar to Model 439, only stainless steel, 8 shot mag., ambidextrous safety became standard 1986, 36 oz. Disc. 1988.

| | $475 | $400 | $350 | $300 | $250 | $200 | $165 | *Last MSR was $523.* |

Add $27 for adj. sights.

MODEL 645 STAINLESS – .45 ACP cal. only, 5 in. barrel, 8 shot mag., squared-off trigger guard, black molded nylon grips, ambidextrous safety, fixed sights, 37 1/2 oz. New 1986. Disc. 1988.

| | $550 | $475 | $400 | $350 | $300 | $250 | $200 | *Last MSR was $622.* |

Add approx. 25% for the approx. 150 Model 645 "Interim" pistols were mfg. in 1988 only.
Add $27 for adj. sight.

MODEL 659 STAINLESS – 9mm Para. cal., similar to Model 459, only stainless steel, 14 shot mag., ambidextrous safety became standard 1986, 39 1/2 oz. Disc. 1988.

| | $475 | $400 | $350 | $300 | $250 | $215 | $180 | *Last MSR was $553.* |

Add approx. 30% for the approx. 150 Model 659 "Interim" pistols were mfg. in 1988 only.
Add $27 for adj. sights.

MODEL 669 STAINLESS – 9mm Para. cal., smaller version of Model 659 with 12 shot finger extension mag., 3 1/2 in. barrel, fixed sights, molded Delrin grips, ambidextrous safety standard, 26 oz. Mfg. 1986-88 only.

| | $450 | $375 | $300 | $250 | $195 | $165 | $140 | *Last MSR was $522.* |

Add approx. 30% for the approx. 150 Model 669 "Interim" pistols were mfg. in 1988 only.

MODEL 908 COMPACT – 9mm Para. cal., compact variation of the Model 909/910, 3 1/2 in. barrel, 3-dot sights, 8 shot mag., straight backstrap, 24 oz. Mfg. 1996-2007.

| | $495 | $355 | $275 | $230 | $195 | $175 | $165 | *Last MSR was $648.* |

MODEL 909 – 9mm Para. cal., 4 in. barrel, traditional double action, large frame, 9 shot mag., fixed sights, single side safety, alloy frame and steel slide, curved backstrap with black synthetic grips, 27 oz. Mfg. 1994-96.

| | $450 | $375 | $300 | $250 | $210 | $190 | $175 | *Last MSR was $443.* |

MODEL 910 – similar to Model 909, except has 10 or 15 shot mag., 28 oz. Mfg. 1994-2007.

| | $455 | $345 | $270 | $230 | $195 | $175 | $165 | *Last MSR was $616.* |

Add $22 for Hi-Viz front sight (disc. 2003).

MODEL 915 – 9mm Para. cal., 4 in. barrel, fixed sights, 10 (C/B 1994) or 15* shot mag., manual safety, aluminum alloy frame, blue finish. Mfg. 1993-94.

| | $425 | $350 | $275 | $225 | $205 | $190 | $175 | *Last MSR was $467.* |

MODEL 1006 STAINLESS – 10mm cal., double action semi-auto, stainless steel construction, 5 in. barrel, exposed hammer, 9 shot mag., fixed or adj. sights, ambidextrous safety. Mfg. 1990-93.

| | $675 | $575 | $425 | $350 | $300 | $245 | $215 | *Last MSR was $769.* |

Add $27 for adj. rear sight.

MODEL 1026 STAINLESS – 10mm cal., 5 in. barrel, traditional double action, features frame mounted decocking lever, 9 shot mag., straight backstrap. Mfg. 1990-91 only.

| | $675 | $575 | $425 | $350 | $300 | $245 | $215 | *Last MSR was $755.* |

MSR	100%	98%	95%	90%	80%	70%	60%

MODEL 1046 STAINLESS – 10mm cal., 5 in. barrel, fixed sights, double action only, 9 shot mag., straight backstrap. Mfg. 1991 only.

| | $675 | $575 | $425 | $350 | $300 | $245 | $215 | Last MSR was $747. |

MODEL 1066 STAINLESS – 10mm cal., 4 1/4 in. barrel, 9 shot mag., straight backstrap, ambidextrous safety, traditional double action, fixed sights. Mfg. 1990-92.

| | $650 | $550 | $425 | $350 | $300 | $245 | $215 | Last MSR was $730. |

Add $75 for Tritium night sights - disc. 1991 (Model 1066-NS).
Only 1,000 Model 1066-NSs were manufactured.

MODEL 1076 STAINLESS – similar to Model 1026 Stainless, except has 4 1/4 in. barrel. Mfg. 1990-93.

| | $700 | $625 | $550 | $450 | $350 | $300 | $245 | Last MSR was $778. |

MODEL 1086 STAINLESS – similar to Model 1066 Stainless, except is double action only.

| | $725 | $600 | $475 | $375 | $300 | $250 | $210 | Last MSR was $730. |

MODEL SW1911 – .45 ACP cal., patterned after the Colt M1911, large frame, SA, 5 in. barrel, 8 shot single stack mag., alloy (disc. 2006), steel or stainless steel frame, steel slide, matte, blue/black (new 2005) or Clear Coat finish, patented S&W firing pin safety release activated by the grip safety, pinned-in external extractor, Wolff springs throughout, Texas Armament match trigger, Hogue rubber (standard) or wood (new 2004) grips, McCormick hammer and thumb safety, Briley barrel bushing, two Wilson magazines, full-length heavy guide rod, high profile Wilson beavertail safety, adj. rear black blade, or Novak Lo-Mount Carry sights, 39 oz. New 2003.

| MSR $1,169 | $940 | $685 | $530 | $425 | $375 | $325 | $295 | |

Add $71 for rear adj. sight.
Add $269 for Doug Koenig Model w/two-tone finish and adj. rear sight (disc. 2007).

* **Model SW1911 Stainless** – features stainless steel frame and slide, checkered wood or black synthetic grips, 39.4 oz.

| MSR $1,153 | $915 | $685 | $500 | $450 | $400 | $350 | $295 | |

Add $127 for adj. sight.
Add $93 for matte finish with black blade front sight (disc. 2006).
Add $324 for wood grips and adj. sights.
Add $72 for tactical lower frame rail w/wood grips (new 2006).
Add $301 for Crimson Trace laser grips (new 2005).

* **Model SW1911 PD (Sc)** – similar to Model SW1911, except has 4 1/4 or 5 (new 2007) in. barrel with small Scandium alloy frame, 8 shot, black finish, and wood grips. New 2004.

| MSR $1,256 | $985 | $730 | $525 | $450 | $400 | $350 | $325 | |

Add $269 for Crimson Trace laser grips.
Add $237 for Gunsite model with gold bead front sight.
Add $40 for tactical lower rail.

* **Model SW1911 w/no firing pin block** – similar to SW1911, except does not have firing pin block, Melonite finish. New 2009.

| MSR $1,240 | $990 | $760 | $530 | $450 | $400 | $375 | $350 | |

* **Model SW1911 Compact ES** – similar to Model SW1911, except has 4 1/4 in. barrel and compact frame, blue/black finish. New 2009.

| MSR $1,288 | $1,025 | $775 | $530 | $450 | $400 | $375 | $350 | |

SW1911 PRO SERIES – .45 ACP or 9mm Para. (new 2009) cal., SA, 8 (.45 ACP) or 10 (9mm Para.) shot mag., 5 in. barrel, 3-dot (9mm Para. cal. only) or Novak front and rear sights, checkered wood grips, stainless steel frame and slide, satin stainless finish, Pro Series features include 300 LPI front strap checkering, hand polished barrel feed ramp, crisp 4 1/2 lb. trigger pull, full length guide rod, oversized external extractor, double sided frame safety, precision crowned muzzle, 41 oz. New mid-2007.

| MSR $1,556 | $1,225 | $1,000 | $875 | $750 | $650 | $550 | $450 | |

Add $127 for 9mm Para. cal. (new 2009).

* **SW1911 Pro Series Subcompact** – similar to SW1911 Pro Series, except has 3 in. barrel, 7 shot mag., and subcompact frame. New 2009.

| MSR $1,304 | $1,025 | $875 | $750 | $650 | $575 | $500 | $450 | |

MODEL 3904 – 9mm Para. cal., double action semi-auto, aluminum alloy frame, 4 in. barrel with fixed bushing, 8 shot mag., Delrin one piece wraparound grips, exposed hammer, ambidextrous safety, beveled magazine well, extended squared-off triggerguard, adj. or fixed rear sight, 3-dot sighting system, 28 oz. Mfg. 1989-91.

| | $450 | $385 | $350 | $325 | $300 | $280 | $265 | Last MSR was $541. |

Add $25 for adj. rear sight.

MSR	100%	98%	95%	90%	80%	70%	60%	

MODEL 3906 STAINLESS – stainless steel variation of the Model 3904, 35 1/2 oz. Mfg. 1989-91.

	$510	$435	$375	$315	$270	$230	$200	Last MSR was $604.

Add $28 for adj. rear sight.

MODEL 3913 COMPACT STAINLESS – stainless steel variation of the Model 3914, 25 oz. Mfg. 1990-99.

	$535	$440	$365	$305	$260	$220	$190	Last MSR was $662.

MODEL 3913TSW TACTICAL – 9mm Para. cal., traditional double action, compact frame, 3 1/2 in. barrel, 8-shot mag., Novak Lo-Mount 2-dot sights, stainless steel slide, aluminum alloy frame, matte stainless finish, straight black backstrap synthetic grips, 24.8 oz. Mfg. 1998-2006.

	$690	$520	$400	$335	$290	$245	$215	Last MSR was $876.

MODEL 3914 COMPACT – 9mm Para. cal., double action semi-auto, aluminum alloy frame, 3 1/2 in. barrel, hammerless, 8 shot finger extension mag., fixed sights only, ambidextrous safety, blue finish, straight backstrap grip, 25 oz. Mfg. 1990-95.

	$495	$425	$350	$325	$295	$280	$265	Last MSR was $562.

This model was also available with a single side manual safety at no extra charge - disc. 1991 (Model 3914NL).

MODEL 3953 COMPACT STAINLESS – 9mm Para. cal., double action only, aluminum alloy frame with stainless steel slide, compact model with 3 1/2 in. barrel, 8 shot mag. Mfg. 1990-99.

	$535	$440	$365	$305	$260	$220	$190	Last MSR was $662.

MODEL 3954 – similar to Model 3953, except has blue steel slide. Mfg. 1990-92.

	$475	$395	$350	$325	$295	$280	$265	Last MSR was $528.

MODEL 4003 STAINLESS – .40 S&W cal., traditional double action, 4 in. barrel, 11 shot mag., white dot fixed sights, ambidextrous safety, aluminum alloy frame with stainless steel slide, one piece Xenoy wraparound grips, straight gripstrap, 28 oz. Mfg. 1991-93.

	$575	$495	$395	$330	$285	$240	$215	Last MSR was $698.

* Model 4003TSW Stainless – similar to Model 4003 Stainless, but has aluminum alloy frame, 10 shot mag., stainless steel slide, S&W tactical features, including equipment rail and Novak Lo-Mount Carry sights, traditional double action only, satin stainless finish, 28 1/2 oz. Mfg. 2000-2004.

	$700	$600	$500	$450	$400	$360	$330	Last MSR was $940.

MODEL 4004 – .40 S&W cal., similar to Model 4003, except has aluminum alloy frame with blue carbon steel slide. Mfg. 1991-92.

	$540	$460	$375	$325	$295	$280	$265	Last MSR was $643.

MODEL 4006 STAINLESS – .40 S&W cal., 3 1/2 (Shorty Forty) or 4 in. barrel, 10 (C/B 1994) or 11* shot mag., satin stainless finish, exposed hammer, Delrin one piece wraparound grips, 3-dot sights, 38 1/2 oz. Mfg. 1990-99.

	$655	$545	$400	$335	$290	$245	$215	Last MSR was $791.

Add $31 for adj. rear sight.
Add $115 for fixed Tritium night sights (new 1992).
The bobbed hammer option on this model was disc. in 1991.

MODEL 4013 COMPACT STAINLESS – .40 S&W cal., semi-auto, standard double action, 3 1/2 in. barrel, 8 shot mag., fixed sights, ambidextrous safety, alloy frame. Mfg. 1991-96.

	$595	$485	$385	$330	$295	$280	$265	Last MSR was $722.

MODEL 4013TSW TACTICAL – .40 S&W cal., semi-auto, standard double action, 3 1/2 In. barrel, 9 shot mag. with reversible mag. catch, aluminum alloy frame with stainless steel slide, satin stainless finish, black synthetic grips, fixed 3-dot Novak Lo-Mount Carry sights, ambidextrous safety, 26.8 oz. Mfg. 1997-2006.

	$825	$630	$450	$385	$335	$280	$235	Last MSR was $1,021.

MODEL 4014 COMPACT – similar to Model 4013, except is steel with blue finish. Mfg. 1991-93.

	$550	$475	$425	$375	$330	$300	$275	Last MSR was $635.

MODEL 4026 STAINLESS – .40 S&W cal., traditional double action with frame mounted decocking lever, 10 (C/B 1994) or 11* shot mag., fixed sights, curved backstrap, 36 oz. Mfg. 1991-93.

	$625	$525	$400	$335	$290	$245	$215	Last MSR was $731.

MODEL 4040 PD – .40 S&W cal., compact frame using Scandium, 3 1/2 in. barrel, Hogue rubber grips, Novak Lo-Mount Carry 3-dot sights, matte black finish, 25.6 oz. Mfg. 2003-2005.

	$625	$525	$400	$335	$290	$245	$215	Last MSR was $840.

MSR	100%	98%	95%	90%	80%	70%	60%	

MODEL 4043 STAINLESS – .40 S&W cal., double action only, aluminum alloy frame with stainless steel slide, 4 in. barrel, 10 (C/B 1994) or 11* shot mag., one piece Xenoy wraparound grips, straight backstrap, white-dot fixed sights, 30 oz. Mfg. 1991-99.

	$635	$510	$390	$325	$280	$240	$210	Last MSR was $772.

Model 4043TSW Stainless – double action only, similar to Model 4043 Stainless, but has S&W tactical features, including equipment rail, 28 1/2 oz. Mfg. 2000-2002.

	$650	$550	$425	$350	$290	$245	$215	Last MSR was $886.

MODEL 4044 – .40 S&W cal., similar to Model 4043, except has carbon steel slide. Mfg. 1991-92.

	$540	$460	$375	$325	$295	$280	$265	Last MSR was $643.

MODEL 4046 STAINLESS – similar to Model 4006 Stainless, except is double action only, 4 in. barrel only. Mfg. 1991-99.

	$655	$540	$400	$335	$290	$245	$215	Last MSR was $791.

Add $115 for Tritium night sights (new 1992).

MODEL 4053 COMPACT STAINLESS – double action only variation of the Model 4013. Mfg. 1991-97.

	$625	$525	$400	$335	$290	$245	$215	Last MSR was $734.

MODEL 4053TSW (TACTICAL) – .40 S&W cal., double action only, 3 1/2 in. barrel, 9 shot mag. with reversible mag. catch, alloy frame with stainless steel slide, satin stainless finish, black synthetic grips, fixed sights, ambidextrous safety, 26.8 oz. Mfg. 1997-2002.

	$730	$580	$425	$360	$315	$260	$225	Last MSR was $886.

MODEL 4054 – double action only variation of the Model 4014. Mfg. 1991-92.

	$650	$550	$425	$350	$290	$245	$215	Last MSR was $629.

MODEL 4056TSW (TACTICAL) – .40 S&W cal., double action only, 3 1/2 in. barrel, 9 shot mag. with reversible mag. catch, alloy frame with stainless steel slide, satin stainless finish, black synthetic grips, fixed sights, ambidextrous safety, 37 1/2 oz Mfg. 1997-2000.

	$675	$575	$450	$350	$290	$245	$215	Last MSR was $844.

MODEL 4505 – .45 ACP cal., carbon steel variation of the Model 4506, fixed or adj. rear sight. 1,200 mfg. 1991 only.

	$650	$550	$425	$350	$290	$245	$215	Last MSR was $660.

Add $27 for adj. rear sight.

MODEL 4506 STAINLESS – .45 ACP cal., 5 in. barrel, 8 shot mag., combat triggerguard, exposed hammer, fixed or adj. rear sight, straight backstrap (curved is optional), Delrin one-piece grips, 40 1/2 oz. Mfg. 1990-99.

	$680	$550	$410	$345	$300	$250	$220	Last MSR was $822.

Add $33 for adj. rear sight.

Approx. 100 Model 4506s left the factory mismarked Model 645 on the frame. In NIB condition they are worth $700.

MODEL 4513TSW – 45 ACP cal., traditional double action, compact frame, 3 3/4 in. barrel, 7 shot mag., 3-dot Novak Lo-Mount Carry sights, stainless steel slide, aluminum alloy frame, satin stainless finish, 28.6 oz. Mfg. 1998-2004.

	$725	$625	$475	$395	$340	$285	$240	Last MSR was $980.

MODEL 4516 COMPACT STAINLESS – .45 ACP cal., bobbed hammer, compact variation of the Model 4506, 3 3/4 in. barrel, 7 shot mag., ambidextrous safety, fixed rear sight only, 34 oz. Mfg. 1990-1997.

	$650	$525	$400	$335	$290	$245	$215	Last MSR was $787.

Original model is marked 4516 while later mfg. changed slide legend to read 4516-1. Original mfg. is more collectible and slight premiums are being asked.

MODEL 4526 STAINLESS – similar to Model 4506 Stainless, except has frame mounted decocking lever. Mfg. 1990-91 only.

	$675	$550	$425	$350	$290	$245	$215	Last MSR was $762.

MODEL 4536 STAINLESS – similar to Model 4516 Compact, except has frame mounted decocking lever only. Mfg. 1990-91 only.

	$675	$550	$425	$350	$290	$245	$215	Last MSR was $762.

MODEL 4546 STAINLESS – similar to Model 4506 Stainless, except is double action only. Mfg. 1990-91 only.

	$675	$550	$425	$350	$290	$245	$215	Last MSR was $735.

MSR	100%	98%	95%	90%	80%	70%	60%

MODEL 4553TSW – similar to Model 4513TSW, except is double action only. Mfg. 1998-2002.

| | $755 | $595 | $450 | $385 | $335 | $280 | $235 | Last MSR was $924. |

MODEL 4556 STAINLESS – .45 ACP cal., features double action only, 3 3/4 in. barrel, 7 shot mag., fixed sights. Mfg. 1991 only.

| | $675 | $550 | $425 | $350 | $290 | $245 | $215 | Last MSR was $735. |

MODEL 4563TSW – .45 ACP cal., traditional double action only, 4 1/4 in. barrel, 8 shot mag., aluminum alloy frame with stainless steel slide, satin stainless finish, includes S&W tactical features, including equipment rail and Novak 3-dot sights, synthetic black straight backstrap grips, 30.6 oz. Mfg. 2000-2004.

| | $750 | $625 | $450 | $390 | $340 | $280 | $235 | Last MSR was $977. |

MODEL 4566 STAINLESS – .45 ACP cal., traditional double action with ambidextrous safety, 4 1/4 in. barrel, 8 shot mag. Mfg. 1990-99.

| | $650 | $550 | $410 | $345 | $300 | $250 | $220 | Last MSR was $822. |

* Model 4566TSW Stainless – similar to Model 4566, except has ambidextrous safety, 39.1 oz. Disc. 2004.

| | $725 | $600 | $450 | $390 | $340 | $280 | $235 | Last MSR was $1,000. |

MODEL 4567-NS STAINLESS – similar to Model 4566 Stainless, except has Tritium night sights, stainless steel frame and carbon steel slide. 2,500 mfg. in 1991 only.

| | $650 | $550 | $425 | $350 | $290 | $245 | $215 | Last MSR was $735. |

MODEL 4576 STAINLESS – .45 ACP cal., features 4 1/4 in. barrel, frame mounted decocking lever, fixed sights. Mfg. 1990-92.

| | $635 | $535 | $410 | $345 | $300 | $250 | $220 | Last MSR was $762. |

MODEL 4583TSW – similar to Model 4563TSW, except is double action only, 30.6 oz. Mfg. 2000-2002.

| | $700 | $575 | $450 | $380 | $330 | $275 | $230 | Last MSR was $921. |

MODEL 4586 STAINLESS – .45 ACP cal., 4 1/4 in. barrel, double action only, 8 shot mag. Mfg. 1990-99.

| | $695 | $575 | $425 | $345 | $300 | $250 | $220 | Last MSR was $822. |

* Model 4586TSW Stainless – similar to Model 4566TSW, except is double action only, 39.1 oz. Mfg. 2000-2002.

| | $700 | $600 | $445 | $380 | $330 | $275 | $230 | Last MSR was $942. |

MODEL 5903 – 9mm Para. cal., double action semi-auto, 4 in. barrel, stainless steel slide and alloy frame, exposed hammer, 10 (C/B 1994) or 15* shot mag., adj. (disc. 1993) or fixed rear sight, ambidextrous safety. Mfg. 1990-97.

| | $650 | $575 | $475 | $395 | $365 | $325 | $300 | Last MSR was $701. |

Add $30 for adj. rear sight (disc).

MODEL 5904 – similar to Model 5903, except has steel slide and blue finish, 26 1/2 oz. Mfg. 1989-98.

| | $535 | $445 | $360 | $330 | $300 | $280 | $265 | Last MSR was $663. |

Add $30 for adj. rear sight (disc. 1993).

MODEL 5905 – 9mm Para. cal., similar to Model 5904, except has carbon steel frame and slide. Approx. 5,000 mfg. 1990-91 only.

| | $650 | $575 | $500 | $440 | $375 | $335 | $300 | |

MODEL 5906 STAINLESS – stainless steel variation of the Model 5904, 37 1/2 oz. Mfg. 1989-99.

| | $615 | $500 | $400 | $335 | $290 | $245 | $215 | Last MSR was $751. |

Add $37 for adj. rear sight.
Add $115 for Tritium night sights.

* Model 5906TSW Stainless – traditional double action only, similar to Model 5906 Stainless, but has S&W tactical features, including equipment rail, 38.3 oz. Mfg. 2000-2004.

| | $650 | $575 | $475 | $350 | $300 | $265 | $235 | Last MSR was $915. |

Add $44 if w/o NLC sight.
Add $132 for night sights (disc.).

MODEL 5924 – 9mm Para. cal., 4 in. barrel, features frame mounted decocking lever, 15 shot mag., 37 1/2 oz. Mfg. 1990-91 only.

| | $625 | $550 | $475 | $375 | $335 | $300 | $280 | Last MSR was $635. |

MODEL 5926 STAINLESS – stainless variation of the Model 5924. Disc. 1992.

| | $600 | $525 | $425 | $350 | $295 | $250 | $210 | Last MSR was $697. |

MSR	100%	98%	95%	90%	80%	70%	60%

MODEL 5943 STAINLESS – 9mm Para. cal., double action only, 4 in. barrel, aluminum alloy frame with stainless steel slide, straight backstrap, 15 shot mag. Mfg. 1990-91 only.

| | $550 | $465 | $390 | $325 | $280 | $235 | $205 | Last MSR was $655. |

* *Model 5943-SSV Stainless* – similar to Model 5943 Stainless, except has 3 1/2 in. barrel, Tritium night sights. Mfg. 1990-91 only.

| | $625 | $550 | $475 | $395 | $330 | $285 | $240 | Last MSR was $690. |

* *Model 5943TSW Stainless* – double action only, aluminum alloy frame with stainless steel slide, includes S&W tactical features, equipment rail, and Novak Lo-Mount Carry sights, 28.9 oz. Mfg. 2000-2002.

| | $650 | $575 | $450 | $375 | $325 | $280 | $265 | Last MSR was $844. |

MODEL 5944 – similar to Model 5943 Stainless, except has blue finish slide. Mfg. 1990-91 only.

| | $625 | $550 | $475 | $400 | $350 | $300 | $280 | Last MSR was $610. |

MODEL 5946 STAINLESS – 9mm Para. cal., double action only, one piece Xenoy wraparound grips, all stainless steel variation of the Model 5943, 39 1/2 oz. Mfg. 1990-99.

| | $615 | $500 | $400 | $335 | $290 | $245 | $215 | Last MSR was $751. |

* *Model 5946TSW Stainless* – 9mm Para. cal., double action only, includes S&W tactical features, equipment rail, and Novak Lo-Mount Carry sights, 38.3 oz. Mfg. 2000-2002.

| | $725 | $600 | $450 | $375 | $315 | $260 | $225 | Last MSR was $863. |

MODEL 6904 COMPACT – 9mm Para. cal., compact variation of the Model 5904, 3 1/2 in. barrel, 10 (C/ B 1994) or 12* shot finger extension mag., fixed rear sight, 26 1/2 oz. Mfg. 1989-97.

| | $550 | $475 | $400 | $350 | $325 | $300 | $280 | Last MSR was $625. |

MODEL 6906 COMPACT STAINLESS – stainless steel variation of the Model 6904, 26 1/2 oz. Mfg. 1989-99.

| | $585 | $470 | $380 | $320 | $275 | $235 | $200 | Last MSR was $720. |

Add $116 for Tritium night sights (new 1992).

MODEL 6926 STAINLESS – 9mm Para. cal., 3 1/2 in. barrel, standard double action, features frame mounted decocking lever, aluminum alloy frame with stainless slide, 12 shot mag. Mfg. 1990-91 only.

| | $650 | $575 | $450 | $375 | $315 | $270 | $230 | Last MSR was $663. |

MODEL 6944 – 9mm Para., double action only, 3 1/2 in. barrel, 12 shot mag., aluminum alloy frame with blue steel slide. Mfg. 1990-91 only.

| | $600 | $525 | $450 | $375 | $325 | $300 | $280 | Last MSR was $578. |

MODEL 6946 STAINLESS – similar to Model 6944, except has stainless steel slide, semi-bobbed hammer, 26 1/2 oz. Mfg. 1990-99.

| | $675 | $575 | $475 | $375 | $315 | $270 | $230 | Last MSR was $720. |

SIGMA MODEL SW9F SERIES – 9mm Para. cal., double action only, 4 1/2 in. barrel, fixed sights, polymer frame and steel slide, striker firing system, blue finish only, 10 (C/B 1994) or 17* shot mag., 26 oz. Mfg. 1994-96.

| | $475 | $400 | $350 | $325 | $295 | $280 | $265 | Last MSR was $593. |

Add $104 for Tritium night sights.

* *Sigma Model SW9C Series Compact* – similar to Sigma Model SW9F, except has 4 in. barrel, 25 oz. Mfg. 1996-98.

| | $450 | $355 | $325 | $295 | $280 | $265 | $240 | Last MSR was $541. |

* *Sigma Model SW9M Series Compact* – features 3 1/4 in. barrel, 7 shot mag., fixed channel rear sight, grips integral with frame, satin black finish, 18 oz. Mfg. 1996-98.

| | $300 | $270 | $240 | $220 | $195 | $175 | $160 | Last MSR was $366. |

SIGMA MODEL SW9VE/GVE (SW9E/SW9P/SW9G/SW9V) – 9mm Para. cal., DAO, features 4 in. standard or ported (SW9P, mfg. 2001-2003) barrel, 10 or 16 (new late 2004) shot mag., 3-dot sighting system, grips integral with grey (disc. 2000), Nato Green (SW9G, disc. 2003) or black polymer frame, black (SW9E, mfg. 1999-2002) or satin stainless steel (SW9VE) slide, 24.7 oz. New 1997.

| MSR $482 | $375 | $325 | $250 | $215 | $185 | $165 | $150 | |

Add $8 for Allied Forces model w/ Melonite slide (mfg. 2007-2009).
Add $380 for SW9VE/SW40VE Allied Forces model w/emergency kit, including space blankets, emergency food, first aid kit, crank radio/ flashlight, multi-tool, and pocket survival pack, cased (mfg. 2007-2009).
Add $48 for SW9P or SW9G with night sights (disc. 2003).
Add $210 for Tritium night sights (disc. 2000).

The Enhanced Sigma Series Model SW9VE was introduced during 1999, after the SW9V was discontinued.

MSR	100%	98%	95%	90%	80%	70%	60%

SIGMA MODEL SW40F SERIES – .40 S&W cal., double action only, 4 1/2 in. barrel, fixed sights, polymer frame, blue finish only, 10 (C/B 1994) or 15* shot mag., 26 oz. Mfg. 1994-98.

| | $450 | $355 | $325 | $295 | $280 | $265 | $240 | Last MSR was $541. |

Add $104 for Tritium night sights (disc. 1997).

* ***Sigma Model SW40C Series Compact*** – similar to Sigma Model SW40F, except has 4 in. barrel, 26 oz. Mfg. 1996-98.

| | $450 | $355 | $325 | $295 | $280 | $265 | $240 | Last MSR was $541. |

SIGMA MODEL SW40VE/SW40P/SW40G/SW40GVE (SW40E/SW40V) – .40 S&W cal., features 4 in. standard or ported (SW40P, mfg. 2001-2005) barrel, 10 or 14 (new mid-2004) shot mag., 3-dot sighting system, grips integral with grey (disc. 2000), Nato green (SW40G) or black polymer frame, black slide with melonite finish (SW40E, mfg. 1999-2002) or satin stainless steel slide, 24.4 oz. New 1997.

| MSR $482 | $375 | $325 | $250 | $215 | $185 | $165 | $150 | |

Add $8 for Allied Forces model w/Melonite slide, (mfg. 2007-2009).
Add $210 for Tritium night sights (disc.).
Add $145 for Model SW40P or SW40G (includes night sights, disc. 2005).
Add $380 for SW9VE/SW40VE Allied Forces model w/emergency kit, including space blankets, emergency food, first aid kit, crank radio/flashlight, multi-tool, and pocket survival pack, cased (mfg. 2007-2009).

The Enhanced Sigma Series Model SW40VE was introduced during 1999, after the SW40V was discontinued.

MODEL SW99 – 9mm Para., .40 S&W, or .45 ACP (new 2003) cal., traditional double action, 9 (.45 ACP cal.), 10 shot mag., similar to the Walther P99, black polymer frame with black stainless slide and barrel, 4, 4 1/8 (.40 S&W cal. only), or 4.25 (.45 ACP cal. only, new 2003) in. barrel, black finish, ambidextrous mag. release, frame equipment groove, interchangeable backstraps, decocking lever, cocking indicator, adj. 3-dot or night sights, 25.4 (9mm Para cal.) or 28 1/2 oz. Mfg. 2000-2004.

| | $565 | $485 | $430 | $380 | $340 | $300 | $275 | Last MSR was $667. |

Add $123 for night sights.
Add $41 for .45 ACP cal. (new 2003).

* ***Model SW99 Compact*** – similar to SW99, except is compact version, not available in .45 ACP cal., 3 1/2 in. barrel, 8 (.40 S&W cal.) or 10 (9mm Para cal.) shot mag. with finger extension, approx. 23 oz. Mfg. 2003-2004.

| | $565 | $485 | $430 | $380 | $340 | $300 | $275 | Last MSR was $667. |

SIGMA MODEL SW357 – .357 SIG cal., 4 in. barrel, 10 shot mag., black finish, stainless steel. Mfg. 1998 only.

| | $525 | $450 | $375 | $325 | $250 | $195 | $165 | |

SIGMA MODEL SW380 – .380 ACP cal., double action only, 3 in. barrel, fixed sights, polymer frame and steel slide, striker firing system, blue finish only, 6 shot mag., shortened grip, 14 oz. Mfg. 1996-2000.

| | $285 | $245 | $210 | $190 | $180 | $170 | $160 | Last MSR was $358. |

MODEL SW990L – 9mm Para., .40 S&W, or .45 ACP cal., DAO, 9 (.45 ACP cal. only), 10 (all cals. except .45 ACP), 12 (.40 S&W cal.) or 16 (9mm Para.) shot mag., similar to the Walther P99, black polymer frame with black stainless Melonite slide and barrel, 4 (9mm Para. cal. only), 4 1/8 (.40 S&W cal. only), or 4.25 (.45 ACP cal. only) in. barrel, black finish, approx. 25 oz. Mfg. 2005-2006.

| | $610 | $515 | $450 | $400 | $350 | $300 | $275 | Last MSR was $729. |

Add $44 for .45 ACP cal.

* ***Model SW990L Compact*** – similar to SW990L, except is compact version with small polymer frame, not available in .45 ACP cal., 3 1/2 in. barrel, 8 (.40 S&W cal.) or 10 (9mm Para cal.) shot mag. with finger extension, approx. 23 oz. Mfg. 2005-2006.

| | $610 | $515 | $450 | $400 | $350 | $300 | $275 | Last MSR was $729. |

MODEL M&P – 9mm Para., .40 S&W, .357 SIG, or .45 ACP (new 2007) cal., DAO, 3 1/2 (new 2007, compact model), 4 (new 2008, .45 ACP cal. only, compact Model 45C), 4 1/4, 4 1/2 (new 2007, .45 ACP cal. only), or 5 (new 2008, 9mm Para. cal. only) in. black Melonite finished stainless steel barrel and slide with twin scalloped slide serrations, large black Zytel polymer frame reinforced with stainless steel chasis, matte black or dark Earth brown (.45 ACP cal. only, new 2007) finish, 10, 12, 15, or 17 shot mag., ramp front sights, Novak Lo-Mount Carry rear sight, ambidextrous manual safety became an option during 2009, 6 1/2 lbs. trigger pull, 18 degree grip angle, Picatinny rail in front of trigger guard, three interchangable grip sizes, 24 1/4-29 1/2 oz. New 2006.

| MSR $719 | $525 | $425 | $350 | $315 | $285 | $260 | $230 | |

Add $111 for night sights (new 2007, full size models only).
Add $269 for Crimson Trace laser grips (new 2008).
Add $39 for .45 ACP cal.
Add $39 for 5 in. barrel.
Add $39 for Model 45C (compact) with 4 in. barrel.

MSR	100%	98%	95%	90%	80%	70%	60%

Add $8 for .357 SIG cal.
Add $71 for ambidextrous manual safety with lanyard loop on non-compact models.

PERFORMANCE CENTER REVOLVER VARIATIONS

MODEL PC-13 – .357 Mag. cal., DA, 6 shot, 3 in. Magna ported barrel, fixed rear w/ramp front sight, Eagle Secret Service boot or Uncle Mike's grips on a K-frame, matte blue finish with beveled cylinder latch, trigger, and charge holes, shrouded extractor rod, trigger has an overtravel stop, 400 mfg., distributed by Lew Horton during 1995.

Last MSR was $760.

Product Code: 170059 (eagle grips) or 170063 (Uncle Mike's grips).

MODEL 19 PERFORMANCE CENTER K COMP – .38 Spl./.357 Mag. cal., DA, blue matte finish, Target K-frame w/ round butt, 6 shot fluted cylinder with counterbores, 3 in. full lug ported barrel, blue matte finish, smooth combat trigger, set back tritium night front sight on post, black blade adjustable rear sight, contoured thumbpiece, rubber combat grips, 36 oz. Mfg. 1994 and 2000.

Last MSR was $800.

Product Code: 170025 (1994 mfg.) and 170163 (2000 mfg.).

MODEL 27-7 – .357 Mag. cal., 8 shot, 100 with 4 in. barrel with black ramp front sight, 100 with 6 1/2 in. barrel with black Patridge front sight, Magna combat grips, 42-45 oz. Distributed by Bangers.

Last MSR was N/A.

Product Code: 170166 (4 in.) or 170167 (6 1/2 in.).

MODEL 66 F COMP – .357 Mag. cal., 3 in. full lug barrel w/ compensator, dovetailed tritium front night sight, tuned action, round butt w/ rubber grips, counterbored cylinder, contoured cylinder latch, "LHF" serial number prefix, approx. 300 mfg. Distributed by Lew Horton, 1993.

Last MSR was N/A.

Product Code: 170024.

MODEL 66 THE SUPER K – .357 Mag. cal., 3 in. specially contoured barrel with 2 port magna porting, white synthetic grip with S&W medallions, Performance Center Tuned action and overtravel trigger stop. Distributed by Lew Horton, 1997.

Last MSR was N/A.

Product Code: 170090.

MODEL 66 F-COMP – .357 Mag. cal., 3 in. full lug ported barrel with drift adj. dovetailed ramp front sight and micrometer click rear sight, 6 shot cylinder with chamfered charge holes, front sight set behind barrel port, glass bead finish, shipped with walnut combat grips and an additional Hogue Bantam monogrip, released during 2003 at the SHOT Show.

Last MSR was $798.

Product Code: 170024FC.

MODEL 67 F-COMP – .38 Spl. cal., 6 shot, SA/DA, 3 in. full lug Power Port barrel, adj. front and rear sights, stainless steel frame, matte black finish, synthetic finger groove grips, 35 oz. Mfg. mid-2007-2009.

	$1,025	$875	$750	$625	$525	$450	$400	Last MSR was $1,311.

Product code: 170234.

MODEL 325 THUNDER RANCH – .45 ACP cal., SA/DA, 6 shot, large frame, interchangeable front sight, adj. rear sight, Scandium alloy frame with stainless steel cylinder, matte black finish, rubber finger groove grips, 31 oz. New 2008.

MSR $1,454	$1,150	$965	$785	$650	$550	$450	$375

Product code: 170316.

MODEL 327 Sc – .357 Mag., 8 shot, 2 or 5 (mfg. 2006-2007) in. barrel with titanium shroud, black finish with natural grey titanium cylinder, Scandium alloy N-frame, teardrop color case hammer and trigger with overtravel stop, Ahrends cocobolo round butt grips with finger grooves (2 in. barrel only) or Hogue rubber (5 in. barrel only) grips, small lanyard pin, PC logo under thumbpiece, fixed or adj. sights, shipped with black PC marked gun rug made by Allen with internal pouch, 2 full moon clips, special ser. no. range, released during 2004 at the SHOT Show.

MSR $1,438	$1,100	$885	$765	$635	$525	$450	$400

Add $16 for 5 in. barrel with adj. sights.

Product Code: 170245FC (black), 170269 (5 in. barrel), or 170251FC (clear).

MODEL 327 TRR8 – .357 Mag. cal., 8 shot, 5 in. barrel, large frame, interchangeable front sight, adj. V-notch rear sight, Scandium alloy with titanium alloy cylinder, synthetic finger groove grips, black finish, equipment rail, 35.3 oz. New mid-2007.

MSR $1,454	$1,150	$965	$785	$650	$550	$450	$375

Product code: 170269.

MSR	100%	98%	95%	90%	80%	70%	60%

MODEL 329-1 AIRLITE PD – .44 Mag. cal. DA, round butt Scandium alloy N-frame, 6 shot titanium cylinder, painted red ramp front sight, serrated and ported 3 in. barrel, adj. black blade front sight, Ahrends cocobolo finger groove wood grips, includes extra Hogue rubber grip, checked teardrop hammer and smooth combat trigger, marked ".44 MAGNUM" on left side of barrel and "PERFORMANCE CENTER" on right, clear or black matte finish, internal key lock, PC logo under thumbpiece, shipped with PC aluminum double lock carry case. Mfg. 2003.

Last MSR was $1,100.

Product Code: 170233 (clear) or 170232FC (black).

All Model 329-1 Airlites were recalled by S&W during July, 2004.

MODEL 625-6 "V COMP" – .45 ACP cal., 4 in. slabside barrel with a removable compensator or a replacement muzzle to protect the crown, 6 shot non-fluted cylinder has a ball-detent lockup in the yoke, Millett dovetailed red ramp front and micrometer click rear sight, Hogue Combat wood grips, semi-target hammer, smooth combat trigger w/ overtravel stop, shipped w/ double combo lock aluminum carry case, 43 oz. Distributed by RSR, 1999.

Last MSR was $925.

Product Code: 170136.

MODEL 625-5 JERRY MICULEK DESIGN – .45 ACP cal., 5 1/4 in. barrel, Patridge front w/ gold bead and adj. black blade rear sight, reduced cylinder freebore, 6 shot fluted cylinder w/ chamfered charge holes, deep cut broached rifling, hand honed bore, satin stainless finish, "Jerry Miculek" Hogue Laminate combat grips, lockable aluminum case, 42 oz. Distributed by Camfour, 2001.

Last MSR was $899.

Product Code: 170176.

MODEL 627-2 STAINLESS – .357 Mag./.38 Spl. cal., DA, stainless steel version of the Model 27, 8 shot cylinder, 5 in. tapered barrel, interchangeable front sights, drilled & tapped for scope mount, chamfered charge holes, flash chrome teardrop hammer, radiused smooth combat trigger with overtravel stop pin, Hogue hardwood combat grips, new thumbpiece, engraved ".357 Magnum 8 Times" on barrel, floating firing pin, RJM prefix, 44 oz. Distributed by Lew Horton, 1997-98.

Last MSR was $1,000.

Product Code: 170089.

MODEL 627-2 1998 LEW HORTON SPECIAL – .357 Mag. cal., 8 shot cylinder, 6 1/2 in. tapered barrel, interchangeable front sights, flash chrome teardrop hammer, radiused smooth combat trigger with overtravel stop pin.

Last MSR was $1,025.

MODEL 627-3 "V-COMP JERRY MICULEK SPECIAL" – 8 shot cylinder, 5 in. barrel, removable compensator, removable/interchangeable cap to protect the rifling, smooth combat trigger w/ overtravel stop pin, TH, drift adj. red ramp front sight, micrometer click rear sight. "Jerry Miculek" design Hogue wooden grips, locking aluminum case, 47 oz. Distributed by RSR, 2000.

Last MSR was N/A.

On July 24th 1999, Jerry Miculek set a world record for firing an S&W 8 shot revolver. The results were: 8 Shots on 1 target in 1.00 seconds and 8 Shots on 2 targets in 1.06 seconds. Both records set using a Model 627 from the Performance Center.

Product Code: 170142.

MODEL 627-PC – .357 Mag. cal., 8 shot, 2 5/8 in. barrel, Millett red ramp drift adj. front sight with micrometer click white outline rear sight, Eagle wood boot grips, flash chromed custom teardrop hammer, smooth combat trigger, full length extractor, stainless steel with glass bead finish, shipped with aluminum double lock carrying case, 37.6 oz. Approx. 302 mfg. 1999-2000.

Last MSR was $1,025.

Product Code: 170133.

MODEL 627-4 – .38 Super cal., 8 shot, black non-fluted cylinder, 5 1/2 in. barrel, angled cut removable compensator and cap, red/white/blue Jerry Miculek designed grip, Patridge front sight with adj. black outline rear sight, chrome teardrop hammer and chrome trigger with overtravel stop, stainless steel, glass bead finish, drilled and tapped. Mfg. for Banger's 2002.

Last MSR was N/A.

Product Code: 170205.

MODEL 627-5 – .357 Mag. cal., 2 5/8 (new 2010), 5 in. tapered and countoured barrel with fluted cylinder, 8 shot, floating firing pin, interchangeable front sight with black blade rear sight, Hogue rubber grips, trigger overtravel stop, internal lock system, new frame design, shipped with black PC marked gun rug, released during 2003.

MSR $1,414	$1,100	$835	$715	$600	$525	$450	$375

Subtract $229 for 2 5/8 in. barrel.

Product Code: 170210.

MSR	100%	98%	95%	90%	80%	70%	60%

MODEL 627 V-COMP – .357 Mag. cal., 8 shot, 5 in. barrel, SA/DA, adj. front and rear sights, stainless steel/alloy frame with two-tone matte or satin stainless finish, synthetic rubber or wood laminate finger groove grips, chrome tear drop hammer, 47 oz. New 2008.

MSR $1,706	$1,360	$1,125	$965	$835	$750	$675	$600

Product code: 170296.

MODEL 629-4 – .44 Mag. cal., 6 1/2 in. barrel, removable muzzle brake with replaceable end cap, rosewood grips. Distributed by Lew Horton, 1998.

Last MSR was N/A.

Product code: 170124.

MODEL 629-5 "V-COMP" – .44 Mag. cal., 4 in. slabside barrel with removable compensator, muzzle cap, non-fluted cylinder, ball-detent lockup in the yoke, flash chromed semi-target hammer, smooth combat trigger w/ overtravel stop, dovetail red ramp front sight, micrometer click rear sight, Hogue wood combat grips w/ S&W Monogram, aluminum carry case, 43 oz. Distributed by RSR in 1999, reintroduced in 2009.

MSR $1,706	$1,360	$1,125	$965	$835	$750	$675	$600

Product code: 170137.

MODEL 629-5 DEFENSIVE REVOLVER – .44 Mag. cal., 2 5/8 in. barrel, ball detent lockup system in the yoke, 6 shot non-fluted cylinder, flash chromed teardrop hammer and smooth combat trigger, Millett dovetailed red ramp front sight, micrometer click rear sight, Hogue wood combat grips, glass bead stainless steel finish, aluminum carry case with the Performance Center logo, 39.6 oz. Distributed by Lew Horton, 1999-2000.

Last MSR was $1,026.

Product code: 170135.

MODEL 646 – .40 S&W cal., 4 in. ribbed slabside barrel, SA/DA, 6 shot fluted titanium cylinder, adj. Patridge front sight, micrometer adj. rear sight, drilled and tapped for scope mount, smooth combat trigger, round butt, L-target frame, "Performance Center" on the left side and "40 S&W" on the right side of barrel, frosted glass bead stainless finish, Performance Center trademark on the frame, Altamont wood combat grips, 2 sets of half moon clips and extraction tool, Performance Center aluminum case with Performance Center trademark, ser. no. prefix "RDA", 36 oz. Mfg. 2000.

Last MSR was $845.

Product code: 170165.

MODEL 657 DEFENSIVE REVOLVER – .41 Mag. cal., 2 5/8 in. barrel, 6 shot non-fluted cylinder, ball detent lockup, full length extractor, round butt, N-frame, adj. Millett red ramp front sight, micrometer adj. white outline rear sight, flash chromed teardrop hammer, chromed trigger with travel overstop, Hogue combat grips, glass bead stainless steel finish, aluminum carry case, 39.6 oz. Distributed by Lew Horton, 1999.

Last MSR was $1,001.

Product code: 170134.

MODEL 686 CARRY COMP – .357 Mag. cal., 4 in. barrel, integral compensator, dovetailed front sight w/ interchangeable post or red ramp, white outline rear sight, Uncle Mike's grips. Distributed by Lew Horton.

Last MSR was $1,000.

Product code: 170016.

MODEL 686 PLUS – .357 Mag. cal., 6 in. tapered barrel, 7 shot fluted cylinder, machined for full moon clips w/ chamfered charge holes, L-frame drilled and tapped for scope mount, round butt, Altamont wood grips, flash chromed semi-target hammer and smooth combat trigger, gold bead Patridge front sight, micrometer adj. white outline rear sight, satin stainless steel finish, 44 oz. Distributed by Lew Horton, 1998.

Last MSR was $929.

Product code: 170103.

MODEL M&P R8 – .357 Mag. cal., 8 shot, SA/DA, 5 in. two-piece barrel, large frame, Scandium alloy frame, stainless steel cylinder, interchangeable dot front sight, adj. V-notch rear sight, accessory rail, 36.3 oz. New mid-2007.

MSR $1,454	$1,150	$965	$785	$650	$550	$450	$375

Product code: 170292.

PERFORMANCE CENTER SEMI-AUTO PISTOL VARIATIONS

MODEL 945 PERFORMANCE CENTER .45 MATCH PISTOL – .45 ACP cal., 5 in. barrel, titanium coated spherical barrel bushing, 8 round mag., Performance Center markings, post front sight, adj. Bo-Mar rear sight, checkered two-piece laminated wood grips, bead blast stainless steel finish, ambidextrous frame mounted thumb safety, grip safety as part of the short beavertail, Master trigger lock, "Performance Center" marked foam-filled aluminum case starting in 1999, 43.5 oz. (1998) 42 oz. (1999 and later mfg.) Mfg. 1998-2000.

MSR	100%	98%	95%	90%	80%	70%	60%

* ***Model 945 Performance Center .45 Match Pistol 170104*** – 5 in. barrel, stainless steel, 8 shot, 43.5 oz. Mfg. 1998.

Last MSR was $1,618.

* ***Model 945 Performance Center .45 Match Pistol 170147*** – 5 in. barrel, two-tone or blue finish, lightened trigger, grip safety, Bo-Mar rear sight, post front sight, stainless steel, ambidextrous frame mounted safety, 42 oz. Distributed by RSR. Mfg. 1998, 1999-2000.

Last MSR was N/A.

* ***Model 945 Performance Center .45 Match Pistol 170152*** – 4 in. barrel, black finish, 8 shot mag., post front and Novak 2 Dot Lo- Mount Carry rear sight, frame mounted safety, titanium coated spherical bushing, 20 LPI checkering front and back strap, extended magazine catch, checkered two-piece wood grips, stainless steel, grip safety, S/N prefix "PCZ", 36 oz. Distributed by Camfour, 2000.

Last MSR was N/A.

* ***Model 945 Performance Center .45 Match Pistol 170153*** – 4 in. barrel, post front and Novak 2 Dot Lo-Mount carry rear sight, grip safety, checkered two piece wood grips, lightened trigger, bead blast stainless steel finish, frame mounted safety, S/N prefix "PCZ", 36 oz. Distributed by RSR, 2000.

Last MSR was N/A.

* ***Model 945 Performance Center .45 Match Pistol 170169*** – 3 3/4 in. barrel, white dot dovetail front and Novak 2 Dot Lo-Mount Carry rear sight, grip and single side frame mounted safety, 7 round mag., checkered laminate wood grips, lightened trigger, black finish alloy frame, stainless steel slide, S/N Prefix "CMF", 28 oz. Distributed by Camfour, 2000.

Last MSR was N/A.

* ***Model 945 Performance Center .45 Match Pistol 170177*** – 3 1/4 in. barrel, white dot dovetail front and Novak 2 Dot Lo-Mount Carry rear sight, beavertail grip and single-side frame mounted safety, 6 round mag., checkered Hogue laminated wood grips, alloy frame with clear glass bead stainless steel slide, Performance Center carry case, 2 mags., 24.5 oz. Distributed by Camfour, 2001.

Last MSR was N/A.

* ***Model 945 Performance Center .45 Match Pistol 170180*** – .40 S&W cal., 3 3/4 in. barrel, white dot dovetail front and Novak 2 Dot Lo-Mount Carry rear sight, beavertail grip and single-side frame mounted safety, 7 round mag., checkered Hogue laminated wood grips, alloy frame w/ glass bead finish stainless steel slide, Performance Center carry case, 2 mags., 25.7 oz. Distributed by Sports South, 2001.

Last MSR was N/A.

* ***Model 945 Performance Center .45 Match Pistol 170184*** – 3 1/4 in. glass bead black barrel, white dovetail front and Novak 2 Dot Lo-Mount Carry rear sight, grip and single side frame mounted safety, 6 round mag., checkered Hogue laminated wood grips, alloy frame with stainless steel slide, lightened trigger, S/N prefix "PCZ", 24 oz. Distributed by RSR, 2001.

Last MSR was N/A.

MODEL 945-1 – .45 ACP cal., 8 shot mag., SA, 5 in. barrel, features scalloped slide serrations, black (disc.) or two-tone finish, checkered front and rear gripstrap, checkered wood panel grips, stainless steel, adj. rear sight, target trigger and bobbed hammer, 40 1/2 oz., released during 2003, reintroduced 2005.

MSR $2,410	$1,925	$1,650	$1,425	$1,225	$1,000	$900	$800

Product codes: 170173 (two-tone) and 170300 (black).

MODEL 1911 (NEW 2004) – .38 Super (new 2005) or .45 ACP cal., 5 in. barrel, single action, black finish, 8 or 10 (.38 Super cal.) shot mag., dovetailed black front sight with adj. micro-click black rear sight, checkered laminate wood grips, stainless steel or stainless Melonite (new 2005) frame/barrel, glass bead finish, full length guide rod, ambidextrous frame mounted safety, 30 LPI front strap checkering, hand lapped and polished fitted barrel, frame and slide, unique front and rear serrations, includes two magazines, 41 oz., released during 2004.

MSR $2,678	$2,025	$1,525	$1,300	$1,100	$900	$800	$700

Add $16 for .38 Super cal. (stainless steel only, new 2005).
Subtract $189 for stainless steel frame/slide.

Product code: 170243 and variations.

* ***Model 1911 (2005)*** – .45 ACP cal., two additional variations of this model were produced during 2005, stainless steel with glass bead satin finish, 8 shot mag., 5 in. barrel, Doug Koenig speed hammer, lightweight match trigger with over travel stop, black dovetail front sight with black micro adj. rear sight, laminate fully checkered front grip, oversized external extractor, full length guide rod and oversized mag. well extension, custom front and rear slide serrations, ambidextrous frame mounted safety, shipped with two 8 shot mags, other variation had high polished flats on the slide and barrel.

Last MSR was N/A.

Product code: 170258 and 170261.

* **Model 1911 .38 Super cal. (2005)** – .38 Super cal., another variation of the original 2004 model, part of Doug Koenig Professional Series, 5 in. barrel, satin stainless steel finish, 10 shot mag., Dou Koenig speed hammer, competition match trigger with overtravel stop, black dovetail front sight, Doug Koenig logo on smooth black Micarta grips, oversized external extractor, full length guide rod, competition mag. well, 30 LPI front strap checkering. Mfg. 2005.

Last MSR was N/A.

Product code: 170257.

THE SHORTY 9 MKIII – 9mm cal., match grade barrel w/ hand fitted titanium bushing, over-size slide rails, ambidextrous safety, Performance Center action tuning job, adj. Novak Lo-Mount sights, included Zippo lighter with Performance Center logo. Distributed by Lew Horton, 1997.

Last MSR was $1,024.

9 RECON – 9mm cal., 3 1/2 in. match grade barrel, titanium coated spherical barrel bushing, double stack 12 + 1 mag., white dot front and Novak 2 Dot Lo-Mount rear sight, traditional DA trigger, hand lapped oversize rails, ambidextrous spring loaded decocker, 20 LPI checkering on the front strap, Hogue wraparound rubber grips, compact frame, two-tone finish with a clear anodized alloy frame and a carbon steel blue slide, aluminum carry case, 27.2 oz. Distributed by RSR, 1999-2000.

Last MSR was N/A.

Product code: 170140.

S&W 4006 SHORTY FORTY – .40 S&W cal., 3 1/2 in. Bar-Sto barrel, spherical bushing, bobbed hammer, Novak Lo-Mount carry sights, 9-round single stack magazine, alloy frame, grips and frame stamped with Performance Center logo, beveled trigger, adj. front dovetail sight, oversize slide rails, 500 mfg., 27 oz. Distributed by Lew Horton, 1992, 1993, and 1995.

Last MSR was $1,500.

* **S&W 4006 Shorty Forty Tactical** – .40 S&W cal., full size companion to Shorty Forty, 5 in. barrel. Distributed by Lew Horton, limited production 1993.

Last MSR was $1,500.

Product code: 170020.

* **S&W 4006 Shorty Forty Compensated** – .40 S&W cal., compensator mounted on ported barrel. Distributed by Lew Horton.

Last MSR was $1,700.

* **S&W 4006 Shorty Forty MK III** – third variation S/N prefix "PCW". Mfg. 1995.

Last MSR was $949.

Product code: 170011.

* **S&W 4006 Shorty Forty MKIII 1997** – ambidextrous safety, low mount adj. sights, hand fitted titanium barrel bushing, precision checkered front strap, hand honed double action S/N prefix "KPC". Distributed by Lew Horton.

Last MSR was $1,025.

Product code: 170061.

* **S&W 4006 Shorty Forty Performance Center .40 S&W Tactical** – .40 S&W cal., 5 in. match grade barrel, fixed tritium night front and Novak 2-dot rear sight, stainless steel frame w/ carbon steel slide materials, tactical black matte slide w/ satin stainless frame finish, 10 round mag., box cut frame and slide rails for 100% contact, balanced slide, ambidextrous decocker, 41.6 oz. Distributed by RSR, 1997.

Last MSR was $1,146.

Product code: 170091.

* **S&W 4006 Shorty Forty Performance Center Compact** – .40 S&W cal., 4 1/4 in. barrel. Mfg. August, 1994.

Last MSR was N/A.

Product code: 170054.

MODEL 4006 SHORTY FORTY Y2000 – .40 S&W cal., 3 1/2 in. barrel, white dovetail front sight, Novak Lo-Mount Carry 2 Dot rear sight, aluminum frame with stainless slide, 9 round mag., two-tone black finish, Performance Center aluminum case. Distributed by Camfour 2000.

Last MSR was N/A.

Product code: 170164.

PERFORMANCE CENTER 40 RECON – .40 S&W cal., 4 1/4 in. match grade barrel w/ compensator, titanium coated spherical barrel bushing, white dot post front and all black Novak Lo-Mount rear sight, 7 round magazine, ambidextrous spring loaded decocker, Hogue wraparound rubber grip, stainless steel material with matte black finish, laser etched with "40 RECON Performance Center" on the left side. Distributed by RSR, 1998.

Last MSR was N/A.

Product code: 170099.

MSR	100%	98%	95%	90%	80%	70%	60%

PERFORMANCE CENTER 45 RECON – .45 ACP cal., 4 1/4 in. match grade ported barrel, titanium coated spherical barrel bushing, white dot post front and black Novak Lo-Mount rear sight, ambidextrous spring loaded decocker, Hogue wraparound rubber grip, 7 round magazine, stainless steel construction, stainless or matte black finish, laser etched "45 RECON Performance Center" on the left side, aluminum carry case, S/N prefix "SFF", 27.8 oz. Distributed by RSR, 1998.

Last MSR was $1022.

Product code: 170098 (matte black), 170141 (stainless finish), or 170128 (includes Recon SWAT knife).

PERFORMANCE CENTER 45 CQB PISTOLS (CLOSE QUARTERS BATTLE) – .45 ACP cal., 4 in. match grade barrel, two variations offered in 1998, Novak Lo-Mount Dot front and Novak Lo-Mount 2 Dot rear sight, 7 round mag., straight backstrap grip, stainless steel slide, titanium coated spherical barrel bushing, alloy frame with a matte black finish (Model CQB-AL) or stainless steel frame with a matte stainless (Model CQB-SS) finish, ".45 C.Q.B. Performance Center" laser etched on the slide's left side. Distributed by Lew Horton, 1998-1999.

Last MSR was $1,235.

Product code: 170106 (alloy) or 170105 (stainless).

THE SHORTY .45 – .45 ACP cal., match grade barrel, ambidextrous safety, adj. sights, hand fitted titanium barrel bushing, oversize frame and slide rails, precision checkered front strap, hand honed double action. Mfg. 1997.

Last MSR was $1,146.

Product code: 170075.

THE .45 LIMITED – 45 ACP cal., match grade barrel, SA trigger, oversize precision cut frame and slide rails, hand fitted titanium barrel bushing and slide lock, adj. sights, oversize mag. well, tuned action, Zippo lighter with Perf. Center logo. Distributed by Lew Horton, 1997.

Last MSR was $1,470.

MODEL 5906 PC-9 – 9mm cal., 3 1/2 in. titanium spherical barrel bushing, 15 shot mag., blue slide with satin stainless frame, smooth trigger, bobbed hammer, dovetail front and Novak Lo-Mount fixed rear sight, 27 oz. Distributed by Lew Horton.

Last MSR was N/A

RIFLES

S&W in 1984 disc. importation of all Howa manufactured rifles. Mossberg continued importation utilizing leftover S&W parts in addition to fabricating their own.

MODEL M&P15 CENTERFIRE SEMI-AUTO SERIES – .223 Rem., 5.45x39mm, or 5.56 NATO cal., gas operated semi-auto, AR-15 style design with 16 in. chrome lined barrel with muzzle brake or 20 in. barrel, 10 or 30 shot mag., one piece, fixed position, skeletonized, or six position CAR collapsible stock, hard coat black anodized finish, features detachable carrying handle, A2 post front sight, adj. dual aperture rear sight, and thinned handguard, M&P15T features extended Picatinny rail on receiver and barrel, in addition to RAS on both sides and bottom of barrel, adj. front and rear folding battle sights, supplied with hard carry case, approx. 6 3/4 lbs. New 2006.

* **Model M&P15** – 5.56 NATO cal., 16 in. carbon steel barrel, 30 shot mag., alloy receiver, black alloy finish, six-position adj. pistol grip stock, adj. rear sight, black post front sight.

MSR $1,406	$1,175	$995	$875	$775	$675	$575	$500

Product Code: 811000.

* **Model M&P15A** – 5.56 NATO cal., gas operated semi-auto, AR-15 style design, 16 in. barrel, 30 shot mag., similar to Model M&P15, except features a receiver Picatinny rail and adj. rear folding battle sight with ribbed handguard.

MSR $1,454	$1,215	$1,000	$875	$775	$675	$575	$500

Product Code: 811002.

* **Model M&P15T** – 5.56 NATO cal., gas operated semi-auto, AR-15 style design, 30 shot mag., 16 in. barrel, similar to Model M&P15A, except features folding rear sight and modular rail.

MSR $1,928	$1,625	$1,395	$1,175	$950	$825	$725	$625

Product Code: 811001.

* **Model M&P15OR** – 5.56 NATO cal., 16 in. carbon steel barrel, 30 shot mag., alloy receiver, black alloy finish, six-position adj. stock, no rear sight.

MSR $1,209	$1,050	$925	$800	$700	$600	$500	$400

Product Code: 811003.

* **Model M&P15FT** – 5.56 NATO cal., gas operated semi-auto, AR-15 style design, 16 in. barrel, 10 shot mag., one-piece pistol grip stock, folding rear and front sights, modular rail, alloy receiver.

MSR $1,928	$1,625	$1,395	$1,175	$950	$825	$725	$625

Product Code: 811004.

MSR	100%	98%	95%	90%	80%	70%	60%

* **Model M&P15X** – 5.56 NATO cal., gas operated semi-auto, AR-15 style design, 16 in. barrel, 30 shot mag., black alloy finish, six-position adj. pistol grip stock, folding rear and black post front sights, modular rail, alloy receiver.

MSR $1,556	$1,275	$1,065	$935	$825	$725	$625	$525

* **Model M&P15I** – .223 Rem. cal., gas operated semi-auto, AR-15 style design, 17 in. barrel, 10 shot mag., black alloy finish, pistol grip stock, adj. rear sight, black post front sight, alloy receiver.

MSR $1,422	$1,185	$1,000	$875	$775	$675	$575	$500

Product Code: 811010.

* **Model M&P15R** – 5.45x39mm cal., gas operated semi-auto, AR-15 style design, 16 in. barrel, 30 shot mag., black alloy finish, pistol grip stock, adj. rear and black post front sight, alloy receiver.

MSR $1,225	$1,060	$925	$800	$700	$600	$500	$400

Product Code: 811011.

* **Model M&P15VTAC** – 5.56 NATO cal., gas operated semi-auto, AR-15 style design, 16 in. barrel, 30 shot mag., black alloy finish, pistol grip stock, modular rail, alloy receiver.

MSR $2,244	$1,925	$1,675	$1,450	$1,225	$995	$875	$725

Product Code: 811012.

* **Model M&P15ORC** – 5.56 NATO cal., gas operated semi-auto, AR-15 style design, 16 in. barrel, 10 shot mag., black alloy finish, pistol grip stock, alloy receiver.

MSR $1,169	$1,025	$900	$800	$700	$600	$500	$400

Product Code: 811013.

MODEL M&P15-22 RIMFIRE SEMI-AUTO – .22 LR cal., gas operated semi-auto, blowback action, AR-15 style design, 16 1/2 in. barrel with or w/o threading, 10 or 25 shot mag., black alloy finish, adj. rear sight, fixed or six position adj. stock, polymer receiver, 5 1/2 lbs. New 2009.

MSR $569	$525	$450	$400	$365	$335	$295	$265

Add $16 for threaded barrel.

SHOTGUNS

S&W in 1984 disc. importation of all Howa manufactured shotguns. Mossberg continued importation utilizing leftover S&W parts in addition to fabricating their own.

MODEL 3000 POLICE – 12 ga. only, blue or parkerized finish, many combinations of finishes, stock types, and other combat accessories were available for this model, 18 or 20 in. barrel.

	$325	$255	$215	$185	$170	$155	$140

Add $125 for folding stock.

SOMMER + OCKENFUSS GmbH

Previous manufacturer located in Baiersbronn, Germany until 2002. Previously imported by Lothar Walther Precision Tool, located in Cumming, GA. Previously imported by Intertex Carousels Corporation during 1998-2000, and located in Pineville, NC.

Sommer + Ockenfuss also produced a bolt adapter to convert the Remington 700 bolt action into a straight pull repeater, enabling the addition of a firing pin safety and firing chamber lock.

PISTOLS: SEMI-AUTO

P21 – .224 HV, 9mm Para., or .40 S&W cal., 3.11 (Combat) or 3.55 (Police) in. rotating barrel, SA/DA operation, release grip safety uncocks the hammer, keyed slide lock blocks firing pin and slide, 10 shot mag., approx. 24 oz. Mfg. 2001.

	$550	$495	$450	$415	$375	$340	$310	Last MSR was $608.

Add approx. $320 for conversion slide assemblies.

RIFLES: SLIDE ACTION

SHORTY – most popular cals., unique slide action rifle in bullpup configuration featuring a straight line design with a grip safety pistol grip which also works the slide assembly, stainless or black coated barrel, compact 6-lug bolt with a locking surface of 0.263 sq. in., with or w/o sideplates inlet into walnut or black synthetic (new 1999) stock. Imported 1998-2002.

* **Shorty Wilderness Rifle** – match trigger, polymer stock, and stainless steel barrel.

	$1,495	$1,275	$1,100	$995	$925	$850	$750	Last MSR was $1,660.

Add $310 for .375 H&H or .416 Rem. Mag. cal. (Shorty Safari).

MSR	100%	98%	95%	90%	80%	70%	60%

Add $200 for walnut stock (Shorty American Hunter).
Add $210 for sight mounts.
Add $88 for recoil brake.

* **Shorty Marksman Rifle** – similar to Wilderness Rifle, except has choice of black coated or fluted heavy match barrel and recoil brake.

	$1,875	$1,675	$1,450	$1,275	$1,100	$995	$850	Last MSR was $2,020.

Add $80 for .308 Win. or .300 Win. Mag. (fluted barrel), $420 for .338 Lapua Mag. with black coated barrel, or $710 for .338 Lapua Mag. with fluted stainless barrel.
Add $80 for stainless barrel.
Add $210 for sight mount, $168 for bipod, $210 for Spigot stock cap.

There were also deluxe variations, limited editions, and Marksman's packages ($4,100-$4,860 MSR) available in this model.

SPECIAL WEAPONS LLC

Previous tactical rifle manufacturer 1999-2002, and located in Mesa, AZ. Previously located in Tempe, AZ.

Special Weapons LLC closed its doors on Dec. 31, 2002. Another company, Special Weapons, Inc., is handling the warranty repairs on Special Weapons LLC firearms (see Trademark Index).

CARBINES: SEMI-AUTO

OMEGA 760 – 9mm Para. cal., reproduction of the S&W Model 76, 16 1/4 in. partially shrouded barrel, fixed wire stock, 30 shot mag., 7 1/2 lbs. Limited mfg. 2002.

	$495	$450	$425	$395	$375	$350	$325	Last MSR was $575.

SW-5 CARBINE – 9mm Para. cal., tactical configuration styled after the HK-94 (parts interchangeable), stainless steel receiver, plastic lower housing, 16 1/4 in. stainless steel barrel, A2 style black synthetic stock with wide forearm, 10 shot mag. (accepts high capacity HK-94/MP-5 mags also), approx. 6 3/4 lbs. Mfg. 2000-2002.

	$1,475	$1,225	$1,025	$875	$800	$750	$695	Last MSR was $1,600.

SW-45 CARBINE – .45 ACP cal., otherwise similar to SW-5 Carbine. Mfg. 2000-2002.

	$1,550	$1,275	$1,050	$895	$825	$775	$725	Last MSR was $1,700.

RIFLES: SEMI-AUTO

SW-3 – .308 Win. cal., tactical configuration styled after the HK-91 (parts interchangeable), tooled receiver, metal steel lower trigger housing, 17.71 stainless steel barrel, A2 style stock, approx. 10 lbs. Mfg. 2000-2002.

	$1,425	$1,175	$995	$850	$800	$750	$695	Last MSR was $1,550.

* **SW-3 SP** – similar to SW-3, except has PSG-1 style trigger assembly, 22 in. custom target barrel and Weaver rail welded to top. Mfg. 2000-2002.

	$2,250	$1,975	$1,700	$1,500	$1,250	$1,050	$895	Last MSR was $2,500.

SPHINX SYSTEMS LTD.

Current manufacturer established in 1876, and presently located in Matten b. Interlaken, Switzerland. Previously distributed until 2009 by Sabre Defence Industries, LLC, located in Nashville, TN. Previously imported by Rocky Mountain Armoury, located in Silverthorne, CO. Previously manufactured by Sphinx Engineering S.A. located in Porrentruy, Switzerland. Previously imported by Sphinx U.S.A., located in Meriden, CT until 1996. Previously imported by Sile Distributors located in New York, NY.

PISTOLS

MODEL 2000S STANDARD – 9mm Para. or .40 S&W (new 1993) cal., semi-auto in standard double action or double action only, 4.53 in. barrel, stainless steel fabrication, 10 (C/B 1994), 15* (9mm Para.), or 11* (.40 S&W) shot mag., checkered walnut grips, fixed sights, 35 oz. Importation disc. 2002

	$965	$750	$625	$525	$450	$410	$375	

Add $117 for .40 S&W cal.

* **Model 2000PS Standard Police Special** – similar to Model 2000S, except has compact slide and 3.66 in. barrel.

	$850	$625	$525	$450	$410	$380	$350	

Add $40 for .40 S&W cal.
Add $87 for N/Pall finish.

* **Model 2000P Standard Compact** – similar to Model 2000 Standard, except has 3.66 in. barrel and 13 shot mag., 31 oz.

	$850	$625	$525	$450	$410	$380	$350	

Add $40 for .40 S&W cal.

MSR	100%	98%	95%	90%	80%	70%	60%

Add $87 for N/Pall finish.

* ***Model 2000H Standard Sub-Compact*** – similar to Model 2000 Compact, except has 3.34 in. barrel and 10 shot mag., 26 oz. Disc. 1996.

| | $850 | $625 | $525 | $450 | $410 | $380 | $350 | Last MSR was $940. |

Add $40 for .40 S&W cal.
Add $87 for N/Pall finish.

MODEL 2000 MASTER – 9mm Para., 9x21mm, or .40 S&W cal., single action only, two-tone finish only, designed for Master's stock class competition.

| | $1,795 | $1,350 | $1,100 | $995 | $895 | $775 | $650 | Last MSR was $2,035. |

MODEL AT-2000 (NEW MODEL) – 9mm Para. or .40 S&W cal., 4.53 in. barrel, 10 shot mag., machined slide with electro deposited finish, decocking mechanism. Limited mfg. 2004-2005.

| | $1,825 | $1,675 | $1,450 | $1,225 | $1,000 | $800 | $675 | Last MSR was $1,995. |

MODEL AT-2000CS COMPETITOR – 9mm Para., 9x21mm, or .40 S&W cal., single or double action, competition model featuring many shooting improvements including 5.3 in. compensated barrel, 10 (C/B 1994), 11* (.40 S&W), or 15* shot mag., Bo-Mar adj. sights, two-tone finish. Imported 1993-96.

| | $1,725 | $1,275 | $1,050 | $950 | $850 | $750 | $675 | Last MSR was $1,902. |

Add $287 for Model AT-2000C (includes Sphinx scope mount).
Add $1,538 for AT-2000K conversion kit (new 1995).
Add $1,490 for Model AT-2000CKS (competition kit to convert AT-2000 to comp. pistol, disc. 1994).

MODEL 2000 COMPETITION – similar to Model 2000 Master, except is SA only and includes more advanced competitive shooting features, Bo-Mar sights, top-of-the-line competition model. Imported 1993-96.

| | $2,475 | $1,925 | $1,725 | $1,500 | $1,250 | $1,050 | $895 | Last MSR was $2,894. |

Add $78 for Model AT-2000GM (includes Sphinx scope mount).

MODEL 3000 SERIES – 9mm Para., 9x21mm (disc.), .40 S&W, or .45 ACP cal., SA/DA, available in standard (4.53 in. barrel), tactical (3 3/4 in. barrel), or competition (4.53 in. barrel, adj. sights), configuration, choice of manual safety or decocker, titanium upper/lower frame with stainless slide, stainless steel slide with titanium lower frame or stainless steel frame/slide, front/rear gripstrap stipling or grooved, two-tone finish, approx. 40 oz. New 2001.

| MSR N/A | $2,525 | $2,275 | $2,000 | $1,800 | $1,575 | $1,375 | $1,150 | |

Add $350 for titanium frame with stainless steel slide.
Add $800 for stainless steel slide with titanium upper/lower frame (disc.).
Add $75 for tactical model.
Add $350 for competition model.

SPHINX .45 ACP – .45 ACP cal., SA/DA, steel construction, 3 3/4 in. barrel, double slide serrations, blue finish, 10 shot mag., fixed Trijicon night sights, black polymer grips, decocker mechanism, approx. 43 oz. New 2007.

| MSR N/A | $2,850 | $2,500 | $2,150 | $1,850 | $1,500 | $1,250 | $1,000 | |

SPIDER FIREARMS

Current rifle manufacturer located in St. Cloud, FL.

RIFLES: SINGLE SHOT

FERRET 50 – .50 BMG cal., single shot bolt action, A2 style buttstock and pistol grip, Picatinny rail, choice of 18, 29, or 36 in. barrel, matte black finish, perforated handguard with bipod, includes muzzle brake. New 2003.

| MSR $3,011 | $2,850 | $2,575 | $2,375 | $2,100 | $1,800 | $1,600 | $1,400 | |

Add $250 for stainless steel barrel (SS Sportsman)
Add $500 for stainless super match barrel (SM Sportsman).

SUPERCOMP FERRET – similar to Ferret 50, except also available in .408 CheyTac and .338 Lapua cal., features solid steel construction, fixed scope rails, 29 or 36 in. Lothar Walther stainless Supermatch barrels, adj. 1 lb. competition style trigger, two-axis cheekrest, and detachable rear monopod. New 2004.

| MSR $3,190 | $2,850 | $2,600 | $2,300 | $2,000 | $1,750 | $1,600 | $1,450 | |

Add $250 for stainless steel barrel.
Add $500 for stainless steel super match barrel.

SPIRIT GUN MANUFACTURING COMPANY LLC

Current manufacturer located in West Palm Beach, FL.

PISTOLS: SEMI-AUTO

SGM9P – 5.56 NATO cal., 7 1/2 in. stainless steel barrel with KX3 compensator, 30 shot mag., black, green, or tan

MSR	100%	98%	95%	90%	80%	70%	60%

finish, pistol length tuned direct gas impingement system, SGM9 lower with integral three position sling mount and swivel, VLTOR custom CASV hand guard, flip up front sight, VLTOR MUR upper receiver, National Match phosphate and chromed custom bolt carrier.

MSR $2,495	$2,200	$1,950	$1,725	$1,500	$1,300	$1,100	$825

RIFLES/CARBINES: SEMI-AUTO

Spirit Gun Manufacturing offers a complete line of AR-15 tactical style rifles and carbines in law enforcement/military and civilian configurations. Current models include: SGM-15, SGM-16, and SGM 17 ($2,495 MSR), SGM-A39, SGM-40, and SGM-41 ($2,495 MSR), SGM-A19 ($2,695 MSR), SGM-A43 ($2,695 MSR), SGM-A23 ($2,795 MSR), SGM-A47 ($2,795 MSR), SGM-A24 ($2,895 MSR), and the SGM-A48 ($2,895 MSR). A variety of options and accessories are available. Please contact the company directly for more information, including pricing and availability (see Trademark Index).

SPORT-SYSTEME DITTRICH

Current manufacturer established in 2003 and located in Kulmbach, Germany. Limited importation in North America by Wolverine Supplies, located in Manitoba, Canada. Previously imported by Marstar Canada, located in Ontario, Canada.

Sport-Systeme Dittrich manufactures high quality semi-auto reproductions of famous military guns, including the MP38 (BD 38), Sturmgewehr 44 (BD 44) and the Gerät Neumünster (BD 3008). Its latest model is a reproduction of the Fallschirmjägergewehr FG42 as the BD42 I. Please contact the importer or the company directly for more information, including pricing and U.S. availability (see Trademark Index).

SPRINGFIELD ARMORY (MFG. BY SPRINGFIELD INC.)

Current trademark manufactured by Springfield Inc., located in Geneseo, IL. Springfield Inc. has also imported a variety of models. This company was named Springfield Armory, Geneseo, IL until 1992.

Springfield Inc. manufactures commercial pistols and rifles, including reproductions of older military handguns and rifles.

COMBINATION GUNS

M6 SCOUT RIFLE – .22 LR, .22 Mag. (disc.), or .22 Hornet cal. over smoothbore .410 bore w/ 3 in. chamber, O/U Survival Gun, 14 (legal transfer needed) or 18 1/4 in. barrels, parkerized or stainless steel (new 1995), approx. 4 lbs. Disc. 2004.

	100%	98%	95%	90%	80%	70%	60%	
.22 LR/.22 Mag. cal.	$425	$375	$325	$275	$250	$225	$195	
.22 Hornet cal.	$775	$725	$650	$550	$475	$400	$325	Last MSR was $215.

Add approx. 10% for stainless steel.
Add 10% for lockable Marine flotation plastic carrying case.

Early mfg. does not incorporate a trigger guard while late production had a trigger guard.

M6 SCOUT PISTOL/CARBINE – .22 LR or .22 Hornet cal. over .45 LC/.410 bore, 16 in. barrels, parkerized or stainless steel. Mfg. 2002-2004.

	100%	98%	95%	90%	80%	70%	60%	
.22 LR cal.	$425	$375	$325	$275	$250	$225	$195	
.22 Hornet cal.	$775	$725	$650	$550	$475	$400	$325	Last MSR was $223.

Add 10% for stainless steel.
Add approx. $200 per interchangeable 10 in. pistol barrel assembly.
Add 15% for detachable stock.

This model was also available with an optional detachable stock ($49-$59 MSR, not legal with a rifled barrel less than 16 in. or smoothbore less than 18 in.).

M6 SCOUT PISTOL – .22 LR or .22 Hornet cal. over .45 LC/.410 bore, 10 in. barrels, parkerized or stainless steel. Mfg. 2002-2004.

	100%	98%	95%	90%	80%	70%	60%	
.22 LR cal.	$425	$375	$325	$275	$250	$225	$195	
.22 Hornet cal.	$775	$725	$650	$550	$475	$400	$325	Last MSR was $199.

Add approx. 10% for stainless steel.
Add approx. $200 per interchangeable 16 in. carbine barrel.

PISTOLS: SEMI-AUTO

OMEGA PISTOL – .38 Super, 10mm Norma, or .45 ACP cal., single action, ported slide, 5 or 6 in. interchangeable ported or unported barrel with Polygon rifling, special lockup system eliminates normal barrel link and bushing, Pachmayr grips, dual extractors, adj. rear sight. Mfg. 1987-90.

	100%	98%	95%	90%	80%	70%	60%	
	$775	$650	$575	$495	$425	$360	$295	Last MSR was $849.

Add $663 for interchangeable conversion units.
Add $336 for interchangeable 5 or 6 in. barrel (including factory installation).

MSR	100%	98%	95%	90%	80%	70%	60%

Each conversion unit includes an entire slide assembly, one mag., 5 or 6 in barrel, recoil spring guide mechanism assembly, and factory fitting.

Pistols: Semi-Auto - P9 Series

MODEL P9 – 9mm Para., 9x21mm (new 1991) .40 S&W (new 1991), or .45 ACP cal., patterned after the Czech CZ-75, selective double action design, blue (standard beginning 1993), parkerized (standard until 1992), or duotone finish, various barrel lengths, checkered walnut grips. Mfg. in U.S. starting 1990.

* **Model P9 Standard** – 4.72 in. barrel, 15 shot (9mm Para.), 11 shot (.40 S&W), or 10 shot (.45 ACP) mag., parkerized finish standard until 1992 - blue finish beginning 1993, 32.16 oz. Disc. 1993.

	$430	$375	$335	$295	$275	$240	$215	Last MSR was $518.

Add $61 for .45 ACP cal.
Add $182 for duotone finish (disc. 1992).
Subtract $40 for parkerized finish.

In 1992, Springfield added a redesigned stainless steel trigger, patented sear safety which disengages the trigger from the double action mechanism when the safety is on, lengthened the beavertail grip area offering less "pinch," and added a two-piece slide stop design.

* **Model P9 Stainless** – similar to P9 Standard, except is constructed from stainless steel, 35.3 oz. Mfg. 1991-93.

	$475	$425	$350	$285	$250	$215	$185	Last MSR was $589.

Add $50 for .45 ACP cal.

* **Model P9 Compact** – 9mm Para. or .40 S&W cal., 3.66 in. barrel, 13 shot (9mm Para.) or 10 shot (.40 S&W) mag., shorter slide and frame, rounded triggerguard, 30 1/2 oz. Disc. 1992.

	$395	$350	$300	$275	$250	$225	$200	Last MSR was $499.

Add $20 for .40 S&W cal.
Add $20-$30 for blue finish depending on cal.
Add $78 for duotone finish.

* **Model P9 Sub-Compact** – 9mm Para. or .40 S&W cal., smaller frame than the P9 Compact, 3.66 in. barrel, 12 shot (9mm Para.) or 9 shot (.40 S&W) finger extension mag., squared-off triggerguard, 30.1 oz. Disc. 1992.

	$395	$350	$300	$275	$250	$225	$200	Last MSR was $499.

Add $20 for .40 S&W cal.
Add $20-$30 for blue finish depending on cal.

* **Model P9 Factory Comp** – 9mm Para., .40 S&W, or .45 ACP cal., 5 1/2 in. barrel (with compensator attached), extended sear safety and mag. release, adj. rear sight, slim competition checkered wood grips, choice of all stainless (disc. 1992) or stainless bi-tone (matte black slide), dual port compensated, 15 shot (9mm Para.), 11 shot (.40 S&W), or 10 shot (.45 ACP) mag., 33.9 oz. Mfg. 1992-93.

	$595	$525	$450	$420	$390	$360	$330	Last MSR was $699.

Add $36 for .45 ACP cal.
Add $75-$100 for all stainless finish.

* **Model P9 Ultra IPSC (LSP)** – competition model with 5.03 in. barrel (long slide ported), adj. rear sight, choice of parkerized (standard finish until 1992 when disc.), blue (disc. 1992), bi-tone (became standard 1993), or stainless steel (disc. 1992) finish, extended thumb safety, and rubberized competition (9mm Para. and .40 S&W cals. only) or checkered walnut (.45 ACP cal. only) grips, 15 shot (9mm Para.), 11 shot (.40 S&W), or 10 shot (.45 ACP) mag., 34.6 oz. Disc. 1993.

	$555	$475	$415	$350	$300	$275	$250	Last MSR was $694.

Add $30 for .45 ACP cal.

* **Model P9 Ultra LSP Stainless** – stainless steel variation of the P9 Ultra LSP. Mfg. 1991-92.

	$675	$525	$425	$360	$315	$260	$225	Last MSR was $769.

Add $30 for .40 S&W cal.
Add $90 for .45 ACP cal.

* **Model P9 World Cup** – see listing under 1911-A1 Custom Models heading.

Pistols: Semi-Auto - R-Series

PANTHER MODEL – 9mm Para., .40 S&W, or .45 ACP cal., semi-auto single or double action, 3.8 in. barrel, hammer drop or firing pin safety, 15 shot (9mm Para.), 11 shot (.40 S&W), or 9 shot (.45 ACP) mag., Commander hammer, frame mounted slide stop, narrow profile, non-glare blue finish only, walnut grips, squared-off triggerguard, 29 oz. Mfg. 1992 only.

	$535	$450	$395	$350	$300	$275	$250	Last MSR was $609.

MSR	100%	98%	95%	90%	80%	70%	60%

FIRECAT MODEL – 9mm Para. or .40 S&W cal., single action, 3 1/2 in. barrel, 3-dot low profile sights, all steel mfg., firing pin block and frame mounted ambidextrous safety, 8 shot (9mm Para.) or 7 shot (.40 S&W) mag., checkered combat style triggerguard and front/rear gripstraps, non-glare blue finish, 35 3/4 oz. Mfg. 1992-93.

	$495	$425	$375	$330	$295	$275	$250	Last MSR was $569.

BOBCAT MODEL – while advertised in 1992, this model was never mfg.

LINX MODEL – while advertised in 1992, this model was never mfg.

Pistols: Semi-Auto - Disc. 1911-A1 Models

MODEL 1911-A1 STANDARD MODEL – .38 Super, 9mm Para., 10mm (new 1990), or .45 ACP cal., patterned after the Colt M1911-A1, 5.04 (Standard) or 4.025 (Commander or Compact Model) in. barrel, 7 shot (Compact), 8 shot (.45 ACP), 9 shot (10mm), or 10 shot (9mm Para. and .38 Super) mag., walnut grips, parkerized, blue, or duotone finish. Mfg. 1985-90.

	$400	$360	$330	$300	$280	$260	$240	Last MSR was $454.

Add $35 for blue finish.
Add $80 for duotone finish.

This model was also available with a .45 ACP to 9mm Para. conversion kit for $170 in parkerized finish, or $175 in blue finish.

* ***Model 1911-A1 Standard Defender Model*** – .45 ACP cal. only, similar to Standard 1911-A1 Model, except has fixed combat sights, beveled mag. well, extended thumb safety, bobbed hammer, flared ejection port, walnut grips, factory serrated front strap and two stainless steel magazines, parkerized or blue finish. Mfg. 1988-90.

	$485	$435	$375	$340	$300	$280	$260	Last MSR was $567.

Add $35 for blue finish.

* ***Model 1911-A1 Standard Commander Model*** – .45 ACP cal. only, similar to Standard 1911-A1 Model, except has 3.63 in. barrel, shortened slide, Commander hammer, low profile 3-dot sights, walnut grips, parkerized, blue, or duotone finish. Mfg. in 1990 only.

	$450	$415	$350	$325	$285	$260	$245	Last MSR was $514.

Add $30 for blue finish.
Add $80 for duotone finish.

* ***Model 1911-A1 Standard Combat Commander Model*** – .45 ACP cal. only, 4 1/4 in. barrel, bobbed hammer, walnut grips. Mfg. 1988-89.

	$435	$385	$325	$295	$275	$250	$230

Add $20 for blue finish.

* ***Model 1911-A1 Standard Compact Model*** – .45 ACP cal. only, compact variation featuring shortened Commander barrel and slide, reduced M1911 straight gripstrap frame, checkered walnut grips, low profile 3-dot sights, extended slide stop, combat hammer, parkerized, blue, or duotone finish. Mfg. 1990 only.

	$450	$415	$350	$325	$285	$260	$245	Last MSR was $514.

Add $30 for blue finish.
Add $80 for duotone finish.

* ***Model 1911-A1 Standard Custom Carry Gun*** – .38 Super (special order only), 9mm Para., 10mm (new 1990), or .45 ACP cal., similar to Defender Model, except has tuned trigger pull, heavy recoil spring, extended thumb safety, and other features. Mfg. 1988-disc.

	$860	$725	$660	$535	$460	$420	$385	Last MSR was $969.

Add $130 for .38 Super Ramped, 10mm was POR.

Pistols: Semi-Auto - 1911-A1 (90s Series)

The initials "PDP" refer to Springfield's Personal Defense Pistol series.

Beginning in 2000, Springfield Armory started offering a Loaded Promotion package on their 1911-A1 pistol line. Many of these features and options are found on the FBI's Hostage Rescue Teams (HRT) pistol contract with Springfield Armory. Standard features of this Loaded Promotion package are hammer forged premium air-gauged barrel, front and rear cocking serrations, Novak patented low profile sights or Bo-Mar type adj. sights, extended thumb safety, tactical beavertail, flat mainspring housing, Cocobolo grips, High Hand grip, lightweight match trigger, full length guide rod, and machine beveled mag. well. This promotion includes all pistols except the Mil-Spec Model 1911 A-1.

In 2001, Springfield's Custom Loaded 1911-A1 Series pistols came equipped standard with Springfield's integral locking system, carry bevel, hammer forged premium air-gauged barrel, front and rear cocking serrations, Novak patented low profile sights (some models come equipped with Tritium sights or Bo-Mar type adj. sights), extended thumb safety, tactical beavertail, flat mainspring housing, cocobolo grips, high hand grip, lightweight adj. match trigger, full length guide rod, machine beveled magwell, and a "loaded" coupon ($600 consumer savings). These Custom Loaded features will vary by model. All models with less than a 5 in. and all alloy pistols supplied with ramped, fully supported barrels.

MSR	100%	98%	95%	90%	80%	70%	60%

Beginning 2002, every Springfield pistol is equipped with a patented integral locking system (I.L.S., keyed in the rear gripstrap) at no extra charge.

In 2007, most models are shipped with an 11 gear system, including one (GI models only) or two mags., belt holster, magazine pouch, and bore brush supplied in a lockable blue plastic case.

PDP DEFENDER MODEL – .40 S&W (disc. 1992) or .45 ACP cal., standard pistol with slide and barrel shortened to Champion length (4 in.), tapered cone dual port compensator system, fully adj. sights, Videcki speed trigger, rubber grips, Commander style hammer, serrated front strap, parkerized (disc. 1992), duotone/bi-tone, or blue (disc. 1993) finish. Mfg. 1991-1998.

	$850	$745	$635	$580	$465	$380	$295	*Last MSR was $992.*

MODEL 1911-A1 90s EDITION (CUSTOM LOADED) – .38 Super, 9mm Para., 10mm (disc. 1991), .40 S&W, or .45 ACP cal., patterned after the Colt M1911-A1, except has linkless operating system, 5.04 (Standard) or 4 (Champion or Compact Model) in. barrel, 7 shot (Compact), 8 shot (.40 S&W or .45 ACP Standard), 9 shot (9mm Para., 10mm, or .38 Super), or 10 shot (.38 Super) mag., checkered walnut grips, parkerized (.38 Super beginning 1994 or .45 ACP beginning 1993), blue or duotone (disc. 1992) finish. New 1991.

* ***1911-A1 90s Edition Mil-Spec*** – .38 Super or .45 ACP cal., blue (disc.), parkerized, bi-tone (new 2004), or OD Green (new 2004) finish, 3-dot Hi-Viz fixed combat sights, includes belt holster and extra set of grips, 35.6 oz.

MSR $696	$595	$515	$445	$395	$320	$265	$205

Add $17 for blue finish (disc. 2001).
Add $21 for OD Green or bi-tone finish (mfg. 2004 only).
Add $57 for .45 ACP cal. with Mil-Spec package (belt holster, double mag. pouch and extra set of grips, new 2009).
Add $631 for .38 Super cal. in High Polish Nickel (Acusport exclusive 2004-2007).

* ***1911-A1 90s Edition Mil-Spec Operator*** – .45 ACP cal. only, similar to Mil-Spec 1911-A1, except has Picatinny light mounting system forged into lower front of frame, parkerized finish only. Disc. 2002.

	$615	$540	$460	$420	$340	$275	$215	*Last MSR was $756.*

* ***1911-A1 90s Edition Loaded Operator*** – .45 ACP cal. only, similar to full size service model, except has Picatinny light mounting platform forged into lower front of frame, checkered hardwood (disc. 2003) or plastic grips, OD Green with black bi-tone Armory Kote finish, Novak low mount tritium (disc.) or Trijicon night sights. New 2002.

MSR $1,387	$1,175	$1,025	$875	$775	$635	$515	$400

* ***1911-A1 90s Edition Lightweight Operator*** – .45 ACP cal. only, 5 in. stainless steel barrel, blue finish, 7 shot mag., fixed low profile combat rear sight, dovetail front sight, cocobolo grips, 34 oz. New 2006.

MSR $1,305	$1,125	$975	$825	$750	$600	$495	$385

* ***1911-A1 90s Edition Standard or Lightweight Model*** – .45 ACP cal. (current mfg.), Standard model has parkerized, blue, or OD Green with Armory Kote (new 2002) finish, Custom Loaded features became standard in 2001, Lightweight Model was introduced 1995 with either matte (disc. 2002), bi-tone (new 2003) or blue (mfg. 1993-disc.) finish, current mfg. is w/ either Novak low mount or Trijicon night sights, 28.6 or 35.6 oz.

MSR $959	$835	$725	$625	$565	$455	$370	$290

Add $74 for Lightweight Model (with Trijicon night sights).
Subtract approx. 10%-25% if w/o Custom Loaded features (new 2001), depending on condition.

* ***1911-A1 90s Edition Stainless Standard Model*** – 9mm Para. (new 1994), .38 Super (disc.), .40 S&W (mfg. 2001-2002), or .45 ACP cal., 7 (.45 ACP cal.), 8 (.40 S&W), or 9 (9mm Para.) shot mag., Custom Loaded features became standard in 2001, wraparound rubber (disc.) or checkered hardwood grips, 11 Gear system holster became standard 2009, Novak Lo-Mount or Bo-Mar type (mfg. 1996-2001) sights, beveled mag. well, 39.2 oz. New 1991.

MSR $990	$885	$775	$660	$595	$480	$395	$305

Add $89 for 9mm Para. cal., or $32 for .40 S&W cal. (disc.).
Add $9 for Tactical Model with combat features and black stainless steel (new 2005).
Add $50 for Bo-Mar type sights (disc. 2001).
Add $202 for long slide variation in .45 Super cal. with V16 porting and Bo-Mar sights (disc.).

* ***1911-A1 90s Edition Stainless Super Tuned Standard*** – .45 ACP cal. only, super tuned by the Custom Shop, 7 shot mag., 5 in. barrel, Novak fixed Lo-Mount sights, 39.2 oz. Mfg. 1997-99.

	$875	$765	$655	$595	$480	$395	$305	*Last MSR was $995.*

* ***1911-A1 90s Edition Standard High Capacity*** – 9mm Para. (disc.) or .45 ACP cal., 5 in. barrel, blue (disc. 2001) or matte parkerized (new 1996) finish with plastic grips, 3-dot fixed combat sights, 10 shot (except for law enforcement) mag. Mfg. 1995-2003.

	$635	$555	$475	$430	$350	$285	$220	*Last MSR was $756.*

Add $50 for blue finish (disc.).

MSR	100%	98%	95%	90%	80%	70%	60%

* ***1911-A1 90s Edition Stainless High Capacity*** – similar to Standard High Capacity, except is stainless steel. Mfg. 1996-2000.

| | $675 | $590 | $505 | $460 | $370 | $305 | $235 | Last MSR was $819. |

* ***1911-A1 90s Edition XM4 High Capacity Model*** – 9mm Para. or 45 ACP cal., features widened frame for high capacity mag., blue (mfg. 1993 only) or stainless finish only. Mfg. 1993-94.

| | $595 | $520 | $445 | $405 | $325 | $270 | $210 | Last MSR was $689. |

MODEL 1911-A1 GI – .45 ACP cal., 5 in. barrel, parkerized, OD Green Armory Kote finish or stainless steel, 7 (standard) or 13 (high capacity) shot mag., low profile military sights, diamond checkered walnut grips with U.S. initials, includes 5.11 Gear belt holster, 36 oz. New 2004.

| MSR $643 | $560 | $485 | $415 | $375 | $300 | $245 | $190 |

Add $50 for stainless steel.
Add $60 for high capacity magazine (parkerized finish, new 2005).

1911-A1 TACTICAL RESPONSE (TRP SERIES) – .45 ACP only, 5 in. standard or bull (Operator Model only) barrel, 7 shot mag., matte Armory Kote finish or stainless steel, checkered rosewood grips, Trijicon (new 2006), Novak or Hi-Viz (disc., Operator Model only) 3-dot Tritium (disc. 2001) sights, 36 oz. New 1999.

| MSR $1,777 | $1,525 | $1,325 | $1,125 | $1,025 | $825 | $675 | $525 |

Add $90 for Operator Model with integral light mounting rail and adj. night sights.

1911-A1 COMMANDER MODEL – .45 ACP cal. only, similar to Standard 1911-A1 Model, except has 3.63 in. barrel, shortened slide, Commander hammer, low profile 3-dot sights, walnut grips, parkerized, blue, or duotone finish. Mfg. 1991-92.

| | $425 | $370 | $320 | $290 | $235 | $190 | $150 |

* ***1911-A1 Commander Model Combat*** – .45 ACP cal. only, 4 1/4 in. barrel, bobbed hammer, walnut grips. Mfg. 1991 only.

| | $425 | $370 | $320 | $290 | $235 | $190 | $150 |

1911-A1 CHAMPION MODEL – .380 ACP (Model MD-1, mfg. 1995 only) or .45 ACP cal., similar to Standard Model, except has 4 in. barrel and shortened slide, blue (disc. 2000) or parkerized (Mil-Spec Champion, new 1994) finish, Commander hammer, checkered walnut grips, 3-dot sights (Novak night sights became standard 2001), 7 shot mag., 33 1/2 oz. Mfg. 1992-2002.

| | $695 | $610 | $520 | $470 | $380 | $315 | $245 | Last MSR was $856. |

Add $30 for Ultra Compact slide (mfg. 1997-98).
Add $79 for ported Champion V10 with Ultra Compact slide (disc.).
Subtract approx. 10%-25% if w/o Custom Loaded features (new 2001), depending on condition.
Subtract approx. $150 for .380 ACP cal. (Model MD-1, disc.).

* ***1911-A1 Champion Model (Custom Loaded)*** – .45 ACP cal. only, stainless steel or Lightweight bi-tone with OD Green finish (new 2004). New 1992.

| MSR $1,051 | $910 | $800 | $675 | $615 | $500 | $400 | $315 |

Add $119 for Ultra Compact slide (mfg. 1997-98).
Add $52 for ported Champion V10 with Ultra Compact slide (disc. 2000).
Subtract $40 for Lightweight Champion with bi-tone OD Green finish (new 2004).
Subtract approx. 10%-25% if w/o Custom Loaded features (new 2001), depending on condition.

* ***1911-A1 Champion Model Lightweight Operator*** – .45 ACP cal., 4 in. stainless steel barrel, blue finish, 7 shot mag., fixed low profile combat rear sight, dovetail front sight, cocobolo grips, 34 oz. New 2006.

| MSR $1,076 | $940 | $825 | $700 | $630 | $510 | $415 | $325 |

* ***1911-A1 Champion Model GI*** – .45 ACP cal., parkerized or blued slide with black anodized frame (Lightweight Model, new 2005), low profile military sights, diamond checkered wood grips with U.S. initials, includes belt holster, 34 oz. New 2004.

| MSR $643 | $555 | $485 | $410 | $375 | $300 | $245 | $190 |

* ***1911-A1 Champion Model TRP*** – .45 ACP cal., 4 in. barrel, otherwise similar to TRP Tactical Response. Mfg. 1999-2001.

| | $1,045 | $915 | $785 | $710 | $575 | $470 | $365 | Last MSR was $1,249. |

* ***1911-A1 Champion Model Lightweight*** – .45 ACP cal., aluminum frame, matte metal finish, night sights became standard during 2001. New 1999.

| | $700 | $610 | $525 | $475 | $385 | $315 | $245 | Last MSR was $867. |

Subtract approx. 10%-25% if w/o Custom Loaded features (new 2001), depending on condition.

* ***1911-A1 Champion Model Comp PDP*** – .45 ACP cal. only, compensated version of the Champion Model, blue. Mfg. 1993-98.

| | $780 | $680 | $585 | $530 | $430 | $350 | $275 | Last MSR was $869. |

MSR	100%	98%	95%	90%	80%	70%	60%

* *1911-A1 Champion Model Super Tuned* – .45 ACP cal., super tuned by the Custom Shop, 7 shot mag., 4 in. barrel, blue or parkerized finish, Novak fixed Lo-Mount sights, 36.3 oz. Mfg. 1997-99.

| | $850 | $745 | $635 | $580 | $465 | $380 | $295 | Last MSR was $959. |

Add $30 for blue finish.

* *1911-A1 Champion Model XM4 High Capacity* – 9mm Para. or .45 ACP cal., high capacity variation. Mfg. 1994 only.

| | $615 | $540 | $460 | $420 | $340 | $275 | $215 | Last MSR was $699. |

1911-A1 COMPACT MODEL – .45 ACP cal. only, compact variation featuring shortened 4 in. barrel and slide, reduced M1911-A1 curved gripstrap frame, checkered walnut grips, low profile 3-dot sights, 6 or 7 shot mag., extended slide stop, standard or lightweight alloy (new 1994) frame, combat hammer, parkerized, blue, or duotone (disc. 1992) finish, standard or lightweight (new 1995) configuration, 27 or 32 oz. Mfg. 1991-96.

| | $415 | $365 | $310 | $280 | $230 | $185 | $145 | Last MSR was $476. |

Add $66 for blue finish.
Add $67 for Compact Lightweight Model (matte finish only).

* *1911-A1 Compact Model Stainless* – stainless steel variation of the Compact Model. Mfg. 1991-96.

| | $495 | $435 | $370 | $335 | $270 | $225 | $175 | Last MSR was $582. |

* *1911-A1 Compact Model Lightweight* – .45 ACP cal., forged alloy frame, matte metal finish, 6 shot mag., Novak night sights became standard 2001. Mfg. 1999-2003.

| | $585 | $510 | $440 | $395 | $320 | $265 | $205 | Last MSR was $733. |

Subtract approx. 10%-25% if w/o Custom Loaded features (new 2001), depending on condition.

»*1911-A1 Compact Model Lightweight Stainless* – similar to Compact Lightweight, except is stainless steel. Disc. 2001.

| | $725 | $635 | $545 | $495 | $400 | $325 | $255 | Last MSR was $900. |

Subtract approx. 10%-25% if w/o Custom Loaded features (new 2001), depending on condition.

* *1911-A1 Compact Model Comp Lightweight* – compensated version of the Compact Model, bi-tone or matte finish, regular or lightweight alloy (new 1994) frame. Mfg. 1993-98.

| | $775 | $680 | $580 | $525 | $425 | $350 | $270 | Last MSR was $869. |

* *1911-A1 Compact Model High Capacity* – blue or stainless steel, 3-dot fixed combat sights, black plastic grips, 10 shot (except for law enforcement) mag. Mfg. 1995-96 only.

| | $540 | $470 | $405 | $365 | $295 | $245 | $190 | Last MSR was $609. |

Add $39 for stainless steel.

* *1911-A1 Compact Model High Capacity PDP Comp* – .45 ACP cal. only, features compensated 3 1/2 in. barrel, 10 shot (except law enforcement) mag., blue finish only. Mfg. 1995-96 only.

| | $830 | $725 | $620 | $565 | $455 | $375 | $290 | Last MSR was $964. |

1911 A-1 ULTRA COMPACT (CUSTOM LOADED) – .380 ACP (lightweight only, mfg. 1995 only), 9mm Para. (new 1998, lightweight stainless only), or .45 ACP cal., 3 1/2 in. barrel, bi-tone (.45 ACP only, disc.), matte (.380 ACP, MD-1), or parkerized (Mil-Spec Ultra Compact) finish, 6, 7 (.380 ACP cal.) or 8 (9mm Para. cal.) shot mag., Custom Loaded features and night sights became standard in 2001, 24 or 30 oz. Mfg. 1995-2003.

| | $680 | $595 | $510 | $460 | $375 | $305 | $240 | Last MSR was $837. |

Add $12 for V10 porting.
Add $12 for Novak Tritium sights (not available on 9mm Para cal.).
Add $110 for bi-tone finish (disc.).
Subtract $50 for MD-1 variation (.380 ACP only).
Subtract approx. 10%-25% if w/o Custom Loaded features (new 2001), depending on condition.

* *1911 A-1 Ultra Compact Mil-Spec* – .45 ACP cal., parkerized (disc.) or blued (new 2004) finish, similar to full size Mil-Spec Model, 6 shot mag., checkered grips, 3-dot fixed Hi-Viz combat sights. Mfg. 2001-2002, reintroduced 2004 only.

| | $550 | $480 | $410 | $375 | $300 | $245 | $190 | Last MSR was $641. |

Subtract approx. 10%-25% if w/o Custom Loaded features (new 2001), depending on condition.

* *1911 A-1 Ultra Compact Stainless Custom Loaded* – 9mm Para. (disc. 2004) or .45 ACP cal., stainless steel, Novak Trijicon night sights became standard 2001. New 1998.

| MSR $1,051 | $915 | $800 | $675 | $615 | $490 | $405 | $315 |

Add $17 for 9mm Para cal. (lightweight, disc. 2004).
Subtract approx. 10%-25% if w/o Custom Loaded features (new 2001), depending on condition.

MSR	100%	98%	95%	90%	80%	70%	60%

* **1911 A-1 Ultra Compact Lightweight** – .45 ACP cal., aluminum frame, matte metal finish, night sights became standard 2001. Mfg. 1999-2001.

| | $695 | $610 | $520 | $470 | $380 | $315 | $245 | Last MSR was $867. |

Subtract approx. 10%-25% if w/o Custom Loaded features (new 2001), depending on condition.

* **1911 A-1 Ultra Compact V10 Lightweight Ported** – .45 ACP cal., bi-tone finish. Mfg. 1999-2001.

| | $750 | $655 | $560 | $510 | $410 | $335 | $260 | Last MSR was $737. |

» **1911 A-1 Ultra Compact V10 Lightweight Stainless** – 9mm Para. or .45 ACP (exclusive) cal., similar to Ultra Combat Lightweight, except is stainless steel, Novak Lo-Mount sights. Mfg. 1999-2002.

| | $725 | $635 | $545 | $495 | $400 | $325 | $255 | Last MSR was $870. |

Add $31 for night sights (.45 ACP cal. only).
Subtract approx. 10%-25% if w/o Custom Loaded features (new 2001), depending on condition.

* **1911 A-1 Ultra Compact High Capacity** – 9mm Para. (disc.) or .45 ACP cal., parkerized (Mil-Spec) or blue (disc.) finish, and stainless steel (disc.) construction, 10 shot mag., 3-dot fixed combat (disc.) or Novak Lo-Mount (new 2002) sights, black plastic grips. Mfg. 1996-2002.

| | $735 | $645 | $550 | $500 | $405 | $330 | $255 | Last MSR was $909. |

Add $98 for stainless steel.
Add $145 for stainless steel with V10 ported barrel (disc.).
Subtract approx. 10%-25% if w/o Custom Loaded features (new 2001), depending on condition.

* **1911 A-1 Ultra Compact V10 Ported** – .45 ACP cal. only, 3 1/2 in. specially compensated barrel/slide, blue (disc.), bi-tone, or parkerized (Mil-Spec Ultra Compact) finish, Novak Lo-Mount or 3-dot combat sights, 30 oz. Mfg. 1995-2002.

| | $690 | $605 | $515 | $470 | $380 | $310 | $240 | Last MSR was $853. |

Subtract approx. 10%-25% if w/o Custom Loaded features (new 2001), depending on condition.

* **1911 A-1 Ultra Compact V10 Super Tuned Ported** – .45 ACP cal. only, super tuned by the Custom Shop, 3 1/2 in. ported barrel, bi-tone finish or stainless steel (exclusive), Novak fixed Lo-Mount sights, 32.9 oz. Mfg. 1997-99.

| | $925 | $810 | $695 | $630 | $510 | $415 | $325 | Last MSR was $1,049. |

Add $70 for stainless steel (exclusive).

1911-A1 MICRO COMPACT – .45 ACP cal. only, 3 in. tapered barrel w/o bushing, matte finish, checkered grips, 6 shot mag., Novak Lo-Mount night sights. Mfg. 2002 only.

| | $625 | $545 | $470 | $425 | $345 | $280 | $220 | Last MSR was $749. |

* **1911 A-1 Micro Compact Lightweight Custom Loaded** – similar to Micro Compact 1911 A-1, except also available in .40 S&W (disc.) cal., bi-tone, OD Green (mfg. 2003 only), or black Armory Kote (mfg. 2003-2004) finish with forged steel slide (grey) and aluminum alloy frame (blue), checkered cocobolo grips, Trijicon night sights, 24 oz. New 2002.

| MSR $1,349 | $1,165 | $965 | $850 | $725 | $600 | $500 | $400 | |

Add $71 for Operator Model with XML X-treme mini light.

* **1911 A-1 Micro Compact Lightweight Stainless Custom Loaded** – .45 ACP cal. only, similar to Micro Compact 1911 A-1 Custom Loaded, except is stainless or black stainless steel slide. Mfg. 2003.

| | $825 | $720 | $620 | $560 | $455 | $370 | $290 | Last MSR was $993. |

* **1911 A-1 Micro Compact GI** – .45 ACP cal., parkerized finish, checkered diamond walnut grips with U.S. initials, includes belt holster, 32 oz. New 2004.

| MSR $693 | $600 | $525 | $450 | $400 | $325 | $270 | $210 | |

1911-A1 TRP (TACTICAL RESPONSE PISTOL) SERIES – .45 ACP cal., 5 in. standard or bull barrel, fixed combat 3-dot tritium or adj. sights, black Armory Kote or stainless steel, checkered front strap, available in Standard, Stainless, and Operator configurations, 4 1/2 - 5 lbs. New mid-2008.

| MSR $1,829 | $1,575 | $1,380 | $1,180 | $1,070 | $865 | $710 | $550 | |

MODEL 1911-A1 EMP (ENHANCED MICRO PISTOL) – 9mm Para. or .40 S&W cal., bi-tone finish, 9 shot mag., 3 in. stainless steel bull barrel, polished stainless slide with blue frame, tritium 3-dot sights, available in Standard or Lightweight configuration, reduced dimensions result in narrower profile, cocobolo or G10 grips, 27 (Lightweight) or 33 oz. New 2007.

| MSR $1,345 | $1,175 | $1,025 | $875 | $785 | $635 | $515 | $400 | |

Add $79 for G10 grips (new 2008).

Pistols: Semi-Auto - 1911-A1 Custom Models

In addition to the models listed, Springfield also custom builds other configurations of Race Guns that are available through Springfield dealers. Prices range from $2,245-$2,990.

Add $100 for all cals. other than .45 ACP.

MSR	100%	98%	95%	90%	80%	70%	60%

CUSTOM CARRY GUN – .45 ACP (other cals. available upon request) cal., similar to Defender Model, except has tuned trigger pull, 7 shot mag., heavy recoil spring, extended thumb safety, available in blue or phosphate (disc.) finish. New 1991.

MSR $1,675	$1,450	$1,150	$950	$800	$700	$600	$550

CUSTOM OPERATOR – .45 ACP cal. New 2001.

MSR $2,595	$2,225	$1,775	$1,400	$1,100	$950	$850	$750

PROFESSIONAL MODEL – .45 ACP cal., FBI contract model, black finish, with or w/o light rail. New 1999.

MSR $2,647	$2,250	$1,775	$1,400	$1,125	$975	$850	$750

1911-A1 CUSTOM COMPACT – .45 ACP cal. only, carry or lady's model with shortened slide and frame, compensated, fixed 3-dot sights, Commander style hammer, Herrett walnut grips, other custom features, blue only.

	$1,615	$1,325	$1,100	$950	$850	$750	$675	Last MSR was $1,815.

1911-A1 CUSTOM CHAMPION – similar to Custom Compact, except is based on Champion model with full size frame and shortened slide.

	$1,615	$1,325	$1,100	$950	$850	$750	$675	Last MSR was $1,815.

CUSTOM HIGH CAPACITY LTD – .40 S&W cal. New 2004.

MSR $2,650	$2,200	$1,775	$1,425	$1,125	$975	$875	$775

OPERATOR LIGHTWEIGHT – .45 ACP cal., 3 in. barrel, bi-tone finish, XML mini-light, includes Novak Trijicon night sights. Limited mfg. 2005.

	$1,050	$925	$800	$700	$600	$500	$400	Last MSR was $1,247.

OPERATOR TACTICAL RESPONSE – .45 ACP cal., 5 in. barrel, black Armory Kote finish, adj. Trijicon night sights. Limited mfg. 2005.

	$1,395	$1,075	$900	$775	$675	$575	$475	Last MSR was $1,639.

LOADED OPERATOR – .45 ACP cal., 5 in. barrel, OD Green or black Armory Kote finish and slide, Novak or Trijicon night sights. Limited mfg. 2005.

	$1,025	$900	$800	$700	$600	$500	$400	Last MSR was $1,218.

Pistols: Semi-Auto - XD Series

All XD pistols were originally shipped with two magazines. Beginning 2005, high capacity magazines are legal for civilian sales in those states that permit high cap. mags. During 2006, all XD pistols are shipped with the XD Gear System, consisting of belt holster, double magazine pouch, magazine loader, two magazines and cable lock.

X-TREME DUTY (XD MODELS) - 5 IN. TACTICAL – 9mm Para., .357 SIG (night sights only beginning 2008), .40 S&W (night sights only beginning 2008), .45 ACP (new 2006), or .45 GAP (mfg. 2005-2007) cal., cold hammer forged 5 in. barrel, 9 (.45 GAP), 10, 12 (.40 S&W or .357 SIG), or 15 (9mm Para.) shot mag., lightweight polymer frame, matte black, bi-tone, Dark Earth (new 2007) or OD Green finish, steel slide, single action striker fired with U.S.A. trigger system, firing pin and loaded chamber indicators, dual recoil spring system, integral accessory rails standard on frame, ambidextrous mag. release, grip safety, front and rear slide serrations, external thumb safety became separate model in 2008, approx. 23 oz. New 2002.

MSR $599	$535	$450	$400	$350	$300	$265	$235

Add $30 for thumb safety (black or bi-tone finish only).
Add $30 for .45 ACP cal. (new 2006), or $80 for bi-tone finish.
Add $92 for Trijicon sights or approx. $90 for Heinie (disc.) tritium Slant Pro sights.
Subtract $7 for .45 GAP cal. black tactical (disc. 2007).

* ***XD Tactical Pro*** – limited mfg. 2003 only.

	$875	$775	$675	$575	$475	$400	$350	Last MSR was $1,099.

X-TREME DUTY (XD MODELS) - 4 IN. SERVICE – 9mm Para., .357 SIG, .40 S&W, .45 ACP (new 2006), or .45 GAP (mfg. 2005-2007) cal., cold hammer forged 4 in. ported or unported barrel, 9 (.45 GAP), 10 (.45 ACP), 12 (.40 S&W or .357 SIG), or 15 (9mm Para.) shot mag., lightweight polymer frame, matte black, bi-tone (new 2003), Dark Earth (new 2007) or OD Green finish, steel slide, single action striker fired with U.S.A. trigger system, firing pin and loaded chamber indicators, dual recoil spring system, integral accessory rails standard on frame, ambidextrous mag. release, grip safety, front and rear slide serrations, thumb safety became seperate model during 2008, approx. 23 oz. New 2002.

MSR $549	$490	$425	$365	$310	$275	$235	$200

Add $29 for .45 ACP cal.
Add $35 for V10 ported barrel (black or OD Green finish, not available in .45 ACP or .45 GAP cal.).
Add $67 for bi-tone finish.

MSR	100%	98%	95%	90%	80%	70%	60%

Add $29 for thumb safety (black or bi-tone finish only).
Add $96 for Trijicon or Heinie tritium Slant Pro night sights (9mm Para., .357 SIG or .40 S&W cal.).
Subtract $7 for .45 GAP cal. (disc. 2007).

X-TREME DUTY (XD MODELS) - 3 IN. SUB-COMPACT – 9mm Para. or .40 S&W (new 2004) cal., cold hammer forged 3 in. barrel, 9 (.40 S&W) or 10 (9mm Para.) shot mag., lightweight polymer frame, bi-tone (new 2004, 9mm Para. cal. only), matte black or OD Green finish, steel slide, single action striker fired with U.S.A. trigger system, firing pin and loaded chamber indicators, dual recoil spring system, integral accessory rails standard on frame, ambidextrous mag. release, grip safety, front and rear slide serrations, 20 1/2 oz. New 2003.

MSR $549	$490	$425	$365	$310	$275	$235	$200

Add $67 for bi-tone finish.
Add $96 for Trijicon or Heinie tritium Slant Pro night sights.
Add $100 for X-treme mini light.

XD COMPACT SERIES – 9mm Para. (mfg. 2007 only), .40 S&W (mfg. 2007 only), or .45 ACP cal., 4 or 5 in. barrel, shortened grip frame, black, OD Green, bi-tone (new 2008), or Dark Earth finish, stainless steel slide (OD Green or Dark Earth only, new 2008), 10 or extended 13 shot mag., 29 or 32 oz. New 2007.

MSR $600	$525	$440	$400	$350	$315	$280	$245

Subtract $30 for 9mm or .40 S&W cal. (4 in. barrel only), w/o night sights.
Add $96 for night sights.
Add $66 for bi-tone finish or stainless steel slide.
Add $46 for 5 in. barrel.

XD CUSTOM SERIES – the Springfield custom shop makes three variations of the XD pistol, including the XD Carry, XD Production, and XD Custom Competition. Most calibers and sizes are available.

Current MSRs on this series are as follows - XD Carry is $895, XD Production is $1,195, and XD Custom Competition is $1,695.

XD(M) SERIES – 9mm Para. or .40 S&W cal., 3.8 (new 2010) or 4 1/2 in. barrel, 16 or 19 shot mag., black, bi-tone, or OD Green, black or stainless steel slide, multi-rail system, interchangeable back straps, includes XD Gear holster and black plastic carrying case. New mid-2008.

MSR $697	$615	$540	$465	$410	$360	$310	$265

Add $66 for bi-tone or $79 for OD Green w/black slide.
Add $118 for Trijicon night sights.

RIFLES: SEMI-AUTO, MILITARY DESIGN

Many models listed below are CA legal, since they do not have a muzzle brake. MSRs are typically the same as those guns available with a muzzle brake. Pricing on CA legal firearms is not included within the scope of this text - please contact the factory directly for this information (see Trademark Index).

M1 CARBINE – .30 Carbine cal., features new receiver on older military M1 GI stocks. Disc.

	$495	$435	$370	$335	$270	$225	$175

M1 GARAND AND VARIATIONS – .30-06, .270 Win. (disc. 1987), or .308 Win. cal., semi-auto, 24 in. barrel, gas operated, 8 shot mag., adj. sights, 9 1/2 lbs.

* ***M1 Garand Rifle*** – .30-06 or .308 Win. cal., mfg. with original U.S. government issue parts, with new walnut stock, 8 shot mag., 24 in. barrel, 9 1/2 lbs. Limited mfg. 2002-2007.

	$1,175	$1,030	$880	$800	$645	$530	$410	Last MSR was $1,439.

Add $30 for .308 Win. cal.

* ***M1 Garand Standard Model*** – supplied standard with camo GI fiberglass stock.

	$725	$635	$545	$495	$400	$325	$255	Last MSR was $761.

Subtract $65 if with GI stock.

* ***M1 Garand National Match*** – walnut stock, match barrel and sights.

	$850	$745	$635	$580	$465	$380	$295	Last MSR was $897.

Add $240 for Kevlar stock.

* ***M1 Garand Ultra Match*** – match barrel and sights, glass bedded stock, walnut stock standard.

	$950	$830	$710	$645	$520	$425	$330	Last MSR was $1,033.

Add $240 for Kevlar stock.

* ***M1-D Sniper Rifle*** – .30-06 or .308 Win. cal., limited quantities, with original M84 scope, prong type flash suppressor, leather cheek pad and slings.

	$1,100	$960	$825	$750	$605	$495	$385	Last MSR was $1,033.

* ***M1 Garand Tanker Rifle*** – similar to T-26 authorized by Gen. MacArthur at the end of WWII, 18 1/4 in. barrel,

MSR	100%	98%	95%	90%	80%	70%	60%	

.30-06 or .308 Win. cal., GI stock standard.

| | $850 | $745 | $635 | $580 | $465 | $380 | $295 | Last MSR was $797. |

Add $23 for walnut full stock.

* **D-Day M1 Garand Rifle** – .30-06 cal., 24 in. barrel, gas operated, military square post front sights, engraved stock, two 8 shot mags., leather sling, cleaning kit, includes wooden crate and limited edition lithograph print, 9 1/2 lbs. 1,944 mfg. 2004-2005.

| | $1,375 | $1,205 | $1,030 | $935 | $755 | $620 | $480 | Last MSR was $1,490. |

BM 59 – .308 Win. cal., mfg. in Italy and machined and assembled in the Springfield Armory factory, 19.32 in. barrel, 20 shot box mag., 9 1/2 lbs.

* **BM 59 Standard Italian Rifle** – with grenade launcher, winter trigger, tri-compensator, and bipod.

| | $1,750 | $1,530 | $1,310 | $1,190 | $960 | $785 | $610 | Last MSR was $1,950. |

* **BM 59 Alpine Rifle** – with Beretta pistol grip type stock.

| | $2,025 | $1,770 | $1,520 | $1,375 | $1,115 | $910 | $710 | Last MSR was $2,275. |

This model was also available in a Paratrooper configuration with folding stock at no extra charge.

* **BM 59 Nigerian Rifle** – similar to BM 59, except has Beretta pistol grip type stock.

| | $2,075 | $1,815 | $1,555 | $1,410 | $1,140 | $935 | $725 | Last MSR was $2,340. |

* **BM 59 E Model Rifle**

| | $1,975 | $1,730 | $1,480 | $1,345 | $1,085 | $890 | $690 | Last MSR was $2,210. |

M1A RIFLES – .243 Win. (disc.), .308 Win., or 7mm-08 Rem. (1991 mfg. only) cal., patterned after the original Springfield M14 - except semi-auto, walnut or fiberglass stock, 22 in. steel or stainless steel barrel, fiberglass handguard, "New Loaded" option (see separate listing) beginning 2001 includes NM air gauged barrel, trigger group, front and rear sights, and flash suppressor or Springfield proprietary muzzle brake, 9 lbs.

* **M1A Standard/Basic Model** – above specifications, choice of Collector (original GI stock, disc. 2001), birch (disc. 2003), walnut (M1A Standard Model beginning 1993), Mossy Oak camo finished (new 2003), black fiberglass (M1A Basic Model), camo fiberglass (disc.), GI wood (disc. 1992), and brown (disc.) or black laminated (M1A Standard Model mfg. 1996-2000) stock, regular or National Match (disc.) barrel.

| MSR $1,649 | $1,425 | $1,250 | $1,050 | $950 | $765 | $630 | $490 | |

Add $90 for new walnut stock.
Add $35 for Mossy Oak camo finished stock.
Add $59 for birch stock (disc. 2003).
Add $44 for stainless steel barrel (disc.), $74 for bipod and stabilizer (disc.) or $159 for brown laminated stock (disc.), $59 for National Match barrel (disc.), $155 for National Match barrel and sights (disc.), $200 for folding stock (disc. 1994).
Subtract $58 for camo fiberglass stock (disc.).

Standard (entry level model) stock configuration for 1996 was black or camo fiberglass.

* **M1A E-2** – standard stock is birch. Disc.

| | $975 | $855 | $730 | $665 | $535 | $440 | $340 | Last MSR was $842. |

Add $30 for walnut stock.
Add $120 for Shaw stock with Harris bipod.

* **M1A Bush Rifle** – .308 Win. cal., 18 in. shrouded barrel, 8 lbs. 12 oz., collector GI, walnut, Mossy Oak camo finished (new 2003), black fiberglass folding (disc. 1994 per C/B), and black fiberglass (disc.) or laminated black (disc.) stock. Disc. 1999, reintroduced 2003 only.

| | $1,300 | $1,135 | $975 | $885 | $715 | $585 | $455 | Last MSR was $1,529. |

Add $29 for walnut stock (disc.), $15 for black fiberglass stock (disc.), $86 for black laminated stock (disc.), $235 for National Match variation (disc.), and $525 for Super Match variation (disc.)

* **M1A National Match** – National Match sights, steel or stainless steel (new 1999) barrel, mainspring guide, flash suppressor, and gas cylinder, special glass bedded oil finished match stock, tuned trigger, walnut stock became standard in 1991, 9 lbs.

| MSR $2,318 | $2,000 | $1,750 | $1,500 | $1,350 | $1,085 | $890 | $690 | |

Add $55 for stainless steel barrel.
Add $155 for heavy composition stock (disc.).
Add $250 for either fiberglass or fancy burl wood stock (disc.).

.243 Win. and 7mm-08 Rem. cals. are also available at extra charge.

* **M1A Super Match** – similar to National Match, except has air-gauged Douglas or Hart (disc.) heavy barrel, oversized walnut or fiberglass super match stock, and modified operating rod guide, rear lugged receiver beginning 1991, approx. 11 1/2 lbs.

| MSR $2,905 | $2,550 | $2,200 | $1,875 | $1,685 | $1,360 | $1,115 | $865 | |

MSR	100%	98%	95%	90%	80%	70%	60%

Add $168 for stainless steel Douglas barrel.
Add $250 for Krieger or Hart barrel (disc.).
Add $664 for McMillan black or Marine Corps camo fiberglass stock.
Add $200 for fancy burl walnut (disc.) stock.
.243 Win. and 7mm-08 Rem. cals. are also available at extra charge.

M1A LOADED STANDARD – .308 Win. cal., 22 in. National Match steel or stainless steel barrel, features shooting upgrades such as National Match trigger assembly, front and rear sights, and National Match flash suppressor, 10 shot mag., black or green fiberglass, Collector GI walnut (disc. 2000), or new walnut stock, approx. 9 1/2 lbs. New 1999.

MSR $1,794	$1,650	$1,425	$1,225	$1,075	$875	$725	$575

Add $114 for new walnut stock.
Add $16 for green stock.
Add $211 for stainless steel barrel and walnut stock.
Add $99 for stainless steel barrel.
Add $525 for extended cluster rail with black fiberglass stock and National Match stainless steel barrel (new 2006).
Add $100 for Collector GI walnut (disc. 2000).

M1A "GOLD SERIES" – .308 Win. cal., heavy walnut competition stock, gold medal grade heavy Douglas barrel. Mfg. 1987 only.

	$1,944	$1,700	$1,460	$1,320	$1,070	$875	$680	Last MSR was $1,944.

Add $126 for Kevlar stock, add $390 for special Hart stainless steel barrel, add $516 for Hart stainless steel barrel with Kevlar stock.

M1A SCOUT SQUAD – .308 Win. cal., 18 in. barrel, choice of GI Collector (disc. 1998), new walnut, green or black fiberglass, Mossy Oak camo finished, or black laminated (disc. 1998) stock, muzzle stabilizer standard, supplied with Scout mount and handguard, approx. 9 lbs. New 1997.

MSR $1,761	$1,550	$1,350	$1,150	$1,050	$840	$685	$535

Add $132 for walnut stock.
Add $87 for Mossy Oak camo finish.
Add $14 for green stock.

M1A SOCOM/SOCOM II – .308 Win. cal., 16 1/4 in. barrel with muzzle brake, black fiberglass stock with steel buttplate, black or urban camo finish, upper handguard has been cut out for sight rail, 10 shot box mag., tritium front sight with ghost ring aperture rear sight, two-stage military trigger, 8.9 lbs. New 2004.

MSR $1,893	$1,725	$1,495	$1,275	$1,150	$925	$750	$585

Add $315 for urban camo stock with cluster rail (Socom II, new 2005).
Add $282 for Generation II black fiberglass stock with cluster rail (Socom II, new 2005) or $393 for extended cluster rail (Socom II, new 2007).

M1A/M21 TACTICAL – .308 Win. cal., Garand action, 22 in. barrel, tactical variation of the Super Match mfg. with match grade parts giving superior accuracy, adj. cheekpiece stock, 11.6 lbs. New 1990.

MSR $3,484	$3,075	$2,700	$2,275	$2,050	$1,645	$1,350	$1,050

Add $411 for Krieger stainless barrrel.

M25 "WHITE FEATHER" TACTICAL – .308 Win. cal., Garand action, includes black fiberglass M3A McMillan stock, 22 in. Kreiger heavy carbon barrel standard, Rader trigger, White Feather logo and Carlos Hathcock II signature, 10 shot box mag., includes Harris bipod, 12 3/4 lbs. Mfg. 2001-2009.

	$4,750	$4,155	$3,560	$3,230	$2,610	$2,135	$1,660	Last MSR was $5,278.

SAR-3 – .308 Win. cal., licensed copy of the pre-import ban HK-91, predecessor to the SAR-8, mfg. in Greece.

	$995	$870	$745	$675	$545	$450	$350

SAR-8 – .308 Win. cal., patterned after the H & K Model 91, roller locking delayed blowback action, fluted chamber, rotary adj. rear aperture sight, 18 in. barrel, recent mfg. incorporated a cast aluminum receiver with integrated Weaver rail, pistol grip, slim forearm, and green furniture (for law enforcement only), supplied with walnut (disc. 1994) or black fiberglass thumbhole sporter stock, 10 (C/B 1994) or 20 (disc. 1994) shot detachable mag., 8.7 lbs. Mfg. in U.S. starting 1990, disc. 1998.

	$1,015	$890	$760	$690	$560	$455	$355	Last MSR was $1,204.

SAR-8 parts are interchangeable with both SAR-3 and HK-91 parts.

* **SAR-8 Tactical Counter Sniper Rifle** – .308 Win. cal., tactical sniper variation of the SAR-8. Mfg. 1996-98.

	$1,325	$1,160	$995	$900	$730	$595	$465	Last MSR was $1,610.

SAR-48 MODEL – .308 Win. cal., authentic model of the Belgian semi-auto FAL/LAR rifle, 21 in. barrel, adj. gas piston operation, 20 shot mag., walnut or synthetic stock, adj. sights, sling, and mag. loader. Mfg. 1985-89.

	$1,675	$1,465	$1,255	$1,140	$920	$755	$585

This model was available in the Israeli configuration with heavy barrel, bipod, flash hider, and flip-up buttplate - add

MSR	100%	98%	95%	90%	80%	70%	60%

approx. 20%. The SAR-48 was disc. in 1989 and reintroduced as the Model SAR-4800 in 1990.

* ***SAR-48 Bush Rifle*** – similar to SAR-48 model, except has 18 in. barrel.

	$1,750	$1,530	$1,310	$1,190	$960	$785	$610

* ***SAR-48 .22 Cal.*** – .22 LR cal., variation of the Sporter Model. Disc. 1989.

	$725	$635	$545	$495	$400	$325	$255	Last MSR was $760.

SAR-4800 SPORTER MODEL – .223 Rem. (new 1997) or .308 Win. cal., authentic model of the Belgian semi-auto FAL/LAR rifle, 18 (.223 Rem. cal. only) or 21 in. barrel, adj. gas piston operation, 10 (C/B 1994) or 20 (disc.) shot mag., walnut (disc.) or black fiberglass thumbhole sporter stock, adj. sights, sling, and mag. loader. Mfg. 1990-98.

	$1,080	$945	$810	$735	$595	$485	$380

All SAR - 4800 parts are interchangeable with both SAR-48 and FN/FAL parts. This model is an updated variation of the pre-WWII FN Model 49.

* ***SAR-4800 Bush Rifle Sporter Model*** – similar to standard model, except has 18 in. barrel.

	$1,085	$950	$815	$735	$595	$490	$380	Last MSR was $1,216.

DR-200 SPORTER RIFLE – while advertised, this model never went into production. ($687 was planned MSR).

STAG ARMS

Current rifle manufacturer located in New Britain, CT.

RIFLES: SEMI-AUTO

All rifles are available in post-ban configuration for restricted states, and include one mag., instruction manual, plastic rifle case, and lifetime warranty.

MODEL 1 CARBINE – .223 Rem. cal., 16 in. chrome lined barrel, A3 forged aluminum upper, standard safety, black anodized finish, six position collapsible stock, removable carry handle, standard GI carbine design, available in right or left (Model 1L) hand, 7.1 lbs.

MSR $949	$860	$750	$645	$585	$475	$385	$300

Add $40 for Model 1L.

MODEL 2 CARBINE – .223 Rem. cal., 16 in. chrome lined barrel, A3 forged aluminum upper, standard safety, black anodized finish, six position collapsible stock, flip up rear sight, tactical top rail, available in right or left (Model 2L) hand, 6.4 lbs.

MSR $940	$850	$745	$635	$580	$465	$380	$295

Add $24 for Model 2L.

* ***Model 2T Carbine*** – .223 Rem. cal., 16 in. chrome lined barrel, A3 forged aluminum upper, ambidextrous (left hand only) or standard safety, six position collapsible stock, flip up rear sight, tactical rail, pistol grip, available in right or left hand, approx. 6.6 lbs.

MSR $1,130	$1,015	$895	$765	$695	$565	$450	$350

Add $25 for left hand (Model 2T-L).

MODEL 3 CARBINE – .223 Rem. cal., 16 in. chrome lined barrel, A3 forged aluminum upper, standard safety, black anodized finish, six position collapsible stock, tactical top rail, available in right or left (Model 3L) hand, 6.1 lbs.

MSR $895	$800	$700	$600	$550	$450	$360	$275

Add $25 for Model 3L.

MODEL 4 RIFLE – .223 Rem. cal., 20 in. heavy barrel, A3 forged aluminum upper, standard safety, black anodized finish, A2 fixed stock, removable carry handle, available in right or left (Model 4L) hand, 7 1/2 lbs.

MSR $1,015	$925	$815	$695	$625	$515	$415	$325

Add $80 for Model 4L.

MODEL 5 CARBINE – 6.8 SPC cal., 16 in. chrome lined barrel, A3 forged aluminum upper, standard or ambidextrous (left hand only) safety, black anodized finish, six position collapsible stock, available in right or left (Model 5L) hand, 7.1 lbs.

MSR $1,045	$940	$825	$700	$635	$515	$415	$325

Add $50 for left hand (Model 5L).

MODEL 6 RIFLE – .223 Rem. cal., 24 1/8 in. stainless steel heavy barrel, A3 forged aluminum upper, standard or ambidextrous (left hand only) safety, fixed A2 buttstock, black anodized finish, tactical top rail, no sights, pistol grip, approx. 10 lbs.

MSR $1,055	$950	$830	$710	$645	$520	$425	$330

Add $40 for left hand (Model 6L).

MSR	100%	98%	95%	90%	80%	70%	60%

MODEL 7 HUNTER – 6.8 SPC cal., 20.8 in. stainless steel barrel, A3 forged aluminum upper, standard or ambidextrous (left hand only) safety, fixed A2 buttstock, black anodized finish, no sights, tactical top rail, two-stage match trigger, Hogue pistol grip, available in right or left hand, approx. 10 lbs.

MSR $1,055	$950	$830	$710	$645	$520	$425	$330

Add $40 for left hand (Model 7L).

STAR, BONIFACIO ECHEVERRIA S.A.

Previous manufacturer located in Eibar, Spain. Star, Bonifacio Echeverria S.A. closed its doors on July 28th, 1997, due to the intense financial pressure the Spanish arms industry experienced during the late 1990s. Previously imported by Interarms, located in Alexandria, VA.

PISTOLS: SEMI-AUTO

MEGASTAR – 10mm or .45 ACP cal., larger variation of the Firestar featuring 4.6 in. barrel and 12 (.45 ACP) or 14 (10mm) shot mag., 47.6 oz. Imported 1992-94.

	$450	$395	$340	$305	$250	$205	$160	Last MSR was $653.

Add $29 for Starvel finish.

ULTRASTAR – 9mm Para. or .40 S&W (new 1996) cal., compact double action design, 3.57 in. barrel, 9-shot mag., blue steel metal, triple dot sights, steel internal mechanism, polymer exterior construction, 26 oz. Mfg. 1994-97.

	$325	$285	$245	$220	$180	$145	$115	Last MSR was $296.

STERLING ARMAMENT, LTD.

Previous manufacturer established c. 1900, and located in Dagenham, Essex, England. Previously imported and distributed by Cassi Inc. located in Colorado Springs, CO until 1990.

CARBINES: SEMI-AUTO

AR-180 – please refer to Armalite section for more information and pricing on this model.

STERLING MK 6 – 9mm Para. cal., blowback semi-auto with floating firing pin, shrouded 16.1 in. barrel, side mounted mag., folding stock, 7 1/2 lbs. Disc. 1989.

N/A	$1,750	$1,500	$1,400	$1,200	$1,000	$795	Last MSR was $650.

PISTOLS: SEMI-AUTO

PARAPISTOL MK 7 C4 – 9mm Para. cal., 4 in. barrel, semi-auto tactical design pistol, crinkle finish, same action as MK. 6 Carbine, fires from closed bolt, 10, 15, 20, 30, 34 or 68 shot mag., 5 lbs. Disc. 1989.

N/A	$1,500	$1,400	$1,200	$1,000	$800	$700	Last MSR was $600.

Add $50 per 30 or 34 shot mag., $125 for 68 shot mag.

PARAPISTOL MK 7 C8 – 9mm Para. cal., similar to C4, except has 7.8 in. barrel, 5 1/4 lbs. Disc. 1989.

N/A	$1,500	$1,400	$1,250	$1,050	$900	$750	Last MSR was $620.

Add $50 per 30 or 34 shot mag., $125 for 68 shot mag.

STEYR MANNLICHER

Currently manufactured by Steyr-Mannlicher AG & Co. KG in Austria. Founded in Steyr, Austria by Joseph Werndl circa 1864. Currently imported beginning mid-2005 by Steyr Arms, Inc., located Trussville, AL. Previously located in Cumming, GA. Previously imported 2004-mid-2005 by Steyr USA, located in West Point, MS. Previously imported 2002-2003 by Dynamit Nobel, located in Closter, NJ. Previously imported and distributed until 2002 by Gun South, Inc. (GSI) located in Trussville, AL.

Note: also see Mannlicher Schoenauer in the M section for pre-WWII models.

For more information and current pricing on both new and used Steyr airguns, please refer to the *Blue Book of Airguns* by Dr. Robert Beeman & John Allen (also online).

PISTOLS: SEMI-AUTO

MODEL GB – 9mm Para. cal., double action, 18 shot mag., gas delayed blowback action, non-glare checkered plastic grips, 5 1/4 in. barrel with Polygon rifling, matte finish, steel construction, 2 lbs. 6 oz. Importation disc. 1988.

	100%	98%	95%	90%	80%	70%	60%	
Commercial	$675	$600	$525	$450	$400	$350	$300	
Military	$795	$725	$650	$600	$525	$450	$400	Last MSR was $514.

In 1987, Steyr mfg. a military variation of the Model GB featuring a phosphate finish - only 937 were imported into the U.S.

MSR	100%	98%	95%	90%	80%	70%	60%

MODEL SPP – 9mm Para. cal., single action semi-auto, delayed blow back system with rotating 5.9 in. barrel, 15 or 30 shot mag., utilizes synthetic materials and advanced ergonomics, adj. sights, grooved receiver for scope mounting, matte black finish, 44 oz. Limited importation 1992-93.

| | $800 | $675 | $600 | $550 | $495 | $450 | $400 | Last MSR was $895. |

MODEL M SERIES – 9mm Para., .357 SIG, or .40 S&W cal., features first integrated limited access key lock safety in a semi-auto pistol, 3 different safety conditions, black synthetic frame, 10 shot mag., matte black finish, loaded chamber indicator, triangle/trapezoid sights, 28 oz. Limited importation 1999-2002.

| | $440 | $395 | $360 | $330 | $300 | $275 | $250 | Last MSR was $610. |

Add $65 for night sights.

M-A1 SERIES – .357 SIG (M357 A-1), 9mm Para. (M9 A-1), or .40 S&W (M40 A-1) cal., DAO, updated Model M with Picatinny rail on lower front of frame, redesigned grip frame, trigger safety and lockable safety system, black polymer frame with matte black finished slide, 3 1/2 (not available in .357 SIG cal.) or 4 in. barrel, 10, 12 (.40 S&W or .357 SIG) or 15 (9mm Para.) shot mag., white outlined triangular sights, approx. 27 oz. Importation began 2004.

| MSR $669 | $550 | $475 | $425 | $375 | $325 | $295 | $275 | |

Add $23 for right angle sights with Trilux (disc.)
Add $40 for night sights.

MODEL S – similar to Model M, except has 3 1/2 in. barrel and shorter grip frame, 10 shot mag., 22 1/2 oz. Limited importation 2000-2002.

| | $475 | $435 | $385 | $350 | $325 | $300 | $280 | Last MSR was $610. |

RIFLES: BOLT ACTION, RECENT PRODUCTION

The Steyr-Mannlicher models were in production 1968-1996.

Current production guns are now called Steyr-Mannlicher models. For models manufactured 1903 - 1971, please refer to the Mannlicher Schoenauer Sporting Rifles

section in this text. All known calibers are listed for each model. Caliber offerings varied often throughout the 28 year run of the Steyr-Mannlicher, stock designs evolved, and sights and magazine styles changed. The only truly rare caliber is the 6mm Rem., which was always special order. Next in North American rarity is the .25-06. Certain additional European calibers are rare in the USA because they were not imported due to lack of popularity - 5.6x57mm, 6.5x57mm, 6x62mm Freres, 6.5x65mm, and 9.3x62mm.

All four action lengths, SL, L, M, S, were offered in numerous deluxe variations with engraving and stock carving on special order blued metal and highly polished engraved actions. Stock carving is heavy and elegant. The "twisted appearance" of the hammer rifles barrels on all firearms of this group lends a unique and unmistakable look to these rifles.

A major irritant for hardcore Steyr-Mannlicher collectors is the continued misidentification of Luxus models by online sellers. First, a standard USA version Luxus has the word "Luxus" engraved on the left side of the receiver. A Luxus also has a steel box magazine instead of a rotary plastic one and a rotary shotgun style safety, although some apparently early Luxus models exist with the sliding side safety.

Pricing shows the result of continued cost increases at Steyr, which finally caused the end of the production run and redesign to the SBS-96 model to save costs, regain competition, and take advantage of improved safety features.

MANNLICHER/STEYR SCOUT – .223 Rem. (new 2000), .243 Win. (mfg. 2000 only, reintroduced 2005), .308 Win., 7mm-08 Rem. (new 2000), or .376 Steyr (mfg. 1999-2000, reintroduced 2005) cal., designed by Jeff Cooper, features grey, black synthetic Zytel or camo (.308 Win. cal. only beginning 2005) stock, 19 1/4 in. fluted barrel, Picatinny optic rail, integral bipod, Package includes Steyr or Leupold (disc. 2005) M8 2.5x28 IER scope with factory Steyr mounts, and luggage case. New 1998.

| MSR $2,099 | $1,850 | $1,575 | $1,375 | $1,125 | $900 | $750 | $650 | |

Add $100 for camo.
Add $600 for Steyr Scout Package with Steyr or Leupold (disc. 2004) scope, mounts and luggage case.

* **Steyr Scout Jeff Cooper** – .223 Rem., .308 Win. or .376 Steyr (disc. 2000, reintroduced 2005) cal., grey synthetic Zytel stock with Jeff Cooper logo and integral bipod, certificate of authenticity with test target, Package (disc. 2004) included Leupold M8 2.5x28 IER scope with factory Steyr mounts, and luggage case. New 1999.

| MSR $2,699 | $2,375 | $2,050 | $1,750 | $1,425 | $1,175 | $1,050 | $900 | |

Add approx. 15% for Steyr Scout Package with Leupold scope, mounts and luggage case (disc. 2004).

* **Steyr Scout** – .243 Win. cal., similar to Jeff Cooper Package, except does not include scope, mounts, or case. Mfg. 1999-2002.

| | $1,525 | $1,350 | $1,200 | $1,050 | $900 | $750 | $625 | Last MSR was $1,969. |

Add $100 for .376 Steyr cal. (black stock only, disc. 2000).
Add $100 for Jeff Cooper grey stock.

MSR	100%	98%	95%	90%	80%	70%	60%

* ***Steyr Scout Tactical*** – .223 Rem. (new 2000) or .308 Win. cal., similar to Steyr Scout, except has black synthetic stock with removable spacers, oversized bolt handle, and emergency ghost ring sights. Mfg. 1999-2002.

| | $1,600 | $1,400 | $1,250 | $1,050 | $900 | $750 | $625 | Last MSR was $2,069. |

»**Steyr Scout Tactical Stainless** – similar to Steyr Scout Tactical, except has stainless steel barrel. Mfg. 2000-2002.

| | $1,650 | $1,425 | $1,150 | $1,025 | $830 | $710 | $590 | Last MSR was $2,159. |

MANNLICHER PRO VARMINT – .223 Rem. cal., 23.6 in. heavy fluted barrel, black synthetic or camo vented stock, includes tactical rail. New 2009.

| MSR $1,799 | $1,600 | $1,450 | $1,275 | $1,075 | $900 | $775 | $650 | |

Add $200 for camo.

SBS TACTICAL – .308 Win. cal. only, 20 in. barrel w/o sights, features oversized bolt handle and high capacity 10 shot mag. with adapter, matte blue finish. Mfg. 1999-2002.

| | $840 | $735 | $625 | $550 | $500 | $450 | $395 | Last MSR was $969. |

* ***SBS Tactical Heavy Barrel*** – .300 Win. Mag. (new 2000) or .308 Win. cal., features 20 (carbine, new 2000, .308 Win. only) or 26 in. heavy barrel w/o sights and oversized bolt handle, matte blue finish or stainless steel (carbine only, new 2000). Mfg. 1999-2002.

| | $865 | $745 | $635 | $550 | $500 | $450 | $395 | Last MSR was $1,019. |

Add $30 for .300 Win. Mag. cal.
Add $40 for stainless steel.

* ***SBS Tactical McMillan*** – similar to SBS Tactical Heavy Barrel, except has custom McMillan A - 3 stock with adj. cheekpiece and oversized bolt handle, matte blue finish. Mfg. 1999-2002.

| | $1,465 | $1,245 | $1,035 | $850 | $725 | $600 | $550 | Last was $1,699. |

Add $30 for .300 Win. Mag. cal.

* ***SBS Tactical CISM*** – .308 Win. cal., 20 in. heavy barrel w/o sights, laminated wood stock with black lacquer finish, adj. cheekpiece and buttplate, 10 shot detachable mag., vent. forend. Mfg. 2000-2002.

| | $3,050 | $2,650 | $2,300 | $1,950 | $1,600 | $1,300 | $1,150 | Last MSR was $3,499. |

This model was also available as a Swiss contract CISM Match in 7.5x55mm cal. with match diopter sights and 23 1/2 in. barrel. Only 100 were imported. NIB Prices are in the $1,850 range.

STEYR ELITE (SBS TACTICAL) – .223 Rem. (disc. 2008) or .308 Win. cal., 20 (carbine, disc.), 22.4 (new 2006) or 26 (disc. 2005) in. barrel with full length Picatinny spec. mounting rail, oversize bolt handle, two 5 shot detachable mags. (with spare buttstock storage), adj. black synthetic stock, matte blue finish or stainless steel. New 2000.

| MSR $2,299 | $1,950 | $1,725 | $1,500 | $1,275 | $1,050 | $875 | $775 | |

* ***Steyr Elite 08*** – .308 Win. cal., 23.6 in. blue or stainless steel barrel, folding stock. New 2009.

| MSR $5,999 | $5,325 | $4,650 | $4,325 | $3,750 | $3,250 | $2,600 | $1,995 | |

MODEL SSG – .243 Win. (disc., PII Sniper only) or .308 Win cal., for competition or law-enforcement use. Marksman has regular sights, detachable rotary mag., teflon coated bolt with heavy duty locking lugs, synthetic stock has removable spacers, parkerized finish. Match version has heavier target barrel and "match" bolt carrier, can be used as single shot. Extremely accurate.

* ***Model SSG 69 Sport (PI Rifle)*** – .243 Win. or .308 Win. cal., 26 in. barrel with iron sights, 3 shot mag., black or green ABS Cycolac synthetic stock.

| MSR $1,989 | $1,775 | $1,500 | $1,225 | $1,000 | $850 | $725 | $650 | |

Add 15% for walnut stock (disc. 1992, retail was $448).

* ***Model SSG PII/PIIK Sniper Rifle*** – .22-250 Rem. (new 2004), .243 Win. (disc.) or .308 Win. cal., 20 in. heavy (Model PIIK) or 26 in. heavy barrel, no sights, green or black synthetic Cycolac or McMillan black fiberglass stock, modified bolt handle, choice of single or set triggers.

| MSR $1,899 | $1,695 | $1,500 | $1,300 | $1,050 | $875 | $750 | $625 | |

Add 15% for walnut stock (disc. 1992, retail was $448).

* ***Model SSG PIII Rifle*** – .308 Win. cal., 26 in. heavy barrel with diopter match sight bases, H-S Precision Pro-Series stock in black only. Importation 1991-93.

| | $2,300 | $1,875 | $1,425 | $1,050 | $825 | $700 | $600 | Last MSR was $3,162. |

* ***Model SSG PIV (Urban Rifle)*** – .308 Win. cal., carbine variation with 16 1/2 in. heavy barrel and flash hider (disc.), ABS Cycolac synthetic stock in green or black. Imported 1991-2002, reimported beginning 2004.

| MSR $1,899 | $1,695 | $1,500 | $1,300 | $1,050 | $875 | $750 | $625 | |

MSR	100%	98%	95%	90%	80%	70%	60%	

* **Model SSG Jagd Match** – .222 Rem., .243 Win., or .308 Win. cal., checkered wood laminate stock, 23.6 in. barrel, Mannlicher sights, DT, supplied with test target. Mfg. 1991-1992.

	$1,550	$1,050	$950	$800	$675	$600	$540	Last MSR was $1,550.

* **Model SSG Match Rifle** – .308 Win. only, 26 in. heavy barrel, brown ABS Cycolac stock, Walther Diopter sights, 8.6 lbs. Mfg. disc. 1992.

	$2,000	$1,500	$1,225	$925	$800	$700	$600	Last MSR was $2,306.

Add $437 for walnut stock.

* **Model SPG-T** – .308 Win. cal., Target model. Mfg. 1993-98.

	$3,225	$2,850	$2,550	$2,200	$1,850	$1,500	$1,200	Last MSR was $3,695.

* **Model SPG-CISM** – .308 Win. cal., 20 in. heavy barrel, laminated wood stock with adj. cheekpiece and black lacquer finish. Mfg. 1993-99.

	$2,995	$2,600	$2,300	$1,950	$1,700	$1,450	$1,200	Last MSR was $3,295.

* **Model SSG Match UIT** – .308 Win. cal. only, 10 shot steel mag., special single set trigger, free floating barrel, Diopter sights, raked bolt handle, 10.8 lbs. Disc. 1998.

	$3,000	$2,500	$2,000	$1,800	$1,500	$1,200	$1,000	Last MSR was $3,995.

UIT stands for Union Internationale de Tir.

* **Model SSG 04** – .308 Win. or .300 Win. Mag. cal., 20 (disc. 2005) or 23.6 heavy hammer forged barrel with muzzle brake, two-stage trigger, matte finished metal, black synthetic stock, adj. bipod, 8 (.300 Win. Mag.) or 10 (.308 Win.) shot mag., Picatinny rail, adj. buttstock, 10.1 lbs. Importation began 2004.

MSR $2,299	$1,950	$1,725	$1,500	$1,275	$1,050	$875	$775	

Add $200 for 16.1 in. barrel.
Add $1,300 for A1 model (new 2009).

HS-50 – .460 Steyr or .50 BMG cal., bolt action, 33 in. barrel with muzzle brake, includes Picatinny rail and bipod. Importation began 2004.

MSR $5,299	$4,850	$4,350	$3,900	$3,500	$3,150	$2,850	$2,500	

RIFLES: SEMI-AUTO

AUG S.A. – .223 Rem. cal., semi-auto tactical design rifle, blowback operation, design incorporates use of advanced plastics, integral Swarovski scope or Picatinny rail (24 in. heavy barrel only), 16, 20, or 24 in. barrel, green composite stock (original bullpup configuration), later mfg. was black or desert tan stock , 30 or 42 shot mag., 7.9 lbs. Importation resumed mid-2006.

MSR $2,295	$2,150	$1,875	$1,600	$1,475	$1,350	$1,100	$995	

Add approx. 10% for 24 in. heavy barrel with Picatinny rail and bipod (disc.).
Add $48 for 42 shot mag.

* **AUG S.A. Commercial** – similar to AUG S.A., grey (3,000 mfg. circa 1997), green, or black finish.

	100%	98%	95%	90%	80%	70%	60%
SP receiver (Stanag metal)	$2,950	$2,750	$2,450	$2,150	$1,750	$1,575	$1,400
Grey finish	$3,150	$2,875	$2,600	$2,250	$1,825	$1,625	$1,450
Green finish (last finish)	$3,400	$2,975	$2,700	$2,300	$1,875	$1,675	$1,500
Black finish	$4,125	$3,750	$3,300	$2,950	$2,750	$2,500	$2,250

Last MSR was $1,362 (1989) for Green finish.

MODEL MAADI AKM – 7.62x39mm cal., copy of Soviet AKM tactical design rifle, 30 shot mag., open sights.

	$2,250	$2,000	$1,800	$1,600	$1,450	$1,250	$1,125	

STOEGER INDUSTRIES, INC.

Current importer/trademark established in 1924, and currently located in Accokeek, MD. Previously located in Wayne, NJ, until 2000. Stoeger Industries, Inc. was purchased by Beretta Holding of Italy in 2000, and is now a division of Benelli USA. Please refer to the IGA listing for currently imported Stoeger shotgun models.

Stoeger has imported a wide variety of firearms during the past seven decades. Most of these guns were good quality and came from known makers in Europe (some were private labeled). Stoeger carried an extensive firearms inventory of both house brand and famous European trademarks - many of which were finely made with beautiful engraving, stock work, and other popular special order features. As a general rule, values for Stoeger rifles and shotguns may be ascertained by comparing them with a known trademark of equal quality and cal./ga. Certain configurations will be more desirable than others (i.e. a Stoeger .22 caliber Mannlicher with double-set triggers and detachable mag. will be worth considerably more than a single shot target rifle).

MSR	100%	98%	95%	90%	80%	70%	60%

Perhaps the best reference works available on these older Stoeger firearms (not to mention the other trademarks of that time) are the older Stoeger catalogs themselves - quite collectible in their own right. You are advised to purchase these older catalogs (some reprints are also available) if more information is needed on not only older Stoeger models, but also the other firearms being sold at that time.

PISTOLS: SEMI-AUTO

COUGAR – 9mm Para., .40 S&W, or .45 ACP (new 2010) cal., SA/DA operation, copy of Beretta, 3.6 in. barrel, matte black finish, 8 (.45 ACP), 11 (.40 S&W) or 15 (9mm Para.) shot mag., ambidextrous safety, 3-dot sights, Bruniton black, silver or two-tone matte finish, checkered plastic grips, blowback action with rotating bolt, removable front sight, mfg. in Turkey. Importation began 2007.

MSR $469	$390	$335	$290	$255	$225	$200	$180

Add $30 for .45 ACP cal. in black finish with accessory rail.
Add $30 for silver or two-tone finish.

STONER RIFLE

Please refer to the Knight's Manufacturing Company listing in this text.

STRAYER TRIPP INTERNATIONAL

Please refer to the STI International listing in this section.

STREET SWEEPER

Previously manufactured by Sales of Georgia, Inc. located in Atlanta, GA.

SHOTGUNS

STREET SWEEPER – 12 ga. only, 12 shot rotary mag., tactical configuration with 18 in. barrel, double action, folding stock, 9 3/4 lbs. Restricted sales following the BATFE classification as a "destructive device." Mfg. 1989-approx. 1995.

	$1,495	$1,350	$1,100	$995	$895	$795	$695

Unless this model was registered with the ATF before May 1st, 2001, it is subject to seizure with a possible fine/ imprisonment.

STURM, RUGER & CO., INC.

Current manufacturer with production facilities located Newport, NH and Prescott, AZ. Previously manufactured in Southport, CT 1949-1991 (corporate and administrative offices remain at this location). A second factory was opened in Newport, NH in 1963, and still produces single action revolvers, rifles and shotguns.

Sturm, Ruger & Co. was founded in 1949 by Alexander Sturm and William B. Ruger to manufacture .22 cal. semi-auto pistols. The original factory was in a wooden structure located across from the train depot in Southport, CT. By 1959, the company moved into a larger modern factory not too far from the original buildings. The product line quickly expanded to a Target Model, single action revolvers, rifles, DA revolvers and shotguns.

From four separate factories, Ruger has manufactured and shipped over 25 million guns. The two Southport, CT facilities are no longer utilized. Guns are manufactured at the two large modern facilities located in Newport, NH and Prescott, AZ. Ruger is America's third largest small arms maker, and offers a complete line of firearms for sportsmen, law enforcement, and military.

Mr. Alex Sturm passed away in November 1951. On July 6, 2002, the legendary William B. Ruger, Sr. passed away in his home in Prescott, AZ.

Beginning 1996, all handguns are supplied with a case and lock.

Please refer to the *Blue Book of Modern Black Powder Arms* by John Allen (also online) for more information and prices on Sturm Ruger black powder models.

Black Powder Revolver Reproductions & Replicas and *Black Powder Long Arms & Pistols - Reproductions & Replicas* by Dennis Adler are also invaluable sources for most black powder reproductions and replicas, and includes hundreds of color images on most popular makes/models, provides manufacturer/trademark histories, and up-to-date information on related items/accessories for black powder shooting - www.bluebookinc.com

The publisher would like to thank John Dougan, Bill Hamm, Richard Machniak and Chad Hiddleson for thier contributions in this and previous editions.

PISTOLS: SEMI-AUTO, CENTERFIRE

LCP (LIGHTWEIGHT COMPACT PISTOL) – .380 ACP cal., DAO, hammerless, black glass filled nylon frame with molded checkering, blued steel slide, 2 3/4 in. barrel, 6 shot mag., .82 in. frame width, black Ruger logos inset in grip panels, includes external locking device, 9.4 oz. New 2008.

MSR $364		$295	$260	$220	$180	$160	$150	$140

P85 – 9mm Para. cal., double action, 4 1/2 in. barrel, aluminum frame with steel slide, 3-dot fixed sights, 15 shot

MSR	100%	98%	95%	90%	80%	70%	60%	

mag., oversized trigger, polymer grips, matte black finish, 2 lbs. Mfg. 1987-1990.

| | $350 | $295 | $265 | $235 | $215 | $200 | $185 | Last MSR was $410. |

Subtract $30 if without case and extra mag.

Any P85 models without the "MKIIR" stamp on either the left or right side of the safety must be returned to the factory for a free safety modification.

* **KP85** – stainless variation of the P85. Mfg. 1990 only.

| | $375 | $315 | $280 | $230 | $200 | $165 | $140 | Last MSR was $452. |

Subtract $30 if without case and extra mag.

Variants included a decocking or double action only version at no extra charge.

P85 MARK II – 9mm Para. cal., double action, 4 1/2 in. barrel, aluminum frame with steel slide, 3-dot fixed sights, 15 shot mag., ambidextrous safety beginning in 1991, oversized trigger, polymer grips, matte black finish, 2 lbs. Mfg. 1990-1992.

| | $350 | $295 | $265 | $235 | $215 | $200 | $185 | Last MSR was $410. |

Subtract $30 if without case and extra mag.

Decocker and DAO models were not available in the Mark II series.

* **KP85 Mark II** – stainless variation of the P85. Mfg. 1990-1992.

| | $375 | $315 | $280 | $230 | $200 | $165 | $140 | Last MSR was $452. |

Subtract $30 if without case and extra mag.

P89 – 9mm Para. cal., improved variation of the P85 Mark II, 10 (C/B 1994) or 15 (new late 2005) shot mag., ambidextrous safety or decocker (Model P89D), blue finish, 32 oz. Mfg. 1992-2007.

| | $380 | $330 | $280 | $250 | $215 | $200 | $185 | Last MSR was $475. |

Variants were available in a decocking (P89DC) or double action only (P-89DAO, disc. 2004) version at no extra charge.

KP89 STAINLESS – stainless variation of the P89, also available in double action only (disc.). Mfg. 1992-2009.

| | $425 | $360 | $305 | $250 | $215 | $200 | $185 | Last MSR was $525. |

Add $45 for convertible 7.65mm Luger cal. barrel (Model KP89X, approx. 5,750 mfg. during 1994 only).

P90 – .45 ACP cal., similar to KP90 Stainless, except has blue finish, 8 shot mag., 33 1/2 oz.

| MSR $591 | $475 | $395 | $335 | $265 | $215 | $200 | $185 | |

Add $50 for tritium night sights (disc. 2006).

P90 models were produced in a variety of models for law enforcement or government contracts and will be found with any combination of safety model, decocker or double action only with fingergroove tactical rubber grip and/or tritium night sights.

KP90 STAINLESS – .45 ACP cal., double action, 4 1/2 in. barrel, oversized trigger, aluminum frame with stainless steel slide, 8 shot single column mag., ambidextrous safety (KP90) or decocking (KP90D), polymer grips, 3-dot fixed sights, ambidextrous safety began approx ser. no. 660-12800. New 1991.

| MSR $636 | $495 | $415 | $360 | $295 | $250 | $225 | $200 | |

Add $50 for tritium night sights (disc. 2006).

KP90 models were produced in a variety of models for law enforcement or government contracts and will be found with any combination of safety model, decocker or double action only with fingergroove tactical rubber grip and/or tritium night sights.

KP91 STAINLESS – .40 S&W cal., similar to Model KP90 Stainless, except is not available with external safety and has 11 shot double column mag. Mfg. 1991-1994.

| | $385 | $335 | $295 | $240 | $210 | $180 | $155 | Last MSR was $489. |

This model was available in a decocking variation (KP91D) or double action only (KP91DAO). Approx. 39,600 of all models were mfg. before being discontinued in favor of the tapered slide KP944 model.

P93D BLUE – similar to KP93 Stainless, except has blue finish, compact model, ambidextrous decocker, 31 oz. Mfg. 1998-2004.

| | $395 | $330 | $285 | $240 | $215 | $200 | $185 | Last MSR was $495. |

Add $50 for tritium night sights.

P93 models were produced in a variety of models for law enforcement or government contracts and will be found with any combination of decocker model or double action only with fingergroove tactical rubber grip and/or tritium night sights.

P93 CHICAGO POLICE SPECIAL CONTRACT – produced in the late 1990s for a Chicago Police Department

MSR	100%	98%	95%	90%	80%	70%	60%

contract, this blued stainless P93 was ordered with a special P89M rollmark on the slide so that those who were concerned about having a "compact" pistol would not be alerted to the fact that it was indeed a P93. Extremely rare in civilian hands.

Extreme rarity precludes accurate pricing on this model, and should be examined for authenticity. NIB specimens have been noted at $500.

KP93 STAINLESS – 9mm Para. cal., compact variation with 3 9/10 in. tilting barrel - link actuated, matte blue or REM (new 1996) finish, 3-dot sights, 10 (C/B 1994) or 15* shot mag., available with DA/SA ambidextrous decocker action or double action only, 31 oz. Mfg. 1994-2004.

| | $450 | $370 | $315 | $260 | $220 | $200 | $185 | Last MSR was $575. |

Add $50 for tritium night sights.

KP93 models were produced in a variety of models for law enforcement or government contracts and will be found with any combination of decocker model or double action only with fingergroove tactical rubber grip and/or tritium night sights.

P94 BLUE – similar to KP94 Stainless, except has blue finish. Mfg. 1998-2004.

| | $395 | $330 | $285 | $240 | $215 | $200 | $185 | Last MSR was $495. |

Add $50 for tritium night sights.

P94 models have been produced in a variety of models for law enforcement or government contracts and will be found with any combination of safety model, decocker or double action only with fingergroove tactical rubber grip and/or tritium night sights.

KP94 STAINLESS – 9mm Para. cal., available with ambidextrous safety, matte blue or REM (new 1996) finish, DA/SA ambidextrous decocker action or double action only, 10 (C/B 1994), or 15* (9mm Para.) shot mag., 33 oz. Mfg. 1994-2004.

| | $450 | $370 | $315 | $260 | $220 | $200 | $185 | Last MSR was $575. |

Add $50 for tritium night sights.

KP94 models have been produced in a variety of models for law enforcement or government contracts and will be found with any combination of safety model, decocker or double action only with fingergroove tactical rubber grip and/or tritium night sights.

P95PR – 9mm Para. cal., available in ambidextrous decocker (D/DPR suffix), ambidextrous safety (new 2001) or double action only configuration (DAO suffix, disc.), polymer frame, 3.9 in. barrel, fixed sights, blue finish, 10 or 15 (new late 2005) shot mag., lower Picatinny rail became standard in 2006, 27 oz. New 1997.

| MSR $393 | $315 | $265 | $230 | $195 | $165 | $150 | $135 |

Add $50 for tritium night sights (disc. 2006).

During 2006, this model's nomenclature changed from P95 to P95PR to reflect the Picatinny style rail.

P95 models have been produced in a variety of models for law enforcement or government contracts and will be found with any combination of safety model, decocker or double action only with fingergroove tactical rubber grip and/or tritium night sights. The P95DAO double action only model was disc. 2004.

KP95PR STAINLESS – stainless variation of Model P95PR. New 1997.

| MSR $424 | $345 | $290 | $245 | $190 | $165 | $140 | $120 |

During 2006, this model's nomenclature changed from KP95 to KP95PR to reflect the Picatinny style rail.

P97D – .45 ACP cal., ambidextrous decocker, 8 shot mag., blue finish, 30 1/2 oz. Mfg. 2002-2004.

| | $370 | $315 | $275 | $235 | $215 | $200 | $185 | Last MSR was $460. |

Add $50 for tritium night sights.

KP97 STAINLESS – .45 ACP cal., similar to KP95 Stainless, except has 8 shot mag., 27 oz. Mfg. 1999-2004.

| | $395 | $315 | $265 | $235 | $215 | $200 | $185 | Last MSR was $495. |

Add $50 for tritium night sights.

P345 – .45 ACP cal., ambidextrous safety or decocker (P345DPR), black polymer frame with matte stainless or blue stainless steel slide, 4.2 in. barrel, fixed sights, polyurethane grips, slimmer profile frame, 8 shot single column mag., with or w/o (disc. 2008) Picatinny rail, loaded chamber indicator, 29 oz. New 2005.

| MSR $577 | $465 | $410 | $335 | $275 | $225 | $210 | $195 |

KP345 – .45 ACP cal., decocker (KP345DPR), similar to P345, except has stainless steel slide, Picatinny rail became standard 2009 (KP345PR), 29 oz. New 2005.

| MSR $617 | $500 | $435 | $345 | $280 | $230 | $210 | $195 |

P944 – .40 S&W cal., similar to P94, ambidextrous safety, blue finish, 34 oz. New 1999.

| MSR $557 | $445 | $360 | $300 | $245 | $215 | $200 | $185 |

Add $50 for tritium night sights (disc. 2006).

MSR	100%	98%	95%	90%	80%	70%	60%

This model has been produced in many versions for law enforcement or government contracts and will be found with any combination of safety type, decocker, or double action only, fingergroove tactical rubber grip, and/or tritium night sights.

KP944 STAINLESS – similar to P944, except is stainless steel, also available as decocker (KP944D). New 1999.

MSR $647	$500	$400	$345	$275	$230	$195	$170

Add $50 for tritum night sights (disc. 2006).

This model has been produced in many versions for law enforcement or government contracts and will be found with any combination of safety type, decocker, or double action only, fingergroove tactical rubber grip, and/or tritium night sights. The KP944DAO double action only model was disc. 2004.

SR9 – 9mm Para cal., striker fired ignition, semi-double action trigger pull, 4 1/8 in. barrel, 10 or 17 shot mag., reversible backstrap, low profile 3-dot sights, glass filled nylon frame, choice of black stainless, brushed stainless steel, or OD Green (new 2009) stainless steel slide, Picatinny rail, ambidextrous safety, 26 1/2 oz. New late 2007.

MSR $525	$450	$400	$350	$315	$275	$240	$210

Add $40 for black stainless or OD Green finish.

Note that all SR9 models serial numbered 330-29999 and earlier are subject to a factory recall at no charge. If your pistol has not yet had the new parts installed, please contact Sturm, Ruger & Company at 1-800-784-3701 or email SR9Recall@ruger.com and they will provide you with shipping instructions.

REVOLVERS: DOUBLE ACTION

During certain years of manufacture, Ruger's changes in production on certain models (cals., barrel markings, barrel lengths, etc.) have created rare variations that are now considered premium niches. These areas of low manufacture will add premiums to the values listed on standard models.

SECURITY SIX (MODEL 117) – .357 Mag. cal., 6 shot, 2 3/4, 3 (late production only), 4, 4 (heavy), or 6 in. barrel, adj. sights, checkered walnut grips, square butt. Mfg. 1970-1985.

			$400	$350	$275	$200	$160	$150	$140	Last MSR was $309.

Add $15 for target grips.

Note that beginning late in the 150- serial number prefix, the grip frame was changed to have a more outward "highback" shape. Revolvers with the earlier "lowback" grip frame are generally considered more collectible. All revolvers having fixed sights and square butt grip frame with "lowback" shape to the backstrap were also marked "SECURITY-SIX". Only when the new highback gripframe came out were the fixed sight and square butt revolvers marked "SERVICE-SIX".

500 of this model were mfg. for the California Highway Patrol during 1983 (.38 Spl. cal.) in stainless steel only. They are distinguishable by a C.H.P. marking. Other Security Six Model 117 special editions have been made for various police organizations - premiums might exist in certain regions for these variations.

POLICE SERVICE SIX – .357 Mag, .38 Spl., or 9mm Para. cal., blue finish only, square butt, fixed sights, checkered walnut grips.

* *Police Service Six Model 107* – .357 Mag, 2 3/4 or 4 in. barrel, fixed sights. Disc. 1988.

			$400	$300	$250	$190	$180	$170	$165	Last MSR was $287.

* *Police Service Six Model 108* – .38 Spl., 4 in. barrel, fixed sights. Disc. 1988.

			$325	$250	$210	$190	$180	$170	$165	Last MSR was $287.

* *Police Service Six Model 109* – 9mm Para., 4 in. barrel, fixed sights. Disc. 1984.

			$600	$550	$500	$400	$275	$195	$175	

POLICE SERVICE SIX STAINLESS STEEL – stainless construction, 4 in. barrel only, fixed sights, checkered walnut grips.

* *Police Service Six Stainless Steel Model 707* – .357 Mag., square butt. Disc. 1988.

			$400	$300	$250	$190	$180	$170	$165	Last MSR was $310.

* *Police Service Six Stainless Steel Model 708* – .38 Spl., square butt. Disc. 1988.

			$325	$250	$210	$190	$180	$170	$155	Last MSR was $310.

GP-100 – .357 Mag./.38 Spl. cal., 3 (new 1990, fixed sights, .357 Mag. only), 4.2, or 6 (.357 Mag. only) in. standard or heavy barrel, 6 shot, strengthened design intended for constant use with all .357 Mag. ammunition, rubber cushioned grip panels with polished Goncalo Alves wood inserts, fixed (mfg. 1989-2006) or adj. sights (standard beginning 2007) with white outlined rear and interchangeable front, 35-46 oz. depending on barrel configuration. New 1986.

MSR $634			$515	$385	$320	$265	$210	$190	$175

MSR	100%	98%	95%	90%	80%	70%	60%

* *GP-100 Stainless Steel* – similar to GP-100, .357 Mag. cal. only, stainless steel. New 1987.

MSR $679	**$540**	**$410**	**$325**	**$260**	**$210**	**$170**	**$140**

Add $22 for adj. sights.

* *GP-100 High Gloss Stainless Steel* – .357 Mag. only, high gloss stainless steel finish, adj. sights, 3 or 4 in. heavy barrel. Mfg. 1996 only.

	$485	**$375**	**$295**	**$250**	**$195**	**$165**	**$140**	Last MSR was $457.

Fixed sights were cataloged but not known to have been produced in this model.

SP-101 STAINLESS STEEL – .22 LR (6 shot - mfg. 1990-2004), .32 H&R (6 shot - new 1991), .327 Federal (6 shot - new 2007), .38 Spl. (5 shot), 9mm Para. (5 shot - mfg. 1991-2000), or .357 Mag. (5 shot - new 1991) cal., 2 1/4, 3 1/16, or 4 (mfg. 1990-2007) in. barrel, small frame variation of the GP-100 Stainless, fixed or adj. (new 1996) sights, 25-34 oz. New 1989.

MSR $607	**$490**	**$365**	**$285**	**$220**	**$175**	**$140**	**$120**

Add $257 for Crimson Trace laser grips (new 2008).
Add $100 for .357 Mag. models with "125 GR. BULLET" rollmarked on barrel lug.
Add $125 for 9mm Para. caliber.
Add $75 for .22 LR caliber.

The .327 Federal caliber configuration will also shoot .32 H&R Mag., .32 S&W, and .32 S&W Long cartridges.

The first few thousand SP-101s in .38 Special had green grip inserts. Also, approximately 3,000 total of the earliest KSP-321 and KSP-331 .357 Mag. models were rollmarked with "125 GR. BULLET" on the barrel under the caliber designation (serial range 570-59359 to 570-67976).

Ruger introduced adj. sights in 1996 available in .22 LR or .32 H&R cal. only.

Ruger introduced a .357 Mag./2 1/4 in. (new 1993) or .38 Spl./2 1/4 (new 1994) in. configuration featuring a spurless hammer, double action only.

SP-101 barrel lengths are as follows: .22 cal. is available in 2 1/4 or 4 in. standard or heavy barrel, .32 H&R is available in 3 1/16 or 4 (new 1994) in. heavy barrel, .38 Spl. is available in 2 1/4 or 3 1/16 in. length only, 9mm Para. is available in 2 1/4 (new 1992) or 3 1/16 in. length only, and .357 Mag. is available in 2 1/4 or 3 1/16 in. length only.

* *SP-101 Stainless Steel High Gloss* – .38 Spl. (disc. 1996), 9mm Para. (disc. 1996), or .357 Mag. cal., similar to SP-101 Stainless Steel, except has high gloss stainless steel finish. Mfg. 1996-97.

	$515	**$475**	**$350**	**$275**	**$225**	**$195**	**$150**	Last MSR was $443.

Add $125 for 9mm Para. cal.

Estimated 100 produced in .38 Spl, 1,500 produced in .357 Mag. and an unknown quantity in 9mm (very rare). Serial range 571-81675 to 572-44777.

Ruger introduced adj. sights in 1996 available in .22 LR or .32 H&R cal. only.

REDHAWK – .357 Mag. (disc. 1985), .41 Mag. (mfg. 1984-1991), or .44 Mag. cal., 6 shot fluted cylinder, redesigned large frame, 5 1/2 and 7 1/2 (disc. 2005) in. barrel, blue finish, square butt, smooth hardwood grips, 49-54 oz. Disc. 2009.

	$615	**$460**	**$375**	**$285**	**$225**	**$180**	**$165**	Last MSR was $789.

Add $40 for scope rings (disc. 2005).

.357 Mag. and .41 Mag. cals. will bring collector premiums if NIB.

* *Redhawk Stainless Steel* – .357 Mag. (mfg. 1984-1991), .41 Mag. (mfg. 1984-1991), .44 Mag or .45 LC (mfg. 1998-2005, reintroduced 2008, 4 in. barrel only) cal., stainless steel construction, 4 (new 2007), 5 1/2, or 7 1/2 in. barrel, choice of regular or Hogue (4 in. barrel only) grips, 49-54 oz.

MSR $887	**$685**	**$535**	**$415**	**$320**	**$275**	**$230**	**$210**

Add $55 for scope rings (Hunter model, .44 Mag. only in 7 1/2 in. barrel).

This model was also available as a KRH-35, and is marked both "Redhawk" and ".357 Magnum". Mfg. was circa 1984-1991.

The 7 1/2 in. barrel was available with or w/o integral scope mounting system.

RIFLES: BOLT ACTION, CENTERFIRE

During certain years of manufacture, Ruger's changes in production on certain models (cals., barrel markings, barrel lengths, etc.) have created rare variations that are now considered premium niches. These areas of low manufacture will add premiums to the values listed on standard models.

Earlier mfg. had flat-bolt handle or hollow round bolt, and will bring $150+ premium, depending on configuration.
Early (pre-1972) mfg. with flat-bolt handle are desirable in the rarer cals. and will command a 100% premium if in 98%+ original condition.

* *Model HM77R Hawkeye Tactical* – .223 Rem., .243 Win., or .308 Win. cal., matte finished blued action and 20 in. bull barrel, no sights, target trigger, black Hogue overmolded stock with bipod, 8 3/4 lbs. New 2009.

MSR $1,172	**$995**	**$865**	**$750**	**$650**	**$575**	**$525**	**$475**

MSR	100%	98%	95%	90%	80%	70%	60%

RIFLES: SEMI-AUTO

During certain years of manufacture, Ruger's changes in production on certain models (cals., barrel markings, barrel lengths, etc.) have created rare variations that are now considered premium niches. These areas of low manufacture will add premiums to the values listed on standard models. The Model 10/22 has been mfg. in a variety of limited production models including a multi-colored or green laminate wood stock variation (1986), a brown laminate stock (1988), a Kittery Trading Post Commemorative (1988), a smoke or tree bark laminate stock (1989), a Chief AJ Model, Wal-Mart (stainless with black laminated hardwood stock - 1990), etc. These limited editions will command premiums over the standard models listed, depending on the desirability of the special edition.

Note: All Ruger Rifles, except Stainless Mini-14, all Mini-30s, and Model 77-22s were made during 1976 in a "Liberty" version. Add $50-$75 when in 100% in the original box condition.

* **K10/22-T Target Tactical** – similar to 10/22-T Target Model, except available in black matte finish, black Hogue overmolded stock, receiver with Picatinny style rail, 16.1 in. barrel with no sights, includes precision adj. bipod, 6.9 lbs. New 2010.

MSR $555	$435	$345	$275	$225	$185	$160	$140

MODEL 44 STANDARD CARBINE – .44 Mag. cal., 4 shot mag., 18 1/2 in. barrel, blowback action, folding sight, curved butt. Mfg. 1961-85.

	$550	$475	$400	$325	$275	$250	$225	Last MSR was $332.

RUGER CARBINE – 9mm Para. (PC9) or .40 S&W (PC4) cal., 16 1/4 in. barrel, 10 (PC4) or 15 (PC9) shot detachable mag., black synthetic stock, matte metal finish, with or w/o sights, with fully adj. rear sight or rear receiver sight, crossbolt safety, 6 lbs. Mfg. 1998-2006.

	$510	$415	$360	$310	$265	$240	$215	Last MSR was $623.

Add $24 for adj. rear receiver sight.

Beginning 2005, this model came standard with an adjustable ghost ring aperture rear sight and protected blade front sight.

MINI-14 – .223 Rem. or .222 Rem. (disc.) cal., 5 (standard mag. starting in 1989), 10 (disc.), or 20* shot detachable mag., 18 1/2 in. barrel, gas operated, blue finish, aperture rear sight, military style stock, approx. 6 3/4 lbs. Mfg. 1974-2004.

	$535	$445	$365	$320	$275	$240	$215	Last MSR was $655.

Add 20% for .222 Rem. cal.
Add $300 for folding stock (disc. 1989).
Add 25% for Southport Model with gold bead front sight.

This model was also available as a Mini-14 GB (primarily used for law enforcement), and was equipped with a flash hider and bayonet lug (blue or stainless, current value is approx. $1,000 if in 95%+ original condition).

* **Mini-14 Stainless** – mini stainless steel version, choice of wood or black synthetic (new 1999) stock. Disc. 2004.

	$565	$445	$380	$320	$275	$230	$200	Last MSR was $715.

Add 20% for .222 Rem. cal.
Add $300 for folding stock (disc. 1990).

MINI-14 RANCH RIFLE – .223 Rem. cal., 5 (standard mag. starting in 1989), 10 (disc.), or 20 shot detachable mag., 18 1/2 in. barrel, hardwood stock, folding rear sight, receiver cut for factory rings, similar to Mini-14, supplied with scope rings, adj. ghost ring aperture rear sight, protected front sight, and flat style recoil pad (became standard 2005), approx. 6 1/2 lbs. New 1982.

MSR $881	$675	$550	$465	$415	$365	$315	$275
Add $17 for 20 shot mag. (2008).
Add $260 for Mini 14 NRA-ILA Limited Edition with 16 1/8 in. barrel and black Hogue overmolded stock (ltd. mfg. 2008-2009).

Due to 1989 Federal legislation and public sentiment at the time, the Mini-14 Ranch Rifle was shipped with a 5 shot detachable mag., 1989-2008.

* **Mini-14 Stainless Ranch Rifle** – .223 Rem. or 6.8mm SPC (new 2007) cal., stainless steel construction, choice of wood (disc.) or black synthetic (new 1999) stock, 6 3/4 lbs. New 1986.

MSR $949	$775	$650	$525	$450	$400	$350	$300
Add $300 for folding stock (disc. 1990).
Add $17 for 20 shot mag. (not available in 6.8mm SPC cal.).

* **Mini-14 Target Ranch Rifle** – .223 Rem. cal., 22 in. stainless steel heavy barrel, ergonomic black or grey laminated thumbhole or Hogue overmolded stock, stainless scope rings, otherwise similar to Mini-14 Stainless Ranch Rifle, 9 1/2 lbs. New 2007.

MSR $1,098	$900	$775	$650	$550	$475	$425	$375
Add $16 for 20 shot mag. (mfg. 2009).

MSR	100%	98%	95%	90%	80%	70%	60%

* *Mini-14 Ranch Rifle w/Collapsible Stock* – .223 Rem. cal., compact 16 1/8 in. blue barrel, 20 shot mag., six position ATI folding/collapsible stock, includes quad Picatinny accessory rails, 7 1/4 lbs. New 2009.

MSR $921	$775	$675	$550	$475	$425	$375	$325

MINI-14 TACTICAL RIFLE – .223 Rem. cal., 16 1/8 in. blue barrel with flash suppressor, synthetic stock, 5 or 20 shot mag., 6 3/4 lbs. New 2009.

MSR $921	$775	$675	$550	$475	$425	$375	$325

MINI-THIRTY – 7.62x39mm Russian cal., 18 1/2 in. barrel, 5 shot detachable mag., hardwood stock, includes scope rings, 7 lbs. 3 oz. Mfg. 1987-2004.

	$540	$450	$405	$375	$335	$300	$260	Last MSR was $695.

* *Mini-Thirty Stainless* – stainless steel variation of the Mini-Thirty, black synthetic stock, adj. ghost ring aperture rear sight and protected front sight became standard 2005, 5 or 20 shot mag. New 1990.

MSR $949	$765	$640	$525	$450	$400	$350	$325

Add $17 for 20 shot mag.

SR-556 – .223 Rem. cal., 30 shot mag., 16.1 in. barrel with muzzle brake, matte black finish, four position chrome plated gas regulator, quad rail handguard, Troy folding sights, six position telescoping M4 style buttstock, Hogue monogrip pistol grip with finger grooves, chrome plated bolt, bolt carrier, and extractor, includes rail covers, soft sided carry case and three magazines, 7.9 lbs. New mid-2009.

MSR $1,995	$1,795	$1,575	$1,375	$1,150	$1,000	$875	$750

SR-22 – .22 LR cal., 10 shot mag., 16.1 in. barrel with muzzle brake, rotary magazine similar to 10/22, Hogue monogrip pistol grip, six position telescoping buttstock, Picatinny rail, mid-length handguard, 6 1/2 lbs. New 2010.

MSR $625	$575	$500	$450	$400	$365	$335	$295

SUPERIOR ARMS

Current manufacturer established in 2004 and located in Wapello. IA.

PISTOLS: SEMI-AUTO

Superior Arms manufactured complete AR-style semi-auto pistols, with either an A4 flattop or A2 carry handle, and 10 1/2 or 11 1/2 in. barrel.

RIFLES: SEMI-AUTO

Please contact the company directly for more information on options, delivery, availability (see Trademark Index).

Add $55 for detachable A2 carry handle.

Due to current high demand and market speculation, consumers may pay a premium over values listed below.

S-15 M4 CARBINE – .223 Rem. cal., A4 flattop receiver with integral rail, 16 in. chromemoly barrel, A2 flash hider, M4 handguard, six position telescoping stock, A2 pistol grip, front sling swivel.

MSR $905	$825	$750	$650	$595	$550	$500	$450

S-15 CARBINE – .223 Rem. cal., A4 flattop receiver with integral rail, 16 in. chromemoly barrel, A2 flash hider, M4 handguard, bayonet lug, six position telescoping stock, A2 pistol grip, front sling swivel.

MSR $905	$825	$750	$650	$595	$550	$500	$450

S-15 MID-LENGTH CARBINE – .223 Rem. cal., A4 flattop receiver with integral rail, 16 in. chromemoly barrel, A2 flash hider, mid-length handguard, bayonet lug, six position telescoping stock, A2 pistol grip, front sling swivel.

MSR $925	$850	$775	$675	$600	$525	$450	$395

S-15 H-BAR RIFLE – .223 Rem. cal., A4 flattop receiver with integral rail, 20 in. chromemoly barrel, A2 flash hider, A2 buttstock, bayonet lug, A2 pistol grip, front sling swivel.

MSR $985	$900	$800	$700	$625	$550	$500	$495

S-15 VARMINT RIFLE – .223 Rem. cal., A4 flattop receiver with integral rail, 20 in. stainless steel bull contour barrel, Picatinny rail gas block, aluminum free floating handguard with sling swivel stud, A2 buttstock, bayonet lug, A2 pistol grip.

MSR $1,075	$975	$850	$775	$675	$600	$550	$495

SURGEON RIFLES, INC.

Current custom rifle manufacturer located in Prague, OK.

Surgeon Rifles manufactures a variety a bolt action rifles, including tactical and long range configurations. Many

MSR	100%	98%	95%	90%	80%	70%	60%

options and accessories are available. Please contact the company directly for more information, including pricing and availability (see Trademark Index).

SURVIVAL ARMS, INC.

Previous manufacturer established in 1990 located in Orange, CT. Previously located in Cocoa, FL, until 1995.

In 1990, Survival Arms, Inc. took over the manufacture of AR-7 Explorer rifles from Charter Arms located in Stratford, CT.

RIFLES: SEMI-AUTO

AR-7 EXPLORER RIFLE – .22 LR cal., takedown or normal wood stock, takedown barreled action stores in Cycolac synthetic stock, 8 shot mag., adj. sights, 16 in. barrel, black matte finish on AR-7, silvertone on AR-7S, camouflage finish on AR-7C, 2 1/2 lbs. Disc.

| | $150 | $125 | $100 | $85 | $75 | $65 | $55 | Last MSR was $150. |

Add 20% for takedown action.

AR-20 SPORTER – similar to AR-22, except has shrouded barrel, tubular stock with pistol grip, 10 or 20 shot mag. Mfg. 1996-98.

| | $195 | $165 | $140 | $120 | $105 | $95 | $80 | Last MSR was $200. |

AR-22/AR-25 – .22 LR cal., 16 in. barrel, black rifle features pistol grip with choice of wood or metal folding* stock, includes 20 (1995 only) or 25 (disc. 1994) shot mag. Disc. 1995.

| | $175 | $150 | $125 | $100 | $80 | $70 | $60 | Last MSR was $200. |

Subtract $50 for wood stock model.

NOTES

T SECTION

TG INTERNATIONAL

Current importer located in Knoxville, TN.

TG International imports a wide variety of firearms, including a FPK Dragunov, Finnish Suomi M31 rifle, Bulgarian AK-74 ($545 MSR), Hungarian AMD rifle ($400-$545 MSR), Bulgarian SSR-85 rifle ($490-$555 MSR), Saiga AK-47 rifle ($490 MSR), and a Saiga shotgun. Pistols include FEG pistols in 9mm and .32 ACP ($275 MSR), and a CZ-82 ($169 MSR). Please contact the company directly for more information and current availability (see Trademark Index).

TNW, INC.

Current rifle manufacturer located in Vernonia, OR. Consumer direct sales.

RIFLES: SEMI-AUTO

TNW makes a belt-fed semi-auto variation of the original Browning M2HB machine gun in .50 BMG cal. Prices were $7,500 - $8,500 until 2009, and are now POR. TNW also makes a semi-auto Model 1919 A4 .30 cal. machine gun - prices range from $2,000 - $2,200, as well as a M230 conversion for $699, and a M37 semi-auto .30 cal. machine gun for $3,995. TNW also manufactures a variation of the German MG-34 semi-auto (POR). Please contact the company directly for more information regarding these semi-auto working replicas (see Trademark Index).

TACTICAL RIFLES

Current rifle manufacturer located in Dade City, FL.

RIFLES

Tactical Rifles makes a complete lineup of bolt action and semi-auto tactical rifles. Current models include the Tactical Long Range ($2,950 MSR), Tactical Para w/ folding stock ($3,550 MSR), Tactical Long Range Magnum ($3,550 MSR), Tactical M40 ($2,795 MSR), Tactical M21 ($4,595 MSR), Dow Custom AR10 (disc. 2004, $2,695 last MSR), Dow FAL15 (disc. 2007, $1,895 last MSR), Tactical AR15 ($2,295 MSR), Tactical Special Varmint ($2,495 MSR), and the Tactical M4C ($1,885 MSR). Please contact the company for more information (see Trademark Index).

TACTICAL WEAPONS

Current law enforcement/military division of FNH USA, located in McLean, VA.

Tactical Weapons currently manufactures machine guns only for law enforcement/military.

TAR-HUNT CUSTOM RIFLES, INC.

Current custom rifled shotgun manufacturer established in 1990, and located in Bloomsburg, PA. Dealer and consumer direct sales.

MSR	100%	98%	95%	90%	80%	70%	60%

SHOTGUNS: BOLT ACTION

The following models are available in left-hand action at no additional charge.

RSG-TACTICAL (SNIPER) MODEL – 12 ga. only, similar to RSG-12, except has M-86 McMillan fiberglass black tactical stock with Pachmayr Decelerator pad and heavy barrel. Mfg. 1992-98.

$1,495	$1,250	$995	$875	$750	$700	$650	Last MSR was $1,595.

Add $150 for Bipod.

TAURUS INTERNATIONAL MFG., INC.

Currently manufactured by Taurus Forjas S.A., located in Porto Alegre, Brazil. Currently imported by Taurus International Mfg., Inc. located in Miami, FL since 1982. Beginning 2007, Taurus Tactical, a separate entity, was created for law enforcement/military sales and service. Distributor sales only.

All Taurus products are known for their innovative design, quality construction, and proven value, and are backed by a lifetime repair policy.

Taurus order number nomenclature is as follows: the first digit followed by a dash refers to type (1 = pistol, 2 = revolver, 3 = rifle/carbine, 5 = magazines, accessories, or grips, and 10 = scope mount bases), the next 2 or 3 digits refer to model number, the next digit refers to type of hammer (0 = exposed, 1 = concealed), the next digit refers to barrel length, the last digit refers to finish (1 = blue, 9 = stainless), and the suffix at the end refers to special features (T = total titanium, H = case hardened, M = matte finish, UL = Ultra-Lite, C = compensator [ported], G = gold accent, R = rosewood grips, PRL = mother-of-pearl grips, and NS = night sights). Hence, 2-941029UL refers to a Model 941 Ultra-Lite revolver in .22 Mag. cal. with an exposed hammer and a 2 in. barrel in stainless steel.

MSR	100%	98%	95%	90%	80%	70%	60%

PISTOLS: SEMI-AUTO

From 1990-92, certain models became available with a Laser Aim LA1 sighting system that included mounts, rings (in matching finish), a 110 volt AC recharging unit, a 9 volt DC field charger, and a high impact custom case.

Taurus incorporated their keyed Taurus security system on most models during 2000, except the PT-22 and PT-25, and this is now available with all models. When the security system is engaged (via a keyed button on the bottom of rear grip strap), the pistol cannot be fired, cocked, or disassembled, and the gun's manual safety cannot be disengaged. This security key also works for the revolvers.

Recent variations that are CA approved are not broken out separately, as pricing is usually the same as the standard model.

Add approx. $30 for the Deluxe Shooter's Pack option (included extra mag. and custom case) on the 92, 99, 100, and 101 Series (disc. 2000).

PT-24/7 – 9mm Para., .40 S&W, or .45 ACP (new 2005) cal., DAO, large black polymer frame with blued steel or satin stainless steel slide, 4 in. barrel with 3-dot sights, grips have Ribber grip overlays, 10, 12 (.45 ACP cal.), 15 (.40 S&W cal.), or 17 (9mm Para. cal.) shot mag., built-in Picatinny rail system on bottom of frame, includes 3 safeties, 27 1/2 oz. Mfg. late 2004-2005.

	$450	$400	$350	$310	$250	$200	$180	Last MSR was $578.

Add $16 for stainless steel.

PT-24/7 PRO FULL SIZE – 9mm Para., .40 S&W, or .45 ACP cal., SA first shot, and follows continually in SA mode, large black polymer frame with blued steel, Duo Tone (new 2009), titanium (9mm Para. cal. only), or satin stainless steel slide, 4 in. barrel with Heinie front and Slant Pro rear sight, Ribber grips (.45 ACP cal.) or Ribber overmold grips (grip inlays), 10, 12 (.45 ACP cal.), 15 (.40 S&W cal.), or 17 (9mm Para. cal.) shot mag., built-in Picatinny rail system on bottom of frame, includes 3 safeties, 27.2 oz. New 2006.

MSR $498	$415	$365	$310	$275	$220	$180	$140

Add $16 for stainless steel or $188 for titanium.

This model uses a SA trigger mechanism. However, if a cartridge does not fire, a DA feature allows the shooter a second firing pin strike via the DA trigger pull. If the cartridge still does not fire, then extraction by slide operation will insert a fresh round while reverting to the SA model automatically.

* **PT-24/7 Pro Long Slide** – similar to Full Size 24/7-Pro, except has 5.2 in. barrel, also available in .38 Super cal. (new 2010), similar mag. capacities, Tenifer finish new 2010, 29.1 oz. New 2006.

MSR $530	$445	$390	$335	$305	$245	$200	$155

Add $15 for stainless steel. Add $31 for Tenifer finish (new 2010). Add $197 for Tenifer finish with night sights (.40 S&W cal. only, new 2010).

* **PT-24/7 Pro Compact** – similar to Full Size 24/7-Pro, except has 3 1/3 in. barrel, similar mag. capacities. New 2006.

MSR $498	$415	$365	$310	$275	$220	$180	$140

Add $16 for stainless steel or $188 for titanium.

PT-24/7 OSS – 9mm Para., .40 S&W, or .45 ACP cal., similar operating system as PT-24/7 Pro Full Size, including SA/DA trigger system, choice of tan or black frame, 5 1/4 in. match grade barrel, Novak sights, lower frame Picatinny rail, 10, 12, 15, or 17 shot mag., ambidextrous decocking safety, black Tenifer steel or stainless (new 2009) slide with front and rear serrations, approx. 32 oz. New 2007.

MSR $623	$475	$425	$365	$325	$260	$215	$190

Add $63 for Novak Lo-Mount night sights.
Add $18 for matte finished stainless steel slide (new 2009).

PT-92(AF) – 9mm Para. cal., semi-auto double action, design similar to Beretta Model 92 SB-F, exposed hammer, ambidextrous safety, 5 in. barrel, 10 (C/B 1994), 15*, or 17 (new late 2004) shot mag., smooth Brazilian walnut (disc.) or checkered rubber (new 1999) grips, blue, nickel (disc.), or stainless steel finish, fixed or night (mfg. 2000-2004) sights, 34 oz.

MSR $609	$475	$410	$350	$310	$260	$210	$155

Add $40 for satin nickel finish (disc. 1994).
Add $415 for Laser Aim Sight (disc. 1991).
Add $78 for night sights (disc. 2004).
Add $266 for blue or stainless conversion kit to convert 9mm Para. to .22 LR (mfg. 1999-2004).

* **PT-92SS (Stainless Steel)** – similar to PT-92AF, except is combat matte (new 2006, high cap. mag. only) or regular stainless steel. New 1992.

MSR $617	$495	$435	$370	$335	$270	$225	$175

Add $78 for night sights (disc. 2004).

* **PT-92AFC** – compact variation of the Model PT-92AF, 4 in. barrel, 10 (C/B 1994) or 13* shot mag., fixed sights. Disc. 1996.

	$335	$295	$250	$225	$185	$150	$115	Last MSR was $449.

MSR	100%	98%	95%	90%	80%	70%	60%

Add $38 for satin nickel finish (disc. 1993).

* *PT-92AFC (Stainless Steel)* – similar to PT-92AFC, except stainless steel. Mfg. 1993-96.

	$400	$350	$300	$270	$220	$180	$140	*Last MSR was $493.*

PT-99 (AF) – 9mm Para. cal., similar to Model PT-92AF, except has adj. rear sight, 10 or 17 shot mag., 34 oz.

MSR $617	$495	$435	$370	$335	$270	$225	$175

Add $45 for satin nickel finish (disc. 1994).
Add $266 for blue or stainless conversion kit to convert 9mm Para. to .22 LR (mfg. 1999-2004) or .40 S&W (mfg. 2000-2004).

This action is similar to the Beretta Model 92SB-F.

* *PT-99SS (Stainless Steel)* – similar to PT-99, except is fabricated from stainless steel. New 1992.

MSR $633	$495	$425	$355	$325	$260	$215	$165

PT-100 – .40 S&W cal., standard double action, 5 in. barrel, 10 (C/B 1994), 11* (reintroduced late 2004) shot mag., safeties include ambidextrous manual, hammer drop, inertia firing pin, and chamber loaded indicator, choice of blue, satin nickel (disc. 1994), or stainless steel finish, accessory rail, smooth Brazilian hard wood (disc.) or rubber grips, 34 oz. Mfg. 1992-97, reintroduced 2000.

MSR $609	$475	$410	$350	$310	$260	$210	$155

Add $40 for satin nickel finish (disc. 1994).
Add $78 for night sights (mfg. 2000-2004).
Add $266 for blue or stainless conversion kit to convert .40 S&W to .22 LR cal. (disc. 2004).

* *PT-100SS (Stainless Steel)* – similar to PT-100, except is fabricated from stainless steel. Mfg. 1992-96, reintroduced 2000.

MSR $617	$495	$435	$370	$335	$270	$225	$175

Add $78 for night sights (disc. 2005).

PT-101 – .40 S&W cal., similar to PT-100, except has adj. rear sight., 11 shot mag. became standard during late 2004, 34 oz. Mfg. 1992-96, reintroduced 2000.

MSR $617	$495	$435	$370	$335	$270	$225	$175

Add $266 for blue or stainless conversion kit to convert .40 S&W to .22 LR cal. (disc. 2004).
Add $45 for satin nickel finish (disc. 1994).

* *PT-101SS (Stainless Steel)* – similar to PT-101, except is stainless steel. Mfg. 1992-96, reintroduced 2000.

MSR $633	$495	$425	$355	$325	$260	$215	$165

PT-111 MILLENNIUM – 9mm Para. cal., double action only, 3 1/4 in. barrel with fixed 3-dot sights, black polymer frame with steel slide, striker fired, 10 shot mag. with push-button release, 18.7 oz. Mfg. 1998-2004.

	$355	$310	$265	$225	$190	$155	$135	*Last MSR was $422.*

Add $78 for night sights (new 2000).
Add $47 for pearl or burl walnut grips (limited mfg. 2003).

* *PT-111 Millennium Stainless* – similar to Model PT-111, except has stainless steel slide. Mfg. 1998-2004.

	$360	$315	$270	$245	$200	$160	$125	*Last MSR was $438.*

Add $78 for night sights (new 2000).
Add $46 for pearl or burl walnut grips (limited mfg. 2003).

* *PT-111 Millennium Titanium* – similar to Model PT-111, except has titanium slide and night or 3-dot (new 2004) sights. Mfg. 2000-2004.

	$415	$365	$320	$275	$225	$185	$165	*Last MSR was $508.*

Add $78 for night sights.

PT-111 MILLENNIUM PRO – 9mm Para. cal., similar to Model PT-111 Millennium, 10 or 12 (new late 2004) shot mag., except has improved ergonomics, Posi-Traction slide serrations, recessed magazine release, manual safety lever, trigger block mechanism, firing pin block, and lightweight frame, 18.7 oz. New 2003.

MSR $467	$375	$325	$270	$245	$200	$160	$125

Add $78 for night sights (disc. 2004).

* *PT-111 Millennium Pro Stainless* – similar to Model PT-111 Millennium Pro, except has stainless steel slide. New 2003.

MSR $483	$395	$330	$285	$260	$210	$170	$135

Add $78 for night sights (mfg. 2004).

* *PT-111 Ti Millennium Pro Titanium* – similar to Model PT-111 Millennium Pro, except has titanium slide, 16 oz. New 2005.

MSR $655	$525	$460	$395	$355	$290	$235	$185

MSR	100%	98%	95%	90%	80%	70%	60%

PT-140 MILLENNIUM – .40 S&W cal., double action only, 3 1/4 in. barrel, black polymer frame, manual safety, 10 shot mag., fixed 3-dot sights, blue steel slide, 18.7 oz. Mfg. 1999-2004.

| | $375 | $335 | $280 | $240 | $200 | $165 | $150 | Last MSR was $461. |

Add $78 for night sights (new 2000).
Add $47 for pearl or burl walnut grips (mfg. 2003).

* **PT-140 Millennium Stainless** – similar to Model PT-140, except has stainless steel slide. Mfg. 1999-2004.

| | $380 | $340 | $285 | $240 | $200 | $165 | $150 | Last MSR was $476. |

Add $78 for night sights (new 2000).
Add $46 for pearl or burl walnut grips (mfg. 2003).

PT-140 MILLENNIUM PRO – .40 S&W cal., similar to Model PT-140 Millennium, except has improved ergonomics, Posi-Traction slide serrations, recessed magazine release, manual safety lever, trigger block mechanism, firing pin block, and lightweight frame, 23 1/2 oz. New 2003.

| MSR $483 | $395 | $330 | $285 | $260 | $210 | $170 | $135 | |

Add $78 for night sights (disc. 2004).

* **PT-140 Millennium Pro Stainless** – similar to Model PT-140 Millennium Pro, except has stainless steel slide. New 2003.

| MSR $498 | $415 | $345 | $295 | $270 | $215 | $180 | $140 | |

Add $78 for night sights (disc. 2004).

PT-145 MILLENNIUM – .45 ACP cal., otherwise similar to Model PT-140 Millennium, 23 oz. Mfg. 2000-2003.

| | $400 | $350 | $300 | $260 | $215 | $175 | $155 | Last MSR was $484. |

Add $79 for night sights (new 2000).

* **PT-145 Millennium Stainless** – similar to Model PT-140, except has stainless steel slide. Mfg. 1999-2003.

| | $400 | $350 | $300 | $260 | $200 | $165 | $150 | Last MSR was $500. |

Add $78 for night sights (new 2000).

PT-145 MILLENNIUM PRO – .45 ACP cal., similar to Model PT-145 Millennium, except has improved ergonomics, Posi-Traction slide serrations, recessed magazine release, manual safety lever, trigger block mechanism, firing pin block, and lightweight frame, 22.2 oz. New 2003.

| MSR $483 | $395 | $330 | $285 | $260 | $210 | $170 | $135 | |

Add $78 for night sights (disc. 2004).

* **PT-145 Millennium Pro Stainless** – similar to Model PT-145 Millennium Pro, except has stainless steel slide. New 2003.

| MSR $498 | $415 | $345 | $295 | $270 | $215 | $180 | $140 | |

Add $78 for night sights (mfg. 2000-2004).

PT-400 – .400 Cor-Bon cal., similar to Model PT-940, except has 4 1/4 in. ported barrel and 8 shot mag., 29 1/2 oz. Mfg. 1999 only.

| | $415 | $365 | $320 | $275 | $225 | $185 | $165 | Last MSR was $523. |

* **PT-400 Stainless** – similar to Model PT-400, except has stainless steel slide. Mfg. 1999 only.

| | $415 | $365 | $320 | $275 | $225 | $185 | $165 | Last MSR was $539. |

PT-609/609TI-PRO – 9mm Para cal., DA/SA, 3 1/4 in. barrel with titanium slide, fixed sights, black polymer grips, lower rail on frame, 13 shot mag., 19.7 oz. New 2007.

| MSR $670 | $535 | $470 | $400 | $365 | $295 | $240 | $185 | |

MODEL 709 SLIM – 9mm Para cal., SA, 3 in. barrel, 8 shot, blue finish, checkered polymer grips, compact frame, fixed front sight, 19 oz. New late 2008.

| MSR $483 | $395 | $330 | $285 | $260 | $210 | $170 | $135 | |

* **Model 709 Slim Stainless** – similar to Model 709, except is matte finished stainless steel, 19 oz. New late 2008.

| MSR $498 | $415 | $345 | $295 | $270 | $215 | $180 | $140 | |

PT-745 COMPACT MILLENNIUM PRO – .45 ACP cal., SA/DA, compact variation of Millennium Pro with 3 1/4 in. barrel, 6 shot mag. with finger extension, matte blue steel slide, loaded chamber indicator, black polymer grip frame, Desert Tan grips were added 2006, 20.8 oz. New 2005.

| MSR $483 | $395 | $330 | $285 | $260 | $210 | $170 | $135 | |

* **PT-745 Compact Millenium Pro Stainless** – similar to PT-745 Compact Millennium Pro, except has stainless steel slide. New 2005.

| MSR $498 | $415 | $345 | $295 | $270 | $215 | $180 | $140 | |

MSR	100%	98%	95%	90%	80%	70%	60%

MODEL 809 – 9mm Para. cal., similar design to the PT-24/7 OSS, 4 in. barrel, SA/DA with Strike Two capability, Novak sights, 17 shot mag., blue or stainless, front and rear slide serrations, lower Picatinny rail, 30.2 oz. New 2007.

MSR $656	$520	$460	$395	$340	$295	$235	$200

Add $18 for stainless steel slide.

MODEL 840 – .40 S&W cal., similar design to the PT-24/7 OSS, 4 in. barrel, SA/DA with Strike Two capability, Novak sights, 15 shot mag., blue or stainless, front and rear slide serrations, lower frame Picatinny rail, approx. 30 oz. New 2008.

MSR $656	$520	$460	$395	$340	$295	$235	$200

Add $18 for stainless steel slide.

MODEL 845 – .45 ACP cal., similar design to the PT-24/7 OSS, 4 in. barrel, SA/DA with Strike Two capability, Novak sights, 12 shot mag., blue or stainless, front and rear slide serrations, lower frame Picatinny rail, approx. 30 oz. New 2008.

MSR $656	$520	$460	$395	$340	$295	$235	$200

Add $18 for stainless steel slide.

PT-908 – 9mm Para. cal., compact version of the PT-92 with 3.8 in. barrel and 8 shot mag., fixed sights, blue or nickel finish. Mfg. 1993-97.

	$330	$290	$250	$210	$180	$150	$130	*Last MSR was $435.*

* **PT-908D SS (Stainless Steel)** – similar to Model PT-908, except is stainless steel. Mfg. 1993-97.

	$385	$345	$295	$250	$215	$170	$150	*Last MSR was $473.*

PT-909 – 9mm Para. cal., DA/SA, 4 in. barrel, lower frame Picatinny rail, 10 or 17 shot mag., blue finish, fixed rear sight, alloy medium frame with steel slide, checkered rubber grips, 28.2 oz. New 2006.

MSR $648	$500	$415	$360	$315	$250	$200	$180

Add $16 for stainless steel slide.

PT-911 COMPACT – 9mm Para. cal., single or double action, 4 in. barrel, 10 or 15 (new late 2004) shot mag., checkered rubber grips, fixed sights, 28.2 oz. New 1997.

MSR $648	$500	$415	$360	$315	$250	$200	$180

Add $79 for night sights (disc. 2004).

* **PT-911 Compact SS (Stainless Steel)** – stainless variation of the PT-911 Compact.

MSR $664	$530	$445	$380	$345	$280	$230	$180

Add $78 for night sights (disc. 2004).

* **PT-911 Compact Deluxe** – choice of blue/gold finish or stainless steel with gold, rosewood, or mother-of-pearl grips. New 2000.

MSR $702	$550	$455	$390	$355	$285	$235	$180

Add $15 for stainless steel with gold or faux mother-of-pearl grips.

PT-917 COMPACT PLUS – 9mm Para. cal., DA/SA, 4 in. barrel with fixed sights, rubber grips, 19 shot mag., medium frame, blue finish or stainless steel, 31.8 oz. New 2007.

MSR $609	$500	$415	$360	$315	$250	$200	$180

Add $18 for stainless steel.

PT-940 – .40 S&W cal., compact version of the PT-100 with 3 5/8 in. barrel and 10 shot mag., fixed sights, 28.2 oz. New 1996.

MSR $648	$500	$415	$360	$315	$250	$200	$180

Add $79 for night sights (disc. 2004).

* **PT-940 SS (Stainless Steel)** – similar to PT-940, except is stainless steel. New 1996.

MSR $664	$530	$445	$380	$345	$280	$230	$180

Add $80 for night sights (disc. 2009).

PT-945 – .45 ACP cal., DA/SA, 4 1/4 in. ported (mfg. 1997-2003) or unported barrel, 8 shot single stack mag., ambidextrous 3 position safety, chamber loaded indicator, 3-dot sights, 29 1/2 oz. New 1995.

MSR $695	$560	$470	$400	$365	$295	$240	$185

Add $78 for night sights (disc. 2004).
Add $39 for ported barrel (disc. 2003).

* **PT-945 SS (Stainless Steel)** – stainless steel variation of the PT-945. New 1995.

MSR $711	$575	$475	$410	$370	$300	$245	$190

Add $78 for night sights (disc. 2004).
Add $39 for ported barrel (disc. 2003).

MSR	100%	98%	95%	90%	80%	70%	60%

PT-957 – .357 SIG cal., compact model with 3 5/8 in. ported (available only with night sights or in 957 Deluxe beginning 2002) or non-ported (new 2002) barrel and slide, 10 shot mag., ambidextrous 3-position safety, blue finish, checkered rubber grips, fixed sights, 28 oz. Mfg. 1999-2003.

	$425	$375	$325	$275	$225	$185	$165	Last MSR was $523.

Add $90 for night sights.
Add $40 for ported barrel (disc. 2002).

* **PT-957 SS (Stainless Steel)** – stainless steel variation of the PT-957. Mfg. 1999-2003.

	$430	$380	$330	$275	$225	$185	$165	Last MSR was $539.

Add $40 for ported (disc. 2001) barrel, or $130 for ported barrel and night sights (disc. 2003).

PT-1911 – .38 Super (mfg. 2006), 9mm Para. (mfg. 2006), .40 S&W (mfg. 2006) or .45 ACP cal., SA, 5 in. barrel, choice of Heinie front and rear sights or Picatinny rail, 8 (.40 S&W or .45 ACP) or 9 (.38 Super or 9mm Para.) shot mag., blue or Duo-tone (new 2008) finish, choice of steel or aluminum (new 2008) frame with steel slide, checkered diamond pattern or bull's head wood grips, bobbed hammer, front and rear serrations on slide, accurized hand tuned action, 32 oz. New mid-2005.

MSR $757	$600	$525	$450	$410	$330	$270	$210	

Add $32 for Picatinny rail.
Add $80 for aluminum frame or Duo-tone finish.

* **PT-1911 Compact** – .45 ACP cal., only, similar to PT-1911, except has 4 1/4 in. barrel, 6 shot mag. Mfg. 2006 only.

	$490	$430	$365	$335	$270	$220	$170	Last MSR was $599.

Add $20 for stainless steel slide.

* **PT-1911 Stainless** – similar to PT-1911, except has stainless steel frame and slide (mirror finished beginning 2008).

MSR $859	$725	$635	$545	$495	$400	$325	$255	

Add $32 for lower frame Picatinny rail.
Add $46 for bull's head grips.

1911B SERIES – .38 Super (1911B-38), 9mm Para. (1911B-9), or .45 ACP (1911BHC-12) cal., 5 in. barrel, blue, stainless, 9, 11, or 12 shot mag., with or w/o Novak night sights, 38-40 oz. New mid-2009.

MSR $677	$535	$470	$400	$365	$295	$240	$185	

Add $103 for stainless steel. Add $17 for 11 shot mag. Add $79 for .45 ACP with 12 shot mag. Add $63 for Novak night sights. Add $93 for Hi-Polish with bull's head walnut grips. Add $16 for pearl grips.

REVOLVERS: RECENT PRODUCTION

From 1990-1992, certain models became available with a Laser Aim LA1 sighting system that included mounts, rings (in matching finish), a 110 volt AC recharging unit, a 9 volt DC field charger, and a high impact custom case.

The following Taurus revolvers have been listed in numerical order. All currently manufactured revolvers listed are rated for +P ammunition.

Tracker model nomenclature refers to a heavy contoured barrel with full shroud, porting, and with or w/o VR.

All currently manufactured Taurus revolvers are equipped with the patented Taurus Security System, introduced in 1998, which utilizes an integral key lock on the back of the hammer, locking the action.

MODEL 45-410 "JUDGE" (44-TEN TRACKER) – .45 LC/.410 shotshell cal., 2 1/2 or 3 (new 2008) in. chamber, SA/DA, 5 shot, 2 1/2 (disc.), 3 (new 2007), or 6 /12 (not available in 3 in. chamber) in. barrel, blue or stainless, fiber optic front sight, Ribber grips, compact frame, 29 or 32 oz. New 2006.

MSR $570	$500	$440	$375	$340	$275	$225	$175	

Add $47 for 3 in. cylinder. Add $39 for 2 1/2 in. cylinder with ported barrel and accessory rail (new 2010).
Add $303 for Crimson Trace laser grips (new 2010).

During late 2007, this model's nomenclature changed to the Model 45-410 Judge.

TECHNO ARMS (PTY) LIMITED

Previous manufacturer located in Johannesburg, S. Africa circa 1994-1996. Previously imported by Vulcans Forge, Inc. located in Foxboro, MA.

SHOTGUNS: SLIDE ACTION

MAG-7 SLIDE ACTION SHOTGUN – 12 ga. (60mm chamber length), 5 shot detachable mag. (in pistol grip), 14, 16, 18, or 20 in. barrel, straight grip or pistol grip stock, matte finish, 8 lbs. Imported 1995-96.

	$795	$675	$625	$550	$500	$450	$400	Last MSR was $875.

MSR	100%	98%	95%	90%	80%	70%	60%

THOMPSON CARBINES & PISTOLS

See Auto Ordnance Corp. section of this book.

THOMPSON/CENTER ARMS CO., INC.

Current manufacturer established during 1967, and located in Rochester, NH. Distributor and dealer sales.

During 2006, Thompson/Center was purchased by Smith & Wesson.

Thompson/Center also has created a custom shop to enable customers to create custom pistols, rifles, shotguns, and muzzleloaders. Please contact the factory for availability and an individualized quotation.

Please refer to the *Blue Book of Modern Black Powder Arms* by John Allen (also online) for more information and prices on Thompson/Center's lineup of modern black powder models.

Black Powder Revolvers - Reproductions & Replicas and *Black Powder Long Arms & Pistols - Reproductions & Replicas* by Dennis Adler is also an invaluable source for most black powder reproductions and replicas, and includes hundreds of color images on most popular makes/models, provides manufacturer/trademark histories, and up-to-date information on related items/accessories for black powder shooting - www.bluebookinc.com

RIFLES: BOLT ACTION

ICON PRECISION HUNTER – .204 Ruger, .223 Rem., .22-250 Rem., .243 Win., 6.5 Creedmoor (new 2010), or .308 Win. cal., 22 in. heavy fluted barrel with 5R button rifling, fat bolt design with tactical style handle, classic varminter style brown synthetic stock with cheekpiece and beavertail forend, detachable 3 shot mag. with single shot adapter, Picatinny rail, adj. trigger, two position safety, sling swivel studs, 8 lbs. New 2009.

MSR $1,299	**$1,150**	**$995**	**$875**	**$750**	**$650**	**$550**	**$450**

ICON WARLORD – .308 Win. or .338 Lapua cal., 5 or 10 shot mag., hand lapped stainless steel fluted barrel, carbon fiber tactical style stock with adj. cheekpiece, available in OD Green, Flat Black, or Desert Sand, Weather Shield finish on all metal, adj. trigger, Picatinny rail, tactical bolt handle, 12 3/4 - 13 3/4 lbs. New 2010.

As this edition went to press, retail pricing was not available on this model.

THUNDER-FIVE

Previous trademark manufactured by MIL Inc., located in Piney Flats, TN. Previous company name was Holston Enterprises, Inc. Previously manufactured by Mil, Inc. located in Piney Flats, TN. Previously distributed by C.L. Reedy & Associates, Inc. located in Jonesborough, TN.

While previously advertised as the Spectre Five (not mfg.), this firearm was re-named the Thunder-Five.

REVOLVERS

THUNDER-FIVE – .45 LC cal./.410 bore with 3 in. chamber or .45-70 Govt. cal. (mfg. 1994-98), single or double action, unique 5 shot revolver design permits shooting .45 LC or .410 bore shotshells interchangeably, 2 in. rifled barrel, phosphate finish, external ambidextrous hammer block safety, internal transfer bar safety, combat sights, hammer, trigger, and trigger guard, Pachmayr grips, padded plastic carrying case, 48 oz., serialization started at 1,101. Mfg. 1992-circa 2007.

	$495	**$450**	**$400**	**$375**	**$350**	**$325**	**$300**	Last MSR was $545.

Sub-caliber sleeve inserts were available until 1998 for 9mm Para., .357 Mag./.38 Spl., and .38 Super cals.

THUREON DEFENSE

Current rifle manufacturer located in New Holstein, WI.

RIFLES: SEMI-AUTO

THUREON DEFENSE CARBINE – 9mm Para. cal., blowback action, 32 shot mag., AR-15 trigger components, integral Picatinny rail, closed bolt, aluminum upper and lower receivers, adj. buttstock, black finish, approx. 6 1/2 lbs.

MSR $660	**$600**	**$550**	**$500**	**$465**	**$435**	**$400**	**$375**

Add $25 for M4 telescoping buttstock.
Add $26 for laser/tactical light mount.
Add $60 for open sights nested in sight rail.

TIKKA

Current trademark imported by Beretta U.S.A. Corp., located in Accokeek, MD. Previously imported until 2000 by Stoeger Industries, located in Wayne, NJ. Tikka rifles are currently manufactured by Sako, Ltd. located in Riihimäki, Finland. Previously manufactured by Oy Tikkakoski Ab, of Tikkakoski, Finland (pre-1989).

During 2000, Tikka was purchased by Beretta Holding of Italy. All currently produced Tikkas are imported by Beretta U.S.A. Corp., located in Accokeek, MD.

Also see listings under Ithaca combination guns and bolt action rifles for older models.

MSR	100%	98%	95%	90%	80%	70%	60%

RIFLES: BOLT ACTION

About 3,000 rifles sold under the Tikka name have been recalled following catastrophic failures, but a small number of guns sold in the American market remain in the hands of consumers who have apparently not heard about the recall. A weakness in the stainless steel used to manufacture rifles during 2003-2004 has lead to ruptured barrels. Consumers are urged to contact the Tikka Recall Center at 800-503-8869 with their rifle's serial number to find out if their firearm is affected.

* **T3 Tactical** – .223 Rem. or .308 Win. cal., T3 action, 20 or 24 (disc. 2007) in. barrel, 5 shot mag., black synthetic stock with adj. comb, Picatinny rail, 7 1/4 lbs. Importation began 2004.

MSR $1,695	$1,425	$1,125	$975	$825	$725	$625	$525

TORNADO

Currently manufactured by AseTekno located in Helsinki, Finland.

RIFLES: BOLT ACTION

TORNADO MODEL – .338 Lapua Mag. cal., unique straight line design with free floating barrel, 5 shot mag., pistol grip assembly is part of frame, limited importation into the U.S.

The factory should be contacted directy regarding domestic availability and pricing (see Trademark Index).

TRANSFORMATIONAL DEFENSE INDUSTRIES, INC.

Current manufacturer of civilian and law enforcement firearms established in 2008 and located in Virginia Beach, VA. Dealer sales.

Transformational Defense Industries, Inc. is part of the Gamma Applied Visions Group SA, an innovative Swiss-based global technology development firm.

TDI, Inc. also offers a Kriss-based semi-auto shotgun. Please contact the company directly for more information, including configurations, availability, and pricing (see Trademark Index).

RIFLES: SEMI-AUTO

KRISS SUPER V VECTOR RIFLE/CARBINE – .45 ACP cal., delayed blowback action, 16 in. steel barrel, Ultramid Nylon 6/6 polymer receiver with A2 steel plates, 30 shot Glock type detachable mag., Picatinny rail, flip up front and rear sights, two-stage trigger, folding vertical forearm grip, rail type folding stock, 5 lbs.

MSR $2,395	$2,250	$1,995	$1,825	$1,650	$1,475	$1,325	$1,125

TRISTAR SPORTING ARMS, LTD.

Current importer established in 1994, and located in N. Kansas City, MO. Distributor and dealer sales.

SHOTGUNS: SEMI-AUTO

PHANTOM SERIES – 12 ga. only, 3 or 3 1/2 (Phantom Field/Synthetic Mag. only) in. chamber, various VR (except Phantom HP) barrel lengths with choke tubes, available in Field (blue metal finish, gold accents, and checkered walnut stock and forearm), Synthetic (black non-glare matte metal and flat black synthetic stock and forearm), or HP (home security with open sights, matte finished metal, and synthetic stock and forearm), 6 lbs. 13 oz.-7 lbs. 6 oz. Italian mfg., limited importation 2001-2002.

		$385	$350	$315	$285	$265	$245	$225	Last MSR was $425.

Subtract $44 for Phantom Synthetic.
Add $74 for 3 1/2 in. Mag. (Field).
Add $44 for Mag. Synthetic.

VIPER SERIES – 12, 20, or 28 (new 2010, wood stock only) ga., 2 3/4 or 3 in. chamber, 24 (Youth), 26, or 28 in. barrel, 5 shot mag., G2 action became standard 2010, brass bead front sight, mag. cut off, vent. rib with matted sight plane, choice of wood, black synthetic, or carbon fiber pistol grip stock, gas operated, choke tubes, approx. 6.2 - 6.8 lbs. Importation began 2007.

MSR $489	$425	$375	$325	$250	$225	$195	$170

Add $30 for synthetic or $90 for wood Youth configuration (20 ga. only).
Add $50 for wood stock.
Add $140 for silver alloy reciever (new 2010).
Add $110 for 28 ga. (new 2010).
Add $120 for carbon fiber stock (disc. 2009).

* **Viper Camo** – 12 ga. only, 26 or 28 in. barrel, G2 action became standard during 2010, similar to Viper Series, except has 100% Mossy Oak Duck Blind camo coverage, 6.8 lbs. New 2008.

MSR $589	$485	$375	$325	$275	$250	$225	$175

Add $50 for Turkey/Waterfowl with 24 or 28 in. barrel.

MSR	100%	98%	95%	90%	80%	70%	60%

VIPER G2 TACTICAL – 12 ga., 20 in. barrel, matte black finish, blade front sight, 5 shot mag., cylinder choke, swivel studs, 6 1/2 lbs. New 2010.

MSR $449	$395	$350	$300	$265	$235	$200	$175

SHOTGUNS: SLIDE ACTION

COBRA SERIES – 12 ga., 20 or 28 in. barrel, 7 shot tube mag., vent. rib with matted sight plane, matte black synthetic stock and forearm, choke tubes, includes two changeable pistol grip style stocks, approx. 7 lbs. Importation began 2007.

MSR $369	$295	$250	$215	$180	$160	$140	$125

Add $70 for tactical style stock with fixed pistol grip and 20 in. barrel.

TROMIX CORPORATION

Current manufacturer established in 1999, and located in Broken Arrow, OK. Dealer or consumer direct sales.

RIFLES: SEMI-AUTO

Tromix manufactured AR-15 style rifles until 2008. Tromix lower receivers bear no caliber designation. Serialization was TR-0001-0405.

The models listed below were also available with many custom options.

TR-15 SLEDGEHAMMER – .44 Rem. Mag. (disc. 2001), .440 Cor-Bon Mag., .458 SOCOM, .475 Tremor, or .50 AE cal., 16 3/4 in. barrel, other lengths and weights available by custom order. Mfg. 1999-2006.

	$1,175	$975	$850	$775	$700	$650	$600	Last MSR was $1,350.

TR-15 TACKHAMMER – various cals., 24 in. bull barrel, other lengths and weights available by custom order. New 1999.

	$1,175	$975	$850	$775	$700	$650	$600	Last MSR was $1,350.

SHOTGUNS

Tromix manufactures Class II short barrel shotguns based on the Saiga model. Please contact the company directly for more information (see Trademark Index).

TRUVELO ARMOURY

Current manufacturer located in Midrand, South Africa. Truvelo Armoury is a division of Truvelo Manufacturers (Pty) Ltd. No current U.S. importation.

Truvelo Armoury manufactures a variety of barrels (.22 to 40mm cal.) and firearms, including the 12 ga. Neostead shotgun, the BXP 9mmP Tactical pistol, custom built hunting and sporting rifles, and military sniper rifles in 7.62x51 NATO, .338 Lapua, 12.7x99mm, 14.5x114mm, 20x82mm, and 20x110mm cals. Truvelo also manufactures the Raptor Infantry rifle and carbine in 5.56 NATO cal. Prices range from $5,200 - $30,000. Please contact the factory directly (see Trademark Index) for more information, including delivery time and availability.

NOTES

U SECTION

U.S. GENERAL TECHNOLOGIES, INC.

Previous manufacturer located in S. San Francisco, CA circa 1994-96.

MSR	100%	98%	95%	90%	80%	70%	60%

RIFLES: SEMI-AUTO

P-50 SEMI-AUTO – .50 BMG cal., includes 10 shot detachable mag., folding bipod, muzzle brake, matte black finish. Mfg. 1995-96.

	100%	98%	95%	90%	80%	70%	60%	
	$5,600	$4,950	$4,475	$3,975	$3,500	$3,050	$2,600	Last MSR was $5,995.

U.S. ORDNANCE

Current manufacturer and distributor located in Reno, NV. Commercial sales through Desert Ordnance, located in Sparks, NV.

U.S. Ordnance is licensed by Saco Defense to be the exclusive manufacturer and distributor for the M60 Series machine gun and spare parts.

RIFLES: SEMI-AUTO

U.S. Ordnance manufactures semi-auto reproductions (BATFE approved) of the M-60/M-60E3 (MSR is POR), M60E4/Mk43 (MSR POR, new 2004). Previous models included the .303 Vickers (MSR was $4,500 w/o tripod), Browning M-1919 (last MSR was $1,995), and the M-1919A4 (last MSR was $2,095). These belt-fed variations are machined to military specifications, and have a 5 year warranty. Please contact the distributor directly for more information, including pricing and availability (see Trademark Index).

USAS 12

Previous trademark manufactured by International Ordnance Corporation located in Nashville, TN circa 1992-95. Previously manufactured (1990-91) by Ramo Mfg., Inc. located in Nashville, TN. Previously distributed by Kiesler's Wholesale located in Jeffersonville, IN until 1994. Originally designed and previously distributed in the U.S. by Gilbert Equipment Co., Inc. located in Mobile, AL. Previously manufactured under license by Daewoo Precision Industries, Ltd. located in South Korea.

SHOTGUNS: SEMI-AUTO

USAS 12 – 12 ga. only, gas operated action available in either semi or fully auto versions, 18 1/4 in. cylinder bore barrel, closed bolt, synthetic stock, pistol grip, and forearm, carrying handle, 10 round box or 20 round drum mag., 2 3/4 in. chamber only, parkerized finish, 12 lbs. Mfg. 1987-1995.

	100%	98%	95%	90%	80%	70%	60%	
	$1,500	$1,250	$1,050	$925	$850	$750	$650	Last MSR was $995.

Add $300-$500 for extra 20 shot drum magazine (banned by the BATF).

Values above are for a semi-auto model. This model is currently classified as a destructive device and necessary federal NFA Class III transfer paperwork must accompany a sale.

UMAREX SPORTWAFFEN GmbH & Co. KG.

Current firearms, airguns, air soft, and signal pistol manufacturer established in 1972 as Uma Mayer Ussfeller GmbH, with headquarters located in Arnsberg, Germany. Initially, the company manufactured tear gas and signal pistols for eastern bloc countries, and then started producing air rifles. After acquiring Reck Sportwaffen Fabrick Karl Arndt, the company was reorganized under the Umarex name.

Umarex purchased Walther during 1996, and also manufactures ammunition, optics, and accessories. During 2006, Umarex purchased Hämmerli, and production equipment was moved from Lenzburg, Switzerland to Ulm, Germany. During 2008, Colt Industries licensed Umarex to manufacture the Colt AR-15 in .22 LR cal., with distribution through Umarex USA. Please refer to the Colt, Hämmerli, and Walther listings for information and values on currently imported firearms.

For more information on currently manufactured (beginning circa 1984) Umarex airguns, including many major U.S. trademark mfg. under license, please refer to the *Blue Book of Airguns* by Dr. Robert Beeman & John Allen (also online).

UNERTL ORDNANCE COMPANY, INC.

Previous manufacturer circa 2004-2006 and located in Las Vegas, NV.

Unertl Ordnance Company manufactured a .45 ACP cal. semi-auto pistol in various configurations, including MEU (SOC) $2,795 last MSR, UCCP $2,195 last MSR, and the DLX $2,195 last MSR. The company also manufactured the UPR bolt action sniper rifle in .308 Win. cal. Last MSR was $5,900.

MSR	100%	98%	95%	90%	80%	70%	60%

UNIQUE-ALPINE

Current manufacturer established in 2002 and located in Bavaria, Germany, with manufacturing sites in Germany and Switzerland. No current U.S. importation.

RIFLES: BOLT ACTION

TPG-1 (TACTICAL PRECISION GEWEHR) – various cals. from .223 Rem. to .300 Win. Mag., modular interchangeable rifle system allows for transfer from single shot to magazine fed rifle, tactical adj. stock available in right hand or Universal configuration and a variety of colors and camo, adj. palm rest, accessory rails.

A wide variety of options are available on this model. Please contact the company directly for more information, including options, pricing, and U.S. availability (see Trademark Index).

UNIVERSAL FIREARMS

Previous manufacturer 1958-1987 and located in Hialeah, FL. Previous company name was Bullseye Gunworks, located in Miami, FL. The company moved to Hialeah, FL in 1958 and began as Universal Firearms.

Universal Firearms M1 carbines were manufactured and assembled at the company's facility in Hialeah starting in the late 1950s. The carbines of the 1960s were mfg. with available surplus GI parts on a receiver subcontracted to Repp Steel Co. of Buffalo, NY. The carbines of the 1970s were mfg. with commercially manufactured parts due to a shortage of GI surplus. In 1983, the company was purchased by Iver Johnson Arms of Jacksonville, AR, but remained a separate division as Universal Firearms in Hialeah until closed and liquidated by Iver Johnson Arms in 1987.

PISTOLS: SEMI-AUTO

MODEL 3000 ENFORCER PISTOL – .30 Carbine cal., walnut stock, 11 1/4 in. barrel, 17 3/4 in. overall, 15, and 30 shot. Mfg. 1964-83. Also see listing under Iver Johnson.

	100%	98%	95%	90%	80%	70%	60%
Blue finish	$450	$375	$325	$275	$235	$200	$185
Nickel-plated	$500	$425	$350	$295	$250	$235	$220
Gold-plated	$500	$425	$350	$275	$250	$225	$200
Stainless	$600	$550	$450	$350	$275	$225	$195

Add $50 for Teflon-S finish.

RIFLES: SEMI-AUTO, CARBINES

1000 MILITARY – .30 Carbine cal., "G.I." copy, satin blue, birch stock, 18 in. barrel. Disc.

	100%	98%	95%	90%	80%	70%	60%
	$375	$325	$275	$235	$200	$180	$170

MODEL 1003 – 16, 18, or 20 in. barrel, .30 M1 copy, blue finish, adj. sight, birch stock, 5 1/2 lbs. Also see listing under Iver Johnson.

	100%	98%	95%	90%	80%	70%	60%	
	$375	$325	$275	$235	$200	$180	$170	Last MSR was $203.

* *Model 1010* – nickel finish, disc.

	100%	98%	95%	90%	80%	70%	60%
	$425	$375	$325	$275	$235	$200	$180

* *Model 1015* – gold electroplated, disc.

	100%	98%	95%	90%	80%	70%	60%
	$425	$375	$325	$275	$235	$200	$180

Add $45 for 4X scope.

1005 DELUXE – .30 Carbine cal., custom Monte Carlo walnut stock, high polish blue, oil finish on wood.

	100%	98%	95%	90%	80%	70%	60%
	$425	$365	$325	$275	$235	$200	$180

1006 STAINLESS – .30 Carbine cal., stainless steel construction, birch stock, 18 in. barrel, 6 lbs.

	100%	98%	95%	90%	80%	70%	60%	
	$475	$425	$375	$325	$275	$235	$200	Last MSR was $234.

1020 TEFLON – .30 Carbine cal., Dupont Teflon-S finish on metal parts, black or grey color, Monte Carlo stock.

	100%	98%	95%	90%	80%	70%	60%
	$425	$375	$325	$275	$235	$200	$180

1025 FERRET A – .256 Win. Mag. cal., M1 Action, satin blue, birch stock, 18 in. barrel, 5 1/2 lbs.

	100%	98%	95%	90%	80%	70%	60%	
	$400	$350	$300	$265	$235	$200	$175	Last MSR was $219.

2200 LEATHERNECK – .22 LR cal., blowback action, birch stock, satin blue, 18 in. barrel, 5 1/2 lbs.

	100%	98%	95%	90%	80%	70%	60%
	$350	$300	$250	$215	$185	$170	$160

5000 PARATROOPER – .30 Carbine cal., metal folding extension or walnut stock, 16 or 18 in. barrel.

	100%	98%	95%	90%	80%	70%	60%	
	$550	$475	$400	$350	$295	$250	$225	Last MSR was $234.

MSR	100%	98%	95%	90%	80%	70%	60%	

5006 PARATROOPER STAINLESS – similar to 5000, only stainless with 18 in. barrel only.

| | $650 | $575 | $500 | $425 | $350 | $285 | $250 | Last MSR was $281. |

1981 COMMEMORATIVE CARBINE – .30 Carbine cal., "G.I Military" model, cased with accessories. Mfg. for 40th Anniversary 1941-81.

| | $700 | $525 | $425 | N/A | N/A | N/A | N/A | |

USELTON ARMS INC
Current manufacturer located in Franklin, TN. Previously located in Madison, TN.

PISTOLS: SEMI-AUTO

Uselton Arms Inc. manufactures M1911-style semi-auto pistols. Models included the Mil-Spec ($2,000 MSR), Compact Classic Stainless ($2,390 MSR), Compact Classic ($2,580 MSR), Carry Classic ($2,400 MSR), Tactical ($2,770 MSR), Tac-Rail ($1,800 MSR, $2,400 with Cerakote finish), Classic National Match ($2,700 MSR), Match Classic Bobtail ($2,840 MSR), and the Double Stack Race Gun ($3,200 MSR).

Limited editions, including the Eagle National Match, 2nd Amendment, and 1911, are also available - prices are POR.

RIFLES: BOLT ACTION

Uselton offers a Warbird Mountain Lite bolt action rifle in 7.82 Warbird cal., with stainless steel long action and choice of Kevlar or laminate thumbhole stock. Additionally, the Warbird is offered in a Tactical configuration with lightweight stock. Other configurations include the Stalker, Stealth, Predator, and Raptor. A variety of options are available. Please contact the company directly for more information, including pricing and delivery time (see Trademark Index).

UZI
Current trademark manufactured by Israel Military Industries (IMI). Uzi America, a partnership between IMI and Mossberg, is currently importing a 9mm Para. and .40 S&W cal. submachine gun carbine built on the mini-Uzi receiver for the law enforcement market.

During 1996-1998, Mossberg imported the Uzi Eagle pistols. These models were imported by UZI America, Inc., subsidiary of O.F. Mossberg & Sons, Inc. Previously imported by Action Arms, Ltd., located in Philadelphia, PA until 1994.

Serial number prefixes used on Uzi Firearms are as follows: "SA" on all 9mm Para. semi-auto carbines Models A and B; "45 SA" on all .45 ACP Model B carbines; "41 SA" on all .41 AE Model B carbines; "MC" on all 9mm Para. (only cal. made) semi-auto mini-carbines; "UP" on 9mm Para. semi-auto Uzi pistols, except Eagle Series pistols; and "45 UP" on all .45 semi-auto Uzi pistols (disc. 1989). There are also prototypes or experimental Uzis with either "AA" or "AAL" prefixes - these are rare and will command premiums over values listed below.

CARBINES: SEMI-AUTO

CARBINE MODEL A – 9mm Para. cal., semi-auto, 16.1 in. barrel, parkerized finish, 25 shot mag., mfg. by IMI 1980-1983 and ser. range is SA01,001-SA037,000.

| | $1,650 | $1,475 | $1,325 | $1,125 | $975 | $875 | $750 | |

Approx. 100 Model As were mfg. with a nickel finish. These are rare and command considerable premiums over values listed above.

CARBINE MODEL B – 9mm Para., .41 Action Express (new 1987), or .45 ACP (new 1987) cal., semi-auto carbine, 16.1 in. barrel, baked enamel black finish over phosphated (parkerized) base finish, 16 (.45 ACP), 20 (.41 AE) or 25 (9mm Para.) shot mag., metal folding stock, includes molded case and carrying sling, 8.4 lbs. Mfg. 1983 - until Federal legislation disc. importation 1989 and ser. range is SA037,001-SA073,544.

| | $1,500 | $1,325 | $1,200 | $1,000 | $950 | $850 | $750 | Last MSR was $698. |

Subtract approx. $150 for .41 AE or .45 ACP cal.
Add $150 for .22 LR cal. conversion kit (new 1987).
Add $215 for .45 ACP to 9mm Para./.41 AE conversion kit.
Add $150 for 9mm Para. to .41 AE (or vice-versa) conversion kit.
Add $215 for 9mm Para. to .45 ACP conversion kit.

MINI CARBINE – 9mm Para. cal., similar to Carbine except has 19 3/4 in. barrel, 20 shot mag., swing-away metal stock, scaled down version of the regular carbine, 7.2 lbs. New 1987. Federal legislation disc. importation 1989.

| | $2,375 | $2,175 | $1,850 | $1,600 | $1,350 | $1,150 | $995 | Last MSR was $698. |

PISTOLS: SEMI-AUTO

UZI PISTOL – 9mm Para. or .45 ACP cal. (disc.), 4 1/2 in. barrel, parkerized finish, 10 (.45 ACP) or 20 (9mm Para.) shot mag., supplied with molded carrying case, sight adj. key and mag. loading tool, 3.8 lbs. Importation disc. 1993.

| | $1,000 | $875 | $795 | $750 | $700 | $650 | $600 | Last MSR was $695. |

MSR	100%	98%	95%	90%	80%	70%	60%

Add $285 for .45 ACP to 9mm Para./.41 AE conversion kit.
Add $100 for 9mm Para. to .41 AE conversion kit.
Add approx. 30%-40% for two-line slide marking "45 ACP Model 45".

UZI EAGLE SERIES – 9mm Para., .40 S&W, or .45 ACP cal., semi-auto double action, various configurations, matte finish with black synthetic grips, 10 shot mag. Mfg. 1997-1998.

* *Uzi Eagle Series Full-Size* – 9mm Para. or .40 S&W cal., 4.4 in. barrel, steel construction, decocking feature, tritium night sights, polygonal rifling. Imported 1997-98.

      $485   **$440**   **$400**   **$365**   **$335**   **$330**   **$275**   Last MSR was $535.

* *Uzi Eagle Series Short Slide* – 9mm Para., .40 S&W, or .45 ACP cal., similar to Full-Size Eagle, except has 3.7 in. barrel. Imported 1997-98.

      $485   **$440**   **$400**   **$365**   **$335**   **$330**   **$275**   Last MSR was $535.

Add $31 for .45 ACP cal.

* *Uzi Eagle Series Compact* – 9mm Para. or .40 S&W cal., available in double action with decocking or double action only, 3 1/2 in. barrel. Imported 1997-98.

      $485   **$440**   **$400**   **$365**   **$335**   **$330**   **$275**   Last MSR was $535.

* *Uzi Eagle Series Polymer Compact* – similar to Compact Eagle, except has compact polymer frame. Imported 1997-98.

      $485   **$440**   **$400**   **$365**   **$335**   **$330**   **$275**   Last MSR was $535.

NOTES

V SECTION

VM HY-TECH LLC
Previous rifle manufacturer located in Phoenix, AZ.

MSR	100%	98%	95%	90%	80%	70%	60%

RIFLES

VM15 – .223 Rem. or 9mm Para. cal., AR-15 style, semi-auto, unique side charging on left side of receiver operated by folding lever allowing easy replacement of scopes, 16, 20, or 24 in. fluted and ported Wilson barrel, aluminum free-floating hand guard, forged lower receiver, A-2 style buttstock with pistol grip, black finish. Mfg. 2002-2009.

| | $800 | $750 | $675 | $600 | $550 | $500 | $400 | Last MSR was $865. |

Add $34 for side-charging loading (new 2005).
Add $310 for 9mm Para. cal.

VM-50 – .50 BMG cal., single shot, 18, 22, 30, or 36 in. Lothar Walther barrel with muzzle brake, aluminum stock, includes bipod, black finish, 22-29 lbs. Mfg. 2004-2009.

| | $2,299 | $2,000 | $1,775 | $1,600 | $1,475 | $1,350 | $1,225 | Last MSR was $2,299. |

Add $40 - $120 for 22-36 in. barrel.

VALKYRIE ARMS LTD.
Current manufacturer located in Olympia, WA. Dealer sales.

Valkyrie Arms Ltd. manufactures semi-auto copies of the M3A1 and DeLisle Commando Carbine. Models include: M3-A1 SA Grease Gun, Delisle Commando Carbine, DeLisle 2000, and the Sten MKII/MKIII pistol and carbine. Custom suppressors are made to order. Currently, Valkyrie Arms is only accepting orders for the Delisle Commando Carbine.

Previously, Valkyrie Arms manufactured the Browning M1919-SA and the DeLisle Sporter Carbine. For more information, including availability and pricing, please contact the company directly (see Trademark Index).

VALMET, INC.
Previous manufacturer located in Jyvaskyla, Finland. Previously imported by Stoeger Industries, Inc. located in South Hackensack, NJ.

The Valmet line was discontinued in 1989 and replaced by Tikka (please refer to the Tikka section in this text) in 1990.

RIFLES: SEMI-AUTO

Magazines for the following models are a major consideration when purchasing a Valmet semi-auto rifle, and prices can run anywhere from $85 (.223 Rem.) up to $250 (.308 Win.). Model 76 .308 mags. will function in a Model 78, but not vice versa.

M-62S TACTICAL DESIGN RIFLE – 7.62x39 Russian, semi-auto version of Finnish M-62, 15 or 30 shot mag., 16 5/8 in. barrel, gas operated, rotary bolt, adj. rear sight, tube steel or wood stock. Mfg. 1962-disc.

| | $2,500 | $2,250 | $1,750 | $1,500 | $1,250 | $1,000 | $900 | |

Add approx. $200 for tube stock.

M-71S – similar to M-62S, except .223 Rem. cal., stamped metal receiver, reinforced resin or wood stock.

| | $1,650 | $1,450 | $1,325 | $1,175 | $975 | $875 | $775 | |

MODEL 76 – .223 Rem., 7.62x39mm, or .308 Win. cal., gas operated semi-auto tactical design rifle, 16 3/4 in. or 20 1/2 (.308 only) in. barrel, 15 or 30 (7.62x39mm only) shot mag., parkerized finish. Federal legislation disc. importation 1989.

	100%	98%	95%	90%	80%	70%	60%	
Plastic Stock	$1,500	$1,250	$1,100	$900	$800	$700	$600	
Wood Stock	$1,700	$1,300	$1,100	$900	$800	$700	$600	Last MSR was $740.

Add approx. 10% for folding stock.
Add 100% for 7.62x39mm cal. with wood stock.
Add 20% for wood stock in .308 Win. cal.

MODEL 78 – .223 Rem., 7.62x39mm, or .308 Win. cal., similar to Model 76, except has 24 1/2 in. barrel, wood stock and forearm, and barrel bipod, 11 lbs. New 1987. Federal legislation disc. importation 1989.

| | $1,750 | $1,525 | $1,375 | $1,175 | $950 | $825 | $700 | Last MSR was $1,060. |

Add 10% for 7.62x39mm cal.

MODEL 82 BULLPUP – .223 Rem. cal., limited importation.

| | $1,675 | $1,425 | $1,200 | $995 | $775 | $650 | $525 | |

MSR	100%	98%	95%	90%	80%	70%	60%

VALTRO

Current manufacturer established during 1988 and located in Brescia, Italy. Currently imported by Valtro USA, located in Hayward, CA. Previously located in San Rafael, CA.

Valtro manufactures both excellent quality slide action and semi-auto shotguns, in addition to a very high quality semi-auto pistol, and a variety of signal pistols. Please contact the importer directly for more product information and availability (see Trademark Index listing).

PISTOLS: SEMI-AUTO

1998 A1 .45 ACP – .45 ACP cal., forged National Match frame and slide, 5 in. barrel, deluxe wood grips, 8 shot mag., ambidextrous safety, blue finish, flat checkered mainspring housing, front and rear slide serrations, beveled mag. well, speed trigger, 40 oz., lifetime guarantee. Very limited importation beginning 1998.

MSR N/A	$5,500	$5,200	$4,950	$4,650	$4,250	$3,850	$3,500

SHOTGUNS: SLIDE ACTION

TACTICAL 98 SHOTGUN – 12 ga. only, 18 1/2 or 20 in. barrel featuring MMC ghost ring sights and integral muzzle brake, 5 shot mag., internal chokes, receiver sidesaddle holds 6 exposed rounds, pistol grip or standard stock, matte black finish, lightweight. Imported 1998 - disc.

	$790	$630	$525	$475	$425	$400	$360

PM5 – 12 ga., 20 in. barrel, 7 shot mag., black synthetic stock with matte black finish, available with or w/o ghost ring sights, optional folding stock. Limited importation beginning 2006.

MSR N/A	$995	$900	$800	$725	$650	$575	$500

VAN DYKE RIFLE DESIGNS

Current rifle manufacturer located in Plainville, KS.

RIFLES: BOLT ACTION

Van Dyke Rifle Designs manufactures bolt action rifles in a variety of configurations, with many options available. Prices listed represent base rifles w/o optics or available options. Please contact the company directly for more information on the variety of available options for each rifle, as well as custom made rifles (see Trademark Index).

DECISION MAKER – .308 Win. cal., 25 in. Shilen stainless steel match grade barrel, teflon coated Earth Tan desert camo finish, A-4 McMillan tactical stock with saddle cheekpiece, three baffle muzzle brake.

MSR $3,425	$3,085	$2,700	$2,315	$2,095	$1,695	$1,395	$1,075

TACTICAL ELIMINATOR SUPER MAGNUM – .338 Lapua cal., Shilen match grade barrel, advanced muzzle brake, designed for extreme distance, wide variety of options available.

Base price on this model is POR.

M24 SUPER MAGNUM – .338 Lapua cal., 28 1/2 or 30 in. Shilen stainless steel free floating barrel, custom chamber dimension, aluminum bedding block, many options available, including rail systems, optics, muzzle brakes, trigger types and stock.

Base price on this model is POR.

REAPER CUSTOM SNIPER – various cals., Shilen stainless steel barrel, Reaper stock design includes aluminum bedding block, three-way adj. buttpad, adj. cheekpiece, long or short action, various options available.

MSR $3,495	$3,150	$2,750	$2,350	$2,150	$1,725	$1,425	$1,100

AI TACTICAL ELIMINATOR I/II – .308 Win. cal., Rem. 700 short action, 22 (Eliminator I) or 24 (Eliminator II) in. Shilen stainless steel match barrel, black matte Teflon finish, multibaffled muzzle brake, Accuracy International stock with adj. cheekpiece and adj. LOP, 5 or 10 shot mag., five sling attachments.

MSR $3,725	$3,360	$2,950	$2,525	$2,285	$1,850	$1,525	$1,175

Subtract $30 for Eliminator II.

* **AI Tactical Eliminator III** – similar to Eliminator I & II, except has Rem. long action, Magnum calibers, longer barrel length.

MSR $3,775	$3,400	$2,975	$2,550	$2,325	$1,875	$1,525	$1,195

DISTANCE DOMINATOR I/II – various cals., Rem. 700 long action, 26 in. Shilen stainless steel barrel (I) or match grade barrel with heavy varmint benchrest contour (II), muzzle brake, H-S Precision heavy Kevlar tactical stock, adj. LOP, variety of options, including floorplate, detachable box mag., and optics.

MSR $3,580	$3,225	$2,820	$2,425	$2,200	$1,775	$1,450	$1,125

Subtract $90 for Distance Dominator II.

MSR	100%	98%	95%	90%	80%	70%	60%

RANGEMASTER SERIES – various cals., designed for long range target shooting.

* ***Rangemaster I*** – M70 short action, controlled round push feed, Shilen stainless steel match grade free floating barrel, glass pillar bedded A4 McMillan tactical stock, adj. cheekpiece, adj. spacer system, sling swivels, deep forend, various finishes.

MSR $3,450	$3,100	$2,710	$2,325	$2,125	$1,700	$1,400	$1,075

* ***Rangemaster II*** – M70 short action, controlled round push feed, 24 in. Shilen stainless steel match grade heavy varmint barrel, stainless bead blast natural texture finish, muzzle brake, A2 McMillan tactical stock, vertical pistol grip, extra high comb, tapered forend, adj. cheekpiece, various finish and available optics.

MSR $3,475	$3,125	$2,735	$2,350	$2,125	$1,725	$1,400	$1,100

* ***Rangemaster III*** – Rem. 700 long action, 26 in. Shilen stainless steel match grade light varmint benchrest contour barrel, triple baffle muzzle brake, bead blast natural stainless color with Teflon silver matte finish, box mag., A3 McMillan lightweight tactical stock, adj. cheekpiece, adj. spacer system, vertical pistol grip, various options and available options.

MSR $3,375	$3,050	$2,675	$2,285	$2,075	$1,675	$1,375	$1,075

* ***Rangemaster IV*** – similar to Rangemaster III, 30 in. Shilen stainless steel barrel, A5 McMillan tactical stock, wider beavertail forend, adj. cheekpiece, Teflon OD green finish, double baffle semi-box muzzle brake, box mag., various options and available options.

MSR $3,575	$3,225	$2,825	$2,425	$2,200	$1,775	$1,450	$1,125

VECTOR ARMS, INC.
Current tactical rifle and parts manufacturer located in N. Salt Lake, UT.

RIFLES: SEMI-AUTO

Vector Arms offers the following semi-auto tactical style rifles currently: V-53 (semi-auto version of the HK53 - $1,350 MSR in 2009), V51 (semi-auto version of the HK-91, $1,024 MSR in 2009). Vector also offered the V-93 (semi-auto version of the HK33 - $1,104 last MSR), Uzi full size post-ban ($595 last MSR), and the RPD (drum or belt fed - $1,999 last MSR). Please contact the company directly for more information on these rifles, including availability and options (see Trademark Index).

VEKTOR
Current trademark established during 1953 as part of LEW (Lyttelton Engineering Work). In 1995, Vektor became a separate division of Denel of South Africa.

Vektor has manufactured a wide variety of firearms configurations, including semi-auto pistols, bolt action and slide action rifles, as well as military arms for South African law enforcement for quite some time. Currently, the company does not make any civilian small arms.

PISTOLS: SEMI-AUTO

All Vektor pistols feature polygonal rifling, excluding the Z88.

MODEL CP1 – 9mm Para. cal., 4 in. barrel, compact model with unique aesthetics and ergonomic design allowing no buttons or levers on exterior surfaces, hammerless, striker firing system, black or nickel finished slide, 10 shot mag., approx. 25 1/2 oz. Imported 1999-2000.

	$440	$400	$360	$330	$300	$280	$260	Last MSR was $480.

Add $20 for nickel slide finish.

This model was recalled due to design problems.

MODEL Z88 – 9mm Para. cal., double action, patterned after the M92 Beretta, 5 in. barrel, steel construction, black synthetic grips, 10 shot mag., 35 oz. Importation began 1999.

	$550	$495	$450	$400	$360	$330	$295	Last MSR was $620.

MODEL SP1 – 9mm Para. cal., double action, 5 in. barrel with polygonal rifling, wraparound checkered synthetic grips, matte blue or normal black finish, 2.2. lbs. Importation began 1999.

	$535	$485	$445	$395	$360	$330	$295	Last MSR was $600.

Add $30 for natural anodized or nickel finish.
Add $230 for Sport Pistol with compensated barrel.

* ***Model SP1 Compact (General's Model)*** – similar to Model SP1, except is compact variation with 4 in. barrel, 25.4 oz. Importation began 1999.

	$575	$510	$460	$410	$360	$330	$295	Last MSR was $650.

* ***Model SP1 Sport Pistol/Tuned*** – similar to Model SP1, except is available with tuned action or target pistol features. Importation began 1999.

	$1,050	$900	$775	$650	$525	$400	$350	Last MSR was $1,200.

Add $100 for Target Pistol with dual color finish.

MSR	100%	98%	95%	90%	80%	70%	60%	

MODEL SP2 – .40 S&W cal., otherwise similar to Model SP1. Importation began in 1999.

| | $575 | $510 | $460 | $410 | $360 | $330 | $295 | Last MSR was $650. |

Add $190 for 9mm Para. conversion kit.

* **Model SP2 Compact (General's Model)** – similar to Model SP2, except is compact variation. Importation began 1999.

| | $575 | $510 | $460 | $410 | $360 | $330 | $295 | Last MSR was $650. |

* **Model SP2 Competition** – competition variation of the Model SP2 featuring 5 7/8 in. barrel, additional magazine guide, enlarged safety levers and mag. catch, and straight trigger, 35 oz. Importation began 2000.

| | $850 | $775 | $675 | $575 | $510 | $460 | $395 | Last MSR was $1,000. |

RIFLES: SLIDE ACTION

H5 – .223 Rem. cal., 18 or 22 in. barrel, rotating bolt, uncheckered forearm and thumb-hole stock with pad, includes 4X scope with long eye relief, 9 lbs., 7 oz.-10 1/4 lbs. Imported 2000-disc.

| | $775 | $650 | $575 | $510 | $460 | $410 | $350 | Last MSR was $850. |

VEPR. RIFLES

Currently manufactured by Molot JSC (Vyatskie Polyany Machine Building Factory) located in Russia. Currently imported by ZDF Import/Export, Inc., located in Salt Lake City, UT. Previously imported during 2004 by European American Armory, located in Sharps, FL.

RIFLES: SEMI-AUTO

VEPR HUNTER (VEPR II) CARBINE/RIFLE – .223 Rem., .270 Win. (new 2004), .30-06 (new 2004), .308 Win., or 7.62x39mm (new 2001) cal., features Vepr.'s semi-auto action, 16 (.223 Rem. or 7.62x39mm cal.), 20 1/2 (carbine, .308 Win. only, disc.), 21.6 or 23 1/4 (disc.) in. barrel with adj. rear sight, scope mount rail built into receiver top, standard or optional thumbhole checkered walnut stock with recoil pad and forend, paddle mag. release, 5 or 10 shot mag., approx 8.6 lbs.

| MSR $550 | $550 | $495 | $440 | $395 | $365 | $335 | $300 | |

SUPER VEPR – .308 Win. cal., thumbhole stock. Limited importation 2001-2007.

| | $950 | $850 | $750 | $650 | $550 | $475 | $400 | |

VICTOR ARMS CORPORATION

Previous manufacturer located in Houston, TX.

Victor Arms Corporation manufactured limited quantities of a .22 LR upper unit for the AR-15. The V22 and its .22 LR cal. magazine replaced the standard .223 upper assembly/magazine. Additionally, a complete protoype gun was also manufactured.

VIGILANCE RIFLES

Current rifle manufacturer located in Redlands, CA.

RIFLES: SEMI-AUTO

VR1 – .338 Lapua, .375 Cheytac, .408 Cheytac, or .505 Gibbs cal., gas operated, stainless steel upper receiver, bull barrel, titanium muzzle brake, premium wood stock in a variety of colors or synthetic tactical stock, two-stage trigger, detachable 5 shot mag., many options available, weights vary according to configuration.

| MSR $7,875 | $7,450 | $6,750 | $5,900 | $5,200 | $4,500 | $3,800 | $2,850 | |

VIPER

Current trademark imported by Tristar, located in North Kansas City, MO. Please refer to the Tristar section.

VOLKMANN CUSTOM, INC.

Current pistol manufacturer established in 2007 and located in Lakewood, CO.

Volkmann Custom, INc. was founded in 2007 by Luke Volkmann and George Horne. Volkmann was formerly a pistol builder for Ed Brown Products.

PISTOLS: SEMI-AUTO

All pistols are hand built, and a variety of options are available. Please contact the company directly (see Trademark Index). Add $100 for ambidextrous safety. Add $250 for custom finish. Add $300 for engraving. Add $250 for custom serial number.

COMBAT CUSTOM – .45 ACP cal., 5 in. barrel, full size frame, black Rockote or blue finish, fixed tritium night sights, 25 LPI checkering.

| MSR $2,395 | $2,395 | $2,150 | $1,900 | $1,650 | $1,425 | $1,275 | $1,050 | |

MSR	100%	98%	95%	90%	80%	70%	60%

COMBATANT – .45 ACP cal., 4 1/4 in. barrel, Commander size frame, black Rockote or blue finish, fixed tritium night sights, 25 LPI checkering.

MSR $2,395	$2,395	$2,150	$1,900	$1,650	$1,425	$1,275	$1,050

COMBATANT CARRY – .45 ACP cal., 4 1/4 in. barrel, Commander size frame and slide with Ed Brown Bobtail mainspring housing, Rockote black, OD green, titanium blue, or desert tan finish, fixed tritium night sights, 25 LPI checkering.

MSR $2,495	$2,495	$2,225	$1,950	$1,675	$1,425	$1,275	$1,050

VOLQUARTSEN CUSTOM, LTD.
Current pistol/rifle customizer and manufacturer established in 1974 and located in Carroll, IA. Dealer sales.

RIFLES: SEMI-AUTO

Current Volquartsen stock configurations include: brown synthetic, grey synthetic, Hogue, McMillan Sporter, and McMillan thumbhole stock. Base values below represent standard Hogue synthetic stock.

Add approx. $183 for grey/brown synthetic stock on most models listed below.
Add approx. $357 for McMillan Sport or thumbhole stock on the models listed below.
Add $291 for laminated thumbhole stock on most models listed below.

EVOLUTION MODEL – .204 Ruger or .223 Rem. cal., gas operated, stainless steel receiver, trigger guard, and bolt, integral machined Picatinny rail on received top, brown laminate stock with extended Monte Carlo cheekpiece, 20 or 24 (.204 Ruger only) in. standard barrel, 10 shot AR-15 style mag., 10 lbs. New 2005.

MSR $2,114	$1,950	$1,700	$1,475	$1,225	$1,000	$850	$725

Add $136 for brown thumbhole stock.
Add $14 for .204 Ruger cal.

VOLUNTEER ENTERPRISES
Previous manufacturer located in Knoxville, TN.
Volunteer Enterprises became Commando Arms after 1978.

CARBINES

COMMANDO MARK III CARBINE – .45 ACP cal., semi-auto, blowback action, 16 1/2 in. barrel, aperture sight, stock styled after the Auto-Ordnance "Tommy Gun." Mfg. 1969-1976.

	$750	$675	$625	$565	$525	$475	$425

Add 10% for vertical grip.

COMMANDO MARK 9 – similar to Mark III in 9mm Para. cal.

	$675	$625	$565	$525	$475	$425	$375

Add 10% for vertical grip.

VULCAN ARMAMENT, INC.
Current rifle manufacturer established in 2003 and located in South St. Paul, MN.

CARBINES/RIFLES: SEMI-AUTO

Vulcan Armament makes a wide variety of AR-15 styled semi-auto carbines and rifles, including configurations for military and law enforcement. Please contact the factory directly for more information about options and availability (see Trademark Index).

All rifles includes sling, manual, cleaning kit, Vulcan knife, and hard case.
Add $20-$25 for removable carry handle.

V15 9MM CARBINE SERIES – 9mm Para. cal., 16 in. chromemoly vanadium steel barrel with threaded muzzle, A2 front sight bases with bayonet lug, all parts manganese phosphate finished, M4 contour, M4 length handguard, full heat shield, A2 upper receiver or A3 flattop receiver, carry handle, adj. sights, Picatinny rail, black anodized hard coat finish, forward assist, hinged ejection port cover, six position adj. buttstock, removable flash hider, accepts Sten magazines, 6 1/2 lbs.

MSR $860	$775	$685	$585	$525	$425	$350	$275

V15 DISPATCHER SERIES – .223 Rem. cal., 16 in. chromemoly vanadium steel barrel with threaded muzzle, gas block mounted under the handguard, A2 flash hider, A2 front sight bases, bayonet lug, fixed A2 stock, A2 or A3 flattop upper reciever, black hard coat anodized finish, 6 1/2 lbs.

MSR $860	$775	$685	$585	$525	$425	$350	$275

V15 M4 CARBINE SERIES – .223 Rem. cal., 16 in. chromemoly vanadium steel button rifled barrel with threaded

MSR	100%	98%	95%	90%	80%	70%	60%

muzzle, A2 flash hider, A2 front sight bases, bayonet lug, A2 or A3 flattop upper reciever, black hard coat anodized finish, M4 length handguard with full heat shields, six position M4 buttstock, 6.4lbs.

| MSR $860 | $775 | $685 | $585 | $525 | $425 | $350 | $275 |

V15 POLYMER SERIES – .223 Rem. cal., 16 or 20 in. chromemoly vanadium steel button rifled H-Bar barrel with threaded muzzle, all parts manganese phosphate finished, A2 flash hider, A2 sight bases, bayonet lug, six position M4 buttstock, Picatinny rail, A2 or A3 polymer receiver, forward assist, hinged ejection port cover.

| MSR $700 | $625 | $550 | $475 | $425 | $350 | $280 | $225 |

V15 TARGET RIFLE – .223 Rem. cal., 20 in. chromemoly vanadium steel threaded button rifled heavy barrel, A2 flash hider, all parts manganese phosphate finished, rifle length handguard, full heat shield, A2 or A3 flattop upper receiver, Picatinny rail, black hard coat anodized finish, fixed A2 buttstock, removable flash hider, aluminum spacer, trap door buttplate.

| MSR $860 | $775 | $685 | $585 | $525 | $425 | $350 | $275 |

Add $25 for A2 carrying handle.

V15 VARMINATOR SERIES – .223 Rem. cal., 20 or 24 in. stainless steel bull barrel, full length aluminum handguard, hard coat anodized finish, aluminum gas block, four Picatinny rails, forged A3 upper receiver, forward assist, hinged ejection port cover, fixed A2 buttstock, aluminum spacer, trap door buttplate, 9.2 lbs.

| MSR $950 | $850 | $750 | $635 | $580 | $465 | $380 | $295 |

V15 200 SERIES – 7.62x39mm cal., 16 in. chromemoly vanadium steel threaded barrel, A2 flash hider, A2 front sight bases, bayonet lug, all parts manganese phosphate finished, M4 length handguard, full heat shields, forged A2 or A3 flattop upper receiver, forward assist, hinged ejection port, six position buttstock, 6.4 lbs

| MSR $900 | $815 | $715 | $615 | $555 | $450 | $365 | $285 |

* **V15 200 Piston Series** – .223 Rem. cal., similar to V15 200 Series, except has proprietary short stroke gas piston operation.

| MSR $950 | $860 | $750 | $650 | $585 | $475 | $385 | $300 |

V15 202 MODULAR CARBINE – .223 Rem. cal., 16 in. chromemoly vanadium steel threaded barrel, A2 flash hider, all parts manganese phosphate finished, A3 flattop upper receiver, four Picatinny rails, black hard coat anodized finish, forward assist, hinged ejection port cover, modular handguard, low profile aircraft aluminum gas block, six position buttstock, 6 1/2 lbs.

| MSR $925 | $835 | $730 | $625 | $565 | $460 | $375 | $295 |

V18 SERIES – .223 Rem. cal., 16 1/2 or 20 in. chrome lined barrel, copy of the AR-180, machined gas block, front sight base, Picatinny rail, FAL style handguard, short stroke gas piston, ambidextrous charging handle, carbon fiber lower, AR pistol grip, polymer FAL stock, rubber buttpad, aluminum recoil plate, last round hold open, 6.8 lbs.

| MSR $689 | $625 | $545 | $475 | $425 | $345 | $280 | $220 |

V73 SERIES – 7.62x39mm, 223 Rem., or .308 Win. cal., copy of Israeli Galil, 100% part interchangeability, including mags. and accessories, machined monoblock receiver, skeletonized black tactical stock, available in AR, ARM, SAR, and Micro configurations.

| MSR $1,550 | $1,395 | $1,220 | $1,050 | $950 | $765 | $630 | $495 |

Add $300 for .308 Win. cal.
Add $100 for ARM model with top carry handle.
Add $449 for SAR or Micro configuration.

RIFLES: BOLT ACTION

All rifles include manual, bipod, removable muzzle brake, gun lock, Vulcan knife, cleaning rod and brush, and scope rail.

V50 SERIES – .50 BMG cal., single shot, 60 degree bolt throw, capable of hits at ranges exceeding one mile, scope mounting rail, standard Mauser pattern trigger, thick recoil pad, "Shark Fin" muzzle brake, available in SS-100 (30 in. barrel, brown laminated thumbhole wood stock), SS-200 (36 in. barrel, grey laminated thumbhole wood stock), SS-300 (30 in. barrel, retractable black tactical stock) or the SS-400 Bullpup (30 in. barrel, bullpup stock).

| MSR $1,900 | $1,725 | $1,525 | $1,295 | $1,175 | $950 | $775 | $600 |

Add $300 for SS-200.

The SS-400 Bullpup model is POR.

W SECTION

WAFFEN HIENDLMAYER

Current manufacturer located in Eggenfelden, Germany. No current U.S. importation.

Klaus Hiendlmayer specializes in custom guns and engraving, and manufactures a version of the SIG 550 sniper rifle and prices range from €1,999-€2,750. Please contact the company directly for more information, including domestic availability (see Trademark Index).

WALTHER

Current manufacturer established in 1886, and currently located in Ulm, Germany 1953 to date. Currently imported and distributed beginning 2002 by Smith & Wesson, located in Springfield, MA. Walther target pistols and target rifles are distributed by Champions Choice located in La Vergne, TN. All target, competiton and service pistols are also currently imported, distributed, and factory serviced by Earl's Repair Service, Inc., located in Tewksbury, MA since 1984. Previously imported and distributed 1998-2001 by Walther USA LLC, located in Springfield, MA, and by Interarms located in Alexandria, VA circa 1962-1999. Previously manufactured in Zella-Mehlis, Germany 1886 to 1945. Walther was sold to Umarex Sportwaffen GmbH circa 1994, and company headquarters are located in Arnsberg, Germany.

The calibers listed in the Walther Pistol sections are listed in American caliber designations. The German metric conversion is as follows: .22 LR - 5.6mm, .25 ACP - 6.35mm, .32 ACP - 7.65mm, and .380 ACP - 9mm kurz. The metric caliber designations in most cases will be indicated on the left slide legend for German mfg. pistols listed in the Walther section.

For more information and current pricing on both new and used Walther airguns, please refer to the *Blue Book of Airguns* by Dr. Robert Beeman & John Allen (also online).

MSR	100%	98%	95%	90%	80%	70%	60%

PISTOLS: SEMI-AUTO, POST-WAR

Smith & Wesson has placed a recall on all Walther PPK and PPK/S pistols manufactured by Smith & Wesson from March 21, 2002-Feb. 3, 2009. Ser. no. ranges subject to this recall are as follows: 0010BAB-9999BAB, 0000BAC-9999BAC, 0000BAD-9999BAD, 0000BAE-999BAE, 0000BAF-9999BAF, 0000BAH-9999BAH, 00000BAJ-9999BAJ, 0000BAK-9999BAK, 0000BAL-5313BAL, 0000BAM-1320BAM, 0000LTD-0499LTD, 0001PPK-1500PPK, 0026REP-0219REP, and 0001WLE-0459WLE. Smith & Wesson has advised all owners to discontinue usage and return the pistol to S&W for free repair. Please contact S&W directly for more information (see Trademark Index).

MODEL P88 & VARIATIONS – 9mm Para. or 9x21mm cal., double action, alloy frame, 4 in. barrel, 15 shot button release mag., fully ambidextrous, decocking lever, matte finish, adj. rear sight, internal safeties, plastic grips, 31 1/2 oz. Mfg. 1987-93.

| | $1,100 | $925 | $750 | $600 | $500 | $450 | $400 | Last MSR was $1,129. |

P88 cutaways were also mfg. in small quantities for instructional use. Current pricing for a mint specimen is approx. $2,000.

* **Model P88 Compact** – 9mm Para. or 9x21mm cal., 3.93 in. barrel, 14* (disc.) or 10 (C/B 1994) shot mag., 29 oz. Imported 1993-2003.

| | $975 | $800 | $650 | $550 | $500 | $475 | $450 | Last MSR was $900. |

Add 25% for 14 shot mag.

P99 & VARIATIONS – 9mm Para., 9x21mm (limited importation 1996), or .40 S&W (new 1999) cal., 4 (9mm Para.) or 4.1 (.40 S&W) in. barrel, polymer frame, 10, 12 (.40 S&W cal. only), 15, or 16 (9mm Para. cal. only, disc. 2006) shot mag., standard, anti-stress (traditional double action, AS Model, new 2004), or quick action (QA, allowing consistent SA trigger performance) trigger, decocking, and internal striker safeties, cocking and loaded chamber indicators, choice of matte black, QPQ (mfg. 1999-2003) finished (silver colored) slide, or titanium coated (mfg. 2003-2006) finish, ambidextrous mag. release, ergonomic black, desert tan (disc. 2008), or green (Military model, new 1999) synthetic grip with interchangeable backstrap, adj. rear sight, 25 oz. Importation began 1995.

| MSR $825 | $695 | $595 | $525 | $475 | $425 | $365 | $315 |

Add $153 for tritium sight set with green 3-dot system or $109 for white 3-dot metal sights.
Add $110 for night sight kit (new 2010).
Add $31 for titanium finish (disc. 2006).
Add $125 for 9x21mm cal. (disc.).

Engraved P99s were also available in the following configurations in 9mm Para. cal. only - Grade I Arabesque ($3,700 last MSR), Grade II Goldline ($4,200 last MSR), Grade III Arabesque w/gold ($4,660 last MSR).

* **P99 Compact** – 9mm Para. or .40 S&W cal., 3 1/2 in. barrel, 8 (.40 S&W cal.) or 10 shot mag. with finger extension, available in QA, AS, or DAO (disc. 2006), Weaver rail, compact frame, blue finish only, 20 oz. New 2004.

| MSR $825 | $695 | $595 | $525 | $475 | $425 | $365 | $315 |

MSR	100%	98%	95%	90%	80%	70%	60%

P990 – similar to P99, except is double action only, features Walther's constant pull trigger system, black, QPQ slide finish, or Military Model (green), 25 oz. Mfg. 1998-2003.

| | $550 | $475 | $425 | $385 | $350 | $325 | $295 | Last MSR was $644. |

RIFLES: DISC.

MODEL WA-2000 – .300 Win. Mag. (55 mfg., standard) or .308 Win. (92 mfg., optional) cal., ultra-deluxe semi-auto, 25.6 in. barrel, 5 or 6 shot mag., optional extras include aluminum case, spare mags., integral bipod, adj. tools and leather sling, regular or night vision scope, special order only, 16 3/4 lbs. Disc. 1988.

| | $36,000 | $32,000 | $29,000 | $27,000 | $25,000 | $22,500 | $20,000 |

A 7.5 Swiss cal. conversion kit was also optional on this model.

RIFLES: CURRENT/RECENT MFG.

Except for the G22 and GSP rifles, the following models are available from Champion's Choice.

MODEL G22 SEMI-AUTO – .22 LR cal., bullpup design with thumbhole stock, fire control and mag. integrated in rear of stock, black synthetic, carbon fiber, or camo (disc. 2006) stock, adj. sliding sights, right or left-hand controls and ejection, blue or military green finish, Weaver style rails on rear sight/carry handle, lower forearm, and on front right mount, 20 in. barrel, 10 shot mag., approx. 6 lbs. New 2004.

| MSR $509 | | $435 | $380 | $330 | $290 | $250 | $225 | $195 |

Add $39 for scope or $67 for laser or $102 for red-dot sights (disc. 2009).
Add $56 for carbon fiber stock (disc. 2007) or $50 for camo stock (disc. 2006).

WEATHERBY

Current trademark manufactured and imported by Weatherby located Paso Robles, CA since 2006. Previously located in Atascadero, CA 1995-2006, and in South Gate, CA, 1945-1995. Weatherby began manufacturing rifles in the U.S. during early 1995. Dealer and distributor sales.

Weatherby is an importer and manufacturer of long arms. Earlier production was from Germany and Italy, and German mfg. is usually what is collectible. Rifles are currently produced in the U.S., while O/U shotguns are made in Italy and semi-autos are mfg. in Turkey.

Weatherby is well-known for their high-velocity proprietary rifle calibers.

Weatherby offers a research authentication service for Weatherby firearms. The cost is $50 per serial number ($75 for custom rifles, $100 for special editions and commemoratives), and includes a certificate signed by Roy Weatherby Jr. and company historian Dean Rumbaugh. Please contact the company directly for more information regarding this service (see Trademark Index).

Early Weatherby rifles used a Mathieu Arms action in the 1950s - primarily since it was available in left-hand action. Right-handed actions were normally mfg. from the FN Mauser type.

RIFLES: BOLT ACTION, MARK V SERIES

Pre-Mark V production started in 1945 and ended in 1961. Initially, rifles were customized from customer supplied guns, and this ended circa 1949. Between 1949-1963, Weatherby manufactured rifles in Southgate from FN Mauser actions in various cals., including the .257, .270, 7mm, .300, and .375 Wby. Mag. cals. From 1955-1959, Southgate also manufactured guns using the Mathieu left-hand action. Additionally, Schultz & Larson from Denmark was subcontracted to make rifles in .378 Wby. Mag. circa 1955-1962. Between 1956-1962, Southgate manufactured a .460 Wby. Mag. cal. using the Brevex Magnum action. Sako of Finland was also subcontracted circa 1957-1961 to produce rifles using a FN Mauser action. Initial Mark V production began in Southgate circa 1958-1959. During 1959-1973, J.P. Sauer of W. Germany was subcontracted to make the Mark V in a variety of calibers up to .460 Wby. Mag. These earlier pre-Mark V rifles will have a 20%-30% premium, depending on original condition and caliber.

In 1992, 24 in. barrels were disc. on most calibers of .300 or greater (including Models Mark V Deluxe, Fibermark, Lazermark, and Euromark). The Mark V action has also been manufactured in Japan.

All recently manufactured Weatherby Magnums in .30-378, .338-378, .378, .416, and .460 cal. are equipped with an Accubrake.

TRR (THREAT RESPONSE RIFLE) – .223 Rem., .308 Win., .300 Win. Mag. (disc. 2002), .300 Wby. Mag. (disc. 2002), .30-378 Wby. Mag. (disc. 2002), or .338-.378 Wby. Mag. (disc. 2002) cal., 22 in. barrel, 5 shot mag., Mark V action with black finished metal and black hybrid composite stock, various barrel lengths, optional Picatinny style ring and base system, 8 1/2-10 1/2 lbs. Mfg. 2002-2005.

| | $1,400 | $1,225 | $1,050 | $950 | $770 | $630 | $490 | Last MSR was $1,737. |

Add $52 for .300 Win. Mag. or .300 Wby. Mag. cals. (disc. 2002).
Add $208 for .30-378 Wby. Mag. or .338-378 Wby. Mag. cals. (disc. 2002).

MSR	100%	98%	95%	90%	80%	70%	60%

RIFLES: BOLT ACTION, CUSTOM SHOP

TRCM (THREAT RESPONSE CUSTOM MAGNUM) – .300 Win. Mag., .300 Wby. Mag., .30-378 Wby. Mag., or .338-.378 Wby. Mag. cal., Mark V action with ergonomic, fully adjustable composite stock, black finished metal, various barrel lengths, optional Picatinny style ring and base system. Mfg. 2002-2009.

| | $2,325 | $2,035 | $1,745 | $1,580 | $1,280 | $1,045 | $815 | Last MSR was $2,899. |

Add $270 for .30-378 Wby. Mag. or .338-378 Wby. Mag. cals.
Add $499 for desert camo stock and titanium nitride coating.

SUB-MOA TRR PACKAGE – .300 Win. Mag., .300 Wby. Mag., .30-378 Wby. Mag., or .338-378 Wby. Mag. cal., 26 in. Kreiger barrel with Accubrake, adj. trigger, laminated stock with T-6 aluminum bedding system with three position buttstock, includes Leupold 4.5-14x50 LRT M1 scope, Talley ring rail, bipod, and hard case. New 2010.

| MSR $3,999 | $3,350 | $2,930 | $2,515 | $2,280 | $1,845 | $1,510 | $1,175 | |

RIFLES: BOLT ACTION, VANGUARD SERIES

All currently manufactured Vanguard rifles are shipped with a factory three shot target, guaranteeing 1.5 in. accuracy at 100 yards.

* **Vanguard Sub-MOA TR** – .223 Rem. or .308 Win. cal., 22 in. countoured barrel with recessed target crown, 5 shot mag., laminated Monte Carlo composite stock with beavertail forearm and Pachmayr Decelerator pad, dual swivel studs, adj. trigger, guaranteed to shoot 3-shoot group of .99 in. or less with factory or premium ammo, 8 3/4 lbs. New 2010.

| MSR $999 | $850 | $745 | $640 | $580 | $470 | $385 | $300 | |

WEAVER ARMS CORPORATION

Previous manufacturer located in Escondido, CA circa 1984-1990.

CARBINES

NIGHTHAWK CARBINE – 9mm Para. cal., semi-auto tactical design carbine, fires from closed bolt, 16.1 in. barrel, retractable shoulder stock, 25, 32, 40, or 50 shot mag. (interchangeable with Uzi), ambidextrous safety, parkerized finish, 6 1/2 lbs. Mfg. 1987-90.

| | $675 | $600 | $525 | $450 | $375 | $325 | $300 | Last MSR was $575. |

PISTOLS: SEMI-AUTO

NIGHTHAWK PISTOL – 9mm Para. cal., closed bolt semi-auto, 10 or 12 in. barrel, alloy upper receiver, ambidextrous safety, black finish, 5 lbs. Mfg. 1987-90.

| | $800 | $700 | $625 | $550 | $475 | $425 | $350 | Last MSR was $475. |

DAN WESSON FIREARMS

Current trademark manufactured by Dan Wesson Firearms beginning 2005, and located in Norwich, NY. Distributed beginning 2005 by CZ-USA, located in Kansas City, KS. Previously manufactured by New York International Corp. (NYI) located in Norwich, NY 1997-2005. Distributor and dealer sales.

PISTOLS: SEMI-AUTO

Until 2005, Dan Wesson manufactured a complete line of .45 ACP 1911 style semi-auto pistols. Previously manufactured models include: Seven (last MSR was $999), Seven Stainless (last MSR was $1,099), Guardian (last MSR was $799), the Guardian Deuce (last MSR was $799), the Dave Pruit Signature Series (last MSR was $899), and the Hi-Cap (last MSR was $689).

PATRIOT 1911 SERIES – .45 ACP or 10mm (Commander slide and frame only) cal., 4 1/4 (Commander) or 5 in. stainless steel match barrel, 1911 Series 70 action, external extractor, fitted parts, and many high-end components by McCormick, Ed Brown, Nowlin, etc., each gun shipped with test target, variations include Patriot Expert (blue or stainless, Bo-Mar style target sights), Patriot Marksman (blue or stainless, fixed sights), AAA cocobolo double diamond checkered grips with gold medallions, 2.3 lbs. Mfg. 2001-2005.

| | $825 | $750 | $650 | $550 | $475 | $425 | $375 | Last MSR was $929. |

Add $20 for 5 in. Patriot with blued action.
Add $70 for 5 in. barrel in stainless steel.
Add $30 for checkered front grip strap.
Add $70 for bobtail frame.

KO3 PANTHER SERIES – .45 ACP cal., full size, 5 in. barrel, Series 70 pistol with cast alloy frame, external extractor, Chip McCormick beavertail with Commander style hammer, forged conventional round top slide, fixed rear sight, matte bead blasted frame and slide top, slide sides are polished, blue or stainless, Hogue rubber grips. Disc.

| | $595 | $525 | $450 | $415 | $385 | $350 | $325 | |

Add $20 for stainless steel.

MSR	100%	98%	95%	90%	80%	70%	60%

PM POINTMAN SERIES – .45 ACP or 10mm cal., full size, 5 in. target barrel, features Chip McCormick beavertail with Commander style hammer, forged conventional round top slide, high target rib or low profile Clark style sights with adj. white outline or Bo-Mar rear sight, blue or stainless, PM1-S is standard gun, checkered exotic hardwood grips. Disc. 2005.

| | $725 | $650 | $575 | $500 | $425 | $385 | $350 | Last MSR was $809. |

Add $50 for checkered front grip strap.
Add $50 for high or Ausi rib (Model PMA-S).
Add $100 for blue finish with Clark/Bo-Mar rib and sights (Model PMA-B, disc.).

POINTMAN SEVEN – .40 S&W (new 2009), .45 ACP or 10mm cal., 5 in. barrel, features stainless steel frame and slide, patterned after the Colt Series 70 semi-auto, 7 shot mag., double slide serrations, many target features, diamond checkered cocobolo grips, 38 oz. Mfg. 2005-2009.

| | $1,050 | $900 | $775 | $700 | $600 | $500 | $400 | Last MSR was $1,158. |

Add $33 for 10mm cal.
Add $31 for .40 S&W cal.
Add $111 for Desert Tan teflon finish with black grips and controls, (.45 ACP cal. only, new 2009).

POINTMAN NINE – 9mm Para. cal., similar to Pointman Seven, 5 in. barrel, stainless steel frame, front strap checkering, fiber optic front sight, cocobolo grips, 38 1/2 oz. Mfg. 2009.

| | $1,095 | $925 | $800 | $700 | $600 | $500 | $450 | Last MSR was $1,247. |

MARKSMAN – .45 ACP cal., stainless steel frame, 5 in. barrel, similar to Pointman, except slimmer design, 38 1/2 oz. Mfg. 2009.

| | $1,225 | $1,000 | $900 | $775 | $650 | $550 | $475 | Last MSR was $1,391. |

PM3-P MINOR SERIES – .45 ACP cal., full size, 5 in. barrel, Series 70 pistol with cast alloy frame, Chip McCormick beavertail with Commander style hammer, forged conventional round top slide, fixed rear sight, matte bead blasted frame and slide top, slide sides are polished, blue or stainless, checkered exotic hardwood grips. Disc.

| | $515 | $450 | $415 | $385 | $350 | $325 | $295 | |

GLOBAL – .45 ACP or 10mm cal., 5 or 6 in. barrel, full size frame, steel or stainless steel, choice of accessory light rail or full length dust cover. Disc. 2005.

| | $1,000 | $900 | $800 | $700 | $600 | $475 | $350 | Last MSR was $1,149. |

RZ-10 RAZORBACK SPECIAL EDITION – 10mm cal., full size, 5 in. barrel, Colt Series 70 design with forged stainless frame and slide, Bo-Mar adj. rear sight, match barrel, bushing, and link, match grade trigger, sear, hammer, and beavertail, checkered synthetic or rubber (new 2006) grips, limited mfg. 2002-2004, and resumed 2006-2009.

| | $1,050 | $900 | $775 | $700 | $600 | $500 | $450 | Last MSR was $1,191. |

Add $257 for Sportsman Model with VZ G10 black operator grips, FO front sights and adj. sights (new 2009).

RZ-45 HERITAGE – .45 ACP cal. only, 5 in. barrel, stainless steel frame, SA, fixed night sights, manual thumb safety, 38 1/2 oz. New 2009.

| MSR $1,275 | $1,050 | $875 | $775 | $700 | $600 | $500 | $400 | |

COMMANDER CLASSIC BOBTAIL – .45 ACP or 10mm cal., 4 1/4 in. barrel, stainless steel frame and slide, Colt Series 70 design, Ed Brown Bobtail mainspring housing, many target features, diamond checkered cocobolo grips, 34 oz. Mfg. 2005-2009.

| | $1,050 | $900 | $775 | $700 | $600 | $500 | $450 | Last MSR was $1,191. |

Add $33 for 10mm cal.
Add $339 for two-tone finish and black ceramic coated slide (10mm cal. only, new 2009).

BOBTAIL CO – .45 ACP cal., similar to Commander Classic Bobtail, except has anodized aluminum frame, stainless steel slide, black ceramic coat finish and fixed night sights. New 2009.

| MSR $1,530 | $1,325 | $1,075 | $950 | $825 | $650 | $550 | $475 | |

VALOR – .45 ACP cal., black ceramic coated finish or stainless steel (new 2010), slimline VZ or GT grips, adj. (disc.) or Heinie Ledge (new 2010) tritium night sights. New 2008.

| MSR $1,594 | $1,425 | $1,150 | $925 | $825 | $725 | $625 | $550 | |

Add $319 for black finish.

* ***Valor Bobtail Commander*** – similar to Valor, except has black or stainless steel frame, bobtail commander style. New 2010.

| MSR $1,658 | $1,450 | $1,165 | $940 | $825 | $725 | $625 | $550 | |

Add $382 for black finish.

SS CUSTOM – .40 S&W cal., stainless steel construction, fiber optic front sight, ambidextrous safety, shark grips. Mfg. 2008-2009.

| | $1,225 | $1,000 | $900 | $775 | $650 | $550 | $475 | Last MSR was $1,389. |

MSR	100%	98%	95%	90%	80%	70%	60%

GUARDIAN – 9mm Para. cal., black light alloy frame, bobtail commander, tritium sight. New 2010.

MSR $1,530	**$1,325**	**$1,075**	**$950**	**$825**	**$650**	**$550**	**$475**

REVOLVERS: DOUBLE ACTION

Dan Wesson has also manufactured a variety of revolver packages that were available by special order only.

MODEL 715 SMALL FRAME SERIES – .357 Mag. cal., 6 shot, stainless steel, 2 1/2, 4, 6, 8, or 10 in. heavy barrel with VR and full ejector shroud, rubber wraparound finger groove grips, interchangeable barrels. Mfg. 2002-2004.

	$625	**$550**	**$475**	**$425**	**$375**	**$325**	**$275**	Last MSR was $709.

Add $50 for 4 in., $90 for 6 in., $150 for 8 in., or $190 for 10 in. barrel.

This model was also available as a pistol pack with 4 barrels and case. MSR was $1,699.

WESSON FIREARMS CO. INC.

Previous manufacturer located in Palmer, MA 1992-95. Previously located in Monson, MA until 1992. In late 1990, ownership of Dan Wesson Arms changed (within the family), and the new company was renamed Wesson Firearms Co., Inc.

REVOLVERS: DOUBLE ACTION

As a guideline, the following information is provided on Wesson Firearms frames. The smallest frames are Models 738P and 38P. Small frame models include 22, 722, 22M, 722M, 32, 732, 322, 7322, 8-2, 708, 9-2, 709, 14-2, 714, 15-2, and 715-2. Large frames include 41, 741, 44, 744, 45, and 745. SuperMag frame models include 40, 740, 375 (disc.), 414 (new 1995), 7414 (new 1995), 445, and 7445. Small frames are sideplate design, while large frames are solid frame construction. Dan Wesson revolvers were mfg. with solid rib barrels as standard equipment.

MODEL 14 (1970s Mfg.) – similar to Model 11, with recessed barrel nut. Mfg. 1971-75.

	$225	**$185**	**$170**	**$160**	**$150**	**$140**	**$130**

MODEL 15 (1970s Mfg.) – similar to Model 14, with adj. sights. Mfg. 1971-75.

	$245	**$200**	**$155**	**$145**	**$135**	**$125**	**$115**

MODEL 9 (1970s Mfg.) – similar to Model 15, except .38 Spl. cal. Mfg. 1971-75.

	$245	**$200**	**$155**	**$145**	**$135**	**$125**	**$115**

Add 20% for 9mm Para Cal.

MODEL 38P – .38+P cal., 5 shot, 6 1/2 in. barrel, fixed sights, wood or rubber grips, 24.6 oz. Mfg. 1992-93.

	$230	**$190**	**$170**	**$150**	**$135**	**$120**	**$110**	Last MSR was $285.

MODEL 14 – .357 Mag. cal., 2 1/2, 4, 6, or 8 (disc. 1994) in. interchangeable barrels, fixed sights, blue. Mfg. 1975-95.

	$215	**$170**	**$150**	**$140**	**$130**	**$120**	**$110**	Last MSR was $274.

Add approx. $7 for each additional barrel length.

MODEL 8 – similar to Model 14, except .38 Spl. cal. Disc. 1995.

	$220	**$170**	**$150**	**$140**	**$130**	**$120**	**$110**	Last MSR was $274.

Add approx. $6 for each additional barrel length.

MODEL 15 – similar to Model 14, except adj. sights, available with 2, 4, 6, 8, 10, 12, or 15 in. barrels. Disc. 1995.

MODEL 15 GOLD SERIES – .357 Mag. cal., 6 or 8 in. VR heavy slotted barrel, "Gold" stamped shroud with Dan Wesson signature, smoother action (8 lb. double action pull), 18kt. gold-plated trigger, white triangle rear sight with orange-dot Patridge front sight, exotic hardwood grips. Mfg. 1989-94.

	$425	**$380**	**$340**	**$300**	**$260**	**$225**	**$185**	Last MSR was $544.

MODEL 9 – similar to Model 15, except .38 Spl. cal. Use same add-ons as in Model 15. Disc. 1995.

	$346	**$285**	**$225**	**$200**	**$190**	**$180**	**$170**	Last MSR was $346.

This model was also available in a Pistol Pac - same specifications and values as the Model 15 Pistol Pac.

MODEL 41 – .41 Mag. cal., double action, 6 shot, 4, 6, 8, or 10 in. barrel VR. Disc. 1995.

	$375	**$305**	**$265**	**$250**	**$230**	**$215**	**$200**	Last MSR was $447.

Add approx. $20 for heavy barrel shroud, approx. $15 for each additional barrel length.

MODEL 45 – .45 LC cal., 4, 6, 8, or 10 in. VR barrel, same frame as Model 44V, blue finish. Mfg. 1988-95.

	$375	**$305**	**$265**	**$250**	**$230**	**$215**	**$200**	Last MSR was $447.

Add $20 for VR heavy barrel shroud, approx. $15 for each additional barrel length.

MSR	100%	98%	95%	90%	80%	70%	60%	

MODEL 45 PIN GUN – .45 ACP cal., competition pin gun model with 5 in. vent. or heavy vent. barrel configuration, blue steel, two stage Taylor forcing cone, 54 oz. Mfg. 1993-95.

	$575	$495	$440	$395	$350	$300	$250	Last MSR was $654.

Add $9 for VR heavy shroud barrel.

REVOLVERS: STAINLESS STEEL

- Models 722, 722M, 709, 715, 732, 7322, 741V, 744V, and 745V were available in a pistol pack including 2 1/2, 4, 6, and 8 in. solid rib barrel assemblies, extra grip, 4 additional sight blades, and fitted carrying case. Last published retail prices were $712 and $785 for the standard and stainless steel models, respectively. VR or full shroud barrels were optional and were approx. priced $103 and $210, respectively.

MODEL 708 – .38 Spl. cal., similar to Model 8. Add approx. $6 for each additional barrel length. Disc. 1995.

	$265	$200	$170	$135	$115	$100	$85	Last MSR was $319.

* **Model 708 Action Cup/PPC** – .38 Spl. cal., extra heavy shrouded 6 in. bull barrel with removable underweight, Hogue Gripper grips, mounted Tasco Pro Point II on Action Cup, Aristocrat sights on PPC. Mfg. 1992 only.

	$725	$650	$550	$460	$395	$335	$285	Last MSR was $857.

Add $56 for Action Cup Model with Tasco Scope.

MODEL 709 – .38 Spl. cal., target revolver, adj. sights. Also available in special order 10, 12 (disc.), or 15 (disc.) in. barrel lengths. Disc. 1995.

	$310	$255	$205	$150	$125	$110	$95	Last MSR was $376.

Add approx. $10 for each additional longer barrel length, approx. $19 for VR, approx. $56 for heavy VR.

MODEL 714 (INTERCHANGEABLE OR FIXED) – .357 Mag. cal., fixed sight Service Model with 2 1/2, 4, or 6 in. barrel, brushed stainless steel. Mfg. 1993-95.

	$260	$200	$160	$125	$110	$95	$85	Last MSR was $319.

Add approx. $6 for 4 or 6 in. barrel.
Subtract $6 for fixed barrel (2 1/2 or 4 in. barrel only).

MODEL 715 INTERCHANGEABLE – .357 Mag. cal., 2 1/2, 4, 6, 8, or 10 in. barrel with adj. rear sight, brushed stainless steel. Mfg. 1993-95.

	$310	$255	$205	$150	$125	$110	$95	Last MSR was $376.

Add approx. $10 for each additional longer barrel length, approx. $19 for VR, approx. $56 for heavy VR.

MODEL 738P – .38 +P cal., 5 shot, 6 1/2 in. barrel, fixed sights, wood or rubber grips, 24.6 oz. Mfg. 1992-95.

	$275	$210	$175	$135	$115	$100	$85	Last MSR was $340.

MODEL 745V – .45 LC cal., similar to Model 45, except in stainless steel. Disc. 1995.

	$430	$345	$285	$235	$200	$170	$145	Last MSR was $524.

Add $20 for heavy full shroud VR barrels, $13 for each additional barrel length.

MODEL .45 PIN GUN – .45 ACP cal., similar to Model 45 Pin Gun, except is stainless steel. Mfg. 1993-95.

	$625	$525	$425	$360	$315	$260	$225	Last MSR was $713.

Add $49 for VR heavy rib shroud.

WILDEY, INC.

Current manufacturer located in Warren, CT. Previously located in New Milford, CT until 1999.

Originally, the company was named Wildey Firearms Co., Inc. located in Cheshire, CT. At that time, serialization of pistols was 45-0000. When Wildey, Inc. bought the company out of bankruptcy from the old shareholders, there had been approximately 800 pistols mfg. To distinguish the old company from the present company, the serial range was changed to 09-0000 (only 633 pistols with the 09 prefix were produced). These guns had the Cheshire, CT address. Pistols produced by Wildey, Inc., New Milford, CT are serial numbered with 4 digits (no numerical prefix).

CARBINES: SEMI-AUTO

WILDEY CARBINE – .44 Auto Mag., .45 Wildey Mag., .45 Win. Mag., or .475 Wildey Mag. cal., features 18 in. barrel with forearm and detachable skeleton walnut stock, polished or matte stainless steel. New 2003.

MSR $3,110	$2,700	$2,225	$1,750	$1,500	$1,235	$1,030	$855	

Add $237 for matte stainless steel finish.

PISTOLS: SEMI-AUTO

Add $585-$1,950 per interchangeable barrel assembly, depending on barrel length and finish.

WILDEY AUTO PISTOL – .45 Win. Mag., .45 Wildey Mag., or .475 Wildey Mag., gas operated, 5, 6, 7, 8, 10, or 14 in. VR barrel, selective single shot or semi-auto, 3 lug rotary bolt, fixed barrel (interchangeable), polished stainless

MSR	100%	98%	95%	90%	80%	70%	60%

steel construction, 7 shot, double action, adj. sights, smooth or checkered wood grips, designed to fire proprietary new cartridges specifically for this gun including the .45 Win. Mag. cal., 64 oz. with 5 in. barrel.

Add $560-$1,148 per interchangeable barrel.

* ***Wildey Survivor Model*** – .357 Mag., .44 Auto Mag. (new 2003), .45 Win. Mag., 45 Wildey Mag., or .475 Wildey Mag. cal., 5, 6, 7, 8, 10, 12, 14 (new 2000), or 18 (new 2003) in. VR barrel, polished stainless steel finish. New 1990.

MSR $1,571 $1,375 $1,025 $800 $665 $560 $465 $410

Add $26 - $125 for 5 in. - 12 in. barrel, depending on length, and $1,206 for 18 in. silouhette model.
Add $26 for .45 Wildey Mag. or .475 Wildey Mag. cal.

The .475 Wildey cal. is derived from a factory cartridge.

* ***Wildey Survivor Guardsman*** – similar to Survivor Model, except has squared-off trigger guard, same options apply to this model as for the Survivor model. New 1990.

MSR $1,571 $1,375 $1,025 $800 $665 $560 $465 $410

* ***Wildey Hunter Guardsman*** – similar to Hunter Model, except has squared-off trigger guard, same options apply to this model as for the Hunter model. New 1990.

MSR $1,829 $1,575 $1,225 $950 $810 $670 $565 $475

Add $100 for 12 in. barrel.
Add $625 for 14 in. barrel.
Add $1,175 for 18 in. silhouette barrel.

WILDEY AUTO PISTOL OLDER MFG. – .475 Wildey Mag. cal. was available in 8 or 10 in. barrel only.

* ***Older Wildey Serial Nos. 1-200.***

  $1,900 $1,700 $1,550 $1,365 $1,125 $950 $775 Last MSR was $2,180.

Add $20 for 8 or 10 in. barrel.

* ***Older Wildey Serial Nos. 201-400.***

  $1,750 $1,550 $1,400 $1,235 $1,000 $870 $700 Last MSR was $1,980.

Add $20 for 8 or 10 in. barrel.

* ***Older Wildey Serial Nos. 401-600.***

  $1,650 $1,375 $1,250 $1,100 $895 $785 $630 Last MSR was $1,780.

Add $20 for 8 or 10 in. barrel.

* ***Older Wildey Serial Nos. 601-800.***

  $1,450 $1,200 $1,000 $885 $715 $610 $515 Last MSR was $1,580.

Add $20 for 8 or 10 in. barrel.

* ***Older Wildey Serial Nos. 801-1,000.***

  $1,100 $925 $800 $695 $585 $485 $415 Last MSR was $1,275.

Add $25 for 8 or 10 in. barrel.

* ***Older Wildey Serial Nos. 1,001-2,489.***

  $1,025 $850 $750 $640 $535 $450 $390 Last MSR was $1,175.

Add $20 for 8 or 10 in. barrel.

WILKINSON ARMS

Previous trademark established circa 1996 and manufactured by Ray Wilkinson circa 1996-1998 (limited production), and by Northwest Arms located in Parma, ID circa 2000-2005.

CARBINES

LINDA CARBINE – 9mm Para cal., 16 3/16 in. barrel, aluminum receiver, pre-ban configuration (limited supplies), fixed tubular stock with wood pad, vent. barrel shroud, aperture rear sight, small wooden forearm, 18 or 31 shot mag., beginning 2002, this model came standard with many accessories, 7 lbs. Mfg. circa 1996-2005.

  $1,295 $1,075 $850 $725 $600 $500 $425 Last MSR was $1,800.

Only 2,200 Linda Carbines were marked "Luger Carbine" on the receiver. The last 1,500 distributed by Northwest Arms include a longer stock, and matched bolt and barrel (Rockwell 57).

TERRY CARBINE – 9mm Para. cal., blowback semi-auto action, 31 shot mag., 16 3/16 in. barrel, closed breech, adj. sights, 7 lbs. Disc.

	100%	98%	95%	90%	80%	70%	60%
With black P.V.C. stock	$475	$395	$325	$295	$260	$230	$200
With maple stock	$625	$525	$400	$350	$340	$325	$300

MSR	100%	98%	95%	90%	80%	70%	60%

PISTOLS: SEMI-AUTO

SHERRY MODEL – .22 LR cal., 2 1/2 in. barrel, aluminum frame, fully machined steel slide, trigger group, and bolt insert, available in various colors, 9 1/4 oz. Mfg. 2000-2005.

	$245	$200	$160	$140	$125	$110	$100

Last MSR was $280.

Add $25 for gold anodized frame.
Add $20 for collector's edition.
Add $100 for Robar coating.

DIANE MODEL – .25 ACP cal., 6 shot, 2 1/8 in. barrel, fixed sight, matte blue, plastic grips. Disc.

	$150	$125	$95	$80	$65	$55	$50

LINDA MODEL – 9mm Para. cal., blowback action firing from closed bolt, 8.3 in. barrel, 31 shot mag., PVC pistol grip, maple forearm, Williams adj. rear sight. Disc.

	$675	$625	$550	$475	$425	$350	$295

WILSON COMBAT

Current firearms manufacturer, customizer, and supplier of custom firearms parts and accessories established in 1978, and located in Berryville, AR.

PISTOLS

Wilson Combat makes a complete range of high quality, semi-auto pistols styled after the M1911 Colt. Current models include: the CQB Series ($2,250-$2,610 MSR), CQB Compact (approx. $2,300 MSR), Classic ($2,345-$2,585 MSR), Compact Carry Comp (approx. $3,000 MSR), Protector ($2,295-$2,380 MSR), KZ Series ($1,325-$1,410 MSR), Classic Super Grade ($3,995-$4,095 MSR), Classic Stainless (approx. $2,450 MSR), Tactical Super Grade ($3,895 MSR), Stealth ($2,495-$2,930 MSR), Professional Series ($2,245-$3,030 MSR), Elite Professional ($3,015-$3,165 MSR), and the Tactical Elite (approx. $3,000 MSR). Please contact the company directly for more information, including a wide variety of options and features.

RIFLES

All rifles come standard with nylon tactical case.

A variety of accessories are available for additional cost - please contact the company directly for more information on available options (see Trademark Index).

UT-15 URBAN TACTICAL CARBINE – .223 Rem. cal., 16 1/4 in. fluted match grade barrel with muzzle brake, aluminum flattop upper and lower receiver, quad rail free float aluminum handguard, black, green, tan or gray anodized finish, 20 shot mag., single stage trigger, ERGO pistol grip, six position collapsible stock, 6.9 lbs.

MSR $2,025	$1,850	$1,625	$1,450	$1,250	$1,050	$875	$675

M4 TACTICAL CARBINE – .223 Rem. cal., 16 1/4 in. fluted match grade barrel with muzzle brake, aluminum flattop upper and lower receiver, quad rail free float aluminum handguard, black, green, tan or gray anodized finish, 20 shot mag., single stage trigger, ERGO pistol grip, six position collapsible stock, 6.9 lbs.

MSR $2,000	$1,850	$1,625	$1,450	$1,250	$1,050	$875	$675

SPR SPECIAL PURPOSE RIFLE – 5.56 NATO cal., 18 in. barrel, rifle length gas system with lo-profile gas block, forged flattop upper and lower receiver, quad rail free float aluminum handguard, black, green, tan or gray anodized finish, 20 shot mag., single stage trigger, ERGO pistol grip, A2 fixed buttstock, 6.9 lbs.

MSR $2,450	$2,225	$1,850	$1,625	$1,450	$1,250	$1,050	$875

SS-15 SUPER SNIPER RIFLE – .223 Rem. cal., 20 in. fluted heavy match grade stainless steel barrel with muzzle brake, aluminum flattop upper and lower receiver, aluminum free float handguard, black, green, tan or gray anodized finish, 20 shot mag., single stage trigger, ERGO pistol grip, fixed A2 stock, 8.7 lbs.

MSR $2,025	$1,850	$1,625	$1,450	$1,250	$1,050	$875	$675

RECON 6.8SPC – 6.8SPC cal., 16 or 18 in. medium weight stainless steel barrel, mid-length gas system with lo-profile gas block, quad rail, flash hider, 15 shot mag., Magpul CTR buttstock with MOE pistol grip and tactical trigger guard, black, green, tan, or grey finish, single stage trigger, 7 1/2 lbs.

MSR $2,350	$2,125	$1,775	$1,550	$1,250	$1,075	$925	$775

SHOTGUNS

Please refer to Scattergun Technologies for complete listing of shotguns and accessories.

WINCHESTER

Current trademark established in 1886 in New Haven, CT. Currently manufactured by Miroku of Japan since circa 1992,

MSR	100%	98%	95%	90%	80%	70%	60%

Herstal, Belgium (O/U shotguns since 2004), and in Columbia, SC (Model 70 only beginning 2008). Previously manufactured in New Haven, CT, 1866-2006, and by U.S. Repeating Arms from 1981-2006 through a licensing agreement from Olin Corp. to manufacture shotguns and rifles domestically using the Winchester Trademark. Corporate offices are located in Morgan, UT. Olin Corp. previously manufactured shotguns and rifles bearing the Winchester Hallmark at the Olin Kodensha Plant (closed 1989) located in Tochigi, Japan, Cobourg, Ontario, Canada, and also in European countries. In 1992, U.S. Repeating Arms was acquired by GIAT located in France. In late 1997, the Walloon region of Belgium acquired controlling interest of both Browning and U.S. Repeating Arms.

For more information and current pricing on both new and used Winchester airguns and current black powder models, please refer to the *Blue Book of Airguns* by Dr. Robert Beeman & John Allen, and the *Blue Book of Modern Black Powder Arms* by John Allen (also online).

RIFLES: BOLT ACTION - MODEL 70, 1964-2006 MFG.

Beginning 1994, Winchester began using the Classic nomenclature to indicate those models featuring a pre-1964 style action with controlled round feeding.

U.S. Repeating Arms closed its New Haven, CT manufacturing facility on March 31, 2006, and an auction was held on Sept. 27-28, 2006, selling the production equipment and related assets.

WSM cals. will bring an approx. 10% premium, and WSSM cals. will bring an approx. 15% premiums on most of the following models, if in 95%+ condition.

MODEL 70 STEALTH – .22-250 Rem., .223 Rem., .308 Win. cal., push-feed action, 26 in. heavy barrel w/o sights, non-glare matte metal finish, Accu-Block black synthetic stock with full length aluminum bedding block, 5 or 6 shot mag., 10 3/4 lbs. Mfg. 1999-2003.

| | $850 | $700 | $650 | $600 | $550 | $500 | $450 | Last MSR was $800. |

MODEL 70 STEALTH II – .22-250 Rem., .223 WSSM, .243 WSSM, .25 WSSM, or .308 Win. cal., push-feed action, 26 in. heavy barrel w/o sights, matte blue finish, redesigned black synthetic stock with aluminum pillar bedding, 3 or 5 shot mag., 10 lbs. Mfg. 2004-2006.

| | $750 | $600 | $500 | $425 | $375 | $325 | $300 | Last MSR was $886. |

Add 10% for WSSM cals.

RIFLES: BOLT ACTION - POST 1964 MODEL 70 CUSTOM GRADES

* **Model 70 Classic Custom Grade Sharpshooter I/II** – .22-250 Rem. (new 1993), .223 Rem. (mfg. 1993-94), .30-06, .308 Win., or .300 Win. Mag. cal., specially designed McMillan A-2 (disc. 1995) or H-S Precision heavy target stock, Schneider (disc. 1995) or H-S Precision (new 1996) 24 (.308 Win. cal. only) or 26 in. stainless steel barrel, choice of blue or grey finish starting 1996. Mfg. 1992-1998.

| | $1,950 | $1,500 | $1,050 | $900 | $850 | $750 | $675 | Last MSR was $1,994. |

Subtract $100 if without stainless barrel (pre-1995).

This model was designated the Sharpshooter II in 1996 (features H-S Precision stock and stainless steel barrel).

This model was also available in left-hand action beginning 1998 (.30-06 and .330 Win. Mag. cals. only).

* **Model 70 Classic Custom Grade Sporting Sharpshooter I/II** – .270 Win. (disc. 1994), 7mm STW, or .300 Win. Mag. cal., 1/2-minute of angle sporting version of the Custom Sharpshooter, custom shop only, Sharpshooter II became standard in 1996. Mfg. 1993-98.

| | $1,875 | $1,425 | $1,000 | $875 | $825 | $750 | $675 | Last MSR was $1,875. |

This model was also available in left-hand action in 1998.

* **Model 70 Classic Custom Grade Sporting Sharpshooter** – .220 Swift cal., 26 in. Schneider barrel, controlled round feeding, available with either McMillan A-2 or Sporting synthetic (disc. 1994) stock. Mfg. 1994-95 only.

| | $1,950 | $1,525 | $1,200 | $975 | $850 | $750 | $650 | Last MSR was $1,814. |

Shotguns: Post-1964, Semi-Auto

Winchester introduced WinChokes in 1969.

* **Super X2 2 3/4 in. Magnum Field Practical MK I** – similar to Super X2 Practical MKII, except is 2 3/4 in. chamber, has regular TruGlo iron sights, and does not have Dura-Touch, cylinder bore Invector choke standard, 8 lbs. Mfg. 2003-2007.

| | $960 | $800 | $675 | $575 | $500 | $465 | $435 | Last MSR was $1,116. |

* **Super X2 3 in. Magnum Field Practical MK II** – home defense configuration featuring black composite stock and forearm, black metal finish, 22 in. barrel with Invector choke system and removable LPA ghost ring sights, 8 shot extended mag., includes sling swivels, Dura-Touch armor coated composite finish became standard during

MSR	100%	98%	95%	90%	80%	70%	60%

2003, 8 lbs. Mfg. 2002-2006.

	$1,075	$885	$715	$635	$550	$495	$440	Last MSR was $1,287.

Subtract 10% if w/o Dura-Touch finished stock and forearm.

SHOTGUNS: SLIDE ACTION, 1964-CURRENT

Winchester introduced WinChokes in 1969.

U.S. Repeating Arms closed its New Haven, CT manufacturing facility on March 31, 2006. There may be some speculation on recently manufactured Model 1300 shotguns. All Model 1300 last MSRs listed are from the Winchester 2006 price sheet, and 60%-100% values reflect today's marketplace with no speculation.

MODEL 1200 POLICE STAINLESS – 12 ga. only, 18 in. barrel, 7 shot mag. Disc.

	$250	$195	$165	$125	$105	$90	$75

MODEL 1200 DEFENDER – 12 ga. only, 18 in. cylinder bore barrel, 7 shot mag., 6 lbs. Disc.

	$250	$200	$180	$155	$140	$125	$110

MODEL 1300 CAMP DEFENDER – 12 ga. only, 3 in. chamber, 8 shot mag., 22 in. barrel with rifle sights and WinChoke, choice of black synthetic (disc. 2000) or hardwood (new 2001) stock and forearm, matte metal finish, 6 7/8 lbs. Mfg. 1999-2004.

	$300	$230	$180	$150	$125	$110	$100	Last MSR was $392.

MODEL 1300 DEFENDER – 12 or 20 (disc. 1996, reintroduced 2001) ga., 3 in. chamber, available in Police (disc. 1989), Practical (new 2005), Marine, and Defender variations, 18 or 24 (mfg. 1994-98) in. cyl. bore barrel, 5 (disc. 1998), 7 (disc. 1998), or 8 shot mag., matte metal finish, choice of hardwood (disc. 2001), composite (matte finish), or pistol grip (matte finish, 12 ga. only) stock, TruGlo sights became standard 1999, 5 3/4 - 7 lbs. Disc. 2006.

	$270	$210	$160	$130	$110	$95	$85	Last MSR was $341.

Add $13 for short pistol grip and full length stocks.
Add approx. $100 for Combo Package (includes extra 28 in. VR barrel - disc. 1998).

* **Model 1300 Defender NRA** – 12 or 20 ga., 18 in. barrel with removable TruGlo fiber optic front sight, composite stock, 8 shot mag., features NRA medallion on pistol grip, also available in 12 ga. combo with pistol grip stock, 6 1/4 - 6 1/2 lbs. Limited mfg. 2006.

	$285	$215	$175	$140	$120	$110	$95	Last MSR was $364.

Add $13 for combo with pistol grip and full length stock.

* **Model 1300 Defender Practical** – 12 ga. only, 3 in. chamber, 8 shot mag., 22 in. barrel with TruGlo adj. open sights, designed for practical shooting events, black synthetic stock and forearm. Mfg. 2005.

	$300	$230	$170	$145	$125	$110	$100	Last MSR was $392.

»**Model 1300 Defender Practical NRA** – 12 ga. only, 3 in. chamber, 8 shot mag., 22 in. barrel with TruGlo sights, black synthetic stock and forearm, Winchoke system, adj. open sights, NRA logo grip cap, 6 1/2 lbs. Limited mfg. 2006.

	$315	$240	$180	$150	$130	$110	$100	Last MSR was $414.

* **Model 1300 Defender Stainless Coastal Marine** – 12 ga. only, 18 in. cyl. bore stainless steel barrel and mag. tube, a Sandstrom 9A phosphate coating was released late 1989 to give long lasting corrosion protection to all receiver and internal working parts, Dura-Touch armor coating stock treatment added 2004, 6 shot mag., synthetic pistol grip (disc. 2001) or full black stock configuration, approx. 6 3/8 lbs. Mfg. 2002-2005.

	$465	$380	$275	$225	$195	$165	$140	Last MSR was $575.

»**Model 1300 Defender Stainless Coastal Marine NRA** – 12 ga. only, 18 in. nickel plated stainless steel barrel, anodized aluminum alloy receiver and plated parts for corrosion resistance, Dura-Touch Armor coating on composite stock, 7 shot mag., sling swivel studs, removable TruGlo fiber optic front sight, 6 1/2 lbs. Limited mfg. 2006.

	$480	$390	$280	$230	$200	$165	$140	Last MSR was $598.

* **Model 1300 Lady Defender** – 20 ga. only, 3 in. chamber, choice of synthetic regular or pistol grip stock, 4 (disc. 1996) or 7 shot mag., 18 in. cyl. bore barrel (new 1996), 5 3/8 lbs. Disc. 1998.

	$235	$190	$150	$120	$105	$90	$80	Last MSR was $290.

SPEED PUMP DEFENDER – 12 ga., 3 in. chamber, side ejection, 5 shot mag., features 18 in. plain barrel with fixed cylinder choke, black composite stock with non-glare finish and ribbed forearm. Mfg. by Miroku during 2008.

	$240	$210	$190	$170	$150	$135	$120	Last MSR was $299.

SXP (SUPER X PUMP) DEFENDER – 12 ga., 18 in. fixed cylinder barrel, 3 in. chamber, non-glare metal finish, 5 shot mag., deep groove forearm, black composite pistol grip stock, 6 1/2 lbs. New 2009.

MSR $319	$255	$225	$200	$185	$170	$160	$150

MSR	100%	98%	95%	90%	80%	70%	60%

WISEMAN, BILL AND CO.

Current custom rifle and pistol manufacturer located in College Station, TX.

Wiseman/McMillan also manufactures rifle barrels and custom stocks.

RIFLES: BOLT ACTION

Add 11% excise tax to prices shown for new manufacture. Some models listed have very limited production.

TSR TACTICAL – .300 Win. Mag., .308 Win., or .338 Lapua Mag., 5 shot detachable mag., or standard floorplate, synthetic stock with adj. cheekpiece, stainless steel fluted barrel with integral muzzle brake, guaranteed 1/2 minute of angle accuracy. Mfg. 1996-2003.

	$2,795	$2,200	$1,700	$1,500	$1,235	$1,030	$855	Last MSR was $2,795.

Add $195 for fluted barrel.
Add $195 for muzzle brake.
Add $150 for 3 position safety.

NOTES

X-Y-Z SECTIONS

XTREME MACHINING

Current rifle manufacturer located in Grassflat, PA. Currently distributed by American Tactical Imports, located in Rochester, NY.

RIFLES: BOLT ACTION

Xtreme Machining also manufactures bolt action target, AK style, AR style, and .50 BMG rifles. Please contact the distributor for options, availability, and pricing.

.338 XTREME – .338 Xtreme cal., single shot or repeater (5 shot detachable mag.) action, choice of laminated wood target, aluminum tactical, or McMillan A-5 stock, stainless steel receiver and 30 in. fluted barrel with 42-port muzzle brake, Picatinny rails, approx. 15 1/2 lbs.

Please contact the distributor directly for availability and pricing on this model (see Trademark Index).

YANKEE HILL MACHINE CO., INC. (YHM)

Current rifle manufacturer established in 1951, and located in Florence, MA. Consumer direct and dealer sales.

MSR	100%	98%	95%	90%	80%	70%	60%

CARBINES/RIFLES: SEMI-AUTO

YHM manufactures a complete line of AR-15 styled tactical rifles and carbines, as well as upper receivers and a wide variety of accessories. Please contact the company directly for more information about available options and dealer listings (see Trademark Index).

BLACK DIAMOND CARBINE – .223 Rem. or 6.8 SPC (new 2010) cal., 16 in. chromemoly vanadium steel barrel, black anodized finish, aluminum lower and flattop upper receiver, mil spec bolt carrier assembly, forward assist, Phantom flash hider, carbine length Diamond handguard, flip up tower front and rear sights, adj. carbine stock, 6.7 lbs.

MSR $1,369	$1,235	$1,080	$925	$845	$680	$550	$425

Add $70 for 6.8 SPC cal.

BLACK DIAMOND SPECTER CARBINE – .223 Rem. or 6.8 SPC (new 2010) cal., 16 in. chromemoly vanadium steel barrel, black anodized finish, aluminum lower and flattop upper receiver, mil spec bolt carrier assembly, forward assist, Phantom flash hider, Specter length Diamond handguard, low profile gas block, flip up front and rear sights, adj. carbine stock, approx. 7 lbs.

MSR $1,407	$1,250	$1,100	$925	$825	$675	$550	$425

Add $70 for 6.8 SPC cal.

BLACK DIAMOND SPECTER XL CARBINE – .223 Rem. or 6.8 SPC (new 2010) cal., similar to Black Diamond Specter Carbine, except has Specter XL length Diamond handguard, approx. 7 lbs.

MSR $1,429	$1,275	$1,100	$950	$835	$675	$550	$425

Add $70 for 6.8 SPC cal.

ENTRY LEVEL CARBINE – .223 Rem. or 6.8 SPC (new 2010) cal., 16 in. chromemoly vanadium steel barrel, black anodized finish, aluminum lower and flattop upper receiver, mil spec bolt carrier assembly, forward assist, Phantom flash hider, carbine length handguard, adj. carbine stock, single rail gas block, 6.4 lbs.

MSR $1,186	$1,075	$915	$785	$715	$575	$475	$365

Add $70 for 6.8 SPC cal.

LIGHTWEIGHT CARBINE – .223 Rem. or 6.8 SPC (new 2010) cal., 16 in. chromemoly vanadium steel barrel, black anodized finish, aluminum lower and flattop upper receiver, mil spec bolt carrier assembly, forward assist, Phantom flash hider, carbine length lightweight handguard, adj. carbine stock, forearm endcap, flip up tower front sight, flip up rear sight, 6.7 lbs.

MSR $1,361	$1,200	$1,050	$895	$815	$650	$535	$415

Add $70 for 6.8 SPC cal.

SPECTER LIGHTWEIGHT CARBINE – .223 Rem. or 6.8 SPC (new 2010) cal., 16 in. chromemoly vanadium steel barrel, black anodized finish, aluminum lower and flattop upper receiver, mil spec bolt carrier assembly, forward assist, Phantom flash hider, Specter length lightweight handguard, adj. carbine stock, forearm endcap, flip up front and rear sights, low profile gas block, 6.9 lbs.

MSR $1,400	$1,215	$1,065	$915	$825	$675	$545	$425

Add $70 for 6.8 SPC cal.

MSR	100%	98%	95%	90%	80%	70%	60%

SPECTER XL LIGHTWEIGHT CARBINE – .223 Rem. or 6.8 SPC (new 2010) cal., similar to Specter Lightweight Carbine, except has XL length lightweight handguard, 7.1 lbs.

MSR $1,418	$1,275	$1,100	$950	$835	$675	$550	$425

Add $70 for 6.8 SPC cal.

SMOOTH CARBINE – .223 Rem. or 6.8 SPC (new 2010) cal., 16 in. chromemoly vanadium steel barrel, black anodized finish, aluminum lower and flattop upper receiver, mil spec bolt carrier assembly, forward assist, Phantom flash hider, carbine length smooth handguard, adj. carbine stock, flip up front tower sight and flip up rear sight, 6.8 lbs.

MSR $1,364	$1,200	$1,050	$895	$815	$650	$535	$415

Add $70 for 6.8 SPC cal.

CUSTOMIZABLE CARBINE – .223 Rem. or 6.8 SPC (new 2010) cal., 16 in. chromemoly vanadium steel barrel, black anodized finish, aluminum lower and flattop upper receiver, mil spec bolt carrier assembly, forward assist, Phantom flash hider, carbine length customizable handguard, adj. carbine stock, flip up front tower sight and flip up rear sight, 6.3 lbs.

MSR $1,366	$1,200	$1,050	$895	$815	$650	$535	$415

Add $70 for 6.8 SPC cal.

BLACK DIAMOND RIFLE – .223 Rem. cal., 20 in. chromemoly vanadium steel barrel, black anodized finish, aluminum lower and flattop upper receiver, mil spec bolt carrier assembly, forward assist, rifle length Diamond handguard, A2 fixed stock, single rail gas block, two mini-risers, 8 lbs.

MSR $1,357	$1,200	$1,050	$895	$815	$650	$535	$415

ENTRY LEVEL RIFLE – .223 Rem. cal., 20 in. chromemoly vanadium steel barrel, black anodized finish, aluminum lower and flattop upper receiver, mil spec bolt carrier assembly, forward assist, rifle length tube handguard, fixed A2 stock, single rail gas block, two mini-risers, 8 lbs.

MSR $1,226	$1,100	$950	$825	$725	$595	$485	$375

LIGHTWEIGHT RIFLE – .223 Rem. cal., 20 in. chromemoly vanadium steel barrel, black anodized finish, aluminum lower and flattop upper receiver, mil spec bolt carrier assembly, forward assist, rifle length lightweight handguard, fixed A2 stock, single rail gas block, two mini-risers, 8 lbs.

MSR $1,347	$1,195	$1,050	$895	$815	$650	$535	$415

SMOOTH RIFLE – .223 Rem. cal., 20 in. chromemoly vanadium steel barrel, black anodized finish, aluminum lower and flattop upper receiver, mil spec bolt carrier assembly, forward assist, rifle length smooth handguard, fixed A2 stock, single rail gas block, forearm endcap, two mini-risers, 8 lbs.

MSR $1,345	$1,195	$1,050	$895	$815	$650	$535	$415

CUSTOMIZABLE RIFLE – .223 Rem. cal., 20 in. chromemoly vanadium steel barrel, black anodized finish, aluminum lower and flattop upper receiver, mil spec bolt carrier assembly, forward assist, rifle length customizable handguard, fixed A2 stock, single rail gas block, two mini-risers, 8 lbs.

MSR $1,350	$1,195	$1,050	$895	$815	$650	$535	$415

Z-M WEAPONS

Current rifle manufacturer and pistol components maker located in Bernardston, MA. Dealer and consumer direct sales.

PISTOLS: SEMI-AUTO

STRIKE PISTOL – .38 Super, .40 S&W, or .45 ACP cal., several configurations available, with or without compensator. Limited mfg. 1997-2000.

	$2,375	$1,825	$1,700	$1,400	$1,150	$995	$750	Last MSR was $2,695.

RIFLES: SEMI-AUTO

LR 300 & VARIATIONS – .223 Rem. cal., modified gas system using AR-15 style action, features pivoting skeletal metal stock, 16 1/4 in. barrel, flattop receiver, matte finish, aluminum or Nylatron handguard, 7.2 lbs. New 1997.

MSR $2,208	$2,100	$1,800	$1,550	$1,300	$1,100	$900	$750

Add $23 for Nylatron handguard.
Add $50 for Military/Law Enforcement model.
Add $75 for Military/Law Enforcement model with Nylatron handguard.

ZVI

Current manufacturer located in Prague, Czech Republic. No current U.S. importation.

MSR	100%	98%	95%	90%	80%	70%	60%

ZVI manufactures the Kevin line of small frame .380 ACP cal. semi-auto pistols. ZVI also manufactures the Falcon, a .50 BMG bolt bolt action repeater (2 shot mag.). Currently, these guns do not have any U.S. importation. Please contact the comapny directly for more information, including pricing and U.S. availability (see Trademark Index).

ZASTAVA ARMS

Current manufacturer established in 1853, and located in Serbia. Currently, certain models are imported by EAA, located in Rockledge, FL. Remington previously imported certain models until 2009, as well as KBI until 2005. Previously distributed by Advanced Weapons Technologies, located in Athens, Greece, and by Nationwide Sports Distributors, located in Southampton, PA. Previously imported by T.D. Arms, followed by Brno U.S.A., circa 1990.

Zastava Arms makes a wide variety of quality pistols, rifles, and sporting shotguns. Zastava Arms was subcontracted by Remington Arms Co. to make certain bolt action rifle models.

HANDGUNS: SEMI-AUTO

MODEL CZ99 – 9mm Para. or .40 S&W cal., double action, 15 shot, 4 1/4 in. barrel, short recoil, choice of various finishes, SIG locking system, hammer drop safety, ambidextrous controls, 3-dot Tritium sighting system, alloy frame, firing pin block, loaded chamber indicator, squared-off trigger guard, checkered dark grey polymer grips, 32 oz.

	100%	98%	95%	90%	80%	70%	60%	
	$450	$395	$365	$330	$300	$285	$265	Last MSR was $495.

While a latter Z9 was advertised, it was never commercially imported. All guns were CZ99 or CZ40.

Zastava CZ99 configurations (with finishes) included matte blue with synthetic grips (500 imported), commercial blue with synthetic grips (750 imported), military "painted finish" with synthetic grips (1,000 imported), matte blue finish with checkered wood grips (115 imported), high polish blue with checkered grips (115 imported), and military "painted finish" with wood grips (2 prototypes only).

MODEL CZ999 SCORPION – 9mm Para. cal., similar to CZ99, except has indicator for the last three rounds in the magazine, fire selector for pistol and revolver mode.

This pistol was imported by K.B.I. as the ZDA model. Please refer to the Charles Daly semi-auto pistol section.

MODEL CZ40 – .40 S&W cal., 55 prototypes were imported for testing, but most had a feeding problem due to improper magazine design, mag. design changes were planned, but were cancelled due to the Serbian/Croatian war.

Suggested retail was $495.

NOTES

FIREARMS TRADEMARK INDEX

The following listings of firearms manufacturers, trademarks, importers, distributors, factory repair centers and parts companies are the most complete and up-to-date ever published. Even more so than last year, you will note additions and substantial changes regarding website and email listings – this may be your best way of obtaining up-to-date model and pricing information directly from some current manufacturers, importers, and/or distributors who don't post retail pricing. When online with the various company websites, it's not a bad idea to look at the date of last web update, as this will tell you how current the online information really is.

For a complete listing of companies and contact information for non-tactical, airguns and modern black powder reproduction industries, please refer to the respective Trademark Indexes in the *Blue Book of Gun Values, Blue Book of Modern Black Powder Arms,* and the *Blue Book of Airguns*. These Trademark Indexes are available online at no charge (**www.bluebookinc.com**).

If parts are needed for older, discontinued makes and models (even though the manufacturer/trademark is current), it is recommended you contact either Numrich Gun Parts Corp. located in West Hurley, NY, or Jack First, Inc. located in Rapid City, SD for domestic availability and prices. For current manufacturers, it is recommended that you contact an authorized warranty repair center or stocking gun shop, unless a company/trademark has an additional service/parts listing. In Canada, please refer to the Bowmac Gunpar Inc. listing.

Hundreds of hours have been spent in this database, and as this edition goes to press, we feel that this information is the most reliable source material available to contact these companies/individuals. However, if you feel that if you have something to add or find an error, we would like to know about it. Simply contact us at: cassandraf@bluebookinc.com.

During the course of the year, after each edition is published, the Trademark Index is constantly updated as more information becomes available. If you should require additional assistance in "tracking" any of the current companies listed in this publication (or perhaps, current companies that are not listed), please contact us and we will try to help you regarding these specific requests. Please visit www.bluebookinc.com for the most current database (available free of charge).

A.M.S.D. (ADVANCED MILITARY SYSTEM DESIGN)
Distributor – Loki Weapon Systems
P.O. Box 383
Coalgate, OK 74538
Phone No.: 580-927-9070
Fax No.: 580-927-9071
Website: www.lokiweaponsystems.com
Email: bashields@lokiweaponsystems.com
Factory
P.O. Box 487
Vernier/Geneva CH-1214 SWITZERLAND
Fax No.: 011-41-223497691
Website: www.amsd.ch
Email: sales@amsd.ch

AR-7 INDUSTRIES L.L.C.
Please refer to Armalite, Inc. listing.

ACCURACY INTERNATIONAL LTD.
U.S. Office
Fredericksburg, VA
Email: aina@accuracyinternational.us
Distributor – Tac Pro Shooting Center
35100 North State Hwy.
Mingus, TX 76463-6405
Phone No.: 907-440-4024
Website: www.tacproshootingcenter.com
Distributor – Mile High Shooting Accessories
14178 Lexington Circle
Broomfield, CO 80023
Phone No.: 303-519-9616
Fax No.: 303-254-6572
Website: www.milehighshooting.com
Distributor – SRT Supply
4450 60th Ave. N.
St. Petersburg, FL 33714
Phone No.: 727-526-5451
Website: www.srtsupply.com
Factory
P.O. Box 81, Portsmouth
Hampshire, U.K. PO3 5SJ
Fax No.: 011-44-23-9269-1852
Website: www.accuracyinternational.com
Email: ai@accuracyinternational.org

ADCO SALES INC.
4 Draper Street
Woburn, MA 01801-4522
Phone No.: 781-935-1799
Fax No.: 781-935-1011
Website: www.diamondguns.com
Website: www.adcosales.com
Email: Dep597@cs.com

ALEXANDER ARMS LLC
U.S. Army - Radford Arsenal
P.O. Box 1
Radford, VA 24143
Phone No.: 540-639-8356
Fax No.: 540-639-8353
Website: www.alexanderarms.com
Email: sales@alexanderarms.com

AMERICAN CLASSIC
Distributor – Eagle Imports, Inc.
1750 Brielle Ave., Unit B-1
Wanamassa, NJ 07712
Phone No.: 732-493-0302
Fax No.: 732-493-0301
Website: www.americanclassic1911.com

AMERICAN PRECISION ARMS
55 Lyle Field Rd.
Jefferson, GA 30549
Phone No.: 706-534-1577
Website: www.americanprecisionarms.com

AMERICAN SPIRIT ARMS
15651 N. 83rd Way, #2
Scottsdale, AZ 85260
Phone No.: 480-367-9540
Website: www.americanspiritarms.com
Email: rifles@americanspiritarms.com

AMERICAN TACTICAL IMPORTS
100 Airpark Drive
Rochester, NY 14624
Phone No.: 800-290-0065
Website: www.americantactical.us

ANZIO IRONWORKS
1905 16th Street North
St. Petersburg, FL 33704
Phone No.: 727-895-2019
Fax No.: 727-827-4728
Website: www.anzioironworks.com
Email: anzioshop@hotmail.com

ARMALITE, INC.
P.O. Box 299
Geneseo, IL 61254
Phone No.: 309-944-6939
Fax No.: 309-944-6949
Website: www.armalite.com
Email: info@armalite.com
Law Enforcement Support Only
P.O. Box 340
Campbellsburg, KY 40011
Phone No.: 502-532-0300
Fax No.: 502-532-0775
Email: toppc@armalite.com

ARMAMENT TECHNOLOGY
(Repair only - no current mfg.)
3045 Robie St., Suite 113
Halifax, N.S. CANADA B3K 4P6
Phone No.: 902-454-6384
Fax No.: 902-454-4641
Website: www.armament.com

ARMS TECH LTD.
5025 N. Central Ave., #459
Phoenix, AZ 85012
Phone No.: 623-936-1510
Fax No.: 623-936-0361
Website: www.armstechltd.com

ARMSCOR (ARMS CORPORATION OF THE PHILIPPINES)
Importer & Distributor - Armscor Precision International
150 N. Smart Way
Pahrump, NV 89060
Phone No.: 775-537-1444
Fax No.: 775-537-1446
Email: armscor@armscor.net

Factory office - Arms Corp. of the Philippines
Parang Marikina 1800
Metro Manilla, PHILIPPINES
Phone No.: 632-942-5936
Fax No.: 632-942-0862
Website: www.armscor.com.ph
Email: armscor@info.com.ph

Executive office - Arms Corp. of the Philippines
6th Floor, Strat 100 Bldg., Emerald Ave.
Ortigas Center, Pasig City, 1600 PHILIPPINES
Fax No.: 632-634-3906
Email: squires@cnl.net

ARSENAL, BULGARIA
Importer - please refer to Arsenal Inc. listing.
Factory - Arsenal 2000 JSCo.
100, Rozova Dolina St.
6100 Kazanlack, BULGARIA
Fax No.: 011-359-431-50001
Website: www.arsenal2000-bg.com
Email: arsenal2000@arsenal2000-bg.com

ARSENAL INC.
5015 West Sahara Ave., Ste. 125
Las Vegas, NV 89146-3407
Phone No.: 888-539-2220
Fax No.: 702-643-8860
Website: www.arsenalinc.com
Email: support@arsenalinc.com

AUSTRALIAN INTERNATIONAL ARMS
North American Importer - please refer to Marstar Arms listing.
Factory
P.O. Box 526
Ashgrove, Brisbane,
Queensland, AUSTRALIA 04060
Fax No.: 011-61-7-3366-7661
Website: www.australianinternationalarms.com.au

AUTO-ORDNANCE CORP.
Please refer to the Kahr Arms listing.
Website: www.tommygun.com
Website: www.tommygunshop.com

BAER, LES
Please refer to the Les Baer Custom listing.

BAIKAL
Importer – please refer to US Sporting Goods listing.
Baikal Factory
Izhevsky Mekhanichesky Zavod
8, Promyshlennaya str.
Izhevsk, 426063 RUSSIA
Fax No.: 011-95-007-341-2765830
Website: www.baikalinc.ru
Email: worldlinks@baikalinc.ru

BARRETT FIREARMS MANUFACTURING, INC.
P.O. Box 1077
Murfreesboro, TN 37133
Phone No.: 615-896-2938
Fax No.: 615-896-7313
Website: www.barrettrifles.com
Email: mail@barrettrifles.com

BENELLI
Importer - Benelli USA
17603 Indian Head Highway
Accokeek, MD 20607-2501
Phone No.: 301-283-6981
Fax No.: 301-283-6988
Website: www.benelliusa.com
Email: benusa1@aol.com
Warranty Repair Address - Benelli USA Corp.
901 Eight Street
Pocomoke, MD 21851

Factory - Benelli Armi S.p.A.
Via della Stazione, 50
I-61029 Urbino (PU) ITALY
Fax No.: 011-39-0722-307-207
Website: www.benelli.it

BERETTA, PIETRO
Importer - Beretta U.S.A. Corp
17601 Beretta Drive
Accokeek, MD 20607
Fax No.: 301-283-0435
Website: www.berettausa.com
Factory - Fabbrica d'Armi Pietro Beretta S.p.A
Via Pietro Beretta 18
25063 Gardone Val Trompia
Brescia, ITALY
Fax No.: 011-39-30-834-1421
Website: www.beretta.it

BERSA
Master Distributor - Eagle Imports, Inc.
1750 Brielle Ave., Unit B-1
Wanamassa, NJ 07712
Phone No.: 732-493-0333
Fax No.: 732-493-0301
website: www.bersafirearmsusa.com
Email: eagle@bersafirearmsusa.com
Factory - Bersa S.A.
Castillo 312
(1704) Ramos Mejia, ARGENTINA
Fax No.: 011-54-1-656-2093

BLACKHEART INTERNATIONAL LLC
RR3, Box 115
Philippi, WV 26416
Phone No.: 877-244-8166
Fax No.: 304-457-1281
Website: www.bhigear.com

BLASER
Importer & Distributor - Blaser USA, Inc.
403 East Ramsey, Ste. 301
San Antonio, TX 78216
Phone No.: 210-377-2527
Fax No.: 210-377-2533
Website: www.blaser-usa.com
Factory - Blaser Jagdwaffen GmbH
Ziegelstadel 1
D-88316 Isny im Allgau, GERMANY
Fax No.: 011-49-75-62702-43
Website: www.blaser.de

BLUEGRASS ARMORY
Good Times Outdoors
4600 West Highway 326
Ocala, FL 34482
Phone No.: 352-401-9070
Fax No.: 352-401-9667
Website: www.bluegrassarmory.com
Email: support@bluegrassarmory.com

BOBCAT WEAPONS INC.
Please refer to Red Rock Arms listing.

BOWMAC GUNPAR INC.
Canadian Parts Supplier
69 Iber Rd., Unit 101
Stittsville, Ontario CANADA K2S 1E7
Phone No.: 800-668-2509
Phone No.: 613-831-8548
Fax No.: 613-831-0530

BREN 10
Distributor - Sporting Products LLC
1919 N. Flagler Dr., Ste. 300
W. Palm Beach, FL 33407
Phone No.: 561-623-5970
Website: www.sportingproducts.com

Factory – Vltor Mfg.
Tucson, AZ
Phone No.: 520-408-1944
Fax No.: 520-293-8807
Website: www.vltor.com
Email: contact@vltor.com

BRILEY MANUFACTURING INC.
1230 Lumpkin Rd.
Houston, TX 77043
Phone No.: 713-932-6995 (Technical)
Phone No.: 800-331-5718 (Orders only)
Fax No.: 713-932-1043
Website: www.briley.com

ED BROWN PRODUCTS, INC.
PO Box 492
43825 Muldrow Trail
Perry, MO 63462
Phone No.: 573-565-3261
Fax No.: 573-565-2791
Website: www.edbrown.com
Email: edbrown@edbrown.com

BROWN PRECISION, INC.
P.O. Box 270 W
7786 Molinos Avenue
Los Molinos, CA 96055
Phone No.: 530-384-2506
Fax No.: 530-384-1638
Website: www.brownprecision.com
Email: info@brownprecision.com

BROWNING
Administrative Headquarters
One Browning Place
Morgan, UT 84050-9326
Phone No.: 801-876-2711
Product Service: 800-333-3288
Fax No.: 801-876-3331
Website: www.browning.com
Website: www.browningint.com
Browning Parts and Service
3005 Arnold Tenbrook Rd.
Arnold, MO 63010-9406
Phone No.: 800-322-4626
Fax No.: 636-287-9751
Historical Research (Browning Arms Co. marked guns only)
Browning Historian
One Browning Place
Morgan, UT 84050-9326
Fax No.: 801-876-3331
Website: www.browning.com

BRÜGGER & THOMET
Importer - please refer to DSA listing.
Factory
Zelglistrasse 10
CH-3608 Thun, SWITZERLAND
Fax No.: 011-41-33-334-6701
Website: www.brugger-thomet.ch

BUEHLER CUSTOM SPORTING ARMS
P.O. Box 4096
Medford, OR 97501
Phone No.: 541-664-9109
Email: rbrifle@earthlink.net

BUL TRANSMARK LTD.
Factory - Bul Transmark Ltd.
10 Rival Street
Tel-Aviv 67778, ISRAEL
Fax No.: 011-972-3-687-4853
Website: www.bultransmark.com
Email: info@bultransmark.com

BUSHMASTER FIREARMS
P.O. Box 1479
999 Roosevelt Trail
Windham, ME 04062
Phone No.: 800-883-6229
Fax No.: 207-892-8068
Website: www.bushmaster.com
Email: info@bushmaster.com

CMMG, INC.
P.O. Box 369
Fayette, MO 65248
Phone No.: 660-248-2293
Fax No.: 660-248-2290
Website: www.cmmginc.com
Email: sales@cmmginc.com

C Z (CESKA ZBROJOVKA)
Importer - CZ-USA
P.O. Box 171073
Kansas City, KS 66117-0073
Phone No.: 913-321-1811
Toll Free No.: 800-955-4486
Fax No.: 913-321-2251
Website: www.cz-usa.com
Email: info@cz-usa.com
Administration Offices - Ceska Zbrojovka
Svatopluka Cecha 1283
CZ-68827 Uhersky Brod CZECH REPUBLIC
Fax No.: 011-420-63363-3811
Website: www.czub.cz
Email: info@czub.cz

CZ (STRAKONICE)
Factory - LUVO Prague Ltd.
Rejskova 7
120 00 Praha 2 CZECH REPUBLIC
Fax No.: 011-420-222-562-238
Website: www.czstrakonice.cz
Email: luvo@iol.cz

CALICO LIGHT WEAPON SYSTEMS
5405 SE Alexander St., Ste. P
Hillsboro, OR 97123
Phone No.: 503-649-3010
Toll free: 888-442-2542
Fax No.: 503-649-3831
Website: www.calicolightweaponsystems.com

CANIK55
Factory - Samsub Domestic Defense and Industry Corporation
Organize Sanayi Bölgesi
No: 28 Kutlukent/SAMSUN TURKEY
Fax No.: 011-90-362-266-6672
Website: www.canik55.com
Email: samsun@canik55.com

CARACAL
Distributor (Italy only) – please refer to Fratelli Tanfoglio listing.
Villa #9 Al Muroor Road
P.O. Box 94499
Abu Dhabi, UNITED ARAB EMIRATES
Fax No.: 011-971-2448-8092
Website: www.caracal.ae
Email: info@caracal.ae

CARBON 15
Please refer to Bushmaster listing.

CAVARLY ARMS CORPORATION
723 W. Commerce Ave. Ste. A
Gilbert, AZ 85233
Phone No.: 480-833-9685
Fax No.: 480-497-4002
Website: www.cavalryarms.com
Email: scout@cavalryarms.com

CENTURY INTERNATIONAL ARMS, INC.
430 Congress Ave., Ste. 1
Delray Beach, FL 33445
Phone No.: 800-527-1252
Phone No.: 561-265-4530
Fax No.: 561-265-4520
Website: www.centuryarms.com
Email: support@centuryarms.com

CHEYTAC
Distributor – SPA Defense
3409 NW 9th Ave., Ste. 1104
Ft. Lauderdale, FL 33309
Phone No: 954-568-7690
Fax No.: 954-630-4159
Website: www.spa-defense.com
Email: contact@spa-defense.com
Distributor - Knesek Guns, Inc.
1204 Knesek Lane
Van Buren, AR 72956
Phone No.: 479-474-1680
Fax No.: 479-471-0377
Website: www.knesekguns.com
Email: sales@knesekguns.com
Factory
185 Arco Ave.
Arco, ID 83213
Toll Free: 888-807-8611
Phone No.: 208-527-8614
Fax No.: 208-527-3328
Website: www.cheytac.com

CHRISTENSEN ARMS
192 East 100 North
Fayette, UT 84630
Phone No.: 435-528-7999
Fax No.: 435-528-5773
Website: www.christensenarms.com
Email: sales@christensenarms.com

CITADEL
Please refer to Legacy Sports listing.

CLARK CUSTOM GUNS, INC.
336 Shootout Lane
Princeton, LA 71067
Phone No.: 318-949-9884
Toll Free Order No.: 888-458-4126
Fax No.: 318-949-9829
Website: www.clarkcustomguns.com
Email: ccgweb@shreve.net

COBB MANUFACTURING, INC.
Please refer to Bushmaster listing.

COLT
Colt's Manufacturing Company LLC
P.O. Box 1868
Hartford, CT 06144-1868
Phone No.: 800-962-COLT
Fax No.: 860-244-1449
Website: www.coltsmfg.com
Colt Defense LLC (Law Enforcement & Rifles)
P.O. Box 118
Hartford, CT 06141
Phone No.: 860-232-4489
Fax No.: 860-244-1442
Website: www.colt.com
AR-15 Rifles, .22 LR cal. only - please refer to Umarex USA listing.
Historical Research - Colt Archive Properties LLC
P.O. Box 1868
Hartford, CT 01644-1868
If mailing in a request, make sure the proper research fee is enclosed (please refer to appropriate Colt section for current fees and related information).

COMPETITIVE EDGE GUNWORKS LLC
17154 CR 180
Bogard, MO 64622
Phone No.: 660-731-5124
Fax No.: 660-731-5091
Website: www.competitiveedgegunworks.com

CORE 15
GTO Guns
4600 West Highway 326
Ocala, FL 34482
Phone No.: 352-401-9070
Fax No.: 352-401-9667
Website: www.core15rifles.com

CZECHPOINT, INC.
103 Stone Road
Knoxville, TN 37920
Phone No.: 865-247-0184
Fax No.: 865-247-0185
Website: www.czechpoint-usa.com

DPMS FIREARMS, LLC
3312 12th Street SE
St. Cloud, MN 56304
Phone No.: 320-258-4448
Fax No.: 320-258-4449
Website: www.dpmsinc.com
Email: dpms@dpmsinc.com

DSA, INC.
P.O. Box 370
Barrington, IL 60011
Phone No.: 847-277-7258
Fax No.: 847-227-7259
Website: www.dsarms.com
Email: customerservice1@dsarms.com

DAEWOO
No current importation

DANIEL DEFENSE
101 Warfighter Way
Black Creek, GA 31308
Phone No.: 866-554-4867
Phone No.: 912-964-4238
Fax No.: 912-851-3248
Website: www.danieldefense.com

DAUDSONS ARMOURY
Industrial Estate, Kohat Road
Peshawar, 25210 PAKISTAN
Fax No.: 011-92-91-276059
Web site: www.daudsons.org
Email: info@daudsons.org
Phone No.: 208-538-6744

DEL-TON, INCORPORATED
Distributor - please refer to American Tactical Imports listing.
218B Aviation Parkway
Elizabethtown, NC 28337
Phone No.: 910-645-2172
Fax No.: 910-645-2244
Website: www.del-ton.com
Email: sales@del-ton.com

DESERT TACTICAL ARMS
P.O. Box 65816
Salt Lake City, UT 84165
Phone No.: 801-975-7272
Fax No.: 801-908-6425
Website: www.deserttacticalarms.com
Email: marketing@deserttacticalarms.com

DETONICS
609 South Breese Street, Ste. 100
Millstadt, IL 62260
Phone No.: 618-476-3200
Fax No.: 618-476-3226
Website: www.detonics.ws
Email: contactus@detonics.ws

DLASK ARMS CORP.
202B 1546 Derwent Way
Delta, British Columbia, V3M 6M4 CANADA
Phone No.: 604-527-9942
Fax No.: 604-527-9982
Website: www.dlaskarms.com

DOMINION ARMS
Factory – Rauch Tactical
250 H Street, Ste. 266
Blaine, WA 98230
Phone No.: 877-829-1050
Fax No.: 866-606-2743
Website: www.rauchtactical.com

DOUBLESTAR CORPORATION
Box 4671
Winchester, KY 40392
Phone No.: 859-745-1757
Fax No.: 859-745-4638
Website: www.star15.com
Website: www.jtdistributing.com
Email: sales@star15.com

E.D.M. ARMS
2410 West 350 North
Hurricane, UT 84737
Phone No.: 435-635-5233
Fax No.: 435-635-5258
Website: www.edmarms.com
Email: sales@edmarms.com

E.M.F. COMPANY
1900 E. Warner Ave., Suite 1-D
Santa Ana, CA 92705
Phone No.: 949-261-6611
Fax No.: 949-756-0133
Website: www.emf-company.com
Email: sales@emf-company.com

EAGLE ARMS
Please refer to Armalite listing.

EAST RIDGE GUN COMPANY, INC.
6319 5th Ave.
Bancroft, WI 54921
Phone No.: 715-366-2006
Website: www.statearms.com
Email: eastrdge@uniontel.net

ENTRÉPRISE ARMS INC.
5321 Irwindale Ave.
Baldwin Park, CA 91706-2025
Phone No.: 626-962-8712
Fax No.: 626-962-4692
Websites: www.entreprise.com

ESCORT
Importer - please refer to Legacy Sports International listing.
Factory - Hatsan Arms Company
Izmir - Ankara Karayolu 28. km. No. 289
Kemalpasa 35170, Izmir - TURKEY
Fax No.: 011-90-232-878-9102-878-9723
Website: www.hatsan.com.tr
Email: info@hatsan.com.tr

EUROPEAN AMERICAN ARMORY CORP.
P.O. Box 560746
Rockledge, FL 32959
Phone No.: 321-639-4842
Fax No.: 321-639-7006
Website: www.eaacorp.com
Email: eaacorp@eaacorp.com

EVOLUTION USA
P.O. Box 154
White Bird, ID 83554
Phone No.: 208-983-9208
Fax No. 208-983-0944
Website: www.evo-rifles.com
Email: evorifles@wildblue.net

FEG
Importer - SSME Deutsche Waffen, Inc.
408 W. Renfro St. #107J
Plant City, FL 33566
Phone No.: 813-598-8438
Fax No.: 813-659-3361
Website: www.ssmedwi.com
Email: ssmedwi@verizon.net
Factory - FEGARMY
1095 Budapest, Soroksari ut 158
Levelcim: H-1440 Budapest Pf. 6 HUNGARY
Fax No.: 011-361-280-6669

FN HERSTAL S.A.
Importer - FNH USA, Inc.
P.O. Box 697
McLean, VA 22101
Phone No.: 703-288-1292
Fax No.: 703-288-1730
Website: www.fnhusa.com
Email: info@fnhusa.com
Military Only
P.O. Box 896
McLean, VA 22101
Phone No.: 703-288-3500
Fax No.: 703-288-4505
Factory - F.N. Herstal S.A.
Voie de Liege, 33
Herstal, Belgium B4040
Fax No.: 011-324-240-8679
Website: www.fnherstal.com

FABARM S.P.A.
Factory - Fabbrica Breciana Armi
Via Averolda 31, Zona Industriale
I-25039 Travagliato, Brescia ITALY
Fax No.: 011-39-030-686-3684
Website: www.fabarm.com

FABRIQUE NATIONALE
Factory - Browning S.A.
Fabrique Nationale Herstal SA
Parc Industriel des Hauts Sarts
3me Ave. 25
B-4040 Herstal, BELGIUM
Fax No.: 011-32-42-40-5212
Email: info@famars.com

FEATHER USA
600 Oak Avenue
P.O. Box 247
Eaton, CO 80615
Phone No.: 800-519-0485
Fax No.: 970-206-1958
Website: www.featherusa.com
Email: featherawi@aol.com

57 CENTER
PMB-603
227 Bellevue Way NE
Bellevue, WA 98004
Phone No.: 888-900-5728
Website: www.57center.com
Email: info@57center.com

FIREARMS INTERNATIONAL INC.
5200 Mitchelldale, Suite E-17
Houston, TX 77092
Phone No.: 713-462-4200
Fax No.: 713-681-5665
Website: www.highstandard.com
Email: info@highstandard.com

FORT SOE SIA
Factory - Science Industrial Association Fort of the Ministry of Internal Affairs of Ukraine
27, 600-letiya str.
Vinnitsa 21027 UKRAINE
Fax No.: 011-380-432-468-016-461-002
Website: www.fort.vn.ua
Email: siafort@ukr.net

FRANCHI, LUIGI
Importer - please refer to Benelli USA listing.
Website: www.franchiusa.com
Factory - Franchi, Luigi, S.p.A.
via Artigiani 1
I-25063 Gardone, VT (Brescia) ITALY
Fax No.: 011-039-030-8341-899
Website: www.franchi.com
Email: info@franchi.com

FULTON ARMORY
8725 Bollman Place #1
Savage, MD 20763
Phone No.: 301-490-9485
Fax No.: 301-490-9547
Website: www.fulton-armory.com

GALIL
No current U.S. importation - semi-auto rifle configuration was banned April, 1998.

GAMBA, RENATO
Exclusive Importer and Distributor - Renato Gamba U.S.A. Corp.
P.O. Box 615
Walnut, CA 91788-0615
Website: www.renatogambausa.com
Email: info@renatogambausa.com
U.S. Service Center
33 Claremont Road
Bernardsville, NJ 07924
Phone No.: 908-766-2287
Fax No.: 908-766-1068
Factory - Bremec srl
Via Artigiani, 93
I-25063 Gardone V.T. (Brescia), ITALY
Fax No.: 011-39-030-891-0265
Website: www.renatogamba.it
Email: infocomm@renatogamba.it

GERMAN SPORT GUNS GMBH
Importer - please refer to American Tactical Imports listing.
Oesterweg 21
Ense-Höingen, D-59469 GERMANY
Fax No.: 011-49-2938-97837-130
Website: www.gsg-5.de

GIRSAN MACHINE & LIGHT WEAPON INDUSTRY COMPANY
Factory
Batlama Deresi Mevkii Sunta Sokak No. 19
Giresun, TURKEY
Fax No.: 011-90-454-215-3928
Website: www.yavuz16.com
Email: satis@yavuz16.com

GLOCK, INC.
Importer
6000 Highlands Pkwy.
Smyrna, GA 30082
Fax No.: 770-433-8719
Website: www.glock.com

Factory - Glock Ges.m.b.H.
Nelkengasse 3, POB 9
A-2232 Deutsch-Wagram AUSTRIA
Fax No.: 011-43-2247-90300312

HE GUN ROOM CO., LLC
5075 Buena Vista Road
Belgrade, MT 59714
Phone No.: 406-586-7383
Website: www.onlylongrange.com

UNCRAFTER INDUSTRIES
171 Madison 1510
Huntsville, AR 72740
Phone No.: 479-665-2466
Website: www.guncrafterindustries.com

-S PRECISION, INC.
1301 Turbine Dr.
Rapid City, SD 57703
Phone No.: 605-341-3006
Fax No.: 605-342-8964
Website: www.hsprecision.com

ALO ARMS, LLC
P.O. Box 552
Phoenixville, PA 19460
Phone No.: 484-614-4860
Fax No.: 610-933-0186
Website: www.haloarms.com
Email: mail@haloarms.com

ECKLER & KOCH, INC.
Importer - Merkel USA
7661 Commerce Lane
Trussville, AL
Phone No.: 205-655-8299
Fax No.: 205-655-7078
Website: www.hk-usa.com
Factory - Heckler & Koch GmbH
Alte Steige 7
P.O. Box 1329
D-78727 Oberndorf Neckar GERMANY
Fax No.: 011-49-7423-7922-80
Website: www.heckler-koch.de

EINIE SPECIALTY PRODUCTS
Repair and Sights only)
301 Oak Street
Quincy, IL 62301
Phone No.: 217-228-952
Fax No.: 217-228-9502
Website: www.heinie.com
Email: rheinie@heinie.com

ENRY REPEATING ARMS COMPANY
59 East 1st Street
Bayonne, NJ 07002
Phone No.: 201-858-4400
Fax No.: 201-858-4435
Website: www.henry-guns.com
Email: info@henryrepeating.com

ENDLMAYER, KLAUS
Please refer to Waffen Hiendlmayer listing.

I-POINT FIREARMS
I.S. Marketer - MKS Supply, Inc.
8611-A North Dixie Drive
Dayton, OH 45414
Phone No.: 877-425-4867
Fax No.: 937-454-0503
Website: www.hi-pointFirearms.com
Email: mkshpoint@aol.com

HIGH STANDARD MANUFACTURING CO.
5200 Mitchelldale, Ste. E17
Houston, TX 77092
Phone No.: 713-462-4200
Fax No.: 713-681-5665
Website: www.highstandard.com
Email: info@highstandard.com

HOWA
Importer - please refer to Legacy Sports listing.

I.O. INC.
P.O. Box 847
Monroe, NC 28111-0847
Phone No.: 866-882-1479
Fax No.: 704-225-8895
Website: www.ioinc.us
Email: uli@ioinc.us

ISSC HANDELSGESELLSCHAFT
Importer – Austrian Sporting Arms
91 W. Main Street
Ware, MA 01082
Phone No.: 800-967-3940
Website: www.austriansportingarms.com
Email: info@austriansportingarms.com
Factory
Hannesgrub 3
A-4910 Ried/Innkreis AUSTRIA
Fax: 011-43-7752-21271
Website: www.issc-handles-gmbh.at

INTERARMS ARSENAL
Please refer to High Standard listing.

INTERSTATE ARMS CORP.
6G Dunham Road
Billerica, MA 01821
Phone No.: 800-243-3006
Phone No.: 978-667-7060
Fax No.: 978-671-0023
Website: www.interstatearms.com

ISRAELI MILITARY INDUSTRIES
Factory
Website: www.imi-israel.com

ITHACA GUN COMPANY
420 N. Warpole St.
Upper Sandusky, OH 43351
Phone No.: 419-294-4113
Fax No.: 419-294-3230
Web site: www.ithacagun.com

IVER JOHNSON ARMS, INC.
1840 Baldwin Street, Unit 10
Rockledge, FL 32955
Phone No.: 321-636-3377
Fax No.: 321-632-7745
Website: www.iverjohnsonarms.com

J.L.D. ENTERPRISES, INC.
Please refer to PTR 91 Inc. listing.

JP ENTERPRISES, INC.
P.O Box 378
Hugo, MN 55038
Phone No.: 651-426-9196
Fax No.: 651-426-2472
Website: www.jprifles.com
Email: service@jprifles.com

J R DISTRIBUTING
15634 Tierra Rejada Rd.
Moorpark, CA 93021
Fax No.: 805-529-2368

JACK FIRST, INC.
Gun Parts/Accessories/Service
1201 Turbine Dr.
Rapid City, SD 57703
Phone No.: 605-343-9544
Fax No.: 605-343-9420
Website: www.jackfirstgun.com

JACKSON RIFLES
(Parts only)
Parton, Castle Douglas
Scotland DG7 3NL U.K.
Fax No.: 011-44-1644-470227
Website: www.jacksonrifles.com

JARRETT RIFLES, INC.
383 Brown Road
Jackson, SC 29831
Phone No.: 803-471-3616
Fax No.: 803-471-9246
Website: www.jarrettrifles.com

JOHNSON AUTOMATIC
Restorations only - Miltech Arms
P.O. Box 322
Los Altos, CA 94023
Phone No.: 650-948-3500
Fax No.: 408-255-7144
Website: www.miltecharms.com

KDF, INC.
(Gunsmithing, Accessories, & Parts)
2485 Highway 46 North
Seguin, TX 78155
Phone No.: 800-KDF-GUNS
Phone No.: 830-379-8141
Fax No.: 830-379-8144
Website: www.kdfguns.com

KAHR ARMS
P.O. Box 220
Blauvelt, NY 10913
Phone No.: 508-795-3919
Fax No.: 508-795-7046
Website: www.kahr.com
Website: www.kahrshop.com

KEL-TEC CNC INDUSTRIES, INC.
1475 Cox Road
Cocoa, FL 32926
Phone No.: 321-631-0068
Fax No.: 321-631-1169
Website: www.kel-tec-cnc.com
Email: ktcustserv@kel-tec-cnc.com

KEPPELER TECHNISCHE ENTWICKLUNG GMBH
Friedrich-Reinhardt Strasse 4
D-74427 Fichtenberg, GERMANY
Fax No.: 011-49-07971-91-1243
Website: www.keppeler-te.de
Email: keppeler.te@t-online.de

KHAN
Importer - please refer to Mossberg listing.
Headquarters
Inkilap Mah. Alemdag Cad.
Site Yolu Sok. No: 3 34768
Umraniye/Istanbul, TURKEY
Fax No.: 011-90-216-632-7444
Website: www.khanshotguns.com
Email: info@khanshotguns.com

KIMBER
Corporate Offices - Kimber Mfg., Inc.
1 Lawton St.
Yonkers, NY 10705
Phone No.: 800-880-2418
Fax No.: 406-758-2223
Custom Shop Phone No.: 914-964-0742
Website: www.kimberamerica.com
Email: info@kimberamerica.com

KNIGHTS MANUFACTURING CO. (KMC)
701 Columbia Blvd.
Titusville, FL 32780
Phone No.: 321-607-9900
Fax No.: 321-268-1498
Website: www.knightarmco.com
Email: civiliansales@knightarmco.com

KRICO
Importer - Northeast Arms LLC
Presque Isle Road, P.O. Box 325
Fort Fairfield, ME 04742
Phone No.: 207-473-7698
Email: info@northeastarms.com
European Sales - please refer to Marocchi listing.
Factory - Krico Jagd-und Sportwaffen GmbH
Nurnberger Strasse 6
Pyrbaum, D-90602 GERMANY
Fax No.: 011-49-091-80-2661
Website: www.krico.de
Email: info@krico.de

KRISS
Please refer to Transformational Defense Industries, Inc.

L.A.R. MANUFACTURING, INC.
4133 West Farm Road
West Jordan, UT 84088-4997
Phone No.: 801-280-3505
Fax No.: 801-280-1972
Website: www.largrizzly.com
Email: guns@largrizzly.com

LRB ARMS
32 Cherry Lane
Floral Park, NY 11001
Phone No.: 516-327-9061
Website: www.lrbarms.com

LWRC INTERNATIONAL, LLC
815 Chesapeake Dr.
Cambridge, MD 21613
Phone No.: 410-901-1348
Fax No.: 410-228-1775
Website: www.lwrci.com

LAKESIDE MACHINE LLC
1213 Industrial Street
Horseshoe Bend, AR 72512
Phone No.: 870-670-4999
Website: www.lakesideguns.com
Email: sales@lakesideguns.com

LARUE TACTICAL
850 Country Road 177
Leander, TX 78641
Phone No.: 512-259-1585
Website: www.laruetactical.com

LEGACY SPORTS INTERNATIONAL LLC
4750 Longley Lane, Ste. 208
Reno, NV 89502
Phone No.: 775-828-0555
Fax No.: 775-828-0565
Website: www.legacysports.com

LEGION
Please refer to Izhmash listing.

LEITNER-WISE DEFENSE
P.O. Box 25097
Alexandria, VA 22313
Phone No.: 703-209-0556
Fax No.: 703-548-1427
Website: www.leitner-wise.com

LES BAER CUSTOM, INC.
803 Iowa Drive
LeClaire, IA 52753
Phone No.: 563-289-2126
Fax No.: 563-289-2132
Website: www.lesbaer.com
Email: info@lesbaer.com

LEWIS MACHINE & TOOL COMPANY
1305 West 11th Street
Milan, IL 61264
Phone No.: 309-787-7151
Fax No.: 309-787-7193
Website: www.lewismachine.net

LUSA USA
1575 Hooksett Road, Ste. 3
Hooksett, NH 03106
Phone No.: 603-485-4800
Website: www.lusausa.com

MG ARMS, INC.
6030 Treaschwig
Spring, TX 77373
Phone No.: 281-821-8282
Fax No.: 281-821-6387
Website: www.mgarmsinc.com
Email: mgarms@swbell.net

MGI
102 Cottage Street
Bangor, ME 04401
Phone No.: 207-945-5441
Fax No.: 207-945-4010
Website: www.mgimilitary.com
Email: sales@mgimilitary.com

MAGNUM RESEARCH, INC.
7110 University Ave. NE
Minneapolis, MN 55432
Phone No.: 763-574-1868
Fax No.: 763-574-0109
Website: www.magnumresearch.com
Email: info@magnumresearch.com

MAJESTIC ARMS, LTD.
101A Ellis St.
Staten Island, NY 10307
Phone No.: 718-356-6765
Fax No.: 718-356-6835
Website: www.majesticarms.com
Email: majesticarms@verizon.net

MARLIN FIREARMS COMPANY
100 Kenna Drive
P.O. Box 248
North Haven, CT 06473-0905
Phone No.: 203-239-5621
Fax No.: 203-234-7991
Website: www.marlinfireams.com

MARSTAR CANADA
R.R. #1, Vankleek Hill
Ontario, CANADA K0B 1R0
Phone No.: 888-744-0066
Fax No.: 613-678-2359
Website: www.marstar.ca

MASTERPIECE ARMS
105A Kingsbridge Dr.
Braselton, GA 30117
Phone No.: 770-832-9430
Phone No.: 866-803-0000
Fax No.: 770-832-3495
Website: www.masterpiecearms.com
Email: darah@masterpiecearms.com

MAUSER
Importer – Mauser USA
403 East Ramsey, Ste. 301
San Antonio, TX 78216
Phone No.: 210-377-2527
Factory - Mauser Jagdwaffen GmbH
Ziegelstadel 1
D-88316 Isny, GERMANY
Fax No.: 011-490-368-4750794
Website: www.mauser.com
Email: info@mauser.com

MAVERICK ARMS, INC.
Please refer to Mossberg listing.

MCCANN INDUSTRIES
132 South 162nd
Spanaway, WA 98387
Phone No. 253-537-6919
Fax No. 253-537-6993
Website: www.mccannindustries.com
Email: mccann.machine@worldnet.att.net

MCMILLAN FIREARMS MANUFACTURING, LLC
1638 W. Knudsen Dr.
Phoenix, AZ 85027
Phone No.: 623-582-9674
Fax No.: 623-581-3825
Website: www.mcmillanusa.com

MICROTECH SMALL ARMS RESEARCH, INC. (MSAR)
300 Chesnut Street
Bradford, PA 16701
Phone No.: 814-363-9260
Fax No.: 814-362-7068
Website: www.msarinc.com

MITCHELL'S MAUSERS
P.O. Box 9295
Fountain Valley, CA 92728 -9295
Phone No.: 800-274-4124
Fax No.: 714-848-7208
Website: www.mauser.org
Email: customerservice@mauser.org

MOSSBERG
O.F. Mossberg & Sons, Inc.
7 Grasso Ave., P.O. Box 497
North Haven, CT 06473-9844
Phone No.: 203-230-5300
Fax No.: 203-230-5420
Factory Service Center - OFM Service Department
Eagle Pass Industrial Park
Industrial Blvd.
Eagle Pass, TX 78853
Phone No.: 800-989-4867
Website: www.mossberg.com
Email: service@mossberg.com

NAVY ARMS CO.
219 Lawn St.
Martinsburg, WV 25401
Phone No.: 304-262-9870
Fax No.: 304-262-1658
Website: www.navyarms.com
Email: info@navyarms.com

NEMESIS ARMS
1090 5th Street, Ste. 110
Calimesa, CA 92320
Phone No.: 909-446-1111
Website: www.nemesisarms.com
Email: david@nemesisarms.com

NESIKA
Please refer to Dakota Arms listing.
Website: www.nesika.com

NEW ENGLAND FIREARMS
Please refer to H&R 1871 listing.

NEXT GENERATION ARMS
Phone No.: 541-336-3336
Website: www.nextgenerationarms.com
Email: info@nextgenerationarms.com

NIGHTHAWK CUSTOM
1306 W. Trimble Ave.
Berryville, AR 72616-4632
Phone No.: 877-268-4867
Fax No.: 870-423-4230
Website: www.nighthawkcustom.com
Email: info@nighthawkcustom.com

NORINCO
Factory - China North Industries Corporation
12A Guang An Men Nan Jie
Beijing 100053 CHINA
Fax No.: 011-86-10-63547603
Website: www.norinco.com
Email: info@norinco.com.cn

NOWLIN MFG. INC.
20622 4092 Rd., Unit B
Claremore, OK 74019
Phone No.: 918-342-0689
Fax No.: 918-342-0624
Website: www.nowlinguns.com
Email: nowlinguns@msn.com

NUMRICH GUN PARTS CORP.
Parts supplier only
226 Williams Lane
P.O. Box 299
W. Hurley, NY 12491
Phone No.: 866-686-7424
Fax No.: 877-486-7278
Website: www.e-gunparts.com
Email: info@gunpartscorp.com

OBERLAND ARMS
Am Hundert 3
D-82386 Huglfing GERMANY
Fax No.: 011-49-8802914-751
Website: www.oberlandarms.com
Email: info@oberlandarms.com

OHIO ORDNANCE WORKS, INC.
P.O. Box 687
Chardon, OH 44024
Phone No.: 440-285-3481
Fax No.: 440-286-8571
Website: www.ohioordnanceworks.com
Email: oow@oowinc.com

OLYMPIC ARMS, INC.
624 Old Pacific Hwy. S.E.
Olympia, WA 98513
Phone No.: 800-228-3471
Fax No.: 360-491-3447
Website: www.olyarms.com
Email: info@olyarms.com

OMNI
Please refer to E.D.M. Arms listing.

PGW DEFENCE TECHNOLOGIES
Importer – Leroy's Big Valley Gun Works
527 2nd Ave. N.
Glasgow, MT 59230
Phone No.: 406-228-4867
Email: leroygun@nemontel.net
Factory
#6-59 Scurfield Blvd.
Winnipeg, Manitoba, CANADA R3Y1V2
Phone No. 204-487-7325
Fax No.: 204-231-8566
Website: www.pgwdti.com

PTR 91 INC.
U.S. Representative - Vincent Pestilli & Associates
193 Sam Brown Hill Rd.
Brownfield, ME 04010
Phone No.: 207-935-3603
Fax No.: 207-935-3996
Email: vapame@fairpoint.net
Factory
P.O. Box 562
Unionville, CT 06085
Phone No.: 860-676-1776
Fax No.: 860-676-1880
Website: www.PTR91.com

PARA USA INC.
10620 Southern Loop Blvd.
Pineville, NC 28134-7381
Phone No.: 704-930-7600
Website: www.para-usa.com
Email: contact@para-usa.com

PATRIOT ORDNANCE FACTORY (POF)
23623 North 67th Ave.
Glendale, AZ 85310
Phone No.: 623-561-9572
Fax No.: 623-321-1680
Website: www.pof-usa.com
Email: sales@pof-usa.com

PETERS STAHL GMBH
Importer - Euro-Imports
412 Slayden St.
Yoakum, TX 77995
Phone/Fax No.: 361-293-9353
Email: mrbrno@yahoo.com
Factory - Peters Stahl GmbH
Friedrich List Strasse 9
33100 Paderborn, GERMANY
Website: www.peters-stahl.com
Email: info@peters-stahl.com

WAFFEN PRECHTL
*Importer - please refer to Mitchell's Mauser's
listing.*
*Factory – Golmatic Werkzeugmaschinen und
Zubehör G. Preschtl*
Auf der Aue 3
Birkenau, GERMANY D-69488
Fax No.: 011-49-6201-182-701
Website: www.golmatic.de

RND MANUFACTURING
14399 Mead Street
Longmont, CO 80504
Phone/Fax No.: 970-535-4458
Website: www.rndedge.com
Email: info@rndedge.com

RPA INTERNATIONAL LTD.
P.O. Box 441
Tonbridge, Kent, U.K. TN9 9DZ
Fax No.: 011-44-8458803232
Website: www.rpainternational.co.uk
Email: info@rpainternational.co.uk

RED ROCK ARMS
P.O. Box 21017
Mesa, AZ 85277
Phone No.: 480-832-0844
Fax No.: 206-350-5274
Website: www.redrockarms.com
Email: info@redrockarms.com

GARY REEDER CUSTOM GUNS
2601 E. 7th Ave.
Flagstaff, AZ 86004
Phone No.: 928-527-4100
Fax No.: 928-527-0840
website: www.reedercustomguns.com
Email: gary@reedercustomguns.com

REMINGTON ARMS CO., INC.
Consumer Services
870 Remington Drive
P.O. Box 700
Madison, NC 27025-0700
Phone No.: 800-243-9700
Fax No.: 336-548-7801
Website: www.remington.com
Email: info@remington.com
Repairs
14 Hoefler Ave.
Ilion, NY 13357
Phone No.: 800-243-9700
Fax No.: 336-548-7801

RHINO ARMS
436 Recycle Dr.
Washington, MO 63090
Phone No.: 636-231-3199
Website: www.rhinoarms.com

ROBAR COMPANIES, INC.
21438 N. 7th Avenue, Ste. B
Phoenix, AZ 85027
Phone No.: 623-581-2648
Fax No.: 623-582-0059
Website: www.robarguns.com
Email: info@robarguns.com

ROBINSON ARMAMENT CO.
ZDF Import/Export
P.O. Box 16776
Salt Lake City, UT 84116-0776
Phone No.: 801-355-0401
Fax No.: 801-355-0402
Website: www.robarm.com
Email: ZDF@robarm.com

ROCK ISLAND ARMORY
Please refer to Armscor listing.

ROCK RIVER ARMS, INC.
1042 Cleveland Road
Colona, IL 61241
Phone No.: 309-792-5780
Fax No.: 309-792-5781
Website: www.rockriverarms.com
Email: info@rockriverarms.com

ROCKY MOUNTAIN ARMS, INC.
1813 Sunset Place, Unit D
Longmont, CO 80501
Phone No.: 800-375-0846
Fax No.: 303-678-8766
Website: www.rockymountainarms.us

ROHRBAUGH FIREARMS CORP.
P.O. Box 785
Bayport, NY 11705
Phone No.: 800-803-2233
Phone No.: 631-242-3175
Fax No.: 631-242-3183
Website: www.rohrbaughfirearms.com

RUSSIAN AMERICAN ARMORY COMPANY
677 S. Cardinal Lane
Scottsburg, IN 47170
Phone No.: 877-752-2894
Fax No.: 812-752-7683
Website: www.raacfirearms.com
Email: info@raacfirearms.com

SOG ARMORY
11707 S. Sam Houston Pkwy. W., Ste. R
Houston, TX 77031
Phone No.: 281-568-5685
Fax No.: 281-568-9191
Website: www.sogarmory.com
Email: sog@sogarmory.com

STI INTERNATIONAL
114 Halmar Cove
Georgetown, TX 78628
Phone No.: 800-959-8201
Fax No.: 512-819-0465
Website: www.stiguns.com
Email: sales@stiguns.com

SWS 2000
Factory – please refer to Peters Stahl listing
Website: www.sws-2000.de

SABRE
Please refer to Mitchell's Mausers listing.

SABRE DEFENCE INDUSTRIES LLC
Sales Office
Sabre House, Belvue Road
Northolt, Middlesex, U.K. UB5 5QJ
Fax No.: 011-44020-8845-4814
Factory
450 Allied Drive
Nashville, TN 37211
Phone No.: 615-333-0077
Fax No.: 615-333-6229
Website: www.sabredefence.com

SAFETY HARBOR FIREARMS, INC.
P.O. Box 563
Safety Harbor, FL 34695-0563
Phone No.: 727-726-2500
Fax No.: 727-797-6134
Website: www.safetyharborfirearms.com
Email: sales@safetyharborfirearms.com

SAIGA
Importer - please refer to Russian American Armory Company listing.

SAKO LTD.
Importer (USA) - please refer to Beretta USA listing.
Website: www.stoegerindustries.com
Importer (Canada) - Stoeger Canada Ltd.
1801 Wentworth St., Unit 16
Whitby, Ontario, L1N 8R6 CANADA
Phone No.: 905-436-9077
Fax No.: 905-436-9079
Email: info@stoegercanada.ca.
Factory - Sako, Limited
P.O. Box 149
FIN-11101 Riihimaki, FINLAND
Fax No.: 011-358-19-720446
Website: www.sako.fi
Email: export@sako.fi

SAMCO GLOBAL ARMS, INC.
6995 N.W. 43rd St.
Miami, FL 33166
Phone No.: 800-554-1618
Phone No.: 305-593-9782
Fax No.: 305-593-1014
Website: www.samcoglobal.com
Email: samco@samcoglobal.com

SAN SWISS ARMS AG
Industrieplatz 1, Postbox 1071
Neuhausen am Rheinfall
CH-8212 SWITZERLAND
Fax No.: 011-41-052-674-6418
Website: www.swissarms.ch
Email: info@swissarms.ch

SARCO INC.
323 Union Street
Stirling, NJ 07980
Phone No.: 908-647-3800
Fax No.: 908-647-9413
Website: www.sarcoinc.com
Email: info@sarcoinc.com

SARSILMAZ
Importer - please refer to Armalite, Inc.
Factory
Nargileci Sk. Sarsilmaz is Merkezi No.: 4
Mercan 34116, Istanbul, TURKEY
Fax No.: 011-90212-51119-99
Website: www.sarsilmaz.com

SAUER, J.P. & SOHN
Importer – Blaser USA, Inc.
403 East Ramsey, Ste. 301
San Antonio, TX 78216
Phone No.: 210-377-2527
Fax No.: 210-377-2533
Website: www.blaser-usa.com
Factory - J.P. Sauer & Sohn GmbH
Sauerstrasse 2-6
D-24340 Eckernförde, GERMANY
Fax No.: 011-49-43-51-471-160
Website: www.sauer-waffen.de

SAVAGE ARMS, INC.
Sales & Marketing
118 Mountain Road
Suffield, CT 06078
Phone No.: 866-312-4119
Fax No.: 860-668-2168
Parts & Service
100 Springdale Road
Westfield, MA 01085
Phone No.: 413-568-7001
Fax No.: 413-562-7764
Website: www.savagearms.com

SCATTERGUN TECHNOLOGIES INC.
Please refer to Wilson Combat listing.

SCHUETZEN PISTOL WORKS, INC.
Please refer to Olympic Arms listing.

SERBU FIREARMS, INC.
6001 Johns Rd., Ste. 144
Tampa, FL 33634
Phone/Fax No.: 813-243-8899
Website: www.serbu.com

SHOOTERS ARMS MANUFACTURING INCORPORATED
Importer - please refer to Century International Arms listing.
Factory
National Highway, Wireless
Mandaue City, Cebu, PHILIPPINES
Fax No.: 011-6032-346-2331
Website: www.shootersarms.com.ph
Email: rhonedeleon@yahoo.com

SIG SAUER
18 Industrial Park Drive
Exeter, NH 03833
Phone No.: 603-772-2302
Fax No.: 603-772-9082
Customer Service Phone No.: 603-772-2302
Customer Service Fax No.: 603-772-4795
Law Enforcement Phone No.: 603-772-2302
Law Enforcement Fax No.: 603-772-1481
Website: www.sigarms.com
Factory - SIG - Schweizerische Industrie-Gesellschaft
Industrielplatz , CH-8212
Neuhausen am Rheinfall, SWITZERLAND
Fax No.: 011-41-153-216-601

SMITH & WESSON
2100 Roosevelt Avenue
P.O. Box 2208
Springfield, MA 01102-2208
Phone No.: 800-331-0852
Website: www.smith-wesson.com
Service email only: qa@smith-wesson.com
Smith & Wesson Research
Attn: Mr. Roy Jinks, S&W Historian
P.O. Box 2208
Springfield, MA 01102-2208
Phone No.: 413-781-8300
Fax No.: 413-731-8980

SPECIAL WEAPONS INC.
Warranty service & repair for Special Weapons LLC
Website: www.tacticalweapons.com

SPHINX SYSTEMS LTD.
Factory
Gsteigstrasse 12
CH-3800 Matten Interlaken SWITZERLAND
Fax No.: 011-41-033-821-1006
Website: www.sphinxarms.com
Email: info@sphinxarms.com

SPIDER FIREARMS
2005-B Murcott Dr.
St. Cloud, FL 34771-5826
Phone No.: 407-957-3617
Fax No.: 407-957-0296
Website: www.ferret50.com
Email" info@ferret50.com

SPIRIT GUN MANUFACTURING COMPANY LLC
1696 Old Okeechobee Road, Bldg. 3F
West Palm Beach, FL 33409
Phone No.: 561-623-5980
Website: www.spiritgunmfg.com
Email: info@spiritgunmfg.com

SPORT-SYSTEME DITTRICH
North American Importer – Wolverine Supplies
Box 729 Virden
Rom2Co Manitoba CANADA
Website: www.wolverinesupplies.com
Burghaiger Weg 20a
D-95326 Kulmbach, GERMANY
Fax No.: 011-49-09221-8213758
Website: www.ssd-weapon.com
Email: sportsysteme.dittrich@t-online.de

SPRINGFIELD ARMORY
Springfield Inc.
420 W. Main St.
Geneseo, IL 61254
Phone No.: 309-944-5631
Phone No.: 800-680-6866
Fax No.: 309-944-3676
Website: www.springfield-armory.com
Email: sales@springfield-armory.com
Custom Shop Email: customshop@springfield-armory.com

STAG ARMS
515 John Downey Dr.
New Britain, CT 06051
Phone No.: 860-229-994
Website: www.stagarms.com
Email: sales@stagarms.com

STEYR MANNLICHER
Importer - Steyr Arms, Inc.
P.O. Box 840
376 Argo Park Ct., Ste. 100
Trussville, AL 35173
Phone No.: 205-467-6544
Fax No.: 205-467-3015
Website: www.steyrarms.com.
Factory - Steyr Mannlicher A.G. & Co. KG
Ramingtal 46
Steyr A-4401 AUSTRIA
Fax No.: 01143-7252-78621
Website: www.steyr-mannlicher.com
Email: office@steyr-mannlicher.com

STOEGER INDUSTRIES
17601 Indian Head Hwy.
Accokeek, MD 20607-2501
Phone No.: 301-283-6981
Fax No.: 301-283-6988
Website: www.stoegerindustries.com

STONER RIFLE
Factory - please refer to Knight's Manufacturing Co. listing.

STRASSER
Please refer to HMS GmbH listing.

STRAYER TRIPP INTERNATIONAL
Please refer to the STI International listing.

STURM, RUGER & CO., INC.
Headquarters
1 Lacey Place
Southport, CT 06490
Phone No.: 203-259-7843
Fax No.: 203-256-3367
Website: www.ruger.com
Service Center for Pistols, PC4 & PC9 Carbines
200 Ruger Road
Prescott, AZ 86301-6181
Phone No.: 928-778-6555
Fax No.: 928-778-6633
Website: www.ruger-firearms.com
Service Center for Revolvers, Long Guns & Ruger Date of Manufacture
411 Sunapee Street
Newport, NH 03773
Phone No.: 603-865-2442
Fax No.: 603-863-6165

SUPERIOR ARMS
836 Weaver Blvd.
Wapello, IA 52653
Phone No.: 319-523-2016
Fax No.: 319-527-0188
Website: www.superiorarms.com
Email: sales@superiorarms.com

SURGEON RIFLES, INC.
48955 Moccasin Trail Road
Prague, OK 74864
Phone No.: 405-567-0183
Fax No.: 405-567-0250
Website: www.surgeonrifles.com
Email: info@surgeonrifles.com

TG INTERNATIONAL
P.O. Box 787
Knoxville, TN 37777
Phone No.: 865-977-9707
Fax No.: 865-977-9728
Website: www.tnguns.com
Email: sales@tnguns.com

TNW INC.
P.O. Box 311
Vernonia, OR 97064
Phone No.: 503-429-5001
Fax No.: 503-429-3505
Website: www.tnwfirearms.com
Email: tnwcorp@aol.com

TACTICAL RIFLES
19250 Hwy. 301
Dade City, FL 33523
Phone No.: 352-999-0599
Website: www.tacticalrifles.net
Email: info@tacticalrifles.net

TACTICAL WEAPONS
Please refer to FNH USA listing.

TANFOGLIO, FRATELLI, S.N.C
Importer - please refer to European American Armory listing.
Factory
Via Valtrompia 39/41
I-25063 Gardone V.T. (BS) ITALY
Fax No.: 011-39-030-891-0183
Website: www.tanfoglio.it
Email: info@tanfoglio.it

TAR-HUNT CUSTOM RIFLES, INC.
101 Dogtown Rd.
Bloomsburg, PA 17815-7544
Phone No.: 570-784-6368
Fax No.: 507-389-9150
Website: www.tarhunt.com
Email: sales@tarhunt.com

TAURUS INTERNATIONAL MANUFACTURING INC.
16175 NW 49th Ave.
Miami, FL 33014-6314
Phone No.: 305-624-1115
Fax No.: 305-623-7506
Website: www.taurususa.com

THOMPSON
Please refer to Auto-Ordnance and Kahr Arms listings.

THOMPSON/CENTER ARMS CO., INC.
P.O. Box 5002
Rochester, NH 03866
Customer Service Phone No.: 603-332-2333
Repair Only Phone No.: 603-332-2441
Fax No.: 603-332-5133
Website: www.tcarms.com
Email: tca@tcarms.com
Custom Shop - Fox Ridge Outfitters
P.O. Box 1700
Rochester, NH 03866
Phone No.: 800-243-4570

THUREON DEFENSE
2118 Wisconsin Ave.
P.O. Box 173
New Holstein, WI 53061
Phone No.: 920-898-5859
Fax No.: 920-898-5868
Website: www.thureondefense.com
Email: info@thureondefense.com

TIKKA
Importer - please refer to Beretta U.S.A. Corp. listing.
Factory - please refer to Sako listing.
Website: www.tikka.fi

TISAS
Importer - please refer to American Tactical Imports. Trabzon Gun Industry Corp.
De Gol Caddesi No. 13/1 Tandogan
Ankara TURKEY
Fax No.: 011-90-312-213-8570
Website: www.trabzonsilah.com
Email: sales@trabzonsilah.com

TRANSFORMATIONAL DEFENSE INDUSTRIES, INC.
P.O. Box 8928
Virginia Beach, VA 23450
Phone No.: 202-659-6888
Fax No.: 202-659-6887
Website: www.kriss-tdi.com

TRISTAR SPORTING ARMS LTD.
1816 Linn St.
N. Kansas City, MO 64116
Phone No.: 816-421-1400
Fax No.: 816-421-4182
Website: www.tristarsportingarms.com
Email: tristarsporting@sbcglobale.net

TROMIX CORPORATION
405 N. Walnut Ave. #8
Broken Arrow, OK 74012
Phone No.: 918-251-5640
Fax No.: 918-806-2087
Website: www.tromix.com
Email: rumore@tromix.com

TRUVELO MANUFACTURERS (PTY) LTD.
Factory - Truvelo Armoury
P.O. Box 14189
Lyttelton 0140 SOUTH AFRICA
Fax No.: 011-27-11-314-1409
Website: www.truvelo.co.za
Email: armoury@truvelo.co.za

TULA ARMS PLANT
Long Gun Importer - SSME Deutsche Waffen, Inc.
408 W. Renfro St. #107J
Plant City, FL 33566
Phone No.: 813-754-8665
Fax No.: 813-659-3361
Website: www.ssmedwi.com
Factory
1 a Sovetskaja Str.
RUS-300002 Tula, RUSSIA
Fax No: 011-70872-27-3439
Website: www.tulatoz.ru
Email: tozmarketing@home.tula.net

U.S. ORDNANCE
Commercial Distributor - Desert Ordnance
1344 Disc Drive #295
Sparks, NV 89436
Phone No.: 775-356-2389
Fax No.: 775-356-2388
Website: www.desertord.com
Email: questions@desertord.com

U.S. SPORTING GOODS
P.O. Box 560746
Rockledge, FL 32956
Phone No.: 321-639-4842
Fax No.: 321-639-7006
Website: www.ussginc.com
Email: ussg@eaacorp.com

UMAREX SPORTWAFFEN GMBH & CO. KG
Importer - Colt AR-15 .22 LR only & Airguns
Umarex USA
6007 South 29th Street
Ft. Smith, AR 72908
Phone No.: 479-646-4210
Fax No.: 479-646-4206
Website: www.umarexusa.com
Factory
Donnerfeld 2
D-59757 Arnsberg GERMANY
Fax No.: 011-49-2932-638224
Website: www.umarex.de

UNIQUE-ALPINE
Postfach 15 55
D-85435 Erding GERMANY
Fax No.: 011-49-08122-9797-23
Website: www.unique-alpine.com

USELTON ARMS INC.
390 Southwinds Dr.
Franklin, TN 37064
Phone No.: 615-595-2255
Fax No.: 615-595-2254
Website: www.useltonarmsinc.com

UZI
Trademark of IMI - no commercial importation.
Repair & Service - please refer to Vector Arms, Inc.
listing.

VALKYRIE ARMS LTD.
120 State Ave. NE, No. 381
Olympia, WA 98501
Phone/Fax No.: 360-482-4036
Website: www.valkyriearms.com
Email: info@valkyriearms.com

VALTRO
Importer - Valtro USA
24800 Mission Blvd.
Hayward, CA 94544
Phone No.: 510-489-8477
Fax No.: 510-489-8477
Website: www.valtrousa.com
Factory - Valtro Europe s.r.l.
Via Capretti 12
I-25136 Brescia, ITALY
Fax No.: 011-39-030-2000869

VAN DYKE RIFLE DESIGNS
101 Colorado Street
Plainville, KS 67663
Phone No.: 785-434-7577
Fax No.: 785-434-7517
Website: www.vandykerifles.com

VECTOR ARMS INC.
270 West 500 North
N. Salt Lake, UT 84054
Phone No.: 801-295-1917
Fax No.: 801-295-9316
Website: www.vectorarms.com
Email: vectorarms@bbscmail.com

VEKTOR
Denel
PO Box 8322
Centurion
0046 South Africa
Fax No.: 011-27-12-428-0651
Website: www.denellandsystems.co.za

VEPR. RIFLES
Importer - please refer to Robinson Armament
listing.

Factory - MOLOT JSC
Vyatskie Polyany Machine Building Plant
135 Lenin St., Vyatski Polyany
RUS-612960 Kirov Region, RUSSIA
Fax No.: 011-007-83334-61832
Website: www.molot.biz

VIGILANCE RIFLES
1653 Plum Lane
Redlands, CA 92374
Phone No.: 909-307-8877
Fax No.: 909-307-8866
Website: www.vigilancerifles.com
Email: affedm@aol.com

VIPER
Please refer to Tristar listing.

VOLKMANN CUSTOM, INC.
1595 Carr Street
Lakewood, CO 80214
Phone No.: 303-888-4904
Fax No.: 303-232-7318
Website: www.volkmanncustom.com

VOLQUARTSEN CUSTOM LTD.
P.O. Box 397
24276 240th St.
Carroll, IA 51401
Phone No.: 712-792-4238
Fax No.: 712-792-2542
Website: www.volquartsen.com
Email: info@volquartsen.com

VULCAN ARMAMENT, INC.
P.O. Box 2473
So. South Paul, MN 55076-8473
Phone No.: 651-451-5956
Website: www.vulcanarms.com

WAFFEN HIENDLMAYER GMBH
Landshuter Strasse 59
D-84307 Eggenfelden GERMANY
Fax No.: 011-49-8721-6451
website: www.waffen-hiendlmayer.de
Email: mail@waffen-hiendlmayer.de

WALTHER
Importer - please refer to Smith & Wesson listing.
www.waltheramerica.com
German Company Headquarters (Umarex)
Carl Walther Sportwaffen GmbH
Donnerfeld 2
D-59757 Arnsberg GERMANY
Fax No.: 011-49-29-32-638149
Website: www.carl-walther.de
Email: sales@carl-walther.de
Factory - Carl Walther, GmbH Sportwaffenfabrik
Postfach 4325
D-89033 Ulm/Donau, GERMANY
Fax No.: 011-49-731-1539170

WEATHERBY
1605 Commerce Way
Paso Robles, CA 93446
Technical Support: 805-227-2600
Service/Warranty: 800-227-2023
Fax No.: 805-237-0427
Website: www.weatherby.com

DAN WESSON FIREARMS
Distributor - please refer to CZ-USA listing.
Factory
5169 Highway 12 South
Norwich, NY 13815
Phone No.: 607-336-1174
Fax No.: 607-336-2730
Website: www.danwessonfirearms.com

WILDEY F.A. INC.
45 Angevine Road
Warren, CT 06754
Phone No.: 860-355-9000
Fax No.: 860-354-7759
Website: www.wildeyguns.com
Email: info@wildeyguns.com

WILSON COMBAT
2234 CR 719
P.O. Box 578
Berryville, AR 72616-0578
Phone No.: 800-955-4856
Fax No.: 870-545-3310
Website: www.wilsoncombat.com

WINCHESTER - U.S.REPEATING ARMS
Administrative Offices
275 Winchester Avenue
Morgan, UT 84050-9333
Customer Service Phone No.: 800-333-3288
Parts & Service Phone No.: 800-945-1392
Fax No.: 801-876-3737
Website: www.winchester-guns.com
Website: www.winchesterguns.com
Winchester Parts and Service
3005 Arnold Tenbrook Rd.
Arnold, MO 63010-9406
Phone No.: 800-322-4626
Fax No.: 636-287-9751

WISEMAN, BILL & CO.
18456 State Hwy. 6 South
College Station, TX 77845
Phone No.: 979-690-3456
Fax No.: 979-690-0156
Email: w.w.wiseman1942@gmail.com

XTREME MACHINING
Distributor - please refer to American Tactical
Imports listing.
500 Cooper Ave.
Grassflat, PA 16839
Phone No.: 814-345-6290
Website: www.xtrememachining.biz

YANKEE HILL MACHINE CO., INC.
20 Ladd Ave., Ste. 1
Florence, MA 01062
Phone No.: 877-892-6533
Fax No.: 413-586-1326
Website: www.yhm.net
Website: www.yildizshotgun.com

ZDF IMPORT EXPORT INC.
Please refer to Robinson Armament listing.

Z-M WEAPONS
203 South St.
Bernardston, MA 01337
Phone No.: 413-648-9501
Fax No.: 413-648-0219
Website: www.zmweapons.com
Email: zm@zmweapons.com

ZVI
MPI Group Ltd.
Holeckova Str. 31
150 95 Prague 5 CZECH REPUBLIC
Fax No.: 044-420-257-325-910
Website: www.zvi.cz
Email: info@zvi.cz

ZASTAVA ARMS
Importer - please refer to European American
Armory listing.
Importer – please refer to USSG listing.
Factory
Trg Topolivaca 4
34000 Kragujevac, SERBIA
Fax No.: 011-381-034-323683
Website: www.zastava-arms.co.rs

Name and Address	Trademarks/ Brand Names	Logos
ALS Technologies, Inc. 1103 Central Blvd. Bull Shoals, AR 72619 **www.lesslethal.com**		
Armas y Cartuchos Del Sur S.L. Ctra. HU-4403 Km. 1,200 Alosno (Huelva), E-21520 Spain **www.delsur.es/index.html**		DELSUR ARMAS Y CARTUCHOS
Arms Corporation of the Philippines 6th Floor, Strata 100 Bldg. Emerald Avenue Ortigas Center Pasig City, 1600 Philippines **www.armscor.com.ph**	ARMSCOR	ARMSCOR
Azot 1 Rdultovskogo Square Krasnozavodsk 141321 Russia **www.azot-patron.ru**	Azot, AZ, Joker, Rex, CSB	AZ AZOT
Barnes Bullets P.O. Box 620 Monda, UT 84645 **www.barnesbullets.com**		BARNES Unleaded. Unfailing. Unbeatable.
Barnaul Machine Tool Plant 28 Kulagina St. Barnaul 656002 Russia **www.ab.ru/~stanok**	Barnaul, Brown Bear, Silver Bear	Barnaul CARTRIDGE PLANT
Baschieri & Pellagri S.p.A. Via frullo 26 Marano di Castenasco (BO) I-40055 Italy **www.bascheri-pellagri.com**	B&P, Gordon System, Gigante, Tricolor, Super Star, Dual-Pigeon, Allodola,	B&P
Black Hills Ammunition P.O. Box 3090 Rapid City, SD 57709-3090 **www.black-hills.com**	Black Hills, Black Hills Gold	The Power of BLACK HILLS Performance
Bornaghi s.r.l. Via dei Livelli Snc 24047 Treviglio (Bg) Italy **www.bornaghi.it**	Bornaghi, FTB, GM 3, S 4, BIOR	FRANCO BORNAGHI FTB TREVIGLIO
Brenneke GmbH Postfach 1646 30837 Langenhagen Germany **www.brenneke.de**	Brenneke, Original Brenneke, SuperSabot, K.O., K.O. Sabot, Black Magic, B.E.T.	ORIGINAL BRENNEKE USA
Bumar ZPS Pionki Ul. Zakladowa 7 26-670 Pionki Poland		

Name and Address	Trademarks/ Brand Names	Logos
Cartuchos Saga S.A. Caparrella, s/n 25192 Lleida Spain **www.saga.es**	Saga, Diana, Munysur, Export, Sur, Partida de la Sierra, Ansar	
CCI Ammunition 2299 Snake River Ave. Lewiston, ID 83501 **www.cci-ammunition.com**	CCI, STINGER, GREEN TAG, MINI-MAG,VELOCITOR, MAXI-MAG, MAXI-MAG TMJ, APS, TNT, Mag-Tip, Plinker, TMJ, GAMEPOINT, SGB, SELECT, POLY-TIP V-MAX, TNT Green, Pistol Match	
Cesaroni Technology Incorporated P.O. Box 246 2561 Stouffville Rd. Gormley, Ontario L0H 1G0 **www.cesaronitech.com**		
Cheddite France S.A. Route de Lyon, 99/Box 112 Bourg-Les-Valence, F-26500 France **www.cheddite.com**		
Cheddite Italy Via del Giaggiolo 189 Livorno, I-5700 Italy **www.chedditeitaly.com**		
CheyTac, LLC 303 Sunset Drive, P.O. Box 822 Arco, ID 83213 **www.cheytac.com**		
Clever Mirage S.r.L. Via A. De Legnago No. 9 37141 Ponte Florio Montorio (VR) Italy **www.clevervr.com**	Clever, Mirage	
Companhia Brasileira de Cartuchos Av. Humberto de Campos, 3220 CEP 09426-900 Guapituba Ribeiro Pires/SP Brasil **www.cbc.com.br**	CBC, Magtech, MAGTECH First Defense, Guardian Gold, Shootin' Size, CleanRange, Featherweight	
Cor-Bon/Glaser 1311 Industry Rd. Sturgis, SD 57785 **www.corbon.com**	CorBon, CorBon/Glaser, DPX, Pow'R Ball, Glaser Safety Slug, Thunder Ranch, Corbon Hunter, U.S. Cavalry Cowboy Action	
DDupleks Ltd. Brivibas Gatve 197 Riga, LV-1039 Latvia **www.ddupleks.lv**		
Dynamic Research Tech. 405 N. Lyon Street Grant City, MO 64456 **www.drtammo.com**		

Name and Address	Trademarks/ Brand Names	Logos
Eley Limited Selco Way Minworth Industrial Estate Sutton, Coldfield West Midlands B76 1BA England **www.eleyammunition.com**	ELEY, Tenex, Match EPS, Club Xtra, Practice 100, Ultimate EPS, Pistol Xtra, Silhouex, Biathlon Match EPS	©**ELEY**
Eley Hawk Ltd. Selco Way, First Ave. Minworth Industrial Estate Sutton Coldfield West Midlands B76 1BA England **www.eleyhawk.com**	Hawk, FIRST, Blue, VIP, Superb, Impax, Hi Flyer, Hymax, Fourlong, Alphamax, Grand Prix, Black Feather, ELEY, Superb Competition, Competition Trap, VIP Sporting, Trainer, HUSH POWER, Grand Prix, Maximum, Alphamax, Alphamax Magnum, Classic Game, Fausteen, Fourlong, Extra Long, VIP Game, HB Pigeon, HI-FLYER, HYMAX, CT GAME, Grand Prix Steel, First Steel, Grand Prix HV, Saluting Blanks, Winchester Cannon Blanks, REALTREE PIGEON	**ELEY**
Environ-Metal Inc. 1307 Clark Mill Rd. Sweet Home, OR 97386 **www.hevishot.com**	HEVI-SHOT, HEVI-SHOT Classic Doubles, HEVI-STEEL, HEVI-13, DEAD COYOTE!	ENVIRON M METAL inc
Estate Cartridge, Inc. 900 Ehlen Dr. Anoka, MN 55303 **www.estatecartridge.com**	ESTATE CARTRIDGE INC.	
Extreme Shock USA Rt. 2, Box 304-N Clintwood, VA 24228 **www.extremeshockusa.com**	Extreme Shock, Tungsten Nytrillium	EXTREME SHOCK
FAM - PIONKI LLC Ul. Zakladowa 7 Pionki PL-26-670 Poland **www.fam-pionki.pl**	ROJ, BAK, CHRABASZCZ 20/30/50, LFT 6.8, W8MP, Olympic, PR-PIK 94/94M/98, SAK, FAM, FAM Plus, W-8 (slug), FS (slug), Dzik (slug), Atut (slug), ONS 2000, CS 94/94M/98	FS
Federal Premium Ammunition 900 Ehlen Dr. Anoka, MN 55303 **www.federalpremium.com**	Premium, V-Shok, Vital-Shok, Cape-Shok, Gold Medal, Personal Defense, Ultra-Shok, Black Cloud, Mag-Shok, High Density, Heavyweight, Wing-Shok, Federal, American Eagle, Champion, Hi-Power, Game-Shok, Power-Shok, Strut-Shok, Top Gun, Speed-Shok, Flitecontrol, Flitestopper, Truball, Hydra-Shok, EFMJ, Spitfire, Prairie Storm, FS Lead, FS Steel	**FEDERAL PREMIUM** AMMUNITION
Fiocchi Munizioni S.p.A. Via Santa Barbara 4 23900 Lecco Italy **www.fiocchigfl.it**	Extrema, Exacta, Shooting Dynamics, Shooting Dynamics Target, Aero Slugs, Golden Pheasant, MAXAC, Helice, X-Low Recoil, White Rino, Super Crusher, Little Rino, Interceptor, Spreader, Power Spreader, Super Match Competition, Golden Goose, Golden Turkey, Rhino 16, Speed Steel, Golden Waterfowl, Golden Trap Evo, Official Trap Evo, Official Skeet Evo, Official Double Evo, PL 32/34, HV 36, GFL 16/20/24/28/32/36/410, TRADITIONAL 34 DISP, TRADITIONAL, BECCACCIA DISP/38 DISP, 12 HV, NOVA SLUG, TRIO A PALLA, NOVA, NOVA BIOR, NOVALLODOLLA, ELLE, EFFE, GI, JK6, CANE, TOP DEFENSE, BLACK MAMBA, TOP TARGET, SUPER MATCH 300/320, BIATHLON S.M. 340, RAPID FIRE S.M. 280, MAXAC SOFT, RAPID FIRE MAXAC, LONG Z, ULTRASONIC, SHORT SUP. MATCH 200, SHORT MATCH 200, 9 P.A. KNALL 9x22	**FIOCCHI**
G&L Calibers LTD P.O. Box 22198 Nicosia, 1518 Cyprus **www.victorycom.com**		Victory Quality Ammunition
Gamebore Cartridge Co. Ltd. Great Union St. GB-Hull HU9 1AR England **www.gamebore.com**	Tradition, Clear Pigeon, Buffalo, Mammoth, Pure Gold, White Gold, Gamebore, Super XLR, White Gold XLR, Blue Diamond, Kent Champion, White Gold F2, White Gold Extreme, Patriot F2, Super Competition, XLR Subsonic, Black Gold, SuperSteel, Super Game Extreme, Pigeon Extreme, Super Game, Mammoth Magnum, Super Game High Bird, Traditional Game, Traditional Hunting, Impact, Impact Mallard, Impact Multi-Shot, Steel-Fibre Game & Wetland Steel	**Gamebore**
GOEX Inc. P.O. Box 659 Doyline, LA 71023 **www.goexpowder.com**	GOEX, Black Dawge Cartridges, GOEX Pinnacle, E-Z Loads, GOEX Pinnacle Replica Black Powder, GOEX Express	**GOEX BLACK POWDER**

Name and Address	Trademarks/ Brand Names	Logos
Hastings 717 4th Street Clay Center, KS 67432 **www.hastingsammunition.com**		*Hastings*
High-Standard Mfg. 5200 Mitchelldale-E17 Houston, TX 77092 **www.highstandard.com**		
Hornady Manufacturing Co. P.O. Box 1848 Grand Island, NE 68802 **www.hornady.com**	Hornady, Frontier, LEVERevolution, For Personal Defense, FPD, TAP, SST, HMR, Varmint Express, V-Max, Custom, InterBond, A-Max, XTP, Evolution, SST Shotgun Slug, Buckshot Light Mag, SST-ML, Lock-N-Load Speed Sabot, FPB, XTP MAG, PowerBelt, Great Plains, SST Interlock, Dangerous Game Series, DGS (Dangerous Game Solid), DGX (Dangerous Game eXpanding), Interlock, Flex-Tip, LIGHT/HEAVY MAG, LIGHT/HEAVY MAG INTERBOND, LIGHT/HEAVY MAG SST, LIGHT MAG, CUSTOM IB, CUSTOM Shot, HAP (Hornady Action Pistol), .17 Mach 2, .17 HMR	**Hornady** *Accurate. Deadly. Dependable.*
Hull Cartridge Co. Ltd. Bontoft Ave., National Ave. Hull, England HU5 4HZ **www.hullcartridge.co.uk**	Sovereign, Elite, Sterling, Imperial, Three Crowns, Hulmax, Solway, Sovereign FITASC, Sovereign Fibre, PRO ONE, PRO ONE DTL300, PRO FIBRE, PRO TWENTY, PROSTEEL, INTERCOMP, CHEVRON, SUBSONIC, SUBSONIC 20, STEEL CLAY, HIGH PHEASANT, ULTRAMAX, SPECIAL PIGEON, GAME & CLAY, STEEL GAME	**H.U.L.L. CARTRIDGE**
Igman d.d. Donje Polje 42 88400 Konjic Bosnia-Herzegovina **www.igman.co.ba**	Igman, Hot Shot	
Impala Europa Dr. Karl Renner Str. 2b Guntramsdorf A-2353 Austria **www.impalabullets.at**	Impala	**IMPALA**
Industrias Tecnos S.A. de C.V. Km. 6 carretera Cuernavaca a Tepoztlan Cuernavaca, Mor. Mexico C.P. 62000 **www.itecnos.com.mx**	Aguila, Colibri, Interceptor, Super Maximum, Sniper Subsonic SSS, Super Colibri, IQ	*Aguila* **AMMUNITION**
Name and Address	Trademarks/ Brand Names	
International Cartridge Corp. 2273 Route 310 Reynoldsville, PA 15851 **www.internationalcartridge.com**	Green Elite TR, Green Elite HP Duty, Green Elite SD, Green Elite FR, Green Elite NT	*International*
ISRAEL MILITARY INDUSTRIES LTD (IMI) Ramat Hasharon 47100 Israel **www.imi-israel.com**	IMI, Action Express	*I.M.I.*
JSC Novosibirsk LVE Plant *(JSC Novosibirsk Cartridge Plant)* Stantsionnaya 30A Novosibirsk 630108 Russia **www.lveplant.ru**	Junior, Sobol, Extra, Korostel, Surok, Kosach	
Kent Cartridge P.O. Box 849 Kearneysville, WV 25430 **www.kentgamebore.com**	Kent, Tungsten Matrix, Fasteel, Precision Steel, Diamond Shot, Velocity, Ultimate Upland, Ultimate Gamebore, White Gold, Blue Diamond, Bio-Wad, Protrial, All-Purpose Diamond Shot, Pure Gold, Traditional Game, Black Gold	**KENT CARTRIDGE**
Kilgore Flares Co. LLC 155 Kilgore Dr. Toone, TN 38381 **contact@kilgoreflares.com** **www.kilgoreflares.com**	Ultra-Frag Enviro-Safe Ammo, Ultra-Frangible	**Kilgore** Ammunition Products

Name and Address	Trademarks/ Brand Names	Logos
Krasnozavodsk Chemical Factory Moscow Region Krasnovavodsk RUSS-141321 Russia **www.khz-record.ru**	Record, Strela, Caban, Poleva, Tandem	
Kynamco Ltd. The Old Railway Station, Station Road Mildenhall, Suffolk IP28 7DT England **www.kynochammunition.co.uk**	Kynoch	
KYRGIAS M.G. S.A. 1 klm. Neochorouda turn Neochorouda Thessaloniki, GR-54500 Greece		
Lazzeroni Arms Company P.O. Box 26696 Tucson, AZ 85726 **www.lazzeroni.com**	Scramjet, Phantom, Firebird, Patriot, Warbird, Titan, Meteor, Tomahawk, Galaxy, Hellcat, Spitfire, Maverick, Lilmufu, Eagle, Saturn, Bibamufu	
Lightfield Ammunition Corp. P.O. Box 162 Adelphia, NJ 07710 **www.lightfieldslugs.com**	Hybred EXP, Commander IDS Lightfield Lites, Hybred-Elite, Lightfield, Star Lite, Alpha Gold 300, Super Star	
Lyalvale Express Ltd. Express Estate Fisherwick Nr. Whittington Lichfield WS13 8XA England **www.lyalvaleexpress.com**	Pro-Fibre, Superfelt, H.V. Fibre, Pro-Comp, Pro-Game, Excel, World Cup, Fibre-Comp, Lyalvale	
MFS 2000 INC. Magyar Loszergyarto ZRt. 3332 Sirok, Pf. 9 Hungary **www.mfs2000.hu**	MFS, MFS 2000	
MagSafe Ammo, Inc. 4700 So. U.S. Hwy. 17-92 Casselberry, FL 32707 **www.magsafeonline.com**	SWAT, Defender, Stealth, Agent, Special Ops, MagSafe, X-Load	
Magtech Ammunition 248 Apollo Dr. #180 Lino Lakes, MN 55014 **www.magtechammunition.com**		
MAXAM Outdoors S.A. Avenida del Partenon, 16 bajo Madrid, E-28042 Spain **www.ueec.es/**		
Mesko S.A. Zaklady Metalowe Ul. Legionow 122 Skarzysko-Kamienna PL-26111 Poland		
Metallwerk Elisenhutte GmbH Nassau (MEN) 10 Elisenhutte Nassau/Lahn D-56377 Germany **Men-info@elisenhuette.de** **www.elisenhuette.de**	QD PEP, QD 1, QD 2, PTP, DK, SFC, MEN	

Name and Address	Trademarks/ Brand Names	Logos
NAMMO Lapua Oy P.O. Box 5 Lapua FIN-62101 Finland **www.lapua.com**	Lapua, Scenar, Midas, Master, Pistol King, Polar Biathlon, D4G, Speed Ace, Rapid Pistol, Mira, SK, Lock Base, Naturalis, CEPP, Hubertus, X-ACT, Midas +, Center-X, Pistol OSP, Bullex-N, Naturalis Long Range, Vihtavuor	
Nike Fiocchi Sporting Ammunition Ltd. Lajos Street 78 H-1036 Budapest Hungary **www.nike-fiocchi.hu**	NF, NIKE, NIKE-FIOCCHI, NIKE sport skeet, NIKE sport trap, NIKE Tracer, NIKE Parcours, NIKE extra, NIKE Mini Magnum, NIKE stren, NIKE Magnum, NIKE Industrial 8 Gauge, NIKE Signal Alarm, NIKE Double Alarm, NIKE Rubber Ball(s), NIKE Voice, NIKE Signal (4-ga.), MONDIAL	
Nitron S.A. Zaklady Tworzyw Sztucznych Krupski Mlyn PL-42693 Poland		
Nobel Sport S. A. 57 Rue Pierre Charron Paris F-75181 France **www.nobelsport.fr**		
NOBEL SPORT ESPANA S.A. Apartado 428 Villacil (Leon), E-24080 Spain **www.excopesa.com/nobel**		
Name and Address	Trademarks/ Brand Names	
Nobel Sport Italia S.r.l. Via di Palazzetto 7/11 San Giuliano (PI) I-56017 Italy **www.nobelsport.it**	Prestige, Migration	
Norma Precision AB Jagargatan SE-67040 Amotfors Sweden **www.norma.cc**	norma, Oryx, Vulkan, Alaska, Plastic Point, Diamond Line, Golden Target, Jaktmatch	
Nosler, Inc. 107 SW Columbia St. Bend, OR 97702 **www.nosler.com**	Nosler, Partition-HG, E-Tip, Nosler Custom, Partition, AccuBond, Ballistic Tip, CT Ballistic Silver Tip, Nosler Solid, Custom Competition, Sporting Handgun, Solid Base	
OJSC "The Tula Cartridge Works" 47-b Marata Tula, 300004 Russia **www.wolfammo.ru**	Wolf, Wolf Gold, Wolf Military Classic, Polyperformance, Wolf Performance Ammunition	
Old Western Scounger/ Navy Arms 219 Lawn St. Martinsburg, WV 25401 **www.ows-ammunition.com**		
Pinnacle Ammunition 111 W. Port Plaza #600 St. Louis, MO 63146 **www.pinnacleammo.com**		

Name and Address	Trademarks/ Brand Names	Logos
Poongsan Metals Corp. (PMC) Keuk Dong Bldg. 60-1 Chungmuro Chung-ku Seoul 100-705 Korea **www.poongsan.co.kr**	PMC, Starfire, eRange, Gold Line, Bronze Line, Zapper, Predator	
Precision Ammunition LLC 5402 East Diana St. Tampa, FL 33610 **www.precisionammo.com**	Copper-Matrix NTF, Firefrangible	
Pretoria Metal Pressings (PMP) Div. of Denel Ltd. Private Bag X334 Pretoria, 0001 Republic of South Africa		
Prvi Partizan Milosa Obrenovica 2 Uzice YU-31000 Serbia **www.privipartizan.com**	Prvi Partizan, PPU, Hotshot, GROM	
Quality Cartridge P.O. Box 445 Hollywood, MD 20636 **www.qual-cart.com**		
Remington Arms Co. P.O. Box 700 Madison, NC 27025 **www.remington.com**	Accelerator, AccuTip/AccuTip-V, Bronze Point, Buckhammer, CBEE 22, Copper-Lokt, Copper Solid, Cyclone, Disintegrator, DriLube, Driving Band, Duplex, ETA, EtronX, Express, Express-Steel, Fireball, Genesis, Golden Saber, Gun Club, Ideal, Hi-Speed, Kleanbore, Lead-Lokt, Core-Lokt, Managed-Recoil, Nitro 27, Nitro CLP, Nitro Mag, Nitro Turkey, Nitro Steel, Peters, Power Level, Power-Lokt, Power Piston, Power Port, R-P, Premier, Rem-Lite, Remington, Remington Leadless, Rustless, Scirocco, Sportsman, ShurShot, Slugger, STS, Subsonic, Super Magnum, Swift-Lokt, Targetmaster, Thunderbolt, UMC, UMC headless, Ultra Mag, Viper, VLS, Vortex, Wetproof, Wingmaster HD, Nitro Pheasant, Yellow Jacket, Gold Box, Short-Action Ultra Mag, Drop Dead Better, Ultra Bonded, Unibody, Zulu	REMINGTON®
Name and Address	Trademarks/ Brand Names	
RUAG Ammotec AG (RWS, norma, Dynamit Nobel, Hirtenberger, GECO, Rottweil, SWISS MATCH) Uttigenstrasse 67 CH-3602 Thun Switzerland **www.ruag.com**	Dynamit Nobel, DN, RWS, Geco, Rottweil, R50, R25, FP50, DE-EVOLUTION, T-Mantel, KS GESCHOSS, ID Classic, UNI Classic, H-Mantel, DK GESCHOSS, V-Mantel, MJ MATCHJAGD, FS GESCHOSS, TMS/TMR GESCHOSS, BIONIC BLACK, BIONIC YELLOW, RWS PREMIUM LINE, RWS PROFESSIONAL LINE, RIFLE MATCH S, RIFLE MATCH, PISTOL MATCH SUPER CLEAN, PISTOL MATCH, PISTOL C 25, RWS SPORT LINE, TARGET RIFLE, TARGET PISTOL, CLUB, RWS FIELD LINE, Z-LANG, SUBSONIC, MAGNUM FMJ, MAGNUM SP, SINOXID, SINTOX, norma, Hirtenberger, Swiss Match, R25, R50, R100, SUPER PISTOL 250, ACTION, GREEN POWER, PENETRATOR, SPECIAL MATCH RUAG, Sintox, Swiss P, Action 1, Action 3, Action 4, Action 5, SeCa, Self, Styx Action	RUAG
SBR Ammunition 1118 Glynn Park Rd. Brunswick, GA 31525 **www.sbrammunition.com**		SBR
SNC Technologies 5 Montee des Arsenaux Le Gardeur Quebec J5Z 2P4 Canada **www.snctec.com**	Greenshield, Short Stop, CQT, FX, Simunition, Dragonfly, SecuriBlank, Sniper Elite	GENERAL DYNAMICS Ordnance and Tactical Systems

Name and Address	Trademarks/ Brand Names	Logos
Sage Control Ordnance 3391 E. Eberhardt St. Oscoda, MI 48750 **www.sageinternationalltd.com**		
Sellier & Bellot JSC Licicka 667 Vlasim CZ-25813 Czech Republic **www.sellier-bellot.cz**	Lord, Fortuna, Mark III, Corona, Junior, Favorit, Tortorella, Black Star, Nontox	
Silver State Armory P.O. Box 962 Packwood, WA 98361 **www.ssarmory.com**		
Name and Address	Trademarks/ Brand Names	
SOTIRIOS NAFPLIOTIS A.B.E.E. P.O. Box 8- Eleon Thiva, GR-32200 Greece		
Speer 2299 Snake River Ave. Lewiston, ID 83501 **www.speer-bullets.com.**	Clean-Fire, Lawman, Speer, Gold Dot, Nitrex, Grand Slam, TMJ, TNT, Uni-Cor, Mag-Tip, Hot-Cor Trophy Bonded, Bear Claw, Lawman RHT, Blazer Clean Fire, Blazer, Flitecontrol	
Swift Bullet Company 201 Main Street Quinter, KS 67752 **www.swiftbullets.com**		
Ten-X Ammunition 5650 Arrow Highway Montclair, CA 91763 **www.tenxammo.com**		
Thifan Industrie S.a.r.l. 275 Rue de Malitorne, B.P. 61 18230 St. Doulchard France **www.sauvestre.com**	Balle Fleche Sauvestre, FIP	
TR&Z USA Trading Corp. 2499 Main St. Stratford, CT 06615		
Trust Eibarres S.A. Murrategui 9 (Azitain) Apartado 32 Eibar ES-20600 Spain **www.trust-eibarres.com**	Trust, Super Halcon, Caza, Galgo Verde, Impulsor, Super Star, Halcon, Semi-Magnum, Caza Slug, Magnum Slug, F-uno, Ujeo Perdiz, Galgo Verde Ecofieltro, Halcon Ecofieltro, Semi-Magnum Ecofieltro, Magnum Ecofieltro, Caza/Bala Star, Pequenos, Sepiol	
UEE Cartucheria Deportiva S.A. Avda. del Partenon, 16 bajo 28042 Madrid - Espana Spain **www.ueec.es**	Rio, Royal, Royal Steel, Starteam, Rio Ammunition	
Ultramax Ammunition 2112 Elk Vale Rd. Rapid City, SD 57701 **www.ultramaxammunition.com**	Ultramax	

Name and Address	Trademarks/ Brand Names	Logos
Ulyanovsk Machinery Plant SUE, PA 2 Metallistov St. Ulyanovsk RUSS-32007 Russia **www.ulmash.narod.ru**		
VAN BRUAENE RIK / VBR-BELGIUM Paralight, VBR Sint Germanusplein 6 B-8800 Roeslare Belgium **Website: www.vbr-belgium.be Phone No.: 0032 051 20 43 20 Fax No.: 0032 051 20 53 20**		
Weatherby, Inc. 1605 Commerce Way Paso Robles, CA 93446 **www.weatherby.com**	Weatherby	
Winchester Div. Olin Corp. Shamrock St. East Alton, IL 62024 **www.winchester.com**	AA, Black Talon, BRI, CXP, Double A, Double X, Drylok Hi-Velocity, Drylok Super Steel, Dynapoint, Fail Safe, Hi-Impact, Lubalox, Lubaloy, Platinum Tip, Popper-Load, Power-Point, Ranger, Silvertip, Super-Handicap, Super-Lite, Super Match, Super Pigeon, Super Steel, Super Unleaded, Super-X, Supreme, SXT, T22, W, Western, Wildcat, Winchester, Xpert, XP3, Xtended Range, Xtra-Lite, XX, Superclean NT, Controlled Expansion Performance, Power-Point Plus, Upland, Winclean, Winlite, Rackmaster, Winglide, Mark 5, E-Tip, AccuBond CT, SRTA (Short Range Training Ammunition), Ranger Law Enforcement, Supreme Elite, Partition Gold, Ranger T-Series, Super Speed, Supersport, USA, Olin, XP^3, Platinum Tip, Dual Bond, Super Pheasant, Super-Target, USA, Bonded PDX1, PHP Bonded, Power Max Bonded, Pointed Soft Point TIN Lead Free Projectiles, Ballistic Silvertip, Xpediter, SXT Design, Power-Point Plus, Super-Target	
WOLF Performance Ammunition P.O. Box 757 Placentia, CA 92871 **www.wolfammo.com**	Wolf Performance Ammunition, Wolf Polyperformance, Wolf Gold, Wolf Military Classic	
YAVASCALAR A.S. Ataturk Mah. Badirma Cad N 49 Balikesir, TR-10100 Turkey **www.yavascalar.com**		

ACCESSORIES TRADEMARK INDEX

The following listings represent manufacturers and companies which specialize in making optics, magazines, upper and lower receivers, stocks, forends/forearms, slides, iron sights, trigger groups, weapon lights, laser sights, accessory rails, metal finishes, slings, and other accessories which enhance the functionality of tactical firearms.

A.R.M.S. INC.
Mounting systems for day optics, night vision, thermal imagers, lasers, and lights, detachable iron sights.
230 West Center St
West Bridgewater, MA 02379
Website: www.armsmounts.com
Phone No.: 508-584-7816
Fax No.: 508-588-8045

ACCUSHOT B&T INDUSTRIES, LLC
Atlas bipods, monopods.
PO Box 771071
Wichita, KS 67277
Website: www.accu-shot.com
Phone No.: 316-721-3222
Fax No.: 316-721-1021

ACT-MAG SRL
Pistol and rifle magazines.
Via Sardegna, 5/F I-25069
Villa Carcina, Brescia Italy
Website: www.act-mag.com
Phone No.: 011-390308980035
Fax No.: 011-390308988833

ADAMS ARMS RETROFIT PISTON SYSTEMS
255 Hedden Ct
Palm Harbor, FL 34681
Website: www.arisfix.com
Phone No.: 727-853-0550
Fax No.: 727-353-0551

ADCO ARMS CO., INC.
Riflescopes, and red dot sights.
4 Draper Street
Woburn, MA 01801
Website: www.adcosales.com
Phone No.: 781-935-1799
Fax No.: 781-935-1011

ADDAX, INC.
AR15 gas piston upper assemblies.
9600 Cozycroft Av, Suite B
Chatsworth, CA 91311
Phone No.: 818-886-5008
Fax No.: 818-886-5007

ADVANCED ARMAMENT CORPORATION
Firearm suppressors.
1434 Hillcrest Rd
Norcross, GA 30093 USA
Website: www.advanced-armament.com
Phone No.: 770-925-9988
Fax No.: 770-925-9989

ADVANCED TECHNOLOGY INTERNATIONAL
Injection-molded synthetic gunstocks and accessories.
2733 West Carmen Ave
Milwaukee, WI 53209
Website: www.atigunstocks.com
Phone No.: 414-464-4870
Fax No.: 414-664-3112

ADVANTAGE TACTICAL SIGHT
"Pyramid Sight Picture" adjustable metallic sights for handguns, rifles, and shotguns.
Wrentech Industries, LLC
7 Avenida Vista Grande B-7, Suite 510
Santa Fe, NM 87508
Website: www.advantagetactical.com
Phone No.: 505-466-1811
Fax No.: 505-466-4735

AE LIGHT
HID and LED lights.
Allsman Enterprises, LLC
PO Box 1869
Rogue River, OR 97537
Website: www.aelight.com
Phone No.: 541-471-8988
Fax No.: 888-252-1473

AIMPOINT, INC.
Electro-optical red dot sights.
14103 Mariah Ct
Chantilly, VA 20151
Website: www.aimpoint.com
Phone No.: 703-263-9795
Fax No.: 703-263-9463

AIMSHOT
Laser and red dot sights, weapon lights, and mounting systems.
340 Dewpoint Lane
Alpharetta, GA 30022
Website: www.aimshot.com
Phone No.: 770-840-8039
Fax No.: 770-840-0269

AIMTECH MOUNT SYSTEMS
Scope mounting systems for handguns, shotguns, and rifles.
PO Box 223
Thomasville, GA 31799
Website: www.aimtech-mounts.com
Phone No.: 229-226-4313
Fax No.: 229-227-0222

AJAX CUSTOM GRIPS, INC.
American made weapon grips.
9130 Viscount Row
Dallas, TX 75247
Website: www.ajaxgrips.com
Phone No.: 214-630-8893
Fax No.: 214-630-4942

ALTAMONT COMPANY
Pistol grips and rifle stocks.
901 North Church Street
PO Box 309
Thomasboro, IL 61878
Website: www.altamontco.com
Phone No.: 217-643-3125
Fax No.: 217-643-7973

ALUMAGRIPS
Ultra high quality handgun grips.
2851 North 34th Place
Mesa, AZ 85213
Phone No.: 602-690-5459
Fax No.: 480-807-3955

AMEGA RANGES, INC.
Picatinny rail systems for Mini-14, M14, M1 Garand, M1 Carbine rifles, and Remington 870 shotguns, and tactical weapon light mounts.
6355 Stinson #202
Plano, TX 75093
Website: www.amegaranges.com
Phone No.: 888-347-0200

AMERICAN TECHNOLOGIES NETWORK, CORP.
Night vision and thermal imaging systems, tactical lights.
1341 San Mateo Ave
South San Francisco, CA 94080
Website: www.atncorp.com
Phone No.: 650-989-5100
Fax No.: 650-875-0129

AMERIGLO
Tritium self-luminous sights for pistols, rifles, and shotguns.
5579-B Chamblee Dunwoody Road, Suite 214
Atlanta, GA 30338
Website: www.ameriglo.com
Phone No.: 770-390-0554
Fax No.: 770-390-9781

AR57/57CENTER
5.7x28mm caliber uppers for AR15 style rifles.
8525 152nd Avenue NE
Redmond, WA 98052
Website: www.57center.com
Phone No.: 888-900-5728

AREA51 PRODUCTS
Tactical weapon accessories.
Taylor, AL 36301
Website: www.area51tactical.com
Phone No.: 908-686-1383
Fax No.: 908-845-0316

ARMAMENT TECHNOLOGY, INC.
ELCAN Optical Technologies sighting systems and related equipment.
3045 Robie Street, Suite 113
Halifax, Nova Scotia, B3K4P6 Canada
Website: www.armament.com
Phone No.: 902-454-6384
Fax No.: 902-454-4641

ARMS TECH, LTD.
5025 North Central Avenue, Suite 459
Phoenix, AZ 85012
Website: www.armstechltd.com
Phone No.: 602-272-9045
Fax No.: 602-272-1922

ASP, INC.
Weapon lights.
2511 East Capitol Dr
Appleton, WI 54911
Website: www.asp-usa.com
Phone No.: 920-735-6242
Fax No.: 920-735-6245

TK LAW ENFORCEMENT
Tactical optics and firearm accessories.
2299 Snake River Avenue
Lewiston, ID 83501
Website: www.atk.com
Phone No.: 208-746-2351
Fax No.: 208-798-3392

WC SYSTEMS TECHNOLOGY
22 to .50 BMG caliber suppressors for pistols, submachine guns, and rifles.
1515 West Deer Valley Road, Suite A-105
Phoenix, AZ 85027
Website: www.awcsystech.com
Phone No.: 623-780-1050
Fax No.: 623-780-2967

ADGER BARRELS, INC.
Cut-rifled and hand-lapped target-grade barrels.
8330 196 Avenue, PO Box 417
Bristol, WI 53104
Website: www.badgerbarrelsinc.com
Phone No.: 262-857-6950
Fax No.: 262-857-6988

ADGER ORDNANCE
Military grade rifle actions, mounting systems, rails, and scope rings.
1141 Swift Street
North Kansas City, MO 64116
Website: www.badgerordance.com
Phone No.: 816-421-4958
Fax No.: 816-421-4958

ARSKA OPTICS
Riflescopes and accessories.
1721 Wright Avenue
La Verne, CA 91750
Website: www.barska.com
Phone No.: 909-445-8168
Fax No.: 909-445-8169

EAMSHOT-QUARTON USA, INC.
Laser sighting systems.
5805 Callaghan Road, Suite 102
San Antonio, TX 78228
Website: www.beamshot.com
Phone No.: 210-735-0280
Fax No.: 210-735-1326

ELL AND CARLSON, INC.
Hand-laminated fiberglass, carbon fiber, and aramid fiber rifle and shotgun stocks and accessories.
101 Allen Road
Dodge City, KS 67801
Website: www.bellandcarlson.com
Phone No.: 620-225-6688
Fax No.: 620-225-9095

ERGARA BARRELS
Barrels, scope mount systems, and rifle slings.
5988 Peachtree Corners East
Norcross, GA 30071
Website: www.bergarabarrels.com
Phone No.: 770-449-4687
Fax No.: 770-242-8546

BLACKHAWK PRODUCTS GROUP
Rifle and shotgun stocks, slings, tactical accessories.
6160 Commander Parkway
Norfolk, VA 23502
Website: www.blackhawk.com
Phone No.: 800-694-5263
Fax No.: 757-436-3088

BLACKTHORNE PRODUCTS, LLC
AR-15, AK47 and Galil parts and accessories
PO Box 2441
Inver Grove, MN 55076
Website: www.blackthorneproducts.com
Phone No.: 952-232-5832
Fax No.: 912-964-7701

BOYDS GUNSTOCK INDUSTRIES, INC.
Walnut and birch laminate replacement stocks.
25376 403rd Ave
Mitchell, SD 57301
Website: www.boydsgunstocks.com
Phone No.: 605-996-5011
Fax No.: 605-996-9878

BRILEY MANUFACTURING, INC.
1911 style pistol accessories.
1230 Lumpkin Road
Houston, TX 77043
Phone No.: 713-932-6995
Fax No.: 713-932-1043

BRITE-STRIKE TECHNOLOGIES, INC.
Tactical weapon lights.
26 Wapping Road, Jones River Industrial Park
Kingston, MA 02364
Website: www.brite-strike.com
Phone No.: 781-585-5509
Fax No.: 781-585-5332

BROWNELLS MIL/LE SUPPLY GROUP
Worldwide distributor of armorers tools, accessories, and OEM parts.
200 South Front Street
Montezuma, IA 50171
Website: www.brownells.com
Phone No.: 641-623-5401
Fax No.: 641-623-3896

BSA OPTICS
Riflescopes and red dot sights.
3911 Southwest 47th Avenue, Suite 914
Ft. Lauderdale, FL 33314
Website: www.bsaoptics.com
Phone No.: 954-581-2144
Fax No.: 954-581-3165

B-SQUARE
Rings, bases, rail mounting systems.
13387 International Pkwy
Jacksonville, FL 32218
Phone No.: 904-741-5400
Fax No.: 904-741-5404

BUFFER TECHNOLOGIES
Recoil buffers for rifles and pistols.
PO Box 105047
Jefferson City, MO 65110
Website: www.buffertech.com
Phone No.: 573-634-8529
Fax No.: 573-634-8522

BULLDOG BARRELS, LLC
OEM barrel blanks and finished barrels.
106 Isabella Street, 4 North Shore Center Suite 110
Pittsburgh, PA 15212
Website: www.bulldogbarrels.com
Phone No.: 412-322-2747
Fax No.: 412-322-1912

BURRIS COMPANY, INC.
Riflescopes, red dot sights, rings, and bases.
331 East 8th Street
Greeley, CO 80631
Website: www.burrisoptics.com
Phone No.: 970-356-1670
Fax No.: 970-356-8702

BUSHNELL OUTDOOR PRODUCTS
Riflescopes, red dot sights.
9200 Cody Street
Overland Park, KS 66214
Website: www.unclemikesle.com
Phone No.: 913-752-3400
Fax No.: 913-752-3550

BUTLER CREEK CORP.
Magazines, replacement barrels, and stocks.
9200 Cody Street
Overland Park, KS 66214
Website: www.butlercreek.com
Phone No.: 913-752-3400
Fax No.: 913-752-3550

BUTTON SLING, INC.
Single point shooting slings.
2913 Northwest 5th Street
Blue Springs, MO 64014
Website: www.buttonsling.com
Phone No.: 816-419-8100
Fax No.: 816-224-4040

C PRODUCTS, LLC
AR platform rifle magazines.
30 Elmwood Court
Newington, CT 06111
Website: www.cproductsllc.com
Phone No.: 860-953-5007
Fax No.: 860-953-0601

CAMMENGA CORPORATION
Rifle magazines, AR15 rifle parts.
100 Aniline North, Suite 258
Holland, MI 49424
Website: www.cammenga.com
Phone No.: 616-392-7999
Fax No.: 616-392-9432

CARL ZEISS OPTRONICS GMBH
Optronic and optical sighting systems.
Gloelstr 3-5
Wetzlar, 35576 Germany
Website: www.zeiss.com/optronics
Phone No.: 011 4964414040
Fax No.: 044 49644140510

CASPIAN ARMS, LTD.
1911 pistol components, replacement slides for Glock pistols.
75 Cal Foster Drive
Wolcott, VT 05680
Website: www.caspianarms.com
Phone No.: 802-472-6454
Fax No.: 802-472-6709

CCF RACE FRAMES, LLC
Replacement frames for the Glock pistols in aluminum, stainless steel, and titanium alloys.
PO Box 29009
Richmond, VA 23242
Website: www.ccfraceframes.com
Phone No.: 804-622-4277
Fax No.: 804-740-9599

CENTURY INTERNATIONAL ARMS, INC.
Importer of firearms parts and accessories.
430 South Congress Drive, Suite 1
Delray Beach, FL 33445
Website: www.centuryarms.com
Phone No.: 561-265-4500
Fax No.: 561-265-4520

CERAKOTE FIREARMS COATINGS
Liquid ceramic coating developed to withstand the most extreme conditions.
NIC Industries, Inc.
7050 Sixth Street
White City, OR 97503
Website: www.nicindustries.com
Phone No.: 541-826-1922
Fax No.: 541-830-6518

CHIP MCCORMICK CUSTOM, LLC
Extra-capacity 1911 pistol magazines, AR-15 match and tactical trigger groups.
105 Sky King Drive
Spicewood, TX 78669
Website: www.cmcmags.com
Phone No.: 830-798-2863
Fax No.: 830-693-4975

CHOATE MACHINE & TOOL
Polymer fixed and folding stocks, and accessories for rifles and shotguns.
116 Lovers Lane
Bald Knob, AR 72010
Website: www.riflestock.com
Phone No.: 501-724-6193
Fax No.: 501-724-5873

C-MORE SYSTEMS
Tubeless ultra-light and miniature red dot sights.
7553 Gary Road PO Box 1750
Manassas, VA 20109
Website: www.cmore.com
Phone No.: 703-361-2663
Fax No.: 703-361-5881

CONETROL SCOPE MOUNTS
Rings, bases.
Hwy 123 South
Seguin, TX 78155 USA
Website: www.conetrol.com

CRIMSON TRACE CORPORATION
Grip-integrated laser sighting systems.
9780 Southwest Freeman Drive
Wilsonville, OR 97070 USA
Website: www.crimsontrace.com
Phone No.: 503-783-5333
Fax No.: 503-783-5334

CYLINDER & SLIDE, INC.
Custom handgun parts and accessories.
245 East 4th Street
Fremont, NE 68025
Website: www.cylinder-slide.com
Phone No.: 402-721-4277
Fax No.: 402-721-0263

D.S.A., INC.
Accessories for AR15 and FAL rifles, B&T rail systems.
27 West 990 Industrial Avenue, P.O. Box 370
Lake Barrington, IL 60011
Website: www.dsarms.com
Phone No.: 847-277-7258
Fax No.: 847-277-7263

DANIEL DEFENSE, INC.
Military small arms upgrade parts, integrated weapon rail systems.
6002 Commerce Boulevard, Suite 109
Savannah, GA 31408
Website: www.danieldefense.com
Phone No.: 912-851-3225
Fax No.: 912-964-3247

DOCTER OPTIC
Riflescopes, red dot sights.
7661 Commerce Lane
Trussville, AL 35173
Website: www.merkel-usa.com
Phone No.: 205-655-8299
Fax No.: 205-655-7078

DOMINION ARMS/RAUCH TACTICAL
Polymer magazines for SIG 550 rifles, M14 and VZ58 rifle upgrade components.
250 H Street, Suite 226
Blaine, WA 98230
Website: www.domarms.com and www.rauchtactical.com
Phone No.: 877-829-1050
Fax No.: 866-606-2743

DUOSTOCK DESIGNS, INC.
Rifle stocks for CQB weapons.
PO Box 32
Welling, OK 74471
Website: www.duostock.com
Phone No.: 866-386-7865
Fax No.: 918-431-3182

DURASIGHT SCOPE MOUNTING SYSTEMS
Scope mounts and rings for center-fire rifles.
5988 Peachtree Corners East
Norcross, GA 30071
Website: www.durasight.com
Phone No.: 770-449-4687
Fax No.: 770-242-8546

EAGLE GRIPS, INC.
Handgun grips.
460 Randy Road
Carol Stream, IL 60188
Website: www.eaglegrips.com
Phone No.: 630-260-0400
Fax No.: 630-260-0486

ELCAN OPTICAL TECHNOLOGIES
Riflescopes and other military grade optics.
1601 North Plano Road
Richardson, TX 75081
Website: www.elcan.com
Phone No.: 972-344-8077
Fax No.: 972-344-8260

ELITE IRON, LLC
Standard and custom caliber suppressors.
1345 Thunders Trail Bldg. D
Potomac, MT 59823
Website: www.eliteiron.net
Phone No.: 406-244-0234
Fax No.: 406-244-0135

ELZETTA DESIGN, LLC
LED weapon lights and accessories.
PO Box 54364
Lexington, KY 40555
Website: www.elzetta.com
Phone No.: 859-707-7471
Fax No.: 859-918-0465

EMA TACTICAL
.223 CountDown magazine, rail systems, stocks, grips, slings, and scope mounts.
1208 Branagan Drive
Tullytown, PA 19007
Website: www.ematactical.com
Phone No.: 215-949-9944
Fax No.: 215-949-9191

EXTREMEBEAM TACTICAL
High-output weatherproof military weapon lights.
2275 Huntington Drive, Suite 872
San Marino, CA 91108
Website: www.extremebeamtactical.com
Phone No.: 626-372-5898
Fax No.: 626-609-0640

FAB DEFENSE
Tactical equipment for military, police, and self-defense weapons.
43 Yakov Olamy Street
Moshav Mishmar Hashiva, Israel 50297
Website: www.fab-defense.com
Phone No.: 011 972039603399
Fax No.: 011 972039603312

FAILZERO
EXO Technology coatings for firearm accessories and parts.
7825 Southwest Ellipse Way
Stuart, FL 34997
Phone No.: 772-223-6699
Fax No.: 772-223-9996

FALCON INDUSTRIES
Ergonomically designed tactical weapon grips and accessories.
PO Box 1690
Edgewood, NM 87015
Website: www.ergogrips.net
Phone No.: 505-281-3783
Fax No.: 505-281-3991

GEISSELE AUTOMATICS, LLC
National Match and combat replacement triggers.
1920 West Marshall Street
Norristown, PA 19403
Website: www.ar15triggers.com
Phone No.: 610-272-2060
Fax No.: 610-272-2069

GEMTECH
OSHA-safe sound suppressors in most defense calibers.
PO Box 140618
Boise, ID 83714
Website: www.gem-tech.com
Phone No.: 208-939-7222

GG&G
Optical mounting systems and tactical weapon accessories.
3602 East 42nd Stravenue
Tucson, AZ 85713
Website: www.gggaz.com
Phone No.: 520-748-7167
Fax No.: 520-748-7583

GRAUER SYSTEMS
IGRS - integrated grip rail system for AR15 style rifles.
303 5th Avenue, Suite 1502
New York, NY 10016
Website: www.grauersystems.com
Phone No.: 202-436-9980

HARRIS ENGINEERING, INC.
Bipods and adaptors for attaching bipods.
999 Broadway
Barlow, KY 42024
Phone No.: 270-334-3633
Fax No.: 270-334-3000

HIVIZ SHOOTING SYSTEMS
Fiber-optic firearm sights, recoil pads.
North Pass, Ltd.
1941 Health Parkway, Suite 1
Fort Collins, CO 80524
Website: www.hivizsights.com
Phone No.: 970-407-0426
Fax No.: 970-416-1208

HOGUE, INC.
Synthetic handgun, rifle, and shotgun grips and stocks.
550 Linne Road
Paso Robles, CA 93447
Website: www.hogueinc.com
Phone No.: 805-239-1440
Fax No.: 805-239-2553

HORUS VISION, LLC
Long range and CQB riflescopes.
659 Huntington Avenue
San Bruno, CA 94066
Website: www.horusvision.com
Phone No.: 650-588-8862; 650-583-5471
Fax No.: 650-588-6264

HYPERBEAM
Riflescopes, night vision scopes.
1504 Sheepshead Bay Road, Suite 300
Brooklyn, NY 11236
Website: www.nightdetective.com
Phone No.: 718-272-1776
Fax No.: 718-272-1797

IC, INC.
All types of aluminum color and graphic anodizing.
12400 Burt Road
Detroit, MI 48228
Website: www.ihccorp.com
Phone No.: 313-535-3210
Fax No.: 313-535-3220

INSIGHT TECHNOLOGY
Tactical lasers and illuminators.
9 Akira Way
Londonderry, NH 03053
Website: www.insighttechgear.com
Phone No.: 877-744-4802
Fax No.: 603-668-1084

INTENSITY OPTICS
Riflescopes.
Onalaska Operations
PO box 39
Onalaska, WI 54650
Website: www.intensityoptics.com
Phone No.: 800-635-7656

IT NIGHT VISION
Generation III night vision sights.
7635 Plantation Road
Roanoke, VA 24019
Website: www.nightvision.com
Phone No.: 540-563-0371
Fax No.: 540-366-9015

JAPAN OPTICS, LTD.
Riflescopes (formerly HAKKO).
2-11-29, Ukima, Kita-ku
Tokyo, 115-0051 Japan
Website: www.japanoptics.co.jp
Phone No.: 011 81359146680
Fax No.: 011 81353922232

JOHN MASEN COMPANY, INC.
Mini 14 and AR-15 accessories, shotgun stocks.
1305 Jelmak Street
Grand Prairie, TX 75050
Website: www.johnmasen.com
Phone No.: 972-790-0521
Fax No.: 972-970-3691

JOHN'S GUNS
Suppressors for military, law enforcement and civilian applications.
Dark Horse Arms Company
1041 FM 1274
Coleman, TX 76834
Website: www.darkhorsearms.com
Phone No.: 325-382-4885
Fax No.: 325-382-4887

JONATHAN ARTHUR CIENER, INC.
.22 LR conversion units/kits for centerfire handguns and rifles.
8700 Commerce Street
Cape Canaveral, FL 32920
Website: www.22lrconversions.com
Phone No.: 321-868-2200
Fax No.: 321-868-2201

KFS INDUSTRIES
Bipods and mounting adaptors, adjustable sights for 1911 style pistols.
875 Wharton Drive Southwest, PO Box 44405
Atlanta, GA 30336
Website: www.versapod.com
Phone No.: 404-691-7611
Fax No.: 404-505-8445

KG INDUSTRIES, LLC
High performance firearm finishes.
16790 US Highway 63 South, Building 2
Hayward, WI 54843
Website: www.kgcoatings.com
Phone No.: 715-934-3566
Fax No.: 715-934-3570

KICK-EEZ PRODUCTS
Sorbothane recoil pads.
1819 Schurman Way, Suite 106
Woodland, WA 98674
Website: www.kickeezproducts.com
Phone No.: 360-225-9701
Fax No.: 360-225-9702

KNIGHTS MANUFACTURING COMPANY
Suppressors in popular calibers, night vision scopes.
701 Columbia Boulevard
Titusville, FL 32780
Website: www.knightarmco.com
Phone No.: 321-607-9900
Fax No.: 321-383-2143

KNS PRECISION, INC.
AR15/M16 tactical accessories.
112 Marschall Creek Road
Fredericksburg, TX 78624
Website: www.knsprecisioninc.com
Phone No.: 830-997-0000
Fax No.: 830-997-1443

KRIEGER BARRELS, INC.
Precision single-point, cut-rifled barrels in calibers ranging from .17 cal. through 4 Bore.
2024 Mayfield Road
Richfield, WI 53076
Website: www.kriegerbarrels.com
Phone No.: 262-628-8558
Fax No.: 262-628-8748

K-VAR CORP.
AK style rifle parts and accessories.
3300 South Decatur Boulevard, Suite 10601
Las Vegas, NV 89102
Website: www.k-var.com
Phone No.: 702-364-8880
Fax No.: 702-307-2303

KWIK-SITE COMPANY/IRONSIGHTER COMPANY
Scope mounts, bases, rings, and extension rings.
5555 Treadwell
Wayne, MI 48184
Website: www.kwiksitecorp.com
Phone No.: 734-326-1500
Fax No.: 734-326-4120

L.P.A. SRL DI GHILARDI
Metalic front and rear sights, sight accessories.
Via Vittorio Alfieri, 26
Gardone, V.T. 25063 Italy
Website: www.lpasights.com
Phone No.: 011 390308911481
Fax No.: 011 390308910951

L-3 COMMUNICATIONS-EOTECH
Holographic red dot weapon sights.
1201 East Ellsworth Road
Ann Arbor, MI 48108
Website: www.l-3com.com/eotech
Phone No.: 734-741-8868
Fax No.: 734-741-8221

L-3 ELECTRO-OPTICAL SYSTEMS
Gen III night vision and thermal imaging weapon sights.
3414 Herrmann Drive
Garland, TX 75041
Website: www.l3nightvision.com
Phone No.: 972-840-5788
Fax No.: 972-271-2195

LANCER SYSTEMS
L5 translucent magazines and other firearms accessories.
7566 Morris Court, Suite 300
Allentown, PA 18106
Website: www.lancer-systems.com
Phone No.: 610-973-2614
Fax No.: 610-973-2615

LARUE TACTICAL
Quick-detach optical sight mounts, rails, AR15 style weapon handguards.
850 CR 177
Leander, TX 78641
Website: www.laruetactical.com
Phone No.: 512-259-1585
Fax No.: 512-259-1588

LASER AIMING SYSTEMS CORPORATION
Viridian brand green laser sights.
5929 Baker Road, Suite 440
Minnetonka, MN 55345
Website: www.viridiangreenlaser.com
Phone No.: 800-990-9390
Fax No.: 952-224-4097

LASER DEVICES, INC.
Visible and infrared laser aiming devices.
2 Harris Court, Suite A-4
Monterey, CA 93940
Website: www.laserdevices.com
Phone No.: 831-373-0701
Fax No.: 831-373-0903

LASERLYTE
Laser sights.
101 Airpark Road
Cottonwood, AZ 86326
Website: www.laserlyte.com
Phone No.: 928-649-3201
Fax No.: 928-649-3970

LASERMAX, INC.
Laser sights.
3495 Winston Place Suite B
Rochester, NY 14623
Website: www.lasermax.com
Phone No.: 585-272-5420
Fax No.: 585-272-5427

LAUER CUSTOM WEAPONRY
Firearms suppressors, Duracoat self-lubricating firearms finish.
3601 129th Street
Chippewa Falls, WI 54729
Website: www.lauerweaponry.com
Phone No.: 715-720-6128
Fax No.: 715-723-2950

LEAPERS, INC.
Electro-optical and tactical scopes, rail mounting systems.
32700 Capitol Street
Livonia, MI 48150
Website: www.leapers.com
Phone No.: 734-542-1500
Fax No.: 734-542-7095

LEATHERWOOD/HI-LUX OPTICS
Rifle scopes, auto-ranging trajectory scopes, 30mm tactical scopes.
Hi-Lux, Inc.
3135 Kashiwa Street
Torrance, CA 90505
Website: www.hi-luxoptics.com
Phone No.: 310-257-8142
Fax No.: 310-257-8096

LEICA SPORT OPTICS
Optical sights.
1 Pearl Court, Suite A
Allendale, NJ 07401 USA
Website: www.leica-camera.com/usa
Phone No.: 201-995-0051
Fax No.: 201-955-1686

LES BAER CUSTOM, INC.
1911 pistol frames, slides, barrels, sights, grips, scope mounts.
1804 Iowa Drive
Leclaire, IA 52753
Website: www.lesbaer.com
Phone No.: 563-289-2126
Fax No.: 563-289-2132

LEUPOLD & STEVENS, INC.
Tactical optical and electro-optical scopes, rings, and bases.
14400 Northwest Greenbriar Parkway 9700,
PO Box 688
Beaverton, OR 97006
Website: www.leupold.com
Phone No.: 503-646-9171
Fax No.: 503-526-1478

LEVELLOK SHOOTING SYSTEMS
Monopods, bipods, and tripods.
105 South 12th Street
Pittsburgh, PA 15203
Website: www.levellok.com
Phone No.: 412-431-5440
Fax No.: 412-488-7608

LEWIS MACHINE & TOOL
Tactical weapon accessories.
1305 11th Street West
Milan, IL 61264
Website: www.lewismachine.net
Phone No.: 309-787-7151
Fax No.: 309-787-7193

LIMBSAVER
LimbSaver recoil pads.
50 West Rose Nye Way
Shelton, WA 98584 USA
Website: www.limbsaver.com
Phone No.: 360-427-6031
Fax No.: 360-427-4025

LINE OF FIRE, LLC
TEGS grip system, 3.2.1. Slings.
3200 Danville Blvd., Suite 220
Alamo, CA 94507
Website: www.loftactical.com
Phone No.: 323-899-3016
Fax No.: 562-424-1562

LONE WOLF DISTRIBUTORS, INC.
Glock pistol accessories.
57 Shepard Road, PO Box 3549
Oldtown, ID 83822 USA
Website: www.lonewolfdist.com
Phone No.: 208-437-0612
Fax No.: 208-437-1098

LRB ARMS
M14 and AR15 receivers.
96 Cherry Lane
Floral Park, NY 11001 USA
Website: www.lrbarms.com
Phone No.: 516-327-9061
Fax No.: 516-327-0246

LUNA OPTICS, INC.
Night vision riflescopes.
54 Columbus Avenue
Staten Island, NY 10304
Website: www.lunaoptics.com
Phone No.; 718-556-5862
Fax No.: 718-556-5869

LWRC INTERNATIONAL, LLC
Tactical firearm accessories.
815 Chesapeake Drive
Cambridge, MD 21613
Website: www.lwrci.com
Phone No.: 410-901-1348
Fax No.: 410-228-1799

LYMAN-PACHMAYR-TRIUS PRODUCTS
Pachmayr synthetic grips, recoil pads, rifle stocks, and sights.
475 Smith Street
Middletown, CT 06457
Website: www.lymanproducts.com
Phone No.: 860-632-2020
Fax No.: 860-632-1699

MAG-NA-PORT INTERNATIONAL INC.
Handgun, shotgun, and rifle barrel porting/muzzle brakes.
41302 Executive Drive
Harrison Twp, MI 48045
Website: www.magnaport.com
Phone No.: 586-469-6727
Fax No.: 586-469-0425

MAGPUL INDUSTRIES CORP.
Fully adjustable buttstocks, magazines, grips, rail covers, and sights for AR15 and other tactical weapons.
PO Box 17697
Boulder, CO 80308
Website: www.magpul.com
Phone No.: 303-828-3460
Fax No.: 303-828-3469

MAKO GROUP
Tactical weapon accessories.
74 Rome Street
Farmingdale, NY 11735
Website: www.themakogroup.com
Phone No.: 631-880-3396
Fax No.: 631-880-3397

MANNERS COMPOSITE STOCKS
Carbon fiber and fiber glass gunstocks.
1209 Swift
North Kansas City, MO 64116
Website: www.mannersstock.com
Phone No.: 816-283-3334

MCMILLAN FIBERGLASS STOCKS
Fiberglass rifle stocks.
1638 West Knudsen Drive, Suite A
Phoenix, AZ 85027
Website: www.mcmillanusa.com
Phone No.: 623-582-9635
Fax No.: 623-581-3825

MEC-GAR SRL
Handgun and rifle magazines.
Via Mandolossa, 102/a
Gussago, Brescia, 25064 Italy
Website: www.mec-gar.it
Phone No.: 011-390303735413
Fax No.: 011-390303733687

MEOPTA USA, INC.
Riflescopes.
50 Davids Drive
Hauppauge, NY 11788
Website: www.meopta.com
Phone No.: 631-436-5900
Fax No.: 631-436-5920

MEPROLIGHT/KIMBER
Tritium night sights and red dot reflex sights.
2590 Montana Hwy 35, Suite B
Kalispell, MT 59901
Website: www.kimberamerica.com
Phone No.: 406-758-2222
Fax No.: 406-758-2223

MEPROLIGHT, LTD.
Electro-optical and optical sights and devices.
58 Hazait Street, Or-Akiva Industrial Park
Or-Akiva, 30600 Israel
Website: www.meprolight.com
Phone No.: 011-97246244111
Fax No.: 011-97246244123

MESA TACTICAL
Telescoping stock systems, shell carriers, rails, and sling loops for tactical shotguns.
1760 Monrovia Ave, Suite A14
Costa Mesa, CA 92627
Website: www.mesatactical.com
Phone No.: 949-642-3337
Fax No.: 949-642-3339

MFI

Rails, risers, scope mounts, and accessories for tactical weapons.
563 San Miguel
Liberty, KY 42539
Website: www.mfiap.com
Phone No.: 606-787-0022
Fax No.: 606-787-0059

MGI

AR-15/M-4/M-16 lower receivers, 90 round magazines, and parts.
102 Cottage Street
Bangor, ME 04401
Website: www.MGImilitary.com
Phone No.: 207-945-5441
Fax No.: 207-945-4010

MIDWEST INDUSTRIES, INC.

Tactical rifle accessories.
828 Philip Drive, Suite 2
Waukesha, WI 53186
Website: www.midwestindustriesinc.com
Phone No.: 262-896-6780
Fax No.: 262-896-6756

MILLETT SIGHTS

Tactical scopes, red dot sights, metallic sights, rings, and bases.
6200 Cody
Overland Park, KS 66214
Website: www.millettsights.com
Phone No.: 913-752-3400
Fax No.: 913-752-3550

MOROVISION NIGHT VISION, INC.

Law enforcement and commercial night vision optical sights.
PO Box 342
Dana Point, CA 92629
Website: www.morovision.com
Phone No.: 949-488-3855
Fax No.: 949-488-3361

MOUNTING SOLUTIONS PLUS

Muzzelite, LightLink, SightLink, and Glock Pistol Fiber Optic Sights,
10655 Southwest 185 Terrace
Miami, FL 33157
Website: www.mountsplus.com
Phone No.: 305-253-8393
Fax No.: 305-232-1247

MURRAYS GUNS

Replacement SKS firing pin kit, Yugoslav SKS gas valve.
12696 FM 2127
Bowie, TX 76230
Website: www.murraysguns.com
Phone No.: 940-928-002
Fax No.: 800-836-7579

NEW CENTURY NCSTAR, INC.

Firearms accessories, optics including precision rifle and pistol scopes, and red dot sights.
10302 Olney Street
El Monte, CA 91731
Website: www.ncstar.com
Phone No.: 626-575-1518
Fax No.: 626-575-2478

NEWCON OPTIK

Electro-optical products, night vision rifle scopes.
105 Sparks Ave
Toronto, ON M2H 2S5 Canada
Website: www.newcon-optik.com
Phone No.: 416-663-6963
Fax No.: 416-663-9065

NIGHTFORCE OPTICS

Nightforce precision rifle scopes.
Lightforce USA, Inc.
1040 Hazen Lane
Orofino, ID 83544
Website: www.nightforceoptics.com
Phone No.: 208-476-9814
Fax No.: 208-476-9817

NIGHT VISION SYSTEMS

Night vision, thermal imaging, combat identification, and lasers.
542 Kemmerer Lane
Allentown, PA 18104
Website: www.nightvisionsystems.com
Phone No.: 610-391-9101
Fax No.: 610-391-9220

NIKON, INC.

Riflescopes.
1300 Walt Whitman Road
Melville, NY 11747
Website: www.nikonhunting.com
Phone No.: 631-547-4200
Fax No.: 631-547-4040

NITREX OPTICS

Riflescopes.
Weaver/ATK Commercial Products
N5549 County Trunk Z
Onalaska, WI 54650
Website: www.nitrexoptics.com
Phone No: 800-635-7656
Fax No.: 763-323-3890

NIVISYS INDUSTRIES, LLC

Night vision weapon sights, and related laser aiming and illumination systems.
400 South Clark Drive, Suite 105
Tempe, AZ 85281
Website: www.nivisys.com
Phone No.: 480-970-3222
Fax No.: 480-970-3555

NODAK SPUD LLC

AKM receivers and fire control parts, AR lowers, Picatinny rails, flash hiders, Benelli 1014/M4 extended mag tubes.
7683 Washington Ave. S.
Edina, MN 55439
Website: www.nodakspud.com
Phone No.: 952-942-1909
Fax No.: 952-942-1912

N-VISION OPTICS

Tactical night vision equipment, thermal imaging devices, and laser sighting systems.
220 Reservoir Street, Suite 26
Needham, MA 02494
Website: www.nvisionoptics.com
Phone No.: 781-505-8360
Fax No.: 781-998-5656

OSPREY INTERNATIONAL, INC.

Laser sights, holographic sights, and daytime riflescopes.
25 Hawks Farm Road
White, GA 30184
Website: www.osprey-optics.com
Phone No.: 770-387-2751
Fax No.: 770-387-0114

PARKER-HALE

Scope mounts, bipods, suppressors, and barrels.
Bedford Road
Petersfield, Hampshire, GU32 3XA United Kingdom
Website: www.parker-hale.co.uk
Phone No.: 011 441730268011
Fax No.: 011 441730260074

PATRIOT ORDNANCE FACTORY

Gas piston weapon systems and uppers, precision sniper stocks, AR rifle magazines, AR rails/forends, and flash hiders.
23623 North 67 Ave
Glendale, AZ 85310
Website: www.pof-usa.com
Phone No.: 623-561-9572
Fax No.: 623-321-1680

PEARCE GRIP

Replacement grips for firearms.
PO Box 40367
Fort Worth, TX 76140
Website: www.pearcegrip.com
Phone No.: 817-568-9704
Fax No.: 817-568-9707

PENTAGONLIGHT

Tactical weapon light systems.
151 Mitchell Ave
San Francisco, CA 94080
Website: www.pentagonlight.com
Phone No.: 650-877-1555
Fax No.: 650-877-9555

PENTAX IMAGING COMPANY

Riflescopes.
600 12th Street, Suite 300
Golden, CO 80401
Website: www.pentaxsportoptics.com
Phone No.: 303-799-8000
Fax No.: 303-460-1628

PHOEBUS TACTICAL FLASHLIGHTS

LED tactical flashlights.
2800 Third Street
San Francisco, CA 94107
Website: www.phoebus.com
Phone No.: 415-550-0770
Fax No.: 415-550-2655

POINT TECH, INC.

1911 type pistol barrels, frames, and slides, Glock barrels, Beretta barrels, Mauser barrels, AR16/M16 barrels, and .50 caliber barrels.
160 Gregg Street, Suite 1
Lodi, NJ 07644
Phone No.: 201-368-0711
Fax No.: 201-368-0133

PRECISION REFLEX, INC.

Custom built AR uppers, rings, bases, carbon fiber forearms, shotgun mounts, charging handles, and auxiliary iron sights.
710 Streine Drive, PO Box 95
New Bremen, OH 45869
Website: www.pri-mounts.com
Phone No.: 419-629-2603
Fax No.: 419-629-2173

PREMIER RETICLES

Tactical riflescopes, scout scopes, owner of patented Gen 2 Mildot reticle.
175 Commonwealth Court
Winchester, VA 22602
Phone No.: 540-868-2044
Fax No.: 540-868-2045

PRIMARY WEAPONS SYSTEMS
Firearm accessories including flash hiders, recoil compensators and retro-fit piston systems.
800 East Citation Court, Suite C
Boise, ID 83716
Website: www.primaryweapons.com
Phone No.: 208-344-5217
Fax No.: 208-344-5395

PROMAG INDUSTRIES, INC.
Rifle and pistol magazines, scope rings, mounts, shotgun stocks, tactical rifle and pistol accessories.
10654 South Garfield Ave
South Gate, CA 90280
Website: www.promagindustries.com
Phone No.: 562-861-9554
Fax No.: 562-861-6377

PSI, LLC
LPA adjustable pistol sights, tactical shotgun sights, ACT-MAG/PSI and Novak pistol magazines.
2 Klarides Village Drive, Suite 336
Seymour, CT 06483
Website: www.precisionsalesintl.com
Phone No.: 203-262-6484
Fax No.: 203-262-6562

QUAKE INDUSTRIES, INC.
Sling swivels, tactical attachments, and parts.
5988 Peachtree Corners East
Norcross, GA 30071
Website: www.quakeinc.com
Phone No.: 770-449-4687
Fax No.: 770-242-8546

RAMLINE
Synthetic gunstocks.
Onalaska Operations
PO Box 39
Onalaska, WI 54650
Website: www.atk.com
Phone No.: 800-635-7656

RANCH PRODUCTS
Scope mounts and other specialty gun parts.
PO Box 145
Malinta, OH 43535
Website: www.ranchproducts.com
Phone No.: 419-966-2881
Fax No.: 313-565-8536

RESCOMP HANDGUN TECHNOLOGIES
Compensators and mounts for all 1911 style pistols as well as AR-15, AK and Galil rifles; magazines for STI and Para Ordnance style hi-cap pistols.
PO Box 11786
Queenswood, 186 South Africa
Website: www.crspeed.co.za
Phone No.: 011 27123334768
Fax No.: 011 27123332112

RIVERBANK ARMORY
Coded oilers, type one bands, flip sights and other parts for M1 carbines and M1 Garands.
PO Box 85
Riverbank, CA 95367
Website: www.riverbankarmory.com
Phone No.: 209-869-5576

ROCK RIVER ARMS, INC.
Parts and accessories for .223, 9mm, .458 Socom, 6.8 SPC, and .308 rifles.
1042 Cleveland Road
Colona, IL 61241
Website: www.rockriverarms.com
Phone No.: 309-792-5780
Fax No.: 309-792-5781

SABRE DEFENCE INDUSTRIES, LLC
Barrels, AR15/M16 style rifle upper and lower receivers.
450 Allied Drive
Nashville, TN 37211
Website: www.sabredefence.com
Phone No.: 615-333-0077
Fax No.: 615-333-6229

SAGE CONTROL ORDNANCE, INC.
EBR Aluminum Chassis Stock for M14 rifles, and accessories for law enforcement/military weapons.
3391 East Eberhardt Street
Oscoda, MI 48750
Website: www.sageinternationalltd.com
Phone No.: 989-739-7000
Fax No.: 989-739-7098

SALT RIVER TACTICAL, LLC
Support items for Combloc and Soviet-era weapons systems.
PO Box 20397
Mesa, AZ 85277
Website: www.saltrivertactical.com
Phone No.: 480-656-2683

SAMSON MFG. CORPORATION
Rail systems and other tactical accessories.
110 Christian Lane
Whately, MA 01373
Website: www.samson-mfg.com
Phone No.: 413-665-1162
Fax No.: 413-665-1163

SCHERER SUPPLIES, INC.
High capacity magazines for Glock pistols.
205 Four Mile Creek Road
Tazewell, TN 37879
Phone No.: 423-733-2615
Fax No.: 423-733-2073

SCHMIDT & BENDER GMBH
High precision rifle scopes for military and law enforcement.
Am Grossacker 42
Biebertal, Hessen, 35444 Germany
Website: www.schmidtbender.com
Phone No.: 011 496409811570
Fax No.: 011 496409811511

SHEPHERD ENTERPRISES, INC.
Riflescopes with integral range finder, bullet drop compensator, and patented dual reticle system.
PO Box 189
Waterloo, NE 68069
Website: www.shepherdscopes.com
Phone No.: 402-779-2424
Fax No.: 402-779-4010

SHERLUK MARKETING
M-16/AR-15 parts and accessories.
PO Box 156
Delta, OH 43615
Website: www.sherluk.com
Phone No.: 419-923-8011
Fax No.: 419-923-812

SHOOTERS RIDGE
Bi-pods, Picatinny rail adaptors, rings, and bases.
N5549 County Trunk Z
Onalaska, WI 54650
Website: www.shootersridge.com
Phone No.: 800-635-7656
Fax No.: 763-323-3890

SI DEFENSE, INC.
AR15 style rifle parts.
2902 Hwy 93 North
Kalispell, MT 59901
Website: www.si-defense.com
Phone No.: 406-752-4253
Fax No.: 406-752-4082

SIGHTMARK
Riflescopes, laser sights, red dot sights, night vision sights, and weapon lights.
201 Regency Parkway
Mansfield, TX 76063
Website: www.sightmark.com
Phone No.: 817-394-0310
Fax No.: 817-394-1628

SIGHTRON, INC.
Tactical and mil-dot scopes, and red dot sights.
100 Jeffrey Way, Suite A
Youngsville, NC 27596
Website: www.sightron.com
Phone No.: 919-562-3000
Fax No.: 919-556-0157

SILENCERCO, LLC
Suppressors.
5511 South 6055 West
West Valley City, UT 84118
Website: www.silencerco.com
Phone No.: 801-973-2023
Fax No.: 801-973-2032

SIMMONS
Rifle, shotgun, and handgun scopes.
9200 Cody Street
Overland Park, KS 66214
Phone No.: 913-782-3131
Fax No.: 913-782-4189

SOG ARMORY, INC.
AR upper and lower receivers, M4 carbine stocks.
11707 South Sam Houston Parkway West, Suite R
Houston, TX 77031
Website: www.sogarmory.com
Phone No.: 281-568-5685
Fax No.: 285-568-9191

SPEEDFEED
Glass-filled polymer shotgun stocks and forends.
13386 International Parkway
Jacksonville, FL 32218
Website: www.safariland.com
Phone No.: 904-741-5400
Fax No.: 904-741-5404

SUN DEVIL MANUFACTURING, LLC
Billet aluminum AR15 components and accessories; hard anodizing, ceramic coating, and nickel teflon finishing.
663 West Second Avenue, Suite 16
Mesa, AZ 85210
Website: www.sundevilmfg.com
Phone No.: 480-833-9876
Fax No.: 480-833-9509

WR MANUFACTURING, LLC
.22, 9mm, .45 ACP, 5.56mm, and .30 caliber
suppressors.
PO Box 841
Pickens, SC 29761
Website: www.swrmfg.com
Phone No.: 864-850-3579
Fax No.: 864-751-2823

ACM III, INC.
Tactical weapon lights and mounts.
2300 Commerce Park Drive, Suite 7
Palm Bay, FL 32905
Website: www.tacm3.com
Phone No.: 321-726-0644
Fax No.: 321-726-0645

ACTICAL INNOVATIONS, INC.
AR15 receivers, .223 suppressors.
345 Sunrise Road
Bonners Ferry, ID 83805
Website: www.tacticalinc.com
Phone No.: 208-267-1585
Fax No.: 208-267-1597

ALLEY MANUFACTURING, INC.
Rings, bases, custom gun parts, and accessories.
9183 Old No. 6 Highway
PO Box 369
Santee, SC 29142
Website: www.talleyrings.com
Phone No.: 803-854-5700
Fax No.: 803-854-9315

ANGODOWN, INC.
Mil-spec tactical weapon accessories.
4720 North La Cholla Blvd., Suite 180
Tucson, AZ 85705
Website: www.tangodown.com
Phone No.: 520-888-3376
Fax No.: 520-888-3787

APCO, INC.
Synthetic stocks and forends, slings, high capacity
magazines, slings, and U.S. "922r" compliance
parts.
PO Box 2408
Kennesaw, GA 30156
Website: www.tapco.com
Phone No.: 770-425-1280
Fax No.: 770-425-1510

.A.S., LTD.
Unique single dot miniature pistol and long gun
sights.
1 Eilat Street
PO Box 84
Tiberias, Israel 14100
Phone No.: 011 972507983433
Fax No.: 011 972467722985

DI ARMS
Camouflage firearms finish, tactical weapon
accessories.
2441 Dakota Craft
Rapid City, SD 57701
Phone No.: 605-415-4910

IMNEY MANUFACTURING, INC.
Replacement triggers for rifles and Rem. 870
shotguns.
3940 West Clarendon Avenue
Phoenix, AZ 85019
Website: www.timneytriggers.com
Phone No.: 602-274-2999
Fax No.: 602-241-0361

TRIJICON, INC.
Night sights, red dot sights, riflescopes, night vision
and thermal imaging systems.
49385 Shafer Avenue
PO Box 930059
Wixom, MI 48393
Website: www.trijicon.com
Phone No.: 248-960-7700
Fax No.: 248-960-7725

TRIPLE K MANUFACTURING COMPANY, INC.
Pistol, rifle, and shotgun magazines.
2222 Commercial Street
San Diego, CA 92113
Website: www.triplek.com
Phone No.: 619-232-2066
Fax No.: 619-232-7675

TROY INDUSTRIES, INC.
Small arms components and accessories, complete
weapon upgrades.
126 Myron Street
West Springfield, MA 01089
Website: www.troyind.com
Phone No.: 413-788-4288
Fax No.: 413-383-0339

TRUGLO, INC.
Tritium fiber-optic aiming systems, red dot sights,
riflescopes.
710 Presidential Drive
Richardson, TX 75081
Website: www.truglo.com
Phone No.: 972-774-0300
Fax No.: 972-774-0323

URBAN-E.R.T. SLINGS, LLC
Custom weapon slings.
PO Box 429
Clayton, IN 46118
Website: www.urbanertslings.com
Phone No.: 317-223-6509
Fax No.: 317-539-2585

U.S. OPTICS, INC.
Riflescopes, mounting systems, custom scopes,
lenses, and mounts.
150 Arovista Circle
Brea, CA 92821
Website: www.usoptics.com
Phone No.: 714-582-1956
Fax No.: 714-582-1959

VALDADA OPTICS
European tactical, precision, and long range
riflescopes.
PO Box 270095
Littleton, CO 80127
Website: www.valdada.com
Fax No.; 303-979-4578
Fax No.; 303-979-0256

VANG COMP SYSTEMS
Barrels, magazine tube extensions, oversized
safeties, and sights for tactical shotguns.
400 West Butterfield Road
Chino Valley, AZ 86323
Website: www.vangcomp.com
Phone No.: 928-636-8455
Fax No.: 928-636-1538

VLTOR WEAPON SYSTEMS
Modular buttstocks, and components and
accessories for AR15/M16/AK rifles.
3735 North Romero Road
Tucson, AZ 85705
Website; www.vltor.com
Phone No.: 520-408-1944
Fax No.: 520-293-8807

VORTEX OPTICS
Red dot sights, riflescopes, rings and mounts.
2120 West Greenview Drive, Suite 4
Middleton, WI 53562
Website: www.vortextactical.com
Phone No.: 800-426-0048
Fax No.: 608-662-7454

WARNE MANUFACTURING COMPANY
Scope rings and mounts.
9057 SE Jannsen Road
Clackamas, OR 97015
Website: www.warnescopemounts.com
Phone No.: 503-657-5590
Fax No.: 503-657-5695

WEAVER OPTICS
Mounting systems, riflescopes, red dot sights.
N5549 County Trunk Z
Onalaska, WI 54650
Website: www.weaveroptics.com
Phone No.: 800-635-7656
Fax No.: 763-323-3890

WILLIAMS GUN SIGHT COMPANY
Pistol, rifle, and shotgun fiber optic sights, scope
mounts, open sights, receiver sights, shotgun
sights, and sling swivels.
7389 Lapeer Road
Davison, MI 48423
Website: www.williamsgunsight.com
Phone No.: 810-653-2131
Fax No.: 810-658-2140

WILLIAMS TRIGGER SPECIALTIES
Sniper grade trigger upgrades for most semi-auto
rifles.
111 SE Second Street
Atwood, IL 61913
Website: www.williamstriggers.com
Phone No.: 217-578-3026

XS SIGHT SYSTEMS, INC.
XS 24/7 tritium night sights for handguns, rifles,
and shotguns; tactical sights for AR15/M16/HK
rifles, and mounting systems.
2401 Ludelle street
Fort Worth, TX 76105
Website: www.xssights.com
Phone No.: 817-536-0136
Fax No.: 817-536-3517

YANKEE HILL MACHINE CO., INC.
Rail systems, forearms, flip-up sights, rifle and
pistol suppressors, flash suppressors,
compensators, and forward grips.
20 Ladd Av, Suite 1
Florence, MA 01062
Website: www.yhm.net
Phone No.: 413-584-1400
Fax No.: 413-586-1326

YUKON ADVANCED OPTICS
Riflescopes and night visions optics.
201 Regency Parkway
Mansfield, TX 76063
Website: www.yukonopticsusa.com
Phone No.: 817-225-0310
Fax No.: 817-394-1628

ZEL CUSTOM/TACTILITE
Bolt-action uppers for AR style rifles in .338 Lapua,
.416 Barrett, and .50 BMG calibers.
11419 Challenger Av
Odessa, FL 33556
Website: www.zelcustom.com
Phone No.: 303-880-8701
Fax No.: 303-353-1473

INDEX

A

P.S.

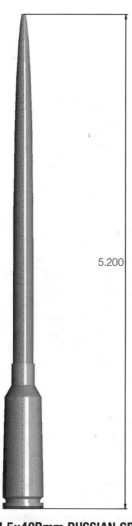

4.5x40Rmm RUSSIAN SPS

5.200

5.450

DBK9067798

Sometimes a 1/4 inch can make all the difference.